ASIAN AMERICAN NOVELISTS
A Bio-Bibliographical Critical Sourcebook

Edited by
Emmanuel S. Nelson

GREENWOOD PRESS
Westport, Connecticut • London

Library of Congress Cataloging-in-Publication Data

Asian American novelists : a bio-bibliographical critical sourcebook /
    edited by Emmanuel S. Nelson.
        p. cm.
    Includes bibliographical references and index.
    ISBN 0–313–30911–6 (alk. paper)
    1. American fiction—Asian American authors Dictionaries.
    2. American fiction—Asian American authors—Bio-bibliography
    Dictionaries.   3. Asian Americans—Intellectual life Dictionaries.
    4. Novelists, American—Biography—Dictionaries.   5. Asian Americans
    in literature Dictionaries.   I. Nelson, Emmanuel S. (Emmanuel
    Sampath), 1954–   .
    PS153.A84A825   2000
    813'.5409895—dc21   99–16099

British Library Cataloguing in Publication Data is available.

Library of Congress Catalog Card Number: 99–16099
ISBN: 0–313–30911–6

First published in 2000

Greenwood Press, 88 Post Road West, Westport, CT 06881
An imprint of Greenwood Publishing Group, Inc.
www.greenwood.com

Printed in the United States of America

The paper used in this book complies with the
Permanent Paper Standard issued by the National
Information Standards Organization (Z39.48–1984).

10 9 8 7 6 5 4 3 2 1

Contents

Preface

Asian American literature, as a distinct area of literary studies, now enjoys a level of critical recognition and institutional legitimacy that was unimaginable when academic interest in the field began on a modest scale about twenty-five years ago. This early interest in Asian American writing during the mid-1970s was generated by a variety of seemingly unrelated developments. A major factor was the Civil Rights movement of the 1960s and the spirit of ethnic nationalism it engendered among various marginalized minority groups in the United States. Student activism, often energized by radical opposition to American military adventurism in Asia, helped create a political climate conducive to ethnicization of curriculum on many influential American campuses. Soon academic programs in Asian American studies, often in embryonic forms, began to emerge on some of the campuses on the West Coast. The Immigration Reform Act of 1965, too, played a role. This bold piece of progressive legislation brought new waves of Asian immigrants to the United States. Because the immigration policy adopted in 1965 gave preference to skilled workers and professionals, the new immigrants tended to be highly educated and solidly middle-class. By the early 1970s anthologies of creative writing by Asian Americans began to appear; these collections provided forums for several young writers to showcase their talent. In 1976, Maxine Hong Kingston published her landmark autobiographical novel, *The Woman Warrior*. It won the National Book Critics Circle Award and soon became one of the most widely taught texts on American campuses.

Since the mid-1970s numerous Asian American writers, such as Amy Tan, Michael Ondaatje, and Bharati Mukherjee, have gained considerable critical as well as commercial success. There are now almost two dozen anthologies of creative works by Asian American artists. Some of these volumes, such as Shawn Wang's *Asian American Literature: A Brief Introduction and Anthology*

(1996), use ethnicity as the primary organizing principle. Other collections—such as Shirley Geok-lin Lim's *The Forbidden Stitch: An Asian American Women's Anthology* (1989) and Elaine H. Kim's *Making More Waves: New Writing by Asian American Women* (1997)—highlight issues of gender. A few anthologies are devoted exclusively to certain topics, such as growing up Asian in America or gay/lesbian sexualities. The Modern Language Association's cumulative bibliography now lists hundreds of scholarly articles on Asian American literature. Almost a dozen book-length studies devoted exclusively to Asian American writing have been published in the last decade alone. This unprecedented interest is also partly a function of the increasing globalization of literary studies in general. Not only can Asian American writing be read as "minority" discourse within the national contexts of multicultural United States and Canada, but large segments of that writing can also be studied in transnational, diasporic, and postcolonial contexts. The growing focus on global approaches to local literatures thus makes Asian American writing a particularly rich and fascinating field.

The publication of this reference volume reflects the new academic status of Asian American literature. The first work of its kind, this sourcebook is designed as a guide to the lives and works of seventy Asian American novelists. The chapters on the authors begin with relevant biographical information, offer interpretive commentary on their major works, provide overviews of the critical reception accorded their works, and conclude with selected bibliographies that list, separately, primary and secondary sources. Advanced scholars will find this a useful reference tool, but its user-friendly style, format, and level of complexity should make it accessible to a much wider audience. To facilitate cross-referencing, whenever a novelist who is also the subject of a chapter in this volume is first mentioned, an asterisk appears next to his or her name.

My use of the terms "American" and "Asian" deserves explanation. For the purposes of this reference work, I have opted to disregard the political boundary between the United States and Canada. Since the historical and current experiences of Asians in Canada and in the United States are substantially similar, it makes little sense to divide them arbitrarily. Therefore, this volume covers both countries. My use of the term "Asian" reflects the definitional changes it has undergone in the last twenty-five years or so. The editors of the earliest anthologies of Asian American writing—for example, Kai-yu Hsu and Helen Palumobinskas's *Asian-American Authors* (1972) and Jeffrey Paul Chan's *Aiiieeeee! An Anthology of Asian American Writers* (1974)—use the term to refer only to Americans of Chinese, Filipino, and Japanese backgrounds. Such a narrow definition is understandable: in the early 1970s, the vast majority of published Asian American writers came from these groups, primarily because these immigrant groups had longer histories in North America than other Asians, and numerically, too, they were more significant. Elaine H. Kim, in her pioneering *Asian American Literature: An Introduction to the Writings and Their Social Context* (1982), slightly expands the definition. She adds Korean Americans to the other three groups. Shirley Geok-lin Lim and Amy Ling's immensely useful *Reading the Literatures of Asian America*, also published in 1992, widens the scope even more: it includes the Vietnamese, Hawaiians, and South Asians as well. Alpana Sharma Knippling's *New Immigrant Literatures of the United States* (1996)—a Greenwood project for which I served as an advisory editor—defines the term even more inclusively. Under the rubric "Asian American," she lists American writers of Arab, Armenian, Chinese, Filipino, Indian, Iranian, Japanese, Korean, and Pakistani backgrounds. Knippling's definition is a bold step in the right direction. Her inclusion of Iranian and Arab writers is simply a recognition of geopolitical realities from a non-Western perspective: that part of the world that is referred to as "the Middle East" in the Western press, for example, is generally called "West Asia" in the Asian media.

I have made a conscious effort to be just as inclusive. A majority of the writers in this volume have East Asian backgrounds; a few have West Asian origins. Several have roots in the countries of the Indian subcontinent; some are Hawaiians. This inclusiveness, however, is not an attempt to conflate disparate identities or to impose artificial homogeneity on distinct cultural groups. Rather, my widening of the definition is based on the recognition of the geographical vastness of the Asian continent, and I suspect that even broader definitions might become necessary in the future. There are, of course, significant and often self-evident differences among Asian Americans, but their shared experiences of migrancy, postcoloniality, and racialized otherness do indeed provide a sufficient basis to establish meaningful lateral connections.

My purpose in editing this volume is not to help define an Asian American literary canon. I am, however, acutely conscious of the fact that a reference work such as this inevitably, even if unintentionally, will be implicated in the process of canon formation. The central objective of this volume is, in fact, to offer reliable, thorough, and up-to-date biographical, bibliographical, and critical information on a range of Asian American novelists. Some of the artists included here are first-generation immigrants; some are third- or even fourth-generation Americans. Some have working-class backgrounds; some are privileged children of affluent parents. Each of them projects his or her singular perspective on a variety of themes. However, all of them, on some level, explore the personal and political implications of being Asian in America. In that process they re-define the very idea of America and who, precisely, is an American.

Let me take this opportunity to thank all the contributors to this volume. Their prompt, enthusiastic, and professional handling of the assignments made my editorial role a genuinely enjoyable one. Many thanks also to Dr. George Butler, senior editor at Greenwood Press, for his unfailing support for this and many other publishing projects.

Meena Alexander
(1951–)

Brunda Moka-Dias

BIOGRAPHY

Born on February 17, 1951, in Allahabad, India, to George and Mary Alexander, Meena Alexander's life journey has moved through many different countries. As a result of her father's government job, she grew up going back and forth, six months in each country, between Kerala, India, and Sudan, North Africa. Entering the University of Khartoum at the early age of thirteen, Alexander finished college in Sudan and went to England for graduate studies at the age of eighteen. At the University of Nottingham, Alexander earned her Ph.D. in English by writing her doctoral dissertation on construction of self-identity in the early English Romantic poets. Enriched by an education, Alexander, however, returned to India to get away from the displacement and discomfort she experienced in England. Back in India at the age of twenty-two, Alexander taught at various universities from 1974 to 1979, including the University of Delhi, Jawaharlal Nehru University, and the University of Hyderabad. In 1979 Alexander left Hyderabad for New York, having married an American she met in India, to start life as a newly married, pregnant wife.

Although her identity remained anchored in India, particularly Kerala, this constant movement through different cultures and continents affected Alexander. As she ponders in *Fault Lines*, her memoir: "And what of all the cities and small towns and villages I have lived in since birth: Allahabad, Tiruvella, Kozencheri, Pune, Delhi, Hyderabad, all within the borders of India; Khartoum in the Sudan; Nottingham in Britain; and now this island of Manhattan? How should I spell out these fragments of a broken geography?" (2). As she continues to explore this notion of creating a life (for her life does not fall into traditional narratives) in her writing, Alexander also has a career in teaching. A resident of New York

City, Alexander currently teaches English and women's studies at Hunter College and the Graduate Center at City University of New York (CUNY). She is also a lecturer in poetry in the Writing Program at Columbia University.

MAJOR WORKS AND THEMES

Alexander started out as a poet but now writes across genres. Having written poetry from the age of fifteen, Alexander's first publication was a collection of poetry titled *The Bird's Bright Ring*. Her poetry appears in many journals and anthologies, including *Critical Quarterly, Chandrabhaga*, and the *Massachusetts Review*, but she has also published several volumes of poetry, including *Stone Roots, House of a Thousand Doors*, and, the latest one, *River and Bridge*. Besides poetry, Alexander has a memoir titled *Fault Lines*. She has also published *The Shock of Arrival: Reflections on Postcolonial Experience*, a collection of poems, essays, anecdotes, imaginary dialogues, and autobiographical explorations. *Nampally Road* was her first novel, followed by her second one, titled *Manhattan Music*. Women's experiences and the diasporic consciousness are major themes in Alexander's works. Specifically, Alexander explores what it means to be cast as woman. In an article titled "Creating a Life through Literature," author Jeffrey R. Young states: "Self-creation is a familiar theme in Meena Alexander's work. For years, she has used her poetry and fiction to piece together a cohesive identity—to figure out what it means to be a woman born in India, educated in England, living in America" (B8). Indeed, images of women and the context of the diasporic consciousness are very important experiential and intellectual topics for the author.

Based on history and on her own experiences (as most of her writing is), Alexander's *Nampally Road* is narrated from the point of view of Mira Kannadical, an English professor in Hyderabad who has returned to India after having been a student in England for four years. Feeling dislocated and out of place in England, the protagonist decides to make a fresh start in her homeland:

I returned to India determined to start afresh, make up a self that had some continuity with what I was. It was my fond hope that by writing a few poems, or a few prose pieces, I could start to stitch it all together: my birth in India, a few years after national independence, my colonial education, my rebellion against the arranged marriage my mother had in mind for me, my years of research in England.(30)

However, Mira returns to an India filled with unrest and turbulence. Mira recognizes that her writing does not hold together and collapses in an environment of "too much poverty and misery," leading her to realize that the world around her does not "permit the kinds of writing" she had "once learned to value" (32). So, recontextualizing her teaching and writing, Mira attempts a definition of herself by getting involved in the society around her. Teaching Wordsworth in Hyderabad, Mira begins to ponder differently on the notions of memory, history, and consciousness in her new, volatile environment. She forms important relationships with Durgabai, a mother figure, and Ramu, her lover. Her bond with Durgabai, which "wove the world together" (69), and her relationship with Ramu, which enhances her social and political awareness, for example, open up new worlds even as they break them apart; the rape of Rameeza Be and the atrocities committed against the weak, whom she sees as pawns in political games, make Mira question her own life and the life of the nation. In this haunting and lyrical novel, Alexander creates Mira, a touching heroine who struggles to piece together a life and bring together her past and her present in the context of contemporary India.

The themes of history, memory, and female dislocation are continued in Alexander's second novel, the focus of which is contemporary America. Unlike the tightly knit *Nampally Road, Manhattan Music*, a sprawling narrative, brings to mind a quote by Saleem Sinai, the protagonist of Salman Rushdie's *Midnight's Children*, who ponders: "Is this an Indian disease, this urge to encapsulate the whole of reality?" (*Midnight's Children*, New York: Knopf, 1980, 84). Alexander's second novel does exactly this by touching on many different topics in many different places via characters who are of many spaces. In the course of her narrative, Alexander weaves into her narrative many social and political incidents from India and America, for example, Hindu-Muslim riots in Hyderabad, the threat of Muslim fundamentalist terrorism in Manhattan, the assassination of Rajiv Gandhi by a Sri Lanka suicide bomber, racism toward Indians in New Jersey, Christian fundamentalism vis-à-vis David Koresh and a Tamilian evangelist named Pirabhakaran in Texas, and the immigrant issues of New York City.

The novel begins with an opening titled "Overture: Monsoon Flood" in the voice of Draupadi, a performance artist of Indo-Caribbean heritage. From then on the chapters are often titled as in "Sitting," "Stirring," "Turning," and so on to indicate stasis and motion as if initiating moves toward negotiation that is an inevitable and integral part of immigrant life. Negotiating identities is a major part of Alexander's work. *Manhattan Music* is a hard novel to sum up, but the gist of the plot goes as follows: Sandhya Rosenblum is an immigrant from India married to an American Jewish man, Stephen Rosenblum. Early on, readers encounter the protagonist's experiencing a sense of dislocation from her homeland while also feeling displaced in her marriage. As the mother of young Dora, Sandhya attempts to identify as a Rosenblum: " 'Rosenblum' is what I am now, this bloom, this life, these roses" (9). Despite this reiteration, the pieces of Sandhya's life do not fit together easily. Unresolved feelings about Gautam, her old love from India, and ambivalence toward her marriage, however, do not keep Sandhya from falling in love with Rashid, an Egyptian immigrant in Manhattan. Furthermore, a sudden trip to Kerala to tend to an ailing father also exposes the protagonist to an indifferent and reclusive sister steeped in Christian evangelism that spans India and America. Questioning the idea of "home" and "return," Sandhya returns to an impatient Stephen and Dora in a fragile condition. Upon her return to Manhattan, Sandhya realizes that Rashid does not want a future with her, and, driven to despair, Sandhya unsuccessfully attempts to kill herself in her friend Draupadi's apartment. The novel ends on a hopeful, though mellow, note, with Sandhya's returning to the city after a period of rest with her cousin Sakhi in New Jersey. Negotiating with, and reconciling to, her new life, Sandhya is "no longer fearful" (227) and realizes: "There was a place for her here, though what it might be she could never have spelled out. And she, who had never trusted words very much, knew she would live out her life in America" (228).

Central to Sandhya's life in Manhattan are other characters such as Draupadi/Dopti, her cousin Jay, and cousin Sakhi. Of the three, Draupadi is probably the most important because she functions as Sandhya's alter ego. Of mixed parentage (an Indo-Caribbean mother and a father of mixed African and Asian heritage), born and brought up in Gingee, New York, Draupadi is able to make it "all up in the present tense" (119), while Sandhya is bogged down by her history and memory. As their friendship grows, so does their understanding of each other, including that of the mythic Draupadi, wife of the Pandavas, who also experienced exile. Finally, the New World, hybrid Dopti, an incarnation of the Old World, mythic Draupadi, saves Sandhya from an attempted suicide, as if to say that the challenge of exile is in survival and not in death. Draupadi's words to Sandhya are poignant: " 'We each have to be many women . . . After all, how many lives did the *Mahabharata* lady have? Crawling through a tunnel to save her life, wasn't she someone quite different from the princess in the palace? And then, the woman bartered in the dice-throw between men, think of her shame, her rage" (222).

Through the characters of Sakhi and Draupadi, Alexander highlights the need to rewrite history from a feminist and diasporic point of view. Sakhi's involvement in antiracist, antisexist work and Draupadi's performance art on subjects as varied as "CC" (Christopher Columbus), "HDT" (Henry David Thoreau and *Walden*), and Draupadi from the *Mahabharata* attempt to bring together the Indian diasporic woman at crossroads in America interrogating what it means to be "American." In coming to terms with ethnicity and femaleness in America, Alexander feels the need to create a wholeness of being that resists the numerous fractures of migration but is left wondering, as she does in *Fault Lines*: "What parts of my past can I hold onto when I enter this life? Must I dump it all? Can I bear to?" (198). As if in answer to this question, Rashid in *Manhattan Music* tells the protagonist, Sandhya that " 'the past is a rough instrument we have to play. People like us have to make up the past from little bits and pieces, play it. Imagine strings running through, playing it" (78). Problematizing the notion of the past by terming it a "rough instrument," Rashid points to underlying elements of memory not as nostalgia or documentation but as a transformative exploration that provides the knowledge through which location is articulated and made to fit the present, multiple, subjective positions. Through her characters who espouse this notion of memory, Alexander puts forth a concept of memory that resists the American transcendentalist notion of the "American self" as without memory, tradition, or history. Thus, memory and history figure in Alexander's work in an important, symbiotic way that connects India and America. Alexander explores self-invention in America vis-à-vis memory and history.

CRITICAL RECEPTION

Most of the criticism of Alexander's work is positive. Her poetry is well received and is often cited for its imagery and lyrical quality. The author's memoir is increasingly anthologized and is on the reading list of courses on women's studies, postcolonial literature, and multicultural literature in America. Alexander's *Shock of Arrival* is seen as an important work in academic circles, with positive comments from literary/cultural critics like Homi K. Bhabha and Gayatri Spiyak. Some of her poetry has been staged as plays, and her poetry is also the subject of a forthcoming documentary film on Asian American women's poetry. *Nampally Road* was named the Editor's Choice in the *Village Voice* and received favorable write-ups in the *Los Angeles Times* and *Publishers Weekly*. *Manhattan Music*, however, has received mixed reviews. A blurb by Chitra Divakarumi on the novel's back over favorably states: "At once violent, erotic and somber, *Manhattan Music* is infused with the power of myth and poetry and the inner life, the electric intersection of characters who illuminate for the reader both the Old World and the New." Reviewer Susheela Rao, however, points out the following:

The coda, consisting of four poems by Arjun Sankaramangalam [the photographer-turned-poet Jay], tries to bring the orchestrated music of Manhattan to a conclusion through sheer, unbridled fancy in its attempt to coalesce widely scattered events and things, even as the story does, and challenges critics to find in these pages reasoned imagination and imaginative reasoning. (456)

In response to this quote, it is necessary to bring one's attention to the "Manhattan" part of the novel. Despite the title, which includes "Manhattan" in it, the novel does not limit itself to this island in New York. In fact, one could say that because of it, the novel (like the city) crosses and questions borders. This "Manhattan" factor supports the "spilling over the edge" aspect of the novel and keeps it from being incoherent and randomly scattered. The stream-of-consciousness style of writing in the novel, especially toward the end and mainly in Draupadi's voice, fits in with the performative attitude of the city and gives credibility to the character of the performance artist Draupadi and the poetry of Arjun Sankaramangalm. The novel is also filled with literary allusions to the Indian epics, Shelley's Frankenstein, the British Romantic poets, Thoreau and Emerson, to name a few; academic language also sporadically appears in the text with references to concepts such as late capitalism and postmodernity. As such, the novel presumes an audience not too far removed from the author's artist/academic location. On the whole, *Manhattan Music* is as intense as its characters who try to make sense of history and memory by attempting to bridge the past and the present.

BIBLIOGRAPHY

Works by Meena Alexander

Poetry

The Bird's Bright Ring. Calcutta: Writers Workshop, 1976.
I Root My Name. Calcutta: United Writers, 1977.
In the Middle Earth. New Delhi: Enact, 1977.
Without Place. Calcutta: Writers Workshop, 1977.
Stone Roots. New Delhi: Arnold-Heinemann, 1980.
House of a Thousand Doors. Washington, DC: Three Continents Press, 1988.
The Storm, a Poem in Five Parts. New York: Red Dust Press, 1989.
Night-Scene, the Garden. New York: Red Dust Press, 1991.
River and Bridge. Toronto: TSAR, 1996.

Memoirs and Reflections

Fault Lines. New York: Feminist Press, 1992.
The Shock of Arrival: Reflections on Postcolonial Experience. Boston: South End Press, 1996.

Novels

Nampally Road. San Francisco: Mercury House, 1991.
Manhattan Music. San Francisco: Mercury House, 1997.

Studies of Meena Alexander

Abraham, Ayisha. "On Writing and Contemporary Issues: Interview with Meena Alexander." *Toronto South Asian Review* (Winter 1993).
Assisi, Francis. "Humane Feminism Incites Poet Meena Alexander." *India West* (February 15, 1991): 1, 44.
Bahri, Deepika, and Vasudeva, Mary. "Interview with Meena Alexander." In *Between the Lines: South Asians on Post-Colonial Identity and Culture*. Philadelphia: Temple University Press, 1996. 35–53.
Bhargava, Tulsi. "Of Earth and Life." Rev. of *Fault Lines*. *The Book Review* (July 1994).
Dave, Shilpa. "The Doors to Home and History: Post-Colonial Identities in Meena Alexander and Bharati Mukherjee." *Amerasia Journal* 19. 3 (1993): 103–111.
Desai, Anita. "Women Well Set Free." *New York Review of Books* (January 16, 1992) 42–45.
Divakaruni, Chitra. "Living in a Pregnant Time: Meena Alexander Discusses Feminism, Literature, Decolonization." *India Currents* (May 1991): 19, 58.
Francia, Luis H. Rev. of *Nampally Road*. *Village Voice* (March 26, 1991): 74.
George, Rosemary. "Displacements and the Place of Literature." In *The Politics of Home:*

Postcolonial Relocations and Twentieth Century Fiction. Cambridge: Cambridge University Press, 1996.

Grewal, Inderpal. "Reading and Writing the South Asian Diaspora: Feminism and Nationalism in North America." In *Our Feet Walk the Sky: Women of the South Asian Diaspora*. San Francisco: Aunt Lute, 1993. 226–236.

Gurleen, Grewal. "Indian American Literature." In *New Immigrant Literature in the United States: A Source Book to Our Multicultural Heritage*. Ed. Alpana Knippling. Westport, CT: Greenwood Press, 1996. 91–108.

Jain, Madhu. "Coming Home: An Expatriate's Lyrical Debut." *India Today* (May 15 1991): 167.

Katrak, Ketu. "The Barbed Wire Is Taken into the Heart." In *An Interethnic Companion to Asian American Literature*. Ed. King-Kok Cheung. Cambridge: Cambridge University Press, 1997.

King, Bruce. Rev. of *House of a Thousand Doors*. *World Literature Written in English* 28. 2 (1988): 379–80.

Knight, Denise. "Meena Alexander." In *Writers of the Indian Diaspora*. Ed. E. Nelson. Westport, CT: Greenwood Press, 1993.

Kumar, Manjushree. "Journey through Time, Meena Alexander's *Fault Lines*." In *Indian Women Novelists*. Ed. R. K. Dhawan. New Delhi: Prestige Books, 1995. 208–221.

Moka-Dias, Brunda. *"Cultural Collage: Narratives of South Asian Women in America."* Diss, Rutgers University, 1997. Ann Arbor, MI: UMI, 1997.

Perry, John Oliver. "Exiled by a Woman's Body: Substantial Phenomena in the Poetry of Meena Alexander." *Journal of South Asian Literature* 12 (Winter/Spring 1986): 1–10.

Rao, Susheela. "Review of *Manhattan Music*." *World Literature Today* 72.2: 456–57.

San Juan E. "From Identity Politics to Strategies on Disruption: USA Self and/or Asian Alter?" In *Asian Americans: Collages of Identity*. Ed. Lee C. Lee. Cornell Asian American Studies Monograph Series no. 1. Ithaca, NY: Cornell University Press, 1992. 122–39.

Stephen, Sumida. "The Pressure of Our Bodies: Different Historics, Gender and Seven Asian American Writers." In *Asian Americans: Collages of Identity*. Ed. Lee C. Lee. Cornell Asian American Studies Monograph Series no. 1. Ithaca, NY: Cornell University Press, 1992. 109–116.

Tharu, Susie. "A Conversation with Meena Alexander." *Chandrabhaga: A Magazine of World Writing* 7 (Summer 1982): 69–74.

Young, Jeffrey R. "Creating a Life through Literature." *Chronicle of Higher Education* (March 14, 1997): B8.

Himani Bannerji
(1942–   )

Geoffrey Kain

BIOGRAPHY

Himani Bannerji was born in Gangatia, Mymensingh district, in what is now Bangladesh. One of seven children, she was educated until high school in Dhaka, then in Calcutta. She received a B.A. degree from Visva Bharati, Santiniketan, then an M.A. in English from Jadavpur University, Calcutta, in 1965. From 1965 to 1969 she served as senior lecturer at Jadavpur University in English and comparative literature. She left India for Canada in 1969 and took an M.A. degree in English from the University of Toronto in 1970. After teaching at Victoria College, Toronto, from 1970 to 1974, she taught as course director in the Department of Social Sciences at Atkinson College, York University (Toronto) from 1974 to 1988. She also began work toward a Ph.D. in sociology at the University of Toronto in 1980. Her major program of study, "Ideology and Social Organization in the Third World," was complemented by two minors, the first in "Theories of Culture and Ideology," the second in "Ideology and Gender Relations." Her Ph.D. dissertation, "The Politics of Representation: A Study of Class and Class Struggle in the Theatre of West Bengal" (1988), sets the stage for much of her subsequent work, focusing as it does on "political art" ("political culture and cultural politics"). The dissertation material has since been revised and published as a book titled *Mirror of Class: Essays on Political Theatre* (1998). Bannerji has taught in the Department of Sociology at York University in Toronto since 1988. She returns to India annually, teaching in Calcutta, speaking at conferences, writing on Indian issues, and organizing projects such as one on attitude toward fertility among slum women in Calcutta, which she directed in the School of Women's Studies, Jadavpur University, from 1994 to 1997. While she divides her time between Toronto and Calcutta, she concedes that she continues to feel most at home in India. As she writes in *Thinking Through* (1995), "I have spent half my life in Toronto, coming no nearer and going no further than I did in the first few years. This journey of mine in Canada is like an arc, suspended, which has not found a ground yet" (1). Her antiracist politics have, in fact, been developed by her experiences as an Indian immigrant in Canada; her Marxist ideals, she maintains, stems from her recognition of her own economically privileged status (G. Kain, personal correspondence, January 5, 1999).

MAJOR WORKS AND THEMES

Himani Bannerji writes in a variety of genres and is perhaps best known for her sociopolitical essays, through which she challenges the dominant culture from an ideological locus of feminism/Marxism/antiracism. She has also published two volumes of poetry (*A Separate Sky*, 1982, and *Doing Time*, 1986) and various short stories, translated a Bengali folktale, and written film reviews. She has published one novel, *Coloured Pictures*, written for an adolescent audience. The short novel is lively and enjoyable in its own right but is certainly best understood within the context of her other antiracist and feminist works.

To clarify Bannerji's sociopolitical perspective, her exposure of, and resistance to, the oppression of race and gender and its relationship to the themes of her fiction (and poetry) and in order to develop a context for her short novel *Coloured Pictures*, reference to some of her critical/theoretical work is especially useful. For example, in the Introduction of her volume of essays *The Writing on the Wall* (1993), she states that she "remain[s] very suspicious, not about naivete, or revolutionary romanticism, but about the pragmatism of our 'postindustrial, postmodern, postsocialist, posthuman' world" and that she attempts "to make sense of culture's (for example theatre, literature, cinema) relationship to what I had grown up calling the realms of the political and historical. Issues spinning out of colonialism, imperialism, class and gender" (ix). Pursuing this ideological end, she maintains in her fiction what may be described as a style of "analytical realism." Her interest in, or commitment to, this narrative method is pointedly described in (among other places) Chapter 7 of her Ph.D. dissertation, "Realism and the Politics of Re-Presentation . . . ," in which she cites Bertolt Brecht's definition of "realism," a definition that clearly describes Bannerji's own authorial position:

Realist means: laying bare society's network/showing up the dominant viewpoint as the viewpoint of the dominators/writing from the standpoint of the class which has prepared the broadest solutions for the most pressing problems afflicting human society/ emphasizing the dynamics of development. (301)

Central to the "dominant viewpoints" Bannerji seeks to "lay bare" in her fiction is what she identifies in her essay "The Passion of Naming" (*Thinking Through*) as a misguided, essentializing notion of the "raced" or colonized peoples.

Through "imposed stereotypes," they "become essentialized, unified or totalized as cultural entities" (26). Resisting the ideology of imperialism, the appropriation of culture by the "so-called West" remains her passion; she is committed to "taking sides, believing that things can change, fighting for it, an activist epistemology grounded in commitment" (*Writing on the Wall* x).

The imposition and impact of cultural stereotypes and methods for facing and resisting these negative social forces are the central themes of *Coloured Pictures*, Bannerji's short novel for young adolescents, which works as a piece with Bannerji's other work concerning racism and sexism. In fact, Bannerji notes that the publisher for whom the novel was originally intended had requested antiracist educational material for the young but then retreated from publishing the book because it "was too political." The novel's central characters are a thirteen-year-old South Asian girl, Sujata, and her social studies teacher, Stephen Stephenson. Sujata bravely stand up to, and physically strikes back at, a local racist bully who attacks her and her friends, while Stephenson is a leading activist organizing the minority communities, in particular, against the increasingly aggressive presence of the Ku Klux Klan (KKK) in Toronto. Sujata first impresses her peers by speaking out in Stephenson's class about racism and KKK violence in her neighborhood, and this encourages an open and ongoing classroom dialogue on racism, cultural misunderstanding, and the ideology of white supremacy.

At one point in the novel, the children, who are of varied ethnic backgrounds, discuss some of the festivals they celebrate, and Sujata refers to the Durga Puja; after she briefly explains who the goddess Durga is, her friend Joe says, "It's interesting . . . that it's a woman who stands for power and evil is a man, and she kills him in a fight. Weird! Where did that come from?" (54). This exchange foreshadows Sujata's violent face-off with the red-haired, white-skinned, racist bully Bob, who taunts her for "smell[ing] like hell. All that curry." Although the bully beats her, Sujata pummels him also, "like a tigress," and "strangely enough she felt no pain, only a feeling of lightness" (58). Sujata and her friends join Mr. Stephenson in a large antiracist rally in the park and a march to the steps of the KKK headquarters in the city. The novel ends positively, with the children's gaining understanding of the power of community organization and the need for unified resistance to intimidation and racial hatred.

CRITICAL RECEPTION

In works on Canadian immigrant writers or Canadian women writers, passages devoted to Himani Bannerji are common, but studies committed exclusively to her work are scarce. Two of these studies are worthy of attention: " 'Some Kind of Weapon': Himani Bannerji and the Praxis of Resistance" by Roshan G. Shahani and "Breaking the Circle: Recreating the Immigrant Self in Selected Works of Himani Bannerji" by Susan Jacob. Both critical essays are contained in the volume of essays *By, For and About: Feminist Cultural Politics* (1994).

Shahani focuses on Bannerji's poetry, emphasizing qualities that also typify her fiction. Her poetry, according to Shahani, is distinguished from much of the other poetry being published by "ethnic" immigrants in Canada that is comfortably sanctioned by the "officially approved policy of multiculturalism" (180). Rather than nostalgia for a lost home or laments over a lost cultural self, Bannerji's work "interrogates the state's cultural and political ideology which under the label of multiculturalism is seen by her to systematically diffuse and dismantle oppositional energies" (181). Her work is "a critique of a system, not a complaint of a localised problem" (183). Shahani points also to Bannerji's insistent realism in her poetry, just as it informs her theoretical work and her fiction.

In "Breaking the Circle . . . ," Susan Jacob surveys the themes of race and gender oppression in Bannerji's fiction, nonfiction, and poetry, offering an introduction to the author by citing various passages that clarify these points of view. Like Shahani, Jacob notes Bannerji's impatience with symbol and metaphor and her reluctance to commit to mainstream notions of the immigrant's travails. Instead, Jacob notes, Bannerji assumes such realities as sexism and racism under the inclusive concept of imperialism, and hers is a thoroughly anti-imperialist ideology and aesthetic.

BIBLIOGRAPHY

Works by Himani Bannerji

Novel

Coloured Pictures. Toronto: Sister Vision Press, 1991.

Poetry

A Separate Sky. Toronto: Domestic Bliss, 1982.
Doing Time. Toronto: Sister Vision Press, 1986.

Essays

(Et al.). *Unsettling Relations: The University as a Site of Feminist Struggle*. Toronto: Women's Press, 1992.
(Ed.). *Returning the Gaze: Essays on Racism, Feminism and Politics*. Toronto: Sister Vision Press, 1993.
The Writing on the Wall: Essays on Culture and Politics. Toronto: TSAR, 1993.
"The Sound Barrier: Translating Ourselves in Language and Experience." In *By, For and About: Feminist Cultural Politics*. Ed. Wendy Waring. Toronto: Women's Press, 1994. 33–52.
Thinking Through: Essays on Feminism, Marxism, and Anti-Racism. Toronto: Women's Press, 1995.
Mirror of Class: Essays on Political Theatre. Calcutta: University of Calcutta Press, 1998.

Selected Short Stories and Fables

The Two Sisters. Toronto: Kids Can Press, 1978. (Folktale in Bengali and English)
"The Story of a Birth." *Fireweed: A Feminist Quarterly* 16 (1983): 123–33.
"On a Cold Day." In *Her Mother's Ashes.* Ed. Nurjehan Aziz. Toronto: TSAR, 1994.
    26–31.
"The Moon and My Mother." In *Contours of the Heart: South Asians Map North Amer-
    ica.* Ed. Sunaina Maira and Rajini Srikanth. New York: Asian American Writers
    Workshop, 1996. 188–96.

Studies of Himani Bannerji

Jacob, Susan. "Breaking the Circle: Recreating the Immigrant Self in Selected Works of
    Himani Bannerji." In *By, For and About: Feminist Cultural Politics.* Ed. Wendy
    Waring. Toronto: Women's Press, 1994. 33–52.
Shahani, Roshan G. " 'Some Kind of Weapon': Himani Bannerji and the Praxis of Re-
    sistance." In *By, For and About: Feminist Cultural Politics.* Ed. Wendy Waring.
    Toronto: Women's Press, 1994, 179–88.

Susham Bedi
(1945–   )

Brunda Moka-Dias

BIOGRAPHY

Susham Bedi is a leading Indian author, writing in Hindi and living in the United States. Bedi was born in Ferozpur, Punjab, on July 1, 1945. She started writing in high school and continued to write in college by taking part in competitions, and some of her early writings were also published in magazines. She studied at Delhi University and Punjab University in India, where she also taught Hindi literature. A scholar of Hindi drama and theater, her Ph.D. thesis, titled "Innovation and Experimentation in Contemporary Hindi Drama," was published as a book in 1984. She was a leading actress and commentator on Indian television in the late 1960s and 1970s. She was also a correspondent for the *Times of India* at Brussels in Belgium (1974–1979). In 1979 Bedi came to the United States because of her husband's job as director of the Indian Tea Board. From 1990 to 1991, she contributed to a BBC weekly program, *Letters from Abroad*, in which she discussed day-to-day issues about life in New York.

Dr. Bedi is a professor of Hindi language and literature at Columbia University. She was also a visiting professor at New York University from 1993 to 1998. Coming to the United States gave Bedi's creative writing a new impetus. As she states in "In the Park":

To write tirelessly free of any questions, of freedom, could only be possible in America. I have found an objectivity which can only be found outside India. . . . My writings have enriched from the point of view of my subjects. I have the freedom to explore the world from both angles; although I have been writing from my childhood, the real voice in my writing came after I left India. (103)

MAJOR WORKS AND THEMES

Bedi has published five novels and a short story collection. Her novels have been translated into other Indian and European languages. Two of her novels (*Havan* and *Lautna*) were translated into Urdu and published in Lahore, Pakistan. Her novels have also been adopted in courses taught at various American and Indian universities. Her first novel, *Havan*, was translated by the reputable translator Dr. David Rubin and published by Heinemann International in 1993 under the title of *The Fire Sacrifice*. This novel sold about 6,000 copies in English and was reviewed favorably in the U.K., India, Pakistan, and the United States. Her other published novels are *Lautna* (Return, 1993), *Itar* (Other, 1997), *Katra-dar-Katra* (Drop by Drop, 1994), and *Gatha Amarbel Ki* (A Song of the Amarbel, to be published). A collection of her short stories entitled *Chiriya Aur Cheel* (Sparrow and the Kite) was published in 1995. Currently, she is working on her sixth novel, entitled *Battlefronts*, and a couple of short stories. Besides the translation of *Havan*, David Rubin has also completed the translation of *Lautna* as *The Portrait of Mira* (to be published) and two other short stories titled "In the Park" and "Death in America." The first is anthologized in *Odyssey*, and the latter is yet to be published. Translations of her other novels (*Itar* and *Gatha Amarbel Ki*) are also in the works by two different translators.

Bedi's works explore the immigrant condition in many ways, often from the point of view of a female protagonist. The central motif of the novel *Havan* or *The Fire Sacrifice* is a Hindu ritual that leads to self-purification and the fulfillment of desires. As the novel begins, Guddo performs this ritual and chants Sanskrit prayers in her New York apartment. Written in the social-realist tradition as pioneered by the famous Hindi writer Premchand, *The Fire Sacrifice* is the story of Guddo the female protagonist, who moves to America from India to make a better life for herself and her family. Invited by her youngest sister, Pinky, Guddo comes to the United States as a widow with a young son, leaving behind two daughters in boarding school, and stays with Pinky and her family. However, the pressures of life in Manhattan and the incompatibility of extended family life with American reality create a rift between the sisters and force Guddo to move in with her other sister, Gita. Thus begins Guddo's story in America, and readers find Guddo making sacrifices and facing difficult situation in order to survive in the New World. Cultural translation does not come easily to Guddo, who is a product of traditional values and religious upbringing; in fact, one could say that the novel makes cultural translation highly questionable in light of the dark events that occur in the lives of Guddo, her sisters, and their families—death, divorce, drug trafficking, and domestic violence, for example— but the absence of a happy ending does not necessarily connote failure in the new land but points to the difficulties involved in the decision to start a new life in a new country. Vis-à-vis Guddo's life and the element of purification and sacrifice so central to the religious "havan," Bedi poses some important questions: Does one hold onto an essence of the pure, the authentic or sacrifice it for the new? How does one negotiate this conflict? Is it possible to bring India and America together?

Through the narrative, dichotomies and dilemmas overwhelm Guddo, and there seems to be nothing redeeming about life in America, but it is important to note that even in such situations Guddo does not set up India as the nostalgic ideal either. While Guddo is able to critically think about nations and ideologies, she has a difficult time getting herself unmoored from "her Arya Samaj moral standards" (92). Unable to reconcile her religious morality with her desire for Dr. Juneja, a married man, Guddo's feelings of guilt constantly torture her and convince her of the futility of the relationship. Her contradictions between the "Indian" and "American" also manifest in her appropriation and abrogation of cultures, thus complicating a simplistic representation of Guddo's identity. For example, even as she lectures to Mr. Batra, an old friend from India, about her purity and her "Indian" morals when he attempts to physically get close to her, she also has an affair with Dr. Juneja, who ends up being very beneficial to her children's future. Yet, when her doctor daughters, Amina and Tanima, face troubled marriages, Guddo is hesistant about the idea of divorce. However, Bedi creates in Guddo a complex character who shows her independent personality when she reprimands her daughters' meekness with their husbands by saying, "You are not inferior to your husbands in any respect" and adds, "so stand up and assert yourselves" (108). Her ideas on citizenship go beyond superficial concerns of money into questions of social commitment, and her analysis of American society vis-à-vis the Indian caste system shows a keen awareness of American notions of race and ethnicity on Guddo's part. According to her, "[T]he WASPS were the Brahmans, the Jews were the Kshatriyas, the Asians were the Vaishyas, the blacks the Shudras" (73).

However, in the end, Guddo is searching, she has many questions and contradictions and not many answers. Performing the ritual of the fire sacrifice, Guddo watches the fire and reflects on the meaning of culture and ritual. Watching the flames engulf the offerings poured into them, the protagonist laments the destructive nature of the fire but also reminds herself about the creative aspect of it. "But the ashes of the sacrificial fire are auspicious, aren't they? Beginnings of new life and new faith, the new generations who will spring up here, flourish here, take root in this new earth" (180). Thus, despite the cultural collision and its negative effects in Guddo's life, her hope for a better life comes through in her fiery, independent spirit.

Like Guddo, Mira, the protagonist of Bedi's soon-to-be-published *The Portrait of Mira*, is also strong-willed. This novel deals with the idea of return that immigrants harbor after they migrate to a new land. In this sense, it looks at the reverse of Guddo's experience. Mira is a classical dancer in India. When Mira comes over to the United States, it means that she loses her world and her culture, thus creating the "Returning Syndrome" in her. She questions societal conventions with regard to herself and her place in the world as an outsider in

American society and Indian society (as an untraditional woman). She never returns to India but does not let go of the possibility of return either.

CRITICAL RECEPTION

While Bedi's enthusiastic and favorable critical reception in India is based on her original writing in Hindi, her reception in the English-speaking world is based on the translation of her works. This difference is an important one to writers like Bedi who write for an audience outside the country they live in. Speaking on this subject with Eileen Tabios in the *Asian Pacific American Journal*, Bedi says: "I do feel it's good for me to have been translated. Writing in a language that is not even spoken by a recognized minority in our country can make a writer absolutely irrelevant. On the other hand, writers hardly have any choice other than writing in the language in which they are born" (91). Being recognized as a writer based only on a translation of her work leaves an entire body of work unknown to Bedi's new audiences, yet she acknowledges:

I have gained from being translated into English, including developing a Western audience. Also, when you are recognized outside India, you become more important within India. I've gotten valued more in my own country. Before, I only reached the Hindi-speaking people. I now have a wider audience within India—its English-speaking public. It is certainly nice to have recognition. (Tabios 92)

However, one needs to be aware that the politics of translation is complex— issues of language, style, and culture have to be carefully negotiated, often with no satisfactory or alternative solutions. As Bedi puts it: "Although the book generally got good reviews, I have some doubts about how certain parts were translated into English. But in those cases, I myself was unable to provide an English alternative" (Tabios 83). In Bedi's case, since her style of writing did not get translated, "criticism arose" that "sections of the writing were flat" (84). Most reviewers, though, have focused on the novel as a whole, with many seeing the novel as an insightful book about psychological transformations. Reviewing the novel in *World Literature Today*, Susheela Rao states: "It is undoubtedly accurate in describing the plight of Indian immigrants in America. It lays bare the tendency of many Indians to cling superficially to Hinduism and to the gradually disappearing Hindu tradition, which is in conflict with the new culture" (429). Applauding the writing of this novel by an Indian for an Indian audience (in India and the West), Professor Emeritus Ainslie Embree of Columbia sees *The Fire Sacrifice* as "breaking new ground" and the creation of Guddo as "a memorable character of quite extraordinary authority" (16).

BIBLIOGRAPHY

Works by Susham Bedi

Novels

Havan. Delhi: Parag, 1989. (*The Fire Sacrifice*. Trans. David Rubin. London: Heinemann, 1993.)
Katra-dar-Katra. Chandigarh: Abhishek, 1994.
Lautna. Delhi: Parag Prakashan, 1993.
Itar. Delhi: National Publishing House, 1997.
Gatha Amarbel Ki. Forthcoming.

Short Story Collection

Chiriya aur Cheel. Delhi: Parag, 1995.

Short Stories

"Ice Armor." *Journal of South Asian Literature* 30.3–4 (1995): 23–27.
"In the Park." In *Odyssey: Stories by Indian Women Writers Settled Abroad*. Ed. Divya Mathur. New Delhi: Star, 1998. 103–11.

Academic Publication

Innovation and Experimentation in Contemporary Hindi Drama. New Delhi: Paraga Prakasana, 1984.

Studies of Susham Bedi

Embree, Ainslie. Rev. of *The Fire Sacrifice*. *Journal of South Asian Literature* 28.1–2 (1993): 357–58.
"The Flames and Ashes of Diaspora." Rev. of *The Fire Sacrifice*. *Asian Times*, February 15, 1994, 13.
"Looking for New Horizons." Rev. of *Havan*. *The Frontier Post* (March 12, 1993): 4.
Rao, Susheela. Rev. of *The Fire Sacrifice*. *World Literature Today* 69.2 (1994): 429.
Sharma, Bulbul. "In Alien Land." Rev. of *The Fire Sacrifice*. *Indian Express*, April 24, 1994, 7.
Tabios, Eileen. "Susham Bedi: A Reconciliation with Translation." *Asian Pacific American Journal* 5.2 (1996): 81–93.
"Writers at Home in the West." Rev. of *The Fire Sacrifice*. *India Mail*, December 14, 1993, 4.

William Peter Blatty

(1928–   )

Rhonda Brock-Servais

BIOGRAPHY

Blatty was born in New York City January 7, 1928, the youngest son of five children, to Lebanese immigrant parents. His father left the family when Blatty was six; his mother, Mary, raised the children alone in perpetual poverty, yet he exclusively attended Catholic schools. Mary was a devout Roman Catholic, as is her son, William Peter, and this early religious grounding is evident in his novels. Blatty was writing young; at age ten he won five dollars in a twenty-five-word-or-less contest for *Captain Future* comic books (Winter 85). With the aid of a scholarship, he attended Georgetown University and received an A.B. in 1950. He returned to Georgetown after some years to complete an MA in English literature.

Blatty has been married three times, most recently to tennis professional Linda Tuero in 1975. He has also held a variety of positions. Upon completing college, he joined the U.S. Air Force and was assigned to the Psychological Warfare Division. Following his military career, Blatty worked for the U.S. Information Agency in Beirut, Lebanon, where his appearance and fluency in Arabic allowed him to move about freely. His most noted career other than as novelist has been as a screenwriter. He has more than nine screenplays to his credit, some based on his own work. His mother passed away in 1967, and this emotionally draining event coincided with a low point in his writing career and sent him seeking isolation. In 1969 he took a cabin and there began to draft his best-known work, *The Exorcist*. Blatty has said that his first interest in the subject came from a newspaper article in 1949 about a local boy who was undergoing the rites of exorcism. From that point, he collected everything he could on the subject and on the Jesuit brotherhood and even contacted the priest involved in the actual case.

Blatty likes to maintain a great deal of control over his artistic output and jealously guards it. Several of his works have been made into movies for which he has written the screenplays. On *The Ninth Configuration* and *Twinkle, Twinkle "Killer" Kane* as well as on *The Exorcist* and *Legion* (the movie was retitled *The Exorcist III*), he maintained creative control. In 1983 he filed an unsuccessful $9 million lawsuit against the *New York Times* because he felt the paper had seriously damaged the sale of *Legion* by not placing it on its best-seller list. This incident is the last time Blatty was in the public eye. No new novels have appeared since then; despite his lack of recent output, his place in contemporary literature has been secure since *The Exorcist*.

MAJOR WORKS AND THEMES

Blatty began his novel-writing career with a series of little-known works: *Which Way to Mecca, Jack?*, *John Goldfarb, Please Come Home!*, and *I, Billy Shakespeare*. Another not very popular work was his follow-up to *The Exorcist*, *I'll Tell Them I Remember You*, a paean to his mother. The earlier three novels all have a comedic slant (also evident in some of his more serious work). *Which Way to Mecca, Jack?* is based on his experiences in Beirut and a particular incident when he posed as the son of King Saud. *John Goldfarb, Please Come Home!* was at the center of a controversy in 1964. In it, a captured American pilot coaches a team of Arabs to victory over the Notre Dame football team. Notre Dame officials accused Blatty of damaging the school's reputation and got an injunction stopping both book and film from distribution. This was overturned the next year. Blatty says he never intended to insult or damage the school.

As opposed to the supernatural horror of *The Exorcist* and *Legion*, *Twinkle, Twinkle "Killer" Kane* and *The Ninth Configuration* are both psychological horror novels. Critic Scott Briggs writes that all four of these books confront "the great mysteries: of life, of God, of humanity's tenuous existence upon the Earth" (13). The latter two are really the same novel written at different points in time. *The Ninth Configuration*, the later one, is generally agreed to have greater character development, a more coherent story, and fewer comedic elements. Noted horror critic Douglas Winter calls it a blend of *Catch-22* and *One Flew over the Cuckoo's Nest* (92). The story is set after the Vietnam War. Colonel Hudson Kane is sent to evaluate a group of servicemen who are being held captive. They may be insane, or they may not be; it is Kane's job to cure them and/or to discover the fakes. Both books are filled with intricate discussions on the nature and meaning of existence. Eventually, Kane commits suicide, and the reader discovers that Kane was not a psychiatrist but his brother is; he is instead a noted guerrilla warrior, the notorious "Killer" Kane who can no longer live haunted by the enemy soldiers he has dispatched.

When *The Exorcist* was published in 1971, Blatty was still primarily known for his comedy writing. This single book changed his reputation. The plot is that of a relatively straightforward supernatural novel (although the supernatural presence isn't absolutely confirmed until the last fifty pages): monstrosity intrudes on normalcy and must be expelled to reestablish the status quo. Divorced Chris MacNeil is a nationally known actress who has come to Georgetown with her twelve-year-old daughter, Regan, to begin a new film. She also has the opportunity to do some directing and realizes that this could be her second big break. First Regan develops a fascination with the Ouija board, and slowly her behavior changes, becoming more and more bizarre. Chris' director is killed in her home while only Regan is present. As the girl's strange behavior escalates, she is taken to a whole host of medical and psychiatric experts. Ironically, one these men of science suggests to Chris, an atheist, that she may want to seek out an exorcist for her child. Chris then takes Regan to Father Damien Karras who is both a Jesuit priest and a psychiatrist. He agrees to evaluate Regan to see whether or not an exorcism should, indeed, be performed. Karras himself is plagued by doubts about his vocation and resists the truth of the girl's possession for some time. Eventually, Father Merrin is brought in to exorcise the demon from the girl. The two priests do battle for the girl's soul, over the course of which Father Karras begins to regain his faith. Father Merrin, although spiritually strong enough for this battle, has kept the secret of his weak heart from everyone. Inevitably, it betrays him, and he dies in Regan's room. The demon is incensed at having its prey taken away, for as Merrin has explained earlier, the target of a possession is not the one possessed but the onlookers. The demon is trying "to make us despair; to reject our own humanity. . . . to see ourselves as ultimately bestial; as ultimately . . . unworthy" (369–70). In a final effort to spare Regan, Karras invites the demon into himself and, once the demon is within him, throws himself from her window to his death. The novel ends with Chris and Regan, apparently fully recovered, preparing to move on. Blatty wrote the screenplay, for which he won an Oscar, for the film and was in close contact with director William Friedkin during filming. One further item needs to be noted: Blatty had nothing whatsoever to do with 1977's *The Exorcist II* and considers the film execrable.

Legion, *The Exorcist*'s sequel, was done twelve years later at the prompting of a friend who wanted to know what happened to her favorite character from the original, the Devil. Although another supernatural novel, *Legion* reads like a police procedural and features two characters from the original: the aging, Jewish police lieutenant William Kinderman and Jesuit priest Father Dyer. Kinderman investigated some of the incidents associated with the first book, while Father Dyer was a friend of Father Karras and arrived at his death scene just in time to perform last rites. Set a few years later, Kinderman is investigating gruesome serial murders that appear to have all the hallmarks of the Gemini killer whom police had shot dead years ago. In due time, Father Dyer falls victim to this new killer, and Kinderman begins to connect the two cases. At the novel's high point, he has Father Karras disinterred and discovers the body of an unknown elderly priest in the coffin. Later, Kinderman goes to a psychiatric facility and learns that an unknown psychotic is indeed Father Karras, evidently still possessed by the demon he invited in at the culmination of the previous book. *Legion* features Kinderman's somewhat discursive musings on the meaning of life and humanity rather than the philosophical discussion of the two priests. This novel, too, was made into a film and was released as *The Exorcist III* (1990). Blatty directed, and it is noticeably free of the pyrotechnic special effects of the first film, excepting the finale, relying more on atmosphere and mood to scare its audience.

CRITICAL RECEPTION

Of all Blatty's works, *The Exorcist* has by far received the lion's share of critical attention. Interestingly, many articles focused on it take time to denigrate the style and to remind their readers that *The Exorcist* was a best-seller. Some writers even go so far as to scorn fans of the work, in one case referring to them as "plebean." These critics are not alone in their dislike of the book. Although called "a page-turner *par excellence*" (*Life*) and said to be well researched and engaging, many early reviews found the work distasteful. The review from *Life* magazine goes on to say that "Faulkner, Blatty is not," criticizing the lack of literary style found in the novel (34). The reviewer from *Time* was considerably harsher, writing that the book is a "pretentious, tasteless, abominably written, redundant pastiche of superficial theology, comic-book psychology, Grade C movie dialogue and Grade Z scatology" (qtd. in "Blatty" 64). *Legion* received many similar reviews; *People* magazine wrote that "it's hard to believe that a worse book will be published in 1983" (Rev. 14).

Whatever one thinks of the novels, there can be no doubt as to their impact on the popular imagination, especially that of *The Exorcist*. Pop culture references abound, particularly to the movie and Linda Blair's revolving head and projectile vomiting. In his article, Bruce Merry points out how masterfully Blatty works the typical horror plot to build suspense and keep the reader wondering whether the danger is really otherworldly. Merry also explains why both Father Merrin and Father Karras must die to restore order to the world of the novel. Many readers felt that the ending allows the Devil, in essence, to win. Robert Geary explains in his work, *"The Exorcist*: Deep Horror?" how this is not the case. Deep horror, according to Geary, has nihilistic implications and a distinctly unhappy ending; it is a genre of despair. *The Exorcist*, on the other hand, ends on a note of love and human connection; Father Karras sacrifices himself precisely because he has once again gained the capacity to love his fellow man unconditionally. Scott Briggs seconds this view when he points out that all Blatty's works have a stable moral center upon which the characters can rely.

Psychoanalytic (Beit-Hallahmi) and Jungian (Burton and Hicks) readings of the novel tend to break it down into a series of tensions or opposites and the eternal battle of chaos versus order. Burton and Hicks note several of these pairs at the outset of their article: order/chans, good/evil, human/beast, male/female, sane/insane, creation/destruction, secular/sacred (118). They then go on to show how these pairs are disrupted through Regan's possession. She is a female child who speaks with a mature, male voice; a human who makes animal noises; and an innocent who utters obscenities (119). Unlike other critics, Burton and Hicks contend that chaos reigns triumphant in the novel and that Father Karras' death fails to reestablish order.

Another common reading of *The Exorcist* is as social horror or a commentary on contemporary social problems. Interestingly, this reading can result in conclusions that are entirely at cross purposes. Stephen King in *Danse Macabre* writes that the story speaks of a pervasive fear of youth evident in the early 1970s. Regan is representative of the youth of the time who experimented sexually and with their lifestyles while her mother, Chris, is the older generation who cannot understand what has "possessed" her child to act in such a fashion. In contrast, Gary Hoppenstand writes that the cultural fear the novel exposes is not that of the child but of the parents: the dissolution of the nuclear family, women's search for personal fulfillment, and single parenting. He suggests that had Chris not been divorced and overly concerned with advancing her career, Reagan would not have been open to the demonic attack. Hoppenstand cites *The Exorcist* along with Tryon's *The Other* and Levin's *Rosemary's Baby* as being the first horror novels based on "grotesque violations of sacred American institutions and traditions" (36). Regardless of which interpretation one prefers, one thing is entirely certain: Blatty's work, especially *The Exorcist*, has become an American institution in and of itself.

BIBLIOGRAPHY

Works by William Peter Blatty

Novels

Which Way to Mecca, Jack? New York: Bernard Geis, 1960.
John Goldfarb, Please Come Home! New York: Doubleday, 1963.
I, Billy Shakespeare. New York: Doubleday, 1965.
Twinkle, Twinkle "Killer" Kane. New York: Doubleday, 1967.
The Exorcist. New York: Harper and Row, 1971.
I'll Tell Them I Remember You. New York: Norton, 1973.
The Ninth Configuration. New York: Harper and Row, 1978.
Legion. New York: Simon and Schuster, 1983.

Studies of William Peter Blatty

Beit-Hallahmi, Benjamin. "*The Turn of the Screw* and *The Exorcist*: Demonical Possession and Childhood Purity." *American Image* 33 (1976): 296–303.

"Blatty, William Peter." In *Contemporary Literary Criticism*. Vol. 2. Ed. Carolyn Riley and Barbara Harte. Detroit: Gayle, 1974. 63–64.

Briggs, Scott. " 'So Much Mystery . . . ': The Fiction of William Peter Blatty." *Studies in Weird Fiction* (Spring 1991): 13–17.

Burton, John, and David Hicks. "Chaos Triumphant: Archetypes and Symbols in *The Exorcist*." In *The American Dimension: Cultural Myths and Social Realities*. Ed. W. Arens and Susan Montague. Port Washington, NY: Alfred, 1976. 117–23.

King, Stephen. *Danse Macabre*. New York: Everest House, 1981.

Geary, Robert. "*The Exorcist*: Deep Horror?" *The Journal of the Fantastic in the Arts* (1993): 55–63.

Hoppenstand, Gary. "Exorcising Devil Babies: Images of Children and Adolescents in the Best-Selling Horror Novel." In *Images of the Child*. Ed. Harry Eiss. Bowling Green, OH: Popular Press, 1994. 35–58.

Merry, Bruce. "The Exorcist Dies So We Can All Enjoy the Sunset Again." *University of Windsor Review* (1975): 5–24.

Rev. of *The Exorcist*. *Life* (October 1972): 34.

Rev. of *Legion*. *People* (August 1, 1983): 14.

Wilson, Michaela Swart. "Blatty, William Peter." In *Contemporary Authors*. Vol. 9. Ed. Ann Evory and Linda Metzgereds. Detroit: Gayle, 1983. 58–59.

Winter, Douglas. "The Horror Fiction of William Peter Blatty." In *A Dark Night's Dreaming: Contemporary American Horror Fiction*. Columbia: University of South Carolina Press, 1996. 84–96.

Vance Bourjaily

(1922–   )

Ymitri Jayasundera

BIOGRAPHY

Born in Cleveland to an immigrant Lebanese father, a noted journalist, editor, and publisher, and a Welsh/"Colonial" American mother, also a journalist and a popular romance novelist, Vance Bourjaily felt he "really had no alternative" (Bruccoli 3) about becoming a writer. His mother's agent sent his first book written at the age of sixteen to Max Perkins, the famed editor of Ernest Hemingway and F. Scott Fitzgerald, at Scribners, who rejected it but felt Bourjaily would become an important future writer. In 1939, at seventeen, he became a copywriter to a prestigious advertising agency in New York through his father's influence. A year later, studying at Bowdoin College in Maine, he wrote mostly one-act plays, which were produced on campus. When World War II began, he volunteered in the American Field Service (ambulance service) in Italy and Syria (1942–1944). Returning home, he was drafted into the army and assigned to Hawaii, where he wrote a three-act play, which his agent sent to Max Perkins at Scribners, who rejected it but gave him an advance to write a novel. Begun in 1946, *The End of My Life* appeared in August 1947, just after Bourjaily's graduation from Bowdoin College. He was married in December 1946 and has two sons; his daughter is now dead.

Bourjaily cofounded with John W. Aldridge, edited, and contributed to *discovery*, an alternative literary magazine that ran from 1951 to 1953 and published such future writers as Saul Bellow, Norman Mailer, and William Styron and poets Adrienne Rich and Louis Simpson. He has also published extensively in major journals and-mainstream magazines, such as *Esquire*, *Harpers*, *New Yorker*, and *Saturday Evening Post*. Most of these articles were collected into two nonfiction books on outdoor life and hunting. Like both of his parents, he has worked as a journalist. In the 1950s he wrote several plays for television that were broadcast from New York. He has been a professor of creative writing (fiction) at the prestigious Iowa Writer's Workshop, University of Iowa, 1958–1980, directed the graduate creative writing program at Louisiana State University in Baton Rouge from 1985, and is currently a professor at the University of Arizona. Since *The End of My Life*, he has published a steady stream of novels, about two every decade. Only *Brill among the Ruins* was nominated for a National Book Award (1970), which led him directly to act as one of the judges for it in 1977.

MAJOR WORKS AND THEMES

Bourjaily's early novels focus on an antiwar theme, reflecting the cynicism and nihilism of post–World War II writers who didn't have the comfort of being disillusioned as Hemingway's young war-torn men. He has experimented widely with form and uses black humor, irony, and absurdity to satirize the modern-day military/ bureaucratic world of his generation that increasingly saw "contemporary society as a warscape of seemingly arbitrary violence and purposeless destruction" (Aldridge, "Vance Bourjaily's *End*" 103). In his first novel, *The End of My Life*, which uses his war experience, a young American ambulance driver stationed in the Middle East and Italy is guilt-ridden for having caused the death of a nurse he had taken joyriding in a jeep in Italy during an enemy attack. His fourth novel, *Confessions of a Spent Youth*, including his experiences of living in New York and his war experiences in the Middle East, is his most autobiographical novel, also his most critically acclaimed, with his narrator, Quincy, having Bourjaily's mixed heritage and "existing in two cultures, [with] each vying for his allegiance" (Shakir, "Pretending to Be Arab" 7). Reflecting on his life, Quincy begins the novel by confessing that he "tells a hundred lies a day" (Bourjaily, *Confessions* 3), which John Muste argues makes him a reliable narrator since the reader is more inclined to believe him ("The Fractional Man as Hero" 76). Structurally, the novel is a series of essays or "confessions" alternating between Quincy's younger and older self.

Bourjaily has experimented not only with different form but also with different subjects. In *Now Playing at Canterbury*, the faculty of a state university produce and act in an opera. Their stories form a present-day American Canterbury tales, reflecting their personalities, and include a collage of narrative and genres, such as cartoons, speech in balloons, an iambic couplet story, and fantasies. For example, in one story a professor fantasizes that F. Scott Fitzgerald visits his Fitzgerald seminar. Incorporating his interest in jazz, Bourjaily essentially writes an epistolary novel, *The Great Fake Book*, which refers to a standard compendium of jazz and swing music of the 1930s–1950s. A young man, Charlie, searches for insights into his dead father through his father's memoirs, notes, and conversations with his father's friends. It also incorporates elements of a detective novel.

Many of Bourjaily's novels react to cataclysmic political events. For example, *Brill among the Ruins*, using his archaeological experiences in Mexico, focuses on the destruction of the native American cultures of South America by Europeans. In *Hound of Earth* a research scientist, disillusioned with his complicity in creating the atom bomb, deserts the army and his family on the day it is dropped in Japan. He eludes the Federal Bureau of Investigation (FBI) by visiting towns/cities with beautiful names, which allow Bourjaily to focus on his theme of the importance of names to origins and on the destruction of native Americans and their culture by European settlers. This is a major theme in Bourjaily's novels—names and their importance to ontology. "To name something is to own it," he once observed (Francis, "A Conversation about Names" 356), and many of his characters' names are allegorical. For example, Brill means fish in British dialect, and Ulysses S. D. Quincy refers to Homer, Grant, the American president, and DeQuincy's *Confessions of an English Opium Eater* (Francis, "A Conversation about Names" 359, 362). *The Man Who Knew Kennedy*, intertextualizing Sinclair Lewis' *The Man Who Knew Coolidge*, begins in the aftermath of the Kennedy assassination and uses the Gatsby/Nick Carraway, observer-narrator, structure, and plotline to evaluate the dark side of the Kennedy era and its consequences to the people of that generation.

CRITICAL RECEPTION

In *After the Lost Generation* (1951), John W. Aldridge highly praises *The End of My Life* for capturing the story of the generation caught between the two world wars. "No book since *This Side of Paradise* has caught so well the flavor of youth in wartime, and no book since *A Farewell to Arms* has contained so complete a record of the loss of that youth in war" (121). In spite of Aldridge's praise and Max Perkins' belief in the 1940s of Bourjaily as a promising young writer, Bourjaily has not achieved the critical fame and stature of his contemporaries, such as Gore Vidal, Norman Mailer, Truman Capote, and so on. Not appreciated by the general public, he seems to be a writer's writer, with his work frequently considered too difficult to read because of his experimental style, although Bourjaily believes a book's "attractions [should be] strong enough to persuade the reader to overcome the difficulties" (Francis, "From Jazz to Joyce" 407). Thomas McCormack, the editor of *Afterwords*, includes Bourjaily with American and British writers such as Norman Mailer, Louis Auchinloss, and John Fowles discussing their writing process and hails *Confessions of a Spent Youth* as "a book of remarkable timeliness for his generation" (xiv).

There have been very few critical articles on Bourjaily's novels, but in 1976 *Critique: Studies in Modern Fiction* devoted most of an issue to Bourjaily's work, including a checklist. Each of four writers discusses a different novel and a wide variety of issues and themes. William Francis, who has twice interviewed Bourjaily, analyzes the allegorical nature of names in *The Hound of Earth*.

Comparing Brill in *Brill among the Ruins* to Saul Bellow's Henderson in *Henderson the Rain King*, Daniel Towner argues that both middle-aged men visit "primitive" cultures to find themselves—a major theme in Bourjaily's work. To find himself, the protagonist in most novels must either travel to the land of his ancestors, as in *Confessions of a Spent Youth*, or, in *The Violated*, discover his origins through his translations of classical languages.

Although Bourjaily's novels, on the whole, do not focus on the traditional ethnic writer's bildungsroman structure of the main character's reconciling with his or her ethnicity and racism in the United States, Evelyn Shakir's two articles in *MELUS* concentrate on a chapter titled "The Fractional Man" in *Confessions of a Spent Youth*, in which Quincy role-plays at being Arab in the Middle East, convincingly to the natives, and discovers that his roots go deeper into his Lebanese heritage than he had believed.

Always experimenting with style, form, and content in each novel, Bourjaily has been praised but frequently criticized for his not always successful narratives and also for the violence and explicit sexual scenes in his novels. Perhaps the reason for his neglect stems from his satirical, nihilistic, experimental, antiwar novels, which require the reader to make a commitment: in the reading.

BIBLIOGRAPHY

Works by Vance Bourjaily

Novels

The End of My Life. New York: Scribners, 1947. Reprinted with Intro. John W. Aldridge. New York: Arbor House, 1984.
The Hound of Earth. New York: Scribners, 1955.
The Violated. New York: Dial, 1958.
Confessions of a Spent Youth. New York: Dial, 1960.
The Man Who Knew Kennedy. New York: Dial, 1967.
Brill among the Ruins. New York: Dial, 1970.
Now Playing at Canterbury. New York: Dial, 1976.
A Game Men Play. New York: Dial, 1980.
The Great Fake Book. New York: Weidenfeld and Nicolson, 1986.
Old Soldier. New York: Donald I. Fine, 1990.

Nonfiction

The Unnatural Enemy. New York: Dial, 1963.
"A Certain Kind of Work: *Confessions of a Spent Youth*." In *Afterwords: Novelists on Their Novels*. Ed. Thomas McCormack. New York: Harper and Row, 1969. 176–91.
Country Matters: Collected Reports from the Fields and Streams of Iowa and Other Places. New York: Dial, 1973.

Anthology

"Dance of the Fireflies," "Not to Confound My Elders," and "Jack and Jill." In *First Words: Earliest Writing from Favorite Contemporary Authors*. Ed. Paul Mandelbaum. Chapel Hill, NC: Algonquin Books of Chapel Hill, 1993. 52–73.

Studies of Vance Bourjaily

Aldridge, John W. *After the Lost Generation: A Critical Study of the Writers of Two Wars*. London: Vision Press, 1951; 2nd ed., London: Vision Press, 1959.

————. "Vance Bourjaily's *The End of My Life*." *Centennial Review* 28.2 (1984): 100–105.

Bruccoli, Matthew J. "Vance Bourjaily." In *Conversations with Writers*. Ed. Matthew J. Bruccoli. Detroit: Gale, 1977. 2–23.

Francis, William A. "A Conversation about Names with Novelist Vance Bourjaily." *Names* 34.4 (1986): 355–63.

————. "From Jazz to Joyce: A Conversation with Vance Bourjaily." *Literary Review* 31.4 (1988): 403–14.

————. "Motif of Names in Bourjaily's *The Hound of Earth*." *Critique: Studies in Modern Fiction* 17.3 (1976): 64–72.

————. "Vance Bourjaily's *The Man Who Knew Kennedy*: A Novel of Camelot." *Literary Onomastics Studies* 14 (1987): 199–211.

McMillen, William. "The Public Man and the Private Novel: Bourjaily's *The Man Who Knew Kennedy*." *Critique: Studies in Modern Fiction* 17.3 (1976): 86–95.

McMillen, William, and John M. Muste. "A Vance Bourjaily Checklist." *Critique: Studies in Modern Fiction* 17.3 (1976): 105–10.

Muste, John M. "The Fractional Man as Hero: Bourjaily's *Confessions of a Spent Youth*." *Critique: Studies in Modern Fiction* 17.3 (1976): 73–85.

————. "The Second Major Subwar: Four Novels by Vance Bourjaily." In *The Shaker Realist: Essays in Modern Literature*. Ed. Melvin J. Friedman and John B. Vickery. Baton Rouge: Louisiana University Press, 1970. 311–26.

Parill, William A. "The Art of the Novel: An Interview with Vance Bourjaily." *Louisiana Literature* 5.2 (1988): 3–20.

Shakir, Evelyn. "Arab Mothers, American Sons: Women in Arab-American Autobiographies." *MELUS* 17.3 (1991–1992): 5–15.

————. "Pretending to Be Arab: Role-Playing in Vance Bourjaily's 'Fractional Man.'" *MELUS* 9.1 (1982): 7–21.

Towner, Daniel. "Brill's Ruins and Henderson's Rain." *Critique: Studies in Modern Fiction* 17.3 (1976): 96–104.

"Vance Bourjaily." *Talks with Authors*. Ed. Charles E. Madden. Carbondale: Southern Illinois University Press, 1968. 201–14.

Cecilia Manguerra Brainard
(1947–   )

Eleanor Ty

BIOGRAPHY

Cecilia Manguerra Brainard was born on November 21, 1947, and grew up in Cebu City, on the island of Cebu in the central Philippines. In an interview with Dana Huebler, she describes her childhood as "paradise" (98). She lived with her family in a Spanish-style villa, tended by servants and surrounded by gardens containing orchids, star apple trees, jasmine, and frangipani. This city appears in her short stories and novel as Ubec (Cebu spelled backwards). Her idyllic childhood is associated with her father, an engineer who was already in his fifties when Cecilia, the youngest of four children, was born. He died when she was nine, and she lost the stabilizing influence of the family. One way of coping with the loss was the writing of a diary, which evolved later into a journal. She attended Maryknoll College in Quezon City from 1964 to 1968 and received a B.A. in communication arts.

In 1969 Brainard immigrated to the United States to study film at the University of California at Los Angeles (UCLA) graduate school. Like many Filipinos at this time, Brainard emigrated to flee the dictatorship of Ferdinand Marcos. She reestablished her friendship with Lauren Brainard, whom she had met in the Philippines when he was serving in the Peace Corps. They eventually married and settled in Santa Monica, where they had three boys—Christopher, Alexander, and Andrew. Between 1969 and 1981 she worked in public relations and as a fund-raiser for a nonprofit organization. In 1981, when she was pregnant with her third child, she took writing classes and began a serious career in writing.

Brainard wrote a bimonthly column, "Filipina American Perspective," for the *Philippine American News* (a now-defunct newspaper published in Los Angeles) from 1982 to 1988. This column gave her the opportunity and stimulus to explore ideas about living in the United States as a Filipina and jogged her memories about growing up in the Philippines. The essays have been collected and published as *Philippine Woman in America*. At the same time, she started publishing short stories and essays in various magazines and journals, first in the Philippines and subsequently in America. Her works can be found in periodicals such as *Focus Philippines, Philippine Graphic, Mr. and Mr. Magazine, Katipunan, Amerasia Journal, Bamboo Ridge Journal, The California Examiner*, and others. Her stories have been included in anthologies, such as *Making Waves* (1989), *Forbidden Fruit* (1992), *Songs of Ourselves* (1994), and *On a Bed of Rice* (1995).

In 1989 Brainard was awarded a California Arts Council Artists' Fellowship in Fiction. Her stories have won the 1985 Fortner Prize and the Honorable Mention Award of the Philippine Arts, Letters, and Media Council in 1989. She has been recognized by the Los Angeles Board of Education in a Special Recognition Award in 1991 and has received the Outstanding Individual Award from the City of Cebu in 1997. Brainard was a founding member and past officer of PAWWA (Philippine American Women Writers and Artists), is a member of Pen America, and teaches creative writing at UCLA Extension.

MAJOR WORKS AND THEMES

What makes the fiction of Cecilia Manguerra Brainard interesting are her creative use of Filipino legends and her rewriting and revisiting of Philippine history. In her short stories and in her first novel, *Song of Yvonne*, which was republished in the United States as *When the Rainbow Goddess Wept*, Brainard integrates the folktales, native traditions, and superstitions that she had heard and seen as a child into twentieth-century settings and contemporary characters. In addition, she is concerned with what postmodernists call historiography, or the ways in which narrative form, strategies of representation, and point of view influence history. In her fiction as well as in her essays, Brainard attempts to find a distinctive voice and style as a Filipina living in America through her handling of these elements.

In her works, she uses the supernatural and writes of her childhood belief in *encantados* (enchanted beings that lived in ancient trees) and in the giant *agta* (mythical giant) in her backyard. With fondness, she describes native traditions, such as the *media noche* banquet on Christmas Eve, which consists of "roasted pig, blood soup, fish rellenos, sansrivals, leche flan" (*Yvonne* 25). At the *sabwag* (a traditional throwing of coins and candy for children), she remembers scrambling for coins and candies that her father would throw on the floor. Filipino foods also play a large role in her evocation of her culture. In an unpublished essay called "A Fulfilling Love Affair," she admits that she has a weakness for Filipino food—for *pusit* (squid), *dinuguan* (pork cooked in blood), *pancit* (noodles), *lechon* (roasted pig), and *adobo* (a sour stew of chicken and pork). In her novel *Song of Yvonne*, the Filipino culture is evoked through foods as well as folktales. The atrocities that happened during World War II in the Philippines are mitigated by the comforting legends told by the epic singer Laydan. Tales of gods and goddesses who deliver the oppressed Ilianon tribe to the promised land are interspersed with narratives of exile that occurred as a result of the Japanese occupation of the country. Problems in the war-torn years are suggestively linked to, and contrasted with, legendary tales of heroic valor and struggle.

Song of Yvonne is a bildungsroman set in 1941–1944. The narrative is told from the point of view of a girl who turns eleven by the end of the war. Yvonne's journey from innocence to experience parallels that of the Filipino people, who also lose their Edenic world as a result of colonization and imperialism—by the Spaniards, the Americans, and, at that period, the Japanese. The novel depicts the suffering and the resistance of the Filipinos against the Japanese. Brainard says that is her "way of documenting the triumph of the Filipino spirit over foreign oppression" (Yvonne 3). She wishes to record the "collective wounding that Filipinos experienced" in World War II (3) and gives vignettes of Japanese cruelties, such as the rape and mutilation of a nurse, the killing of Doc Mendez's family, the massacre of entire towns, the bayonet beating and killing of prisoners. As Leonard Casper notes, "Brainard prevents the novel from descending into either melodrama or polemic by maintaining young Yvonne as her singular narrator throughout" (252). She gives her version of the events where "her share of . . . pain is naturally scaled down" (Casper 252). Eventually, Yvonne takes over the role of epic singer. Her stories and singing become the means by which the nation and tribe recover.

In the same way that Song of Yvonne attempts to pay attention to the lives of ordinary people affected by a particular moment in history, Acapulco at Sunset and Other Stories, Brainard's most recent collection of short stories, focuses on a Filipina who marries a South American and lives in Mexico. It is set in the era that linked the Philippines to Acapulco during the Galleon trade. In an essay written for the Pacific Enterprise called "Another Look at Magellan's Journey around the World," Brainard revisits the history concerning Ferdinand Magellan and argues that he was not the first person to circumnavigate the world but that Magellan's Malay slave, Enrique, a native of Sumatra, should be given this credit. Brainard argues that Enrique spoke the same language as the people of Samar and Cebu, which makes him her kababayan (fellow countryman). This essay, based on historical fact and research, reveals Brainard's continuing fascination with history and what official recorded history often leaves out.

CRITICAL RECEPTION

The reception of Brainard's fiction has been very positive, especially by readers and reviewers in the Philippines. Her life and career are viewed as something of a success story, as there is only a handful of Filipino writers who are published in the United States. Isagani Cruz notes that her "short stories are refreshingly new, therefore comfortably old-fashioned; they are delightfully conventional, therefore startlingly innovative" (20). Hidalgo's critical chapter on Brainard does not discuss the novel, but she points out that Brainard writes as an "expatriate" and sees the past nostalgically. The most sustained study of the novel to date is the review by Leonard Casper, who praises the work for its "controlled resonance" (252).

BIBLIOGRAPHY

Works by Cecilia Manguerra Brainard

Novels

Song of Yvonne. Quezon City: New Day, 1991.
When the Rainbow Goddess Wept. New York: Dutton, 1994; reprinted, New York: Plume, 1995.

Essays and Essay Collection

Philippine Woman in America. Quezon City: New Day, 1991.
"Another Look at Magellan's Journey around the World." *Pacific Enterprise: A Magazine for Enterprising Filipinos and Friends* (Fall 1998): 13–17.

Short Story Collections

Woman with Horns and Other Stories. Quezon City: New Day, 1987.
(Coed.). *Seven Stories from Seven Sisters: A Collection of Philippine Folktales.* Los Angeles: Philippine American Women Writers and Artists, 1992.
(Ed.). *Fiction by Filipinos in America.* Quezon City: New Day, 1993.
Acapulco at Sunset and Other Stories. Manila: Anvil, 1995.
(Coed.). *The Beginning and Other Asian Folktales.* Los Angeles: Philippine American Women Writers and Artists, 1995.
(Ed.). *Contemporary Fiction by Filipinos in America.* Manila: Anvil, 1997.
Banna the Python and Other Stories. Tahanan, forthcoming.

Studies of Cecilia Manguerra Brainard

Aubry, Erin. "A Child's Vision of Life during Wartime." *Los Angeles Times*, November 15, 1994, E-8.
Beltran, Marie G. "Woman with Stories and Other Concerns." *Filipinas* (May 1995): 29, 56.
Casper, Leonard. Rev. of *Song of Yvonne*. *Philippine Studies* 41 (2d Quarter 1993): 251–54.
Cruz, Isagani R. "The Pleasures of Ubec, Otherwise Known as Cebu." *Starweek: The Sunday Magazine of the Philippine Star* (October 29, 1995): 20.
Hidalgo, Cristina Pantoja. *Filipino Woman Writing: Home and Exile in the Autobiographical Narratives of Ten Writers.* Manila: Ateneo de Manila University Press, 1994.

Huebler, Dana. "An Interview with Cecilia Manguerra Brainard." *Poets and Writers Magazine* (March/April 1997): 96–105.

Ty, Eleanor. " 'Never Again Be the Yvonne of Yesterday': Personal and Collective Loss in Cecilia Brainard's *Song of Yvonne*." In *Writing Dispossession, Writing Desire: Asian-American Women Writers*. Ed. Srimati Mukherjee. Forthcoming.

Theresa Hak Kyung Cha
(1951–1982)

Yi-Chun Tricia Lin

BIOGRAPHY

Theresa Hak Kyung Cha was born on March 4, 1951, in Pusan, Korea. In 1962, with her family's relocation to Hawaii, Cha began two decades of odyssey in the West, which is partially recounted in *Dictée*. In 1964 the Chas moved to San Francisco. There, Theresa Cha attended Catholic school. At Convent of the Sacred Heart, San Francisco, she started her education in Western classics and languages. In addition to singing in the school choir, Cha studied French and Greek and Roman classics. This period laid a profound foundation for her creation of *Dictée*.

Her education at the University of California at Berkeley completed her formation as an artist and writer. As an undergraduate student in comparative literature at Berkeley (1969–1973), Cha read widely, from Korean poetry to European modernist and postmodern literature. She was especially drawn to the writings of Samuel Beckett, Nathalie Sarraute, Monique Wittig, and so on. In addition, she studied art and received encouragement to work in performance. In 1974 she began her career as a performance artist, producer, director, and writer. She received her second B.A. from Berkeley in art in 1975. In 1976 Cha went to Paris to study film theory with Christian Metz, Raymond Bellour, and Thierry Kuntzel. After she returned to Berkeley, Cha continued her creative production and performance and received an M.A. and M.F.A. in art, also from Berkeley, in 1977 and 1978.

In 1980 Cha moved to New York to continue her pursuit as a performance artist. That year she edited *Apparatus/Cinematographic Apparatus: Selected Writings* to "reveal the process of film and make accessible the theoretical writings and materials of filmmakers," according to Cha in the Preface. The volume was one of the first anthologies of writings on film theory. In 1982 Cha married Richard Barnes in May and published *Dictée*. In November 1982, she was killed in Soho, New York City. At the time of her death, Cha was working on multiple projects, including a film and another book.

MAJOR WORK AND THEMES

Not exactly famed as a novelist, Cha distinguished herself as a performance artist. *Dictée*, Cha's preeminent literary presentation, should be considered in the context of her performance art. Her book performs with fragmented tales, irregular spacing, pictures, maps, ideographs, official correspondence/documents, and seemingly irrelevant language exercises. Its form and content together weave a rich postcolonial, postmodern, multilingual feminist text and arguably one of the most challenging texts in Asian America. Its signification process is much like an "archaeological" excavation of meanings of a palimpsest.

Albeit void of one single controlling narrative or voice, *Dictée* charts histories and diasporas of the Korean people. Its fragmented narratives recapture and reenact the fragmentation of postcolonial Korean American female subjectivity. The main body is divided into nine sections, each entitled with the one Muse and her attribute, such as "Clio—History," "Calliope—Epic Poetry," and "Melpomene—Tragedy." The book begins with French and English dictation (*dictée*) exercises, which gradually move and merge with fragments about struggles of Korea. Language acquisition and national identity, two seemingly disparate themes, are gracefully joined in Cha's narrative.

Cha's "national" discourse must be examined, however, in the postcolonial and feminist context. *Dictée* is much less about Korea than about the effect its colonization and separation have on its subjects. All Cha's "subjects," to be exact, are women—mothers, daughters, lovers, and sisters—which departs from the male-centered national discourse. The quintessential female figure, "the mother," occupies the central stage of *Dictée*, taken to embody one's origin, home, language, and nation. The mother is Hyung Soon Huo, Cha's mother, and she symbolizes the emotional link between one's language and nation: the mother tongue and motherland. Cha's text moves from mother, to mother tongue, to motherland. Such "movement," one key word in the book to denote that fluidity from the text to the nation and from the mother to the tongue, fuses two entities—the mother and nation—in one space:

You leave you come back to the shell left empty all this time. To claim to reclaim, the space. Into the mouth the wound the entry is reverse and back each organ artery gland pace element, implanted, housed skin upon skin, membrane, vessel, waters, dams ducts, canals, bridges. (57)

Closely connected with the symbolic imagery of the mother is language. Language makes coherent the fragmented, nonlinear narratives, which reflect the alienated, scarred, and wounded female subjects. To be sure, the absence of Korean language and employment of Chinese, English, and French form one powerful statement about colonialism and Western imperialism. No one single language is sufficient to bear the tales of Cha's narrator, nor is she anywhere at home in one tongue. Through the use of language, the narrator is able to debunk Western cultural imperialism. In "Diseuse," language is likened, subtly, to (political) occupation in a female body:

She allows others. In place of her. Admits others to make full. Make swarm. All barren cavities to make swollen. The others each occupying her. . . . Now the weight begins from the uppermost back of her head, pressing downward. It stretches evenly, the entire skull expanding tightly all sides toward the front of her head. She gasps from its pressure, its contracting motion. (3–4)

Dictée is a multilayered, plural text. The book is Cha's own historiography, both history and comment on history at once. More so, on a different level, *Dictée* can be treated as a treatise on writing, memory, and time. The memory that Cha intends to restore is a differential one; it cannot be contained within the past, and it is as alive as the moment we live in. Such is why Cha resists the "grammar" of historical writing. For her, the only memory that is alive is carved in the present time. Therefore, Cha writes against time, against oblivion:

She says to herself if she were able to write she could continue to live. Says to herself if she would write without ceasing. To herself if by writing she could abolish real time. She would live. (141)

If we remember that Cha died right after publishing *Dictée*, her writing, indeed, seemed also Cha's performance of her own immortality.

CRITICAL RECEPTION

Dictée represents a new breed of literary production in Asian America: it departs from the American-centered narrative. This difference explains partly the somewhat slow recognition of *Dictée*. The decade after Cha's death, it was circulated and studied among small, but steady, groups of Cha's art admirers and Asian American scholars. There were more than a dozen posthumous shows on her (literary and visual) art; however, in literature, Walter K. Lew's collage, *Excerpts from: ΔIKTH DIKTE for* DICTEE *(1982)*, is the first full-length dedication to Cha from the postcolonial Korean perspective, and *Dictée* was not fully understood for a long time. Elaine H. Kim remarks, for example, "The first time I glanced at *Dictée*, I was put off by the book. I thought that Theresa Cha was talking not to me . . ." (3). Although there was critical and scholarly interest in *Dictée*, perchance the key factor that salvaged Cha's long out-of-print text was the redefining of Asian Americans and widening of Asian America. In

1994 *Dictée* was reprinted by Third Woman Press. With its reprint came also *Writing Self/Writing Nation*, Kim and Alarcón's collection of critical essays on *Dictée*. This critical volume, for sure, affirms the importance of Cha's book and, uncannily, assures Cha's "self-prophecy": *"She says to herself . . . by writing she could abolish real time. She would live"* (141).

BIBLIOGRAPHY

Works by Theresa Hak Kyung Cha

(Ed.). *Apparatus/Cinematographic Apparatus: Selected Writings*. New York: Tanam, 1980.
Dictée. New York: Tanam, 1982.

Studies of Theresa Hak Kyung Cha

Kim, Elaine H. "Poised on the In-between: A Korean American's Reflections on Theresa Hak Kyung Cha's *Dictée*." In *Writing Self/Writing Nation: A Collection of Essays on* Dictée *by Theresa Hak Kyung Cha*. Ed. Elaine H. Kim and Norma Alarcón. Berkeley: Third Women Press, 1994. 3–69.
Kim, Elaine H., and Norma Alarcón, eds. *Writing Self/Writing Nation: A Collection on Theresa Hak Kyung Cha's* Dictée. Berkeley: Third Women Press, 1994.
Lew, Walter K. *Excerpts from: ΔIKTH DIKTE for* DICTEE *(1982)*. Seoul, Korea: Yeul Eum, 1992.
Rinder, Lawrence. "The Theme of Displacement in the Art of Theresa Hak Kyung Cha and a Catalogue of the Artist's Oeuvre." M.A. thesis, Hunter College, City University of New York, 1990.
Sakai, Naoki. "Distinguishing Literature and the Work of Translation: Theresa Hak Kyung Cha's *Dictée* and Repetition without Return." In *Translation and Subjectivity: On "Japan" and Cultural Nationalism*. Minneapolis: University of Minnesota Press, 1997. 18–39.
Siegle, Robert. *Suburban Ambush: Downtown Writing and the Fiction of Insurgency*. Baltimore: Johns Hopkins University Press, 1989.
Stephens, Michael. "Korea: Theresa Hak Kyung Cha." *The Dramaturgy of Style: Voice in Short Fiction*. Carbondale: Southern Illinois University Press, 1986. 184–210.
Wilson, Rob. "Falling into the Korean Uncanny: On Reading Theresa Hak Kyung Cha's *Dictée*." *Korean Culture* 12 (Fall 1991): 33–37.
Wolf, Susan. "Theresa Cha: Recalling Telling Retelling." *Aferimage* 14.1 (Summer 1986):11–13.

Diana Chang
(1934–   )

Carol Roh-Spaulding

BIOGRAPHY

Diana Chang is regarded as the first American-born Chinese to publish a novel in the United States. She was born in New York City in 1934 to a Chinese father and an American-born Eurasian mother, but her parents moved to China when she was an infant. Chang was raised in various cities, including Beijing, Peking, Nanking, and Shanghai, the latter city becoming the setting for her best-known work, *Frontiers of Love*. Her formative years as a writer, however, were spent in the United States. Chang completed high school following the end of World War II and then returned to the United States, where she graduated from Barnard College in 1949. She lived in New York City, where she worked as an editor in book publishing and wrote *Frontiers of Love*, published in 1956. She went on to write five more novels between 1959 and 1978: *A Woman of Thirty* (1959), *A Passion for Life* (1961), *The Only Game in Town* (1963), *Eye to Eye* (1974), and *A Perfect Love* (1978), but only *Frontiers of Love* has received extensive critical attention, especially since its republication by the University of Washington Press in 1974, with an Introduction by Asian American writer and critic Shirley Geok-lin Lim. Four years after the publication of her last novel, Chang went on to publish three volumes of poetry, *The Horizon Is Definitely Speaking* (1982), *What Matisse Is After* (1984), and *Earth, Water, Light* (1991). She has also collaborated on two translated volumes of poetry by Chinese women, *Approaching* in 1989 and *Saying Yes* in 1991.

Chang is the recipient of several awards, including a Fulbright and the John Hay Whitney Fellowship. She served for a time as editor of the *American Pen* and was invited to join the faculty in English at Barnard College, where she taught creative writing for many years. Her stories and poems have appeared in a number of literary journals, and she continues to attract critical attention from critics in Asian American literature. She is active in the Asian American Writer's Workshop, based in New York City, where she gives readings of her work. Chang is also an accomplished painter and is regularly featured both in joint and single-artist showings of her work. She currently lives in Manhattan and Water Hill, Long Island.

MAJOR WORKS AND THEMES

Central to the novels of Diana Chang is the belief that individuals have the terrifying freedom and responsibility to create their own identity. This fundamentally existentialist idea is the major theme of Chang's first novel, *Frontiers of Love*. Set in the "Eurasian" city of Shanghai near the end of the war, the novel depicts the identity crises of three young Chinese Eurasians, nineteen-year-old Mimi Lambert, twenty-six-year-old Feng Huang, and twenty-year-old Sylvia Chen. Each character represents three possible responses to the conflict of a biracial and bicultural subjectivity. Mimi identifies with her Caucasian side, rejecting the part of her that is Chinese by becoming obsessed with Robert Bruno, her wealthy white lover, whose father forbids his son's marriage to a Eurasian and whose eventual rejection of Mimi leads to her downfall. Passionate and impulsive, Feng Huang becomes caught up in subversive communist activities with his Chinese comrades, rejecting both his Chinese father's wealth and the love and care of his divorced English mother. For a time he becomes Sylvia's lover, but ultimately, his desperate need to create an unambivalent and "pure" identity as a Chinese leads to Feng's downfall. Only the intensely self-conscious and ambivalent Sylvia is able to fashion for herself an identity that goes beyond nationality, ethnicity, parentage, or other social or political definitions to a strong and mature sense of self. She comes to believe that she must become "her own witness" and that forming one's own identity was "a responsibility and a gift you could not evade. No one else could supply one's own center" (239).

Chang's subsequent novels also take on the theme of existential responsibility toward one's self, although the focus on Eurasian identity does not appear again in her fiction. Instead, the later novels, with the exception of her fourth, *The Only Game in Town* (1963), feature only Caucasian characters and what Chang refers to as "universal" themes of identity and maturation. In *A Woman of Thirty*, young Emily Merrick's infatuation with the married architect who becomes her lover leads her to a crisis of identity in which she feels trapped between her own narrowly moral, white, Protestant upbringing and the human desire to remain open to the fullest possibilities in life. The scope and intensity of this crisis of identity are magnified in Chang's later novels, *A Passion for Life* and *Eye to Eye*. In these novels, as well, the characters must grapple with the socially enforced limitations of a white Protestant upbringing that has kept them from mature self-knowledge. In each case, the conflict arises from a consuming passion that launches the protagonist beyond conventional social codes, so that, ultimately, they gain the ironic insight achievable only by an outsider.

In contrast to her portrayal of Caucasian characters for the purpose, as Chang describes it, of portraying "Everyman" rather than the particular viewpoint of a Chinese or Chinese American, the author's published poetry continues the deeply ambivalent themes of biracial and bicultural identity that preoccupied the characters of her first novel. In one poem titled "An Appearance of Being Chinese," the speaker calls herself a "tall tale" who can never be authentically Chinese. (65). In another poem, "Second Nature," Chang seems to refer to her nationless status, writing, "I shuttle passportless within myself" (Wand 138). That there may be a price to pay for this fundamental identity disequilibrium, even if it is the wiser choice, is suggested in "The Horizon Is Definitely Speaking," when Chang writes, "We have practiced too well a partial living" (*Horizon* 29).

Just one of Chang's published stories, "The Oriental Contingent" deals with Chinese American identity and, as such, has been the subject of much recent critical attention. But, for the most part, the work of Diana Chang portrays "universal" characters and themes, allowing her to address the themes of most importance to her in her fiction—the individual's obligation to become himself on herself most fully and authentically despite his or her ethnicity. As Chang herself once explained, "I cannot present a more Chinese self because it may be expected of me; that would be jumping through ethnic hoops held up by majority, Caucasian or Chinese, conceptions and assumptions leading directly to a stereotyping we all know, nor can I not reveal a self who, though complex and very confusing often, is the self that I am." Notable in this stated defense of her subject matter is the declaration that, while Chang refuses to write from a recognizably Asian or Asian American perspective, she also refuses to reduce the complexity of issues of identity to a question of either/or, Caucasian or Chinese. In her poetry those themes are addressed personally, while in the majority of her novels and in most of her short fiction, Chang strives to make identity conflict and the resolution of that conflict relevant to the widest possible audience by subsuming "aspects of her background in the interest of other truths" (Ling, *Between Worlds* 119).

CRITICAL RECEPTION

Diana Chang began writing and publishing in 1956, prior to the advent of civil rights-era consciousness and the study of what has come to be referred to as "multicultural" literature. This is one reason that placing Chang's novels within the field of Asian American literature has proved difficult for critics: although her work has been claimed—and justifiably so—for the field of Asian American literature, the novels do not, for the most part, address Asian American themes or portray Asian American characters or settings, at least not in ways that most critics agree upon as recognizably Asian American. Original reviews of *Frontiers of Love* regard the book as a novel of war without calling into question Chang's own Asian or American status. In fact, Kenneth Rexroth's admiring review states quite simply, "She's one of ours" (273). No reviewer in 1956 regarded the identity conflict of Sylvia Chen as in any way transposable to issues of American ethnic identity. When Asian American literary criticism turned to consideration of Chang's work, however, response differed widely. Early nationalist-inspired Asian American critics such as Frank Chin were scornful of Chang's apparent refusal to address the themes of her people. Later, roughly parallel to the development of Asian American literary criticism as a whole, critics like Amy Ling, Shirley Geok-lin Lim, and Cynthia Sau-ling Wong began to recognize that the very notion of a diasporic identity and the consequent calling into question of what constituted the boundaries of Asian American literature and identity were precisely the themes that made Chang a contemporary Asian American writer. Shirley Lim regards Chang as a "protean author, a master of disguises whose authorial identity cannot be fixed by ethnicity" ("Twelve" 73). Such readings were followed by the latest generation of Asian American critics, who have found Chang's work rewarding for discussions of postmodern and "hybrid" identity. At the same time, however, critical response is limited almost exclusively to Chang's work that deals with recognizably Asian American characters or themes—her first novel, *The Frontiers of Love*, the body of her poetry, and her short story "The Oriental Contingent." Recent work on the "white" novels of Diana Chang (specifically, *A Woman of Thirty*, *A Passion for Life*, *Eye to Eye*, and *A Perfect Love*) has continued with the trend in Asian American literary criticism of addressing issues of individual subjectivity in addition to (Lowe, Wu), or, in some cases, as opposed to (Spaulding), identifiably "Asian American" content.

BIBLIOGRAPHY

Works by Diana Chang

Novels

The Frontiers of Love. New York: Random House, 1956; Seattle of University of Washington Press, 1994.
A Woman of Thirty. New York: Random House, 1959.
A Passion for Life. New York: Random House, 1961.
The Only Game in Town. New York: Signet, 1963.
Eye to Eye. New York: Harper and Row, 1974.
A Perfect Love. New York: Grove, 1978.

Short Stories

"Falling Free." *Crosscurrents: A Quarterly* 5.3 (1985): 55–72.
"Getting Around." *North American Review* (December 1986): 46–49.
"The Oriental Contingent." In *The Forbidden Stitch: An Asian American Women's An-*

thology. Ed. Shirley Geok-lin Lim, Mayumi Tsutakawa, and Margarita Donnelly. Corvallis, OR: Calyx Books, 1989.

"Once upon a Time." *North American Review* (March 1991): 50–51.

Poetry

"Otherness." In *Asian American Heritage.* Ed. David Hsin-fu Wand. New York: Washington Square Press, 1974. 135–138.

"Saying Yes." In *Asian American Heritage.* Ed. David Hsin-fu Wand. New York: Washington Square Press, 1974. 135–138.

"Second Nature." In *Asian American Heritage.* Ed. David Hsin-fu Ward. New York: Washington Square Press, 1974. 138.

"An Appearance of Being Chinese." *New York Quarterly* 17 (1975): 65–67.

The Horizon Is Definitely Speaking. Port Jefferson, NY: Backstreet Editions, 1982.

What Matisse Is After. New York: Contact House, 1984.

"In Two." *Ms.* (July–August 1988): 83.

"On Being in the Midwest." In *The Forbidden Stitch: An Asian American Women's Anthology.* Ed. Shirley Geok-lin Lim, Mayumi Tsutakawa, and Margarita Donnelly. Corvallis, OR: Calyx Books, 1989.

"On the Fly." In *The Forbidden Stitch: An Asian American Women's Anthology.* Ed. Shirley Geok-lin Lim, Mayumi Tsutakawa, and Margarita Donnelly. Corvallis, OR: Calyx Books, 1989.

Earth, Water, Light: Poems Celebrating the East End of Long Island. Brentwood, NY: Binham Wood Graphics, 1991.

Translations

Approaching. Ed. Parker P. Huang, Diana Chang, and Stanley H. Barker. Merrick, NY: Cross Cultural Communications, 1989.

Saying Yes. Ed. Parker P. Huang, Diana Chang, and Stanley H. Barker. Merrick, NY: Cross Cultural Communications, 1991.

Articles

"Why Do Writers Write?" *American Pen* (Summer 1969): 1–3.

"Wool Gathering, Ventriloquism, and the Double Life." *American Pen* (Summer 1970): 1–4.

Studies of Diana Chang

Bowers, Faubion. Rev. of *Frontiers of Love. Saturday Review* 39 (1956): 13.

Cheung, King-Kok. *An Interethnic Companion to Asian American Literature.* New York: Cambridge University Press, 1997. 297, 299.

Gelfant, Blanche H. Rev. of *Eye to Eye. The Hudson Review* 28 (1975): 313–14.

Hamalian, Leo. "A MELUS Interview: Diana Chang." *MELUS: The Journal of the Society for the Study of the Multi Ethnic Literature of the United States* 20.4 (1995): 29–43.

Lease, Benjamin. "Struggle and Love in Shanghai." Rev. of *Frontiers of Love. Chicago Sun-Times,* September 23, 1956, sec. 2:4.

Leebove, Patricia Harusame. Rev. of *Frontiers of Love*. *Belles Lettres: A Review of Books by Women* 10.2 (1995): 66.

Lim, Shirley Geok-lin. "Introduction." *The Frontiers of Love*. Seattle: University of Washington Press, 1994. v–xxiii.

———. "Twelve Asian American Writers in Search of Self-Definition." *MELUS: The Journal of the Society for the Study of the Multi Ethnic Literature of the United States* 13.1–2 (1996): 57–77.

Ling, Amy. *Between Worlds: Women Writers of Chinese Ancestry*. New York: Pergamon Press, 1990.

———. "Writer in the Hyphenated Condition: Diana Chang." *MELUS: The Journal of the Society for the Study of the Multi Ethnic Literature of the United States* 7.4 (1980): 69–83.

Lowe, Lisa. *Immigrant Acts: On Asian American Cultural Politics*. Durham, NC, and London: Duke University Press, 1996. 63–64.

Prescott, Orville. Rev. of *Frontiers of Love*. *New York Times*, September 24, 1956, 25.

Rexroth, Kenneth. Rev. of *Frontiers of Love*. *Nation* (September 29, 1956): 271–73.

Spaulding, Carol Vivian. "Blue-Eyed Asians: Eurasianism in the Work of Edith Eaton/Sui Sin Far, Winnifred Eaton/Onoto Watanna, and Diana Chang." Diss., University of Iowa, 1997. Ann Arbor, MI: DAI DA9640020.

Wong, Cynthia Sau-ling. *Reading Asian American Literature: From Necessity to Extravagance*. Princeton: Princeton University Press, 1993. 98.

Wu, Kitty Wei-hsuing. "Cultural Ideology and Aesthetic Choices: A Study of Three Works by Chinese American Women: Diana Chang, Bette Bao Lord, and Maxine Hong Kingston." Diss., University of Maryland, 1989.

Evelina Chao
(1949–)

Wentong Ma

BIOGRAPHY

Born in Chicago in 1949, Evelina Chao belongs to the second-generation Chinese Americans. Not much biographical information has been made available about the author of *Gates of Grace* except a short Introduction that appears in *Contemporary Authors*. According to *Contemporary Authors*, Evelina Chao, daughter of Edward C. T. and Vera Lin, attended Oberlin College from 1968 to 1969. She got her bachelor of music, however, from Juilliard School in 1972. Later on, she completed her master of music at the State University of New York at Binghamton in 1974.

Chao played the first violin from 1972 to 1974 at Binghamton's Amici Quartet. After leaving Binghamton in 1974, she became a freelance musician and teacher in both New York and Pennsylvania. In 1977 she joined Indianapolis Symphony as the first violin. She left Indiana in 1980 to become a member of the St. Paul Chamber Orchestra in Minnesota, where she has been an assistant principal viola since.

In an interview with *Contemporary Authors*, responding obviously to a question as regards musicianship and authorship, Chao has this to say: "The fact that I am a professional musician has helped me greatly in becoming a writer. The hours I have spent alone practicing and working on violin/viola technique, the development of discipline, concentration, love of solitude, and dealing with anxiety and rejection have all been of immeasurable help" (77). Chao knows from experience anxiety and rejection and, most importantly, perseverance in the face of all that negative situation a person of color has to encounter. To be a writer, to get published, Chao has to overcome the same level of difficulty and rejection as she obviously did in the music world.

Chao personally experienced discrimination, which led to her writing (*Contemporary Authors*). She attributes that discrimination not only to Americans' having a limited view of Asians due to their naïveté and inexperience but also to Asians' own unwillingness to divulge their lives. To do something about this drives Chao to write *Gates of Grace*: in her own words, she "seeks to explore and possibly illuminate the stereotypical view held of Asians by Westerners" (*Contemporary Authors* 77).

MAJOR WORK AND THEMES

Exploration the novel certainly is, but one is puzzled as to what kind of illumination one could possibly have on discrimination. Or does this illumination lie in attributing the fault of discrimination to both the Westerners and Asians, as cited earlier? In other words (for this could be exactly the subtext of Chao's novel under discussion), if the limited views of Asians held in the West are expanded, and the unwillingness to divulge their lives on the part of Asians is dispelled (for instance, through volitionally writing a novel called *Gates of Grace*), then everything will be fine or can be worked to a kind of optimum state in which the novel ends. Undoubtedly, Chao advocates the principle of great reconciliation for ethnic harmony, the hallmark of "melting pot" logic, which has failed to work in recent decades, having served its limited historical function.

But to judge *Gates of Grace* purely on the level of pro-"melting pot" will be a little unfair, as mixed in the novel are elements that Chao had already alluded to in the interview with *Contemporary Authors*. One of the elements is the notion of mythology, which Chao characterizes as follows: "I feel the Chinese experience is infused with a particularly vivid and deep-rooted mythology. The collision of this spectacular mythology with American life and values creates a complex moral dilemma for all Chinese, and it is this dilemma that I am compelled to examine and describe" (77).

For now, one can only cite *Gates of Grace* as the evidence of Chao's examination and description, because the announced work in progress titled *The Return of Hoping* has been abandoned, while the work to replace that, *The River of Years*, still awaits a publisher. Let's first take a look at the published novel.

Gates of Grace sets its background against the surprising events in the late 1940s in China, when Mao's communists, pushing forward on all fronts, drove the ever-disintegrating KMT (Nationalist Party) troops to the south. Under this circumstance of imminent takeover by a new regime, people had many ways of escape. For those who were sick and tired of the corrupted KMT government, the incoming communists, who avowed to serve the interest of the people, bolstered their hope for a fair and just government. These people therefore stayed on. Those die-hard KMT cronies fled with their boss to the small island of Taiwan. Those who were more resourceful, though disillusioned about any politics, sought their escape elsewhere; they sailed across the ocean to the other side of the world. This last resort became the fate of Kung-Chiao and Mei-Yu, an intellectual couple who left China on the eve of revolution.

The novel opens on the scene of departure on an ocean liner. Like thousands of others, Kung-Chiao and Mei-Yu were fleeing the country. But the couple also had their personal predicament. They fled the country also to seek a marital freedom that their parents denied them, so the departure was in the meantime an elopement. Once settled in New York, Kung-Chiao went to school at New York University, and Mei-Yu worked as a dressmaker. Kung-Chiao was then mysteriously murdered, leaving Mei-Yu with their daughter. The community of Chinatown extended a helping hand, led by an old lady, Ling, the widow of a warlord.

Ling brought Mei-Yu under her own roof. She arranged for Mei-Yu several good business deals, the profit from which enabled the latter to survive and support her daughter. Ling then drew Mei-Yu's attention to a business venture in Washington, D.C. Through the connection of her son, a practicing lawyer, Ling opened a garment factory where Mei-Yu assumed the position of the head seamstress. It so happened that Ling's son, Richard, abandoned his former lover, a Taiwanese, and fell for Mei-Yu, who was still considered young and pretty. They married and had a son. Richard, unsatisfied with the law firm with which he was associated, finally opened his private firm. The story would be much too bland if it just ended there.

The surprise came with the revelation of Madame Ling's will, in which she confessed orchestrating the death of Mei-Yu's husband, Kung-Chiao. Ling had arranged both the waylay and the murder but got away scot-free, as she was clever enough to lay the blame on another Chinese whom she recognized as the murderer of her own husband in wartime China. With a move like this, Ling got rid of her enemy, avenged herself, and further put under her roof a woman whom she would like her son to marry. Richard suspected as much but, out of devotion to his mother and lacking hard proof, never questioned her. Mei-Yu took the news with equanimity, in order to keep the status quo. The second generation, however, revolted, being less forgiving. The daughter of Mei-Yu found it hard to reconcile with her stepfather. When choosing a college, she picked Columbia University in New York, away from both her parents.

The novel serves to vindicate Chao's characterization of Chinese people who came to settle in a new country. These people brought with them mythology and mystery. Chao has done much to either dispel or clarify that mystery. But due to lack of a sense of history, the effort to dispel and illuminate falls short of being satisfactory. This is clear on several occasions. The first occurs in the beginning of the novel, the part of the book that deals with a historical period that Chao presents with limited understanding. Therefore, her account is stamped with the mark of hearsay and incomprehension (5). The incomprehension is inherited from a class of intellectuals in contemporary China who have never studied the problems of the Chinese people. The result is that they always look at the epoch-making event of communism with distaste. Communists are looked upon as a force that both thrives and is supported by the mobs of desperately poor people, like the mob we encounter in the beginning of the novel. What is revealed is an uncalled-for arrogance toward the poor and the unfortunate to whom, up till 1949, no one but radical communists could render some help.

On another occasion, Chao makes greater efforts to illuminate Chinese mythology. When Mei-Yu's daughter encountered racism at school, the mother followed the well-intentioned suggestion of letting students know more about China. She put on a *qipao* (traditional close-fitting dress with high neck and slit skirt) and delivered a speech, complete with exotic exhibits. Thereafter, her daughter was looked on with respect and understanding.

Living in the late 1990s, many people know that an endeavor like this is not likely to work anymore, though it is being pursued just as much now as it was in the old days. Whether it reinforces the stereotypes or builds cultural understanding and harmony, such an endeavor, looked at through historical lenses, deserves some praise only insofar as it is regarded as no more than a historical expediency, the practice of which requires care and new awareness of the roots of racism. In this regard, the effort to dispel and clarify a mythology or mystery appears misguided. It is misleading because it leads people to believe that skin-deep clarification will heal the wounds of racism. History—material history, to be exact—on the contrary, is going to clarify everything, history from which, in this sense, not even the fabrication of art, for instance, the novelistic art, can get away.

CRITICAL RECEPTION

Evelina Chao's work is not widely publicized and has received no scholarly attention beyond some favorable reviews that are not accessible. The entry in *Contemporary Authors* is the only published record available so far.

BIBLIOGRAPHY

Works by Evelina Chao

Novel

Gates of Grace. New York: Warner Books, 1985.

Articles and Reviews

"Come Watch the Sun Go Home." Rev. of *Come Watch the Sun Go Home*. *Minneapolis Star Tribune*, December 6, 1998. C3.
"A Look inside the World of Four Passionate Musicians." *Minneapolis Star Tribune*, January 31, 1999. C9.
"SPCO Plays in Hong Kong, Singapore." *Minneapolis Star Tribune*, February 20, 1999. A6.

Study of Evelina Chao

Contemporary Authors. Vol. 120. Detroit: Gale Research, 1987. 76–77.

Frank Chin
(1940–   )

Guiyou Huang

BIOGRAPHY

Frank Chin was born in 1940 in Berkeley, California. At an early age he moved to Oakland to realize "big ideas." Chin graduated from the University of California at Berkeley. He claims to be the first Chinese American brakeman on the Southern Pacific Railroad, a personal and professional experience that he masterfully sketches in various works. Chin was also the first Asian American playwright to have a play produced at the American Place Theatre in New York, in 1972, when Asian American writing as literature had hardly been heard of, not to mention recognized.

Chin did not start out as a playwright, which he became by pure accident. In 1970 he went to Maui, Hawaii, where he worked with friends in construction. When the East/West Players in Los Angeles held a playwriting contest, prompted by an urge to get off the island, Chin wrote *The Chickencoop Chinaman* in six weeks, won the $500 contest, and left the island. Then Chin met Randy Kim, a Chinese/Korean American actor who made his writing "fast, fun, and sharp" (Davis, *Amerasia* 86), and with Kim in mind he wrote his second play, *The Year of the Dragon*, which was also staged at the American Place Theatre in New York.

After the plays, Chin produced a collection of eight short stories and published them under the title *The Chinaman Pacific and Frisco R. R. Co.* in 1988, which received the American Book Award from the Before Columbus Foundation. In the early 1990s Chin devoted a considerable amount of creative energy to writing novels, publishing *Donald Duk* in 1991 and *Gunga Din Highway* in 1994. Chin's novels were influenced by black writers such as Reed as well as by classical Chinese writers such as Luo Guanzhong and Shi Nai'an, respective authors of *Romance of the Three Kingdoms* and *Water Margin*. Chin is also considerably immersed in other Chinese classics such as Wu Cheng'en's *Journey to the West* and the must-read for all Chinese military academies and many U.S. military institutions, Sun Tzu's *The Art of War*, the all-time masterpiece on warfare. In fact, Chin's thinking on social, cultural, religious, intellectual, and racial issues has benefited from his studies of these classics. To say that Chin emulates the 1960s black revolutionaries is to underestimate the shaping power of these Chinese masterpieces on war and warfare.

Chin is a controversial figure in the Asian American literary and cultural communities. He is recognized by some as the "Godfather" of Asian American writing (*The Big Aiiieeeee!* 529); others have called him an acrimonious critic. Indeed, Chin can be anything but boring, and he has contributed something to almost every Asian American literary genre as playwright, novelist, essayist, critic, and editor. He was the first editor of the groundbreaking Asian American anthology entitled *Aiiieeeee!* and second editor of *The Big Aiiieeeee!*, though he has been primarily regarded as a playwright and, in recent years, a novelist.

MAJOR WORKS AND THEMES

"Frank Chin is known for uncompromising portrayals of Chinese Americans and for incorporation of Chinese mythology into his works," comments *Asian American Voices* (a Coffee House Press sampler) on Chin's thematic concerns in both his drama and fiction (186). The themes that Chin hammers at in his plays, novels, short stories, and even his poignant essays all concern Asian America, and he handles them in such a way that they do not seem to be intended to please any one particular racial group or another. Reviewing *Donald Duk*, Robert Murray Davis writes, "Chin seems in all his prose to write best about railroads, intellectual guerrilla warfare, and eating" (715), an observation that aptly sums up some of Chin's themes.

In his novels Chin also pursues historical, social, and intellectual issues relevant to Chinese American and Asian American cultural heritages. He seems pointedly interested in the way mainstream American media—Hollywood film industry in particular—represent the yellow man in predominantly white America. Chin appears to be the only Asian American writer who all too often resorts to the term "yellow" that so many other Asian American writers have shunned. Aside from energetically assaulting the media—and the Charlie Chan movies— Chin picks personal fights with nonwhite print media that, he believes, either contribute to the stereotyping of the yellow man by mainstream writers and the film and television industries or are accomplices in various forms of victimization of Asian Americans.

Chin's first attempt at fiction resulted in *Donald Duk*, a novel that portrays a twelve-year-old Chinatown boy comically called Donald Duk, who wants to be a dancer like Fred Astaire and who hates his name and things Chinese, more so because Chinese New Year is around the corner, which means ethnic Chinese

cultural traditions (represented by Cantonese opera) and family unions will be
highlights of celebration in Chinatown, accompanied by elaborate preparing and
eating of Chinese food. The novel delves into Chinese American history through
the dreams of Donald Duk, which all revolve around one monumental event in
the nineteenth-century history of the United States: the building of the transcontinental railroad. Donald's knowledge of the Chinese participation in the development of the American West—acquired through reading or learned from his
older relatives such as Uncle Donald—enables him to catch errors in his history
teacher Mr. Meanwright's classroom presentation of the Chinese, therefore challenging the stereotypical and bookish views of his race.

The teacher reads from a history book written by his Berkeley professor, who
thus characterizes the Chinese:

"The Chinese in America were made passive and nonassertive by centuries of Confucian
thought and Zen mysticism. They were totally unprepared for the violently individualistic
and democratic Americans. From their first step on American soil to the middle of the
twentieth century, the timid, introverted Chinese have been helpless against the relentless
victimization by aggressive, highly competitive Americans." (2)

The teacher's appreciative way of reading from his professor's book angers
Donald, who whispers to his white pal Arnold Azalea, "Same thing as everybody—Chinese are artsy, cutesy and chickendick" (3). Donald's father, King
Duk, and his Uncle Donald are, however, not openly critical of such demeaning
of their race; instead, they teach him more subtle ways of defending himself
and averting racial violence.

Chin's frequent invocations of the 108 outlaws so heroically depicted in Shi
Nai'an's *Water Margin* are intended as counterevidence (cultural and historical)
against racial theories that portray Chinese as nonassertive and passive. These
108 outlaw heroes, known to every Chinese literate and illiterate, asserted themselves by rising up against government's cruel taxation and tyrannical oppression
and in the end became heroes praised and emulated by subsequent generations
of Chinese at home and abroad. In addition to this textual and historical evidence
meant to contradict the stereotyping of Chinese as passive and nonassertive,
Chin digs up evidence from the forgotten leaves of American history—the building of the railroad in which Chinese laborers not only participated but were the
most competitive workforce. In the tracklaying contests, Chinese laborers beat
their Irish counterparts by laying ten miles in one day and set a world record.
The leader of the Chinese gangs was Kwan the Foreman, who not only shared
the family name of Kwan Kung of *Romance of the Three Kingdoms*—the god
of war and literature—but indeed lived up to the reputation of a people whose
accomplishments can be judged by qualities pertaining only to competitive, courageous heroes who represent "the heroic tradition" Chin so admiringly writes
about in his works.

But in the "official" American history annals, only the names of the Irish railroad builders were recorded, not the Chinamen's, which bothered Donald but not his father, who told him, " 'They don't want our names in their history books. So what? You're surprised. If we don't write our history, why should they, huh?' " He advised his son to "keep the history yourself or lose it forever, boy. That's the mandate of heaven" (122). Donald and his friend Arnold Azalea conducted library research for factual information on Chinese railroad builders and found books and photos that exposed the lies about the Chinese, so that Donald was able to correct his history teacher of his erroneous knowledge about who really built the railroads. Donald therefore rediscovered a Chinamen's history, exposed historical lies told by the whites, and dispelled the myth of Chinese as being passive, nonassertive, and noncompetitive; ultimately, he gained racial pride in himself, his family, and his Chinese race.

Frank Chin continues his mission as an Asian American writer working on racial and cultural issues in his second novel, *Gunga Din Highway*. This title was adapted from Rudyard Kipling's ballad about the Indian water boy who helped the British fight his own people. Chin is convinced that of contemporary Asian American writers, some have taken the Gunga Din Highway in their eagerness to gain mainstream acceptance and willingness to assimilate into the dominant white culture. In his famous and controversial "This Is Not an Autobiography" and "Come All Ye Asian American Writers of the Real and the Fake" Chin angrily attacks what he believes to be "fake" Asian American writers—Maxine Hong Kingston,* David Henry Hwang, Betty Bao Lord,* and Amy Tan,* though it would be next to impossible to determine how one Asian American writer is fake, and another is real. Broadly stated, in Chin's opinion, these writers all conspire with the white Establishment in order for their works to be marketable and for themselves to be accepted, by "selling out" real Chinese and Chinese American cultures and histories. Or, to phrase it in Saidian terms, these writers Orientalize Asian cultures and peoples. In *Gunga Din Highway* Chin consciously resists such representations.

Gunga Din Highway is a complex novel blending Chinese myth and classics with American pop culture and Hollywood movies. Unlike Kingston and Tan, who concentrate on mother–daughter relationships, Chin focuses on the tensions of father–son relationships, which is intended to showcase opposing views of racial and cultural stereotyping and victimization of Chinese Americans, deployed around the notorious, familiar screen image of the Chinese detective Charlie Chan, whom the father, Longman Kwan, wants to be the first Chinese to play and whom Ulysses the son (the protagonist) hates as much as he does his father. To satirize the hypocrisy of Christianity and to parody its structural hierarchy, Chin breaks his long narrative into four sections. In the first section, "The Creation," Chin recounts the Chinese mythic story of creation and proceeds to set up Charlie Chan—indeed, his white player Anlauf Lorane—as the father and Longman Kwan—Chan's Number Four Son and the Chinaman Who Dies— as the son, and if there is a ghost, that may well be Hollywood.

Longman Kwan's lifelong ambition is to become the first Chinese to play

Charlie Chan, not to break Hollywood's preference for Caucasian males for the role of an Oriental man but rather to fulfill his own desire for fame. In his son Ulysses' mind, however, Longman Kwan only reinforces the stereotyping of Chinese by wanting to play and *be* Charlie Chan, while the "real" Chan (the white player) is getting decrepit, fat, obscene, all symptoms of health declining toward death. Ulysses S. Kwan, on the other hand, was named after James Joyce's novel as well as Kwan Kung, the archetypal male who represents freedom, rebellion, and creativity. We might as well add that his name also resembles that of the former U.S. president, Ulysses S. Grant. Ulysses is an actor in his friend Benedict Han/Mo's plays, leading a picaresque life of his own while remaining an observer and perhaps judge of his father's moral and professional conduct.

Chin satirizes Charlie Chan and his white players as well as his four sons, all Chinese and all hoping to play Chan some day. He also mocks Charlie Chan admirers and supporters, most noteworthy of whom is Pandora Toy, author of film reviews, essays, and a book called *The Conqueror Woman*, an obvious reminder of Kingston's *The Woman Warrior*. Pandora Toy is a dynamic character in part 3, "The Underworld." Her essay, "A Neurotic Exotic Erotic Orientoxic," seems to be used as a reified instance of the practice of Orientalism by an American Oriental, who, as a Chinese woman who loves sex but unfortunately was born in an "unmanly culture" (251), is appalled by the nonsexiness and lack of attraction of Chinese men. Pandora Toy and her husband, Benedict Han (Ulysses' blood brother), and Longman Kwan (who admires Toy's review of his cinematic performances, among other things) all are admirers of Charlie Chan and therefore represent "fake" Asian Americans.

Longman Kwan dies in the end, as does his wife, Hyacinth. Perishing with him is his hope of becoming the first Chinese to play Charlie Chan, just like some wishes of Pandora Toy, whose name suggests nothing more than a tantalizing sign of hope. Longman Kwan's death signals the end of the Charlie Chan era, if not that of all racial stereotyping and misrepresentation.

CRITICAL RECEPTION

Chin's plays and short stories seem to have received more critical attention than his novels, and it may be fair to say that his creative writings have, overall, been underestimated, though as editor and critic he has been extensively quoted by scholars and critics. His novels *Donald Duk* and *Gunga Din Highway* have been reviewed in many journals, magazines, and newspapers, and most reviews are relatively short notices. Like most book reviews, some reviews of his novels are lukewarm; others commend him for his creative energy and uncompromising portrayals of characters; but little has been said that is totally negative.

In her review of *Donald Duk* Janet Ingraham writes, "Chin spices his first novel with a flip, clipped, present-tense narrative voice, slapstick dialog, and kinetic dreamscapes. The result is a tart social comment packed into a cartoon, with verbal energy verging on hyperactivity" (220). Robert Murray Davis commends Chin for producing a more accessible work in *Donald Duk* than most of the stories in *The Chinaman Pacific and Frisco R. R. Co*. Davis suggests, "*Donald Duk* can be read as an introduction to Chin's more difficult work or as an example of Asian-American narrative that takes a perspective very different from Maxine Hong Kingston's. More important, it deserves to be read on its own merits as a lively and masterful piece of storytelling" (715). *Donald Duk* seems easier reading, perhaps because it is short and has one major story line.

Tom De Haven notices a common quality that Donald Duk shares with his cartoon namesake, and that is a "truculent disposition" that manifests itself in the boy's despising an ethnic culture "he finds ludicrous and deeply embarrassing" (9). Donald's character changes as a result of the education he receives. That education goes beyond what is taught in the classroom by white teachers; it comes in a series of haunted dreams, in which Donald lived and toiled as a railroad builder among his fellow Chinamen in the spring of 1869. De Haven further writes, "Throughout 'Donald Duk,' Mr. Chin's energy is high and his invention lively, but all too often the narrative seems rushed, filled with first-draft bursts of staccato prose. For every scene that reads true or funny, there's another that seems arbitrary or forced, and occasionally—as in the diatribe against the television newswoman Connie Chung—downright meanspirited" (9). Despite its crammed and unsorted nature, De Haven asserts, "Donald Duk, and his eponymous novel, come vigorously, even heroically, alive" (9).

Gunga Din Highway, a much longer work, has received similar responses. According to Donna Seaman, Chin's second novel is "a frenetic, irreverent, and episodic father-and-son saga that encompasses some five decades of American clichés, moviemaking, and image bashing." Seaman recognizes the hero Ulysses' alienation from both his father and "authentic Chinese culture," or Hollywood's "warped version of it." Regarding Chin's narrative techniques, Seaman comments, "Chin sets Ulysses' serendipitous adventures within a comic book-style cultural survey that mocks everything American, from movies to music, drugs, politics, the media, pornography, and racism" (111).

Robert Murray Davis reviewed *Donald Duk* and once also interviewed Chin for *Amerasia*. In his notice of *Gunga Din Highway*, Davis suggests a few pre-requisites for reading the novel, including real and made-up American movies, Chinese classics, W. H. Auden and Hemingway, and some knowledge of Chin's life, all of which suggest the richness and complexity of the novel. But Davis himself falls prey to not being conversant in Chinese classics, as is obvious in his failure to explain the relationships among Ulysses; his father, Longman Kwan; Charlie Chan; and Sun Tzu. Davis writes, "Ulysses, the strategist, tries to avoid becoming the grandson of Chan, but, ironically, the pseudonym of the author of *The Art of War* is 'the Grandson' " (361). "Tzu" in Sun Tzu, like in Lao Tzu or Kong Tzu (Confucius), is a respectful vocative used to address a highly venerable worthy, especially an ancient, having nothing to do with the notion of grandson; though the two pairs of ideograms are identical, their pronunciations have different intonations. (Sun Tzu's real name is Sun Wu.)

Rebecca Stuhr-Rommereim agrees with other reviewers and adds, "Despite the odd pedantic paragraph, descriptions are vivid and arresting and the writing is convincing. Chin is an important writer, and this new book should be added to all collections" (111). Claudia Ricci, on the other hand, speaks of the novel less positively and recognizes its satirical intent as well as its preoccupation with Hollywood's condescending portrayals of Asians. Ricci also faults Chin for his poor characterization: "Mr. Chin presents us with a huge cast of characters, most of whom, alas, never manage to evoke deep sympathy or concern. His prose deftly combines humor with deadly cynicism, but its disdainful tone keeps the reader at a distance" (16).

By far the most comprehensive evaluation of *Gunga Din Highway* is provided by Wen-ching Ho. Ho calls it "an ambitious novel of satire and protest" that "deals mainly with Chinese America's predominant attitude toward Hollywood film industry's deliberate misrepresentation and underrepresentation of Chinese Americans and their culture" (158). Ho also identifies Pandora Toy in the novel as a parody of Maxine Hong Kingston, so "*Gunga Din Highway* is a rejoinder to Kingston's parody of Frank Chin in *Tripmaster Monkey*" (159). Ho reads the novel as Ulysses Kwan's awakening realization of the precariousness of his racial identity, which then set him "on a quest for his cultural and racial identity" (160).

Ho nevertheless shares Claudia Ricci's reservation about Chin's methods of characterization. "Besides its grand-scale temporal and spatial design, the novel also contains an imposing array of characters, but most of them appear only a couple of times" (161). Ho finds weakness in its narrative structure caused partly by seemingly random use of subtitles that she believes are "translations of well-known Chinese idioms" and writes that "it is sometimes difficult to decipher the connection between a subtitle and the episode proper" (161). In fact, most of the subtitles Ho refers to are not just well-known idioms; they are some stratagems expressible in four-word Chinese collocations developed and expounded by Sun Tzu in *The Art of War*, one of several Chinese classics that Chin seems most familiar with and never tires of quoting in almost all his works.

BIBLIOGRAPHY

Works by Frank Chin

Novels

Donald Duk. Minneapolis: Coffee House, 1991.
Gunga Din Highway. Minneapolis: Coffee House, 1994.

Short Stories

The Chinaman Pacific and Frisco R. R. Co. Minneapolis: Coffee House, 1988.

Plays

The Chickencoop Chinaman and The Year of the Dragon. Seattle: University of Washington Press, 1981.

Edited Work

(with Jeffery Paul Chan, Lawson Fusao Inada, and Shawn Wong). *Aiiieeeee!* Washington, DC: Howard University Press, 1974.

The Big Aiiieeeee! (With Jeffrey Paul Chan, Lawson Fusao Inada, and Shawn Wong). New York: Meridian, 1991.

Essays and Articles

"This Is Not an Autobiography." *Genre* 18 (Summer 1985): 109–30.

"Who Runs Asian American Studies?" *Amerasia* 16.2 (1990): 143–45.

"Come All Ye Asian American Writers of the Real and the Fake." In *The Big Aiiieeeee!* Ed. Jeffrey Paul Chan, Frank Chin, Lawson Fusao Inada, and Shawn Wong. New York: Meridian, 1991. 1–92.

"Uncle Frank's Fakebook of Fairy Tales for Asian American Moms and Dads." *Amerasia Journal* 18.2 (1992): 69–87.

Studies of Frank Chin

Davis, Robert Murray. "Frank Chin: An Interview with Robert Murray Davis." *Amerasia* 14.2 (1988): 81–95.

———. Rev. of *Donald Duk. World Literature Today* 65.4 (Autumn 1991): 715.

———. Rev. of *Gunga Din Highway. World Literature Today* 69.2 (Spring 1995): 360–61.

De Haven, Tom. Rev. of *Donald Duk. New York Times Book Review* (March 31, 1991): 9.

Ho, Wen-ching. Rev. of *Gunga Din Highway. Amerasia Journal* 22.2 (1996): 158–61.

Ingraham, Janet. Rev. of *Donald Duk. Library Journal* 116 (February 15, 1991): 220.

Ricci, Claudia. Rev. of *Gunga Din Highway. New York Times Book Review* (January 29, 1995): 16.

Seaman, Donna. Rev. of *Gunga Din Highway. Booklist* 91.2 (September 15, 1994): 111.

Shervington, Sharon L. "Not by Shakespeare Alone." *New York Times Book Review* (March 31, 1991): 9.

Stuhr-Rommereim, Rebecca. Rev. of *Gunga Din Highway. Library Journal* 119 (October 1, 1994): 111.

Sook Nyul Choi
(1937–)

Mara Scanlon

BIOGRAPHY

Sook Nyul Choi was born in 1937 in Pyongyang in what is now North Korea. Although Choi refers to her novels as "fictional history," many critics see them as autobiography, and their major events correlate to Choi's own tumultuous youth. During World War II in Japanese-occupied Korea, Choi's family (like that of Sookan Bak, the heroine of her novels) suffered great losses at the hands of the occupiers. When Japanese control gave way to the authority of the Soviet communists, Choi, her mother, and her younger brother escaped across the 38th parallel to South Korea, seeking the safety of American protection. Their life in Seoul was disrupted again in 1950, when the Korean War ravaged the nation. In the midst of trauma and dislocation, Choi's writing began: "In grammar school and high school I wrote short stories, poetry, and newspaper articles in Korean," the author reports (qtd. in Vandergrift 3). In 1958 Choi immigrated to the United States to attend Manhattanville College in New York. Choi married a Korean businessman, and, after his sudden death, she worked in his export-import business before going into teaching. She taught in the New York City school system for almost twenty years while raising her two daughters, before turning to writing. Now retired from teaching and living in Cambridge, Massachusetts, Choi devotes her energies to writing fiction and children's literature.

Choi's first novel, *Year of Impossible Goodbyes*, was published in 1991 in the United States. In the intervening years, it has also been translated into Korean, French, Italian, and Japanese. This story of Sookan Bak's childhood was followed by the sequels *Echoes of the White Giraffe* in 1993 and *Gathering of Pearls* in 1994. Choi has also written three books for younger children, each of which identifies the cultural tensions and richness of the Korean American experience. *Halmoni and the Picnic* was published in 1993, followed by *The Best Older Sister* and *Yummi and Halmoni's Trip* in 1997.

Despite the close ties to Korea evidenced in Choi's fiction, the author considers herself " 'an American, not an Asian-American. . . . I wrote [*Year*] as an American educator, as an American citizen,' " she says, in response to students' requests to write a book about her experiences when they found a dearth of Asian texts on World War II. Choi explains, " 'As my grandfather said, you contribute to where you live. The United States embraced me. I embrace it back' " (qtd. in McCabe 66).

MAJOR WORKS AND THEMES

The three autobiographically based novels that form the series on Sookan Bak represent Choi's major works. Each, along with Choi's picture books for smaller children (such as *Halmoni and the Picnic*, in which a traditional Korean grandmother is welcomed by her American granddaughter's classmates), includes themes of maintenance and respect for tradition and its sometimes uneasy relationship to individualism. With the tone of a memoir, *Year of Impossible Goodbyes* chronicles the tenacity of the Bak family's preservation of Korean ethnicity during Japanese occupation. Ten-year-old Sookan's absent father is working in the Korean independence movement; her brothers and uncle are in labor camps. At home, Sookan learns Hangul (the Korean script) and Buddhist practice from her grandfather, the character who most embodies tradition. He fights to preserve national and family history, even the memory of torture, in the face of systematic efforts to obliterate it. Finding that the family retains some semblance of hope or pleasure, the Japanese punish them by forcing the girls who work in their sock factory to become "spirit girls" for the Japanese army and by cutting down the pine tree in the yard, a violation of beauty that leads to Grandfather's shock and death. When the Japanese surrender, the Baks rejoice in the reestablishment of their Korean culture, but they are disappointed when the Soviet communists come to organize locals into party members. In a terrifying attempt at escape to South Korea, Sookan and her brother Inchun are separated from their mother and must cross the 38th parallel alone. The family is eventually reunited in Seoul.

Echoes of the White Giraffe again finds Sookan, Inchun, and their mother as refugees in Pusan during the Korean War around 1950. The White Giraffe is an old poet who calls the refugees each morning to awake to a new and better day, a sound Sookan treasures. Concentrating on the adolescent Sookan's innocent, but forbidden, relationship with a young man and her hopeful preparation for school in America, this novel begins to focus more clearly on Sookan's growing independence. *Gathering of Pearls*, which follows Sookan to college in the United States in 1954, chronicles her struggles to reconcile the traditional expectations of her family at home with the independence and challenges of her new American life, a task made harder by her mother's death.

Choi's theme of individualism manifests itself as an unconventional feminist independence for girls and women. A sense of autonomy marks the Western spirit for Choi: "Growing up under Japanese rule, we were told that the individual is nothing. Over here, the individual person has value" (qtd. in McCabe 66). Sookan, Choi's heroine, exhibits this sustaining individualism during her escape from South Korea, through her hope and determination as a refugee, and in her tenacious resolve to pursue an education in the United States despite its violation of appropriate feminine roles. The feminist aspect of Choi's novels is also developed through the strong community of girls and women with whom Sookan finds support, especially in the character of her understanding and enduring mother. Choi's picture book *The Best Older Sister*, in which Sunhi learns that she is just as loved as her new brother Kiju, carries a similar theme of (re)valuing girls to younger readers.

CRITICAL RECEPTION

Choi's classification as a writer of children's and young adult fiction is a possible explanation for the absence of any serious critical attention to her work. The awards she has garnered for her writing, however, indicate the positive reception the books have had and her strong reputation among educators and experts in juvenile fiction. This is especially true for *Year of Impossible Goodbyes*, probably Choi's best work to date, which was awarded the Judy Lopez Book Award for the National Women's Book Association (1992), among other honors.

Book reviews for Choi's novels and stories also have been generally positive and suggest the books' broader appeal. A reviewer in the *Korean Quarterly*, for instance, writes that "Choi's novels are anything but childlike and speak powerfully and intensely to older readers as well" (Winzig 1). As Choi's awards might suggest, praise has been especially high for *Year*, including for its simple and poetic prose. Writes one reviewer, "Choi's story deepens with every turn of the page. Her characters are touching, her plot gripping, her tone honest and compassionate. *Year of Impossible Goodbyes* is a compelling novel" (Sheanin 10). Similar acclamation is given at times to *Echoes of the White Giraffe* for its universal appeal, descriptions of nature, and unconventional romance. But praise for *Year*'s sequels often has been more reserved. Critics who applaud *Year* have been disappointed by its sequels' flatter characters, disruptive movement of time, and lack of exciting story lines. Of *Gathering of Pearls*, for instance, two reviewers say that even Sookan "plays an almost martyrly role here. . . . [H]er strength and spunk are conspicuously absent" (Devereaux and Roback 440). Despite varying assessments of the novels' prose and plots, critics seem generally agreed that Choi is successful in her goal of writing to "foster greater understanding about her homeland's 'sad history' " (Zahner 18).

BIBLIOGRAPHY

Works by Sook Nyul Choi

Novels

Year of Impossible Goodbyes. Boston: Houghton Mifflin, 1991.
Echoes of the White Giraffe. Boston: Houghton Mifflin, 1993.
Gathering of Pearls. Boston: Houghton Mifflin, 1994.

Picture Books

Halmoni and the Picnic. Illus. Karen M. Dugan. Boston: Houghton Mifflin. 1993.
The Best Older Sister. Illus. Cornelius Van Wright and Ying-Hwa Hu. New York: Delacorte, 1997.
Yummi and Halmoni's Trip. Illus. Karen M. Dugan. Boston: Houghton Mifflin, 1997.

Studies of Sook Nyul Choi

Day, Frances Ann. "Sook Nyul Choi: Korean American." In *Multicultural Voices in Contemporary Literature: A Resource for Teachers.* London: Heinemann, 1994: 32–34.
Devereaux, Elizabeth, and Diane Roback. "Children's Books." Rev. of *Gathering of Pearls. Publishers Weekly* (August 8, 1994): 440.
Helbig, Alethea, and Agnes Regan Perkins. Rev. of *Echoes of the White Giraffe.* In *This Land Is Our Land: A Guide to Multicultural Literature for Children and Young Adults.* Westport, CT: Greenwood Press, 1994: 118.
McCabe, Bruce. "Author's Korean Novel Embraces Her Two Homes." *Boston Globe,* December 3, 1991, city ed., 66.
Philbrook, John. "For the Younger Reader: Strangers in a New Land." Rev. of *Gathering of Pearls. San Francisco Chronicle Sunday Review* (December 11, 1994): 10.
Roback, Diane, and Richard Donahue. "Children's Books." Rev. of *Echoes of the White Giraffe. Publishers Weekly* 240. 12 (March 1993): 80.
Sheanin, Wendy. "A Girl's Tale of Wartime Occupation and Hope." Rev. of *Year of Impossible Goodbyes. San Francisco Chronicle Sunday Review* (March 29, 1992): 10.
Vandergrift, Kay E. "Learning about Sook Nyul Choi." January 7, 1999 ⟨http://www.scils.rutgers.edu/special/kay/choi.html⟩.
Winzig, Jerry. "Discovering Sook Nyul Choi's Autobiographical Novels for Young Adults." *Korean Quarterly* (January 7, 1999) ⟨http://www.menet.umn.edu/~pchung/KoreanQuarterly/ISSUE2/revchoi2.html⟩.
Zahner, Cathy Karlin. "Korean Girl's Travails Put Life in Perspective." Rev. of *Year of Impossible Goodbyes. Kansas City Star,* March 1, 1992, 18.

Susan Choi
(1969–   )

Elizabeth Fitzpatrick

BIOGRAPHY

Susan Choi is at the beginning of a promising writing career. Her short fiction and her distinguished first novel, *The Foreign Student* (1998), treat some of the subtler aspects of the immigrant experience with complexity and sensitivity. She was born in Indiana in 1969 to a Korean immigrant father and a first-generation American, Russian Jewish mother. She attended Yale University, where she won the Wallace Prize for Fiction in 1990. Her determination to become a writer crystallized while at Yale as an undergraduate, and after completing a degree in literature there in 1990, she went on to Cornell University's master's program in creative writing. In 1991 she won the Henfield Foundation Transatlantic Review Award. While at Cornell she taught literature courses and creative writing at the undergraduate level and was awarded Cornell's Wallace Prize for Distinguished Teaching in 1995.

In 1995 and again in 1997 she was a fellow at the Fine Arts Work Center in Provincetown, Massachusetts. She currently lives and writes in New York, where she is also a fact-checker at the *New Yorker* magazine. She's working on a second novel.

MAJOR WORKS AND THEMES

Choi is a young writer who published eight short stories between 1992 and 1998 and a recent, well-received first novel. *The Foreign Student* concerns the relationship between the Korean student Ahn Chang and the self-identified southern belle Katherine Monroe, both traumatized children of relative privilege in their late twenties, as it unfolds in a mountaintop southern college town. It is set in Sewanee, Tennessee, in 1955, with alternating episodes from Chang's memories of Korea during the war years and Katherine's childhood in Sewanee. Choi's American South gains its reality from well-rendered voices and fine images of clean, empty spaces—early morning bus stops, houses reopened after the winter, noontime, small-town market streets. Taken together, the descriptive settings form a background of blankness and silence, against which Chuck—Chang's Americanized name—and Katherine make known to each other, or at least open up to themselves, the respective traumas that made them the wary, elusive figures they are. Both characters are paralyzed in the present until the ghosts of the past can be confronted or at least acknowledged.

If Choi can be said to be investigating some aspect of Asian Americanness in her work, it would seem to be in her explorations of her characters' silences about the past and how such silences distance her characters from each other. In the short fiction, the gulf is often between American children and their immigrant parents. Choi has said that the impetus for her novel came from conversations with her father, who somewhat unwillingly told her stories about his experiences in Seoul during the Korean War. In the short story "Memorywork" (1992) a mother's "enforced amnesia" is challenged by her daughter: "She is flabbergasted by my disregard for the past, for what she thinks is her past." Sometimes the silences are breached, almost anticlimactically, as in "Seven" (1994) when a father reveals a secret to his daughter: "He gives this to me so easily, this revelation, I feel like I've stepped through a door. As if it were never a matter of keys and locks, only the simple task of finding where it was: that mythical closet where the secrets of the years are ranged on slumping shelves, dusty and somehow diminished. And my father there, wearing a SHIT HAPPENS T-shirt, unsurprised and even pleased at my arrival."

But unlike novelists like Toni Morrison, in whose *Beloved*, for example, speech becomes a sort of sacrament of confession by which the past is exorcised, Choi most often distrusts the spoken word as a means of communicating experience. Indeed, woven through the novel and the short fiction are many observations about the power of language, not to put the past to rest but rather to dazzle, obfuscate, and conceal. Katherine says in *The Foreign Student*, "Speaking English is far more difficult than reading it or writing it. One must be spontaneous, witty and charming *sans cesse*. It's a tall order even for those of us who were raised to do nothing but" (10). In "Seven" a Korean scholar uses language that acquires a meaning all its own: "In 1961 he writes an essay called 'The Art of Shakespeare and the Order of Life,' in an English full of such inexplicable passion and grammatical ignorance that its many mistakes are inadvertent poetry, and its confusion of tenses transcendent. No one who reads it can doubt his achievement. His English bursts forth in blossoms that have no root, no basis in knowledge, no clear notion of structure" (108).

In Choi's world, then, language is ultimately to be distrusted as a means of communicating feelings, especially between immigrants and "Americans." Chuck and Katherine seem to understand each other by osmosis. Communication occurs by way of small acts that take the place of language—feeding, providing ashtrays, sitting in silence with a bedridden uncle—and it is left to the novelist to go below the smooth silences to recuperate the stories beneath the surface.

CRITICAL RECEPTION

Since Choi is only at the beginning of her career as a novelist, critical response at present is confined to reviews of her novel, *The Foreign Student*. Reviewers generally praise Choi's understanding of the human condition, ability to inhabit her characters, and especially her eye. For example, Jill Smolowe, writing in *Time*, says Choi "writes gracefully, insightfully and with striking maturity as she explores the lives of these two outcasts." The reviewer for *Publishers Weekly* mentions Choi's "keen eye" for the landscape and manners of the South and says that "it is in her beautifully detailed evocation of the rich, albeit scarred emotional landscapes that she is at her best—grave, clear-eyed and artless." Kimberly B. Marlowe, writing in the *New York Times*, praises the way Choi "catches such moments in a very clear glass."

The novel is a romance in that its main characters manage to recognize an affinity and fall in love despite their very different origins. Reviewers are struck by the somewhat jarring contrast between the novel's setting in a sleepy, social southern college town and Chang's horrific memories of wartime Seoul. The juxtaposition is mostly seen as a strength. In prepublication remarks, Arthur Golden, author of *Memoirs of a Geisha*, says, "Two very unlikely worlds intersect in *The Foreign Student*, war-ravaged Korea and the genteel culture of Sewanee, Tennessee. In gracious prose, Susan Choi renders their cruelties, their lies, and their beauty." But Shirley N. Quan, writing for *Library Journal*, finds Choi's structure too challenging, claiming that "the reader is unable to gain a strong sense of a single character before being moved to the next. Hence when the story lines shift, the individual reader is left with a sense of confusion and disconnection."

In one review of the novel, the *Houston Chronicle*'s Elizabeth Haas oddly claims Choi as a southern novelist with ties to Flannery O'Connor: "(B)aroque social rules, racial obsessions and eccentric ideas of femininity . . . from this contradictory yet glistening web of experience, Southern writers have crafted graceful stories of treachery and mercy." Richard Eder's long and thoughtful review in the *Los Angeles Times*, on the other hand, positions Choi's protagonist as a mediator between Korean and American culture: "Wrestling with the strangeness of the American South after living through the horrors of the Korean War, this seemingly awkward and diffident young man does more than give the American reader a view of a foreign place and foreign mind. He implants this foreignness in our American self; in the best of senses, he colonizes us."

BIBLIOGRAPHY

Works by Susan Choi

Novel

The Foreign Student. New York: HarperCollins, 1998.

Short Stories

"Memorywork." *The Iowa Review* 23.2 (Spring 1992): 83–94.
"The Way to Live Wisely." *Epoch* 41.2 (Spring 1992): 180–86.
"Heir." *Documents.* No. 4/5 (Spring 1994): 83–94.
"Seven." In *Writing Away Here: A Korean-American Anthology.* N.p, 1994. 107–26.
"The Runner." *The Iowa Review* 25.1 (Winter 1995): 127–31.
"Memorywork." In *Hard Choices: An Iowa Review Reader.* Ed. David Hamilton. Iowa City; University of Iowa Press, 1996. 420–33.
"Harbor Deep." *Shankpainter.* No. 38 (Spring 1998): 9–15.
"The Dark Ages." *Epoch* 47.1 (Fall 1998): 178–96.

Studies of Susan Choi

Eder, Richard. "Crossing Borders." Rev. of *The Foreign Student. Los Angeles Times Book Review* (August 30, 1998): 2.
Haas, Elizabeth. "Good County People: Southern Drama Draws Strength from Enigmatic Pair." Rev. of *The Foreign Student. Houston Chronicle*, September 20, 1998, 18.
Leber, Michele. Rev. of *The Foreign Student. Booklist* 94.22 (August 1998): 1960.
Marlowe, Kimberly B. "Chang Chuckified." Rev. of *The Foreign Student. New York Times Book Review* (October 18, 1998): 29.
Quan, Shirley. Rev. of *The Foreign Student. Library Journal* 245.13 (September 1998): 129.
Rev. of *The Foreign Student. Publishers Weekly* (July 6, 1998): 47.
Smolowe, Jill. Rev. of *The Foreign Student. Time* (September 7, 1998): 83.

Denise Chong
(1953–   )

Nikolas Huot

BIOGRAPHY

Born in Vancouver, British Columbia, Denise Chong was raised in Prince George, a town 500 miles north of Vancouver, where she moved when she was five years old. Chong left that little town, where she had to endure name-callings and physical abuse, to attend a university and later established residence in Ottawa. First employed as an economist with the Department of Finance, Denise Chong became an economic adviser to Prime Minister Trudeau between 1980 and 1984. In 1985, following her husband, she traveled to Peking, where she stayed for two years. Denise Chong now lives in Ottawa with her husband and two children.

Although Chong had always been curious about her family history and the possibility of having relatives in China, the death of her grandmother and the silence of her mother hindered her every effort to find out more. Unwilling to give up, Chong started her research in her parents' dresser with an old photograph of two little Chinese girls (her mother's sisters) and began to reassemble piece by piece the history of her family on both sides of the Pacific Ocean. This arduous reconstruction produced encouraging results in 1987, when Chong and her mother had the chance to meet for the first time their relatives still living in China. This reunion of a family kept apart by war, racist legislation, and geography not only gave Chong the chance to learn about the other half of her family but also provided her with the material for an article that eventually appeared on the cover of the October 1988 issue of *Saturday Night Magazine*. After the publication of the article and numerous offers for her to write a book, Chong started to press her mother for more information, even sending her monthly questionnaires to fill in the gaps. Slowly, her mother began to share her experiences and her memories more openly; "it was important for her to tell me the story and confide in me," said Chong (qtd. in Soo). Six years later, after much research and many heart-to-heart conversations with her mother, Chong produced a book-length version of her article entitled *The Concubine's Children: The Story of a Chinese Family Living on Two Sides of the Globe.*

MAJOR WORKS AND THEMES

Through the tracing of her family history over the best part of the twentieth century and across two continents, Denise Chong describes the hardships endured by Chinese immigrants who came to seek their fortunes in North America ("Gold Mountain") and by those who remained at home to face war, poverty, and political unrest. She not only presents the living conditions in the early days of the Chinatowns but also explains the complexities of Chinese traditions, culture, and family structure.

The Concubine's Children mainly recounts the tumultuous lives of May-ying and Chan Sam, Chong's maternal grandparents. In 1924 Chan Sam, who had left China eleven years before to seek his fortune in Gold Mountain, arranges for the passage of a seventeen-year-old concubine to join him in Canada. Upon arrival, May-ying, the concubine from China, is put to work in a teahouse in order to pay off the price of her travel. While her wages go to the teahouse owner, who paid for her passage, May-ying gives her tips to her "husband," who regularly sends money to his first wife in China. In 1928 a visit to China is organized, but, believing a soothsayer who said the concubine was carrying a son, Chan Sam and May-ying leave their two daughters to the care of the first wife and precipitantly return to Vancouver. May-ying's third child is born in Canada, but, to the despair of the mother, it is another girl. From the Depression onward, May-ying's earnings as a waitress become the main (when not the sole) income for the Canadian and Chinese family. Slowly growing resentful toward the husband she never loved, May-ying eventually leaves Chan Sam and starts to drink, gamble, and sleep with various teahouse customers.

Still trying to prove she can be a good mother, May-ying raises Hing, her daughter and Denise Chong's mother, very strictly, allowing her few liberties and fewer pleasurable moments. May-ying, "dressed [Hing] as a boy, . . . spanked her and ordered her to kneel in obedience afterwards"; all the while, Hing was cleaning up after her mother's alcoholic vomiting and lovemaking (219). The only solace Hing can find is her schoolwork, but she must leave high school and find a job in order to support her mother, whose health and income are rapidly declining.

The complicated family story continues with the marriage of Hing, the deaths of Chan Sam and May-ying, and the misadventures of the Chinese family. Chong concludes her narrative with her mother's meeting of her sister and half brother in China. Only by meeting them did Chong learn how the Chinese members of her family perceived the events in Canada and how they struggled through China's many political torrents. This meeting not only gave the opportunity for Chong to learn about her Chinese family but also allowed her to get in touch with her roots and heritage and, at the same time, allowed her mother to reconcile herself with the memory of May-ying.

Leaving her grandmother and mother's stories aside, Denise Chong in her second book turned to the life story of another strong Asian woman. The well-known Pulitzer Prize-winning photograph of the nine-year-old girl running naked in terror after a napalm strike hit her village is the origin of Chong's latest initiative. In her second hook-length project, published late in 1998, *The Girl in the Picture: The Story of Kim Phuc Whose Image Altered the Course of the Vietnam War*, Denise Chong presents the sensitive life story of Phan Thi Kim Phuc, the "napalm girl." Following Phuc's journey from Vietnam to Cuba and her "defection" to Canada, Chong reveals the struggle and the great odds Phuc had to overcome in order to reclaim her life.

CRITICAL RECEPTION

In *The Concubine's Children*, Denise Chong "details the treatment of women in her family without trivializing Chinese culture or underestimating its internal logic" and is remarkably open in her portrayal of her lonely grandmother, her irresolute grandfather, and her abused mother (Guterson). However, because of this frankness and candid nature of her book, Chong has been questioned by some who feel that she betrayed her family secrets and her grandmother by divulging her alcoholism and promiscuity. To those critics, Chong replied that her journey into the past was worthwhile because "I did it as an act of love to the family. . . . When my mother picked up the book and said aloud, 'I forgive my mother,' I knew right then and there, it was worth it" (qtd. in Kumagai).

A national best-seller in Canada, *The Concubine's Children* has been acclaimed by critics and reviewers across Canada and the United States. Praised as an "engaging and compelling" narrative (Yogi) and as a "beautiful, haunting, and wise" portrait (Guterson), *The Concubine's Children* has been called "an exceptional work of family history" and a "perfectly wonderful book . . . [that] has the flow of fiction" (Yardley). Across America, critics commended her treatment of this difficult story, her approach to her origins, and her narrative style.

Not only did Chong receive great reviews, but she also amassed many honors for her autobiography. In 1994 she collected the City of Vancouver Book Prize and the Van City Book Prize, and in 1995 she received the Edna Staebler Award for Creative Non-Fiction. The same year, *The Concubine's Children* was short-listed for the Governor General's Award and the Hubert Evans Non-Fiction Prize.

BIBLIOGRAPHY

Works by Denise Chong

Autobiography

"The Concubine's Children." In *Many-Mouthed Birds: Contemporary Writings by Chinese Canadians*. Ed. Bennett Lee and Jim Wong-Chu. Vancouver: Douglas and McIntyre, 1991. 59–78.

The Concubine's Children: The Story of a Chinese Family Living on Two Sides of the Globe. Toronto: Penguin, 1994.

Biography

The Girl in the Picture: The Story of Kim Phuc Whose Image Altered the Course of the Vietnam War. New York: Viking, 1998.

Anthology

(Ed.). *The Penguin Anthology of Stories by Canadian Women*. Toronto: Penguin, 1997.
(Intro.). *The Penguin Anthology of Stories by Canadian Women*. Toronto: Penguin, 1997.

Article

"The Concubine's Children." *Saturday Night Magazine* (October 1988): 1–8.

Studies of Denise Chong

Guterson, David. "Oceans Apart." Rev. of *The Concubine's Children*. *New York Times Book Review* (January 15, 1995): late ed., 7.24.

Hai-Jew, Shalin. Rev. of *The Concubine's Children*. *Northwest Asian Weekly* (February 3, 1995): PG.

Kumagai, Naoko. "Denise Chong." May 2, 1996. ⟨http://www.peak.sfu.ca/the-peak/96–1/issue5/chong.html⟩ (February 5, 1999).

"New This Week." Rev. of *The Concubine's Children*. *Newsday* (January 26, 1995): B02.

Soo, Jacalyn. "Interview with Author Denise Chong." ⟨http://www.asian.ca/media/china-city/jsoo.htm⟩ (February 5, 1999).

Van Hertbruggen, Maddy. Rev. of *The Concubine's Children*. June 28, 1998. ⟨http://www.clark.net/~bell/eibr/bio/chong_concubines_children.html⟩ (October 3, 1998).

Yardley, Jonathan. "New World, Old Ties." Rev. of *The Concubine's Children*. *Washington Post*, January 8, 1995, Book World X03.

Yogi, Stan. Rev. of *The Concubine's Children*. *San Francisco Chronicle*, February 19, 1995, 5.

Louis Hing Chu
(1915–1970)

Shunzhu Wang

BIOGRAPHY

Now hailed by Chinese American scholars and critics as a novelist of pivotal importance in the development of Chinese American literary traditions, Louis Chu was never recognized as such during his own time. In fact, he was hardly known as a novelist. When he died on February 27, 1970, an obituary notice in the March 2 issue of the *New York Times* announced his death as that of a "Broadcaster and Social Worker" (37:2). Indeed, in spite of his education and literary ambition, Chu's life experience had much in common with the life struggle of the ordinary Chinese immigrants he portrayed in his novel.

Born on October 1, 1915, in Toishan (Taishan County), Canton (Guangtong Province), China, Chu immigrated with his family to Newark, New Jersey, in 1924. After graduating from high school, he attended Upsala College, where he graduated in 1937 with a major in English and a minor in sociology. He then went to New York University and earned an M.A. in sociology in 1940. During World War II he served for two years, from 1943 to 1945, in a unit of the U.S. Army Signal Corps stationed in Kunming, southwestern China. After the war, he went back to China to seek a wife as a result of the War Brides Act of 1945. He married Kang Wong, a woman born and raised in China, and took her to the United States, where they settled in New York's Chinatown and eventually raised their four children.

Life was hard for them. In order to support his family, Chu opened a record shop, Acme Co., in 1950. A year later, he and his wife started a Chinese radio program, *Chinese Festival*, which aired ninety minutes each weekday on WHOM-FM. The program, which remained on the air until 1961, included news, interviews, commercials, and Chinese recorded music and was very popular among Chinese laundrymen and restaurant workers.

While struggling with the hardships of life, Chu also became an active member of the New York Chinese community. He served as executive secretary of a social center, the Soo Yuen Benevolent Association, and as director of the Golden Age Club, a day center for the elderly funded by the New York Department of Welfare. He remained in the two positions, respectively, from 1954 and 1961 until his death.

In addition, Chu sustained a strong interest in social studies and in writing, particularly about life in Chinatown. This was clearly indicated by the fact that a decade after he received his M.A. in sociology and at a time of financial difficulties, he made the decision to enroll for two years of postgraduate training at the New School for Social Research and take creative writing courses. "I always had a desire to write," he told an interviewer. "In prep school I used to write poetry. I remember writing furiously during the dead of night while on night duty as a switchboard operator in the army. In Kunming, China, in 1944, I bought an old beat-up typewriter with borrowed money. . . . and tried to resume writing" (Rev. *Library Journal* [hereafter, *LJ*] 604–5). His efforts at publishing, however, were met with frequent rejections. In 1947 he finished a book-length manuscript, which was subsequently turned down by five different publishers. In spite of that, his desire "to portray a very small segment of human life," as he termed it, remained strong. His solid training in sociology and creative writing, his personal experience of life in Chinatown, and his strong determination to tell that lived experience finally resulted in the fine classic piece, *Eat a Bowl of Tea*.

MAJOR WORK AND THEMES

At the time of the publication of *Eat a Bowl of Tea*, Chu was reportedly "working on a second novel" and planning to "do a play" (*LJ* 605). Unfortunately, they never appeared before the public. Whether they were not completed or not accepted for publication is not known. But what we know about Chu and the unappreciative times he lived in seems to suggest that the latter is likely the case. At least, it is safe to say that Chu must have written more than just one novel. This is suggested by the fact that his short story, "Bewildered," which tells of the bewilderment a new Chinese immigrant experiences with the U.S. immigration offices, was posthumously published in an Asian American journal, *The East Wind*, in 1982. For those interested in the study of Chu or Chinese American literature, an effort to rediscover his lost pieces would be well worthwhile.

The "very small segment of human life" that Chu longed to describe is the life of ordinary Chinese immigrants in their adopted country, as is evidenced in all his known works: *Eat a Bowl of Tea*, "Bewildered," and his master's thesis,

"Chinese Restaurants in New York City." This was not by any means a new theme. But with this theme, Chu honestly and accurately articulated a new Chinese American sensibility. In *Eat a Bowl of Tea*, he presents us a picture of Chinese and Chinatown distinctly different from the stereotypes that had already existed and been accepted as the standard images of Chinese and Chinese community.

American literature before Chu, particularly popular literature, abounded with caricatures of "Orientals." Anglo-American writers were largely responsible for the construction of these stereotypes. According to Elaine H. Kim, stereotypes in their writing usually fall into two basic kinds: "[T]he 'bad' . . . sinister villains and brute hordes, neither of which can be controlled by the Anglos and both of which must therefore be destroyed. The 'good' . . . helpless heathens to be saved by Anglo heroes or the loyal and lovable allies, sidekicks, and servants" (4). Both kinds function to establish a racial hierarchy in which the "Orientals" are inferior and marginal, while the white is superior and central. Whether "good" or "bad," the Oriental people remain the unspoken Other, to be appreciated or condemned by the white Self.

Early Asian American writers, although strikingly smaller in number in comparison with Anglo-American writers, also helped, whether consciously or not, to reaffirm these stereotypes. Pardee Lowe's *Father and Glorious Descendant* denigrates everything Chinese or Chinese American and praises everything American. Both the Father and the descendant are "glorious" precisely because they are non-Chinese-like. Jade Snow Wong,* in *Fifth Chinese Daughter*, does not reject everything Chinese, but her "assertion of Chinese identity was restricted to identification with whatever was acceptable about it to white society" (Kim 66). Lin Yutang's *Chinatown Family* presents an idealized picture of Chinese community inhabited by Chinese who are "docile, grateful" and "accept brutality, injustice, and hardships cheerfully" (Kim 104). Implicitly or explicitly in all three is the message that America is a land of equal opportunity, that the mass Chinese living in the ghetto have only themselves to blame for their suffering. This is certainly not a perspective that provides any insider's depth, nor is it objective. Rather, it is an outsider's view, mirroring the opinions of the white supremacists about American society and people of Chinese descent.

In Chu's *Eat a Bowl of Tea* we see a Chinatown faithfully portrayed: nonexotic, realistic with its weaknesses and strengths. Its inhabitants are not measured according to the white standards of "good" or "bad." Neither are they presented as objects along with other exotic items in Chinatown, subject to the appreciation of the curious whites or those who pass for white. Rather, they are flesh-and-blood human beings, invested with feelings and emotions reflective of a full consciousness of self. Instead of seeing their problems as merely caused by the negative aspects of Chinese culture and tradition, Chu sees them as conditioned by the historical, social, and cultural forces that shaped the Chinese American community. In other words, he sees them not as Chinese problems but as Chinese American problems.

In *Eat a Bowl of Tea* the biggest problem facing bachelor society in New York's Chinatown is lack of women. Around this problem a number of themes—racial oppression, patriarchal oppression, marriage crisis, Tong (clan association) maneuvers, and so on—are intricately interwoven and played out via their spatial and temporal sequences.

First and foremost is the theme of racial discrimination. Although this remains an unspoken issue throughout the novel, the temporal framework of the narrative invites the reader to situate the related events in actual historical contexts. For example, Wang Wab Guy, an older member of the New York Chinatown bachelor society, last visited his wife in China in 1924, the year when the National Origins Law, which is also known as "Second Exclusion Act," was enforced. Under this law, Chinese wives of U.S citizens were denied entry to the United States. Ben Loy, Wang's son, who is a World War II veteran, went to China to seek a wife in 1948, five years after the National Origins Law had been lifted and three years after the War Brides Act had come into effect. These historical events certainly explain the lack of women in New York's Chinatown and help the reader to better understand emotional experiences the members of the bachelor society undergo during the lonely years of longing and struggling.

The spatial framework of the narrative, working in line with the temporal referents, evokes in the mind of the reader an image of an invisible white wall looming around Chinatown, cold and insurmountable, separating its inhabitants from the dominant society beyond and the rest of the world. The noisy restaurants and the steamy laundry houses where they work long hours, the dark mahjongg clubhouse where they gamble, and the dingy and suffocating dormitories and apartments where they live all indicate their unspeakable entrapment, their separation from the outside world in both physical and psychological senses.

Patriarchal oppression is an explicit theme of *Eat a Bowl of Tea*. But Chu skillfully interweaves this issue with that of racial oppression and thus gives it a new spin, compelling the reader to see it in both literal and figurative terms. On the literal level, Wang Wah Guy is a repressive father figure. In the name of providing for, and protecting, his son, he arranges his marriage and controls his life, thus depriving him of his independence. Ben Loy's impotence is largely a result of living a passive life strictly controlled by his father. Finally "tired of playing the role of the dutiful son, keeping silent while his father told him what to do" (240), he moves out of reach of his father, and with the help of Chinese herbal medicine, he claims his independence and manhood at the same time.

While an oppressive father, Wah Guy is also the oppressed, for there is another repressive father figure, the faceless white Father. Just as Wah Guy controls Ben Loy's life, the faceless white Father controls Wah Guy's fate and that of the entire Chinese community with an equally firm hand. The ways in which the two exercise control, however, are strikingly different. Wang controls as provider and protector, with a sense of parental love and pride, whereas the white Father controls by exploiting and rejecting, with contempt and disgust for his "adopted," or "illegitimate" children. If Wah Guy deprives his son of his adulthood unintentionally and temporarily, the white Father deprives him of his husbandhood and manhood intentionally and permanently. The entire Chinatown bachelor society speaks directly to this deprivation. For Wah Guy, life under the control of white Father means long, hard labor and separation from his wife. The result is a sense of guilt toward his wife, which in turn makes him all the more determined to take good care of their son, to make him the husband and family man that he himself has failed—or rather, not been allowed—to be.

Against such a dark background of dual oppression the comic events of marriage crisis and Tong maneuver unfold. The newlyweds Ben Loy and Mei Oi love each other very much. But the bridegroom, under the shadow of two oppressive fathers, finds himself impotent in front of his beautiful wife. Torn between love for her husband and frustration at his impotence, Mei Oi allows herself to be seduced by Ah Song, an older bachelor of the community. Wah Guy, after learning that his daughter-in-law is bearing a child of the infamous womanizer, attacks him and slices off his ear. Ah Song files a charge against him, and Wah Guy goes into hiding. The Tong leaders intervene, forcing Ah Song to withdraw his charge and to leave the community for five years.

Everyone involved in the scandal then finds it necessary to relocate. Wah Guy and Lee Gong, his longtime friend and father of his daughter-in-law, have to leave New York, for they are too ashamed of the scandal of Mei Oi's adultery. Wah Guy goes to work in his brother's restaurant in Chicago, and Lee in his cousin's poultry market in Sacramento. Ben Loy and Mei Oi, too, decide to leave New York, the place that would remind them of the scandal and of their expected roles as dutiful son and daughter-in-law. For a new beginning, they go to San Francisco. Ben works in a restaurant, where he is soon promoted from waiter to assistant cook. In letting go of the past, he recovers his manhood and becomes a happy and responsible father.

A question arises from this relocation episode: have they thus surmounted the white "wall" surrounding the Chinese community? The places where they go and work seem to suggest a negative answer. Ah Song's reaction after hearing the order of exile illustrates vividly a sense of deep entrapment in the Chinese community, a sense that is paradoxically coupled with a sense of rootlessness—a sense of being alienated from both the white and Chinese communities: "Go away? But where could he go? He had been to a lot of places, Vancouver . . . Seattle . . . Montreal . . . San Antonio . . . San Francisco . . . Las Vegas. . . .All the places he wanted to go in New York would be barred to him" (227). Although a social outcast of the community, Ah Song's stream-of-consciousness-like reflection can be said to be representative of a moral dilemma in which all Chinese Americans are caught.

CRITICAL RECEPTION

Eat a Bowl of Tea, as mentioned before, received little critical attention upon its publication in 1961. The few reviews it had at the time were very brief and negative. Curtis W. Stucki, for example, commented in *Library Journal* that "neither its treatment of characters nor the writing is of sufficient quality to recommend its purchase." The book was soon buried, along with its author, in oblivion until its rediscovery in the early 1970s by a group of Asian American scholars who included Chu in their book *Aiiieeeee! An Anthology of Asian-American Writers*. In this first anthology of its kind, Chu's book is praised as "the first Chinese-American novel" to portray Chinatown realistically as "non-exoticized" (xxxi). The critical anthology thus establishes for Chu a place he deserves in Asian American literary tradition, but it does not go into any actual discussion of the book besides suggesting a "politically correct" direction for future scholarship on him.

The book has gone through two reprints since its rediscovery, one in 1979 by University of Washington Press with an Introduction by Jeffery Chan; the other in 1993 by its original publisher, Carol Publishing Group. Chan's Introduction, while echoing the previously-mentioned anthology's evaluation of Chu, makes a neat argument about Chu's ability to "make English out of Cantonese" (2), a linguistic merit that gives his book an authentic Chinatown flavor.

One of the most valuable works of scholarship on Chu in the early 1980s is Elaine H. Kim's *Asian American Literature*. In Chapter 4, "Portraits of Chinatown," she devotes a section to *Eat a Bowl of Tea* and gives a fairly comprehensive analysis of the book. By carefully situating the book in its social and historical context, she was able to render her analysis smoothly nonpolitical and make her points without resorting to critical jargon.

Cheng Lok Chua is another scholar whose criticism on Chu in the early 1980s is worth mentioning. In addition to a book review, which, like Chan's Introduction, stresses its linguistic merits, he wrote "Golden Mountain: Chinese Versions of American Dream in Lin Yutang, Louis Chu, and Maxine Hong Kingston.*" In comparing the three authors, he concludes that "Chu sees Chinese tradition as oppressive and champions the American aspiration" (33). This conclusion captures half of the truth but misses an ambivalence embedded in the narrative toward both traditions.

Critical interest in Chu continues in the 1990s. Shu-yan Li's "Otherness and Transformation in *Eat a Bowl of Tea* and *Crossings*" is worth mentioning. Li's comments on Chu's use of language, his literal translation of Cantonese dialect into English, are informative and objective. While considering Chu's language helpful in revealing the speakers' "exclusion from the mainstream" (102), he also points out that some of the renditions cry for explanatory notes and that a few make little sense in immediate context, which "may partly explain why *Eat a Bowl of Tea* did not immediately appeal to American readers outside the culture" (102). Finally, Li also suggests some connections between Mei Oi and Pan Jin Lian, a fictional figure that appears in two Chinese classics—Shih Nai-an's *Water Margin* and Hsiao-hsiao-Sheng's *Jin Ping Mei* (*The Golden Lotus*).

The two most theoretically and politically informed essays on Chu in the 1990s are Ruth Y. Hsiao's "Facing the Incurable: Patriarchy in *Eat a Bowl of*

Tea" and Jinqi Ling's "Reading for Historical Specificities: Gender Negotiations in Louis Chu's *Eat a Bowl of Tea*." Hsiao is among the very few who have negative things to say about the book since its rediscovery. Critiquing the book from a feminist perspective, she argues that if we consider Chu's book "as the herald of the new Asian American sensibility," this new sensibility he heralds is not free of patriarchy, one of "the twin evils" the book supposedly subverts (153). Ling's essay serves as a comment on Hsiao's, moreover. By evoking Frederic Jameson's notion of interpretation as "a historical/political act" to "[re-store] to the surface of the text the repressed and buried reality" (Hsiao 153) he argues that an awareness to historical specificities would allow us to see clearly the disruptive potentials that Chu invests in the female character Mei Oi. Ling's argument is sharp and well grounded but heavily loaded with critical jargon. What is revealing about these two essays is that Hsiao's argument is also made by "plac(ing) the novel in its historical context" (Hsiao 153). This tells us that different readers may interpret reality in different ways and that *Eat a Bowl of Tea* is a rich and powerful text that evokes different, even contradictory interpretations.

BIBLIOGRAPHY

Works by Louis Hing Chu

Novel

Eat a Bowl of Tea: A Novel of New York's Chinatown. 1961. Seattle: University of Washington Press, 1979.
"Eat a Bowl of Tea." (excerpt from *Eat a Bowl of Tea: A Novel of New York's China-town*). In *Aiiieeeee! An Anthology of Asian-American Writers*. Eds. Frank Chin et al. Garden City, NY: Doubleday, 1974. 76–87.

Short Stories

"Bewildered." *The East Wind* (1982). 72–79.

Master's Thesis

"The Chinese Restaurants in New York City." New York University, 1939.

Studies of Louis Hing Chu

Chan, Jeffery. "Introduction." In *Eat a Bowl of Tea*. Seattle: University of Washington Press, 1979. 1–5.
Chua, Cheng Lok. "Golden Mountain: Chinese Versions of American Dream in Lin Yutang, Louis Chu, and Maxine Hong Kinston." *Ethnic Groups* 4 (May 1982): 33–59.
———. Rev. of *Eat a Bowl of Tea*. *Explorations in Ethnic Studies* 3.1 (1980): 67–69.
Hsiao, Ruth Y. "Facing the Incurable: Patriarchy in *Eat a Bowl of Tea*." In *Reading for*

Literatures of Asian American. Ed. Shirley Geok-lin Lim and Amy Ling. Philadelphia: Temple University Press, 1992. 151–62.

Kim, Elaine H. *Asian American Literature: An Introduction to Their Writings and Their Social Context.* Philadelphia: Temple University Press, 1982. 109–121.

Ling, Jinqi. "Reading for Historical Specificities: Gender Negotiations in Louis Chu's *Eat a Bowl of Tea.*" *MELUS* 20.1 (Spring 95): 35–52.

Li, Shu-yan. "Otherness and Transformation in *Eat a Bowl of Tea* and *Crossings.*" *MELUS* 18.4 (Winter 1993/1994): 99–111.

Prig, Benson Webster. "Transactional Analysis: A Viable Approach for Discussing Human Autonomy in Fictional Texts." Diss., Bowling Green State University, 1990.

Rev. of *Eat a Bowl of Tea.* "New York's Chinatown." *Library Journal* (February 1, 1961): 604–5.

Rev. of *Eat a Bowl of Tea. Literature and Its Times.* Vol. 4: *World War II to the Affluent Fifties (1940–1950s).* Ed. Joyce Moss and George Wilson. Detroit: Gale, 1997. 124–30.

Rev. of *Eat a Bowl of Tea. Kliatt Young Adult Paperback Book Guide* 14 (Winter 1980): 5.

Rev. of *Eat a Bowl of Tea. Asian American Literature: Reviews and Criticisms of Works by American Writers of Asian Descent.* Ed. Lawrence J. Trudeau. Detroit: Gale, 1999. 61–70.

Stucki, Curtis W. Rev. of *Eat a Bowl of Tea. Library Journal* (March 15, 1961): 1157.

Richard Crasta (also Avatar Prabhu)
(1952–)

Barry Fruchter

BIOGRAPHY

Richard Crasta, also known as Avatar Prabhu (for publications in the United States and Germany), was born in 1952 in Bangalore, India, the son of John and Christine (née D'Souza) Crasta, Roman Catholics of Mangalore, Karnataka state; he grew up in and around the latter town. An all-important factor in his development was the church, in the form of family devotions, the convent school to which he was sent as a boy, and the secondary school or "college" of his adolescence. It is the "motor" of the narrative in *The Revised Kama Sutra* and accounts for much of his career.

After attending school and receiving the B.A. from the University of Mysore (1972), Crasta was eventually accepted into the Indian Administrative Service (IAS), through whose ranks he rose to become the deputy commissioner of a large south Indian district. However, this position suited him neither professionally, as a creative writer, nor socially—he had few opportunities to meet the woman of his dreams. He served in the IAS for thirteen years.

Crasta traveled to the United States in 1979, enrolling in American University in Washington, D.C., where he remained through 1981, earning an M.A. After a short return to India and the IAS, Crasta emigrated in 1984 to the New York City area. He and his wife, Jovita (née Peris), another south Indian emigrant and a psychiatrist at a local hospital, live in suburban Rockville Centre, New York, with their three children. In 1987 Crasta received an M.F.A. from the program in Creative Writing at Columbia University.

After more than eight years of work, *The Revised Kama Sutra: A Novel of Colonialism and Desire* appeared in India in 1993. Subsequent editions appeared in Britain, the United States, and Germany. A collection of critical essays,

Beauty Queens, Children and the Death of Sex, appeared in India in 1997. Finally, Richard Crasta edited and contributed essays to *Eaten by the Japanese: The Memoirs of an Unknown Indian Soldier*, by John Baptist Crasta, his father, in India in 1998. In 1998, too, he began publishing under the name Avatar Prabhu.

MAJOR WORK AND THEMES

Revised Kama Sutra follows the youth of one Vijay Prabhu of Mangalore, south India. The first-person narrative is picaresque in its broadly comic sensibility, along with many passages of unadulterated longing, disappointment, rage, and/or political commentary. The book is organized in four parts named after the four Vedic qualities associated with the stages of life: "The Beginnings of Wisdom, or, Encounters with Dharma," "Turning Away the Dogs of God, or, in the Time of Artha," "Delicious Undertakings, or, the Rule of Kama," and "Endless Laughter, or, The Moksha Express." So Crasta/Prabhu, unlike Vatsayana, does not limit himself to guiding readers through the realm of *kama* or sexuality: he goes the original work three better and "covers" all four realms of the mind-body state.

The first part, "The Beginnings of Wisdom, or, Encounters with Dharma," follows the protagonist from his earliest childhood memories—the bite of a neighborhood dog, the food of the south Indian plantations—into the trauma of separation, first to the limbo of a convent school, then the purgatory of boarding with a mercenary "granny," and finally the hell of a Jesuit "college." Vijay lives in a world of the senses into which is belatedly introduced a puritanism that will haunt him throughout his childhood, whether via his rejection by an auntie shocked by his forwardness in snuggling against her breasts in bed, the loss of a sybaritic holiday diet in favor of the miserable food of the convent or the yearlong regime of *boblem* (pumpkins) imposed by a father trying to save money, or in the form of the Five Pillars of Oppression, the young Mangalorean Catholic lad's version of T.E. Lawrence's *Seven Pillars of Wisdom*. Young Vijay also learns how to wash without being naked, how to compare sexual organs with young girls right under the noses of nuns, how to survive the end of the world by praying, and how to admire Jackie Kennedy, wife and then widow of the world's most powerful Catholic leader. Armed with this wisdom, Vijay Prabhu escapes an Indian Catholic education every bit as intact as Stephen Dedalus does the Irish equivalent.

In "Turning Away the Dogs of God, or, In the Time of Artha," he is reeducated into the wider world of India, all the while struggling with his awakening sexuality and his disapproving parents. Typical of this section are the chapters "Prometheus Unzipped," "How to Succeed," and "Love in the Region of Filaria," which details the elegiac first love for Deepa, his friend Shekhar's sister (the equal of Mangan's sister in James Joyce), her sweet sixteen party, and the anguish and anger of realizing that "apple-cheeked beauties, even pseudo apple-cheeked beauties, were not to be won with Rs. 3.45 tins of Parry's Sweets; for godsake; they were won with elephantloads of emeralds and rubies . . . and above all with a Poppy who is rolling in dough" (122), two conditions alien to the young Vijay. Before, during, and after his obsession with the beauteous Deepa, Vijay steeps himself in the fonts of bodily wisdom, both native ones such as Vedic tracts on diet and foreign ones such as the pages of *Reader's Digest*, Dale Carnegie, and Charles Atlas. The search for physical fulfillment is rivaled by endless projects for getting rich, usually involving the aid of generous Americans; in this section Vijay begins his lifelong habit of writing to Jackie Kennedy, his admiration for whom is equaled only by his boundless faith that she will come to his aid and transport him to the land of Hollywood and advertising, where waiters earn enough to become latter-day caliphs of Baghdad.

The third section, "Delicious Undertakings, or, the Rule of Kama," is arguably the book's center. The peripatetic Vijay moves to Bombay, to Lucknow, to Calcutta, to distant Shillong; at each stop he ascends another rung on the ladder of erotic satisfaction—such as it is for the church-disabled Vijay. Bombay is identified with the jovial radical Jawahar, whose experience with his girl has convinced him that "if you kiss a girl down there, she'll do anything for you" (174). Lucknow, the "City of Nawabs," becomes the scene of a fiasco in which Vijay contracts with a Muslim for the favors of his "magnificent-busted" daughter, only to discover that the "dream princess" is menstruating and ready for sleep. "The Real Thing" is an encounter with an "English" (as it turns out, light-skinned Punjabi) prostitute inclined to think of the evening as "kaam," or work, rather than "kama," or love, but after this undertaking the hapless Vijay has graduated from autoerotic to actively heterosexual status, even though his fair lady tells him his time is up while he is still in full fettle. Finally, in "Shillong," be achieves erotic greatness and reconnects with his ancient heritage of kama, with a local beauty: "Dr. Love was a Nepali, a mixture of Indian and Mongolian, lithe, tough, extremely vigorous. . . . Watching the quickening in my face . . . she said cheerfully: 'Like fuckee-fuckee?' " (207–8) The third book ends in a "frame" conversation with "the pulchritudinous Pam Gardner," American golden girl and Vijay's editor, some ten years later, who is equally moved by the narrative and the sexual description in this last chapter. With the introduction of this contemporary American girl, who embodies the four Vedic realms in comic-pornographic fashion, we are launched into the final section of the novel.

"Endless Laughter, or, the Moksha Express" bridges the gap between an Indian adolescence and young adulthood and a maturity that flickers back and forth between the Indian and American worlds. In it Vijay experiences the pleasures, pains, and, above all, the boredom of the life of an IAS administrator; the turmoil of an erotic friendship with Maya, a girl from university days now living as a "liberated" woman; the upwelling of the desire to write. He confronts and rejects his parents' world of arranged marriages, all the while noticing more and more the aging, the vulnerability of his parents. Finally, he has his first taste of Washington, D.C., in subfreezing temperatures, of America in the grip of the racist frenzy of the Iran crisis, and of American beauties whose sophisticated behavior is marched by their sexual ambivalence.

Returning to India, he revisits his mentor, Father Maximus, formerly a font of *Reader's Digest*-inspired wisdom, now "a shrunken man, a shred of his former self" (316). Let down gently by a changed Maya, brought up short by his altered friends, he discovers a new bond of sympathy for the old Mangalore and indeed for the poverty and sorrow of India. He also bonds with his father as the two break into laughter at the thought of the television Vijay promises to buy for the old man. In a brief Epilogue, Vijay returns to America and to the delights of Pam, his editor and a veritable Eden of pleasure and promise. He sees America as "a quiet country, a country of almost unnatural, comforting, solipsistic peace" (322), where the artist can dream without interference from the cries and shouts of the distant India, which is his theme.

CRITICAL RECEPTION

A number of reviews of *The Revised Kama Sutra* (*RKS*) have appeared since its release in 1993, the majority, of course, in India. *India Today*'s Bindu Menon describes *RKS* as "a rambunctious and hilarious book," while Mahesh Nayak and Vikas Kumar in *Mangalore Today* note that although "it has nothing to do with Vatsayana or the delicate art which he professed . . . it is no less steamy. Very much so. Also irreverent, comical, hilarious, and, at times, hysterical" (18).

British reviewers were also generally favorable. More recent reviews in the United States, while generally positive, were mixed. *Publishers Weekly* praises *RKS* as "[a]n exuberant, unabashedly raunchy picaresque novel," adding that though the narrative critiques the effects of colonialism, "Vijay's account of his single-minded pursuit of sex is more often fueled by pure apolitical lust." This reviewer was put off by the "intrusive commentaries by author and editor" but allows that "readers will find these minor annoyances superseded by Prabhu's considerable, irreverent charm" (54). In addition, there have been several interviews with the author and reviews of his second book, *Beauty Queens, Children and the Death of Sex*. To date, there have been no full-length critical analyses.

BIBLIOGRAPHY

Works by Richard Crasta/Avatar Prabhu

The Revised Kama Sutra: A Novel of Colonialism and Desire. New Delhi: Viking India, 1993; New Delhi: Penguin India, 1994; Manchester: Fourth Estate, U.K., 1994, 1995; New York: Sunstar, 1998; Vienna: Deuticke Verlag, Austria, 1998.
Beauty Queens, Children and the Death of Sex. Bombay: HarperCollins India. 1997.
Editor and contributor of essays to *Eaten by the Japanese: The Memoirs of an Unknown Indian Soldier*, by John Baptist Crasta. Invisible Man, 1998.

Studies of Richard Crasta/Avatar Prabhu

Menan, Bindu. "A Small-Town Voice." Rev. of *The Revised Kama Sutra. India Today* (December 29, 1997): 81.

Nayak, Mahesh, and Vikas Kumar. "Hamburgers Can Never Taste the Same as *Idlis* to an Indian." *Vikas Kumar Mangalore Today*, January 1998, 18–20.

Rev. of *Beauty Queens, Children and the Death of Sex. Femina*, (December 1997): 86.

Rev. of *The Revised Kama Sutra. Publishers Weekly* (October 27, 1997): 54.

Thapur, Sumita. "All One Writes Is Autobiographical." *The Pioneer*, March 22, 1994, 13.

Kiran Desai

(1972–   )

Sarala Krishnamurthy

BIOGRAPHY

Kiran Desai was born in India in 1972. At the age of sixteen she immigrated
to the United States and studied for a B.A. degree at Bennington College in
Vermont. At present she is enrolled for a master's in fine arts at Columbia,
where she is a recipient of a Woolrich Fellowship. She is the daughter of a very
famous Indian novelist, Anita Desai, who teaches creative writing at Massachusetts Institute of Technology.

MAJOR WORK AND THEMES

Kiran Desai has written only one novel, *Hullabaloo in the Guava Orchard*,
which she says was inspired by a news item that she read in the *Times* of India
about a holy man who climbed a guava tree and refused to get down. She
explains, "I'm interested in what makes people eccentric, and how important
eccentrics are in making other people's life rich and meaningful" (Mallay 33).

Hullabaloo is a delightful and ironic tale told of an idiot, full of wit and
humor signifying nothing. It concerns the withdrawal of a human being from
the chaos of everyday life to lead an indolent life unfettered by mundane
thoughts. The novel gives us a glimpse into the chaotic milieu of a small town
in north India, Shahkot, which is caught between tradition and modernity, between fable and faith, between science and superstition. Sampath Chawla, the
protagonist of the novel, is catapulted into fame when he decides to settle down
on a guava tree far away from home. The people of Shahkot form a hubbub of
activity around the "Monkey Baba," as Sampath is called in the novel, and what
transpires is described in a delectable manner by Kiran Desai. She is able to

capture the idiosyncrasies of humankind and the culpability of human nature in the face of odd or unusual circumstances.

Sampath Chawla is born to Kulfi, an addlepated woman, at the end of a long period of drought. The whole town of Shahkot is gasping for a spell of rain and relief from the inclement weather during the hot, dry, and dusty months of summer. The newspaper carries reports of the various ways by which nature can be induced to shower bountiful rain over Shahkot. Suggestions are made by the townsfolk to draw the rain clouds over their parched town. At the end of this long season come the rains, bringing with them, as fate would have it, a supply of baby food, medicines, and other interesting items found in a pack thrown down by the Red Cross Society and a newborn baby, Sampath.

From these propitious beginnings, Sampath wends his way through school and college in a dreamlike trance, with his education culminating in his appointment as a junior clerk at the post office. Though he is envied for having a job in a government office, Sampath's life is terribly monotonous, and to fight boredom he steams open letters to read their contents. Life becomes interesting for him when the letters reveal a world of fantasy and romance, joy and sorrow, humor and pathos, which hitherto was denied to him. Life goes by in all its enchantment in the company of Miss Jyotsana and other colleagues till such a time as he makes a spectacle of himself in the wedding of his boss' daughter by stripping and exposing his derriere to the guests, and he is promptly dismissed from his job. Everybody is very upset with Sampath, and only his grandmother has faith in him. She states, "Even if he appears he is going downhill, he will come up on the other side. Yes, on the top of the world. He is just taking the longer route" (26).

Sampath soon embarks on a journey that takes him out of Shahkot to a guava orchard, which becomes his haven of peace. He climbs up a guava tree and is struck by the calm that pervades the atmosphere. Here, at last, away from tremendous familial pressures to perform well and from societal expectations, he finds tranquility in the lap of Mother Nature in communion with the creatures of the earth. By and by, his anxious family hear of his ascent up the tree and arrive at the orchard to coax him to come down. But all to no avail. Finally, they are advised to get him married. The dreams of Mr. Chawla, Sampath's ambitious and greedy father, of obtaining a fat dowry go up in a smoke when the bride-to-be, while attempting to reach Sampath, tumbles down the tree and falls down in heap. The townsfolk of Shahkot visit Sampath out of curiosity and are amazed at what they believe are his clairvoyance and his ability to look into their innermost thoughts but what is simply the knowledge gained from reading their private letters in the post office. Mr. Chawla, swift as lightning, spotting an excellent opportunity to turn his son's whimsical act into one of gain, is quick to capitalize on his popularity. Soon, Mr. Chawla has made arrangements for his family's accommodation in the watchman's shed in the orchard; a cot is raised up for Sampath to recline on comfortably, a garden umbrella spruced up to block out the sun above Sampath's cot, a pulley system installed to carry up his food, and the services of a potter requisitioned for a regular supply of pots to enable him to answer nature's call.

As Sampath's fame spreads through Shahkot and beyond, two people's lives swirl out of control: his mother, Kulfi, and his sister, Pinky. Kulfi, always and already a little soft in the head, finds comfort in cooking exotic dishes for her son, foraging in the forest for herbs, spices, birds and fowl, and other weird ingredients. Pinky, on the other hand, ever the practical one, feeling neglected by all the adulation directed toward her moron of a brother, promptly falls in love with the Hungry Hop, the ice cream vendor, because he rescues her grandmother's dentures from the vicious Cinema Monkey. Later, in a fit of passion, she proceeds to bite off his ear. Subsequently, she carries on a full-blown affair with him by exchanging gifts and letters, even though he is under the supervision of his numerous aunts. Soon they decide to elope, because Hungry Hop is being pressured to marry a girl chosen by his people.

The Cinema Monkey and his troop of monkeys find their way to the orchard and settle down around Sampath, in whom they identify a sympathetic soul. Sampath's cogitations attract many devotees and some skeptics, like the disguised spy from the Atheistic Society who is also a member of the Branch to Uncover Fraudulent Holy Men (BUFHM). This spy is nonplussed by the homage that Sampath receives and is determined to expose him for the charlatan he imagines him to be. The spy believes that Sampath's otherworldliness is because of the ingredients that his mother adds to the dishes that she concocts for him and secretly dips his finger into the pot that is simmering with food.

Matters come to a head when the monkeys, always an excitable lot, chance upon a bag containing five bottles of rum. Having acquired a taste for alcohol, the monkeys become habitual drunkards, always scrounging for hard liquor and disrupting the assembly that gathers under Sampath. Mr. Chawla, who has made sufficient money out of his son's asceticism, grows worried at the prospect of his resources dwindling. He planned to move Sampath out of the tree and to build a proper hermitage for him. The monkeys grow more and more disruptive as time passes. Finally, the people of Shahkot decide to take the matter into their own hands and after a lot of argument finalize a plan of capturing the monkeys and transporting them to a far-off forest in the Himalayas. A day is fixed for this plan of action, the army personnel and police officers enlisted, and the new district commissioner apprised. It is the same day that Pinky plans to elope with Hungry Hop.

Hungry Hop is to come and pick her up at an appointed spot. Meanwhile, Hungry Hop has been introduced to a beautiful girl as his prospective bride. Hungry Hop is in a dilemma whether to marry Pinky, who is an aggressive and dominating girl, or the sweet, pink, and birthday cake girl who is so docile and charming that she will give in to his every whim and fancy. Hungry Hop drives his van through the town, and he is caught and trussed up in the nets meant to catch the monkeys.

Kulfi, who has her enormous cauldron ready and bubbling with spices that she has put in, sets off to catch the most vital ingredient for her dish—a monkey. The spy positions himself on a tree above the cauldron to spot the concoction that she is making. The Brigadier, who is leading the march, the district commissioner, Mr. Vermaji the scientist, Mr. Chawla, the army, and the towns people move toward Sampath's tree and, to their great consternation and alarm, find him missing. They find however, a big guava, a single guava, on his cot. The Cinema Monkey grabs the guava and with it leaps and bounds and makes its way to the mountaintop, chased by all the people. As the people reach the mountaintop, they hear the crack of a broken branch and find Kulfi's cauldron with its delicious gravy bubbling and seething with something in it.

Hullabaloo captures the essence of an Indian countryside and the eccentricities of the people who live in Shahkot with rare sensitivity and dry humor. The novel has the quality of a fable and is frothy and light in touch, with no great moral to expound. While the characters are delineated in quite some detail, the vignettes of Pinky, Hungry Hop, Jyotsana, the Brigadier, Vermaji, and others form the backdrop against which the drama of Sampath is played out. The question that is to be asked is whether Sampath is a real hermit—a seer in the true sense of the word. Desai obviously suggests that he is dim-witted fool who has been mistaken for one by the gullible people of Shahkot. One can compare Sampath to the other charlatan in Indian fiction—Raju, the guide, the eponymous hero of the novel by R. K. Narayan. Raju is also a fraud and takes on the mantle of a guru in order to make his living easier. At the end of the novel, Raju collapses in hunger with the vision of rain in his eyes. R. K. Narayan introduces an ambiguous element at the end of the novel, creating a situation that defies resolution. Desai has attempted to do the same in *Hullabaloo*. But whereas Raju in *The Guide* is a criminal and a charlatan, Sampath in *Hullabaloo* is a protagonist whose disarming simplicity and naïveté are charming in his innocence. While he does not carry the weight of his illustrious predecessor, he is disengaged from worldly affairs, treading a lonely path divested of chicanery and dishonesty. Sampath represents the holy men of India, who find God in their uprightness and fidelity and are revered for the same qualities. In a world of deceit, chaos and confusion, ugliness and hostility, Sampath is an ocean of mercy, forgiveness, and light. He is a true recluse, and when his natural hermitage is invaded by the money-mongers, he remains unaffected. He finds true companionship with the monkeys and peace in the guava orchard. When he realizes that his platitudinous life is being encroached upon by a sea of humanity, he disappears. Sampath is not born great; he does not achieve greatness; but he has greatness thrust upon him. Desai has succeeded in creating a great character and an interesting fable.

CRITICAL RECEPTION

Kiran Desai's maiden attempt has been greeted with great aplomb everywhere. Salman Rushdie has included a chapter from *Hullabaloo* in a collection of Indian writing in English that he edited for *New Yorker*. The reviews of the book have been very favorable, boosting the sales figures very high. Reviewers have praised Kiran Desai for the comical look that the novel offers of the people and situations in the imaginary Indian village, Shahkot. While all the critics agree that the novel does not propound any grand idea or take up for discussion any great mythic vision, it stands as a "meticulously crafted work of gently comic satire!" (Kakutani 45). Desai is lauded for being an "impeccable stylist, full of deliciously amusing, irreverent observations on India's rampant religiosity, self-involved families, monumental inefficiencies, stiff relations between sexes and life's toe stubbing limitations." (Rev., *Atlantic Monthly*). Critics point out that even though nobody remembers the plot because of the inherent flimsiness of the tale, still the novel is a pleasure to read and should be recommended for all libraries.

BIBLIOGRAPHY

Work by Kiran Desai

Novel

Hullabaloo in the Guava Orchard. New York: Atlantic Monthly Press, 1998.

Studies of Kiran Desai

Carnell, Simon. "Out on Limb in India." Rev. of *Hullabaloo in the Guava Orchard. The Spectator* (May 30, 1998): 34.

Charters, Mallay. Rev. of *Hullabaloo in the Guava Orchard. Publishers Weekly* 245.2 (January 12, 1998): 32–33.

Chew, Shirley. "The Wise Man Sitting up a Tree." Rev. of *Hullabaloo in the Guava Orchard. Times Literary Supplement* 4963 (May 14, 1998): 21.

Dwarakanath, Kala. "Monkeys, Mischief in the Guava Tree 'Hermitage.' " Rev. of *Hullabaloo in the Guava Orchard. India Abroad* (November 6, 1998): 48.

Jaffrey, Zia. "The Prophet in the Tree." Rev. of *Hullabaloo in the Guava Orchard. New York Times Book Review* (August 9, 1998): 2.

Kahn, Meredith. Rev. of *Hullabaloo in the Guava Orchard. Harper's Bazaar* 3438 (May 1998): 131.

Kakutani, Michiko. "Celebrity Frenzy Invades a Sleepy Indian Village." Rev. of *Hullabaloo in the Guava Orchard* by Kiran Desai. *New York Times*, June 12, 1998, E45.

Mulrine, Anna. Rev. of *Hullabaloo in the Guava Orchard. U.S. News and World Report* 125.2 (July 13, 1998): 61.

Nathan, Paul. "Up a Tree." Rev. of *Hullabaloo in the Guava Orchard. Publishers Weekly* 245.4 (January 26, 1998): 24.

Quinn, Judy. "Rushdie Causes Rush for First Novel." Rev. of *Hullabaloo in the Guava Orchard. Publishers Weekly* 244.15 (April 14, 1998): 24–25.

Rev. of *Hullabaloo in the Guava Orchard. Atlantic Monthly* (May 1998). 48.

Rev. of *Hullabaloo in the Guava Orchard*. *Library Journal* (May 1, 1998): 136.

Rev. of *Hullabaloo in the Guava Orchard*. *New Yorker* 74.17 (June 22–29, 1998): 150.

Seaman, Donna. Rev. of *Hullabaloo in the Guava Orchard*. *Booklist* 94.16 (April 15, 1998): 1427.

Steinberg, Sybil. Rev. of *Hullabaloo in the Guava Orchard*. *Publishers Weekly* 245.12 (March 12, 1998): 77.

Stuhr, Rebecca A. *Rev. of Hullabaloo in the Guava Orchard*. *Library Journal* 123.8 (May 1, 1998): 136.

Chitra Banerjee Divakaruni
(1956–   )

Brunda Moka-Dias

BIOGRAPHY

Chitra Banerjee Divakaruni was born July 1956 in Calcutta, India. Having attended institutions such as Loreto House and Presidency College in Calcutta, she came to Wright State University in Dayton, Ohio, to get an M.A. in 1977. Interestingly, corporate America played a role in the author's move to America. Employment with Esso, an American Oil company, fueled Divakaruni's father's curiosity about America, and thus the family moved to Oklahoma. In 1978 Divakaruni enrolled in the University of California at Berkeley to receive her Ph.D. and after doing so lived and taught in the Bay Area for many years.

Divakaruni's writing has come late in life and is directly tied to her migrant condition. Studying Renaissance literature and writing a dissertation on Christopher Marlowe seemed inadequate and distant from her life as a female immigrant in the United States. As she states in an interview by Joan Smith in the *San Francisco Examiner Magazine*:

I think that in some ways being an expatriate made me want to write, because it is such a powerful and poignant experience when you live away from your original culture and this becomes home, but never quite, and then you can't go back and be quite at home there either, so you become a kind of outsider to both cultures. Which is hard, but very good for writers, I think, to be in the position of looking in from the outside observing.

While expressing her immigrant experience in writing, Divakaruni has also helped other women cope with this "powerful and poignant experience" by founding a help line for South Asian women called MAITRI (18). Working in collaboration with mainstream women's organizations, Divakaruni and her friends assist South Asian women and "act as a bridge" linguistically, socially and culturally (18). She continues to teach and write and currently lives in Houston, Texas, with her husband and two sons.

MAJOR WORKS AND THEMES

Divakaruni's writing sets forth impulses of oral traditions and possesses the lyrical quality and the vibrant, descriptive imagery of poetry and oral storytelling. Having started out as a poet, she has also successfully included fiction—short stories and novels—into her oeuvre, thus writing across genres. Moving and beautifully written, her early collections of poetry like *Dark like the River, Reason for Nasturtiums, and Black Candle* were published by smaller presses and are not as well known as her later works. Most of her poetry and prose mainly deals with the theme of gender and migration, though her writing style varies based on the genre. *Arranged Marriage* is filled with stories that are simply told, in a heartfelt, realistic, and contemporary way. *Arranged Marriage* is thematically unified and explores, questions, rearticulates, and redefines the South Asian cultural construction of the feminine. That is, the characters, the imagery, the setting, and the themes deepen their significance as they recur with variation, in completely different ways, through each story, thus highlighting the reader's experience of the whole, which is greater than the sum of its parts. Similarly, her collections of poems titled *Leaving Yuba City* pays homage to the first wave of Asian Indian immigrants to America. Imagining the lives of Punjabi farmers who came to Yuba City, California, in the early 1900s, the author's prose poems and image-filled poetry tell stories of women's experiences against varying cultural backgrounds. In this collection, she also draws on various cultural artifacts like photography, film, and paintings by American artist Francesco Clemente.

The author's *Mistress of Spices* is a novel that strings magic, memory, and immigrant life into a tale of love and survival. In this novel, set in a sacred, mythical frame, the conflict is between desire and duty in the life of the protagonist, Tilo, the spice-Mistress, the healer. Divakaruni's protagonist is an ageless wisewoman clothed in an ancient body. Tilo is a spice-Mistress and healer who is supposed to lead an ascetic life by helping people with her knowledge of the magical properties of spices in her dusty little shop in Oakland, California. Abandoning her own desires in order to please the spices and win their power and approval, Tilo abides by the rules. She tries not to become overly involved with the customers for fear of the spices' wrath until she meets Raven, the handsome Native American. For Raven's love, she defies the patriarchal strictures of the spices and is ordered by them to choose between love and power. Raven, like Tilo's immigrant customers and the mistress of spices herself, is torn between two opposing identities, and in Raven and Tilo's relationship, Divakaruni explores what it means to be Indian—of America and India. Largely allegorical and mythic in its conscious structure, this novel does not repudiate the social; instead, it makes a case for the integration of the sacred and the social aspects of life. Tracing the protagonist's development through her various incarnations as Nayantara, Bhagyavati, Tilo, and finally Maya, the author dramatizes the conflict between the community and the individual and transforms the feminine into an empowered individual in connection with the community. In creating a woman-centered novel that embodies the element of choice, the author emphasizes power.

Power is also an integral issue in her depiction of immigrant cultures in the United States. In portraying the South Asian community in the novel, Divakaruni points to the diversity in the South Asian population in the United States and writes about characters of different classes and backgrounds. Exposing the "model minority" myth of the South Asian immigrants, she depicts abused, marginalized women, the middle class, and the working class. In elaborate characterizations, readers encounter Lalita, the battered victim of domestic violence; Haroun, a Kashmiri Muslim who drives cars for a living; Geeta Bannerjee, who is well educated and wants to marry her colleague Juan Cordero, who "came out of the barrio;" and Jagjit, the turbaned, Punjabi boy who is harassed in school and thus joins a gang (145). In brief references, the author gives glimpses of the rich Indians who, despite being rich, have problems: the sexy, young, "bougainvillea girls" (50); the Indian nurse who works with AIDS patients; the young Indian man with AIDS; and South Asian men who work as mechanics and own motels. Incorporating hate crimes perpetrated on Asian Indians—by the gang called the Dotbusters—into the novel, the author re-creates in the characters of Mohan and Veena the violence and prejudice suffered by virtue of ethnicity, a threat to mainstream America. In all these descriptions, the author points to the diversity and the difficulties of being South Asian in the United States.

In proposing an honest, community-based vision of a multicultural United States, Divakaruni creates a novel that addresses the problems of current-day America and its nonwhite populations. Divakaruni portrays a positive aspect of America by depicting marginalized communities of the United States, mainly the South Asian immigrants and the Native Americans but also in the portrayal of Kwesi, the African immigrant, and Juan Cordero, the Chicano American. In writing about "American" communities that are not perceived as "American" by the dominant white majority, the author redefines "America" as human and connected in contrast to capitalistic and isolated. Tilo's life in America shifts from a solely South Asian context to an interethnic, interracial context, as seen especially in Tilo's love for Raven (the Native American). The author portrays the complexities in forging interethnic and interracial relationships. Divakaruni highlights the need to get away from polarizations of races and ethnicities, from a notion of power that conquers and divides to understand power as that which includes the individual and the community.

Her latest novel, *Sister of My Heart*, is the story of two cousins who grow up as sisters in the same household in Calcutta. Having grown out of her short story "The UltraSound" (in *Arranged*), this novel traces the life of Anju and Sudha since their birth on the same day, a day that killed their fathers mysteriously in their quest for a cave full of rubies. The sisters grow into womanhood under the care of three mothers: two mothers and an aunt. Bonded in very special ways due to dire circumstances, the novel spends a lot of time testing this bond between the unusually beautiful Sudha and the ordinary, but ambitious, Anju. Dark family secrets, unrequited love, arranged marriages, and familial obligations of duty separate the sisters, with Anju bound for America and Sudha for provincial Bengal. The conflict over old and new ways comes to a climax when Sudha is told to get an abortion by her husband's family since she is carrying a girl-child. In addressing this issue of gender-biased abortions, Divakaruni creates a contemporary drama that forces women to take a stand on age-old injustices against gender. The close bond and strength of the sisters' relationship stand out in the tragedy of Anju's miscarriage and the triumph of Sudha's decision to leave her husband's house to save her unborn daughter.

Having grown up believing that her father had brought ruin on her cousin and the entire Chatterjee household, Sudha's discovery of the truth surrounding her father makes for a touching ending to the story as Sudha also leaves for America. Told in chapters written alternately in the voices of the sisters, the novel uses a fairy-tale structure filled with rhymes and stories within stories and moves at a fast pace with a plot that thickens with the turn of every page. While the story of the Chatterjee men going to search for a cave of rubies adds a sense of adventure and intrigue to the plot, it may come across as a forced fit into the fairy tale mold of the novel, but part of Divakaruni's skill is her ability to juxtapose the extraordinary with the ordinary. The strength of this novel is its characterization of women's relationships on many levels. The author's deep understanding of woman's world filled with emotions of sacrifice, desire, obligation, loss, jealousy, forgiveness, friendship, rivalry, and, most importantly, love is beautifully rendered. The birth of Sudha's daughter Dayita (Beloved) anticipates renewal, hope, and healing, but the novel is open-ended and does not provide closure. Sudha's life in America in all its complexity is left as a story to be imagined.

CRITICAL RECEPTION

Divakaruni has been critically very well received. She is an award-winning poet. Her collection of poetry titled *Black Candle* received the Hackney Literary Award in 1988 and the Barbara Deming Memorial Award in 1989. In 1990 she was the recipient of the Santa Clara Arts Council Award, California, for parts of *Black Candle*, which also received an honorable mention for the Paterson Poetry Prize. She won the Allen Ginsberg Poetry Prize and the Gerbode Foundation Award for *Leaving Yuba City*. In the same year, 1994, she won the Pushcart Prize for parts of the same collection. Her poetry also attracts performance artists who choreograph it for women's causes.

She was also awarded the PEN Oakland Josephine Miles Prize for Fiction, the Bay Area Book Reviewers Award for Fiction, and an American Book Award from Before Columbus Foundation for her collection of short stories titled *Arranged Marriage*. Critics have compared Divakaruni's *Mistress of Spices*, a best-selling novel, to works by Garcia Marquez and Laura Esquivel. Divakaruni's book tours attract a lot of attention, and she has been reviewed in a variety of print material, from newspapers to scholarly journals.

While most of the reviews are positive, she has also been critiqued by readers for stereotyping and exoticizing Indian women. Such criticisms may occur partly because of Divakaruni's use of Indian fairy tales, myths, and legends, which audiences may view as "exotic," and because Divakaruni's writing style explores and reveals the different experiences of women without dogmatically taking sides on women's issues. Yet anyone who reads her highly nuanced writing realizes that women's struggles are always at the core of her works. In a recent review of Divakaruni's second novel, *Sister of My Heart*, writer Cathy Grossman states: "*Sister* is a more mature and accessible book, less exotic than Mistress", she adds: "Its boundaries are neat and Time stays chronological." Highlighting her preference for Western ways of knowing and seeing the world, this writer categorizes Divakaruni's novels into separate divisions. On the contrary, Divakaruni's works are complex and rich precisely because they explore different ways of knowing and seeing the world, which go beyond binary divisions and categories. As the author herself puts it in an edited collection of South Asian fiction and poetry titled *Living in America*:

The challenge lies in trying to bring alive, for readers from other ethnic backgrounds, the Indian—and Indian American—experience, not as something exotic and alien but as something human and shared. It lies in getting my own community to see the subject of my work (often the plight of women of Indian origin struggling within a male-dominated culture, even here in America). It is necessary and important and not, as many have complained, a betrayal of my people, an exposure of secrets that create a "bad impression" of Indians in American society. But the opportunities are more important: to be able to straddle two distinct cultures and depict both with the relatively objective hand of the outsider; to destroy stereotypes and promote understanding between different sectors of the multicultural society in which we live; to paint the complex life of the immigrant with its unique joys and sorrows, so distinct from those of people who have never left their native land. (Rustomji-Kerns 47)

Divakaruni attempts to do all of this by creating characters with what she calls, in a conversation with Rajini Srikanth, a "writer's responsibility" that does not concern itself with "the majority culture's reaction" (99). She adds: "We've got to work with truth and honesty and care for our characters. When we care for our characters, the readers will start to care for and about them, as well. And when the reader connects with the characters in this emotional way, *that's* when the stereotypes break down" (99).

BIBLIOGRAPHY

Works by Chitra Banerjee Divakaruni

Novels

Mistress of Spices. New York: Doubleday, 1996.
Sister of My Heart. New York: Doubleday, 1999.

Short Stories

Arranged Marriage. New York: Doubleday, 1995.

Poetry

Dark like the River. Calcutta: Writer's Workshop Press, 1987.
Reason for Nasturtiums. Berkeley: Berkeley Poets Workshop and Press, 1990.
Black Candle. Corvallis: OR: Calyx Books, 1991.
Divakaruni, Chitra. "Chitra Divakaruni." In *Living in America: Poetry and Fiction by South Asian American Writers*. Ed. Roshni Rustomji-Kerns. Boulder, Co: Westview Press, 1995. 28–30.
Leaving Yuba City. New York: Anchor Books, 1997.

Studies of Chitra Banerjee Divakaruni

Adil, Alev. "Magic Amreekah." Rev. of *Mistress of Spices*. *The Times Literary Supplement* (March 21, 1997): 24.
Dijkstra, Sandra. Rev. of *Sister of My Heart*. *Publishers Weekly* (November 9, 1998): 55.
Grossman, Cathy Lynn. "Mystical 'Mistress of Spices' Casts a Subtle, Seductive spell." Rev. of *Mistress of Spices*. *USA Today*, June 26, 1997, 5.
———. "Rich Voices from the Heart." Rev. of *Sister of My Heart*. *USA Today*, February 4, 1999, 6D.
Guy, David. "Could a Little Fenugreek Hurt?" Rev. of *Mistress of Spices*. *New York Times Book Review* (April 13, 1997): 21.
Merlin, Lara. Rev. *of The Mistress of Spices*. *World Literature Today* 72.1 (1998): 207.
Moka-Dias, Brunda. "Cultural Collage: Narratives of South Asian Women in America." Diss., Rutgers University, 1997. Ann Arbor, MI: UMI, 1997.
Smith, Joan. "The Spices of Life." *San Francisco Examiner Magazine* (February 16, 1997): 7–18.
Srikanth, Rajini. "Chitra Banerjee Divakaruni: Exploring Human Nature under Fire." *Asian Pacific American Journal* 5.2 (1996): 94–101.
Tharoor, Shashi. "Currying Flavor." Rev. of *The Mistress of Spices*. *Los Angeles Times*, March 9, 1997, 10.

Winnifred Eaton
(1875–1954)

Lisa Botshon

BIOGRAPHY

Winnifred Eaton is thought to be the first Asian American novelist and, despite her relative obscurity today, was a well-known author in the early part of this century. She was the eighth child of sixteen born to a Chinese mother, Grace Trefusis, and a white English father, Edward Eaton. Raised in Montreal, the Eaton children were not taught much of their mother's language and culture. Additionally, they were largely able to pass as white. Of the extensive Eaton family, two were to become important writers: Winnifred and her older sister Edith. The trajectories of the two sisters' careers, however, took different courses. While Edith took on the Chinese pseudonym Sui Sin Far and wrote primarily of Chinese immigrants on the West Coast, Winnifred adopted a Japanese-sounding pseudonym, Onoto Watanna, and made her fame writing Japanese romances.

Winnifred Eaton placed her first story in a Montreal newspaper at the age of fourteen. When she was twenty, she traveled to Jamaica, where she worked as a stenographer for a year. She later moved to Chicago, where she wrote her first novel, *Miss Numè of Japan* (1899); this is thought to be the first novel ever published by an Asian American.

Publicity for Winnifred Eaton as Onoto Watanna claimed that she was a Japanese noblewoman from Nagasaki, and photos of the author showed her dressed in a kimono, as in the frontispiece for her novel *The Wooing of Wisteria* (1902). As Onoto Watanna, Eaton published at least ten Japanese-situated romance novels, several of which became best-sellers. One of her most popular works, *A Japanese Nightingale* (1901), was made into a Broadway play as well as a film and was translated into other languages.

After her initial success, Eaton moved to New York City, where in 1901 she married Bertrand Babcock. The couple had four children. During her time in New York, she published nearly a novel a year with major presses, including *The Wooing of Wisteria* (1902), *The Heart of Hyacinth* (1903), and *The Love of Azalea* (1904). In 1907 she departed from her successful Japanese formula and wrote a novel from the perspective of an Irish immigrant cook, *The Diary of Delia: Being a Veracious Chronicle of the Kitchen, with Some Side-Lights on the Parlour*. This she submitted to the *Saturday Evening Post* under the pseudonym Winnifred Mooney, but the *Post* elected to publish it under her by-then-recognizable Japanese pseudonym instead. In 1915 and 1916 she wrote two semiautobiographical narratives, both of which were published anonymously: *Me: A Book of Remembrance* and *Marion, the Story of an Artist's Model*. The latter was cowritten with her sister, Sara Bosse, with whom she wrote *Chinese-Japanese Cook Book* in 1914.

In 1917 Winnifred Eaton divorced Babcock and married Francis Fournier Reeve. The Reeves settled on a cattle ranch in Alberta, Canada; this setting inspired the novels *Cattle* (1923) and *His Royal Nibs* (1925). Between 1924 and 1931 Eaton worked in Hollywood, where she wrote and edited numerous screenplays, including *Mississippi Gambler* (1929) and *Shanghai Lady* (1930). Many of the films she worked on, however, did not credit her. She later returned to Canada, where she lived until her death on April 8, 1954. Her papers are housed at the University of Calgary.

MAJOR WORKS AND THEMES

Many of Eaton's best-known novels are romances set in Japan that focus on Japanese or mixed-race heroines who become involved with white American or English men. Her romances are traditional in many aspects; they feature beautiful, imperiled heroines who are rescued by handsome heroes. The couples face serious obstacles before they are able to unite. However, Eaton is one of few popular authors of her era who depict interracial romance without disastrous results. She does not employ racial identity as a plot device to separate lovers; rather, her novels tend to normalize relations between nationally and racially diverse characters. In *Sunny-San* (1922), for example, the only real deterrent in a romance between a white American man, Jerry, and a Eurasian woman from Japan, Sunny, is the hero's preexisting white fiancée. Once this fiancée is disposed of, Sunny joyfully reunites with Jerry and is smoothly incorporated into a white American family. Sunny's race and heritage do not prevent this union.

While a perusal of Eaton's Japanese heroines may reveal them to have stereotypical features, such as charming exoticism or beguiling naïveté, her women characters also share characteristics more typical of the American "new woman." They are often feisty and resist convention in their insistence on self-determination. In the novel *Tama*, Tama, for example, a blind mixed-race heroine marginalized by her neighbors for her difference, becomes a self-sufficient forest dweller rather than suffer the abuse of her society. In Eaton's first novel published after the ratification of the Nineteenth Amendment in 1920, which gave women the right to vote, Sunny-San makes her own way to New York from Japan, having decided that she is tired of her repressive guardians. Once in New York, she is made aware that women "have got the francheese [*sic*], we got the right to vote and be nachelised [*sic*] if we want to" (230).

Eaton's genre of choice, the popular romance, afforded the author financial stability, fame, and a chance to promote the idea of mixed-race unions, a subject that obviously had personal relevance. Nonetheless, her Japanese persona and trade in popular Orientalism are perceived to have taken a toll. In her fiction-alized anonymous memoir, *Me, a Book of Remembrance* (1915), the narrator, Nora Ascough, a stand-in for Eaton, mentions that she has a foreign-born mother but refuses to reveal her precise origins. Later in the narrative, Nora thinks about her success as an author and laments, "My success was founded upon a cheap and popular device. . . . Oh, I had sold my birthright for a mess of potage!" (154). Here, through a removed nostalgic narrator, Eaton articulates a profound ambivalence about her public persona and her work, both based on the creation of Onoto Watanna.

CRITICAL RECEPTION

Winnifred Eaton's novels were fairly well reviewed by prominent newspapers and journals of her time. These reviews most often praised her "realistic" render-ings of Japanese culture. *The Heart of Hyacinth* (1903), for example, was com-mended in the *New York Times* for the way it conveyed "an impression of a real people, as distinct from a people made up of fans, sashes, and kimonos" (Brownell 685). Several years later a *Times* review of *Tama* (1910) deemed the novel "[c]harmingly Japanese in form as well as atmosphere."

Despite her fame and popularity in the early part of this century, Winnifred Eaton's work has received little scholarly attention to date. Amy Ling was the first scholar to publish a discussion of Eaton in the 1980s as part of an early venture to uncover an Asian American literary history. In this 1984 *MELUS* article, she unveils Eaton as "Ethnic Chameleon and Popular Success" and champions her as "the first Chinamerican fictionist and something of a feminist" (7). Ling followed this article with others on Winnifred Eaton and her sister Edith. In 1990 she devoted a substantial chapter to the Eaton sisters in her book *Between Worlds: Women Writers of Chinese Ancestry*. This work provides bio-graphical material on the Eatons and surveys their writings.

Until recently, Winnifred has been unfavorably compared to her sister Edith. Because Edith assumed a pseudonym and persona that matched their mother's national and racial origins, she has been perceived to be more "authentic" than Winnifred, who decided to create a persona that was completely invented. Addi-tionally, critics have found Winnifred's popular writing difficult to assess. In *Between Worlds* Amy Ling writes that Winnifred Eaton's "personal integrity did not match up to Edith's" (49). James Doyle, whose 1994 essay recovers both Eaton sisters as Canadian authors, argues that although Winnifred is a "fluent stylist," she is "the less capable of the two sisters" as well as less "sincere" (57).

In the last few years, however, scholars have begun to evaluate Winnifred Eaton on her own terms. Pat Shea, for example, argues that Eaton challenges convention by incorporating controversial issues of race and sex into her formulaic romances. Yuko Matsukawa views Eaton as a "tricksterlike figure who assumes multiple identities in order to straddle different spheres and disrupt the sense of reality and complacency in those worlds" (107). An increasing interest in her writings is also evident in the reissue of two of her works since 1997— *Me: A Book of Remembrance* (University Press of Mississippi) and *Miss Numè of Japan* (Johns Hopkins). A full biography of Winnifred Eaton written by her granddaughter, Diana Birchall, is forthcoming from University of Illinois Press.

BIBLIOGRAPHY[1]

Works by Winnifred Eaton

Novels (as Onoto Watanna)

Miss Numè of Japan: A Japanese-American Romance. 1899. Baltimore: Johns Hopkins University Press, 1999.
A Japanese Nightingale. New York: Harper, 1901.
The Wooing of Wisteria. New York: Harper, 1902.
The Heart of Hyacinth. New York: Harper, 1903.
Daughters of Nijo. New York: Macmillan, 1904.
The Love of Azalea. New York: Dodd, Mead, 1904.
A Japanese Blossom. New York: Harper, 1906.
The Diary of Delia: Being a Veracious Chronicle of the Kitchen, with Some Side-Lights on the Parlour. New York: Page, 1907.
Tama. New York: Harper, 1910.
The Honorable Miss Moonlight. New York: Harper, 1912.
Sunny-San. New York: George H. Doran, 1922.
Cattle. London: Hutchinson, 1923.
His Royal Nibs. New York: W. J. Watt, 1925.

Short Stories (as Winnie Eaton)

"A Poor Devil." *Metropolitan Magazine* (n.d., 189?).
"A Half Caste." *Frank Leslie's Popular Monthly* 48 (September 1899): 489–96.
"Two Converts." *Harper's Monthly Magazine* (September 1901): 585–89.
"Kirishima-San." *The Idler* 20 (November 1901): 315–21.
"Margot." *Frank Leslie's Popular Monthly* 53.2 (December 1901): 202–9.

1. I thank Diana Birchall and Elizabeth Rooney for their help in compiling this bibliography.

(With Bertrand W. Babcock). "Eyes That Saw Not." *Harper's Monthly Magazine* (June 1902): 30–38.
"A Contract." *Frank Leslie's Popular Monthly* 54.4 (August 1902): 370–77.
"The Loves of Sakura Jiro and the Three-Headed Maid." *Century Magazine* 65.5 (March 1903): 755–60.
"Miss Lily and Miss Chrysanthemum." *Ladies Home Journal* (August 1903): 11–12.
"The Flight of Hyacinth." *Current Literature* 35 (October 1903): 437–40.
"The Wrench of Chance." *Harper's Weekly* (1906): 1494+.
"Maneuvers of O-Yasu-san." *Saturday Evening Post* 25 (January 1908): 9+.
"A Neighbor's Garden, My Own and a Dream One." *Good Housekeeping* (April 1908): 347–53; (May 1908): 484–90.
"Delia Dissents." *Saturday Evening Post* 22 (August 1908): 22–23.
"Lend Me Your Title." *Maclean's Magazine* (February 1919): 13+; (March 1919): 16+.
"Starving and Writing in New York." *Maclean's Magazine* (October 15, 1922): 66–67.
"Elspeth." *The Quill* (January 1923): 23–30.

Autobiographies (as Anonymous)

Me: A Book of Remembrance. 1915. Jackson: University Press of Mississippi, 1997.
(With Sara Bosse). *Marion, the Story of an Artist's Model by Herself and the Author of Me.* New York: W. J. Watt, 1916.

Nonfiction (as Onoto Watanna)

"The Half Caste." *Conkey's Home Journal* (November 1898): N.p.
"The Life of a Japanese Girl." *The Ladies Home Journal* 16 (April 1899): 7.
"New Year's Day in Japan." *Frank Leslie's Popular Monthly* 49.3 (January 1900): 283–86.
"The Japanese Drama and the Actor." *Critic* 41 (September 1902): 230–37.
"Every-day Life in Japan." *Harper's Weekly* 2 (April 1904): 500+.
"Marvellous Miniature Trees of Japan." *Woman's Home Companion* 31 (June 1904): 16.
"The Japanese in America." *The Eclectic Magazine* 148 (February 1907): 100–104.
(With Sara Bosse). *Chinese-Japanese Cook Book.* Chicago: Rand-McNally, 1914.
(As Winnifred Reeve [Onoto Watanna]). "The Candian Spirit in Our Literature." *Calgary Daily Herald*, March 24, 1923. 11.

Studies of Winnifred Eaton

Bloom, Harold, ed. *Asian American Women Writers.* Philadelphia: Chelsea House, 1997.
Doyle, James. "Sui Sin Far and Onoto Watanna: Two Early Chinese-Canadian Authors." *Canadian Literature* 140 (Spring 1994): 50–58.
Howells, William Dean. "A Psychological Counter-Current in Recent Fiction." *North American Review* (December 1901): 872–88.
Ling, Amy. *Between Worlds: Women Writers of Chinese Ancestry.* New York: Pergamon, 1990.
———. "Creating One's Self: The Eaton Sisiters." In *Reading the Literatures of Asian America.* Ed. Shirley Geok-lin Lim and Amy Ling. Philadelphia: Temple University Press, 1992. 310–13.

————. "Revelation and Mask: Autobiographies of the Eaton Sisters." *a/b: Auto/Biography Studies* 3.2 (Summer 1987): 46–52.

————. "Winnifred Eaton: Ethnic Chameleon and Popular Success." *MELUS* 11.3 (Fall 1984): 5–15.

Matsukawa, Yuko. "Cross-Dressing and Cross-Naming: Decoding Onoto Watanna." In *Tricksterism in Turn-of-the-Century U.S. Literature*. Ed. Elizabeth Ammons and Annette White-Parks. Hanover: University Press of New England, 1994. 106–25.

Moser, Linda Trinh. "Afterword." In *Me, a Book of Remembrance*, by Winnifred Eaton. Jackson: University Press of Mississippi, 1997, 357–72.

Oishi, Eve. "Introduction." In *Miss Numè of Japan: A Japanese-American Romance*, by Onoto Watanna. Baltimore: Johns Hopkins University Press, 1999, xi–xxxiii.

Rev. of *Heart of Hyacinth*, by Winnifred Eaton, and *The Heart of Japan*, by Clarence Ludlow Brownell. *New York Times*, October 3, 1903, 685.

Rev. of *A Japanese Nightingale*. *New York Times*, November 9, 1901, sec. 8:19.

Rev. of *Sunny-San*. *Times Literary Supplement* (July 13, 1922): 462.

Rev. of *Tama*. *New York Times*, January 14, 1911, sec. 2: 16.

Shea, Pat. "Winnifred Eaton and the Politics of Miscegenation in Popular Fiction. *MELUS* 22.2 (Summer 1997): 19–32.

"A Writer from Japan." *New York World* (February 6, 1898): N.p.

Indira Ganesan

(1960–   )

Harish Chander

BIOGRAPHY

Indira Ganesan was born on November 5, 1960, at her grandparents' home in Srirangam, a small town in the southern Indian state of Tamil Nadu. She spent her early childhood in northern India, in Uttar Pradesh, where her father worked as a statistician. Her father left for the United States in the mid-1960s for his graduate studies and then called his wife and two children to join him. Ganesan was then five and came to the United States just in time to start first grade in Rockland County, New York. Initially, blending the Eastern and Western cultures was a challenging experience for her. After she finished high school, her parents sent her to India to study at a Catholic women's college in Madras, but she found the adjustment difficult and the educational environment restrictive and returned a year later to the United States. In 1979 she entered Vassar College in New York and graduated with a major in English in 1982. She was elected to the Phi Beta Kappa honor society. She then attended the Writers' Workshop at the University of Iowa, receiving her M.F.A. degree in 1984. She received fellowships the next two years to attend the MacDowell Colony and the Fine Arts Work Center in Provincetown, Massachusetts. For a number of years after the fellowships, she supported her writing by taking various jobs, from personal assistant of the late painter Myron Stout, to an art gallery director, to a visiting instructor. Ganesan published her first novel, *The Journey*, in 1990.

The following year Ganesan was appointed assistant professor of English at the University of Missouri for the academic year 1991–1992. This led to a string of teaching appointments in the succeeding years, at the University of California, San Diego, from 1992 to 1995; at the University of California, Santa Cruz, from 1995 to 1996; at the Bunting Institute, Radcliffe College, from 1997 to 1998;

and at Southampton College of Long Island University, from 1998 to present. Her second novel, *Inheritance*, was published in 1998.

MAJOR WORKS AND THEMES

Ganesan is the product of both East and West, finding inspiration from a variety of sources: "From Shakespeare and James Joyce and Virginia Woolf. From Isaac Babel and Vladimir Nabokov and Gabriel Garcia Marquez. From fairy tales and fables and Greek mythology. From the Indian stories. From picture books and nursery rhymes and names" (Morrison). Comparing writing to a metaphorical island, she says: "Writing is more outward, a reflection of all that is outside too, music, light, and landscape. It's a beautiful state to enter . . . a kind of enchantment. A good country to visit" (Morrison). Like Toni Morrison, Zora Neale Hurston, and Maxine Hong Kingston,* Ganesan writes from a "double perspective of ethnicity and gender" (Telephone interview with Indira Ganesan by Marilou Briggs Wright, May 8, 1991).

In *The Journey*, nineteen-year-old Renu Krishnan returns from America to Pi, a fictional island in the Bay of Bengal that serves as the setting for both of Ganesan's novels, with her mother and younger sister Meenakshi to grieve for her "twin" cousin Rajesh, who died in an Indian train accident. Renu and her sister are creatures of two cultures, having been born on Pi but raised in Long Island. Renu is deeply affected by her cousin's passing. Ganesan herself describes the book as "a coming of age story about a young girl who triumphs over the disaster of her cousin's death" (Nair).

Fed on Indian superstitions and old wives' tales and worried about retribution from the gods, Renu harbors irrational fears. With her cousin's passing, she fears that her own death is imminent. She often dreams of three giantesses who appear before her bed, "place stones in their mouths and swallow" (33). She fears that if she returns to the American way of life, she will suffer divine sanction: "Whenever she slipped into the American way of life, when she stopped wearing the red *tikka* on her forehead, when she stopped going to temple, she could not free herself of the idea that the gods were still hunting her, that they were waiting to seek retribution" (14). She is so haunted by these images that she is fearful of going to bed. She even contemplates "sati"—the despised practice of the widow's throwing herself into her husband's funeral pyre—and she has visions of Rajesh seated in the fire and hears the fire calling her (158).

The prejudices of Westerners against Indians and of Indians against Westerners provide another theme of the story. When Renu's uncle Adda Krishnamurthi seeks the permission of the father of the European Alphonsa, the father refuses: "No citizen would rest knowing a brown man sweeps a white woman into his arms at night" (65). When Adda brings his European wife to his parents' home in India, she receives a cold reception, the old women of the village warning, "To marry out of caste was to stick a tongue out at the gods" (66). The look that Adda's mother gave her made Alphonsa lose her voice, and becomes largely reticent. Ultimately, Alphonsa is driven to enter a convent, where she kills herself.

But the irrational prejudice of Westerners and Indians is contradicted by the irrational partiality of each to the other's culture. Ganesan ridicules people like Freddie Flat, an American hippie, who loves all things Indian: "He'd come to India for adventure. He wanted to forget about classes, about his parents, about a life too tangled even at eighteen—free himself from the conventions of Western materialism. . . . [H]e adopted Eastern ways, gave up meat for a while, exchanged his mother's blue-eyed Madonna for a goddess sitting on an open, perfumed lotus" (93–94). Meenakshi, Renu's fifteen-year-old sister, loves all things American, which leads her to have an affair with Freddie, though he is twice her age.

Arranged marriages are also a target of criticism in the novel. The narrator observes that many women in Renu's family passively accepted arranged marriage and "disappointments were not uncommon" (46), even though matchmakers tried to match the bride's and groom's heights, their tastes in food, and horoscopes. Renu finds arranged marriages to be a source of unhappiness: "No wonder the women in her family photographs looked so grim, thought Renu—imagining Heathcliff and discovering only Kumar or Anand" (46–47). Renu clearly resists arranged marriages, though she allows her mother to search-for a match for her when her mother insists that marriage is the only solution to her problems.

The novel also criticizes a society that does not sanction widows' remarrying but cannot tolerate an unattached woman. Renu journeys to the interior of Pi to a place called Trippi, where she meets Marya the Seer, who offers the possibility of self-creation. Marya explains that she "nearly died of neglect" when she left her husband because of his infidelity (127). She remarks: "Not everyone will agree that it was a good choice, but I chose my light" (127). She asks Renu "why she is stuck with the memory of the dead, this necrophilia" (126). When Renu answers that "Rajesh is my twin," she exclaims: "But he doesn't exist as he was, only as you have created him" (126). The Seer advises Renu that "each one of us can be our own light. You can even be the Light of the World" (126). "Be your own light" seems to be the author's creed as well.

The novel ends optimistically with Renu free from her debilitating grief, ready to return to the United States: "Renu Krishnan stood on the beach on the island of Pi, ready for her journey," "away from her superstitions and fears, away from her self-wrought sickness," "stepping away from her inherited weights" (173–74).

In Ganesan's second novel, *The Inheritance*, fifteen-year-old Sonil narrates the story of her stay at her grandmother's home on Pi, where Sonil has come to recover from a chronic illness. Sonil, who has been brought up by her aunts in mainland India, is eager to learn about her aloof mother, Lakshmi, who lives on Pi, and her father, who departed India before she was born and who she later discovers is white. A bildungsroman, the novel describes Sonil's experiences of love, rejection, and loss and her eventual self-realization and emancipation.

Inheritance owes its power to the strong female characters who populate it, including Sonil's mother, Lakshmi, her aunts, who run their joint household without their husbands who work abroad, her beloved grandmother, and Sonil herself. The only man in the house is her opium-addicted great-uncle, a "wraith-like man" (41) whose goings and comings are imperceptible. Sonil does not seem to mind the absence of a male presence: "We were a family of women, without a strong man to give us buoyancy in the social waters. . . . I didn't think we needed men. My aunts largely managed without them and prospered. In fact, I think, without men we were stronger" (43).

When Sonil's cousin Jani leaves their grandmother's house to enter a convent, Sonil finds companionship in Richard, a thirty-year-old American who is seeking spiritual enlightenment in India. They begin an intense affair, described in sensuous terms in the novel. Kissing and being kissed by Richard give her a dizzy sensation and make her feel as if she were "transported in another world" (91). Renu says about Richard: "He was everything that no one in my family was; it was everything I wanted to be" (146). When Richard abruptly ends the affair, Renu begins to understand her mother and to forgive her mother's neglect of her. Having once compared her mother to "the bird which abandoned her young in other birds' nests" (117), Renu now realizes that her mother has perhaps herself been abandoned by Renu's American father. When her mother's second lover, Ashoka Ram, visits on the death of Sonil's grandmother, her mother begins to reveal her past to Sonil. Having refused Ashoka's offer of marriage, she tells her daughter that she will not marry any man because of how men have treated her.

Renu's cousin Jani also refuses to marry, in this case a man suggested by her parents. Jani escapes the arrangement by entering a convent. When Renu visits her at the convent, Renu begins to learn why Jani would not marry the man, who is nicknamed "C.P.": "Loving Asha, she couldn't love C.P." (156). Renu herself feels the urge "to kiss Jani, pull her toward me, make her leave the convent. Who needed boys anyway?" (156–57).

The inheritances of the title are evident in the lives of the younger generation, which often follow the same troubled paths as those of the older generation but at the same time allow the young the freedom to choose. Sonil recognizes her inheritance: "My family is ingrained in my actions. . . . Yet there are parts of me that are nothing like them. . . . I do not have to be like my mother. . . . Yet a shard of her exists in everything I do. My grandmother is in my heart a mandala I never part with, and my mother is a necklace I never take off" (192).

CRITICAL RECEPTION

Ganesan's novels have received, in the main, generous, but qualified, praise from critics. Mark Dery in the *New York Times Book Review* writes about *The Journey*: "Indira Ganesan's first novel is a symphony for the senses. The pages teem with unforgettable images, rendered in clean, economical prose. . . . For all her metaphysical fireworks, Ms. Ganesan maintains a wry sense of humor that prevents her story from collapsing under its own weight." *The New Yorker* reviewer observes: "The book occasionally has the haphazard feel of a first novel, but Ms. Ganesan . . . writes nimble prose that promises good things to come." (108). Annie-Marie Conway, writing for the *Times Literary Supplement*, says: "*The Journey* is rich in local color, perceptive about childhood fears and adolescent sureties, often droll, undeniably inventive but somehow fails to engage." *Publishers Weekly* writes: "While the charm of the writing and observations about East and West engage the reader, Renu's story drifts into an arbitrary half-resolution."

Inheritance has received more critical attention than *The Journey*. According to Sarah Curtis, the *Times Literary Supplement* reviewer, "Indira Ganesan's writing is direct but sometimes almost embarrassingly lush. She is best in describing the details of a young girl's day, such as how Sonil makes mandalas to restore her grandmother to health; less good when she tries to convey the mysticism that pervades India." Donna Seaman in her *Booklist* review observes: "Ganesan accomplishes so much in this gracefully sensual tale, pondering questions of spirituality and forgiveness and taking the measure of just how much we inherit from our family, no matter how unconventional its configuration may be." Ganesan, like Arundhati Roy and Chitra Divakaruni,* is part of a glorious flowering of contemporary Indian literature" (776). The *Library Journal* reviewer, Beth E. Andersen, writes about *Inheritance*: "Lush and stylish, this gentle, if idealized, story of a first love affair by the author of *The Journey* is perhaps a more dazzling international version of Judy Blume's perennially popular *Forever* (1975), but it is well worth reading." Edward Hower, in the *New York Times Book Review*, says that in *Inheritance*, "Ganesan has created an appealing young heroine whose determination and sensitivity win us over in the end."

BIBLIOGRAPHY

Works by Indira Ganesan

"The Wedding" (a short story). *Seventeen* 48 (February 1989): 110–11.
The Journey. New York: Alfred A. Knopf, 1990.
"Food and the Immigrant." In *Half and Half: Writers on Growing Up Biracial and Bicultural*. Ed. and intro. Claudine Chiawei O'Hearn. New York: Pantheon, 1998. 170–80.
The Inheritance. New York: Alfred A. Knopf, 1998.

Studies of Indira Ganesan

Andersen, Beth E. Rev. of *Inheritance*. *Library Journal* (November 15, 1997): 76.
Conway, Annie-Marie. Rev. of *The Journey*. *Times Literary Supplement* (April 12, 1991): 18.

Curtis, Sarah. Rev. of *Inheritance*. *Times Literary Supplement* (July 18, 1997): 22.

Dery, Mark. Rev. of *The Journey*. *New York Times Book Review* (September 9, 1990): 26.

Hower, Edward. "Spice Island." Rev. of *Inheritance*. *New York Times Book Review* (March 29, 1998): 16.

Nair, Hema. "Interview with Indira Ganesan by Hema Nair." *Little India* (June 1998): 8.

Rev. of *The Journey*. *New Yorker* (September 1990): 108.

Rev. of *The Journey*. *Publishers Weekly* (April 27, 1990): 52.

Seaman, Donna. Rev. of *Inheritance*. *Booklist* 94.9 (January 1998): 776.

Wright, Marilou Briggs. "Indira Ganesan." In *Writers of the Indian Diaspora*. Ed. Emmanuel S. Nelson. Westport, CT: Greenwood, 1993. 115–21.

Stephen Gill
(1932–)

Anita Mannur

BIOGRAPHY

Stephen Gill was born in 1932 in Sialkot, Punjab, an area that is now a part of Pakistan. After Pakistan was formed in 1947, Gill's family moved to India. He attended Khalsa Higher Secondary School in Delhi, where his mother was also a teacher. He received his B.A. from Punjab University and his M.A. in English literature from Meerut College (Agra University). Gill spent the next few years traveling and working outside India. During the three years that he taught at a high school for the Ministry of Education in Ethiopia, one of his first books. *English Grammar for Beginners*, was published. He then moved to Italy, where he worked both as a translator and as a teacher.

Gill arrived in Canada in 1965 to pursue a graduate degree in English at the University of Ottawa. After three years, Gill left graduate school to devote more time to his writing but remained in Canada. Over the next two years he alternated between Ottawa and Montreal, where he resumed teaching at the high school level. In 1971 he moved to Cornwall, Ontario. Finding that Cornwall lacked the literary scene that could be found in larger Canadian cities, Gill tried to establish a literary association for prospective writers and authors in the area. In 1973 the Cornwall Writer's Guild was formed with Gill's help. By May 1977 it became affiliated with the Canadian Authors' Association with Gill at the helm, but it dissolved within two years of its inauguration. Despite the fact that Cornwall was unable to provide the same literary networks and stimuli as cities such as Toronto, Gill lives there partly because of the small-town feel of Cornwall and also because it provides him with the atmosphere to produce creative work.

In the late 1970s Gill established Vesta Publications: a small-scale publishing house largely run by Gill (apparently from the basement of his house) that is committed to publishing new authors.

Although most of his work is written in English, he occasionally translates his poetry into Urdu, Hindi, and Panjabi. Gill's first published work appeared in the mid-1970s. At present, Gill continues to write, translate, and edit collections of writings, but his primary focus is on publishing and helping new writers find their voice. He currently resides in Cornwall with his wife and children.

MAJOR WORKS AND THEMES

Gill's novels and poetry address a variety of themes and issues. Alienation, in numerous forms, is a driving thematic in much of Gill's fiction, particularly in his novels *Why*, *Immigrant*, and *The Loyalist City*. These texts present protagonists in similar dilemmas: Christy Springer in *The Loyalist City*, Ruben Motard in *Why*, and Reghu Nath in *Immigrant* are young men who are estranged and lonely in the setting of large cities such as Ottawa and Montreal. In all three novels, the characters live in hostile societal milieus, often characterized as "racist," "unfriendly," "competitive," "materialistic," and suspicious of "others." Gill's characters are consistently unable to find meaning in their lives. Interestingly, this is intimately connected with the notion that they are unable to establish successful heterosexual relations. Unwilling to accept responsibility for their own actions, Gill's protagonists are also quick to blame others—particularly women—for their problems.

Immigrant will be of interest to readers concerned with Gill's depiction of South Asians in Canada. Published in 1977, this novel offers one of the earliest imaginative accounts of South Asians in North America, preceding Bharati Mukherjee's* frequently cited *Jasmine* (1989) in publication by twelve years. Focusing on the experiences of a young Indian man, Reghu Nath, who initially comes to Canada to pursue graduate studies, Gill's novel obliges readers to reflect on the place of South Asians in Canadian cities. The protagonist quickly abandons his studies because his progress is impeded by hostile and racist professors. The rest of the narrative sees him unsuccessful in attempts to secure gainful employment or establish meaningful relations with people. His latent misogyny and inability to accept responsibility for his own failings, however, make it difficult to empathize with his character. The use of an unsympathetic protagonist places the reader in an interesting situation: do we dismiss his complaints about racial and ethnic injustices because he appears to be lazy and misogynistic?

On the whole, Gill's writings are informed by his interest in world peace, pro-humanism, the experience of people of color in North America, and world injustices. His antiwar sentiment and interest in human interactions are also important concerns of his writings. Although his style is often not innovative, his writing, including the works discussed earlier (and his poetry and short stories that are not included in my analysis), directly addresses some of these concerns, which Gill views as central problems of contemporary Canadian society.

CRITICAL RECEPTION

Although in recent years there has been a growing critical awareness of literary works by writers of South Asian origin, Stephen Gill's writings in general
have received little critical attention in scholarly journals or book-length studies.
One of the few book-length studies that discuss Gill's fiction is Arnold Harichand Itwaru's study of Canadian immigrant fiction, *The Invention of Canada:
Literary Text and the Immigrant Imaginary*. Itwaru's text, however, does not
focus exclusively on Gill's writing: rather, he analyzes Gill's work along with
writings by other Canadian immigrant writers such as Austin Clarke, Brian
Moore, and Ved Devajee. Gill's work is discussed in the final chapter of the
text, "Antinomian Cyphers in Jan Drabek, Stephen Gill and Ved Devajee." Itwaru, however, does not seem impressed by either the form or content of Gill's
novel *Immigrant*.

Although he notes that *Immigrant* raises important questions pertaining to the
situation of the newly arrived immigrant in Canada, he adds that Gill "details
expectations and failures which by now we would deem common place in the
immigrant experience in Canada" (134). Itwaru does not find Gill's style aes-
thetically pleasing, noting that Gill's novel stands out from other works because
"the writer seems not to have entered the literary style of the art form of the
novel" and that "Gill repeats too much for a satisfactory literary rendering of
the problematic he sees" (135).

Diametrically opposed to this is the most extensive critical source on Stephen
Gill that has been published so far: a study titled *Stephen Gill and His Works*
by George Hines. Although the author provides in-depth descriptions of Gill's
major works with thorough plot summaries, he does not provide strong literary-
critical analyses of Gill's writings. For example, he notes that "as a writer, Gill
is primarily concerned with basic human emotions, about which his poems make
forceful statements" (44): this vague commentary, which does not subject Gill's
work to rigorous analyses, is characteristic of Hines' text. A more useful feature
of Hines' text is the extensive bibliography of newspaper articles written by
Gill. Included in this list is bibliographic information about various reviews of
his books as well as articles on his work that appear in newspapers and magazines.

Although Gill's work has received little attention in literary-critical arenas, it
has been extensively reviewed in many smaller newspapers and journals in Can-
ada and India. Hines' text provides a list of some of these articles, but with
Gill's help, I was able to examine a forthcoming volume on Gill's work,
Glimpses: A Selection of Published Articles about Stephen Gill and His Books.
Many of the reviews (originally published in smaller newspapers in Canada and
India) comment on the clarity of Gill's writing and his keen eye for noting the
details of human existence. Bluebell S. Phillips notes that in *Immigrant* and
Why, "the reader will find herself/himself much more knowledgeable about not
only the physical aspects of the country, but also of the social, political, moral
and living conditions that prevail" (87). Robert Durrell praises *Life's Vagaries*

for "demonstrat[ing] that people in various parts of the world have the same hopes, fears, problems and ambitions" (88). Praise for Gill's work abounds in this text, but again, I was struck by the overall lack of rigorous literary analysis that would perhaps allow us to better understand how Gill's work functions in relation to South Asian American literature.

BIBLIOGRAPHY

Works by Stephen Gill

Edited Collections

(Coeditor). *Poets of the Capital*. Ottawa: Borealis Press, 1973.
(Coeditor). *Seaway Valley Poets*. Cornwall: Vesta, 1975.
Green Snow: Anthology of Canadian Poets of Asian Origin. Cornwall: Vesta, 1976.
Tales from Canada for Children Everywhere. Cornwall: Vesta, 1979.
Anti-War Poems. Vol. 1. Cornwall: Vesta, 1984.
Anti-War Poems. Vol. 2. Cornwall: Vesta, 1986.
Vesta's Who's Who of North American Poets. Cornwall: Vesta, 1990.

Nonfiction

English Grammar for Beginners. New Delhi. S. Chand, 1968.
Six Symbolist Plays of Yeats. New Delhi: S. Chand, 1970.
Discovery of Bangladesh. Melksham: Colin Venton, 1975.
Scientific Romances of H. G. Wells. Cornwall: Vesta, 1977.
Political Convictions of G. B. Shaw. Cornwall: Vesta, 1980.
Sketches of India. Cornwall: Vesta, 1980.

Novels

Immigrant Cornwall: Vesta, 1977.
Why. Cornwall: Vesta, 1977.
The Loyalist City. Cornwall: Vesta, 1979.

Poetry

Reflections and Wounds. Cornwall: Vesta, 1978.
Moans and Waves. Cornwall: Vesta, 1982.
The Flowers of Thirst. Cornwall: Vesta, 1991.
Songs for Harmony. Cornwall: Vesta, 1992.
The Dove of Peace. New York: MAF Press, 1993.
Divergent Shades. India Writers Forum, 1995.

Short Stories

Life's Vagaries: Fourteen Short Stories. Cornwall: Vesta, 1974.

Young Adult Literature

Simon and the Snow King. Cornwall: Vesta, 1981.
The Blessings of a Bird. Cornwall: Vesta, 1983.

Studies of Stephen Gill

Hines, George, *Stephen Gill and His Works*. Cornwall: Vesta, 1982.

Itwaru, Arnold Harichand. *The Invention of Canada: Literary Text and the Immigrant Imaginary*. Toronto: TSAR, 1990.

Millward, Rekha. *A Checklist of Works by and about Stephen Gill*. Cornwall: Vesta, Forthcoming.

Samal, S. *Love and Harmony in Stephen Gill's Poetry*. Cornwall: Vesta, Forthcoming.

Sass, Tish. *Glimpses: A Selection of Published Articles About Stephen Gill and his Books*. Cornwall: Vesta, Forthcoming.

Jessica Tarahata Hagedorn
(1949–)

Ruby S. Ramraj

BIOGRAPHY

Jessica Tarahata Hagedorn, poet, playwright, and novelist, was born in Manila, Philippines, in 1949 and immigrated to San Francisco with her mother and brother when she was fourteen. At an early age, following in the footsteps of her grandfather, who was a writer, she began writing. On coming to the United States, her cultural interests broadened to include performance art, poetry, and rock-and-roll music. She was the lead singer and songwriter of the Gangster Choir for several years. She studied theater at the American Conservatory Theatre in San Francisco. All the while, she continued to write poetry and short fiction.

In 1978 she moved to New York and began writing and performing plays professionally. Her play *Tenement Lover: no palm trees/in new york city* was staged in 1981. This work focuses on themes that have continued to interest her: the import of revolution, the othering of minorities, the power of dominant cultures, and the conception of home and exile. A performance artist, she has rendered her own work in various experimental theaters and dance workshops. She made her mark also on television: *A Nun's Story*, on which she collaborated with Blondall Cummings, and *Holy Food* were broadcast on public television in 1988 and 1989, respectively.

Her first novel, *Dogeaters* (1990), earned her the distinction of being a finalist for the National Book Award. Set in the Philippines of the 1950s, it recalls the life of an upper-class Filipino now living in the United States. The novel reveals the gap between the privileged class and the poor. Her second novel, *The Gangster of Love* (1996), enlarges on the themes and concerns raised in the first. Set almost wholly in the United States, it explores more extensively than her first novel the confusion about cultural identity, ambivalent feelings toward families and friends, and the hold—for better or worse—that art can have on people's lives. Compared to the earlier novel, the tone of this text is more pessimistic and the characters more bohemian and unethical. Both novels use the montage effect of film to create rapidly shifting scenes and the rhythm of music to portray elusive qualities of people and places. Hagedorn's talents as performance poet, playwright, and musician are very much in evidence in her novels, and this genre has brought to the fore her multifaceted artistic attributes.

MAJOR WORKS AND THEMES

In her two novels to date, *Dogeaters* and *The Gangster of Love*, Hagedorn focuses on themes that are recognizably postmodern and postcolonial in her exploration of the lives of characters in multicultural and multiracial worlds. She tries to come to terms with hybridity and multiplicity, revealing the difficulties her characters feel living in worlds that reject or marginalize them, feeling alienated in their original and adopted societies. Her characters—often misfits— experience feelings of displacement and exile wherever they are, in the Philippines or the United States. They struggle to discover their own identity and sense of belonging. Hagedorn has a sympathetic bond with ordinary people and their lot in life. In an interview with Kay Bonetti, she describes herself as "an underdog person" who aligns herself "with those who seem to be not considered valuable in polite society" (220). In these two texts, she explores as well the identity of women, artists, revolutionaries, and rebels and the tragic consequences of challenging existing social norms.

In addition to questions of identity in *Dogeaters*, Hagedorn discusses current issues of postcolonialism, neocolonialism, and historical representation. The Philippine people are described as suffering "collectively from a cultural inferiority complex." One of the characters claims that they belong to "a nation doomed . . . baptized and colonized to death by the Spaniards and the Americans" (101). This is a society that is still suffering the consequence of Spain's harsh colonialism—the Spanish, for instance, look down on the mestizos (Spanish Asian)—and now is subjected to U.S. neocolonialism, particularly in the area of culture—witness the impact of Hollywood films on the Filipinos. Movies are not merely entertainment but a colonizing medium that, as John Updike says in his review of the novel, invades "the young minds of the Third World . . . without the corrective reality of North America upon emerging from the theatre" (105). Hagedorn points up this cultural domination of the local culture by setting the opening scene of *Dogeaters* in the "air-conditioned darkness of Avenue Theater" (3).

Dogeaters, set in Manila between the 1950s and 1980s, is a series of juxtaposed, loosely related accounts of the lives of a large gallery of characters. While the main sections of the text are given from the perspective of the upper-class, first-person female narrator, Rio Gonzaga, some of the other sections are seen through the eyes of the poverty-stricken homosexual prostitute, cocaine addict, and disc jockey Joey. Other narratives recount the lives of politicians, criminals, television personalities, and ordinary citizens. Interspersed among these "chapters" are historical documents (real and invented), radio dramas, songs, and prayers.

The fragmented structure of the text appropriately conveys the discordant, disjointed lives of the two narrators, Rio and Joey, and their sense of alienation from their Philippine society. They are both suffocated by their respective social milieu: Rio by her upper-class life of country clubs, beauty parlors, enforced marriages, and overt sexual indiscretions; and Joey by his squalid underworld life where he is at the mercy of his demanding pimp and clients. His paltry efforts at rebellion take the form of stealing or using cocaine. Hagedorn's Manila of the 1950s is a despairing city of social and political turmoil over which no one seems to have any control.

Hagedorn eschews the traditional linear novel form for what could be termed fragmentary memories and flashbacks. She uses this technique effectively, particularly when she has Rio recall her life in Manila after "all these years in America" (6). These are some of the more compelling scenes in the novel. Living in a world of family feuds, social disruptions, and political upheavals, she is ready to immigrate to the United States with her mother, who is herself eager to leave her unfaithful husband. Once in the United States, Rio initially revels in her newfound freedom from her restrictive Manila life. Joey, too, escapes the debilitating squalor of his life by joining a band of guerrillas—after he witnesses the assassination of the opposition leader. He begins to see himself afresh as a kind of hero, a fighter for his country.

In subverting the traditional cause-and-effect, linear narrative structure in *Dogeaters*, Hagedorn is very much a postmodern writer. She has acknowledged the profound influence of Gabriel García Márquez's *One Hundred Years of Solitude* on her first attempt at extended fiction (Bonetti 229). There is a feel of spontaneity to the novel, and this, together with the personal, lyrical, often elegiac tone, produces some remarkably haunting passages:

In my recurring dream, my brother and I inhabit the translucent bodies of nocturnal moths with curved, fragile wings. . . . Raul and I embrace our destiny: we fly around in circles, we swoop and dive in effortless arcs against a barren sky, we flap and beat our wings in our futile attempts to reach what surely must be heaven. (247)

Here Rio's desire to escape her mother's dominance, to be free and gain her eventual independence is evoked by the image of translucent moths, fragile and beautiful, striving heavenward to the light.

Alienation, identity, and nomadism are recurring themes in her second novel, *The Gangster of Love*. Hagedorn follows an immigrant family—mother and two children—who immigrate to the United States from Manila because of a father's infidelity—as in *Dogeaters*. The first-person narrator, Raquel (Rocky) Rivera, a fervent rock-and-roll fan, arrives in San Francisco on the day that Jimmy Hendrix dies. Hagedorn establishes the importance of music in Rocky's life in the opening paragraph and subsequently in two imaginary encounters with the dead singer. Rocky's brother, Voltaire, feeling alienated in his new environment, withdraws into himself, a silent, sad youth. Soon he returns to the Philippines. Rocky, on the other hand, initially involves herself in the glitzy aspects of her new home. She goes off with a fellow musician, Elvis Chang, to New York, where they form a band, "the Gangster of Love." Even though she achieves some success with the band, she eventually leaves the United States, returning to Manila with her baby daughter. But she is not happy here either. Dissatisfied with both Manila and the United States, she seems doomed to drift aimlessly between them. Hagedorn underscores her vacillation and ambivalence toward her birth and her adopted countries, designating it as "Yo-Yo," a term that she introduces and defines toward the end of the novel.

Hagedorn portrays with graphic details the New York experiences of Rocky and Elvis (and their friends Keiko, a photographer, and Sly, a member of the band) with contemporary, drug-infused, pop rock culture. She describes a lifestyle of extremes—of alternating ennui and franticness, of sexual extravagance and nostalgic innocence. What appears to be missing in these scenes is any clear moral stance on the part of either the characters or the text itself. Their lives are empty and meaningless, but they are not aware of this. Sex is impersonal and loveless. Rocky tells Elvis (speaking about Keiko), "I wish you'd both get in bed and get over it" (110). Rocky at times seems to have some awareness of her meaningless life and yearns for some kind of fulfillment as a woman and an artist. She perceives this longing only vaguely; she never articulates it, and in the end it seems unconvincing.

In relating the events in the novel, Hagedorn uses (as in *Dogeaters*) two first-person narrative voices: the primary voice is Rocky's, which alternates in a few sections with Elvis'. This technique is effective in giving the reader two different views of the same crucial incidents and relationships. For instance, we get both sides of Rocky's relationship with Keiko and their ongoing conflict. Hagedorn also employs a fragmented structure similar to that of *Dogeaters*—perhaps even more so as she intersperses the already disjointed narratives with dreams, jokes, and definitions. If the intention is to create a milieu of chaos, it is not wholly successful. It appears to be contrived, a deliberate attempt at being unnecessarily avant-garde.

The protagonists of *The Gangster of Love* are not as engaging as in *Dogeaters*. Both Rocky and Elvis lack depth; they are more stereotypes of the narrow, spoiled, and self-indulgent. Unlike *Dogeaters*, the writing is prosaic, devoid of striking imagery and rhythm, and the narrative is scant, reflecting little character development. Hagedorn's second novel certainly does not measure up to her first.

CRITICAL RECEPTION

Hagedorn initially made her name as a performance artist, musician, poet, and playwright. Her music, poetry, and drama (which focus, like her novels, on violence, revolt, gender and ethnic discrimination, alienation, and hybridity) have been praised for their honesty and passion. With the publication of *Dogeaters* and *The Gangster of Love*, she is now being recognized as one of the new wave of fiction writers to focus on the experience of recent immigrants to the United States. *Dogeaters* received, for the most part, favorable reviews in the United States and Britain in such periodicals as *American Book Review*, *Commentary*, *New York Times Book Review*, *New Yorker*, and the *Times Literary Supplement*. John Updike, in the *New Yorker*, wrote an incisive analysis of the text, praising it for its rich characterization and the "immediacy of its personal witness" (104). Blanche D'Alpuget echoed his sentiments, calling it "a rich small feast of a book." (1). Carol Iannone, however, felt that "the disparate materials of *Dogeaters* were not very skilfully handled." (50).

The Gangster of Love did not enjoy the positive critical reception of *Dogeaters*, eliciting mixed reviews. Some reviewers admit that the novel does capture the dark mood and the fastpaced, carefree life of American pop rock culture; however, they criticize it as a "novel without much of a plot or memorable characters" (Corrigan 66). On the other hand, Francine Prose of *New York Times Book Review* is "exhausted by the book's manic drive," yet she finds in it characters "to care about deeply." Most critics have noted Hagedorn's eye for detail, her honest concern with crucial questions of identity and security. Hagedorn's work already has been the subject of dissertations, one on her poetry and two on *Dogeaters*. Her contributions as a performance artist, musician, playwright, and novelist have been written about in newspapers and analyzed in scholarly articles in books and journals. Evidently, Hagedorn has begun to find a prominent place for herself among contemporary Asian American novelists.

BIBLIOGRAPHY

Works by Jessica Tarahata Hagedorn

Novels

Dogeaters. New York: Pantheon Books, 1990.
The Gangster of Love. New York: Houghton Mifflin, 1996.

Poetry

Four Young Women: Poems. Ed. Kenneth Rexroth. New York: McGraw-Hill, 1973.
Dangerous Music: The Poetry and Prose of Jessica Hagedorn. San Francisco: Momo's Press, 1975.
Pet Food and Tropical Apparitions. San Francisco: Momo's Press, 1981.
Early Ripening: American Women's Poetry Now. Ed. Marge Piercy. Pandora Press, 1987.

Plays

Tenement Lover: no palm trees/in new york city. Between Worlds: Contemporary Asian-American Plays. Ed. Misha Berson. New York: Theatre Communications Group, 1990. 81–90.

Edited book

Charlie Chan Is Dead, an Anthology of Contemporary Asian-American Fiction. New York: Penguin, 1993.

Studies of Jessica Tarahata Hagedorn

Bonetti, Kay, et al., eds. *Conversations with American Novelists.* Columbia: University of Missouri Press, 1997. 217–33.

Chang, Juliana Chu. "Word and Flesh: Materiality, Violence and Asian-American Poetics." Diss., University of California at Berkeley, 1995.

Corrigan, Maureen. "Yo-Yo in a Rock Band." Rev. of *The Gangster of Love. The Nation* 263 (October 28, 1996): 64–66.

Covi, Giovanna. "Jessica Hagedorn's Decolonialization of Subjectivity: Historical Agency beyond Gender and Nation." In *Nationalism and Sexuality: Crisis of Identity.* Ed. Yiorgos Kalogeras and Domna Pastourmatzi. Thessalonici, Greece: Aristotle University, 1996. 63–80.

D'Alpuget, Blanche. Rev. of *Dogeaters. New York Times Book Review* (March 25, 1990): 1.

De Manuel, Maria Teresa. "Jessica Hagedorn's *Dogeaters*: A Feminist Reading." *Likha* 12.2 (1990–1991): 10–32.

Evangelista, Susan. "Jessica Hagedorn and Manila Magic." *MELUS: The Journal of the Society for the Study of the Multi-Ethnic Literature of the United States* 18.4 (Winter 1993–1994): 41–52.

———. "Jessica Hagedorn: Pinay Poet." *Philippine Studies* 35.4 (1987): 475–87.

Gillian, Jennifer. "Border Perceptions: Reading U.S. Intervention in Roosevelt and Hagedorn." In *The Image of the Frontier in Literature, Media, and Society.* Ed. Will Wright et al. Pueblo: University of Southern Colorado, 1997. 121–25.

Gima, Charlene Setsue. "Writing the Pacific: Imagining Communities of Difference in the Fiction of Jessica Hagedorn, Keri Hulme, Rodney Morales, and Gary Pak." Diss., Cornell University, 1997.

Iannone, Carol. Rev. of *Dogeaters. Commentary* 91 (March 1990): 50.

Knippling, Alpana Sharma. *New Immigrant Literatures in the United States.* Westport, CT: Greenwood Press, 1996. 81–83.

Lee, Rachel C. "The Americas of Asian-American Literature: Nationalism, Gender and Sexuality in Bulosan's *America Is in the Heart*, Jen's *Typical American*, and Hagedorn's *Dogeaters*." Diss., University of California at Los Angeles, 1995.

Lee, Robert A. "Eat a Bowl of Tea: Asian Americans in the Novels of Jish Jen, Cynthia Kadohata, Kim Ronyoung, Jessica Hagedorn, and Tran Van Dinh." *Yearbook of English Studies* 24 (1994): 263–80.

Ling, Jinqi. "Identity Crisis and Gender Politics: Reappropriating Asian American Masculinity." In *An Interethnic Companion to Asian American Literature.* Ed. King-kok Cheung. Cambridge: Cambridge University Press, 1997. 312–37.

Lowe, Lisa. "Decolonization, Displacement, Disidentification: Asian American 'Novels' and the Question of History." In *Cultural Institutions of the Novel.* Ed. Deidre Lynch and William B. Warner. Durham, NC: Duke University Press, 1996. 96–128.

Manuel, Dolores de. "Marriage in Philippine-American Fiction." *Philippine Studies* 42.2 (1994): 210–16.

Ostriker, Alicia. *Stealing the Language: The Emergence of Women's Poetry in America.* Boston: Beacon Press, 1986.

Prose, Francine. Rev. of *The Gangster of Love. New York Times Book Review* (September 15, 1996): 14.

Updike, John. Rev. of *Dogeaters. New Yorker* 67. 102 (March 18, 1991): 102–6.

Chuang Hua

(?–)

Hailing Xiao

BIOGRAPHY

Chuang Hua was born in China. She first went to England with her family at an early age and then to the United States. The author lived in New York City in the 1980s and in Connecticut. Further information about the author is not available at this time.

MAJOR WORK AND THEMES

Chuang's autobiographical novel, *Crossings*, is sometimes considered one of the first Asian American modernist works. The novel deals with the female protagonist Fourth Jane's cultural identity and her self-searching journey. Under the influence of her father's strong Chinese traditional thinking, which is often in conflict with the practice of the New World, Fourth Jane finds herself in a constant struggle to define her true self.

Crossings is a novel filled with memories, dreams, fantasy, and myths of China. Fourth Jane often recalls scenes of Chinese landscape: "the farm house, field, solitary tree, the distant mountains have fused, have become one with the American landscape. I can't separate anymore" (125). In one paragraph, Chuang described Fourth Jane's nostalgic feelings in the following way:

One evening she visited Dyadya and found in his study a magazine sent from China. On the first page was a poorly reproduced photograph of a farmer's house built up of mud and rushes and roofed in tile standing in the middle of a neatly tilled field. A tree clung by the wall of the house, a line of mountains beyond the fields. With a shock she recognized the landscape, could smell the tilled soil, felt the embrace of the house, climbed the mountains. Unguarded, a seizure of loss struck her. (123–24)

Fourth Jane often participates in traditional family rituals to keep old Chinese customs alive.

Fourth Jane's many crossings of different cultures are depicted in the novel as she went from China to England and then the United States and stayed in France for a long time. Also, Fourth Jane was raised by nurses from China, Scotland, and Ireland during different periods of her early years. As Amy Ling states in her essay "A Rumble in the Silence: *Crossings* by Chuang Hua," "Many physical dislocations may also result in a psychic loss of orientation, of identity, and of clear direction" (31). Therefore, *Crossings* may be considered a novel that best reflects the theme of a Chinese female self-exploration and search for identity in Western cultures.

CRITICAL RECEPTION

Crossings received hardly any critical attention until the novel was republished in 1986 with a Foreword by Amy Ling. Since then, three brilliant essays have been published on the study of *Crossings* dealing with the theme and style of the novel.

The first study on *Crossings* is conducted by Ling, who focuses on the "forces of fragmentation" (32) in both Fourth Jane's personality as well as in Chuang's experimental style. Ling argues, "In addition to the confusing ordinal and sexual position in the family, Jane has experienced many geographical moves, which have created their own confusions" (30). Furthermore, Ling points out that Chuang's method of narration is fragmented: "[T]he narration is broken into small segments from paragraph to paragraph, even from sentence to sentence" (33). Finally, Ling demonstrates that Chuang "creates artistic coherence" (36) through the use of appropriate images in the novel. Later in her Foreword to *Crossings*, Ling reiterates that the fragmentation of the book is a reflection of the author's mental state. Ling points out, "Its prose is often elegantly spare, its punctuation and syntax often unconventional. Quotation marks may be omitted; fragments and run-on sentences abound, and characters are unspecified, and chronological leaps may occur, even within a single paragraph" (2).

Another critic, Veronica C. Wang, did a comparative study of Chuang's *Crossings* with Anzia Yezierska's autobiographical novel *Bread Givers* and Maxine Hong Kingston's* *The Woman Warrior* and *China Men*. Wang argues that a study of Yezierska's and Kingston's portrayal of immigrant experience will "sharpen for the reader the physical, cultural, and psychological displacement uniquely felt by the protagonist in *Crossings*" (23). According to Wang, all the protagonists in these novels start their "self-transformation toward some measure of personal equilibrium" (34) through their realization of the dilemma and the conflicts within and without (34). In addition, Wang demonstrates that Fourth Jane leads a more "diasporic and fragmented" (35) life due to her intense feelings of "uprootedness and lack of an anchor" (35).

Like Ling and Wang, Shu-yan Li argues that *Crossings* should be given "a special place in the study of Chinese-American literary tradition" (99). Li illustrates "otherness and transformation" (99) embodied in Louis Chu's* *Eat a Bowl of Tea* and *Crossings* by analyzing the elements of Chinese heritage in the novels. Moreover, Li explores Chuang's effective use of "images of architectural closure" (107), which helps to reveal Fourth Jane's "disorientation and mental disturbance" (107).

All these critics seem to state that Fourth Jane appears to be leading a wandering existence without a central purpose in her life, as one can see from the fragmented narrative and her alienated life. However, Lesley Chin Douglass argues that Fourth Jane is "attempting to rediscover a Chinese identity and a way of embracing life, through a Taoist tradition which has been lost to her" (55). Perhaps Douglass best summarizes Fourth Jane's seemingly aimless life through his observation that Fourth Jane represents "a Taoist return to her roots (ken), through the seemingly passive act of countless crossings or uprootings (fei)" (56).

BIBLIOGRAPHY

Work by Chuang Hua

Crossings. Boston: Northeastern University Press, 1986.

Studies of Chuang Hua

Douglass, Lesley Chin. "Finding the Way: Chuang Hua's *Crossings* and Chinese Literary Tradition." *MELUS* (Spring 1995): 53–65.

Li, Shu-yan. "Otherness and Transformation in *Eat a Bowl of Tea* and *Crossings*." *MELUS* (Winter 1993–1994): 99–110.

Ling, Amy. "Foreword." In *Crossings*. Boston: Northeastern University Press, 1986.

———. "A Rumble in the Silence: *Crossings* by Chuang Hua." *MELUS* (Winter 1982): 29–37.

Wang, Veronica C. "In Search of Self: The Dislocated Female Émigré Wanderer in Chuang Hua's *Crossings*." In *Multicultural Literatures through Feminist/ Poststructuralist Lenses*. Ed. Barbara Frey Waxman. Knoxville: University of Tennessee Press 1993. 23–36.

Cynthia Kadohata
(1956–　)

Su-lin Yu

BIOGRAPHY

Born in Chicago in 1956, Cynthia Kadohata is a third-generation Japanese American. She spent most of her early childhood traveling with her family. Her family moved to Arkansas, Georgia, Michigan, and back to Chicago before finally settling in Los Angeles, the city Kadohata has called her home. At eighteen, Kadohata enrolled in Los Angeles City College and then transferred to the University of Southern California, where she earned a degree in journalism. After being injured in a car accident in 1977, Kadohata relocated to Boston, where she began to develop her interest in writing short stories and fictions. She then briefly attended the writing programs at the University of Pittsburgh and Columbia University. With the publication of her first novel, *The Floating World*, in 1989 Kadohata established her reputation as a writer. Her short fiction has appeared in the *New Yorker*, *Grand Street*, and *Pennsylvania Review*, and her second novel, *In the Heart of the Valley of Love* (1992), has been widely reviewed. She has also received grants from the National Endowment for the Arts and a prestigious Whiting Award.

Kadohata's family background and life experience figure prominently in her works. Her experience of constantly being on the road with her family constitutes not only a basic element of *The Floating World* but also a source of inspiration to her writing. Kadohata has stated that she likes traveling because it creates a new perspective from which she contemplates ordinary things. In *In the Heart of the Valley of Love* Kadohata deals with a major traumatic experience, a car accident. At age twenty-one, she was severely injured while walking down a street in Los Angeles when a car jumped the curb and smashed into her, leaving her with a broken collarbone and mangled right arm. Francie, the nineteen-year-old protagonist, has a crushed arm resulting from a similar accident. This accident convinced Kadohata that life is transient and unpredictable. Writing her stories in response to such events, Kadohata has sometimes blurred the division between life and fiction. In an interview with Lisa See, she acknowledged, "Sometimes I can't remember if something has happened to me or to my character. My memories become their memories, and their memories become mine" (48).

MAJOR WORKS AND THEMES

Kadohata's two novels not only follow the long literary tradition of stories of coming-of-age but also contribute to a postmodern form of fiction. Cast within a loose and free-associative structure, both narratives stitch together a series of disjointed episodes and render a seemingly progressive journey. Although their settings are different, the stories are told through young female narrators who share similar personalities: perceptive, playful, and deceptively naive. *The Floating World* centers on Olivia, a twelve-year-old Japanese American girl who develops her cultural identity in the 1950s, when the horror of the mass internment of Japanese was still in the air, when it was hard for Japanese Americans to find jobs, and when Japanese Americans were still discriminated against as "Japs." Set in Los Angeles in the year 2052, *In the Heart of the Valley of Love* portrays Francie, a nineteen-year-old orphan of Asian and African descent who searches for the meaning of her existence in a chaotic city where riots and arrests are daily occurrences, where law-breaking is rampant, and where everyone carries a gun for self-protection. In a similar way, both stories show how the protagonists become more mature and independent through their journeys. Nevertheless, as *The Floating World* validates the anchor of family in an unstable world, *In the Heart of the Valley of Love* celebrates human capacity to love and hope in a wasteland.

In *The Floating World*, Olivia's identity is greatly shaped by her family's floating existence. Looking for jobs in the 1950s, Olivia and her family are constantly on the move in what her grandmother Obasan called the floating world: "The Floating World was the gas station attendants, restaurants, and jobs we depended on, the motel towns floating in the middle of fields and mountains. In old Japan, Ukiyo meant the districts full of brothels, teahouses, and public baths, but it also referred to change and the pleasures and loneliness change brings" (3). Although Olivia and her family lived an uprooted and displaced life, the three generations try to sustain themselves by achieving a sense of stability and continuity. To Olivia, Obasan represents the issei generation, which endeavors to pass on the Japanese cultural heritage. Olivia's attitude toward Obasan is ambivalent. She takes much of her knowledge of life from her grandmother, but she hates the old woman's meanness, cruelty, and insults. Olivia tells us how Obasan demands she be hostile to white people and thus asks her to resist assimilation into American society. Unable to fully understand Obasan's hostility and alienation, Olivia declared, "I want to be opposite to Obasan. Anything she does, I never will" (18). Yet, her life turns out to be "intertwined" with Obasan's. As the oldest child in the family, Olivia must accept her responsibility to take care of Obasan. Olivia reveals her inner struggle: "Sometimes I ran from her, but I never ran hard. I didn't want her to catch and hit me, but I didn't want to lose her either" (20–21). The tension of Olivia's continuous struggle with Obasan reaches its climax in the scene when Olivia lets her die without helping her. There Olivia finally vents her rage toward her grandmother, and later she tries to justify her deed. She tells her mother, "She [Obasan] made me kill her!" (26). But her justification cannot free her from her guilt. Indeed, even by killing Obasan, Olivia cannot completely free herself from the ethnic heritage represented by Obasan. As a matter of fact, after Obasan's death, Olivia is haunted by the spirit of Obasan throughout her life. She begins to express a desire to know more about her, to tell stories about her, to search for advice from her diary, and to accept the "magic purse" that contains Obasan's life experience. As a result, Olivia inherits Obasan's legacy without acknowledging it.

In contrast to Obasan's resistance to the dominant white culture, Olivia's parents desperately seek to assimilate themselves into American society. Because of their own failures and unhappiness, Olivia's parents expect their daughter to become happy and to find a place in that society. They praise Olivia's ability to speak fluent English because they believe that assimilation requires good English: "If you couldn't see her [Olivia], you wouldn't even know she was Japanese" (8). Olivia appears to follow her parents' beliefs and expectations but rebels inwardly. She insists, "I would do many things that were contrary to my upbringing" (83). When she leaves her family, Olivia reveals her determination to abandon some of her parents' teachings. She states, "My parents had taught me many things they hadn't meant to teach me and I hadn't meant to learn. One of those things was fear; their big fear, during the war; and when my father was arrested" (121). Olivia's refusal to accept the fear caused by racism implies that she will erase her Japanese identity. But as soon as Olivia starts life on her own in Los Angeles, she turns out to be as displaced as her parents. Apparently, Olivia's identity is based less on the mainstream concept of freedom than on her home culture.

Olivia's home culture, however, is not formed by itself. It comes from a larger social and historical context—the fragmenting effects of internment on the Japanese American community. In Gibson, where an exclusively Japanese community is located, Olivia appears to find a stable locale as home. Olivia not only realizes that her bond to the community is as important as her bond to her family but also emphasizes a sense of safety provided by the Japanese community. But even there, as one reviewer says, her family has "as marginalized and exiled an existence as life on the road" (Ong). The family are still floating in a condition of perpetual marginality. One reason Olivia feels marginalized is that their rented house, which is located near the outside of the town, reflects their diminished status as social rejects. It is, at best, a temporary retreat into an isolated state of near-invisibility. Yet another reason Olivia and the other Japanese feel alienated in Gibson is that in public they must keep silent. Olivia recalls, "When my family was out with a relative's family, you always felt people were staring if you weren't looking. There were no blacks living in Gibson; only whites and the few Japanese. We were all very quiet in public" (60). The extremely static social structure and oppressive public attitudes toward Japanese Americans inevitably enhance Olivia's desire of freedom represented by the concept of America.

Kadohata nevertheless challenges the notion that Japanese identity can properly belong only to childhood, to be gradually and inevitably replaced by an "American" identity as the child becomes an adult. Instead, she constructs for Olivia an identity that can be free and belong to the world at the same time. She chooses to end her novel with a floating existence in which Olivia is able both to maintain her Japanese heritage and to enjoy her freedom. Kadohata uses the vending-machine route of Jack, her stepfather, to signify a journey for Olivia's returning to the floating world. On the route, Olivia finds a fluid movement quite similar to what she had experienced before. But Olivia's ride soon turns into a solitary quest for herself. Probing into Jack's floating world, Olivia ultimately invokes Jack's specter. Through this figure she is able to vent her feeling of pity and anger and, finally, to accept her own floating existence. At the end, Olivia is emphatically alone. As she walks off into the future, her solitary, vanishing figure seemingly diminishes the novel's initial implication of return. Nevertheless, it actually suggests a return to her home culture.

As a sequel to Kadohata's first novel, *In the Heart of the Valley of Love* starts where *The Floating World* ends. At the beginning of the novel, Francie, like Olivia, is nourished and protected by her family. Because she has lost both parents to lung cancer, her family is her Aunt Annie and Annie's boyfriend, Rohn, with whom she lives after her parents' death. Living in a city where gas and water are rationed and where people disappear and die abruptly, they have tried to make the best of their lives by showing love for each other. Inspired by the love of Annie and Rohn, Francie is generally strong and optimistic. Even in depression, she is still able to find beauty, to see promise, and to imagine love among chaos and decay. After Rohn's mysterious disappearance, she survives with two stones representing her parents, a twig from a plant Annie and Rohn had given her along with a Mace gun and watercress. As she ventures into the outside world on her own, Francie recalls the scenes of Annie and Rohn's dancing in their living room. Because they were unhappy until they fell in love with each other, their dancing makes her "secretly optimistic about the world." Witnessing the power of their love, Francie says, "So I believed anything was possible. Everything always worked out. And that was how I met the world that autumn" (32).

When she decides to enter college, Francie, however, encounters a world more complicated than it seems. It is a multicultural world where class difference is prominent. The society is divided between the inhabitants of the "richtowns," who go to universities and into business, and everyone else—the "non-whites and poor whites [who] made up sixty-four percent of the population but made only twenty percent of the legal purchases" (33). For the first time, Francie recognizes that she belongs to the lower-class community, where half the adults can't read, and all have been excluded from the nation's economy. But, after she meets her friends, she notes that they possess "a cunning," "a sword against the world, the way wealth was a shield for the people of richtown. What lay underneath all the cunning was hope" (34). The capacity to hope enables them to endure increasing violence, economic stagnation, police corruption, and moral degradation. For instance, their hope for justice is articulated in two stories appearing in their school newspaper. In one story, Francie and her friends try to defend Matt Burroughs, who is charged with murder but who is possibly innocent; in the other story, they attempt to reveal the scandal of a school administrator who has allegedly been sleeping with students in exchange for passing grades and parking passes. Eventually, their hope leads them to the discovery of love represented by the two rings in a box left by Jewel's grandfather in 1998. With her grandfather's love, Jewel is able to break the abusive relationship and move on with her life. For Francie, the box becomes a sanctuary where she and Mark, Francie's boyfriend, may protect their most precious possessions and pass on their love as they face an unpredictable future. Consequently, the narrative suggests a return to the theme of the importance of ancestral legacy in *The Floating World*.

In her experimentation with the futuristic novel, Kadohata not only produces a chilling prognostication of what lies in store for Americans but also provides social commentary on America today as in the year 2052. As she has said, "Everybody thinks about race and ethnicity, and if it's set in the future, maybe you won't look at it in the same way" (Pearlman 119). Apparently, in her second novel she is less concerned with racial than with class differences. But, as in her first novel, Kadohata also creates powerful characters whose love and hope triumph over the destructive forces of their lives. When violence has become a part of their everyday life, Kadohata emphasizes that love and hope lend them purpose and enable them to function and to see life as worthwhile. Like Olivia at the end of *The Floating World*, Francie stays where she belongs. Because she believes that love can turn a dangerous city into a home. Francie, in the last scene, envisions nightmarish pictures with hope: "Los Angeles was the only home either of us had ever known, and maybe this would be the only love we would ever know. For those reasons, I knew I would never leave Los Angeles" (225).

CRITICAL RECEPTION

Although there have been no extensive critical or scholarly examinations of Kadohata's works to date, *The Floating World* has been critically acclaimed by major Asian American scholars. Elaine H. Kim gives a brief examination of the relationship between Olivia and her mother in her study of the gender relationship between Asian men and women. Sau-ling Cynthia Wong mentions the theme of mobility in *The Floating World* in her discussion of the politics of mobility in Asian American writings. The novel has also met with favorable reviews. Reviewers have uniformly praised her distinctive style in the book. Diana O'Hehir describes the narrative as "straightforward and direct . . . [Kadohata's] aim and the book's seem to be one: to present the world affectionately and without embroidery." Caroline Ong notes that *The Floating World* is "haunting because of its very simplicity and starkness, its sketchy descriptions fleshing out raw emotions and painful truths." Some commentators, however, debate the portrayal of Japanese Americans in the narrative. Acknowledging Kadohata's contribution to the diversity of Japanese American experience, Stan Yogi claims, "Kadohata's characters, who engage in premarital sex, behave cruelly and crudely, and speak eloquently, often defy impressions of Japanese Americans as a 'model minority' " ("Japanese American Literature" 147). One Japanese interviewer, however, complains that because Kadohata is not historically correct about Japanese American experience, she is socially irresponsible. In her response to this controversy, Kadohata emphasizes that she does not attempt to speak for all Asians in her work.

Kadohata's second novel was not as well received as her first. Barbara Quick argues that the novel lacks conviction and imagination and finds the narrative "haphazardly constructed out of [the main character's] deadpan stream of consciousness observations, which read like a bad translation of Camus. The result is like listening to someone describe a long and pointless dream." Michiko Kakutani points out that "*Heart of the Valley* is an uncomfortable hybrid: a pallid piece of futuristic writing, and an unconvincing tale of coming of age." Other reviewers are impressed by her work. Susan Heeger asserts, "The message of this marvelous though often painful book is that our capacity to feel deep emotion—our own and others'—just might bind us together, and save us from ourselves" (8). Although not all aspects of her works would captivate her readers, Kadohata is receiving increasing critical attention for the magic of her style and the importance of her thematic concerns.

BIBLIOGRAPHY

Works by Cynthia Kadohata

The Floating World. New York: Ballantine Books, 1989.
In the Heart of the Valley of Love. 1992. Los Angeles: University of California Press 1997.

Studies of Cynthia Kadohata

Edwards-Yearwood, Grace. "Growing Up Japanese-American." Rev. of *The Floating World. Los Angeles Times Book Review* (July 16, 1989): 12.

Ehrlich, Gretel. "A Japanese Girl Wistfully Drifts across America." Rev. of *The Floating World*. *Chicago Tribune*, July 23, 1989, 6.

Heeger, Susan. "Los Angeles: 2050." Rev. of *In the Heart of the Valley of Love*. *Los Angeles Times Book Review* (August 23, 1992): 1, 8.

Henry, Jim. "Cynthia Kadohata." In *Notable Asian Americans*. Detroit: Gale, 1995. 142–43.

Innes, Charlotte. "Asian-American Family Finds a Life on the Road." Rev. of *The Floating World*. *Philadelphia Inquirer*, July 30, 1989, 12.

Kakutani, Michiko. "Growing Up Rootless in an Immigrant Family." Rev. of *The Floating World*. *New York Times*, June 30, 1989, 27.

———. "Past Imperfect, and Future Even Worse." Rev. of *In the Heart of the Valley of Love*. *New York Times*, July 28, 1992, 15.

Kim, Elaine H. " 'Such Opposite Creatures': Men and Women in Asian American Literature." *Michigan Quarterly Review* 29 (1990): 68–93.

Moore, Susanna. "On the Road with Charlie-O." Rev. of *The Floating World*. *Washington Post*, June 25, 1989, 5–7.

O'Hehir, Diana. "On the Road with Grandmother's Magic." Rev. of *The Floating World*. *New York Times Book Review* (July 23, 1989): 16.

Ong, Caroline. "Root Relations." Rev. of *The Floating World*. *The Times Literary Supplement* (December 29, 1989–January 4, 1990): 1447.

Pearlman, Mickey. "Cynthia Kadohata." In *Listen to Their Voices: Twenty Interviews with Women Who Write*. New York: W. W. Norton, 1993. 112–20.

Quick, Barbara. Rev. of *In the Heart of the Valley of Love*. *New York Times Book Review* (August 30, 1992): 14.

Roth, John K., ed. "Cynthia Kadohata." In *American Diversity, American Identity*. New York: Holt, 1995. 603–6.

Sassone, Ralph. "The Wander Years." Rev. of *The Floating World*. *The Village Voice* (September 19, 1989): 55.

See, Lisa. "Cynthia Kadohata." *Publishers Weekly* (August 3, 1992): 48–49.

Smith, Wendy. "Future Imperfect: Los Angeles 2052." Rev. of *In the Heart of the Valley of Love*. *Washington Post Book World* (August 16, 1992): 5.

Spurling, John. "East, West, Which Is Best?" Rev. of *The Floating World*. *The Observer* (October 1, 1989): 49.

Wong, Sau-ling Cynthia. "The Politics of Mobility." In *Reading Asian American Literature: From Necessity to Extravagance*. Princeton: Princeton University Press, 1993. 118–65.

Yogi, Stan. "Japanese American Literature." In *An Interethnic Companion to Asian American Literature*. Ed. King-Kok Cheung. Cambridge: Cambridge University Press, 1997. 125–55.

———. Rev. of *The Floating World*. *Amerasian Journal* 16.1 (1989): 261.

Younghill Kang
(1903–1972)

James Livingston

BIOGRAPHY

Younghill Kang was born on May 10, 1903, in Song-Dune-Chi, Hamkyung Province, a small village 300 miles north of Seoul, Korea. Before the age of ten, Kang became educated in classic Korean and Chinese literatures. During this time, Kang's family was victimized by the political persecutions of the colonizing Japanese government. Due to the tumultuous political environment, Kang left his father's farm and traveled to Seoul to further his education, focusing on science. This early loss of domestic stability contributed to his sense of being an exile; his exilic sensibility would eventually surface with insistence in many of his works. Indeed loss, alienation, and disconnection are among his major themes.

At the age of eleven, Kang secretly traveled to Japan to study Western science. In pursuit of his academic ambitions, he was willing to live among the colonizers who destroyed his domestic harmony. Ultimately, Kang dreamed of traveling to America to study, yet he was unable to secure the means for such a journey. In spite of his misfortune, Kang graduated from Youngsaing School in 1918 and began teaching math in Japan. A year later, he returned to Korea and became involved in a political protest, ending up imprisoned by the Japanese police. After he was released, Kang wrote for a Korean newspaper and worked on translations of Keats, Browning, and Shakespeare.

After a failed attempt to escape from Korea and with the help of a missionary, Kang immigrated to the United States in 1921. At the age of eighteen, he moved to Canada and began studying at Dalhousie Missionary College in Nova Scotia. A year later, Kang attended Harvard University. Three years later he received a bachelor of science from Boston University. Subsequently, he found his true ambitions in literature, not science, so he continued to study, receiving a master's degree in English education from Harvard University. During that time, he began to write solely in English and took a job with the publishers of *Encyclopedia Britannica*, editing submissions on Asian art and literature.

At the age of twenty-seven, in 1929 Kang began work on his first autobiographical novel, *The Grass Roof*. Meanwhile, Kang met and married Frances Keely, a poet (with whom he had three children, Lucy Lynn, Christopher, and David), and began to teach in the Comparative Literature Department at New York University. There, a fellow teacher, Thomas Wolfe, befriended Kang. In addition to new social opportunities, Kang's writing career advanced significantly due to the help of Wolfe. With Wolfe's help, Maxwell Perkins, editor for Charles Scribner's Sons, reviewed and accepted Kang's manuscript of *The Grass Roof*, it was published in 1931, a year after his first child, Lucy Lynn, was born.

With the positive reviews it generated, *The Grass Roof* gave Kang the confidence he needed to function as an Asian writer in the Western world. The book recorded his experiences of early childhood growing up in Korea, his hatred of Japanese colonization of Korea, and his journey to Japan seeking education yet finding exile in the process.

In 1933 Kang published *The Happy Grove*, a children's version of *The Grass Roof*; in addition, *The Grass Roof* is translated and published in Germany. That same year, Kang received a Guggenheim Foundation Fellowship for a sequel to *The Grass Roof*; it also sparked interest in Hollywood for a motion picture based on his story.

In 1934 Kang moved to Rome and then to Germany while attempting to finish his book. A year later, he returned to the United States. Meanwhile, *The Grass Roof* was translated and published in France. In 1937 *East Goes West: The Making of an Oriental Yankee* was published. That same year his son Christopher was born, and he accepted an assistant professorship at New York University's (NYU) Washington Square College.

Kang earned wide recognition as an author and educator. Furthermore, he was awarded the Halperine Kaminsky Prize in France for the translation of *The Grass Roof*, the Louis S. Weiss Memorial Prize in 1953, and an honorary doctorate in literature from Koryo University in 1970. In addition, Kang has taught at NYU, Yale University (1950), Long Island University (1952), and the Asia Institute in New York (1950–1951). Kang worked for the Metropolitan Museum of Art in the 1930s, and during the 1940s he worked in Korea for the U.S. Military Office of Publications and later as the adviser to the director of the Corps Office of Civil Information. Many of his major works are autobiographical, yet he also published extensive translations, as well as articles for newspapers and journals.

MAJOR WORKS AND THEMES

First and foremost, Younghill Kang was faced with a formidable challenge: it was a matter of necessity for Kang to write a story that was palatable to the

American public during a period of American nationalism and parochialism during the 1930s and 1940s. Kang's *The Grass Roof* (1931) gave the American readers what they wanted—a picturesque story of a Korean boy, his small farming village, and his fight to escape the "uncivilized" nation of grass-roofed huts. Moreover, Kang's story appeals to the American sensibility by criticizing arranged marriages and confirming certain Asian stereotypes. His hostility toward the Japanese and his pro-Christian stance also probably appealed to American readers. However, many American readers failed to discern a subtle aspect of Kang's work: his subdued criticism of certain American institutions and cultural practices. In addition, *The Grass Roof* allows insight into Kang's religious and political idealism. By gaining American sympathy and encouraging the readers to forge a rapport with him, Kang empowers himself to launch a bold critique of American materialism and racism in his next major work, *East Goes West: The Making of an Oriental Yankee*.

Kang's *The Happy Grove* (1933) is a children's adaptation of *The Grass Roof*; it is a portrayal of the author's boyhood story linking Korean and Chinese ideals, undermining the myth of the savage warrior, and confirming the value of scholarship within the culture. It is a story of a young Korean boy trying to find himself in the middle of conflicting cultures—the ancient culture of his parents and competing Western ideals.

East Goes West: The Making of an Oriental Yankee (1937) is not a straightforward autobiography; it is a novel based loosely on the life of author Younghill Kang. A reader who sees it simply as a discovery text by an immigrant author could easily misinterpret the chronicled events as nonfiction, yet this recollective narrative works on two levels: it can be considered a bildungsroman since it maps the protagonist's maturation; it can also be read as an account of the author's development as a poet—a *Kunstlerroman*. The protagonist, Chungpa Han, leaves Korea bewildered, seeking scholarship in America yet facing exile in the process. Following a linear pattern, Han leaves and does not look back. He persistently pushes forward, seeking the American Dream, so the theme becomes distinctly an American theme—the protagonist's movement from rags to riches and a cautious celebration of American individualism. As Han acculturates, his idealism forces him to confront American materialism and modernity. In stark contrast, Han senses the pain associated with straddling conflicting cultures; he remains alone and exiled. He examines American nationalism, intellectual chauvinism, misguided missionary work, and the social necessity of assimilation. With Han's incremental Americanization, he becomes increasing critical of certain aspects of traditional Korean culture, such as the practice of arranged marriages. Yet Han's unique observations of American values become a satiric commentary on modernity and Western civilization.

CRITICAL RECEPTION

The Grass Roof, Kang's first book, received considerable publicity. Lady Hosie of *The Saturday Review of Literature*, claims that Kang's work "is a tremendous achievement" and that "Mr. Kang has a true poet's love of the country." Later she adds, "His book is a real contribution to literature and to our understanding of his countrymen and women." It seem, however, that she credits Kang for having created an anthropological work, not a literary text. In contrast, as Sunyoung Lee points out, distinguished writers such as Rebecca West and H. G. Wells speak with the highest regard for Kang's literary work (375). In addition, *The Grass Roof* drew the attention of Hollywood; a motion picture was proposed based on Kang's story.

Kang's second book, *The Happy Grove*, received a favorable review from *The Saturday Review of Literature* (1933). Bertha Mahony concludes that *The Happy Grove* is a story about "a rich and ancient culture with the making of beautiful things inherent in it."

Kang's last novel, *East Goes West: The Making of an Oriental Yankee*, by far, is Kang's most widely read and praised work. The book has been reprinted three times (1937, 1965, 1997). It has been praised by *The Saturday Review* (1937) as being "one of the best books in the world, for it is by a classical scholar for the Far East" ("Korean in America"). Recently, it has been resurrected; its newest edition contains editorial notes, an Afterword, and Kang's most complete biography. In addition, an essay by Sunyoung Lee, "The Unmaking of an Oriental Yankee," is included; here, he closely examines and praises Kang's work. Lee asserts:

Kang's most accomplished work, *East Goes West* is a unique and vividly realized account of the heady cultural mix taking place on the margins of early twentieth-century America's growing prosperity. In its portrait of a young man's fracturing idealism, it is also an extraordinary, if coded, critique of American materialism. (377)

Kang is by far a visionary; he is just beginning to be truly appreciated for his insightful views of America. With the current academic trend toward multiculturalism, Kang's work is bound to receive greater scholarly attention.

BIBLIOGRAPHY

Works by Younghill Kang

The Grass Roof. New York: Scribner's, 1931.
The Happy Grove. Illus. Leroy Baldridge. New York: Scribner's, 1933.
East Goes West: The Making of an Oriental Yankee. New York: Scribner's, 1937. Chicago: Follett, 1965. Kaya, 1997. Excerpt reprinted in *Asian-American Heritage: An Anthology of Prose and Poetry*. Ed. David Hsin-Fu Wand. New York: Washington Square, 1974. 217–50.

Studies of Younghill Kang

Hosie, Lady. "A Voice from Korea." *The Saturday Review of Literature* (April 4, 1931): 707.

Jones, F. C. "The Tragedy of Korea." *Pacific Affairs* 41 (1968): 71.

"A Korean-Born Lad Ventures into the West." *The Boston Transcript*, September 18, 1937, books sec.: 3.

"Korean in America." *The Saturday Review of Literature* (September 18, 1937): 15.

Lee, Sunyoung. "Afterword." In *East Goes West*. Chicago: Follett, 1965. 373–79.

Mahony, Bertha. "Apprentices to Life." *The Saturday Review of Literature* (December 9, 1933): 341.

Thompson, Ralph. "Books of the Times." *New York Times*, September 18, 1937, L 17.

Woods, Katherine. "Making of an Oriental Yankee." *New York Times Book Review* (October 17, 1937): 11.

"Younghill Kang, Writer, 69, Dies." *New York Times*, December 14, 1972, 14.

Richard E. Kim

(1932–)

Jae-Nam Han

BIOGRAPHY

Richard E. Kim was born in Hamhung, a city in northern Korea, on March 13, 1932, while the Korean peninsula was under Japanese colonial rule. His father, Chun-Do, was a fighter for national independence, and Kim and his family had to live a few years in Manchuria, avoiding the Japanese persecution. These childhood experiences instilled in him strong nationalist sentiments, which he would later recollect in his third novel, *Lost Names: Scenes from a Korean Boyhood* (1970). Kim grew up in the city of Hwangju and attended Second Pyongyang Middle School, located in the capital city of North Korea. After Korea was divided into the North and the South after its liberation in 1945, Kim and his family came to the South, this time fleeing the communist persecution of landowners.

After finishing high school in the southwestern city of Mokpo, he entered Seoul National University as an economics major. In 1950, while he was a freshman at the university, the Korean War broke out. His active involvement in this war would later provide material for his first novel, *The Martyred* (1964). An anticommunist, he volunteered to serve in the South Korean army. He became a reserve officer in the marine corps before he was discharged due to pneumonia. He later volunteered to become a liaison officer between the U.S. and South Korean forces. After serving as an aide-de-camp to General Arthur Trudeau, then commander of the U.S. Seventh Army, he was honorably discharged from the army in December 1954.

Thanks to General Trudeau and Charlotte D. Meinecke of New York University, Kim came to Middlebury College in Vermont in 1955 to finish his college studies, majoring in political science and philosophy of history. Without receiving his bachelor's degree, he earned an M.A. degree in creative writing at Johns Hopkins University in 1960. Then Kim studied in the University of Iowa Writer's Workshop, earning an M.F.A. in creative writing in 1962. The next year he earned an M.A. degree in Far Eastern studies at Harvard. In 1960 Kim married Penelope Ann Groll, a Caucasian who was a fellow student at Middlebury, and became a naturalized citizen in 1964. From 1962 till 1977 he taught college English at various institutions, including Long Beach State College, the University of Massachusetts at Amherst, Syracuse University, and San Diego State University. In 1981–1983 he also taught British and American literature as a Fullbright scholar at Seoul National University. Since 1985, Kim has been president of the Trans-Literary Agency in Shutesbury, Massachusetts. Kim is a recipient of the Ford Foundation Foreign Fellowship and the Guggenheim Foundation Fellowship.

Kim is probably the best-known novelist among Korean American writers, his fame resting chiefly on three novels, *The Martyred*, *The Innocent* (1968), and *Lost Names*. He also published two nonfiction books written in Korean, *In Search of Lost Years* (1985) and *In Russia and China: In Search of Lost Koreans* (1989). Published in Seoul, these books record Kim's encounters with the Koreans living in China and Russia, who are the "lost" souls living on foreign soil, not unlike his own experience. At the time of *Lost Names*' publication Kim was at work on a new novel; however, he has yet to publish it.

MAJOR WORKS AND THEMES

Kim is a diaspora writer who finds his subject matter in the major historical events of twentieth-century Korea. He once remarked, "Korea is the foundation of my literature, my eternal pursuit of my literary way and all of my literary sources" (qtd. in Choy 284). Unlike most of the other Korean American writers who deal with the Korean immigrant life in the United States, Kim limits the physical boundaries of his fiction entirely within Korea: the physical setting is Korea, the characters are all Koreans, and the actions loosely follow the historical events of Korea, such as the Japanese occupation (*Lost Names*), the Korean War (*The Martyred*), and the May 16, 1961, military coup d'état (*The Innocent*). In *The Martyred* and *The Innocent*, the author draws on the historical events in Korea to delve into the issues of the individual's place in an apathetic universe, the paradoxical nature of good and evil, the use (or uselessness) of religious faith, human suffering, and the finality of death. *Lost Names*, a quasi autobiography, contains the author's personal observations of the hard life of Koreans living under Japanese colonial occupation.

Kim made it clear that his first novel, *The Martyred*, was informed by existentialism: he dedicated his novel to "the memory of Albert Camus, whose insight into 'a strange form of love' overcame for me the nihilism of the trenches and bunkers of Korea." The story about the mystery of the Christian faith, *The Martyred* centers on the execution of twelve Christian ministers in Pyongyang by the North Korean communists and the mysterious survival of two others, Mr. Hann and Mr. Shin, during the Korean War. When the South Koreans and the United States forces briefly occupy Pyongyang, Captain Lee, an intelligence officer in the South Korean army and the narrator of the novel, is ordered to investigate the case. A captured Red intelligence officer, Major Jung, informs Captain Lee that among the twelve executed ministers, only one died as a martyr; the other eleven died like dogs, begging for their lives at the hands of contemptuous executioners. Reportedly, Mr. Shin was spared because he was courageous enough to spit in the major's face; Mr. Hann for reasons of insanity.

Although he has lost his Christian faith, Mr. Shin continues to minister to his followers, promising a better life, because he does not want to leave them in hopelessness. Finally he confesses to the clergy that he was a Judas betraying the twelve in order to save his own life. Before he dies, Mr. Shin leaves the narrator his last words: "Love man, Captain. Help him! Bear your cross with courage, courage to fight despair, to love man, to have pity on mortal man" (*Martyred* 286). Rumor has it that Mr. Shin has resurrected and now is a faithful minister in different parts of Korea.

The Innocent and *Lost Names* complete Kim's trilogy of modern Korean history. *The Innocent* draws on the South Korean military coup d'état of 1961 in order to explore the question, Is murder a necessary evil? The novel focuses on how brutal reality forces the "innocent" Major Lee to renounce his idealistic humanitarianism and recognize the use of ruthless action. A group of young Korean officers plot to overthrow the corrupt civilian government. The leader of the coup, Colonel Min, believes in the use of bloody actions for higher aims. In contrast, Major Lee, a moralist and peace-lover, envisions a bloodless overthrow of the government. The coup is carried out successfully, largely thanks to Colonel Min's belief in the use of force. After the coup Colonel Min is killed by thugs in the narrator's presence. The narrator tells the dying Colonel Min, holding him in his arm: "You are not a criminal, Colonel Min. You are not a murderer like other common criminals and murderers. You have work to do. You have a task to fulfill. You have a destiny to live with, Colonel. You have a higher purpose in your life and in this world, this maddening world as you say" (*Innocent* 369). The conversion has taken place: the narrator renounces his idealism. The author implies that idealism without action is futile.

In his *Lost Names*, Kim covers the years 1932 and 1945, when he was a child in Japan-occupied Korea. The title of the book refers to the Koreans' forced adoption of Japanese names by their Japanese rulers. The novel has seven sections: "Crossing," "Homecoming," "Once upon a Time," "Lost Names," "An Empire for Rubber Balls," "Is Someone Dying?," and "In the Making of History—Together," each of which focuses on how a Korean family, not unlike Kim's own at the time, struggles against the foreign occupier. In the beginning of the novel, the protagonist as a baby and his family cross the frozen Tuman River in search of safety in Manchuria. After a few years' sojourn in Manchuria, the family returns to Pyongyang. On the first day of school there, the boy is beaten up by a Japanese teacher who wrongly accuses him of lying: "He slaps me on the cheek, so hard that I stagger and crumple back into my seat. He pounces at me, pulls me up by the back of my neck, and when I am on my feet again, he slaps me again on the other check" (*Lost* 41). By the end of the novel, the Koreans take over their town after the Japanese surrender to the United States. The narrator declares, "Today, this night, the town is at last OURS. Today, this night, I join the ranks of men in the making of history—together" (*Lost* 195). The Koreans finally regain their Korean names, their religious freedom, their cultural identity, and their dignity as a people.

CRITICAL RECEPTION

Kim's first novel, *The Martyred*, was rejected by many American publishers before it was finally accepted by Braziller. Once published, it became an instant best-seller. The reviews of his first novel were overwhelmingly positive. In his article "The Love Stance: Richard E. Kim's *The Martyred*," for instance, David D. Galloway found numerous parallels between the novel and Camus' works, such as *The Plague* and *The Stranger*. Chad Walsh pointed out that Kim's book was "written in the great moral and psychological tradition of Job, Dostoevski and Albert Camus" (35). As an English-as-a-second-language (ESL) writer, Kim was also likened to Joseph Conrad, who was Kim's literary model (Engle). The reviewer for *Choice* stated, "Joseph Conrad became English in his use of his adopted language. Kim, a Korean-American, has brought to his adopted language much of the feel and sensitivity of Korea" ("Kim" 216). Many other critics praised Kim for his superior writing ability. Philip Roth said that the novel is "written in a mood of total austerity; and yet the passion of the book is perpetually beating up against its seemingly barren surface" (qtd. in Engle). *The Martyred*, a final nominee for the National Book Award, sold over 150,000 copies and was translated into over ten languages. Lan Cao and Himilce Novas, in their *Everything You Need to Know about Asian-American History* (1996), rated *The Martyred* as the ninth best work among the books written by Asian Americans (181). While the general reaction to the novel was highly favorable in America, South Korean Christians responded differently. Some of the Christian leaders and laymen were so outraged by Kim's apparently demeaning portrayal of Christian Koreans that they denounced him as "Satan" (Kim, *Search* 260).

The Innocent has received mixed reactions. In his review of the novel, Hassell A. Simpson praised it, alongside *The Martyred*, as being "superior to most of those written by Americans in the same period" (67). Kim has been praised for his skillful use of suspense. *Publishers Weekly* commented that the novel is "a worthy successor to the widely acclaimed "The Martyred' " ("*Innocent*" 46). It is "an awfully good suspense story. Betrayals and counter-betrayals, intrigues, and executions, the unravelling of the mysterious past, keep the reader going" ("*Innocent*" 46). Overall, however, *The Innocent* received more unfavorable criticisms than favorable ones. Christopher Nichols sharply attacked Kim for his defense of the bloody South Korean military coup, his lack of moral vision, and his "departure from" his first novel (183). Colin Clark's assessment of the novel was not favorable, either. According to him, this is "the dullest of novels," for it "has little action, background, or development, and it is made up almost entirely of long, stilted conversations on ideology" (3578). Richard M. Elman's evaluation of *The Innocent* was along the same lines. To him, this novel was a failure due to its dubious moral position and its lack of particular details: "If one wishes to make theological noises any empty lot won't do; one has to invest one's theology with a sense of a particular moral world inhabited by morally possible men." Finally, Stuart Hood found this work "an excessively boring book" with many superfluous dialogues and other unnecessary details (120). While he was acclaimed as a brilliant writer in the United States, Kim was denounced among South Korean intellectuals as a sympathizer with the military dictator, the late South Korean president Park Chung Hee.

With the publication of *Lost Names*, Kim's reputation has been salvaged. The novel impressed the reviewer Brooke Anson, who commented, "This is a well-written book which should be read because it deals with a neglected area of modern history and explores without preaching, a near-universal problem of man" (2253). In a review of *Lost Names*, J. McRee Elrod observed, "Although a shorter work, *Lost Names* gives a much truer picture of Korean life than Pearl Buck's *Living Reed*" (161). J. M. Elrod also commented: "*Lost Names* is to be preferred to the equivalent portion of Pearl Buck's *Living Reed* as parallel reading for the student of Asian Studies seeking a feeling for this time in Korea" (162). Regarding *Lost Names*, Pearl S. Buck herself had nothing but praise: "I think it is his best-book. He writes of a period in Korean history which I know very well from my own research, and it is remarkable that through the scope of one family he conveys the feelings of a nation when it is captured by alien military force, suffers, and is freed. It is the best piece of creative writing I have read about Korea. If this young man continues to do as well as this, he will some day be worthy of the Nobel Prize for Literature."

BIBLIOGRAPHY

Works by Richard E. Kim

Novels

The Martyred. New York: Braziller, 1964.
The Innocent. Boston: Houghton, 1968.
Lost Names: Scenes from a Korean Boyhood. New York: Praeger, 1970.

Essay

"Notes from the Underground." *Koreana Quarterly* 12.3 (1970): 24–27.

Nonfiction in Korean

In Search of Lost Years. Seoul: Somundang, 1985.
In Russia and China: In Search of Lost Koreans. Seoul: Uryu Munhwasa, 1989.

Studies of Richard E. Kim

Anson, Brooke, Rev. of *Lost Names: Scenes from a Korean Boyhood. Library Journal* (September 15, 1970): 2253.

"Best-Selling Korean." *Life* (March 20, 1964): 125–126.

Cao, Lan, and Himilce Novas. *Everything You Need to Know about Asian-American History.* New York: Plume/Penguin, 1996.

Chang, Yunshik, Rev. of *The Martyred. Pacific Affairs* 40 (1967–1968): 387–90.

Choy, Bong-youn. *Koreans in America.* Chicago: Nelson, 1979.

Clark, Colin. Rev. of *The Innocent. Library Journal* (October 1, 1968): 3578–3579.

"The Courage to Be." Rev. of *The Martyred. Time* (February 28, 1964): 108.

Elman, Richard M. "A Coup D'etat in Korea and Much Theological Noise." Rev. of *The Innocent. New York Times Book Review* (November 10, 1968): 4.

Elrod, J. McRee Rev. of *Lost Names. Pacific Affairs* 44.1 (1971): 161–62.

Engle, Paul. "The Story of Kim." Rev. of *The Martyred. New York Times Book Review* (February 16, 1964): 35.

Galloway, David D. "The Love Stance: Richard E. Kim's *The Martyred.*" *Critique* 7 (1964–1965): 163–71.

Hill, William B. Rev. of *The Martyred. America* (February 22, 1964): 264–65.

Hood, Stuart. "Incestuous Brood." Rev. of *The Innocent. Listener* (July 24, 1969): 119–20.

"The Innocent. Richard E. Kim." *Publishers Weekly* (August 2, 1968): 46.

"Kim, Richard E. *The Innocent.*" Rev. of *The Innocent. Choice* 6.2 (1969): 216.

Klausler, Alfred P. "Unbeliever as Saint." Rev. of *The Martyred. Christian Century* (May 6, 1964): 639.

Lash, Richard G. " 'The Martyred' in Theological View," Rev. of *The Martyred. Korea Journal* 5.3 (1965): 55+.

McCune, Evelyn. Rev. of *Lost Names. Journal of Asian Studies* 30 (1971): 472–73.

Nichols, Christopher. "The Tough and the Tender." Rev. of *The Innocent. National Review* (February 25, 1969): 183–84.

O., S. K. "Korean Memories," Rev. of *Lost Names. Newsweek* (July 13, 1970): 100.

Simpson, Hassell A. "A Bitter Lesson of Brutal Passion." Rev. of *The Innocent. Saturday Review* (November 23, 1968): 66–67.

Wade, James. "Author Richard Kim Looks Homeward." *Korean Journal* 5.3 (1965): 53–54.

Walsh, Chad. "Another War Raged Within." Rev. of *The Martyred. New York Times Book Review* (February 16, 1964): 1+.

Maxine Hong Kingston
(1940–   )

Guiyou Huang

BIOGRAPHY

Maxine Hong Kingston (Hong Ting Ting is her name in Chinese) was born on October 27, 1940, in Stockton, California, the eldest of six children, to parents of Chinese origin. Before she could even talk, she heard her parents reciting Chinese poetry, including Tu Fu and Li Po, the two most acclaimed poets in Chinese history. Her mother chanted the story of Fa Mu Lan, China's legendary heroine who inspired her own *The Woman Warrior*. Kingston started to write at the age of eight, telling her parents that she was doing homework. She attended the University of California at Berkeley and first majored in engineering before changing to English. After graduation in 1962 Kingston taught English and mathematics in high schools in California and Hawaii. In 1977 she assumed duties of an English professor at the University of Hawaii. Now she is professor of English at her alma mater, Berkeley. In the past quarter century Kingston has published nonfiction, fiction, poetry, and prose in different venues, but she is primarily regarded as a novelist.

Since the publication of her first nonfiction work, *The Woman Warrior: Memoirs of a Girlhood among Ghosts*, Kingston has won several major literary awards; these include the National Book Critics Circle Award for *The Woman Warrior* in 1976; the *Mademoiselle* magazine award in 1977; the National Book Award for *China Men* in 1981; the Stockton, California, Arts Commission Award in 1981. In 1980 she was named "Living Treasure of Hawaii." Besides, Kingston has been widely acclaimed as one of the most read contemporary American writers, her *The Woman Warrior* being the most taught work in universities and colleges across the country; it was a major factor in the Modern Language Association's (MLA) decision to publish *Approaches to Teaching*

Kingston's The Woman Warrior (1991), one of a series of approaches to teaching English, American, and word masterpieces.

Kingston has acknowledged influences from mainstream American and English writers such as Nathaniel Hawthorne, Walt Whitman, William Carlos Williams, and Virginia Woolf, though she has also shown interest in other writers such as Mark Twain and Gertrude Stein. These, of course, are not the only sources that impacted her creative efforts. Asian literatures and cultures, especially classical and folkloric Chinese writings, have also left deep imprints on her works. Even though the scope of Kingston's knowledge of East Asian cultures and literatures seems narrower than that of some other Asian American writers, she peppers her texts with Romanized Chinese phrases and sentences—usually in Cantonese pronunciation—a fact that comments on the bilingual nature of her work.

The Woman Warrior first appeared in 1976, an autobiographical work that has generated an enormous amount of interest among literary critics, sociologists historians, anthropologists, feminists, and others. As its title clearly indicates, it is a work about women. In 1980 Kingston boosted her first success with a second autobiographical book, titled *China Men*, which deals with her male ancestors and Chinese American history. Together, the two nonfiction works provide the reader with multiangle looks into the family history of the Hong family dating back to the mid-nineteenth century. However, although some teachers in universities and high schools teach *The Woman Warrior* and *China Men* as novels—indeed, they do possess obvious novelistic characteristics—Kingston did not produce her first real novel, *Tripmaster Monkey: His Fake Book*, until 1989. The first chapter of the novel, "Trippers and Askers," was anthologized in its entirety in the fifth edition of the *Norton Anthology of American Literature* (vol. 2). These three works, along with some short stories, poems, and miscellaneous essays, have secured Kingston a solid reputation as a major contemporary American writer who has been heavily anthologized in textbooks of many kinds.

Kingston now lives in Oakland, California, with her husband, Earll Kingston, an actor, and continues to write and teach.

MAJOR WORKS AND THEMES

According to her way of calculating the number of years of writing, by 1999 Kingston had been writing for forty years. Even though she does not stand out as a most prolific writer on the contemporary scene in literary America, she is indisputably among the most formidable writers dealing with timely issues in the late twentieth century. All her three major works are different with respect to themes and narrative techniques. However, her principal themes concern race and gender, the mother–daughter relationship, racial and cultural identities, and Chinese American history, of which the most salient seem to be racism and sexism, which she confronts with narrative strategies that were not in vogue in American literature before.

The Woman Warrior, by far the most acclaimed of all Kingston's works, deals with several important themes: racial clashes and cultural differences, politics of sex and gender, family history, and self-identity. Even though this work is heavily autobiographical, a considerable portion of it is fiction and fictionalized history. It breaks down into five sections—each with its own title—that do not appear to be directly related to one another. As a whole, *The Woman Warrior* blends fiction, history, myth, autobiography, and legend to examine vital issues that intimately concern Kingston, who grew up as an ethnic American woman.

The opening chapter, "No Name Woman," focuses on her suicide aunt, her father's sister back in China. The conventional mode of autobiographical writing is immediately displaced by Kingston's quoting and questioning her mother's injunction, " 'You must not tell anyone,' my mother said, 'what I am about to tell you' " (3). The breach of the family taboo and divulging of a family secret promise the unfolding of a tragedy that could happen only to women. Writing as a nonviolent act is productively utilized to counter violent acts such as the birth of a child, a masked raid on her family, and the drowning of mother and child in the family well. No Name Woman's sexual trespassing is punished both by her own disgraced family and by fellow villagers who judged adultery as an unforgivable crime in times of poverty ("Adultery, perhaps only a mistake during good times, became a crime when the village needed food" [13]). Kingston's mother intends to use the aunt's story to educate her maturing daughter, forewarning her about the dangerous consequences of sex outside marriage, but the daughter-narrator takes her mother's telling of the story as an invitation for her to participate in her aunt's punishment by keeping silence.

Writing the story, then, not just violates her mother's injunction but also protests oppression of women and assaults Confucian sexism in the early years of twentieth-century China. By writing it, Kingston gives voice to the voiceless and life to the dead. As she remarks to Shelley Fisher Fishkin in a 1991 interview, "I realized that by writing about her I gave her back life and a place in history and maybe immortality. And then I thought, it's a duty of mine to save her in this way. There's a redemption that takes place in art, and I had resolved questions that would not resolve in life" (786). Other unresolved questions Kingston attempts to resolve in part two, "White Tigers," where the author displays a fantastic show of imaginative powers.

"White Tigers" dispels the depressive tone of "No Name Woman" and acutely contrasts the weak image of a suicide housewife with an able-bodied woman warrior/avenger. Kingston transforms the millennium-old legend of China's Hua Mulan to suit her narrative needs in order to advocate a feminist agenda. To undo the victimization of women—in Chinese or American or any other culture—women must be empowered. Kingston's Fa Mu Lan fulfilled a man's role in battle and accomplished heroic deeds that had been claimed only by men. To subvert the stereotyping of women as passive and powerless and to expose the oppressive nature of sexism, Kingston presents a woman who, at the age of seven, followed a bird up to the mountains, where she acquired two kung fu teachers who trained her to be a warrior so that some day she would be able to avenge the draft of her father by the baron and the emperor. Unlike the famous patriot Yue Fei, who had words carved into his back by his mother alone, Kingston's woman warrior was carved by both parents as a way of empowerment, just as she was trained by both a man and a woman who may or may not be husband and wife.

Unlike the Chinese Hua Mulan, who marched and fought in a man's disguise for twelve years and was not married, Kingston's Fa Mu Lan had a baby and a husband who wept uncharacteristically when he saw the scar words on her back; and instead of being ordered around in a male-dominated culture, the woman warrior gave orders to her husband. At the end of her military crusade, Fa Mu Lan led her army into Peiping (Beijing), beheaded the emperor, and crowned a peasant before she triumphantly returned to her parents-in-law, to whom she said: "I will stay with you, doing farmwork and housework, and giving you more sons" (45). As the woman warrior achieved her end of avenging herself and her family, her author accomplished her own goal of creating a feminist heroine in the Americanized Fa Mu Lan, different from the Chinese Mulan, who, instead of beheading the emperor as her American counterpart did, paid her loyalty to him and returned home and to her female identity.

The second half of "White Tigers" is purely autobiographical and contrasts starkly with the thrilling adventures of the fantasized woman warrior. "My American life has been such a disappointment," declares the narrator to her reader (45). Their hard immigrant life is made doubly excruciating due to the ubiquitous presence of racism. Young Maxine was fired twice because of her protest over her bosses' use of racial slurs as well as their racist behavior. When racism is coupled with sexism and poverty and becomes cripplingly oppressive, Maxine entertains dreams of becoming a swordswoman for the mere sake of seeking justice from racist America and sexist China, though such consciousness remains only in the deep recesses of dreams. An alternative to being a swordswoman is to become a writer as a way of combating sexist and racist evils:

The swordswoman and I are not so dissimilar. May my people understand the resemblance soon so that I can return to them. What we have in common are the words at our backs. The idioms for *revenge* are "report a crime" and "report to five families." The reporting is the vengeance—not the beheading, not the gutting, but the words. And I have so many words—"chink" words and "gook" words too—that they do not fit on my skin. (53)

This reporting is writing that represents a different type of fighting.

The middle chapter, "Shaman," is a biographical sketch of the narrator's mother, Brave Orchid, who is woman warrior, medicine woman, exorcist, and storyteller. In Brave Orchid's life in China, two events stood out: defeating a ghost and purchasing a slave girl. Brave survived famine and war in China, and after emigrating to America, she had to undergo new ordeals. She called her adopted country a ghost country while continuing to hold China as home. The daughter, on the other hand, refused to take China as home because China to her was a ghost country that sold girls as slaves, and she did not want to go there for fear of being sold. The mother and daughter's interlocutions bear out differing, often conflicting perceptions of national and cultural identities of the self, and their views are hardly reconcilable. The mother seems to represent a remote, lost East, while the daughter stands for a "ghost-free" country that is America.

The Woman Warrior, however, does not exclusively focus on heroines and warriors. In "At the Western Palace," the fate of their opposites—women victims of sexual manipulation—is presented in black humor and realistic details. Moon Orchid, Brave's sister, is in almost every way her sister's opposite: weak, passive, timid, and submissive—all characteristics of *yin*, as is suggested by her name. Moon was abandoned in Hong Kong by her husband, who emigrated to America, where he became a doctor and bigamously married a young Chinese American woman. At Brave's instigation, Moon arrived in America to reclaim him; Brave even devised a plan for their reunion in Los Angeles, where the bigamist husband worked, but the carefully hatched plan unclimactically ended in the husband's agreeing to buy them lunch but not taking Moon back.

Moon's sojourn in her sister's house sets the stage for the dramatization of cultural differences and clashes. Moon came to America with deep-rooted, inveterate Chinese habits that Brave's children failed to appreciate or comprehend. For example, when she praised the children for being smart or pretty, they would either say thank you or simply agree with her; "Not once did she hear a child deny a compliment" (134). So she marveled at what she thought was their vanity. The total Americanization of American-born Chinese children also comments on the Americanization of Moon's husband, who told her, "I'm living like an American" (153). Moon's inability to negotiate a settlement with him and her disinterest in the American style of life, along with her gradual loss of sanity and self-identity, eventually drove her crazy and caused her death. Brave used the incident to educate her children, telling them that "they must help her keep their father from marrying another woman because she didn't think she could take it any better than her sister had"; and "Brave Orchid's daughters decided fiercely that they would never let men be unfaithful to them. All her children made up their minds to major in science or mathematics" (160)—Kingston herself tried engineering.

Even though *The Woman Warrior* is about a woman warrior who defines her self-identity with the succor of her sword, Kingston apparently realizes the unlikelihood of becoming a warrior in the soldier sense of the word. So in the concluding segment of her book, "A Song for a Barbarian Reed Pipe," she moves toward identifying with a warrior in the fighter sense of the term. The famous, talented woman poet Ts'ai Yen now becomes the controlling image displacing the swordswoman Fa Mu Lan. In the silent Chinese girl whom she tortured for not having a voice, Kingston sees the danger of losing not only one's voice but also one's identity if one does not speak up. The narrator even tries to settle scores with her parents for acting Chinese and imposing silence on her. She battles silence with deliberate articulateness. To express her feelings about growing up Chinese American and to combat Chinese sexism and American racism—indeed, they are present in both countries—Fa Mu Lan's sword is inadequate; in times of peace and under the rule of law, a pen seems a more effective weapon in changing human consciousness.

Ts'ai Yen lived among "barbarians" in humiliating conditions for twelve years. Upon her return to China she expressed her suffering and exotic experiences through writing autobiographical poems, by which she set a usable example for Kingston from nearly 2,000 years ago. Ts'ai Yen is thus a very different type of woman warrior, with whom Kingston shares some commonalities such as living among people not of their own race and using writing as a necessary means of reclaiming self-identity. *The Woman Warrior* represents female warriors who fight for vital causes such as political equality and survival in native as well as foreign cultures, against female oppression in the forms of sexism and racism, often under extreme circumstances. But *The Woman Warrior* presents only "half" of Kingston's family history and focuses only on women members. The other half is narrated in *China Men* and is about male heroism, as the book's original title, "Gold Mountain Heroes," indicates.

Kingston's perception of the American nation seems inseparable from her understanding of one of nineteenth-century America's greatest miracles—the building of the transcontinental railroad, in which Chinese laborers, among others, heavily participated. *China Men* represents this period of American history from a purely Chinese American perspective. William Carlos Williams inspired Kingston with his *In the American Grain*, a historical book without a second volume. Kingston started her *China Men* where Williams closed his *In the American Grain*, as a sequel to it as well as to her own *The Woman Warrior*. In her interview with Marilyn Chin, Kingston relates the importance of the Chinese contribution to the building of the railroad: "They bind the country together with steel, the bands of steel that are the railroads" (71). While the building of the railroad remains a major concern of the narrative, the cultivation of Hawaiian sugarcane fields, also by Chinese laborers, constitutes another significant story line.

Although *China Men* almost exclusively deals with the narrator's male ancestors, its narrative unfolds with a discourse on "discovery," where Tang Ao, a China man looking for the Gold Mountain, stumbles into the Land of Women, where he is captured, has his feet bound, and is made into a female servant to the queen of the land that was said to have been discovered in North America. This episode is told in a fairy-tale fashion, but critics are quick to point out that Tang Ao's experience epitomizes the feminization of Asian males in North America, where they emigrated and were figuratively emasculated because they were forced to seek and hold jobs that were traditionally female domains such as the kitchen and the laundry. Nevertheless, many Chinese left their mothers and wives for the utopianized land called America, where gold awarded its diligent, sincere seekers. Kingston's father, grandfather, uncles, and granduncles made America their destination because it held a dream they could not realize in poverty-stricken China due to wars and famines.

But Kingston is not primarily concerned with why her forefathers decided to leave China; she is more interested in what these Chinese did to earn their right to be Americans. *China Men* is very compelling in its presentation of Chinese Americans' participation in the building of America. While this work is a family narrative with an emphasis on males, it is also a narration of the nation. Kingston examines several issues: the law (especially immigration laws), the nation, and, again, race relations. Much as Fa Mu Lan and Ts'ai Yen—two archetypal female figures—are the guiding light in *The Woman Warrior*, Tu Fu and Guan Goong—two archetypal male figures in Chinese literature and folklore—are the controlling images in *China Men*.

Tu Fu, the great realist poet of the Tang dynasty, represents the elite Chinese intellectual who ultimately made a name for himself. The dream of Kingston's father was to become a Tu Fu, but it was shattered when he failed the imperial examinations and became a schoolteacher instead, in the role of which he failed even more miserably because he could not properly discipline his pupils. When livelihood was threatened because of the loss of his job, he took off to America with other male family members. How he came to America, however, remains a mystery to the daughter-narrator because he refused to talk ("No stories, No past. No China" [14]). As a result Kingston works up two conflicting versions of the father's passage to America: the legal father and the illegal father—one who came through proper immigration channels and one who was smuggled in without legal papers.

Kingston's reconstruction of the legal father's entry at Angel Island attacks governmental racism and comments on post–World War I power relations among nations. At the detention center on Angel Island off the coast of San Francisco, the Chinese immigrants were kept for months and even years before they were let into the country. "The demons did not treat people of any other race the way they did Chinese. The few Japanese left in a day or two. It was because their emperor was strong" (55). The snobbish way the Immigration and Naturalization Service handled Japanese immigrants reflects not only the U.S. government's anti-Chinese practice in implementing immigration policies but also its reluctance to offend Japan, which was emerging as an international power to be wrestled with, especially after Japan had won several wars with both China and Russia at the turn of the century.

In *China Men* Kingston devotes an entire chapter titled "The Laws" to expose the hypocritical nature of these laws and the inconsistency in its implementation by government agencies. Despite the signing of the Burlingame Treaty between the United States and the emperor of China, which promised free migration and emigration from and to one another's country, Chinese workers were driven out.

The anti-Chinese campaign culminated in the creation and passage of the first Chinese Exclusion Act in 1882. The 1924 Immigration Act worsened the problem by specifically banning "Chinese women, wives, and prostitutes" from entering the country. But even if a Chinese was fortunate enough to successfully enter the country, life would be ineluctably hard due to racial problems.

In New York Kingston's father lost his laundry to the machinations of fellow Chinese immigrants; then he was ruthlessly exploited by a fellow villager for whom he ran a gambling house. When he finally owned his own laundry and house, his dream of returning to China was dashed, and his sojourner status gave way to an ethnic American identity. This identity was also fought for by Kingston's other forefathers, notably, the great grandfather of the Sandalwood Mountains and the grandfather of the Sierra Nevada Mountains. These men were Cantonese—ocean people; "the ocean and hunger and some other urge made Cantonese people explorers and Americans" (91). The great-grandfather, Bak Goong, came to Hawaii at the invitation of the Royal Hawaiian Agricultural Society; his settlement was therefore not only legal but from the beginning a form of aid as well as an act of contribution to the agricultural development of the United States' latest state. However, even though Bak Goong, Bak Sook Goong, and others came as guests or, indeed, agricultural experts, they had to work under "the rule of silence" (100), a theme Kingston also explores in *The Woman Warrior*. The workers defied the rule by inventing a "talk" therapy, including shouts in order not to be silenced into nonexistence.

These Chinese plantation workers not only helped turn Hawaii into a modern agricultural state, but also created a new culture unique to it: as Bak Goong said of their talking and shouting into the earth, "We made it up. We can make up customs because we're the founding ancestors of this place" (118): they established new rituals, fathered children, and set up tribes. Bak Sook Goong even became a Paké godfather. Though in the end both Bak Goong and Bak Sook Goong returned to China, many another Paké godfather stayed, and "the king and queen of the Sandalwood Mountains had ruled that a China Man who married a Hawaiian would be called Hawaiian" (118)—hence their Hawaiian and, later, American status.

Kingston recognizes not just Chinese workers' contribution to America's agricultural economy; in "The Grandfather of the Sierra Nevada Mountains" she goes on to delineate Chinese laborers' building of the transcontinental railroad. Ah Goong, the grandfather, was hired along with other Chinese to build the railroad because "Chinamen had a natural talent for explosions. Also there were not enough workingmen to do all the labor of building a new country" (128). Chinamen handled dynamites, won tracklaying contests against Welshmen and Irishmen, and staged strikes for an eight-hour workday. The transcontinental railroad would not have been possible without these Chinamen, and when it was finished, the white demon officials declared it "the Greatest Feat of the Nineteenth Century" and "the Greatest Feat in the History of Mankind" and said, "Only Americans could have done it." Kingston comments, "Even if Ah Goong had not spent half his gold on Citizenship Papers, he was an American for having built the railroad" (145).

In "Cultural Mis-readings by American Reviewers" Kingston writes, "Chinese-American history has been a battle for recognition as Americans; we have fought hard for the right to legal American citizenship" (59). *China Men* was apparently written in that spirit and should be read as an effort to justify the legal citizenship of the narrator's forefathers. Unfortunately, racist America started driving out Chinese laborers soon after the completion of the railroad. As Frank Chin* also makes it clear in his novel *Donald Duk*, though the Chinese were the main workforce that built the railroad, when photos were taken to celebrate its completion, no Chinese workers were included: a significant page in American history, largely written by the Chinese, was erased. Kingston's *China Men* and Chin's *Donald Duk* were both written to reinstate the Chinese segment of American history.

The building and development of the modern American nation also owed to contemporaries, such as Kingston's brothers, who took part in the Vietnam War and other similar ventures in order to defend America's freedom and interests. They were sent on military missions on America's behalf because they were Americans, and as such they have every right to be Americans, their true national and cultural identity.

The Vietnam War is the concern of the chapter "The Brother in Vietnam" in *China Men*. In her next major work, *Tripmaster Monkey*, Kingston makes it the background against which the rebellious and obnoxious male protagonist Wittman Ah Sing puts on a one-man show. *Tripmaster Monkey* bears limited resemblance to Kingston's autobiographical works for obvious reasons: it is narrated in the third-person omniscient; it uses a male protagonist and follows one principal story line; it is fiction set exclusively on American soil; it is, ultimately, an Asian American novel. In *The Woman Warrior* and *China Men* the spirit of the warrior looms large, be it the revengeful Fa Mu Lan or Guan Goong, the God of Literature and War; in *Tripmaster Monkey*, however, one finds a different kind of guiding spirit, a combination of the rebellious, mischievous, and obnoxious fictional Monkey King of China and the garrulous, all-embracing, innovative, and free-spirited quintessential poet of nineteenth-century America, Whitman.

The title of the novel, *Tripmaster Monkey*, is adapted from the sixteenth-century Chinese masterpiece called *Journey to the West* (also translated *Monkey King* by Arthur Waley) by Wu Cheng'en. Wu's Monkey is admired for his adept ability to transform into seventy-two forms in emergent circumstances for the purpose of defeating or confusing or deceiving his enemies, mostly demons, goblins, and spirits, on their perilous quest to India for the Sutra. But Monkey, like Achilles, has severe limitations: he can be controlled and subdued by his master Tripitaka (Tang Seng) using certain prayers, and, no matter how fast and far he can hop, he can never escape beyond the fingertips of the huge palm of Tathagata. Wittman Ah Sing shares Monkey's restless nature as well as his audacity to bring chaos to the Establishment, a trait that informed the turbulent 1960s, especially in the San Francisco Bay Area, where the University of California, Berkeley is located, which both Wittman in the novel and Kingston the novelist attended, also in the heady 1960s.

Then there is the never-ending, never-stopping Whitman. Kingston titles more than half of her novel's nine chapters with phrases taken from Whitman's *Leaves of Grass*, noticeably from "Song of Myself," "Song of the Open Road," and "Song for Occupations." Kingston told Shelley Fisher Fishkin about her admiration of Whitman: "I like the freedom that Walt Whitman was using to play with and shape the American language. . . . I like the rhythm of his language and the freedom and the wildness of it. It's so American. And also his vision of a new kind of human being that was going to be formed in this country" (784). Wittman Ah Sing had wanted to be a poet, like Whitman, and did write poems and read some to his first love, Nanci Lee (but he does not seem to be *her* first love), to which she offered no enthused compliments. Though Wittman shares Whitman's garrulous and free-spirited disposition, he also reads Rilke both in private and public, even on public transportation.

While American authors lurk over Wittman's head, Chinese classics also lend him power in his creative endeavors. While Wu Cheng'en's *Journey to the West* provides the grain of the rebellious/mischievous spirit, Luo Guanzhong's *Romance of the Three Kingdoms* and Shi Nai'an's *Water Margin* offer him basis for his play's characters. Being a poet does not give Wittman the desired opportunities of being heard by, and interacting with, his audience, so he chose to be a playwright, a more social function. His determination to write a play is further resolved after being fired from the toy store where he worked for obscene behavior in front of customers. His great dream now is to write and direct a play based on the famous *Romance of the Three Kingdoms*, of which he makes a considerable success.

Individual freedom—even when it means unemployment—is of utmost importance to Wittman. But this freedom is constantly being threatened because external social forces—including the actors and audience that he must have to stage his play—both disrupt and make his freedom. Marriage is another factor that affects his career as a free-spirited playwright. Taña, a blond, is not exactly his dream girl; marrying her instead of the beautiful Nanci Lee, a Chinese American, is not a choice but a necessity. Wittman thus lives in the tension between hankering for Nanci Lee and being married to Taña, who likes to stay married to him but refuses to be *the* wife (she is employed).

Wittman also lives in the shadows of a group of matriarchs, those "Flora Dora" girls who are also his aunts and mother, somewhat like Jia Baoyu, the male protagonist in Cao Xueqin's *Dream of the Red Chamber*, who is almost always between and among matriarchs and girls. These novels—*Romance of the Three Kingdoms*, *Water Margin*, *Journey to the West*, and *Dream of the Red Chamber*—collectively called the Four Masterpieces of Chinese fiction, all seem to have left their imprints on *Tripmaster Monkey*, and the influences are not limited to the characters and plots; they are also quite noticeable in the way Kingston constructs her narrative frame and makes transitions between chapters.

With respect to narrative structure, all of these four novels fall into the category of Chinese fiction called *zhanghui xiaoshuo*—novels that break into chapters, each with its own title and each closing with a fixed formula of words that foretells the reader about the content of the ensuing chapter. The end of Chapter 1 of *Tripmaster Monkey* utilizes such a closural procedure: "If you want to see whether he [Wittman] will get that play up, and how a poor monkey makes a living so he can afford to spend the weekday afternoon drinking coffee and hanging out, go on to the next chapter" (35). So do all other chapters.

Wittman is a product of the hip 1960s, an Asian American who cannot separate himself from the politics of the time or from the racial groups that practice different politics and beliefs. He makes friends with blacks, Japanese, Filipinos, dates Chinese, and marries a Caucasian; he loathes FOBs (fresh off the boat); and he speaks the language of the 1960s. Alongside the representation of 1960s language, Kingston offers an encyclopedic view of Asian America in that particular era. All the important issues concerning Wittman—race relations, culture, marriage, women's liberation, war—are panoramically recapitulated in the final three chapters, most funnily in Wittman's harangue on a series of unrelated topics ranging from his thought on racial stereotyping in American culture and society, to his loathing of women's using cosmetic surgery to achieve a double eyelid to look pretty, to his questioning about the accuracy of hyphenated names of ethic groups, to his own marriage with Taña, his unemployment, and his antiwar stance.

Tripmaster Monkey uses the merciful Kuan Yin as narrator, the Bodhisattva goddess that sits back, watches, and blesses. Kuan Yin is, of course, also among Wittman's audience. Having seen the play and heard the playwright's harangue, she makes these observations about Wittman:

He had staged the War of the Three Kingdoms as heroically as he could, which made him start to understand: The three brothers and Cho Cho were masters of war; they had worked out strategies and justifications for war so brilliantly that their policies and their tactics are used today, even by governments with nuclear-powered weapons. And they *lost*. The clanging and banging fooled us, but now we know—they lost. Studying the mightiest war epic of all time, Wittman changed—beeen!—into a pacifist. (340)

Of course, one pacifist cannot stop all wars, and wars of all kinds—military, religious, cultural, and racial—rage on and continue to dominate the concerns of the media, the writer, and the average citizen.

CRITICAL RECEPTION

Kingston remains one of the most formidable of ethnic writers in America today. Even though she has authored only three book-length works, they have generated a great many reviews, essays, and articles in books, journals, and magazines, not to mention translations in various foreign languages. Indeed, the amount of critical acclaim Kingston has garnered may make any serious writer jealous. The Modern Language Association of America has up to now selected only sixty-one writers of the world for whose works it has published approaches of how to teach them, of which Kingston's *The Woman Warrior* makes number thirty-nine. This fact alone proves the high level of significance of her works.

While reviews and critical studies of Kingston's works are largely positive, some are mixed and even negative. A considerable number of reviews and studies raise concerns about the generic nature of Kingston's first two works, though some readers simply call them novels. Indeed, *The Woman Warrior* and *China Men*, while considerably autobiographical, can be justifiably called autobiographical novels or fictionalized autobiographies. Kingston's own article "Cultural Mis-readings by American Reviewers," published in *Asian and Western Writers in Dialogue*, sums up these mixed reviews and offers her exasperated responses and refutations. *The Woman Warrior*, perhaps because of its pioneering status as the first Asian American feminist work, understandably has been approached by both Asian American and mainstream American critics.

Kingston had expected her first work to be read from the women's lib angle, the Third World angle, and the *Roots* angle ("Cultural Mis-readings" 55). Indeed, substantial evidence can be found in *The Woman Warrior* that sustains such readings and interpretations. But many Asian American critics consider the work a resounding challenge to the existing canon of traditional American literature hitherto defined and dominated by the white, male writer. As Shirley Geok-lin Lim, editor of *Approaches to Teaching Kingston's* The Woman Warrior, points out, "*The Woman Warrior* is a complex, highly inventive, historically embedded work. It is part biography, part autobiography, part history, part fantasy, part fiction, part myth, and wholly multilayered, multivocal, and organic" (x). This statement aptly sums up the generic complexity and textual exuberance of the work.

One element widely noted by reviewers and critics is Kingston's exploration and representation of identity. Elaine H. Kim, greatly credited for authoring the first scholarly book on Asian American literature, observes that Kingston's book represents an attempt to sort out a Chinese American identity: "*The Woman Warrior* is also a landscape of the consciousness and experience of the contemporary American-born daughter of Chinese immigrant parents. *The Woman Warrior* is about women, but it is primarily about the Chinese American's attempt to sort fact from fantasy in order to come to terms with the paradoxes that shape her life as a member of a racial minority group in America" (199). The process of growing up Chinese American for the daughter-narrator is one of finding and asserting herself by creating distance between her and her parents, who continue to think *à la mode chinois*. As Suzanne Juhasz writes, "*China Men* demonstrates that finding the father, for the daughter, means finding what one has always known: that distance" (187). Juhasz probes into the structural design of both of

Kingston's autobiographical works to make this point: "Such narrative structures suggest the evolution of female identity, which is formed in relation to the mother through the achievement of individuation in the context of connection, in relation to the father through the understanding of separation, the creation of substitutes for connection" (173). Chen Lok Chua makes a similar comment: "[T]he ancestral dream has metamorphosed into a contemporary pursuit of identity—of identity as woman, as writer, as American" (63).

Overall, most Asian American critics, especially Asian American women critics, view *The Woman Warrior* and *China Men* as compelling creations that break and subvert mainstream America's stereotypes of the Asian American. These critics include Shirley Geok-lin Lim, King-Kok Cheung, Elaine Kim, Sau-ling Cynthia Wong, Linda Ching Sledge, and Amy Ling, all of whom have published extensively on Asian American writers and paid enormous attention to Kingston, her *The Woman Warrior* in particular.

Although *China Men* has been less studied, it has nonetheless captured the attention of a great number of teachers and students of literature. Linda Ching Sledge calls Kingston "the family historian as epic poet" who in *China Men* "attempts an imaginative reconstruction of one particular Cantonese family's emigration to America as the prototypical history of all immigrant American Chinese" ("Maxine" 3). Now that the author is an epic poet, her work has to be a celebration of heroes—the Chinese workers on Hawaii's sugarcane fields and along the laid tracks of the transcontinental railroad. "The two founding fathers in *China Men*, Bak Goong of the Hawaiian Islands and Ah Goong of California," argues Sledge, "are prototypes of the family hero, fashioned in the image of the valiant, long-suffering Prometheus" (7). In this epic, Sledge ultimately informs us, "Maxine Kingston raises private experience to the level of American myth" (19). David Leiwei Li, on the other hand, reads *China Men* as a challenge to "the problematic democratic nationalism of the canonical paradigm" as well as an effort "to write into the existing canon the possibilities of change within the canon itself" (482). That is, Kingston's talk-stories in *China Men* have created a shocking impact on the established norms of canonical American literature and thus sign themselves in as a new segment of the American canon.

Donald C. Goellnicht starts his study of *China Men* with a discussion of Tang Ao, the feminized Chinaman in the Land of Women. "The feminization of Tang Ao acts metonymically for the emasculation of China Men in white America" (193). Goellnicht examines what he calls the "double-edged antiracist, antisexist sword wielded by the narrator": Kingston both deplores the emasculation of Chinamen by mainstream America and critiques the Confucian patriarchy of traditional family life (194). *China Men*, then, should be read in the context of history-based discourse on American racism and Chinese sexism/patriarchy. Kingston attacks and indicts both. Along lines of politicized and historicized arguments, Goellnicht concludes that "*China Men* is to some extent an act of revenge on the father; but it is also an act of attempted reconciliation between daughter and father, just as *The Woman Warrior* was an act of reconciliation between daughter and mother" (205).

In the personal statement she contributed to *Approaches to Teaching Kingston's* The Woman Warrior, Kingston reminds her readers:

To best appreciate *The Woman Warrior*, you do need to read *China Men*. You'll see that "I" achieve an adult narrator's voice. And you'll find out what else the people do. Brave Orchid comes to New York and takes up the role of wife. The feminist narrator journeys to the Land of Men. She finds the ancestors and sympathetically follows the brothers to Vietnam. "I" am nothing but who "I" am in relation to other people. In *The Woman Warrior* "I" begin the quest for self by understanding the archetypal mother. In *China Men*, "I" become more whole because of the ability to appreciate the other gender. (Lim 23)

Not only does the female narrator become "more whole" by learning to appreciate the father's gender *in China Men*, but Kingston's two-volume autobiography achieves completeness *with* it, and this completeness enabled her to leave behind personal and familial subject matters appropriate for autobiographies and charge into the world of fiction that yielded *Tripmaster Monkey*.

So far the only novel Kingston has authored, *Tripmaster Monkey* has garnered much critical acclaim, though the breadth and depth of studies on it have been limited compared with her first two books, perhaps due to the fact, among other things, that it was her latest publication. As Shelley Fisher Fishkin comments on the novel: "Kingston made her debut as a novelist in 1989 with a wild and exuberant novel set in San Francisco in the 1960s about a hip, word-drunk, fifth-generation Chinese American poet, playwright, and nonstop talker named Wittman Ah Sing. *Tripmaster Monkey: His Fake Book* has received enormous critical acclaim and has also earned a place on the bestseller list" (782). Marilyn Chin praises the novel as "encyclopedic" (57).

Nicci Gerrard tells prospective readers of *Tripmaster Monkey*: "If at first you don't succeed: try, try and try again," apparently aware of the difficulty of reading such a wildly imaginative work. Gerrard sums up the concerns of the novel around Wittman's virtuoso performance: "It loops around the playfulness of imagination, responsibility of love, pervasive and crass nature of prejudice, cruelty of American individualism and power of language. It is a bitter and delirious talk story." Perhaps due to the novel's sweeping presentation of these topics, Gerrard complains, "Only halfway through the freewheeling narrative does a sense of control weight Wittman's flights of fancy. Eventually his fake book settles into a rhythm and direction that the reader can follow." Despite the novel's labyrinthine structure, Gerrard concludes that Wittman Ah Sing is "an extraordinary and unforgettable creation."

Tom Wilhelmus buys into George Steiner's theory that a dual cultural or linguistic background often stimulates the success of some of the best writers, and he believes this scenario happened to Kingston's *Tripmaster Monkey*. Wilhelmus finds the novel both familiar and exotic, imposing and encompassing, like Joyce's *Finnegans Wake* or Nabokov's *Ada*. He writes, "The book's real power lies in its storytelling, in the ability of its incredibly rich narrative thrust to borrow the riches not only of English and American idiom, literature, drama, and film, but also from Chinese novels, poems, and epics . . . in order to create an all-inclusive narrative framework, whose dimensions are mythic, within whose structure all stories and characters—and races—are equal" (150). But Wilhelmus does not just praise the novel, for he finds Kingston's use of Wittman's harangue at the audience unfortunate, charging her for lacking trust in the medium "she herself sought to create in a novel which otherwise carried its message on every page" (151).

In a more sophisticated and spoofing-toned review, John Leonard calls *Tripmaster Monkey* "another dreambook, like *The Woman Warrior*. Or another history lesson, like *China Men*" (768). Leonard does not seem to be impressed by Kingston's protagonist or the organizational framework or the style of her language, and he satirizes her art as sneaky and for inventing a language of her own that "she'd no place to put [it] in her first two books"; so "[t]o sing herself, she needed someone like the unbuttoned Wittman" (769). Leonard considers the novel less charming but more exuberant than her two nonfiction works; nonetheless, he tells the reader: "You can stop looking for the Novel of the Sixties. It took 3,000 years on its journey to the West. But here are the peaches and the Sutras" (772).

Leonard's review represents the lukewarm, middle-ground responses to Kingston's works. Other responses, such as Sheryl A. Mylan's "The Mother as Other: Orientalism in Maxine Hong Kingston's *The Woman Warrior*," locate a visible grain of Orientalism: "Out of ignorance and misunderstanding of her mother's life in China, Maxine constructs a framework by which to judge her; her standards for judging her mother are, if not manifest Orientalism, at least latent or unconscious demonstrations of Orientalism" (133). Other white critics have labeled Kingston a "Chinese woman writer," "inscrutable," "exotic," the very same labels that have been stamped on the Chinese.

However, the most poignant, negative, and, according to some scholars, even acrimonious reviews seem to have come from Asian American male critics, most vocally the playwright and novelist Frank Chin, who, some believe, provided the prototype of Wittman Ah Sing in *Tripmaster Monkey* and who later wrote *Gunga Din Highway* to counterattack Kingston. Interestingly, perhaps also ironically, Chin and Kingston were both born in 1940, both were English majors at UC-Berkeley, both lived in the Bay Area, both worked in Hawaii, both write about the same things and people, and both write about each other in their works. The fundamental charge Chin makes on Kingston is what he calls her "fakeness." In his eyes, Kingston misrepresents and distorts not only Chinese culture and history but also Chinese American culture and history. Chin's more detailed critiques of Kingston can be found in his often quoted "This Is Not an Autobiography," "Come All Ye Asian American Writers of the Real and the Fake," and "Frank Chin: An Interview with Robert Murray Davis," among others.

Debates on, and studies of, Kingston's works show no significant signs of diminishing, but Kingston has not written a new novel since *Tripmaster Monkey*. In 1992, however, she revealed a hint at what her next novel would be like in "The Novel's Next Step," where she indicates, "We need to write the Global Novel" (63), which could be a sequel to *Tripmaster Monkey*, in which the Whitmanian Monkey or the monkeyish Wittman—a genuine Asian American combination of an Asian and an American cultural icon—has grown up. That Global Novel perhaps is being written, but it's not here yet.

BIBLIOGRAPHY

Works by Maxine Hong Kingston

Autobiographies

The Woman Warrior: Memoirs of a Girlhood among Ghosts. New York: Alfred A. Knopf, 1976; New York: Vintage International, 1989.
China Men. New York: Alfred A. Knopf, 1980; New York: Vintage International, 1989.

Novel

Tripmaster Monkey: His Fake Book. New York: Alfred A. Knopf, 1989; New York: Vintage International, 1990.

Prose

Hawai'i One Summer. San Francisco: Meadow, 1987.

Poems

"Absorption of Rock." *Iowa Review* 12 (1981): 207–8.
"Restaurant." *Iowa Review* 12 (1981): 206.

Short Story

"Duck Boy." *New York Times Magazine* 12 (June 1977): 54–55, 58.

Articles

"Literature for a Scientific Age: Lorenz' *King Solomon's Ring*." *English Journal* 62 (January 1973): 30–32, 36.
"On Understanding Men." *Hawaii Review* 7 (1977): 43–44.
"Reservations about China." *Ms.* 7 (October 1978): 67–68.
"San Francisco's Chinatown." *American Heritage* 30.1 (December 1978): 36–47.
"The Making of More Americans." *New Yorker* 55 (February 11, 1980): 34–42.
"The Coming Book." In *The Writer on Her Work*. Ed. Janet Sternburg. New York: Norton, 1980. 181–85.
"Cultural Mis-readings by American Reviewers." In *Asian and Western Writers in Dialogue: New Cultural Identities*. Ed. Guy Amirthanayagam. London: Macmillan, 1982. 55–65.
"A Writer's Notebook from the Far East." *Ms.* 11 (January 1983): 85–86.

"The Novel's Next Step." *Small Press* (Winter 1992): 63–64.
"A Letter to Garrett Hongo upon the Publication of *The Open Boat*." *Amerasia Journal* 20.3 (1994): 25–26.

Studies of Maxine Hong Kingston

Chen, Lok Chua. "Two Chinese Versions of the American Dream: The Golden Mountain in Lin Yutang and Maxine Hong Kingston." *MELUS* 8.4 (1981): 61–70.

Cheung, King-Kok. "Provocative Silence: *The Woman Warrior* and *China Men*." In *Articulate Silences: Hisaye Yamamoto, Maxine Hong Kingston, Joy Kogawa*. Ithaca, NY: Cornell University Press, 1993. 74–125.

———, ed., *An Interethnic Companion to Asian American Literature*. Cambridge: Cambridge University Press, 1997.

Chin, Frank. "Come All Ye Asian American Writers of the Real and the Fake." In *The Big Aiiieeeee!*. Ed. Jeffery Paul Chan, Frank Chin, Lawson Fusao Inada, and Shawn Wong. New York: Meridian, 1991. 1–92.

———. "This Is Not an Autobiography." *Genre* 18 (Summer 1985): 109–30.

Chin, Marilyn. "A Melus Interview: Maxine Hong Kingston." *MELUS* 16.4 (Winter 1989–1990): 57–74.

Chun, Gloria. "The High Note of the Barbarian Reed Pipe: Maxine Hong Kingston." *The Journal of Ethnic Studies* 19.3 (Fall 1991): 85–94.

Dasenbrock, Reed Way. "Intelligibility and Meaningfulness in Multicultural Literature in English." *PMLA* 102.1 (January 1987): 10–19.

Davis, Robert Murray. "Frank Chin: An Interview with Robert Murray Davis." *Amerasia* 14.2 (1988): 81–95.

Fishkin, Shelley Fisher. "Interview with Maxine Hong Kingston." *American Literary History* 3.4 (Winter 1991): 782–91.

Gerrard, Nicci. "Wittman Ah Sing." *New Statesman and Society* 25 (August 1989): 28.

Goellnicht, Donald C. "Tang Ao in America: Male Subject Positions in *China Men*." In *Reading the Literatures of Asian America*. Ed. Shirley Geok-lin Lim and Amy Ling. Philadelphia: Temple University Press, 1992. 191–212.

Holaday, Woon-Ping Chin. "From Ezra Pound to Maxine Hong Kingston: Expressions of Chinese Thought in American Literature." *MELUS* 5.2 (1978): 15–24.

Juhasz, Suzanne. "Maxine Hong Kingston: Narrative Technique and Female Identity." In *Contemporary American Women Writers: Narrative Strategies*. Ed. Catherine Rainwater and William J. Scheick. Lexington: University Press of Kentucky, 1985. 173–89.

Kim, Elaine H. *Asian American Literature: An Introduction to the Writings and Their Social Context*. Philadelphia: Temple University Press, 1982.

Leonard, John. "Of Thee Ah Sing." *The Nation* (June 5, 1989): 768–72.

Li, David Leiwei. "*China Men*: Maxine Hong Kingston and the American Canon." *American Literary History* 2.3 (1990): 482–502.

Lim, Shirley Geok-lin. "Assaying the Gold: Or, Contesting the Ground of Asian American Literature." *New Literary History* 24.1 (1993): 147–69.

———, ed. *Approaches to Teaching Kingston's* The Woman Warrior. New York: MLA, 1991.

Lin, Patricia. "Clashing Constructs of Reality: Reading Maxine Hong Kingston's *Trip-*

master Monkey: His Fake Book as Indigenous Ethnography." In *Reading the Literatures of Asian America*. Ed. Shirley Geok-lin and Amy Ling. Philadelphia: Temple University Press, 1992. 333–48.

Lin Blinde, Patricia. "The Icicle in the Desert: Perspective and Form in the Works of Two Chinese-American Women Writers." *MELUS* 6.3 (1979): 51–71.

Ling, Amy. *Between Worlds: Women Writers of Chinese Ancestry*. New York: Pergamon Press, 1990.

———. "Chinese American Women Writers: The Tradition behind Maxine Hong Kingston." In *Redefining American Literary History*. Ed. A. LaVonne Brown Ruoff and Jerry W. Wand Jr. New York: MLA, 1990. 219–36.

Mylan, Sheryl A. "The Mother as Other: Orientalism in Maxine Hong Kingston's *The Woman Warrior*." In *Women of Color: Mother-Daughter Relationships in 20th-Century Literature*. Ed. Elizabeth Brown-Guillory. Austin: University of Texas Press, 1996. 132–52.

Sledge, Linda Ching. "Maxine Kingston's *China Men*: The Family Historian as Epic Poet." *MELUS* 7.4 (1980): 3–22.

———. "Oral Tradition in Kingston's *China Men*." In *Redefining American Literary History*. Ed. A. LaVonne Brown Ruoff and Jerry W. Wand, Jr. New York: MLA, 1990. 142–54.

Slowik, Mary. "When the Ghosts Speak: Oral and Written Narrative Forms in Maxine Hong Kingston's *China Men*." *MELUS* 19.1 (Spring 1994): 73–88.

Skandera-Trombley, Laura E., ed. *Critical Essays on Maxine Hong Kingston*. Boston: G. K. Hall, 1998.

Smith, Sidonie. "Maxine Hong Kingston's *Woman Warrior*." In *A Poetics of Women's Autobiography: Marginality and the Fictions of Self-Representation*. Bloomington: Indiana University Press, 1987. 150–73.

Wilhelmus, Tom. "Various Pairs." *The Hudson Review* 43.1 (Spring 1990): 147–54.

Wong, Sau-ling Cynthia. *Reading Asian American Literature: From Necessity to Extravagance*. Princeton: Princeton University Press, 1993.

Bharti Kirchner
(1940–   )

Krishna Lewis

BIOGRAPHY

Bharti Kirchner was born June 1, 1940, in Calcutta, India. In 1962, after receiving B.A. and M.A. degrees in mathematics at Presidency College in Calcutta, Kirchner came to Seattle for further studies at the University of Washington. Her academic interests shifted to computer science, subsequently, her first professional positions upon leaving the university were in Chicago as a computer programmer, then as a systems analyst and consultant. Later she worked in the Middle East and Europe for several years before moving in 1977 to San Francisco to work as a systems programmer at Levi Straus; as systems manager at Bank of America from 1980 to 1984; and then as an advisory systems engineer for IBM from 1984 to 1989. In 1985, while still with IBM, she returned to Seattle.

The writing career of Bharti Kirchner began in earnest in 1990, when she left IBM to devote herself to doing full-time course work in the writing program at the University of Washington. Earlier, she had taken writing classes at the university and elsewhere, frequently publishing her class assignments in local and regional publications. Indeed, Kirchner, a voracious reader of fiction from childhood, had always wanted to be a writer. Currently an award-winning cookbook author and novelist, Kirchner has written over fifty articles on food, travel, and fitness in such publications as *Food and Wine*, *Writer's Digest*, *Vegetarian Times*, *Eating Well*, *Simply Seafood*, *Northwest Travel*, *Seattle Weekly*, *Seattle Times*, and *Fitness Plus*. She has appeared on many radio and television shows. She conducts writing classes in Seattle and at writers' conferences nationally; and she has been on the faculty of the Pacific Northwest Writers' Conference for six years. While working for IBM, Kirchner taught cooking classes in her spare time and planned on writing on Bengali cooking and culture. Kirchner's first publications are successful, well-received cookbooks that continue to sell well in paperback. Her previous work in computer science and her multicultural interests as a cookbook author are important influences on her fiction.

MAJOR WORKS AND THEMES

Kirchner's *The Healthy Cuisine of India* (1992) was an alternate selection of *Better Homes and Gardens* Book Club and named by *Food Arts* magazine as one of the best cookbooks of 1992. Her second volume, *The Indian Inspired Cookbook, International Table* (1993), was selected among top ten cookbooks of 1993 by *USA Today* and deemed one of the best cookbooks of 1993 by the *Chicago Tribune*. She is the author of two other cookbooks, *The Bold Vegetarian* (1995) and *Vegetarian Burgers* (1996). The cookbooks carry innovative agendas, including the introduction of Indian cuisine coupled with healthy cooking as well as eclectic, multicultural meal preparations. *The Healthy Cuisine of India*, for example, filled a gap in the market for books that combined Indian with low-fat cooking; as suggested by its title, *The Indian Inspired Cookbook, International Table*, while retaining the emphasis on health, focuses on eclectic dishes drawn from world cuisines, many of which Kirchner experienced during her various travels (2). Through different textures and tastes of food, Kirchner evokes and blends the richness of diverse cultures.

Bharti Kirchner's first novel, *Shiva Dancing* (1998), is shaped by the author's knowledge of the software industry, health, and world cuisines. The main character, Meena Gossett is a software engineer and a distance runner, as well as a connoisseur of food. The novel's strong points include its portrayal of a cutthroat software industry, its meticulous descriptions of cuisines and customs, and its evocation of a "globalized" world, all the while providing intimate, detailed narrations of place, particularly village Rajasthan, the San Francisco Bay Area, and urban Calcutta. *Shiva Dancing* engages these places as the protagonist Meena Gossett undertakes a journey from her home in San Francisco to India; thematically, the novel rehearses concerns that occupy much of contemporary Asian American fiction: it inquires into search for roots, the relations that obtain between location and identity, and the means by which ethnic American identity is maintained.

The novel begins in village Rajasthan, where Meena and her childhood playmate Vishnu are born and spend their childhood. When both Vishnu and Meena are seven years old, they are married; immediately after the completion of the marriage ceremony, Meena is kidnapped by marauding bandits on camels. Arriving by train in Delhi with her captors, she manages to elude them but then cannot find her way back to her village home. An American couple comes to Meena's aid, taking her to their home in San Francisco. In the United States Meena grows into a beautiful, well-educated, and successful computer scientist. After not having any contact with Vishnu since her abduction many years earlier, at age thirty-five Meena is able to locate Vishnu through her cybernetwork and engages in an e-mail correspondence with him. Unfortunate circumstances of her American life, such as her foster mother's death, being unjustly laid off at work, and a complicated romantic relationship with an American, contribute to her resolve to return to India to find both her mother and Vishnu.

Arriving in Rajasthan, she discovers that her mother had died at the time of her kidnapping at the hands of the same bandits and, significantly, realizes that though the village of her childhood will always be an important memory, it is no longer home to her. She then flies to Calcutta to find Vishnu caught in the midst of Bengal ethnic politics and violence, obliquely mirroring the backstabbing and corruption of her San Francisco workplace. The adult, still-single Vishnu is a prominent Calcutta reporter who also has been unjustly fired from his job. By the end of her Calcutta visit, Meena recognizes that she cannot fulfill the expectations of an Indian wife, despite the strange intersections of their fates, their comfortable companionship, and Vishnu's desire to honor their marriage.

In Asha, a Bengali college student who is obviously in love with Vishnu and with whom Vishnu is in love, Meena sees the ideal Indian wife. The differences between Meena and Asha are rendered by consciously exotic descriptions of Asha:

The door opened slowly on an exquisite young woman in a pale blue sari, her silken black hair in a coil that seemed ready to collapse. . . . How terribly young she was. . . . Asha's voice was even younger than her years. Her clipped English accent was charming to the ear. She was polished in a pure, unspoiled way. . . . Asha was tranquil, Meena noticed. No doubt she had been raised to accept people and situations, even a rival, with equanimity (310–11)

By revealing Meena's idealization of Indian women, this ironic narrative makes clear the irrevocability of migration: she cannot return. Indeed she proclaims, "Vishnu and I are on different paths now. . . . I guess I have to make a fresh start. Let my past go" (315). On the other hand, Meena realizes that San Francisco is also not home, and her American boyfriend, Antoine (who has also arrived in Calcutta), says, "We're both wandering in search of a home or maybe ourselves" (323). The end of the journey is always the beginning of yet another, hence, the title of the novel; Asha, appropriately given the philosopher's voice, explains: "Lord Shiva danced. And the world changed under his feet. He does this periodically to bring the world back to order, to get us out of our rut" (315). In *Shiva Dancing* ethnic identity is ultimately that which is continually relocated and revised. However, there remains a need for a stability concomitant with a dynamic ethnicity such as this; it is met through the adoption of an American self, which in Meena's case occurs in her romantic relationship with Antoine.

As made evident by the glossing of Indian terms, cultures, and customs throughout the novel, Kirchner has in mind a broad readership, extending beyond an audience of Indians and Indian Americans. Kirchner takes pains to educate her reader: she chronicles a successful Indian American woman's life, thus resisting the frequent depiction of such a life as victimized by American culture; demonstrates changing positions of women both in India and in the United States; makes tribal politics the subject of serious inquiry; writes against stereotypical images of India by emphasizing the modernity of India; and explores the configurations of hybrid identity in Indian American and other communities. The latter theme is an important topic in her most recent novel, *Sharmila's Book*, as she repeats the plot of "return to India" and further investigates the strategies by which an Indian American woman would straddle two worlds.

CRITICAL RECEPTION

At this time the critical reception of *Shiva Dancing* is confined to book reviews. These, for the most part, emphasize the novel's compelling plot structure, particularly its dramatic tension, and point to its engagement of contemporary issues in multiculturalism, ethnicity, and women's lives. The difficulties of the protagonist's journey reproduce the travails of identity formation; thus, one reviewer writes: "The tense climax finds Meena choosing between her 'promised land' and her escalating feelings for Antoine, as well as her growing acceptance of her 'American-ness' (Jana). Another sees Meena's "rare pathway through life" as drawing upon the author's "bicultural life and the sometimes-jarring East-West juxtapositions she has experienced" (Fry). Though sometimes Kirchner's "metaphors and sentence structure lack sophistication" (Jana), the critics would agree that the "intriguing journey" (Sengupta) that she plots makes her novel "accessible and entertaining" (Jana) as well as a compelling read. Kirchner is currently at work on a third novel tentatively entitled *Darjeeling*. With three novels contributing to the genre of Asian American fiction, she will surely be the subject of much critical discussion.

BIBLIOGRAPHY

Works by Bharti Kirchner

Novels

Shiva Dancing. New York: E. P. Dutton, 1998.
Sharmila's Book. New York: E. P. Dutton, 1999.

Cookbooks

The Healthy Cuisine of India. Los Angeles: Lowell House, 1992.
The Indian Inspired Cookbook, International Table. Los Angeles: Lowell House, 1993.
The Bold Vegetarian. New York: HarperCollins, 1995.
Vegetarian Burgers. New York: HarperCollins, 1996.

Studies of Bharti Kirchner

Fry, Donn. "In Life and in Art—In Her First Work of Fiction, Bharti Kirchner Straddles Two Cultures." *Seattle Times*, March 15, 1998, 14.

Jana, Reena. "San Francisco Overachiever Longs for Simpler Life in India." *San Francisco Chronicle*, March 15, 1998, 5.

Rubin, Merle. "Migration That Leads to Self-Discovery." *Christian Science Monitor*, March 10, 1998, 14.

Sengupta, Shivaji. "In the Backdrop of Terrorism, Ethnic Violence." *India Abroad* (February 13, 1998): 44.

Joy Kogawa
(1935–)

Cynthia F. Wong

BIOGRAPHY

A second-generation Japanese Canadian, or nisei, Joy Nakayama was born in Vancouver, British Columbia, on June 6, 1935. Her parents, Lois Yao Nakayama and Gordon Goichi Nakayama, were issei, or first-generation Japanese Canadians, in a predominantly white, middle-class community. She married David Kogawa in 1957, had two children, and divorced in 1978.

Kogawa's childhood experiences were shaped by the apparent and widespread racism arising from World War II, when all persons of Japanese descent in both Canada and the United States were interned. At age six, Kogawa and her family were evacuated to Slocan, which one critic described as "a ghost town in the old silver-mining region of eastern British Columbia" (Cheung 129). Her main character, Naomi, in the novel *Obasan* (1981) is about the same age as Kogawa when she was relocated.

After relocation, the family settled in Coaldale, Alberta, where Kogawa attended the University of Alberta in 1954. She also attended the Women's Training College, the Conservatory of Music, and the University of Saskatchewan. Her first job as a staff writer for the Office of the Prime Minister in Ottawa, Ontario, began in 1974.

Kogawa's literary work began in poetry, with her first collection, *The Splintered Moon*, appearing in 1968. These were followed by *A Choice of Dreams* (1974), *Jericho Road* (1977), and *Six Poems* (1978), before she tried her hand at fiction.

Obasan was published in the early 1980s, when Canadians of Japanese descent were beginning their fight for reparation for internment from the Canadian government. *Itsuka* (1992), which is a sequel to *Obasan*, documents the reparation process and the hard-won fight for recompense. As expected, Naomi—who appears in both novels—undergoes important emotional and psychological changes in the course of the two novels.

The 1980s for Kogawa was a fertile period. She was the recipient of the Books in Canada First Novel Award in 1981 and in 1982 was recognized by the Authors Association Book of the Year Award and the Before Columbus Foundation American Book Award. *Obasan* was rewritten for a younger audience, and that book was entitled *Naomi's Road*, which was then translated into Japanese as *Naomi no Michi*, published in Tokyo by Shogakkan Press in 1988. In 1985 Kogawa published another volume of poetry entitled *Woman in the Woods*.

Though occupied by her historical rendering of the internment in her fiction, Kogawa continued to actively educate people firsthand about the devastation that governmental policy caused Japanese Canadians. She has written a couple of essays on her views. In interviews, she shares the fact that Naomi in *Obasan* was largely an autobiographical portrait of her own experiences.

In 1995 Kogawa published another intensively rendered novel, *The Rain Ascends*, a tale about a grown woman who discovers that her minister father had abused young boys. Millicent Shelby makes the discovery in middle age, at a time when her father's own career is already in decline, and she faces the difficult decisions of both confronting him and making public her realizations. Although her own father was a minister—probably the rich source of her setting and characterization—it is not apparent that Kogawa's own father was the model for the Reverend Charles Shelby, a Church of England clergyman.

Kogawa is a member of the Order of Canada and the recipient of numerous honorary degrees. She has made Toronto her home since 1979.

MAJOR WORKS AND THEMES

The best-known and most widely received novel by Kogawa is *Obasan*. In that book, which is alternatively about silence and the critical emotional moment when silence must be broken in order that some form of liberation might begin, Kogawa writes about Naomi's painfully evolving consciousness. The title character, Obasan, is her aging aunt who has maintained a stoical reserve about the tragedies of wartime and the devastation of internment. Raised by Obasan since a child, Naomi is closer in mind-set and spirit to Obasan than she is to her mother's sister, Aunt Emily, who has determined that the historical facts should never die with the silence of those who underwent the experience.

Critics note that "Obasan" also means "woman" in Japanese and that the novel's dual reference is a rich source of feminist awakening in Naomi as well. At the beginning of the novel, Naomi is a thirty-six-year-old schoolteacher who has to endure the activist encouragements of Aunt Emily; Naomi is clearly uncomfortable with her aunt's determination to make private experience into a public record.

In the background of the story, which is ostensibly about Naomi's return to her hometown of Granton, Alberta, in order to help Obasan grieve over the death of her husband, Naomi's Uncle Isamu, Naomi confronts her past. In that period, Naomi begins to learn her mother's fate and the historical reason she and her brother Stephen were left in Obasan's care. The quick succession of deaths—her father and her grandparents—in that childhood period, along with another horrible realization of childhood molestation, only adds to the grave discovery at novel's end.

When Naomi opens the letters, documents, and journals left for her by Aunt Emily, she also opens the old wounds and peels back the old scabs that never truly healed.

This skeletal story is conveyed with all the cadence and intonation of poetry; the powerful evocation of imposed silence is rendered with aching beauty in Kogawa's prose. Naomi's pathos is never exaggerated, and her pain—while muted—is real and rooted in the author's own consciousness of what happened to her family and other Japanese Canadians in wartime.

Itsuka, which takes place some ten years after the events in *Obasan*, picks up Naomi's desire eventually to learn about the historical circumstances of her mother's death. The death of Obasan has compelled Naomi to leave Granton for good and to locate Aunt Emily in Toronto. One critic described this novel as one that "traces the development of Naomi's political consciousness, following the story of her growing involvement in the pursuit of historical truth and her investment in the dream that '*itsuka*'—someday—'the time for laughter will come' " (Kanefsky 19).

These two major novels deal with recurrent themes that are rooted in the historical situation of internment. Both establish the importance of family honor and endurance in the face of gravest circumstances. Naomi's identification with Obasan's moral reserve directly contrasts with Aunt Emily's activism; by the second novel, however, Naomi is swayed toward her aunt's views about history, particularly about the tenuousness of human experiences in the face of its eradication if people do not choose to remember and record their significance. In manifesting her own complex desire to merge Aunt Emily's social revolt with Obasan's stance on maintaining silence, Naomi demonstrates that it is necessary to also accept the dignity that silence has guarded in propounding a view of outspokenness.

Naomi's own grief about her mother's death by nuclear disfigurement and suffering is always in the background of the two novels. Working through that grief is one crux of her own evolving political awareness, for she begins to associate the personal loss with a larger communal meaning. In other words, the relationships of the personal, public, and political find fruition in her developing self-knowledge and need to take ostensible action to counter the ills that history has fostered.

Kogawa's next novel, *The Rain Ascends*, considers similar concerns of family loyalty and family history-making, although its subject matter of pedophilia produces a different set of stakes. Also told from a daughter's point of view, the story centers on Millicent Shelby's horrifying discovery about her father's sexual abuses. That the abuses occurred under the auspices of his work as clergyman adds a dimension of social responsibility to Millicent's decision about whether or not to denounce him to the public.

Millicent's adoration and loyalty to her father produce an interesting set of moral challenges. Kogawa does not simplify the questions for her readers; rather, she leaves them to ponder the multifaceted dimensions of the way human beings are interrelated in their destinies and fates: Who becomes responsible for the weakest and most vulnerable members of society when the strongest and morally righteous have failed them? Or, to put the question in the frame of the earlier two novels, What reparation is available to those so deeply wronged?

Kogawa's writings are insightfully conceived and skillfully rendered pieces about those darker terrains of human consciousness and experience. Her queries about the burden, as well as the liberation, of history are insightful and provocative.

CRITICAL RECEPTION

Critical acclaim for Kogawa's *Obasan* is widespread. B. A. St. Andrews notes that writers like Kogawa "are not only continuing Canada's leap into literary greatness; they are recording the changing identity of the nation" ("Co-Wanderers" 56). Erika Gottlieb and Lynne Magnusson celebrate the novel's ability to speak the unspeakable, with the latter declaring that the novel is "a political speech act [which is] a strong protest against the treatment of Japanese Canadians in the years of and following the Second World War" (59).

In analyzing the power of Kogawa's prose, critics have focused on her unique ability to let silence speak the horror of Naomi's experiences. How these opposing realms manage to do so in such eloquent manner is the subject of King-Kok Cheung's groundbreaking study in the essay "Attentive Silence." Cheung interprets the dichotomy of speaking and not-speaking as inseparable doubles: "In writing a quiet book, one that is attentive to image and to nuances of feeling, the author also vindicates Obasan's silence" (167). The contrast of Emily's more open discourse about history provides evidence of the ways both the resilience of issei and the resolve of nisei are needed to effect change, or what Cheung more modestly calls "a change of heart" in key characters (167).

Focusing on the relationship of fiction to the historical events, Mason Harris, Donald C. Goellnicht, and Manina Jones argue that the novel is "historiographic metafiction." The term derives from Linda Hutcheon's definition of a genre that "inscribes and then subverts its mimetic engagement with the world. It does not reject [mimesis] . . . but it does irrevocably change any simple notions of realism or reference, by confronting the discourse of art with the discourse of history" (qtd. in Cheung 127).

An argument about the novel's expressive realism (a term used by Catherine Belsey) concerns the work of the preceding critics and of Marilyn Russell Rose;

all see the relationship of fiction and art as irrevocable, but the degree to which either realm can express what "really happened" to Japanese Canadians distinguishes each critical view.

In other words, what is the relationship of the novelist concerned with the aesthetic goals of silence to those real individuals who have lived with the actual experience of keeping silent about internment?

Rachelle Kanefsky offers a fascinating reading of this postmodern query in her essay "Debunking a Postmodern Conception of History: A Defense of Humanist Values in the Novels of Joy Kogawa" (1996). Beginning her essay with an epigraph from Kogawa's *Itsuka*— "To be without history is to be unlived crystal, unused flesh; is to live the life of the unborn" (280)—Kanefsky takes issue particularly with Goellnicht's view that Kogawa represents different versions of history through the various characters. The competing views of Obasan, Aunt Emily, and Naomi sustain a notion that no version of history is either absolute or complete. Only in acknowledging the limits of a private reality can dialogue about truth among the principals begin.

For Kanefsky, such dialogues as envisioned by critic Goellnicht reiterate the "anything goes" mode of subjectivity that only endangers a possibility of discovering any truth. Rather, Kanefsky eloquently notes, "Through Naomi's evolving philosophical and political consciousness, Kogawa demonstrates that the struggle for legitimacy in historical representation takes place not in the deconstruction of truth but in the collective defence of truth" (29). The goal of both *Obasan* and *Itsuka*, according to Kanefsky, is the effort to clarify truth, not obfuscate it under the auspices of postmodern views about history.

Such clarification of themes, for instance, is well explored in essays by Shirley Geok-Lin Lim, who examines maternal bonds in the novel, by Cheng Lok Chua, who examines Christian and Asian motifs and symbols, and by Teruyo Ueki, who considers the "scheme of disclosure" (8) set up by the "nested riddles" of *Obasan*.

How individuals survive the horror of historical knowledge is the basis of Heather Zwicker's essay; the relationship of a colonial version of history against the "authority and universality of Western historicism" (21) is the subject of Sonia Snelling's fascinating article.

Briefly, there is no shortage of engaged and rigorous analyses of *Obasan*, while work on *The Rain Ascends*, for instance, is more sparse. The variety of background information provided by the critics for the first two novels indicates the richness of Kogawa's work. While not outright didactic, *Obasan* and *Itsuka* offer provocative accounts of the struggle endured by Japanese Canadians during and after World War II. *Naomi's Road*, a school textbook used in Japan, confirms, in Kanefsky's words, "that Kogawa's words are understood as relevant, accurate, and, finally, as signifiers of truth" (15). The compelling power of Kogawa's prose is therefore part of the fictional and historical discourses from which truth is eventually found.

BIBLIOGRAPHY

Works by Joy Kogawa

Fiction

Obasan. Harmondsworth, England: Penguin, 1981; Boston: Godine, 1982; New York:
     Anchor Doubleday, 1994.
Woman in the Woods. Oakville, Ontario: Mosaic Press, 1985.
Naomi's Road. Toronto: Oxford University Press, 1986.
Itsuka. Toronto: Viking Press, 1992; New York: Anchor Doubleday, 1994.
The Rain Ascends. Toronto: Knopf, 1995.

Poetry

The Splintered Moon. Fredericton: University of New Brunswick Press, 1968.
A Choice of Dreams. Toronto: McClelland and Stewart, 1974.
Jericho Road. Toronto: McClelland and Stewart, 1977.
Woman in the Woods. Oakville: Mosaic, 1985.
Six Poems. Toronto: League of Canadian Poets, 1978.

Essays

"Is There a Just Cause?" In *Up and Doing: Canadian Women and Peace*. Ed. Janice
     Williamson and Deborah Gorham. Toronto: Women's Press 1989. 157–62.
"From the Bottom of the Well, from the Distant Starts." In *Telling It: Women and
     Language across Cultures*. Ed. the Telling It Book Collective. Vancouver: Press
     Gang, 1990. 95–97.

Studies of Joy Kogawa

Cheung, King-Kok. "Attentive Silence: *Obasan*." In *Articulate Silences: Hisaye Yama-
     moto, Maxine Hong Kingston, Joy Kogawa*. Ithaca, NY: Cornell University Press,
     1993. 126–67.
Chua, Cheng Lok. "Witnessing the Japanese Canadian Experience in World War II:
     Processual Structure, Symbolism, and Irony in Joy Kogawa's *Obasan*." In *Read-
     ing the Literatures of Asian America*. Ed. Shirley Geok-lin Lim and Amy Ling.
     Philadelphia: Temple University Press, 1992. 97–108.
Fairbanks, Carol. "Joy Kogawa's *Obasan*: A Study in Political Efficacy." *Journal of
     American and Canadian Studies* 5 (1990): 73–92.
Fujita, Gayle K. " 'To Attend the Sound of Stone': The Sensibility of Silence in *Obasan*."
     MELUS 12 (1985): 33–42.
Goellnicht, Donald C. "Father Land and/or Mother Tongue: The Divided Female Subject
     in Kogawa's *Obasan* and Hong Kingston's *The Woman Warrior*." In *Redefining
     Autobiography in Twentieth Century Women's Fiction*. Ed. Janice Morgan and
     Colette T. Hall. New York: Garland, 1991. 119–34.
Gottlieb, Erika. "The Riddle of Concentric Worlds in *Obasan*." *Canadian Literature* 109
     (1986): 34–53.

Harris, Mason. "Broken Generations in *Obasan*: Inner Conflict and the Destruction of Community." *Canadian Literature* 127 (1990): 41–57.

Jones, Manina. "The Avenues of Speech and Silence: Telling Difference in Joy Kogawa's *Obasan*." In *Theory between the Disciplines: Authority/Vision/Politics*. Ed. Martin Kreiswirth and Mark A. Cheetham. Ann Arbor: University of Michigan Press, 1990. 213–29.

Kanefsky, Rachelle. "Debunking a Postmodern Conception of History: A Defence of Humanist Values in the Novels of Joy Kogawa." *Canadian Literature* 148 (Spring 1996): 11–36.

Lim, Shirley Geok-Lin. "Japanese American Women's Life Stories: Maternity in Monica Sone's *Nisei Daughter* and Joy Kogawa's *Obasan*." *Feminist Studies* 16 (1990): 289–311.

Magnusson, A. Lynne. "Language and Longing in Joy Kogawa's *Obasan*." *Canadian Literature* 116 (1988): 58–66.

Merivale, P. "Framed Voices: The Polyphonic Elegies of Hebert and Kogawa." *Canadian Literature* 116 (1998): 68–82.

Potter, Robin. "Moral—in Whose Sense? Joy Kogawa's *Obasan* and Julia Kristeva's *Powers of Horror*." *Studies in Canadian Literature* 15 (1990): 117–39.

Rose, Marilyn Russell. "Politics into Art: Kogawa's *Obasan* and the Rhetoric of Fiction." *Mosaic* 21 (1988): 215–26.

Snelling, Sonia. " 'A Human Pyramid': An (Un)Balancing Act of Ancestry and History in Joy Kogawa's *Obasan* and Michael Ondaatje's *Running in the Family*." *Journal of Commonwealth Literature* 32 (1997): 21–33.

St. Andrews, B. A. "Co-Wanderers Kogawa and Mukherjee: New Immigrant Writers." *World Literature Today* 66 (1992): 56–58.

———. "Reclaiming a Canadian Heritage: Kogawa's *Obasan*." *International Fiction Review* 1311 (1986): 29–31.

Turner, Margaret E. "Power, Language and Gender: Writing "History" in *Beloved* and *Obasan*." *Mosaic* 25 (1992): 81–97.

Ty, Eleanor. "Struggling with the Powerful (M)Other: Identity and Sexuality in Kogawa's *Obasan* and Kincaid's *Lucy*." *International Fiction Review* 20 (1993): 120–26.

Ueki, Teruyo. "*Obasan*: Revelations in a Paradoxical Scheme." *MELUS* 18 (1993–1994): 5–20.

Williamson, Janice. "Biocritical Essay on Joy Kogawa." In *Sounding Differences: Conversations with Seventeen Canadian Women Writers*. Toronto: University of Toronto Press, 1993. 352–54.

Willis, Gary. "Speaking the Silence: Joy Kogawa's *Obasan*." *Studies in Canadian Literature* 12 (1987): 239–49.

Zwicker, Heather. "Canadian Women of Color in the New World Order: Marlene Nourbese Philip, Joy Kogawa, and Beatrice Culleton Fight Their Way Home." In *Canadian Women Writing Fiction*. Ed. Mickey Pearlman. Jackson: University Press of Mississippi, 1993. 142–54.

Alex Kuo

(1939–)

Douglas Sugano

BIOGRAPHY

In 1939 Alex Kuo was born in Boston, where his father, Z. Y. Kuo, was teaching psychology at Harvard University. During World War II, from 1942 to 1945, Kuo's family moved to China, living in Chongqing and Shanghai. Kuo completed his primary and secondary education in Hong Kong, receiving a General Certificate of Education from London University at the age of sixteen. In 1955 his family moved to Windsor, Connecticut, where Kuo repeated the last two years of high school because his parents thought him too young to enter college. He went on to complete his B.A. degree in writing at Knox College (Galesburg, Illinois) in 1961 under the tutelage of Carroll Arnett and Samuel Moon. Kuo went on to study creative writing with other notable Asian American writers Frank Chin* and Lawson Inada at the University of Iowa's M.F.A. program under Donald Justice and Philip Roth.

After completing his M.F.A., Kuo taught creative writing and literature at South Dakota State University for a year and received tenure at the University of Wisconsin at Oshkosh, where he taught for five years, until 1969. Kuo resigned his position to protest the expulsion of African American students from the university, and he was determined to effect change through administrative means. He moved on to direct the Creative Writing Program and the Fine Arts Division at Roger Williams College as well as the Communications Program at Northern Illinois University. Kuo went to the Pacific Northwest in 1971 to direct and to teach in the Ethnic Studies Program at Central Washington University, a position he held for three years. During the next five years Kuo served as vice chancellor for academic affairs and taught in the departments of black studies and English.

In 1979, disenchanted with academics, Kuo worked for the U.S. Forest Service for half a year. Nearly broke, Kuo resumed teaching at Washington State University, where he established the Comparative American Studies Program in 1984. He still teaches creative writing, Asian American literature, American Indian literature, comparative American cultures, environmental literature, and the American West. Since 1989 Kuo has traveled three times to China: the first time to teach at Beijing University and the Forestry University; the second occasion to teach as a senior Fulbright scholar at Jilin University, 1991–1992; and most recently, in 1998–1999, as the Lingnan Visiting Scholar in American studies at Hong Kong Baptist University. Since the late 1960s, over eighty of Kuo's poems and over thirty short stories have appeared in journals such as *Arts in Society, Shenandoah, Poetry Northwest, The Wisconsin Review, The Yardbird Review, The Greenfield Review, The Journal of Ethnic Studies,* and *Boundary2.* Kuo's poetry has also appeared in fourteen anthologies and in three volumes. Kuo's *The Window Tree* (1971) was the first volume of poetry published by an Asian American. *Chinese Opera* is his first published novel.

MAJOR WORK AND THEMES

Kuo's novel explores the ambiguities in the term "multicultural" as he presents settings, situations, and characters that all belie facile categorization. It is 1989, when Sissy George, a cross-blood Native American singer from eastern Washington, visits her fiancé, Sonny Ling, a Chinese American pianist who has a teaching residency in Beijing. The rather straightforward plot premises, that of Sonny's Beijing concert and Sissy's singing the title role of *Carmen* (sung in French, directed by a Russian-trained Chinese opera star), are complicated by Sonny's desire to find his father, the Communist Party's ubiquitous security measures, the party's fear of cultural contamination, and a student-faculty underground that is mounting a fateful demonstration at Tiananmen Square. In the middle of the novel, Cao Feng, a journalist and would-be novelist, considers if he should review Ling's recital as an individualistic and Western cultural demonstration. Feng and perhaps the narrator contemplate the best way to describe a contemporary Chinese culture that is still reeling from the Cultural Revolution:

He thought that only fiction could understand and explain how a revolution could culminate in a nation that colonized itself, unfit for death, day by day little wisps of hope evaporating into instant lies four hundred times every day, and feigned exaggerations in the burgeoning bureaucracy. If the truth be discovered . . . within such a context, then ideology has no compelling urgency. (86)

In essence, the novel explores the relationships among foreigners and natives in a society where such labels are no longer meaningful. Kuo posits a multicultural world in which the characters share the experiences of Bizet's *Carmen* and Schumann's *Kreisleriana,* aesthetic spaces that may be, in some regard, just as significant as Tiananmen Square in 1989. While the Chinese characters behave in a "traditionally" guarded fashion because they know they are being watched, the American characters slowly learn how to encrypt their own messages and how to decipher their hosts' behavior. Through the rehearsals for the performances and the performances themselves, through their art, all of the characters find "free spaces" to speak and to act honestly. Kuo's novel, at least in part, weighs the power of action, the power of words (through the journalist Feng and the math professor Luo), and the power of the unspoken understanding that transcends culture or may even embody culture itself. In this way, the Chinese find some measure of freedom in their art, and the Americans find some measure of freedom in their budding political awareness that this "foreign" culture is not so strange after all. An epigram on the novel's title page describes:

> that irremediable space
> between performance and consequence
> between trailing images of the same person
> framed moments apart, at once magnificent and insignificant.

These lines may, indeed, embody the spirit of this Chinese opera.

CRITICAL RECEPTION

Because the book was published late in 1998, it is too early to expect many critical responses. Two book reviewers noted the novel's desire to study the complexity of ethnic and cultural identity, the relationship between knowledge and power, and human rights issues as symptoms rather than ends in themselves. Both reviewers appreciated Kuo's poetic language as well as Kuo's ability to avoid simplistic cause-and-effect relationships. One reviewer observed that some characters, particularly Professor Luo, Madame Zhou, and Zheng Xiaomei, are all underdeveloped, but perhaps that understatement is part of Kuo's point. The playful narrator, who flits in and out of the novel, admits that he is somewhat of an outsider; and as we know from the intricate plot, perhaps those Chinese characters do not wish to be "known" in a Western fashion. Perhaps those characters, used to constant surveillance, understand that they can make themselves known to Sissy and Sonny through subtler means—encoded words in passing, graceful gestures, and courageous, but small, acts.

BIBLIOGRAPHY

Works by Alex Kuo

Novel

Chinese Opera. Hong Kong: Asia 2000, 1998.

Short Stories

"Where Are You Really From?" *Greenfield Review* 4 (1975): 99–102.
"Dates/80." *Tin Can Journal* 1 (1980): 5–9.
"Statements/81." *Journal of Ethnic Studies* 10 (1982): 83–84.
"Statements/81.2." *Journal of Ethnic Studies* 10 (1982): 85–88.
"Why He Did What He Did." *Wisconsin Review* 17 (1983): 24–25.
"Did You Not See?" *The Literary Review* 28 (1984): 70.
"It's the Third Embrace." *The Malahat Review* 69 (1984): 59–61.
"Does Anything Come Out Alive?" *Journal of Ethnic Studies* 12 (1985): 65–86.
"Something's Wrong with This Picture." *Wisconsin Review* 19 (1986): 46–47.
"Cicadas." *Chicago Review* 36 (1990): 85–86.
"Eggs." *Chicago Review* 36 (1990): 80–81.
"Growing Tomatoes." *Chicago Review* 36 (1990): 84.
"Morning Stars." *Caliban* 10 (1991): 37–39.
"Past Perfect Tense." *Redneck Review of Literature* 21 (1991): 11–12.
"Reductions." *Ergo!* 6 (1991): 52–54.
"Relocation." *Redneck Review of Literature* 21 (1991): 11.
"Smoke." *Caliban.* 10 (1991): 35–36.
"Captured Horses." *Ergo!* 7 (1992): 9–10.
"Exit, a Chinese Novel." *Universe* 5 (1992): 24–25.
"Of Politeness and Psychs in China." *The Bulletin* (1992): 60–61.
"The Peking Cowboy." *Blue Mesa Review* 4 (1992): 78–81.
"The Connoisseur of Chaos." In *Charlie Chan Is Dead: An Anthology of Contemporary Asian American Fiction.* Ed. Jessica Hagedorn. New York: Penguin, 1993. 201–3.
"Definitions." *Green Mountains Review* 6 (1993): 47–49.
"The Catholic All-Star Chess Team." *The Redneck Review of Literature* 29 (1995): 27–32.
"The Temptation of China." *Many Mountains Moving* 1 (1995): 99–106.
"American Visitor." *The Bridge Bulletin* 63 (1997): 55–57.
"Friends." *The Bridge Bulletin* 64 (1998): 104–5.
"Shanghai Solution." *The Bridge Bulletin* 64 (1998): 86–87.

Poetry

The Window Tree. Peterborough, NH: Windy Row Press, 1971.
New Letters from Hiroshima and Other Poems. New York: Greenfield Review, 1974.
Changing the River. Berkeley, CA: Ishmael Reed, 1986.

Studies of Alex Kuo

Huntington, Rebecca. Rev. of *Chinese Opera. Seattle Times*, September 20, 1998, weekend ed., B5.
Rev. of *Chinese Opera. International Examiner*, September 2–16, 1998, 17.
Webster, Dan. Rev. of *Chinese Opera. Spokane Spokesman-Review*, September 20, 1998, E7, E8.

Helena Kuo
(1911–   )

Jean Amato

BIOGRAPHY

The title of Helena Kuo's 1942 autobiography, *I've Come a Long Way*, echoes her journeys as an overseas Chinese writer and journalist. Kuo was born in Macao in 1911 to a large, upper-class Chinese family. Because her progressive father believed in modern education, she left home for Canton at an early age to be one of the only two girls accepted into middle school at Lingnan University. Later she uprooted herself again to attend Shanghai University. During the Japanese occupation, her growing disillusionment with a sheltered university life led her to look for work and financial independence.

Referring to herself as a "feminist as well as being feminine," Kuo is caught between the pull of a career and traditional codes for a woman (5). Realizing that "[she] could be a good woman only if [she] could be a free woman," she decided against a marriage that would have denied her independence (50). Propelled by an adventurous and patriotic spirit, she then traveled to the West "to help build a new China and promote friendliness toward China and other nations" (248). She came to the United States in 1939 at Eleanor Roosevelt's personal invitation; there she became a minor celebrity and lecturer, eventually settling in New York.

MAJOR WORKS AND THEMES

As a single woman stubbornly trying to gain entry into the male-dominated field of journalism, she faced difficulties in both the West and the East. When she began writing in the 1930s, a period when Chinese women were moving out of traditional patriarchal roles while gaining access to higher education. Kuo still faced a Chinese society that offered women few opportunities. In her first attempts at journalism, she was locked into secretarial roles but did not give up until she was offered a low-paying position as editor of a weekly women's page on the *China Evening News*. Her career as a writer and journalist was often blocked by her race and gender. Once, in London, she was offered a column in the *Daily Mail*, but after realizing that the editors wanted only curious and exotic anecdotes from a Chinese woman, she eventually "gave up and wrote what they expected" (277). In 1940 she published *Peach Path*, a collection of her candid feminist essays. She also wrote *Giants of China* in 1944, a collection of biographical sketches of Chinese individuals who shaped Chinese culture, and later translated two novels by the Chinese novelist Lao She.

Helena Kuo's 1944 novel, *Westward to Chungking*, centers around the courage and strength of an ordinary Chinese family uprooted by the ravages of the Sino-Japanese War. The novel opens in 1937 Soochow, where the protagonist, Lee Tien-min, lives a well-off life of contentment with five successful children. After Japanese attacks, they undertake a treacherous journey to Chungking. Forced to leave behind everything, including his ancestral home, Tien-min eventually discovers that he has lost nothing; instead he gained the ideals of patriotism, perseverance, and simple living. Tien-min stands as an allegorical figure for modern China. "Tien-min was old, but he was fighting. . . . Tien-min was China at war" (297). He stands as a juxtaposition of traditional Confucian, patriotic, and progressive ideals. He raises and educates his daughters to be independent and allows them to serve the country at great risk because he "[sees] in his children the fighting spirit of China" (100).

While the novel is centered in China, letters home from the eldest son, studying in the United States, provide commentary on Asian American issues such as racial prejudice, limited opportunities for educated Chinese Americans, and Japanese American internment camps. While the novel includes positive portrayals of American characters helping with the war effort in China, it also makes bold statements chastising the West for supplying Japan with weapon materials.

CRITICAL RECEPTION

According to Amy Ling, Helena Kuo belongs with the educated, upper-class Chinese American immigrant writers of the World War II period who were "prepared to be unofficial diplomats and bridges between the East and West . . . fueled by patriotic ardor, they felt impelled to make friends for China through the vivid stories of suffering and heroism that each had to tell" (54).

Without falling into simple East versus West binaries, Kuo does not merely embrace the modern and dismiss the traditional but reveals their interplay in both Chinese and Western culture. Regarding the character Tien-min in *Westward to Chungking*, a reviewer in the *New York Times* noted that "Miss Kuo shows it is the combination of the new and old that will be China's future strength" (Parke). In addition, "her revealing glimpses of home life" and the social upheavals of war impart a stamp of authenticity. One reviewer from the *Weekly Book Review* points out that Kuo "achieves sure and vivid authenticity" with her protagonist, "Tien-min who is real and fascinating" (Cooper).

When examining the body of Kuo's writings, Amy Ling argues that her early work, especially *Peach Path*, had an "outspoken, confident, at times deliberate stance," while her later work became increasingly less feminist and more "subdued by masculine and Western dominance" (65).

BIBLIOGRAPHY

Works by Helena Kuo

Fiction

Westward to Chungking. New York: D. Appleton-Century, 1944.

Autobiography

I've Come a Long Way. New York: D. Appleton-Century, 1942.

Essay Collection

Peach Path. London: Methuen, 1940.

Nonfiction

Giants of China. New York: E. P. Dutton, 1944.
Dong Kingman's Watercolors. New York: Watson and Guptil, 1981.

Translations

The Quest for Love of Lao Lee, by Lao She. New York. Reynal and Hitchcock, 1948.
The Drum Singer, by Lao She. New York. Harcourt, Brace, 1952.

Studies of Helena Kuo

Cooper, Page. Rev. of *Westward to Chungking*. *Weekly Book Review* (September 10, 1944): 4.
Ling, Amy. *Between Worlds: Women Writers of Chinese Ancestry*. New York: Pergamon Press, 1990.
Parke, Andrea. Rev. of *Westward to Chungking*. *New York Times*, October 15, 1944, 26.
Strobel, Marion. Rev. of *Westward to Chungking*. *Booklist* (November 1, 1944): 78.
Swing, Sally. Rev. of *Westward to Chungking*. *Boston Globe*, September 20, 1944, 15.

Chang-rae Lee
(1965–   )

Martin Kich

BIOGRAPHY

Chang-rae Lee was born in Korea on July 29, 1965. When he was three years old, his parents, Young Yong and Inja (Hong) Lee, emigrated to the United States. They settled in metropolitan New York, where his father established a successful psychiatric practice. In contrast, his mother was a homemaker and never mastered English. Although the family lived first on the Upper West Side of Manhattan and then in New Rochelle, they attended a Korean Presbyterian church in Flushing. So, almost from the start, the spheres of Lee's life were clearly demarcated between a professional father and a homebound mother, between their own family life in prosperous suburban neighborhoods and life in the ethnic, inner-city neighborhoods of most Korean American immigrants. Lee's mother died in 1992 from cancer, but his father is still practicing psychiatry.

After graduating from Phillips Exeter Academy, Lee received a B.A. from Yale University in 1987, worked for a short time as an analyst on Wall Street, and then pursued a graduate degree in creative writing at the University of Oregon, receiving an M.F.A. in 1993. He has since taught in the Creative Writing Program at the University of Oregon. In June 1993, he married Michelle Branca, an architect.

Several reviewers have asserted that Lee is the first Korean American to have a novel published by a major American publisher. More widely, he has been hailed as the first major Korean American novelist. Lee has been both flattered and humbled by such claims, which have been based, after all, on his only novel to date, *Native Speaker*. Likewise, Lee has expressed his concern that a novelist who chooses to focus on his ethnicity or region is too readily categorized as "ethnic" or "regional"—with both terms suggesting works with less than universal themes and less than lasting import. Lee, however, feels certain that novelists' treatment of their materials—in particular, novelists' sense of language—rather than the materials themselves, ultimately determines the impact and worth of a work.

For *Native Speaker*, Lee received the PEN/Hemingway Award for Best First Fiction and the 1995 Discover Award. In addition, *Native Speaker* was named a finalist for the 1995 Oregon Best Book Award; the American Library Association Reference Service Association included the novel on its list of "Notable Books 1993–1996," and the literary journal *Granta* included Lee in its list of the fifty best American writers under the age of forty. Lee's essays and excerpts from his novel have begun to appear in such collections as *Rest American Essays 1996, Under Western Eyes*: *Personal Essays from Asian America, Family*: *American Writers Remember Their Own, Making Contact*: *Readings from Home and Abroad*, and *Against the Current: Readings for Writers*. Moreover, Lee has become a popular lecturer, speaking at campuses such as the University of Colorado at Boulder and Claremont-McKenna College.

His second novel, *A Gesture Life*, has just been published.

MAJOR WORK AND THEMES

The protagonist of *Native Speaker* is Henry Park, a relatively young Korean American who works for a shadowy spy-for-hire company specializing in ethnic and racial investigations. At a point when Park's few, fragile personal relationships have come apart, he is assigned to infiltrate the organization of a popular Korean American city councilman from Flushing who is being touted as a New York mayoral candidate. Almost inevitably, Park's identity as a spy is revealed, causing him to confront profound questions about his identity apart from his spying.

Native Speaker has been justly praised for its convincing synthesis of a broad variety of themes. The immigrant's experience is presented as being, at once, archetypally American and marginalizing. The native language is integral to the immigrant's sense of identity, to a feeling of personal continuity and stability in the midst of tremendous changes in circumstance, and yet it is also the major obstacle to assimilation and success in America. The difficult transition from one culture to another involves continual compromises between very different expectations and between very different ways of articulating them. On the simplest level, the word "native" becomes itself paradoxical, designating both the immigrants' "native" tongue and the new language that their children need to learn to speak as the "natives" do.

For the children of immigrants, neither their parents' language nor English is truly a "native" tongue. Questions of identity, which are here clearly reducible to issues of meaning—that is, traceable to semantic and syntactical ambiguities—are as central to the children's experience as survival and success have been to their parents'. The children are truly "hyphenated Americans." The cultural compromises of the parents have served to define the totality of the children's experience: the parents have made some difficult cultural choices, but their children have been left to consider the consequences of choices whose contexts they cannot fully comprehend, and thus they sometimes question even the necessity of the choosing, rather than just the rightness of a particular choice.

Henry's marriage provides an intensely personal parallel to the broader bicultural conflicts of the novel. Their separation is linked thematically, if not always causally, to three deaths, all of which have occurred previous to the main action of the story—that of Henry's mother from cancer when he was still a young boy, that of his father from a series of debilitating strokes when Henry was just entering full maturity, and that of their seven-year-old son, who suffocated in a tragic accident. The deaths of Henry's mother and son are especially traumatic and terribly ironic when considered together. Yet Henry's response to even this poignantly personal combination of events is colored by his pointed sense of the broader issues in his identity: his grief is all the more genuine and profound because he has great difficulty articulating it; in a very real sense, it is also "hyphenated."

Henry's occupation is both a fortuitous opportunity and a dangerous entanglement for someone whose sense of identity is fluid at best and tenuous at worst. Inevitably, Henry's "spying" transforms his personal issues into much broader political, social, and cultural issues. In fact, in an acutely ironic way, Henry's personal issues are both extended and subsumed in the broader issues. His starting place is the continuing question of who he is; but, for most others, the essential question is what, given who he is, should be expected of him. So Henry faces a version of the immigrant's dilemma of mixed expectations, but here the expectations themselves are much more ambiguous on both sides and levels of the conflict.

Chang-rae Lee's style is a compelling blend of relatively straightforward observation and sudden insight. There is a Hemingwayesque quality to the prose—and especially to the dialogue—that is appropriate given Hemingway's great influence on subsequent hard-boiled novelists, including those working in the mystery, suspense, and spy genres. But there is also a great lyricism to the prose, a feel for when and how to introduce the quietly startling image or figure of speech, and these qualities are traceable to other, earlier "immigrant" novels (such as Henry Roth's *Call It Sleep*). That Lee should write so well adds another layer of irony to a novel that keeps returning to the theme of what it means to express yourself in English when you don't feel as if you are entirely living in English.

CRITICAL RECEPTION

Writing for *Library Journal*, Janet Ingraham describes *Native Speaker* as a "first novel of impressive poetic and psychological accomplishment." In *New*

Statesman and Society, Ruth Pavey asserts that "language is the heroine of this novel: language spoken, written, stumbled over, learnt, misunderstood, found wanting." In a review for the quarterly *MELUS*, Tim Engles describes Lee's novel as a "graceful, multilayered, and at times poignantly affecting novel" in which "the lack of a unified narrative voice, while bothersome to some critics, subtly signals the linguistic flexibility of a person who has grown up working to develop an identity largely by trying on those of others" (140–41).

In a review in the *New York Times Book Review*, Rand Richards Cooper comments: "*Native Speaker* brims with intrigue and political high jinks, but Mr. Lee . . . is no spy novelist. His interest lies in language, culture, and identity; for him, the spy makes a convenient symbol for the American immigrant. . . . [Lee covers] familiar immigrant ground with skill and feeling, showing how father and son wield their respective languages to wound each other" (32). Reviewing the novel for the *New Yorker*, Verlyn Klinkenborg calls Lee's prose "elliptical, riddling, poetic, often beautifully made," adding. "Every sentence is a climax and an understatement, a koan of his own. It's the right language for insight, . . . but it's the wrong language for telling a spy story. . . . Spying seems, after all, like too small a vehicle for ambitions of the kind that Chang-rae Lee rightly harbors."

BIBLIOGRAPHY

Works by Chang-Rae Lee

Novels

Native Speaker. New York: Putnam/Riverhead, 1995.
A Gesture Life. New York: Riverhead, 1999.

Periodical Articles

"The Faintest Echo of Our Language." *New England Review* 15 (Summer 1993): 85–92.
"Coming Home Again." *New Yorker* (October 16, 1995): 164–68.
"Mute in an English-Only World." *New York Times*, April 18, 1996, A21.
"Uncle Chul Gets Rich," *New York Times Magazine* (May 12, 1996): Sec. 6, 44.

Studies of Chang-Rae Lee

Belluck, Pam. "Being of Two Cultures and Belonging to Neither." *New York Times*, July 10, 1995, B1.
Dezell, Maureen. "The Two Worlds of Chang-rae Lee." *Boston Globe*, May 11, 1995, 65.
Garner, Dwight. "Lucky Chang." *Vanity Fair* (March 1995): 115.
Monaghan, Peter. "A Korean-American Novelist's Impressive Debut." *Chronicle of Higher Education* (April 7, 1995): A6.
Pandiscio, Richard. "Great New Stories." *Interview* 25 (September 25, 1995): 136–39.

Reviews of Native Speaker

Annichiarico, Mark. *Library Journal* (May 15, 1996): 28.
Augenbraum. Harold. *Library Journal* (December 1995): 192.
Booklist (March 15, 1996): 1272.
Burkhardt, Joanna M. *Library Journal* (July 1995): 140.
Cooper, Rand Richards. *New York Times Book Review* (April 9, 1995): 24.
Eder, Richard. *Los Angeles Times Book Review* (March 19, 1995): 3.
Engles, Tim. MELUS 22 (Summer 1997): 140–42.
Entertainment Weekly (March 24, 1995): 60.
Flusfeder, David. *Times Literary Supplement* (October 27, 1995): 23.
Golden, Arthur. *Boston Globe*, April 16, 1995, B27.
Hong, Catherine. *Vogue* (April 1995): 236.
Ingraham, Janet. *Library Journal* (February 1, 1995): 98.
James, Kim. *U.S.A. Today*, May 12, 1995, D5.
Jones, Tony. *Denver Post*, May 21, 1995, E10.
Kirkus Reviews (December 1, 1994): 1565.
Kliatt Young Adult Paperback Book Guide (November 1995): 52.
Kliatt Young Adult Paperback Book Guide (May 1996): 46.
Klinkenborg, Verlyn. *New Yorker* (July 10, 1995): 76.
Lambert, Pam. *People* (June 5, 1995): 35–38.
Library Journal (March 1, 1995): 91.
London Observer, November 24, 1996, 18.
Mallon, Thomas. *GQ* (April 1995): 90.
Min, Song. *Amerasia Journal* 23.2 (1997): 185+.
Mong, Adrienne. *Far Eastern Economic Review* (April 4, 1996): 48+.
Morton, Brian. *Times Educational Supplement* (November 3, 1995): 11.
O'Farrell, Maggie, *New Statesman* (July 24, 1998): 48.
Pavey, Ruth. *New Statesman and Society* (August 25, 1995): 32.
Richmond, Dick. *St. Louis Post-Dispatch*, May 18, 1995, G4.
Solomon, Charles. *Los Angeles Times*, April 21, 1996, BR15.
Steinberg, Sybil. *Publishers Weekly* (January 9, 1995): 54.
Sullivan, Mary Ellen. *Booklist* (February 15, 1995): 1059.
Times Educational Supplement (December 29, 1995): 13.
Treat, John Whittier. *World & I* (June 10, 1995): 338–41.
Village Voice Literary Supplement (December 1995): 23.
Washington Post Book World (December 15, 1996): 4.
Wood, James. *Guardian*, (August 4, 1995): 28.
Yang, Jeff. *Village Voice* (March 1995): 26–28.

C. Y. Lee
(1917–)

Luchen Li

BIOGRAPHY

Chin-Yang Lee was born December 23, 1917, in Hunan Province, China. When he was ten, his family moved to Beiping (Beijing), where Lee finished middle school and then enrolled in Jinan's Shandong University. Soon after he entered college, China was invaded by Japan. As he recalls in an autobiography included in *World Authors (1950–1970)*, "[T]he entire institution was forced to flee southwest to Yunnan to escape the Japanese" (Wakeman 847). He went to Southwest Associated University in Kunming, Yunnan Province, and earned his bachelor's degree in 1942, after which he decided to sell his possessions in order to study in the United States.

Lee arrived in the United States in 1942 and enrolled in the graduate comparative literature program at Columbia University in New York City. Later he transferred to Yale to study drama at Yale's Drama School. He received an M.F.A. degree in 1947.

After his graduation from Yale in 1947, Lee remained in the United States and worked on different jobs. He edited a Chinese-language newspaper and was a daily columnist for *Chinese World*, a newspaper published in San Francisco's Chinatown. He also taught Chinese at the Monterey Army Language School and contributed to Radio Free Asia. In 1949 Lee won a contest sponsored by *Reader's Digest* for his short story "Forbidden Dollar," which was anthologized in *Best Original Short Stories* that same year. This further encouraged Lee to apply for permanent residence in America and continue his career as a writer. Also in 1949 he became an American citizen.

Lee's dream to be a professional writer was realized in 1957, when his first novel, *The Flower Drum Song*, was published by Farrar, Straus, and Cudahy.

This novel was later made into a Broadway musical by Rodgers and Hammerstein. The success of the novel was followed immediately by the publication of four more novels—*Lover's Point* (1958), *The Sawbwa and His Secretary: My Burmese Reminiscences* (1959), *Madame Goldenflower* (1960), and *Cripple Mah and the New Order* (1961). Lee published two more books in the 1960s, *The Virgin Market* (1964) and *The Land of the Golden Mountain* (1967), after which he did not publish any major novel for ten years until *China Saga*, a family epic, came into print in 1987. In the 1990s, Lee published two more novels, *The Second Son of Heaven* (1990) and *Gate of Rage: A Novel of One Family Trapped by the Events at Tiananmen Square* (1991). These two books further show the writer's profound interest and strong passion in the past and contemporary history of his home country.

MAJOR WORKS AND THEMES

Most of Lee's novels, different from many other Asian American literary works, are exclusively related to the historical events in the author's home country, China. Although an American citizen, Lee has remained considerably involved and interested in the events of his native land. Much of his fiction details life in China rather than the experience of the Chinese immigrants in America. Most of his stories have their roots, connections, and impacts in China. Discussing his position as a Chinese writer living as an American citizen with a *Publishers Weekly* interviewer in 1987, Lee said, "I am an American citizen and my loyalties are here in this country, but I have always hoped that China would become prosperous and raise its standard of living. . . . But in order to catch up with Western countries, the government will have to continue to encourage free enterprise and personal freedom" (See 84–85).

Comparison and contrast between the East and the West are apparent in his first novel, *The Flower Drum Song*. This is a slight, but irresistibly charming, story of San Francisco's Chinatown. The main character in the novel, Mr. Wang, a guardian of the rigid morals of old China, comes into conflict with his Americanized son. In this novel, the author describes Chinatown in San Francisco from several perspectives: "To the casual tourists," the author writes, "Grant Avenue is Chinatown, just another colorful street in San Francisco; to the overseas Chinese, Grant Avenue is their showcase, their livelihood; to the refugees from the mainland, Grant Avenue is Canton" (1). Such convenience makes a Chinese immigrant like Mr. Wang feel at home because he can find herb medicine and Chinese food as he would in China. But this old-fashioned Chinese refuses to put his money in the bank; instead, he "saves" his money under his bed in his bedroom. Refusing to wear Western dress, he wears "long gowns, silk gowns in the summer, satin gowns in the spring or autumn, fur gowns or cotton-padded gowns in the winter" (5). Mr. Wang doesn't like even children born in America. In his thinking, "[C]hildren born in a foreign land always lack filial piety," so "it is better not to have them" (72). In an attempt to keep the

Chineseness in his own children, Mr. Wang disciplines his boys and feeds them with the fundamental morals and virtues of Confucius (73). He wants to make his boys talk and act like a Chinese.

Lee's illuminating reflections on the differences in values and morals between the Chinese and Americans can also be found in his second novel, *Lover's Point*. But in his other novels, Lee tells the stories that took place in China. His stories are closely related to the ups and downs in Chinese history, both past and contemporary. *Cripple Mah and the New Order*, for example, satirizes the new government's rule in Red China. *The Second Son of Heaven* traces the events of the Taiping rebellion in China during the mid-nineteenth century and reveals the details of a turbulent era in Chinese history. Filled with action, emotion, passion, and humanity, the novel vividly captures Hung Xhiu-ch'uan's fights against tyranny, which becomes an example not only for his own people and time but for all later uprisings in China. This theme of fighting the ancient tyranny is consistent with Lee's concern about China's current movement for democracy and freedom. His *Gate of Rage*, for example, narrates the experience of a family who was trapped in Beijing during the Tiananmen Square massacre in 1989. Some critics call it Lee's epic novel, which beautifully integrates highly credible characterization with turbulent Chinese political history (See). The novel tells the story of one family torn by ideologies, borders, and times ranging from Mao Zedong's Cultural Revolution to Deng Xiaoping's modernization program and open policy. In this novel Lee presents China's contemporary political history until the fateful day, June 4, 1989, when tanks ran over the students in Tiananmen Square. The Gate of Heavenly Peace took a new meaning in Lee's novel—it has become the Gate of Rage, which places China's younger generation on the edge of bravery and death.

Taken as a whole, Lee's writing appears to be so closely tied with Chinese history and current events that his novels may sound too foreign to many readers.

CRITICAL RECEPTION

Lee's works have not received much attention in literary criticism. Even *The Flower Drum Song*, which was adapted into a musical and then a Universal film, did not draw the most favorable reviews upon its publication. Some reviewers pointed out that the book was "simple, even clumsy" in its structure and style (Seaman 558).

Lee's second novel, *Lover's Point*, did not receive many positive comments either. The reaction to the novel was basically negative, sometimes with patronizing compliments. For example, R. T. Bresler comments, "As is usual with second novels, the book, in comparison with its predecessor, suffers slightly in originality; and at times Mr. Lee writes like a fugitive from an amateur literary group. But all this is more than redeemed by his sympathetic, original picture of people—the protagonists and the various others who cross their paths—and the delightful viewpoints on customs and ideas that pop up throughout the story"

(1230). Donna Seaman comments, "While Lee's heavy-handed political commentary is countered with a busy and romantic plot, it still doesn't add up to great fiction, though it does provide accessible, even enjoyable vehicle for understanding their grievous events" (2030).

Positive comments tend to focus on Lee's talent of characterization and his knowledge of the Chinese sense of humor. As William Hogan has commented, Lee "has a keen eye for the engaging waywardness of human behavior, and a relaxed gift for storytelling. He has an uninhibited liking for uninhibited people, and enjoys their and even his own frustrations" (24). The best gift Lee possesses as a writer, according to Lewis Gannett, that he "expresses his enjoyment of them with a wry, deadpan sense of humor; and the reader shares his enjoyment." But Lee's characterization, his talent with the native Hunan Flower Song, and the theatrical attributes in the novel are most valuable to critics. Gannett comments, "It [*The Flower Drum Song*] is called novel though some day it will undoubtedly make a play. It presents, with lingering charm and affection, a preposterous cast of characters, in San Francisco's Chinatown" (1).

"Lee's stories show the conflict and blending of East and West in a delightful fashion that proves love and desire for freedom to be a wonderful thing in any language" (Hogan). Dishearteningly enough, the exoticism of his works often provokes certain resistance among readers. But as China is becoming more and more familiar to people in the West, readers are apt to find Lee's writing more approachable and more valuable than it has been perceived. Lee's works are sure to receive more and more attention when China and the Chinese stories are no longer exotic to English readers.

BIBLIOGRAPHY

Works by C. Y. Lee

The Flower Drum Song. New York: Farrar, Straus, and Cudahy, 1957.
Lover's Point. New York: Farrar, Straus, and Cudahy, 1958.
The Sawbwa and His Secretary. New York: Farrar, Straus, and Cudahy, 1959.
Madame Goldenflower. New York: Farrar, Straus, and Cudahy, 1960.
Cripple Mah and the New Order. New York: Farrar, Straus, and Cudahy, 1961.
The Virgin Market. New York: Farrar, Straus, and Cudahy, 1964.
The Land of the Golden Mountain. New York: Farrar, Straus, and Cudahy, 1967.
China Saga. New York: Weidenfeld and Nicolson, 1987.
The Second Son of Heaven. New York: William Morrow, 1990.
Gate of Rage: A Novel of One Family Trapped by the Events at Tiananmen Square. New York: William Morrow, 1991.

Studies of C. Y. Lee

Bresler, R. T. Rev. of *Lover's Point*. *Library Journal* (April 27, 1958): 1230.
Gannett, Lewis. Rev. of *The Flower Drum Song*. *New York Herald Tribune Book Review* (June 2, 1959): 1, 3.

Hogan, William. Rev. of *Lover's Point*. *San Francisco Chronicle*, April 13, 1958, 24.

Seaman, Donna. *Booklist*. 87 (July 1991): 558.

See, Lisa. "C.-Y. Lee Interview." *Publishers Weekly* (August 14, 1987): 84–85.

Wakeman, John. *World Authors: 1950–1970*. New York: H. W. Wildon, 1975.

Zia, Helen, and Susan B. Gall, eds. *Notable Asian Americans*. Detroit: Gale Research, 1995.

Gus Lee

(1946–   )

John C. Hawley

BIOGRAPHY

Augustus Samuel Mein-Sun Lee was born in San Francisco on August 8, 1946, the only son of Tsung-Chi Lee and Da-Tsien Tsu. His three sisters had been born in mainland China and accompanied his mother on the difficult trek across China to India and then to the United States in 1944. There, the family rejoined Tsung-Chi, who had once been a major in the Kuomintang army and who, since 1939, had been working in San Francisco for the Bank of Canton. When Gus was only five, his mother died of breast cancer, and his father, two years later, married a severe Pennsylvania Dutch woman. Gus grew up in the Panhandle and the Haight, a predominantly African American area of San Francisco, and he had a difficult time becoming accepted. He joined the Young Men's Christian Association (YMCA) and learned to box. Later, with the strong encouragement of his father, he attended West Point but did not complete the program. He received his bachelor's degree from the University of California at Davis in 1969 (where he was named Distinguished Military Graduate), and a J.D. in 1976. He worked for the army's Judge Advocate General's Corps from 1977 to 1980 (receiving a Meritorious Service Medal and First Oak Leaf Cluster for criminal investigation and trial advocacy and an Army Commendation Medal for legal advising) and then for the Sacramento County District Attorney's office from 1980 to 1984. In the latter capacity he became a member of the Order of the Silk Purse for trial advocacy. In subsequent years he worked for the California District Attorneys Association and as director of legal education for the State Bar of California, receiving in 1988 the Outstanding Instructor Award. In recent years he moved to Colorado Springs and retired from the law to devote himself full-time to writing. He is married to Diane Elliott, a psychiatric nurse and educator.

The topics of Lee's novels have tended to follow his career. *China Boy*, published in 1991, tells of his boyhood in San Francisco. *Honor and Duty* (1994) recounts his struggles at West Point. *Tiger's Tail* (1996) draws on Lee's assignment in postwar Korea as one of ten army attorneys in the Connelly Commission that investigated illegal recruiting practices. *No Physical Evidence* (1998) is set in the law courts of Sacramento.

MAJOR WORKS AND THEMES

Gus Lee's thematic preoccupations seem to stem from two sources: his as a Chinese American to find a niche in the larger and potentially dismissive American society and his desire to identify and cultivate the characteristics of masculinity as traditionally defined in Chinese tradition and, more importantly, in contemporary American culture. Along the way, especially in the first two books, Lee carries on a one-sided conversation with his surprisingly invisible father, who is bound and determined that his family will establish its American credentials.

The novels are decidedly autobiographical, though less so in the last two. In the first two, the protagonist is Kai Ting, almost a dead-ringer for Lee. In the third he is Jackson Hu-chin Kan, and in the fourth, Joshua Jin. In the most recent novels Lee is perhaps signaling that he has said enough about himself, and now, while incorporating the knowledge he has gained in his military and legal careers, he does not wish to write confessionally. In the four novels published to date, one can notice Lee's focus shifting gradually away from his early abiding sense of alienation. In its place have appeared more haunting questions of responsibility that the author, having himself come to terms with his own cultural assimilation as an Asian American, is apparently allowing to rise to fuller consciousness and examination—questions that are less ethnically based than were his earlier questions of identity.

A haunting presence in the novels is the author's mother, whose remembered warmth carries with it the Chinese wisdom that Lee attempts to salvage, along with the respect for scholarship that was a tradition in her family ("I was so happy to be her son, her strength and beauty a shield against the glare of complicated and misunderstood days" [*China Boy* 30]). Her courage in leading her three daughters out of China becomes symbolic for the author of a fortitude he seeks to emulate in the personal challenges of his early years ("She refused obsequiousness, rejected submission, and exchanged restraint for spontaneity. . . . She acted as if she were an enfranchised male" [*China Boy* 18]). Recognizing her importance in their younger brother's life, Lee's sisters hid from him for several months their mother's death from cancer—even writing him letters in her name. But it was not until he had become an adult that he felt a strong need to recover his memories of her. His sisters were the depository of those memories, and he quizzed them thoroughly before beginning his writing career.

Lee's stepmother, on the other hand, is portrayed in his novels as "Edna

Madalyn McGurk Ting," who, he writes in *China Boy*, "liked me until she heard me speak, watched me walk, saw my clothing, observed my skinniness, and realized that I ate Chinese food willingly" (67). She is everything that Cinderella might have wanted in a wicked stepmother, and in this first novel Lee does his best to punish her for her total rejection of all that the children associate with their natural mother—affection, storytelling, a warm home, self-affirmation, and, most pointedly, anything that would identify the children with their Chinese roots. Lee casts his father's relationship with his new wife in terms of the man's determined embrace of Americanism, and this complicates the author's own self-definition. "Father's heart belonged to Lillian Gish, the Barrymores, Thomas Jefferson, Joseph Stilwell, H. Norman Schwarzhedd [*sic*], the Springfield '03, the T-2 parachute, the Vought O2U pursuit biplane, C-rations, and the hot dog" (*China Boy* 33). It is this father whom Lee attempts to embrace and emulate, with only partial success, in *Honor and Duty*, his compelling account of his years at West Point. He describes it as "a process of attrition that would last for over three years," adding with trepidation that "I was the only Chinese I saw" (*Honor and Duty* 2).

With a somewhat distant father and as an only son with three older sisters, it is not surprising that Lee speaks through protagonists who valorize male friendship. In the first novel Kai Ting finds solace in an African American friend, Toussaint, who was important enough in his life that the author as recently as 1995 enlisted his wife's help in successfully locating his former friend, now a family practitioner in the Kaiser hospital system. At the YMCA he idolizes his boxing instructors, Hector Pueblo and Anthony Barraza, and in the Chinese community he finds a substitute for his mother's civilizing efforts in "Uncle" Shim. At West Point he seeks the attention of General Schwarzhedd, who had played a significant role in Lee's father's life and who has a better knack at accepting human failure. Ting responds with emotion to acceptance by an older male: "He gently took his eyes away from mine when he noticed that mine were wet, that I was losing control. I had experienced an urge to hug him" (*Honor and Duty* 400–401).

In *Tiger's Tail* the theme of male bonding plays itself out against the backdrop of espionage and consequent paranoia. Loyalty takes on personal importance for the protagonist, who is investigating the possible murder of his predecessor in the job. Much like the war movies that Lee's father found so compelling, in this novel the exigencies of battle force the men to forge friendships that last until death and even beyond. In *No Physical Evidence* the battle has shifted to the courtroom, and the intensity of the friendships seems consequently less significant. Nonetheless, even here the theme assumes an importance that suggests that the young boy who wanted so much to find a formula that would mitigate his daily beatings on the street continues to test the waters in any new setting. He wishes to fit in and remains aware that he stands out.

Questions of ethics and spirituality have assumed a larger role in the third and fourth novels. In the early books there was unfair suffering by the protagonist, but he is presented as too young to step outside the situation and ask how responsibility should be assigned. In the last two books, on the other hand, there are bad men and good men. There are some, like the two protagonists, who are a little of both. This growing sophistication in addressing ethical questions has its roots in Lee's relationship with his mother, who converted to Christianity in China. This was not of much immediate importance to the author as a young boy, who was sent by public transit to a new church each weekend by his wicked stepmother, but as an adult it has assumed a more prominent role. In talking about his mother with his sisters, Lee writes that "I discovered . . . how far away I had traveled from her hopes. The last thing she wanted me to be was an agnostic and I was" (Stone 48). At the time, he had been having trouble with his marriage, and his wife was concerned that he had become overly stern with their son. Entering therapy, he was led to a men's group at his local church, and a deeper form of male bonding began to change his life. "Christianity," he recently remarked, "gave me a sense of genuine humility and hope for my children. I no longer have the things I feared most in myself, attitudes that I saw in my father and stepmother. Without my faith, I couldn't have done it. In my original culture, Chinese fathers literally have the power of life and death. What I found through faith is that children learn respect if you respect them" (Stone 48).

The role of father, in fact, assumes increasing importance in the novels. In the first two, Lee speaks as a child who must come to terms with his own early struggles with his father's severe expectations and apparent emotional distance. In the two more recent novels, however, he writes from the viewpoint of an adult protagonist who is haunted by the loss of a daughter. In *Tiger's Tail*, the story of espionage is bracketed by Jackson Kan's nightmarish memory of a young girl dying in his arms, a girl he had mistakenly shot. As the story progresses, this dream reasserts itself at troubling times, until Kan is able to sublimate his anguish and offer compensatory love to a young Korean girl whose life is precarious, at best. In *No Physical Evidence* the central case that is being brought to trial is one of rape of a young teenage girl, and prosecutor Joshua Jin finds himself learning as much about himself as about the criminals as he assumes the role of foster father to the thirteen-year-old victim. "In the United States and Canada," he writes, "six hundred thousand kids were in the six-billion-dollar-a-year child sex industry, perishing before they died" (*No Physical Evidence* 385). The reader recognizes that Jin's obsession with the case springs less from this appalling statistic than from the fact that he is estranged from his wife following the death of their eleven-year-old daughter. The fact that the personal crises are finding manifestations and even salvation in the external world seems, now, less ethnically based—and simply American.

CRITICAL RECEPTION

Although Lee has had enough financial success from his books that he is finally able to devote himself full-time to his writing, and even though he has met with quite favorable reviews in the press, he is only now beginning to figure prominently in critical literary studies of Asian American writers. Perhaps this is because he was not trained as a novelist and, as Kiki Olson remarked in the *New York Times Book Review* regarding the voice in *China Boy*, "Kai's voice is original, elegantly naive. His conflicts are narrated in a direct, affecting, unique language, an abracadabra stew of metaphors, aphorisms, hyperbole, a patois of American, Chinese and Mexican words and street lingo." In other words, the voice is hard to pin down as "typically" Asian American: Lee's autobiographical writing reflects, like a chameleon, the hybrid culture in which he shaped his identity as an American.

But reviewers universally agree that, as Andrea Kempf notes in *Library Journal*, "Lee is a born storyteller." She is speaking, in particular, of *Honor and Duty*, which John Mort describes as "a great leap forward from Lee's first novel, the endearing but clunky *China Boy*" (*Booklist*). This is his best book, to date. Kathleen Norris evaluates this second novel as "a big book, and at times Mr. Lee seems too bent on getting it all in," but like so many others she is impressed by the strong characterization and the often moving descriptions of memories ("Maybe all families seek to hide precisely those things that writers must embrace. Gus Lee embraces even the most painful circumstances in a spirit of forgiveness").

In the third and fourth novels the malleability of Lee's narrative voice continues to draw comment. *Tiger's Tail* incorporates a M.A.S.H.-like familiarity with army language that can be off-putting for the civilian reader, despite its obvious success in placing us in the scene. "At times," writes Scott Martelle for the *New York Times Book Review*, "the dialogue is so filled with military jargon that the book almost needs English subtitles." Others object to an uneven tone, as in Emily Melton's criticism in *Booklist* that "Lee's writing is a curious hybrid, interspersing hard-core military jargon and in-your-face violence with often heavy-handed and perhaps intentionally overdone attempts at lyrical descriptive passages." It may be too strong to describe the novel as a genre-bender, yet some of the confusion over the tone may well arise from Lee's attempt to write a thriller through the eyes of a protagonist with the hard-bitten attitude we have come to expect from army novels, tempered by a sensitive underside that has been influenced by an Asian American cultural heritage and a traumatic experience in an earlier war. As the discerning writer for the *Sewanee Review* notes, "[T]he bitter agnosticism that resulted from his Vietnam experience (and that has alienated him from his family's values) is challenged, and to some degree overcome, by the mystical culture of Korean female shamanism that he has to rely on in his investigation. A resonantly complex work, *Tiger's Tail* is less a detective story than a serious and effective novel that happens to have a plot based on criminal investigation" (461).

That sort of investigation and Lee's genre manipulation continue in *No Physical Evidence*, with a similar fluctuation of tone and skewing of reader expectations. He plays with the hard-bitten Jack Webb jargon ("just the facts, ma'am") that readers of detective fiction recognize, and even the novelist's use of an intriguing (and hopeless) case to lift his protagonist from the depths of depression will be familiar. But the fact that the detective in question is Chinese American breaks the stereotype, as other writers of detective fiction have done by casting a gay male in the role. The book is overplotted, as *Tiger's Tail* may have been, but reviewers praise it for strong atmospheric passages and for its compelling depiction of the misuse of children.

Christine So observes that the shifts in voice in Lee and other Asian American writers suggest "breaks in traditional American narratives of belonging" (So 141). What she finds notable in Lee, however (and this may be what others decry as a weakness), is the use of jokes. "In the process," she writes, "he also complicates our understanding of ethnic humor and its correlation to acculturation by drawing comedy not only from the tension between the majority and minority, but also from the relationships between minority cultures" (143). Lee is, thus, typical of ethnic writers who use humor to extend the moment of potential assimilation "indefinitely, even as the novel moves towards establishing belonging" (143). She is speaking of *China Boy*; in reviewing all four novels, however, one can see two movements: the humor broadens beyond the ethnic joke, and the protagonist's sense of assimilation asserts itself with greater assurance.

John C. Hawley investigates the role played by sexuality in *Honor and Duty*, asking if "Lee is seeking to right the balance in the sexual politics that have cast Asian men as unattractive to Caucasian women, and Asian women as delightfully submissive to Caucasian men" (187). Hawley's principal aim, however, is to compare Lee's troubled relationship with his disapproving father with those of other Asian American male writers. He concludes that "Gus Lee's protagonist, intent on building up his muscles and becoming a man, nonetheless admits in a quiet moment that 'for all the gahng and shiao, the math and Confucius, the hunger and hard times, I just wanted my dad to like me' " (194). The early consensus seems to be that Gus Lee is surely among the most important Chinese American novelists and that many more books are in the works.

BIBLIOGRAPHY

Works by Gus Lee

Novels

China Boy. New York: Dutton, 1991.
Honor and Duty. New York: Knopf, 1994.
Tiger's Tail. New York: Knopf, 1996.
No Physical Evidence. New York: Columbine, 1998.

Studies of Gus Lee

Hawley, John C. "Gus Lee, Chang-Rae Lee, and Li-Young Lee: The Search for the Father in Asian American Literature." *Ideas of Home: Literature of Asian Migration.*

Ed. Geoffrey Kain. East Lansing: Michigan State University Press, 1997. 183–95.

Kempf, Andrea. Rev. of *Honor and Duty*. *Library Journal* 119 (January 1994): 162.

Martelle, Scott. Rev. of *Tiger's Tail*. *New York Times Book Review* 101 (April 21, 1996): 26.

Melton, Emily. Rev. of *Honor and Duty*. *Booklist* 90 (January 1, 1994): 90.

Mort, John. Rev. of *Tiger's Tail*. *Booklist* 92 (February 1, 1996): 899.

Norris, Kathleen. Rev. of *Honor and Duty*. *New York Times Book Review* (February 20, 1994): 8.

Olson, Kiki. Rev. of *China Boy*. *New York Times Book Review* (July 21, 1991): 11.

Rev. of *No Physical Evidence*. *Kirkus* 66 (August 1, 1998): 1059.

Rev. of *Tiger's Tail*. *Sewanee Review* 104 (July 1996): 461.

So, Christine. "Delivering the Punch Line: Racial Combat as Comedy in Gus Lee's *China Boy*." *MELUS* 21.4 (Winter 1996): 141–55.

Stone, Judy. "Gus Lee: A China Boy's Rites of Passage." *Publishers Weekly* (March 18, 1996): 47–48.

Marie G. Lee
(1964–)

Rhonda Brock-Servais

BIOGRAPHY

In Bob Dylan's hometown of Hibbing, Minnesota, a small, predominantly Scandinavian community, Marie G. Lee's family was the only one of Korean descent. Her parents emigrated from Korea in 1953, and she was born April 25, 1964. Lee's father, like her character Ellen Sung's, is a physician. She has described herself as a shy, bookish child who spent many hours reading because it was easier than interacting with her schoolmates. As a youth, her favorite books featured alienated characters to whom she could relate: *The Outsiders* and *The Catcher in the Rye* were two favorites. Her own work for young readers features characters who are such outcasts as a result of race. She says further that much of her childhood was spent "just dreaming" (Jones 112), and she credits this time and the support of her parents (who are nontraditional) with turning her into a writer. Although she was writing during her childhood and adolescence, no one saw her stories and poems. Lee believes Nancy Willard, a teacher, was one of the first to confirm the value of her writing and to give her confidence to continue.

As an adult, Lee leads an active and involved life. She likes to ski and rollerblade and practices tae kwon do, a Korean martial art. She graduated from Brown University in 1986 with an A.B. in economics and did a variety of jobs before becoming a full-time author. She married Professor Karl Jacoby (another Brown graduate) in June 1997. During the spring 1997 semester, she was a visiting lecturer in American studies at Yale University. The following academic year, she was a Fulbright scholar at Seoul Women's University. Lee is also a member of various groups designed to support and promote Asian American arts, a member of the Society of Children's Book Writers, and a volunteer for

New York City's Read Aloud Program. She sums up her work by saying, "I believe literature can be transformative because it can help develop people's humanity by literally putting themselves in other people's shoes. . . . Even opening the eyes of one person is worth it" (qtd. in Jones 117).

MAJOR WORKS AND THEMES

Lee has written novels for both middle-grade and young adult readers. *Night of the Chupacabras* and *If It Hadn't Been for You, Yoon Jun*, as well as the most recent *F is for Fabuloso*, are all for younger readers. *F is for Fabuloso* centers on what it is like to grow up as an immigrant in America. *Night of the Chupacabras* is a light, multicultural mystery involving Mexican folklore and a visiting Korean protagonist determined to figure out what or who is killing his host's goats. Lee has said visiting her husband's family ranch in Sonora gave her the idea.

If It Hadn't Been for You, Yoon Jun was Lee's second novel, and it comments on all the same themes as her works for more mature readers: the internal turmoil of the outsider, growing up in those circumstances, and the desire to fit in. In this novel, cheerleader Alice Larson, a Korean who was adopted by a white couple as a baby, must come to terms with her own unconscious racism when a Korean family moves to her small, midwestern town. Alice, like her older cousin, Ellen Sung, thinks of herself as culturally white. Yoon Jun is the same age and grade as Alice, who sees him as "dork" and a "dweeb" and doesn't want to be associated with him: " 'Hey, you're Korean, aren't you, Alice?' Minna said suddenly. Alice's mouth went dry, like sandpaper, for a second. 'No,' she said quickly. 'I'm not the same kind—I'm American' " (18). Later, not too surprisingly, Alice is assigned to be Yoon Jun's partner for a research project on other nations that will end in an international food festival. Through working with him, she learns about her heritage and comes not only to accept her difference but to take pride in it. At the novel's end, Yoon Jun saves Alice from being hit by a car. In praising him, another cheerleader calls him "that Japanese kid": " 'He's Korean,' Alice correct[s]. 'Like me' " (131).

Lee has noted that she's been asked when she'll move from race to more "universal themes." Her answer is "probably never" (Jones 112). All three young adult novels, *Finding My Voice* (her first), *Saying Goodbye* (its sequel), and *Necessary Roughness*, feature protagonists who are facing the consequences of being different in small-town America. *Finding My Voice* is about fitting in and peer and parental pressure. The novel, Lee says, is, to an extent, autobiographical. Ellen Sung is a senior who is competing on the gymnastics team, maintaining high grades (her father has determined that she will attend Harvard and become a doctor), and trying to manage her relationship with her first boyfriend (Tomper, the local football hero). In addition, her gymnastic rival, Marsha, is a racist who insults Ellen at every turn, particularly after Ellen and Tomper become romantically involved. The book follows Ellen as she learns self-confidence and individual freedom. She is hospitalized at the end as a result of an attack made by the drunk Marsha but still ready to move out into the wider world.

Saying Goodbye follows Ellen's fortune during her first year as a premed freshman at Harvard. Here not only does she face academic pressures, but race becomes an even more prominent issue. Ellen's roommate, Leecia, is African American and active in a black campus group. She assumes that Ellen is equally as involved in her own heritage. Over the course of the novel, Ellen does become involved with the Korean group on campus. She also begins learning tae kwon do and uses her creative writing class to try to understand her personal history and that of her friends. The climax of the book comes when Leecia's group brings a rap performer to campus whose lyrics advocate violence against Koreans. At first, Ellen tries to remain apart from the planned demonstration, but her new boyfriend, Jae, is the son of Korean shop owners whose livelihood was destroyed in the Los Angeles riots of 1992. As a result of her involvement in the demonstration, Ellen's friendship with Leecia ends badly. Although the novel is ostensibly about college, the true focus is the racial attitudes and relations between the various characters and within the larger society that surrounds them.

Similarly, *Necessary Roughness* features a protagonist, Chan Kim, who is not only trying to be accepted as an Asian American in a small midwestern town but also trying to overcome the personal tragedy of his twin sister, Young's, death. Further, Chan's relationship with his father, who is strict and overbearing, but loving, is difficult. Chan, who was a noted soccer player in Los Angeles, finds an outlet in football; the game becomes "the central metaphor for how a Korean family confronts life, death, and assimilation" (Rev., *Kirkus*). Lee says, "Asian Americans inhabit a tricky place because while our looks will always deny us from looking totally 'American,' we do not have that 'angry minority' spot to identify with. Black Panthers, A.I.M., La Raza—but Angry Asian?" (Jones 112). Coming to terms with just such an anger is only one of the tasks of growing up that Chan must master during the novel.

Additionally, Marie G. Lee has short stories in several adult anthologies: *Making New Waves: New Writing by Asian American Women* and *New Worlds of Literature* are among them. Her current project is a collection of short stories for adult readers.

CRITICAL RECEPTION

Lee's first four books have been well received by the children's and young adult reading, communities and educators alike. All four have been noted in "best of" lists and/or have won awards. Lee is particularly recommended for reluctant readers because her books are fast-paced, episodic, and accessible. However, at least one reviewer has complained that *Necessary Roughness* "is a bit disappointing in comparison" to the two novels featuring Ellen Sung (Rev., *Notes*). Still, this same reviewer praises Chan's character for not being "divided." That is, he is comfortable with both his Korean heritage and with being an American. Problems arise when other characters insist that he must be one or the other.

Another reviewer notes that the way Lee deals with racism is both "explicit and sensitive" (Ray). A reviewer of *Finding My Voice* seconds this praise by saying that the book is "filled with searing truths about day-to-day racism" (Rev., *Kirkus*). *If It Hadn't Been for You, Yoon Jun* is particularly praised as "one of the few elementary grade novels that deal with racial pride and prejudice in an accessible fashion" (Del Negro).

Ellen Sung, especially, is a strongly drawn and individual character that almost any young reader could relate to. In particular, she and other Lee's characters truthfully portray a difficult, yet loving, relationship with their parents. Hearne writes that in *Finding My Voice* the reader can witness Ellen's character "deepen[ing] credibly" and goes on to say that readers can empathize with her and celebrate her "emerging confidence" (48). Another reviewer points out the universality of the work by saying it "addresses issues of growing independence and self-awareness faced by young people as they begin to cross the threshold into adulthood" (Knoth): Along these lines, Hearne ends her review of *Saying Goodbye* by wondering if a third novel is forthcoming, for she feels readers will be interested to see what happens to "these honest and interesting personae."

Lee's work has been cited by the National Conference of Christians and Jews in *The Human Family . . . Learning to Live Together*. Although this is without a doubt an honor, unfortunately, like many other writers who feature minority protagonists, Lee's works are seen primarily as multicultural and are frequently used as teaching tools rather than recommended as good novels in their own right. Her stories are consistently noted for "giv[ing] voice to a point of view that has been wanting until recently in fiction about Asian-Americans" (White 144). Even her thriller, *Night of the Chupacabras*, is subject to this classification in reviews. *Booklist* touts the novel as an introduction to two cultures, customs, and languages and makes special note of the glossary provided. However, with continued exposure and similar high-quality work, some day, hopefully not too far off, Marie G. Lee will become known as an author not just of good multicultural books but of good books, period.

BIBLIOGRAPHY

Works by Marie G. Lee

Novels

Finding My Voice. New York: Houghton Mifflin, 1992.
If It Hadn't Been for You, Yoon Jun. New York: Houghton Mifflin, 1993.
Saying Goodbye. New York: Houghton Mifflin, 1994.
Necessary Roughness. New York: HarperCollins, 1997.
Night of the Chupacabras. New York: Avon, 1998.
F is for Fabuloso. New York: Avon, 1999.

Studies of Marie G. Lee

Del Negro, Janice. Rev. of *If It Hadn't Been for You, Yoon Jun. Booklist* (July 1993): 1966.

Hearne, Betsy. Rev. of *Finding My Voice. Bulletin of the Center for Children's Books* (October 1992): 47–48.

———. Rev. of *Saying Goodbye. Bulletin of the Center for Children's Books* (July/August 1994): 364.

Jones, J. Sydney. "Marie G. Lee." In *Authors and Artists for Young Adults.* Vol. 25 Ed. Thomas McMahon. Detroit Gale, 1998. 111–17.

Knoth, Maeve Visser. Rev. of *Saying Goodbye. Horn Book* (July/August 1994): 458.

Lee, Marie. "How I Grew." *ALAN Review* (Winter 1995): 8–11.

"Marie G. Lee's Official Homepage." http://www.geocities.com/Athens/Acropolis/4416.

Ray, Karen. "Children's Books." *New York Times*, June 27, 1993, late ed., sec. 7: 21.

Rev. of *Finding My Voice. Kirkus Reviews* (September 15, 1992): 1190.

Rev. of *Necessary Roughness. Kirkus Reviews* (November 1, 1996): 1602.

Rev. of *Necessary Roughness. Notes from the Windowsill.* (a Web site of book reviews for young readers) http://lib.nmsu.edu/subject/childlit/reviews/notes/6_1.html.# necessary.

Rev. of *Night of the Chupacabras. Booklist* (November 15, 1998): 501.

White, Libby K. Rev. of *Finding My Voice. School Library Journal* (October 1992): 143–44.

SKY Lee
(1952–   )

Martin Kich

BIOGRAPHY

SKY Lee was born Sharon Lee in 1952 in Port Alberni, a milltown in northern British Columbia. In her interview with Noami Guilbert, she recounts some of the events of her childhood. One of the most poignant anecdotes concerns her mother's practice of gathering watercress from a stream near the elementary school that Lee attended. Although she was embarrassed when some of the other-children wondered if her family routinely ate weeds, she also realized that few, if any, of her classmates had even an inkling of how delicious the water-cress was.

After receiving a B.A. in fine arts from the University of British Columbia, Lee worked for a while on the feminist magazine *Makara*. Then she enrolled in Douglas College to pursue a diploma in nursing. Since graduating, she has worked as a nurse in several settings, migrating to working with alcoholics. Despite the success that she has achieved with *Disappearing Moon Cafe*, she has continued to work as a nurse while maintaining a disciplined writing routine. In *Telling It*, she comments on this dual focus: "I have worked very hard and . . . every bit of it has contributed to my writing. Yes it's hard, you have to ream out the last of your energy to also write on top of that but ultimately that is, as I say, my way of striving for freedom and I don't resent having to do, you know, work to enhance my writing and I don't see the two as conflictive" (133).

Lee has described herself as a lesbian and as a Maoist, though she has ob-jected to the common perception that such terms are reductive—that anyone who embraces them as self-descriptive is necessarily submitting to some sort of prescriptive categorization. In *Telling It*, she states: "My guerrilla base is my garden, where I escape to rest. Come home to your garden, your collective plot, someone else's garden; just get in touch again! To heal is often the hardest thing to do, especially when we have gotten so used to being ill or injured. It is a way of fighting for our humanness. The vision of a woman in her garden is to me a very important one. Ultimately, the vision of a woman tilling and culti- vating her garden called earth is the only one I want to pass on unsullied to my great granddaughters. Remember, Mao only went a little ways with his revo- lution. Now as women, we must regain the initiative and go much farther. We must go where no man has gone before" (108–9).

Disappearing Moon Cafe took Lee fifteen years to write. For the novel, Lee received the City of Vancouver Book Award. The novel was also short-listed for the Governor General's Award and was included in Erica Bauermeister's *500 Great Books by Women: A Reader's Guide.* For her master's degree in Canadian studies at Carleton University, Tina Dunlop-Addley has recently com- pleted the first graduate thesis on Lee's work: "The Politics of Location in Canadian Women's Novels by Daphne Marlett, SKY Lee, and Joy Kogawa."

Published by a small press, Lee's collection of short stories, *Bellydancer*, has received less attention than the novel but more attention than it would have received had it been published previous to the novel. Although the stories in *Bellydancer* treat many of the same themes as Lee's novel, the female protag- onists are not all Chinese Canadians.

Lee lives in Vancouver with her two children—a son, Nathan, and a daughter, Mayan.

MAJOR WORK AND THEMES

Disappearing Moon Cafe is a challenging and rewarding novel. It traces the often-tormented experiences of four generations of the Wong family, who are prominent among, and in many ways representative of, the Chinese community in Vancouver. The focus is especially on the women, whose infatuations, mar- riages, and illicit affairs transform the simple principle of a direct line of inher- itance into something more resembling Chinese boxes.

On a first reading, however, the novel may be somewhat daunting. The rel- ative obscurity and foreignness of the immigrant experience of the Chinese Canadians, the sheer number of characters in the novel and the sketchy intro- ductions of many of them, and the sudden shifts in time back and forth among a half-dozen periods ranging from the late nineteenth century to the late twen- tieth all combine to make the reader feel adrift in the narrative. In addition, although most of the sections of the novel are titled to indicate the perspective from which events are being perceived and related (typically either from the first-person or the third-person-limited points of view), some sections are more ambiguously or variously focused. Since the style is often more oblique than direct, more poetic than expository, the reader has to proceed on faith, believing that most elements of the plot and the major characters will eventually sort themselves out—or become easier to sort out.

In fact, by about the halfway point of the novel, everything does seem to become somehow more accessible and coherent: the characters become distinguishable by their eras and personalities; the significant events begin to emerge from the jumbled fragments of family lore, communal rumors, and personal suppositions; and the ramifications of the novel's being the construction of Kae, one of the great-granddaughters, begin to provide a purposeful shape and rhythm to the narrative as a whole.

Curiously, in a novel in which the threat of unintentional incest begins to hang over each character like the potential for some sort of genetic malady, almost all of the sexual involvements occur offstage. Lee seems very hesitant to intrude on the genuinely loving intimacies between her characters, however illicit they may be; the only explicit scenes are very pointedly mercenary and more sordidly erotic—which is an odd way to describe relationships other than those that are, very ironically, nearly incestuous. If the novel did present these materials more directly, it would seem much more a potboiler dressed up with postmodern narrative gimmicks. Instead, Lee recognizes the primal impulses revealed in, rather than driven by, the melodrama, and she provocatively explores the universal truths inherent in the story of a small and relatively closed community. The greatest, but quietest, irony in this beautifully ironic novel is that despite—or perhaps because of—the efforts to maintain a racially untainted Wong family line, these Chinese Canadians are gradually assimilated into a sort of racial melting pot, with Native American and French Canadian bloodlines mixing in.

CRITICAL RECEPTION

In the criticism of *Disappearing Moon Cafe*, three misleading observations about the novel recur rather frequently. First, the novel has been credited with renewing interest in the historical contributions of Chinese immigrants to the construction of the trans-Canadian railroads and to the general development of the Pacific provinces. But the novel does not itself directly focus on the lives of those early laborers. Instead, we learn about them only in a fragmented manner through recollections of other characters such as the patriarch Gwei Chang Wong and his long-unacknowledged, part Native American son, Ting An Wong. So the laborers' experience provides more of a broad backdrop to the story than an integral element of its development.

Second, while the characters naturally think often of China, of relatives left behind, and of return visits that might be made—and a few that actually have been made—the novel does not really range in its spatial settings from western Canada to China. For the characters in the novel, China is always—and often poignantly—more of a transformed memory or a dream-place than a real alternative to their Canadian circumstances. Eventually, it becomes the "foreign" place.

Third, the Disappearing Moon Cafe provides a lyrical title for the novel, but

it is not a particularly dramatic locus for the action and themes of the novel—
except perhaps in the ironic sense that it is the origin of the family's fortune,
and most of its misfortune is played out elsewhere. Beyond these three points,
the critics and reviewers have generally focused on the novel's narrative structure and style and on its themes—variously finding fault with some aspects of
its development but typically emphasizing other aspects that more than com-
pensate.

In his profile for *Contemporary Authors*, Stephen Milnes provides this suc-
cinct description of the novel's narrative structure and style: "Powerful vignettes,
flashbacks, multiple perspectives, and temporal juxtapositions are features of
[Kae's] narrative as she wrestles with the problems of knowing and representing
the past" (601).

In reviewing *Disappearing Moon Cafe* for *Canadian Literature*, Joshua S.
Mostow criticizes the lack of cohesion among the "vignettes that switch from
character to character" in the novel (174). Although he also finds fault with the
surprisingly slight suspense generated by a plot structured around a web of
secrets and partial revelations, he does find the novel almost singularly lacking
in the sentimentality and nostalgia that have characterized and often undermined
some of the most noteworthy novels written by Asian American women. Mostow comments, in sum, that Lee's novel "is a uniquely Canadian and uniquely
feminine consideration of the Chinese immigrant experience" (175).

Writing in the *New York Times Book Review*, Angela Jabine remarks on the
novel's subject and style: "From the vantage point of a bustling restaurant in
Vancouver's Chinatown, SKY Lee sketches in the harsh and boisterous environment surrounding it. Ms. Lee's slapstick lyricism at times undercuts the del-
icacy with which she reveals the tragic aspects of her story, but it also tempers
Kae's harsh judgment of her forebears, particularly the husbands who preserved
their husbands' families at the expense of their own integrity."

The reviewer for *Kirkus Reviews* presents a very pithy description of the
novel's stylistic mix: "Lee successfully combines magic realism and epic sweep
in the fast-moving story."

Reviewing the novel for the *Women's Review of Books*, Marina Heung finds
much to praise in Lee's development of the novel's themes: "Intricately plotted,
with its shifting narrative perspectives, [the novel] re-aligns family relationships
to reveal a web of submerged alliances; it acknowledges the historical restraints
on Chinese women while powerfully asserting the potential of female agency
and commonality." But Heung argues that the novel's conclusion is inherently
flawed: "Throughout the novel, Kae has attended almost exclusively to the past;
we learn relatively little about her present life and circumstances. It remains
unclear, then, how she herself will 'give meaning' to the lives and struggles of
her foremothers."

In her review of *Bellydancer* for *Quill and Quire*, Julie Adam asserts: "Lee's
anger at the economic basis of relationships, the destructive nature of patriarchy,
the struggle for the ownership of women's bodies . . . is cloaked in the ironic

and the macabre." This broad appraisal is a fair description of the themes of *Disappearing Moon Cafe* as well as those of the stories.

Lien Chao's "As Agents and as Perspective: Female Characters in *Disappearing Moon Cafe*" is very much an analysis of the novel from a feminist perspective. Decrying the general "lack of representation of Chinese Canadian women in Canadian discourse," Chao commends Lee's novel as a dramatic statement against this trend: "Lee deconstructs gender/race stereotypes of the silent and submissive Oriental women and foregrounds her female characters as agents in the families as well as in family-owned business. Lee effectively constitutes Chinese Canadian women's sub-culture as a historical part of the community history, in which the female characters interpose their distinctive voices. . . . [Lee's novel] breaks through the silence in the following two areas: first, the hundred year collective silence of the Chinese community in Canadian history and culture; second, Chinese Canadian women's double silence as racial minority women" (220, 221)

In "The Latitudes of Romance: Representations of Chinese Canada in Bowering's *To All Appearances a Lady* and Lee's *Disappearing Moon Cafe*," Graham Huggan classifies the two novels as examples of "exoticist romance" and then describes the category as "dangerously double-sided," for "in exotic literature, . . . the tendency is to glorify foreigners, [whereas] in colonial literature, it is to denigrate them" (35). Specifically, he examines how Lee's choice of this literary form complements the process of ethnic, racial, and cultural assimilation that she represents in her novel: "Lee uses the *inclusiveness* of romance—its capacity to combine aspects of tragedy and comedy within an interwoven pattern—as a means of transforming a divisive history into unifying myth" (38). Later, Huggan adds: "Kae's search for 'authenticity' indicates the temptation that exists within beleaguered ethnic communities to fall back on nostalgic myths of pure identity which only replicate the structure of the dominant culture. . . . This dilemma is addressed . . . by providing a series of contending—often contradictory—narratives. None of these narratives is authentic or complete, or even reliable: none can be traced back to a single source, or to an identifiable point of origin" (41).

BIBLIOGRAPHY

Works by SKY Lee

Novel

Disappearing Moon Cafe. Vancouver: Douglas and McIntyre, 1990; Seattle: Seal, 1991.

Other Works

Bellydancer: Stories. Vancouver: Press Gang, 1994.
(With Lee Maracle, Daphne Marlatt, and Betsy Warland). *Telling It: Women and Lan-*

guage across Cultures—The Transformation of a Conference. Vancouver: Press Gang, 1990.

(With Paul Yee). *Teach Me to Fly Skyfighter! and Other Stories*. Juvenile fiction. Toronto: Lorimer, 1983.

Studies of SKY Lee

"Anarchy in Print: Writer SKY Lee Challenges Canadian Literary Norms." *Asian Week*, November 4, 1994, 14.

Chao, Lien. "As Agents and as Perspective: Female Characters in *Disappearing Moon Cafe*." In *Intersexions: Issues of Race and Gender in Canadian Women's Writing*. Ed. Coomi S. Vevaina and Barbara Godard. New Delhi: Creative, 1996. 219–30.

Conde, Mary. "Visible Immigrants in Three Canadian Women's Fictions of the Nineties." *Etudes Canadiennes/Canadian Studies* 19 (June 1993): 91–100.

Darias-Beautell, Eva. "Displacements, Self-Mockery, and Carnival in the Canadian Postmodern." *World Literature Today* 70 (Spring 1996): 316+.

Guilbert, Naomi. "Interview with Sharon Lee." In *Jin Guo: Voices of Chinese Canadian Women*. Ed. Momoye Sugiman. New York: Women's Press, 1993. 91–98.

Huggan, Graham. "The Latitudes of Romance: Representations of Chinese Canada in Bowering's *To All Appearances a Lady* and Lee's *Disappearing Moon Cafe*." *Canadian Literature* (Spring 1994): 34–48.

Larson, Jesse. "*Disappearing Moon Cafe*, by SKY Lee." In *500 Great Books by Women: A Reader's Guide*. Ed. Erica Bauermeister. New York: Penguin, 1994. 162–63.

Milnes, Stephen. "SKY Lee." In *Contemporary Novelists*. 6th ed. Detroit: St. James, 1996. 601–2.

Reviews of Bellydancer: Stories

Children's Book Review Service 94 (1995): 190.

Prasarttongosoth, Pam. *Sojourner: The Women's Forum* 31 (August 1995): B9.

Smucker, Ronica Sanders. *Lambda Book Report* (January-February, 1995): 24.

Williams, Mary Elizabeth. *Belles Lettres* 10 (Spring 1995): 76–77+.

Reviews of Disappearing Moon Cafe

Adam, Julie. *Quill and Quire* 61 (January 1995): 38.

Allen, Bob. *Washington Post*, November 3, 1991, WBK 10.

Belles Lettres 7 (Fall 1991): 20.

Books in Canada 23 (November 1994): 36+.

Ferber, Elizabeth. *Utne Review* (November 1991): 148.

Finetti, Scilla. *Amerasia Journal* 22.3 (1996): 171–73.

Heung, Marina. *Women's Review of Books* 9 (November 1991): 23.

Ingraham, Janet. *Library Journal* (September 15, 1991): 110.

Jabine, Angela. *New York Times Book Review* (February 9, 1992): 18.

Johnson, Angela. *Off Our Backs* 22 (December 1992): 13.

Kendall, Elaine. *Los Angeles Times*, November 15, 1991, E12.

Kim, David D. *Village Voice Literary Supplement* (September 10, 1991): S6.

Kirkus Reviews (August 15, 1991): 1034.

Lim, Shirley Geok-Lin. *San Francisco Chronicle*, September 29, 1991, REV8.

Mostow, Joshua S. *Canadian Literature* (Spring 1992): 174+.
Ms.. (November 1991): 76.
Multicultural Review 1 (January 1992): 47+.
Ott, Bill. *American Libraries* 23 (Spring 1992): 720.
Pool, Gail. *Houston Post*, November 17, 1991, C5.
Publishers Weekly (August 17, 1992): 498.
Rapport: West Coast Review of Books 16.4 (1992): 20.
Seaman, Donna. *Booklist* (October 15, 1991): 408.
Steinberg, Sybil. *Publishers Weekly* (August 23, 1991): 42.
Washington Post Book World (November 3, 1991): 10.

Adet Lin (also Tan Yun)
(1923–1971)

Jean Amato

BIOGRAPHY

Daughter of Dr. Lin Yu-tang, the prominent overseas Chinese writer and unofficial spokesperson for China in the 1930s and 1940s, Adet Lin was part of a group of highly educated, worldly, and upper-class Chinese American immigrant writers of her era whose works promoted China and its people to Western readers with moving and heroic stories of the Sino-Japanese War. Born in Amoy, China, in 1923, Adet was thirteen when she immigrated to the United States with her family.

Although she spent the majority of her life in the United States, Adet identified more with China (Ling 62). As a teenager, she was discontented with her safe and easy life in the United States while her homeland was being torn apart by the Sino-Japanese War. After attending Columbia University from 1941 to 1943, she joined the American Bureau for Medical Aid to China to serve in the Chinese army medical service in Kunming, China, from 1943 to 1946. Once back in the States, she remained politically active, working for the United States Information Service and the Voice of America.

MAJOR WORKS AND THEMES

At age sixteen, Adet and her sisters, Lin Tai-yi and Mei Mei, collaborated on a 1939 collection of unedited diary entries entitled *Our Family*, where they discussed family life and impressions of Europe, the United States, and China. While generally light in tone, the work addresses complex issues of war, patriotism, class, stereotypes, and racism with candid honesty. In these youthful entries, Adet's idealism, fervent patriotism, and romantic, yet solemn, tendencies clearly reveal themselves. In 1941 Adet, Mei Mei Lin, and Lin Tai-yi published a second autobiographical collection, *Dawn over Chungking*, which tells of their six-month visit to a small village in their homeland, where they were under constant danger of Japanese bombing raids. Surrounded by war's destruction, the text continually affirms a hope in humanity and "the birth of a new nation" (70). In 1940 Adet and Lin Tai-yi translated *Girl Rebel: The Autobiography of Hsieh Pingying with Extracts from New War Diaries*. This work provided Western readers with their first introduction to a Chinese woman warrior; it also roused the patriotism that compelled Adet to return to China.

Adet's experiences in war-torn China provided the background for her first novel, in 1943, *Flame from the Rock*, set in China during the Sino-Japanese War. The novel mixes "patriotic ardor and youthful idealism with a love story" between an unlikely pair (Ling 69). Through a fateful accident that almost takes her life, twenty-year-old Kuanpo Shen, a volunteer nurse from a scholarly family, is saved by a blood transfusion from the taciturn and coarse soldier Wang Tsai. The novel is framed by the patriotism of a war that brings the couple together to overcome class, education, and ideological differences and eventually takes their lives with a tragic ending. Eighteen years later, Adet published *The Milky Way and Other Chinese Folk Tales*. In 1970 she translated Tang dynasty poems in *Flower Shadows*.

CRITICAL RECEPTION

Amy Ling points out that in *Dawn over Chunking*, the Japanese air raids, with their "socially leveling and community-strengthening effect," reconnected Adet to her homeland and reaffirmed simple truths (60–61). In *Dawn over Chunking*, Adet's undying patriotism reveals itself in her certainty that "victory should emerge from this suffering and courage (112). Adet also questions her own privileged position in a war that always "demanded more from the poor" (112).

The *Saturday Review of Literature* praises *Dawn over Chunking's* role in bringing the vivid realities of war to the American reader (Maybon). In a similar fashion, a *Book Week* reviewer of *Flame from the Rock* notes that with its realistic portrayal of peasant life it "should do much to develop sympathetic understanding for this ally nation" (Litten). While acknowledging the novel's somber tone, reviewers from the *New York Times* (Maher) and *New Yorker* (Rev.) praise *Flame from the Rock's* authentic portrayal a youthful patriotism. A few reviews convey a patronizing tone that seems overly centered on the curious novelty of the author's age, ethnicity, and English-language ability. Amy Ling points out that many reviews of *Flame from the Rock* also praise its unique blending of romanticism and social realism (69). Ling goes on to claim that the protagonist's romantic bond to the soldier, Wang Tsai, "can be read as an allegory of Adet Lin's love for the land of her birth; backward and stolid though it may be, the blood bond is there in her veins and it is ineradicable" (70). Ling also reads the novel as a criticism of those from Adet's own intellectual and privileged class background who, although more removed from the bloody struggle, might still look down upon coarse Chinese soldiers such as Wang Tsai, upon whose strength rests the fate of the nation and its people (70).

BIBLIOGRAPHY

Works by Adet Lin/Tan Yun

Novel

Flame from the Rock. New York: John Day, 1943.

Autobiographies

(And Lin Tai-yi and Mei Mei Lin). *Our Family*. Ed. LinTai-yi. New York: John Day, 1939.
(And Lin Tai-yi and Mei Mei Lin). *Dawn over Chungking*. New York: Van Rees Press, 1941.

Nonfiction

The Milky Way and Other Chinese Folk Tales. New York: Harcourt, Brace, 1961.

Translations

(And Lin Tai-yi). *Girl Rebel: The Autobiography of Hsieh Pingying with Extracts from Her New War Diaries*. New York: John Day, 1940.
Flower Shadows: 40 Poems from the Tang Dynasty. [Tangshih Hsüani]. Taipei: Taiwan Chunghua Shuchü, 1970.

Studies of Adet Lin/Tan Yun

Bisson, T. A. Rev. of *Dawn over Chunking*. *Saturday Review of Literature* (April 5, 1941): 20.
Ling, Amy. *Between Worlds: Women Writers of Chinese Ancestry*. New York: Pergamon Press, 1990.
Litten, F. N. Rev. of *Flame from the Rock*. *Book Week* (November 28, 1943): 6.
Maher, Catherine. Rev. of *Flame from the Rock*. *New York Times*, November 21, 1943, 34.
Maybon, Richie, Rev. of *Flame from the Rock*. *Saturday Review of Literature* (January, 1944): 20.
Rev. of *Flame from the Rock*. *New Yorker* (November 20, 1943): 108.

Steven C. Lo
(1949–   )

Jeffrey Partridge

BIOGRAPHY

Similar to the narrator of his 1989 novel, Steven C. Lo moved to Lubbock, Texas, from his native Taiwan to pursue graduate studies in business and eventually founded a consulting firm specializing in joint-ventures with China. Lo obtained a B.B.A. from the National University of Taiwan (1972), subsequently pursued graduate studies at Texas Technological University, and completed his M.S. at Northwestern University in 1974. Since 1979 Lo has represented major U.S. and Asian companies in negotiating, developing, executing, and managing a wide range of major business projects in China.

The sardonic edge to his novel's fictional world appears in contrast with Lo's actual business achievements. His impressive track record in Sino-American business relations has made him a sought-after lecturer on the subject. He has served as visiting professor in a Shanghai university and is active in numerous Chinese and American business associations.

Lo's interest in writing extends back to grade school and university years in Taiwan. He won prizes for his Chinese writing exercises and served as editor of class journals in the university. This early interest, coupled with a lack of confidence in English, prompted him to take up a creative writing course offered by a community college in Texas. Lo developed his skills by writing stories and poems in his spare time. Although *The Incorporation of Eric Chung* is his only major publication to date, Lo remains active as a writer and is a member of the Authors' Guild.

Lo's wife is a Texas Tech graduate and, like him, an immigrant from Taiwan. They live in Texas with their three sons.

MAJOR WORK AND THEMES

The Incorporation of Eric Chung is structured on two plots, or "incorporations." One is the tale of Eric Chung as a young Taiwanese national adjusting to American university life and the peculiarities of Texan culture. In this, the novel fits well within the *Liu-hsueh-shen wen-hsueh* (or, overseas student literature) genre of Taiwanese immigrant texts, with the significant exception that it is written in English. The foibles of cross-cultural blunders and miscommunication are a humorous veneer, under which lies a subtext of lonely, desperate anxiety.

The other plot is the story of Eric Chung as a budding businessman seeking his fortune in American business. The humor of this plot lies in the absurdity of Eric's situation. He is sucked into, and soon made president of, a nonviable company aimed at doing business with communist China in the 1970s. The business is losing millions of dollars a year for the parent company, despite the promise of a big payoff through a budding (but doomed) relationship with a group of Chinese delegates. Eventually, Eric is ordered to fire all his employees except his secretary and move to an empty office until his fate is decided. From here, Eric tells his story.

While it would not be inaccurate to describe these plots (as most reviewers did) as parallel or interweaving, it is perhaps more interesting to see the "business incorporation" as a parable of the "immigrant incorporation." Eric is valued by the parent company only for his status as a cultural representative. His inexperience in business and his ignorance of mainland China and communist bureaucracy do not impede his speedy rise to the presidency. What matters is that he looks Chinese and speaks Chinese. In short, Eric's cultural identity legitimates the company, and he is therefore no more than symbolically useful. Thus, what appears to be perfect assimilation—Chinese American rises to the leadership of an international company—is, in fact, cultural tokenism and cold-hearted manipulation. Eric's physical alienation from the parent corporation, while still technically a member of that corporation, is indeed a parable of the Asian immigrant's alienation in a society that incorporates, but never embraces, that immigrant.

Language—its appropriation, usage, and codedness—plays significantly in the novel. In the first chapter, Eric admits his uneasiness with the English language as he looks back on his early experiences with business communication: "English hadn't become *easy* for me at the time (to my great disappointment), despite it was already my fifth year here in the States" (3). Mistakes like "despite it was" occur only occasionally throughout the novel, prompting some reviewers to see them as textual flaws (see Critical Reception). However, in this case, the "mistake" is highly ironic if read as intentional. To say the language "hadn't become *easy*" for him implies that he believes himself to be highly proficient now. This, of course, is inherently mocked in the dependent clause where the ungrammatical "despite it was" appears. In this way, the text reveals a dialogic interplay of the past Eric Chung and the present Eric Chung, each, to use Bakhtin's idea, "ironizing" the other.

This dialogic interplay is complicated by another: the appropriation of the immigrant story by the cold language of business. In the preceding passage, Eric explains that what he will express about his experience in America could be related in a concise telegraph, the kind he learned to write as a businessman: "COLDWELL COMPANY-EXECUTIVE, ERIC CHUNG, REMOVED FROM JOB, STRIPPED OF DUTIES, SOON TO BE CANNED" (3). Eric then suggests a few alterations to this text to make it even more concise and businesslike: "COLDWELL COMPANY EXECUTIVE REMOVED FROM JOB/SOON TO BE CANNED" (3). The first version reduces one man's life to fifteen words in the interest of concise, businesslike communication. The "improved" version reduces it to ten words by removing the man's personal identity—his name. Business-speak unmasks the meaninglessness and loneliness of Eric's immigrant life, while the act of reduction unmasks the coldness of business culture.

In short, alienation, manipulation, cultural commodification, and the utter strangeness of the Asian immigrant's life are themes that Lo makes central not only to the novel's narrative but to the very language of that narrative.

CRITICAL RECEPTION

The Incorporation was reviewed by more than thirty publications when it was released by Algonquin Books in 1989, including the *Los Angeles Times*, *Fortune*, and *Mother Jones*. Most of the reviews were favorable, with even the more critical ones expressing respect for Lo's first novelistic effort. For instance, Phillip Lopate, writing for *Mother Jones*, calls the characters "lightweight" and bemoans a lack of plot tension, among other criticisms. Yet, his overall impression is that the novel is "likable and amusing" and that Lo "demonstrated plenty of comic talent and sociological acumen in this first novel."

Reviewers varied in their response to what the reviewer for the *Dallas Morning-News* called "curiosities of grammar and punctuation" (Compton). Some suggested that this was a flaw. Most, however, saw certain quirks of the prose as appropriate for an immigrant narrator like Eric Chung. "I passed in flying colors" is an example from the novel that Lopate highlights to show the "color" of Eric's use of the English language.

The novel's humor featured largely in its reviews, eliciting descriptions like "charming," "entertaining," and "amusing." Former *Fortune* editor Wyndham Robertson called it "wry and canny" (qtd. on dust jacket), and Amy Tan, in a letter to the publisher, says she found herself "laughing out loud" (qtd. on dust jacket). While some saw the humor as pointing to darker insights, others seemed unable to get past it. The reviewer for the *Library Journal*, for instance, claimed that *The Incorporation* was "less dramatic than the recent best seller *The Joy*

Luck Club, but its quiet humor is appealing" (Wilhelm; emphasis added). Some of the less savvy reviews seemed to see no deeper than the "funny look at cultural differences" (Herring).

The preoccupation with *The Incorporation*'s humor in its reception and marketing came under criticism in Carolyn See's review in the *Los Angeles Times*. In a highly positive review (she calls it "a wonderful, wonderful novel"), See asks whether the novel was being misread and misrepresented. Calling *The Incorporation* "heartbreaking and profound," See denotes the alienation and wastefulness expressed through the lives of the immigrant characters who are "cut loose in the meaninglessness of America." Keith S. Graham of the *Atlanta Journal* shared See's view, saying, "For all the book's lighthearted style, Chung's gloomy but ultimately disturbing view is effectively presented."

Given its mostly positive reception and thematic/linguistic richness, it is surprising that *The Incorporation* has been so quiet in the works of Asian American scholarship.

BIBLIOGRAPHY

Work by Steven C. Lo

The Incorporation of Eric Chung. Chapel Hill, NC: Algonquin, 1989.

Studies of Steven C. Lo

Compton, Robert. Rev. of *The Incorporation*. *Dallas Morning News*, November 6, 1989, 5C.

Deutschman, Alan. Rev. of *The Incorporation*. *Fortune* (February 26, 1990): 113.

Graham, Keith S. Rev. of *The Incorporation*. *Atlanta Journal*, October 29, 1989, N8.

Herring, Neill. Rev. of *The Incorporation*. *Macon Telegraph and News*, December 24, 1989: B2.

Lopate, Phillip. Rev. of *The Incorporation*. *Mother Jones* (December 1989): 45.

Rev. of *The Incorporation*. *Publishers Weekly* (August 18, 1989): 51.

See, Carolyn. Rev. of *The Incorporation*. *Los Angeles Times*, October 30, 1989, E8.

Wilhelm, Albert E. Rev. of *The Incorporation*. *Library Journal* (October 15, 1989): 103.

Bette Bao Lord
(1938–   )

Jean Amato

BIOGRAPHY

Bette Bao Lord, novelist and international activist, was born in Shanghai, China, in 1938. She immigrated to the United States with her family in 1946, during China's civil war. She grew up in Brooklyn, New York, and New Jersey and later attended Tufts University. She received an M.A. from the Fletcher School of Law and Diplomacy, where she met her husband, Winston Lord. They have two children.

Lord served on the boards of many international organizations such as the Asia Foundation and the National Commission on U.S.–China Relations. In 1993 she was named chair of the Freedom Foundation. She received a number of honorary doctorates and distinguished awards, including the American Women for International Understanding Award, the United States Information Agency Award, and membership into the International Women's Hall of Fame.

In 1946 the Nationalist government sent her father and his family to the United States. Assuming they would be gone for less than two years, they left their infant daughter. San San, with family in China. Once the People's Republic of China (PRC) was established, and the United States severed diplomatic relations, they were unable to return home. Thus, San San was separated from her family for seventeen years. In 1964, at age twenty-three. Lord wrote *Eighth Moon* her sister San San's account of her life in the PRC from 1946 to 1961, when she was finally reunited with her family in America.

MAJOR WORKS AND THEMES

In 1981 Lord wrote her first novel, *Spring Moon*, based on her visits to the PRC in the 1970s and the stories of her ancestors that she grew up with. *Spring*

Moon follows five generations of a prominent family from the late nineteenth century through 1927, with an Epilogue set in the 1970s. Through the eyes of Spring Moon, a strong-willed daughter raised in the traditional roles for women, it attempts to bear witness to the political and social upheavals of modernizing China on both a personal and public scale.

In 1984 Lord published a children's book, *The Year of the Boar and Jackie Robinson*, a fictionalized account of her own first year in America. While in Beijing from 1985 to 1989, where her husband served as the U.S. ambassador, Bette Bao Lord served as a CBS special news consultant for the 1989 Tiananmen Square movement. In 1990 Lord published *Legacies: A Chinese Mosaic*, a diverse collection of first-person accounts of PRC citizens from the last ten years that reveal personal and sociopolitical currents that led up to the Tiananmen incident.

Lord's 1964 novel, *Eighth Moon*, centers around an alliance between three characters: Steel Hope, heir to a once-powerful family; Mountain Pine, his disabled and intellectual servant; and a poor grave keeper's daughter posing as a boy named Firecrackers. In an idealistic, patriotic pact that begins during the Japanese occupation and survives fifty years of revolutionary chaos, loss, and triumph, the novel traces the social/political upheavals from the Cultural Revolution to Tiananmen Square that the characters face. They call themselves "Brothers of the Middle Heart," vowing to defend their country and each other to the end. Enmeshed in a love triangle, their loyalty to each other is repeatedly tested by the ongoing waves of revolution, reform, and violence of the times.

CRITICAL RECEPTION

Amy Ling points out that Lord's novel *Spring Moon* paints a China typical of Chinese Americans who were not recent immigrants [97]. "Theirs is a China recollected from memory or never known personally, but pieced together from the reminiscences of elders or from romanticized images prevalent in the West" (97).

Both Charlotte Curtis and Wei-hsiung Kitty Wu point out that Lord's narrative form is modeled after classical Chinese novels, such as *Dream of the Red Chamber*. This classical flavor, along with Lord's uncontextualized English translations of exotic-sounding Chinese names, may have the effect of unintentionally reinforcing an Orientalizing nostalgia for a timeless exotic China, one that "serves as an indelible reminder of a way of life that has very nearly vanished" (Curtis). Ronald Nevans' review in *Saturday Review* is an example of how readers may focus only on the novel's exotic portrayal of traditional Chinese life and leave out its modern and political aspects. "Through *Spring Moon*," writes Nevans, "we see the beauty of the inner courtyard society. But we see, too, how Chinese society's rigid etiquette hobbles the lives of its women as surely as their bound feet." *Spring Moon*, which took Lord six years to write, remained on the best-seller list for thirty-one weeks, a time when narratives that seemed to lament a lost glory for a Chinese past and voice discontent toward the stark realities of life in communist China were popular.

Many reviewers comment on both novels' rich character portrayals and dramatic movement through modern Chinese history. Jan Alexander's review of *The Middle Heart* calls it a "revolutionary epic" or romantic "multi-generational saga" with an "appealing cinematic quality" that "continues a genre made popular by Jun Chang's *Wild Swans* and Anchee Min's *Red Azalea*."

BIBLIOGRAPHY

Works by Bette Bao Lord

Novels

Eighth Moon. New York: Harper and Row, 1964.
Spring Moon. New York: Harper and Row, 1981.
The Year of the Boar and Jackie Robinson. New York: HarperCollins, 1984.
The Middle Heart. New York: Alfred A. Knopf, 1996.

Nonfiction

Legacies: A Chinese Mosaic. New York: Alfred A. Knopf, 1990.

Studies of Bette Bao Lord

Alexander, Jan. "Casualties of History: The Middle Heart by Bette Bao Lord." *Far Eastern Economic Review-Interactive Edition* (May 30, 1996). *http://www.feer. com/Restricted/china/bkb530.html* (March 3, 1999)
Curtis, Charlotte. Rev. of *Spring Moon*. *New York Times Book Review* (October 25 1981): 15.
Fox, Mary Virginia. *Bette Bao Lord: Novelist and Chinese Voice for Change*. Chicago: Children's Press, 1993.
Guleff, E. B. Rev. of *Spring Moon*. *Library Journal* (October 15, 1981): 2049.
Lamb, Brian. Interview. *Booknotes*. C-SPAN. May 27, 1990. *http://www.booknotes.org/ transcripts/50013.html* (March 3, 1999)
Ling, Amy. *Between Worlds: Women Writers of Chinese Ancestry*. New York: Pergamon Press, 1990.
Nevans, Ronald. Rev. of *Spring Moon*. *Saturday Review* (October 1981): 75.
Wu, Wei-hsiung Kitty. "Cultural Ideology and Aesthetic Choices: A Study of Three Works by Chinese American Women: Diana Chang, Bette Bao Lord, and Maxine H. Kingston." Diss., University of Maryland, 1989.

Anchee Min
(1957–)

Shunzhu Wang

BIOGRAPHY

Anchee Min was born into a teacher's family on January 14, 1957, in Shanghai, China. Like most people of her generation, she "was raised on the teachings of Mao and the operas of Madam Mao, Comrade Jiang Qing" (*Red* 3). Red was her color, and the tough heroines of the revolutionary operas were her role models. Being the oldest of the four children, she began baby-sitting her siblings when she herself was only five. At the age of ten, when the Cultural Revolution was under way, she became a leader in her school's Little Red Guard. By twelve she was so well versed in Mao's quotations that she was able to use them cunningly in a speech of self-criticism that saved her mother from being condemned. But with this audacity and "political awareness," she also denounced one of her favorite teachers as an enemy of the proletarian dictatorship.

In 1974 Min was sent along with many other city youths to Red Fire Farm, where they were supposed to become peasants. The farm was administered much like a military camp. Living the disciplined life of a soldier, Min worked in fields from five in the morning till nine at night. Here, despite knowing that it is a crime punishable by death, she fell in love with the commander of her company, whom she admired as a living opera heroine. When the Shanghai Film Studio came looking for potential actors and actresses, she was luckily chosen and soon had the rare chance of playing the lead role in *Red Azalea*, a propaganda film about the life of Madam Mao. Her lucky star fell, however, with the downfall of the "Gang of Four" following Mao's death in 1976. She lost her lead actress position and was demoted to set clerk for six years before finally coming to the United States under the sponsorship of Joan Chen, her studio friend who had come to America to seek an acting career.

Min attended the Art Institute of Chicago from 1985 to 1991, earning a B.F.A. and M.F.A. there. Before being accepted as a degree-seeking student, however, she had to improve her English. Failure to do so within six months would mean deportation from the country. While working at several odd jobs, as waitress, assistant plumber, delivery messenger, and baby-sitter, to support herself, she took English-language courses in earnest. What she wrote for English-as-a-second-language (ESL) classes formed the basis for her first book, *Red Azalea*, an immediate hit memoir that won her the Quality Paperback Club's 1994 non-fiction award. Her second book, *Katherine*, came out a year later in 1995.

Min married Qigu Jiang in 1991, an artist from Shanghai who came to study at the Art Institute of Chicago and became a professor there upon graduation. They had a daughter but got divorced in 1994. Min now lives with her daughter alternately in Shanghai and Los Angeles.

MAJOR WORKS AND THEMES

The thematic concern of both *Red Azalea* and *Katherine* is the psychic wounds the Cultural Revolution inflicted upon the Chinese people. Both seem to convey the message that the depth and width of the wounds are beyond measure and that Maoist revolutionary discourse has largely dehumanized the entire nation, leaving its people deformed and perverted.

Red Azalea is classified as autobiography, but it might be more appropriately called a "fictional autobiography." As some critics have rightly noted, while the first and second parts of the book are plausible as accounts of Min's painful experience of coming-of-age during the Cultural Revolution, the third part "suggests something approaching fantasy" (Evans 852). In the first part, we see an innocent teenager girl corrupted by a crazy environment completely devoid of human affection. Through the telling of her lesbian relationship with Yan and of Little Green's excessive show of femininity in the second part, Min tells how the official suppression results in an exaggerated and distorted expression of desire and human relations. The third part treats her relationship with the mystified and feminized "supervisor." Here Min shows that the psychological trauma extends to the victims as well as the beneficiaries of the revolution.

Min's second book, *Katherine*, is a novel that tells "the story of a traumatized nation through the desperate lives of the students" (MacDougall) of a young American who comes to teach English in China in the early 1980s. "The picture of China as a country that has lost all morality" (MacDougall 23) is made all the bleaker through the cultural clashes sparked by the appearance of the energetic, innocent, and warmhearted American named Katherine in the midst of her disillusioned, cold, and manipulative Chinese students. As Zebra, the student narrator, contemplates: "Do you [Katherine] know that just by standing in front of us you show us how deformed we are?" (*Katherine* 12). Through *Katherine*, Min shows that although the Cultural Revolution is officially over, its catastrophic effect upon the Chinese mind is far from being over. It has left the

Chinese people psychologically so deeply warped that they are still living in the mental prisons constructed for them and by themselves.

Indeed, Min believes that while the Chinese people are victims of the Cultural Revolution, many of them (including people such as the teenager Min and the disillusioned Zebra) are also victimizers. The Cultural Revolution and the repressive cultural tradition have turned China into "a land that produced evil personalities" (*Katherine* 182). Both *Red Azalea* and *Katherine* embody Min's conviction that this "Chinese shame" must be confronted honestly and boldly before we can envision any positive changes. The real hope and possibility for such changes, as Min sees it, obviously lie with China's willingness to embrace Western morals and values.

One aesthetic device worth noting is the narrative point of view. On the surface, both stories are narrated by a Chinese insider. But the "objectiveness" with which the Chinese mind is examined betrays a "subjective" view from an Americanized Min. As Min honestly admits: "My American education helped me write the book" and "get under the skin" of the matter (O'Hara 16).

CRITICAL RECEPTION

Like other books about contemporary Chinese politics, such as *Wild Swan* and *Life and Death in Shanghai*, Min's books caused quite a buzz in America as well as other Western countries. (Interestingly, though, Chinese American scholars and critics have been silent.) While both *Red Azalea* and *Katherine* have drawn numerous reviews, most of which are positive, the first is generally considered the better of the two.

While almost all the reviews sing *Red Azalea*'s praise, not many provide valuable comments. An exception is Orville Schell's review, which maintains that although Min's "language is sometimes imprecise and confusing," it is nevertheless "a small masterpiece" (282). Judy Polumbaum's review, although a bit overboard in its praise, is perhaps the most valuable and substantial one. She reads its theme as "less a manifesto against rigid sexual mores than a study in the ways people construct, deconstruct and reconstruct mental prisons for each other and themselves" (3). Min's style is regarded as "almost Whitman-esque," even though it "startles with slightly off-key phrases, beckons with unlikely analogies, endears with minor grammatical violations," whereas "her obstreperous declarations and incongruous juxtapositions work" (3). Less substantial, but worth mentioning, is Rhoda Koenig's review, which regards the simple declarative sentences (of which almost the entire book is composed) as "a style that suits the brutality of Min's story as well as her own childlike frankness and ferocity."

Elizabeth Ward is one of the few who have only positive things to say about *Katherine*. She praises it for its "simple, but effective structure," then makes an argument that "what is admirable about Katherine . . . is Min's refusal to make her warring opposites completely black and white, the 'bad' Chinese vs. the 'good' American." This argument, however, is not well supported in her review. Most reviewers are more critical of *Katherine*. Sybil Steinberg, who holds that it "is less successful on a number of fronts than her outstanding memoir, *Red Azalea*," finds it sensuality "forced," its characters lacking "the tight focus," its writing "off-key," and its climax "rushed." This kind of harsh, yet insightful, comment is echoed in Sarah Smith's review. She considers the novel as having several flaws—Katherine is "improbably naïve and ignorant of Chinese mores," "the sway of Min's romantic language and the perniciously hopeful influence of Katherine wreck the novel's finer points," and the narrative "is marred by . . . infelicitous enthusiasms" of flirtations with America. Thus, she concludes that this "is a guileless book about a far from guileless time, and a difficult story, too simply told." Smith is a bit too harsh, but her points are well made. Beverly Lowry, who believes Min exhibits in *Red Azalea* an "amazing ability to see her own life within the framework of history and still provide meticulous emotional and sensory details," is also less enthusiastic about *Katherine*: She thinks that Katherine, "the visiting professor is a mess," and Zebra is a "dandy" narrator who is too "repetitive." *Red Azalea* "brought us news and . . . touched our hearts," she writes, while *Katherine* only "brings us news."

Studies of Min in forms other than book review are very rare. An-chi Lin did her master's thesis on Min's use of Chinese metaphors and idioms in *Red Azalea*. In addition to that, Wendy Somerson's "Under the Mosquito Net: Space and Sexuality in *Red Azalea*" is perhaps the single most important and valuable piece of literary criticism on Min thus far. Examining the book in a transnational frame, Somerson gives an enlightening analysis of the issues concerning the production and reception of the book. She argues that, with this transnational and feminist narrative, Min "disrupts both U.S. Orientalist discourse about the Cultural Revolution and Chinese masculinist national discourse," but, on the other hand, "on the level of textual production, Min has to negotiate with Orientalist construction of China to produce her text within a 'Western' frame" (100, 104). The latter point perhaps also partly explains why Chinese American scholars and critics have remained silent in the midst of Min's popularity.

BIBLIOGRAPHY

Works by Anchee Min

Memoir

Red Azalea. New York: Pantheon, 1994.

Novel

Katherine. New York: Riverhead Books, 1995.

Studies of Anchee Min

Evans, Harriet. Rev. of *Red Azalea*. *The China Quarterly* 139 (September 1994): 852–23.

Koenig, Rhoda. Rev. of *Red Azalea*. *New York* 27.5 (January 31, 1994): 63.

Lin, An-Chi. "The Figurative Languages of Anchee Min: Cross-Cultural Meaning and Schemata in the English Prose of a Non-Native Writer." Master's thesis, University of California, 1996.

Lowry, Beverly. Rev. of *Katherine*. *Los Angeles Times*, July 30, 1995, 11.

MacDougall, Colina. "Culture Clashes." Rev. of *Katherine*. *Times Educational Supplement* 4830 (October 27, 1995): 23.

O'Hara, Delia. "Author Anchee Min's Book Weaves Her Story and History of China." *Chinatown News*, December 18, 1994, 16.

Polumbaum, Judy. "The Cultural Contradictions of Communism." Rev. of *Red Azalea*. *The Women's Review of Books* 11:8 (May 1994): 1–3.

Rev. of *Red Azalea*. *Contemporary Literary Criticism* Vol. 86, (1994): 83–97.

Schell, Orville. "Stolen Kisses." Rev. of *Red Azalea*. *Vogue* 184.3 (March 1994): 278, 282–83.

Shapiro, Judith. "Counterrevolutionary Sex." Rev. of *Red Azalea*. *New York Times* Book Review (February 27, 1994): 11.

Smith, Sarah A. "Interesting Times." Rev. of *Katherine*. *New Statesman and Society* 8.367 (August 25, 1995): 33.

Somerson, Wendy. "Under the Mosquito Net: Space and Sexuality in *Red Azalea*." *College Literature* 24.1 (February 1998): 98–115.

Steinberg, Sybil. Rev. of *Katherine*. *Publishers Weekly* 242 (March 13, 1995): 58.

Wilson, Kathleen. "Interview with Anchee Min." *Contemporary Literary Criticism* Vol. 86, Detroit: Gale, 1994: 94–97.

Ward, Elizabeth. "Anchee Min's Quiet Stiletto Stabs at Modern China." Rev. of *Katherine*. *Japan Times*, March 12, 1996, 16.

Yang, T. H. "I ko chung kuo tu che k'an Min Anchee ti ch'ang hsial shu: Hung Tu Chuan." *Chinese Daily News*, January 28, 1996, Sec. C: 12.

Rohinton Mistry
(1952–   )

Bindu Malieckal

BIOGRAPHY

Rohinton Mistry was born in Bombay in 1952. He spent his childhood and some of his adult life there, and as a result, Mistry makes Bombay the locale for his fiction. In fact, in an interview, Mistry clarifies why he writes about India rather than Canada: "I am still more concerned with the lives of those children in the old world" (Hancock 144). Mistry immigrated to Canada in 1975. He started to write short stories in 1983, and in 1985 he won two Hart House literary prizes and *Canadian Fiction Magazine*'s Annual Contributor's Prize. Mistry published his first work of fiction, a collection of short stories titled *Tales from Firozsha Baag*, in Canada and England in 1987. The volume was later published as *Swimming Lessons and Other Stories from Firozsha Baag* in the United States in 1989. Mistry's first novel, *Such a Long Journey*, was published in 1991 and earned the Governor General's Award, the Commonwealth Writers Prize for Best Book, and the W. H. Smith/*Books in Canada* First Novel Award. Mistry's second novel is *A Fine Balance*, published in 1996. Presently, he is working on a third novel, which will be published by Alfred A. Knopf in the United States and by Faber and Faber in England.

MAJOR WORKS AND THEMES

Swimming Lessons and Other Stories from Firozsha Baag is a collection of eleven tales set in a Bombay apartment complex that is chiefly inhabited by Parsis or Zoroastrians. To an extent, the stories are self-contained, but Mistry interlocks the narratives, allowing intersections of ideas and characters. The volume shows the progression of time from the first story to the last—about ten years pass between "Auspicious Occasion" and "Swimming Lessons"—so the intermediate accounts relate the developments, disintegrations, and deaths of certain characters during the period. Each story deals with a unique motif, such as Dr. Mody's disappointment with his rapscallion son Pesi in "The Collectors" or Khorshedbai's descent to madness in "The Paying Guests"; however, the unifying theme of *Swimming Lessons and Other Stories from Firozsha Baag* concerns the dilemma of choosing between two opposing sides: between the past and the present, afterlife and earthly existence, parents and lovers, hate and guilt, Canada and India.

In "Exercisers," Jehangir Bulsara's dilemma is his inability to choose between his parents and his girlfriend, Behroze. His parents, particularly his mother, hate Behroze and suspect her intentions. For her part, Behroze finds Jehangir's parents controlling and unfair. At his parents' insistence, Jehangir visits a holy man, who confirms that he is trapped between loyalty and rebellion, conformity and freedom. In "Condolence Visit," Daulat Mirza has lost her ailing husband, Minocher, to sickness and is coping with the loss, but Najamai's frequent reminders on how to conduct death rituals stunt Daulat's progress. The conflict comes to a head when Daulat decides to sell Minocher's traditional headdress, or *pugree*, a choice that Najamai opposes. For Daulat, the Parsi bridegroom who wishes to buy the *pugree* symbolizes rejuvenation in the cycle of life; for Najamai, the sale of the *pugree* signifies a premature end to Daulat's mourning: "in the middle an embarrassed young man pulled two ways, like Minocher Mirza's soul, in a tug-of-war between two worlds" (75). In "The Squatter," Sarosh immigrates to Canada, Anglicizes his name to "Sid," and vows to return to India in ten years if he cannot fully assimilate. After disastrous attempts to use a Western commode (Sarosh is dependent on the Indian style of squatting for defecation), he returns to India, broken, confused, and conscious of his hybrid identity as both Indian and Canadian. Sarosh-Sid's story shows the dualism that develops from immigration and cultural conflict. Likewise, in "Lend Me Your Light," Kersi Boyce relocates to Canada but considers the move in the context of two disparate events: his brother Percy's selfless assistance of Indian farmers victimized by corrupt moneylenders and his friend Jamshed's constant depreciation of India and pursuit of materialism in the United States. Kersi clearly prefers Percy's charity to Jamshed's crassness, but since he lives in Canada, he must negotiate a middle ground.

A fascinating aspect of the book is Mistry's comments on storytelling through Nariman Hansotia, the Firozsha Baag raconteur who recounts the fantastical adventures and exploits of one Savukshaw, and Kersi, one of Hansotia's young listeners, whose medium is the written word. The last story from the volume, "Swimming Lessons," describes how Kersi, now living in an apartment complex in Toronto, publishes a set of stories about Firozsha Baag. Kersi sends his work to his parents in Bombay, who after reading the tales, discuss strategies of writing, artistic distance, and fiction versus nonfiction. Hansotia's sagas and Kersi's chronicles add to the palimpsest that is *Swimming Lessons and Other*

Tales from Firozsha Baag. Like Dr. Mody's prized, shimmering, Spanish dancing lady stamp, Mistry's short stories are the ultimate product of a finely honed
craft converging the real and the imagined.

Mistry's first novel, *Such a Long Journey,* narrows its scope and focuses on
one family in Khodadad Building, also a Parsi development. The protagonist is
Gustad Noble, a middle-aged and devout Parsi whose decency contrasts with
the decadence of the Indian government in 1971, the scene of the novel. The
historical context covers West Pakistani aggression in East Pakistan, the Refugee
Relief Tax, Indira Gandhi's corruption, and the general shortage of amenities,
such as water, that defines postcolonial India. The title describes Gustad's personal struggle to reach beyond the disappointments of his life: his father's in-
solvency, his son Sohrab's refusal to attend the prestigious Indian Institute of
Technology, the disappearance and death of his friend Major Jimmy Bilimoria,
the demise of another confidant, Dinshawji, and his daughter Roshan's chronic
illness. Gustad contrasts his problems with wistful memories of a prosperous
childhood, of his grandmother's fattened chicken dinners, of creating lasting
furniture with his grandfather, of venturing into the world of his father's bookstore, and of soulful vacations to hilly Matheran.

In keeping with the discrepancy between Gustad's past and present, *Such a
Long Journey* contains symbols of melancholy and joy. The blackout paper that
Gustad preserves on the apartment windows denotes his depression. He posi-
tioned the paper during the Indochina War of 1962 but retains it past usefulness
because the artificial darkness comforts and represents him. Another symbol of
Gustad's gloom is his weak hip, which he obtained after saving Sohrab's life
during a traffic accident. While Madhiwalla Bonesetter, an unconventional doctor with magical hands and mysterious remedies, healed the injury, Gustad's
lingering limp indicates that Bonesetter cannot cure enduring anguish. A black
wall that separates the compound from the busy street also signifies Gustad's
despair. Passersby use the structure as a public latrine, causing the proliferation
of mosquitoes that plague Gustad's ground-floor apartment. Gustad stops the
wall's defamation by commissioning an artist to draw pictures of religious figures on the structure. The wall transforms from an icon of depravity to a representation of India's secularism. Gustad finds temporary succor also from other
artistic/spiritual endeavors: his grandfather's sturdy and fine furniture, literary
masterpieces reminiscent of his father's collection, and the observance of Parsi
customs, such as the recitation of *kusti* prayers every morning.

Apart from Gustad Noble, a crucial character in *Such a Long Journey* is
Tehmul-Lungraa, who represents both Gustad's damnation and his salvation.
Like Gustad, Tehmul has a hip injury, but while Gustad's accident left only a
limp, Tehmul is physically and mentally crippled. Gustad sees Tehmul as a more
unfortunate version of himself, so he treats Tehmul like a son and with gentle-
ness. Gustad and Tehmul's lives parallel each other in their respective secret
dealings. Bilimoria involves Gustad, against his will, in a Research and Analysis
Wing (RAW) plot designed by the crooked Indira Gandhi, while Gustad's wife,

Dilnavaz, and her reclusive friend, Miss Kutpitia, initiate the innocent Tehmul in their dangerous, superstitious rites. Gustad and Tehmul's fates diverge during a confrontation between the municipality, which wants to destroy the wall of all religions to widen the road, and a *morcha*, or procession of people disgruntled with the municipality's mediocre maintenance of roadside gutters. In the midst of the melee, Tehmul sustains a fatal head injury and unwittingly becomes the agent of Gustad's salvation. Just as Bilimoria carried Gustad to Bonesetter's clinic after his accident, Gustad conveys Tehmul to his deathbed and prays and cries over his broken body. Tehmul's tragedy dissolves Gustad's disappointment and sorrow, all of which Tehmul embodied but which seem inconsequential in the light of Tehmul's death. Gustad's tears cleanse and signify rebirth, and he reconciles with Sohrab. Thus, at the end of the novel, Gustad removes the black-out paper from the windows and allows the sunlight into his dwelling for the first time in many years.

A submotif of *Such a Long Journey* is the war for space and legitimacy that takes place between regionalists and Bombay's immigrant populations. Gustad paints a grim picture of the conflict: "No future for minorities, with all these fascist Shiv Sena politics and Marathi language nonsense. It was going to be like the black people in America—twice as good as the white man to get half as much" (55). Politics, racism, and caste violence come to a head in Mistry's second novel, *A Fine Balance*. Dina Dalal (a widow), Ishvar and Omprakash Darji (low-caste cobblers turned tailors), and Maneck Kohla (a student) struggle to preserve a fine balance between survival and squalidness. Dina spends her life on the verge of economic ruin; Ishvar, Om, and their Chamaar family are always one step away from caste violence; Maneck Kohla's house balances on a hillside, as does his depression. During the Emergency of 1975, which forms the backdrop of the novel, even the government of India, led by Indira Gandhi, falters between democracy and absolutism. Valmik, a lawyer/ proofreader/ rally organizer whose name alludes to the ancient Sanskrit writer Valmiki, explains the dynamics of life among the unprivileged in India: "You have to maintain a fine balance between hope and despair. . . . In the end, it's a question of balance" (229). Maneck, in contrast, believes that "[e]verything ends badly" (330), and indeed, there are many tragedies in *A Fine Balance*.

Eventually, Dina loses her battle for independence and moves in with her abusive brother, and Maneck's despair drives him to commit suicide, but Ishvar and Om's story is the most tragic and most gripping of the novel, because catastrophes occur in their lives, as well as in the lives of their ancestors, with disturbing inevitability. Ishvar and Om belong to the Chamaar caste, a low caste of tanners and leather workers. The caste prejudices that their family faces through the generations are well documented. Ishvar's father, Dukhi Mochi, has listened to his own father narrate a litany of horrible, but established, injustices at the hands of upper-caste peoples. To save his sons from constraints, Dukhi apprentices Ishvar and Narayan with Ashraf, a friend who is a Muslim and a tailor. The close and mutually respectful relationships between Ashraf, Dukhi,

Ishvar, Narayan, and eventually Narayan's son, Om, defy generations of Hindu–Muslim violence. In fact, when a Hindu mob threatens to kill Ashraf and his family, Ishvar and Narayan bravely defend them; caste violence among Hindus, however, persists unabated. As Dukhi states, "Years pass, and nothing changes" (142). Indeed, when Narayan decides that he wants to vote, a right taken away by the high-caste Thakur Dharamsi, who traditionally rigged the elections, Dharamsi orders the torture and lynching of Narayan and then proceeds to murder the entire family. Dharamsi rationalizes the reasons for the murders: "What the ages had put together, Dukhi had dared to break asunder; he had turned cobblers into tailors, distorting society's timeless balance. Crossing the line of caste had to be punished with the utmost severity" (147). Though Ishvar and Om are spared their lives, several years later, Dharamsi arranges Om's castration, thereby demonstrating his dogmas of segregation.

Though Ishvar and Om migrate to Bombay in search of a better life, they come across similar cruelties, though the aggressor is the government, which uses the Emergency to sequester the poor of Bombay. Despite being trained tailors, Ishvar and Om struggle to find work and are forced to sleep in the streets, where they pay tribute to street tyrants like Beggarmaster, a nefarious individual who disfigures children in the name of "professional alterations," so that they will elicit sympathy and obtain more alms. In addition, the decrees of the Emergency make them targets for forced attendance at political rallies and the destruction of their hut as per the legislative plan to eliminate slums. For a brief time, Ishvar and Om find work with Dina and live comfortably in her flat along with Maneck, Dina's paying guest, but their tranquillity is transitory. Government agents force Ishwar to undergo sterilization. He develops complications, and his legs are amputated. By the end of the novel, Mistry describes how Ishvar, who had previously risen beyond caste limitations, faces a degrading future. An amputee who can no longer sew, he is relegated to moving himself around on a small, wheeled platform. Finally, Ishvar and Om are forced to forsake their hard-earned profession and become beggars.

In anticipation of the criticism that would follow regarding the relentless tragedies in Ishvar and Om's lives and his descriptions of beggars' realities, Mistry offers the following quotation from Balzac to introduce A Fine Balance, part of which reads, "And after you have read this story of great misfortunes, you will no doubt dine well, blaming the author for your own insensitivity, accusing him of wild exaggeration and flights of fancy. But rest assured: this tragedy is not fiction. All is true." While the actual characters are fictitious, each character exemplifies a type: the destitute widow; the family destroyed by caste war; the student agitator tortured and killed in the name of national security; the homeless. A Fine Balance narrates the historical events of the Emergency with accuracy, and Mistry's writing blends fact and fiction and attains a subtle, successful poise. Like the novel's Monkey-Man, a juggler and entertainer whose act involves tying two children to the end of a stick and balancing the switch on the tip of one finger, Mistry portrays poverty, political policies, corruption, and caste wars with sympathy and realism but without melodrama. It is no wonder, then, that *A Fine Balance* is a novel of tremendous power, compassion, and balance, a true epic.

CRITICAL RECEPTION

In an interview for *Canadian Fiction Magazine* in 1989, Mistry elucidates his philosophy of composition: "One must write for the sake of writing, to create good literature. The other things follow in a very natural way. I grew up in Bombay. Now I am here. I'm a writer. I am determined to write good literature. That is my primary concern. But to write well, I must write about what I know best. In a way, I automatically speak for my 'tribe' " (Hancock 145). Later, he adds, "I suppose I am a traditional writer. I am not trying to break new ground or pioneer new techniques" (148). To a question on archetypes, Mistry responds, "The Parsi characters in my stories, and their dreams, ambitions, and fears are as accessible to the Western reader as the Indian reader. The universalities of the story are sufficient" (147). Mistry conveys his conviction that any good story has worldwide appeal and that literary pursuits are vital in "A Fable of Lost Dreams," a speech that he gave upon being awarded an honorary doctorate from the University of Ottawa. In the fable, Mistry implies that creative writing, which he compares to dreams and to "having a glimpse of paradise" (20), is enriching not only for authors but also for readers. Of federal cutbacks on the arts, Mistry predicts, "Without dreams, people perish" (20).

To be sure, the importance that Mistry bestows on fiction corresponds to the attention literary critics grant Mistry's creations. Many analyses single out Mistry's portrayal of the Parsi community. Keith Garebian heralds *Swimming Lessons and Other Stories from Firozsha Baag* as "the first significant collection of short fiction that expresses the Parsi sensibility. Mistry's apartment complex of Firozsha Baag is but a microcosm of Indian life, but, more particularly, (as a Parsi colony) it is a microcosm of a highly defined sect that has managed to keep its own customs, language, and religion intact while becoming a vital part of the Indian scene" (25–26). Nilufer Bharucha historicizes Mistry's narratives as literature of the Parsi diaspora. Even though Mistry has stated that he expounds universal, not specifically Parsi themes, Bharucha States. "in spite of this disclaimer, Mistry's discourse does revolve around the detailing of Parsi identity. It also reveals how Parsis are learning to cope with the reality of post-colonial India and how they are coming to terms with their new lives in the West" ("When Old Tracks" 59). She argues that in *Swimming Lessons and Other Stories from Firozsha Baag*, the tenants, who prefer their status in colonial India, resist postcolonial India and conduct an almost ethnocentric lifestyle ("When Old Tracks" 59). In *Such a Long Journey*, Bharucha notices the opposite: "The Parsi world gradually moves out of its self-imposed isolation and interacts at the highest levels of finance and politics with the post-colonial Indian world" ("When Old Tracks" 61). However, Bharucha reprimands Mistry for drafting female stereotypes in *Such a Long Journey*. She argues that Roshan is "a doll-like creature, sickly and fragile," Miss Kutpitia is "the archetypal spinster," and Dilnavaz is the typical, superstitious wife, a foil to the more rational hero Gustad ("From behind a Fine Veil" 182). Bharucha shrewdly comments, "In a novel entitled *Such a Long Journey*, the female characters do not journey at all" ("From behind a Fine Veil" 183).

Articles also study the stylistic devices of Mistry's books. Using the "Swimming Lessons" as a cue, Silvia Albertazzi depicts the entire collection as metafiction (65). Amin Malak posits that Mistry's artistry is his "unassuming ironic stance" ("Insider/Outsider" 189). In his dissection of Mistry's layered narratives, Malak investigates such characteristics as heritage, private and collective memory, digression, orality, and literacy ("The Shahrazadic Tradition"). Along the same lines, Ajay Heble scrutinizes Hansotia's tale of Sarosh-Sid's aborted attempt at Westernization. As with any framed account, Hansotia's particularities interfere in the story's elucidation and explication (Heble 53); thus, while Sarosh-Sid's experiences forward cultural dualism, the tale itself is also hybrid in form (Heble 54). Heble notices similar "discursive strategies" (55) in "Auspicious Occasion" and "Lend Me Your Light." He concludes that Mistry is "working from within in order to subvert" (Heble 55). In another interesting critique, David Williams points out that in 1970s India, tangible implements of writing and identification, such as Gustad's cache of ink pens and nibs or Dr. Paymaster's incorrectly labeled sign, evoke nostalgia and security that cannot be supplanted with electronic mediums (60–61).

Reviews of *Swimming Lessons and Other Stories from Firozsha Baag* are overwhelmingly positive. Hope Cooke compliments the "antic humor" that Mistry endows to the otherwise gloomy lives of the characters, compares Firozsha Baag to a beehive, and commends the locking imagery. Sybil Steinberg, who portrays the collection as "an elegant mosaic that should confirm Mistry as a rising star in the literary firmament," records that the tales "evoke brilliantly the textures of this exotic yet startlingly knowable setting." Correspondingly, Elizabeth Shostak observes that the stories are "rich in the concrete details of daily life" (129) and admires the work's "wonderfully eccentric array of characters" (128). Additionally, Shostak extols Mistry's presentation of Parsi culture: "Mistry shows himself to be connected to the heritage he has so successfully transmuted into art" (129).

Assessments of *Such a Long Journey* combine commendation and criticism. Mistry's language and humor are subjects of admiration. Andrew Robinson summarizes, "Mistry has a fine, comic inventive ear for dialogue, and a fastidious, penetrating eye for detail. The energy, squalor and frequent cruelty of life in a big Indian city have seldom been more pungently conveyed." Pico Iyer assesses, "Mistry catches the pungent cadences of Indian English as they have seldom been caught before" ("Close" 76). Some reviewers define Mistry's comic techniques. T. L. Craig identifies it as "black humor" (22), while David Ray classifies Mistry's style as "erotic satire." Criticism of *Such a Long Journey* concerns its political component. Ray remarks, "Many of the novel's passionate political concerns seem warmed over." Aamer Hussein finds the grouping of humor and politics "ineffective." Hussein rationalizes, "Mistry seems to be a victim of the NRI [Non-Resident Indian] syndrome; his vision is the expatriate's offering a reading of the real as pure text, to be erased and rewritten in the service of a narrative design." Robinson admits that the intersection of Gustad's domestic dilemmas with political issues "sits uncomfortably." Although Robinson categorizes *Such a Long Journey* as "one of the best novels about India in recent years," he also points out its failing: "It finally falls short of the Great Bombay Novel that it promises."

Evaluations of *A Fine Balance* probe Mistry's intentions. Germaine Greer, for instance, fumes, " 'I hate this book. It is a Canadian book about Indian' " (qtd. in Kagal 29). While Ann Diamond's and A. G. Mojtabai's reviews are generally complimentary, they question the novel's tone: Diamond records, "At times Mistry's storytelling is more theatrical than novelistic" (37); Mojtabai believes that the work's "imbalance" is both the lack of the characters' inner lives as well as Mistry's attention to the marginalized poor, "a disproportion of background to foreground." Other commentators marvel at the compassion Mistry's characters induce. Patricia Goldblatt congratulates the characters' "human spirit" and "tenacity and courage." Pico Iyer pronounces Mistry a "rigorous humanitarian" ("Down" 90) and explains, "He gives faces and voices to suffering and takes us into the lives and huts of dirt-poor souls we usually regard only with pity or suspicion" ("Down" 91). Iyer nominates Mistry as the foremost of India's many illustrators: "The field of candidates for the title of Great Indian Novelist is as crowded these days as for its American equivalent, but few have caught the real sorrow and inexplicable strength of India, the unaccountable crookedness and sweetness, as well as Mistry. And no reader who finishes his book will look at the poor—in any street—in quite the same way again" ("Down" 91).

BIBLIOGRAPHY

Works by Rohinton Mistry

Short Stories

Swimming Lessons and Other Stories from Firozsha Baag. Boston: Houghton Mifflin, 1989.

Novels

Such a Long Journey. New York: Vintage, 1991.
A Fine Balance. New York: Alfred A. Knopf, 1996.

Speeches

"A Fable of Lost Dreams." *The Canadian Forum* 75 (1996): 18–20.

Studies of Rohinton Mistry

Albertazzi, Silvia. "Passages: The 'Indian Connection,' from Sara Jeanette Duncan to Rohinton Mistry." In *Imagination and the Creative Impulse in the New Literatures in English*. Ed. M. T. Bindella and G. V. Davis. Amsterdam: Rodopi, 1993. 57–66.

Bharucha, Nilufer E. "From behind a Fine Veil: A Feminist Reading of Three Parsi Novels." In *Margins of Erasure: Purdah in the Subcontinental Novel in English*. Ed. Jasbir Jain and Amina Amin. New Delhi: Sterling, 1995. 174–185.

———. " 'When Old Tracks Are Lost': Rohinton Mistry's Fiction as Diasporic Discourse." *Journal of Commonwealth Literature* 30 (1995): 57–64.

Cooke, Hope. "Beehive in Bombay." Rev. of *Swimming Lessons and Other Stories from Firozsha Baag*. *New York Times*, March 5, 1989, 26.

Craig, T. L. "Fiction." *University of Toronto Quarterly* 62.1 (1992): 21–53.

Diamond, Ann. "Indira's Web." Rev. of *A Fine Balance*. *Canadian Forum* (1996): 36–37.

Dodiya, Jaydipsinh, ed. *The Fiction of Rohinton Mistry*. London: Sangam, 1998.

Garebian, Keith. "In the Aftermath of Empire: Identities in the Commonwealth of Literature." *The Canadian Forum* 68 (1989): 25–33.

Goldblatt, Patricia. Rev. of *A Fine Balance*. *English Journal* 86.2 (1997): 94.

Hancock, Geoff. "An Interview with Rohinton Mistry." *Canadian Fiction Magazine* 65 (1989): 143–50.

Heble, Ajay. " 'A Foreign Presence in the Stall': Towards a Poetics of Cultural Hybridity in Rohinton Mistry's Migration Stories." *Canadian Literature* 137 (1993): 51–61.

Hussein, Aamer. "With an Exile's Eye." Rev. of *Such a Long Journey*. *The Times Literary Supplement* (March 1, 1991): 20.

Iyer, Pico. "Close Quarters." Rev. of *Such a Long Journey*. *Time* (April 8, 1991): 76–77.

———. "Down and Really Out." Rev. of *A Fine Balance*. *Time* (April 22, 1996): 90–91.

Kagal, Carmen. "An Accidental Family." Rev. of *A Fine Balance*. *New York Times*, June 23, 1996, 29.

Malak, Amin. "Insider/Outsider Views on Belonging: The Short Stories of Bharati Mukherjee and Rohinton Mistry." In *Short Fiction in the New Literatures in English*. Ed. J. Bardolph. Nice: Faculte des Lettres et Sciences Humaines de Nice, 1989. 189–196.

———. "The Shahrazadic Tradition: Rohinton Mistry's *Such a Long Journey* and the Art of Storytelling." *Journal of Commonwealth Literature* 29.2 (1993): 108–18.

Mojtabai, A. G. "An Accidental Family." Rev. of *A Fine Balance*. *New York Times*, June 23, 1996, 29.

Ray, David. "Under Her Thumb and in Her Pocket." Rev. of *Such a Long Journey*. *New York Times*, July 7, 1991, 13.

Robinson, Andrew. "Happiest within the Family." Rev. of *Such a Long Journey*. *The Spectator* (March 2, 1991): 31.

Shostak, Elizabeth. Rev. of *Swimming Lessons and Other Stories from Firozsha Baag*. *Wilson Library Bulletin* 63.9 (1989): 128–29.

Singh, Amritjit. "Rohinton Mistry." In *Writers of the Indian Diaspora: A Bio-Bibliographic Critical Sourcebook*. Ed. Emmanuel S. Nelson. Westport, CT: Greenwood, 1993. 207–18.

Steinberg, Sybil. Rev. of *Swimming Lessons and Other Stories from Firozsha Baag*. *Publishers Weekly* (December 9, 1988): 43.

Williams, David. "Cyberwriting and the Borders of Identity: 'What's in a Name' in Kroetsch's *The Puppeteer* and Mistry's *Such a Long Journey*?" *Canadian Literature* 149 (1996): 55–71.

Kyoko Mori
(1957–   )

Rhonda Brock-Servais

BIOGRAPHY

Born March 9, 1957, in Kobe, Japan, Kyoko Mori is now an American citizen. Her tragic and difficult childhood is the core of her literary work to date. Her mother, Takako, committed suicide at age forty-one, when Mori was only twelve. Her father quickly remarried a cold and difficult woman, as does the fictional father in both young adult novels (*Shizuko's Daughter* and *One Bird*). These painful events as well as the emotional and physical violence and the separation from her maternal family are all issues that surface time and again in her works. During her junior year of high school, she was an exchange student with a sister school in Mesa, Arizona. She left Japan permanently after two years of college when she received a scholarship to Rockford College, where she was awarded a B.A. in 1979. Mori attended graduate school at the University of Wisconsin, Milwaukee, where she earned both master's and doctoral degrees in 1981 and 1984. Her first book, *Shizuko's Daughter* is based on the group of short stories that constituted her doctoral dissertation. Currently, she resides in De Pere, Wisconsin, where she is an associate professor and writer in residence at St. Norbert's College. She was married to Charles Brock in 1984 and amicably divorced in 1996. During her 1990 sabbatical, she returned to Japan to travel and visit with both sides of her family. This trip is the basis of *The Dream of Water* and figures largely in *Polite Lies*.

Mori attributes her love of beauty, reading, and writing to her mother and her mother's family. Her mother created a cultured home for her children, reading to Mori and her brother since they were small. She also took them to art displays and on nature walks. Her grandfather kept a daily journal, which inspired Mori to discipline her own writing. As a young person, she reports that she was drawn to Western literature for its emotional content, a sharp contrast to the restraint commonly found in Japanese literature (Shelton 182). She maintains artistic pursuits other than writing and lists knitting, spinning, and weaving among her hobbies (181). Both Megumi (*One Bird*) and Yuki (*Shizuko's Daughter*) also rely on artistic pursuits to help maintain their connections with the world.

MAJOR WORKS AND THEMES

Mori's two novels and autobiographical memoir (*The Dream of Water*) as well as her nonfiction collection of essays, *Polite Lies*, all have similar themes. The various characters found in her works are all reflections of persons and situations she knew growing up or experienced traveling as a foreigner in what was once her homeland. Mori herself says that the two young adult works, *Shizuko's Daughter* and *One Bird*, are the same story told from different points of view. She further comments that she believes the later novel, *One Bird*, to have more humor and "irreverence" (Shelton 184). Mori says that she doesn't exclude or include something from her work because of the young readers. Rather, she adds, thinking about her young adult audience helps her to "deal more directly with character and plot, instead of always relying on style and imagery" (interview, February 2, 1999).

Both works begin with the female protagonist's loss of her mother. Yuki, Shizuko's daughter, arrives home from piano lessons to find her mother dead from inhaling gas fumes. Megumi, fifteen to Yuki's twelve, watches as her mother packs to go back to her native village, ostensibly to help her aging father. Megumi realizes her mother will not be coming home and is understandably angry. In both works, the father is distanced and dictatorial and quickly installs a replacement for the girl's mother in the house. These former mistresses are fairy-tale stepmothers, finding nothing but fault with their adoptive daughters and causing them difficulty at every turn. Growing up without a mother and learning to mother oneself form the core of both works. Megumi has learned from a spinster veterinarian that baby birds left by their mothers often die; however, Megumi is older than Yuki and considerably more assertive. Megumi's main concern is that she will not have the strength to continue on without her mother. By the novel's end, she has reached an agreement with her father that will allow her to visit her mother once a year. Yuki's story, on the other hand, is considerably sadder. The collection of vignettes follows her from age twelve to eighteen or so. Yuki, after the loss of her mother, retreats into herself, and her few ventures to make human connection (for instance, a friendship with another schoolgirl, Sachiko) are awkward and painful. However, the ending does provide both a sense of hope and renewal. Despite the hopeful endings, both novels are pervaded with a sense of loss.

Also emphasized in both novels are the effect of Japanese society on a sensitive, self-aware woman and the difficulty of growing into just such a woman.

In *One Bird*, Megumi's mother explains that if she hadn't left, she would surely have killed herself. She further explains why she leaves Megumi behind:

When a woman leaves her husband, the children must stay with their father, especially if the woman's parents are poor. The woman must go live with her parents for the rest of her life, giving up her children until they are old enough—full-grown adults—to visit on their own; the father usually does not allow any visits. The children, she said, would be better off with the father. Growing up poor and fatherless means growing up in shame, being despised by strangers and neighbors alike. (5–6)

In fact, it is clearly shown in both works that neither of the girls is better off living with the father (except financially, and this is not an issue). Mori believes the demands of the Japanese patriarchy are overwhelming, leaving little room for a woman's thoughts and feelings. Both Yuki and Megumi are talented— Yuki draws and later becomes a photographer, while Megumi's essays win awards. These artistic pursuits allow them to maintain a sense of self in their oppressive worlds.

Mori's memoir, *The Dream of Water*, can be read as a potential sequel to either or both of these novels as, in fact, it is in some ways. Its core is Mori's visit to Japan made during her 1990 sabbatical. The work actually covers a span of seven weeks; however, not all of this is narrated. Instead, the focus is solely on Mori's interaction with family and friends and rediscovering Japanese culture. Mori finds she is more comfortable with the American expatriate family she stays with than with her own family. Like both works for younger readers, *The Dream of Water* is a carefully crafted work filled with loving natural description. It is, in some ways, more disturbing than the novels, for here the reader sees a young Mori taping her light switch off, covering her bedroom floor with things to trip up her father, and practicing an escape route over the roof in response to her fear of his physical violence (neither Megumi or Yuki is physically abused). This adult work denies the sense of closure and reconciliation found in the other two novels. By the work's end, Mori has not come to accept her father and stepmother as one might assume, but she has come to an understanding that allows her to legitimate her anger and hurt. A further theme found in *The Dream of Water* is the inability to speak as an adult does. While convention and their age bind both younger protagonists, Mori, here, finds that she never learned to speak as an adult in Japanese, her native tongue.

CRITICAL RECEPTION

Mori's work for young adult readers has been widely praised, appearing, on numerous state and national "best" lists: her "first novel, *Shizuko's Daughter*, set in modern Japan, is a jewel of a book, one of those rarities that shine out only a few times in a generation" (Rosenberg). Still, reviewers of both *Shizuko's Daughter* and *One Bird* tend to emphasize the import of the books as excellent examples of multiculturalism rather than as artistic works in their own right. For instance, the *New York Times* reviewer wrote that *One Bird* "is so lively and affecting that one imagines its readers will be too engaged by its heroine situation to notice how much—and how painlessly—they are learning about another culture" (Prose). The paperback edition of *Shizuko's Daughter* bears an advertisement inside the front cover. "Look for these other fine novels about teens growing up in other cultures." On this topic, Mori says she believes that young people are sometimes encouraged "to read books in a very purely instructional way.... As an author, I don't think people should read literature to glean information or conclusions about culture or anything else" (interview, February 2, 1999).

Mori's prose is frequently praised for its poetry and careful description, especially of natural scenes. However, reviewers have complained about its restraint and lack of drama. Further, Harris of the *Los Angeles Times* writes that the dialogue can be stiff and sounds translated. *The Dream of Water* received mixed reviews, although for the most part they were positive. *Polite Lies*, on the other hand, has been panned as being "strident" and "shrill" (Barton). Of course, at the same time, at least one reviewer wrote that despite her background Mori's *Polite Lies* proceeds "without ever becoming shrill or bitter" (Sandin).

One review of *One Bird*, entitled "Shizimu's Daughter," perhaps best captures the most frequently heard complaint about Mori's writing—that the subject matter is the same for each work and that the characters are more or less interchangeable with those the author has known in her life (Prose). Perhaps Bruce Corson summed it up best when reviewing *The Dream of Water*; he asks Mori for more good writing on a different topic. Mori admits the truth of this to some extent; she says her first novel was "a way of admitting the pain in my life perhaps. And then when I wrote *One Bird*, it was a way of being able to look at that same story with more irreverence and humor" (Shelton 184). In another interview she adds, "I don't really know too many authors who don't write the same thing over and over in some way" (February 2, 1999). Currently, Mori is working on another novel set in Milwaukee, Wisconsin, and featuring a weaver in her mid-thirties as the protagonist. Readers can expect it to be full of beauty and the carefully crafted prose for which Kyoko Mori has been so rightfully noted.

BIBLIOGRAPHY

Works by Kyoko Mori

Novels

Shizuko's Daughter. New York: Holt, 1993.
One Bird. New York: Holt, 1995.

Autobiography

The Dream of Water. New York: Holt, 1995.

Nonfiction

Polite Lies: On Being a Woman Caught between Cultures. New York: Holt, 1998.

Poetry

Fallout. Chicago: Ti Chucha Press, 1994.

Studies of Kyoko Mori

Barton, Emily. Rev. of *Polite Lies: On Being a Woman Caught between Cultures*. *New York Times*, March 8, 1998, late ed., sec. 7: 19.

Blinkhorn, Lois. "Out of Tragedy, a Quiet Pursuit of Truth." *Milwaukee Journal Sentinel*, March 22, 1998, C1.

Corson, Bruce. "Fading Memory, Lingering Pain." (*Cleveland*) *The Plain Dealer* April 23, 1995, 12J.

Harris, Michael. Rev. of *Shizuko's Daughter*. *Los Angeles Times*, June 13, 1993, Book Review Section: 6.

Heller, Amanda. Rev. of *Polite Lies: On Being a Woman Caught between Cultures*. *Boston Globe*, February 8, 1998, G2.

Prose, Francine. "Shizimu's Daughter." *New York Times*, November 12, 1995, late ed., sec. 7: 50.

Rosenberg, Liz. Rev. of *Shizuko's Daughter*. *New York Times*, August 22, 1993, late ed., sec. 7: 19.

Sandin, Jo. "Caught between Cultures: In the Mid-West, a Japanese-American Finds Her Voice." *Milwaukee Journal Sentinel*, January 25, 1998, C11.

Shelton, Pamela. "Kyoko Mori." In *Authors and Artists for Young Adults*. Vol. 25. Ed. Thomas McMahon. Detroit: Gale, 1998. 181–86.

Toshio Mori
(1910–1980)

Sarah Catlin Barnhart

BIOGRAPHY

Toshio Mori was born in San Leandro, a community now overcome by the sprawling metropolis of Oakland, California, on March 20, 1910. He was the American son of Japanese parents, Hidekichi and Yoshi (Takaki) Mori. Upon arrival in America, his parents worked in plant nurseries, a profession that Mori would adopt as an adult. He attended public schools, eventually earning a high school diploma. Although he did not receive additional formal schooling, he continued to educate himself, frequenting bookstores and libraries. He read French and Russian writers, as well as Americans such as Sherwood Anderson. At night, after a full day of work in the nursery, he wrote. In 1941 Mori's first book, *Yokohama, California*, was accepted for publication; however, the book was set aside by the publisher during World War II due (at least in part) to anti-Japanese sentiment. Because the book was written by a Japanese American, it was suspect. In the mid-1940s, Mori and his family were relocated to Topaz Camp, Millard County, Utah, by the War Relocation Authority, Department of the Interior. Mori was named "camp historian." Ironically, Mori had a brother who had been serving voluntarily in the American army before the war broke out. He was later injured in Europe while defending the very country that had incarcerated his family. On June 29, 1947, Mori married Hisayo Yoshiwara. They had one son, Steven. By 1949 Mori had returned to his native Oakland, and *Yokohama, California* was finally being published after a seven-year postponement with one difference: two stories had been added to the already complete manuscript.

After the war, readers no longer cared to read stories written by a Japanese American, but in 1985 renewed interest in Asian American writers spurred the publication of a new edition of *Yokohama, California* with a second Introduction. Mori published two other books in his lifetime, *Woman from Hiroshima*, a novel, and *The Chauvinist and Other Stories*, both in 1979. Both books were largely ignored by critics and are now out of print. Mori also published short stories in anthologies such as *Speaking for Ourselves* (1969), *Japanese Americans: Untold Story* (1971), *Asian-American Authors* (1972), *Asian-American Heritage* (1974), *Aiiieeeee! Anthology of Asian-American Writers* (1974), and *Counterpoint* (1976).

MAJOR WORK AND THEMES

Toshio Mori introduced himself to the reading public with the publication of his first book, *Yokohama, California*, in 1949. Although he wrote two other books, this is the one that receives critical attention and for which he is known and remembered. The book comprises several sections that could better be described as vignettes than short stories. The volume is unified as a whole by its focus on a specific time, place, and people, making it read more like a novel than a collection of unrelated stories.

Mori's tales are set in either his own California hometown or in the Topaz Center, a World War II detention camp. The original manuscript of the book was set entirely in Yokohama, California, but two stories were added to the collection after World War II and before the book was published, one of which is set in a relocation camp. In the Introduction to the 1985 edition, Lawson Fusao Inada best captures the reigning tone of the original stories in the collection:

There is . . . a burnished glow to the book which simply reflects the actual atmosphere of the time, the way the people felt, saw, and lived. Not that the book is gilded with goodness from cover to cover; on the contrary, the people and incidents portrayed are very real, with more aspirations than outright successes. But there are no failures, no real losers and victims. This was, after all, a time of hope and optimism, of established communities, of flourishing culture, of the new generation getting on with America. This was a time of pride and accomplishment. The people quite obviously believed in themselves, in what they could do, were doing, in America. (ix–x)

The book is infused with hope that is often unfulfilled but continues, unchecked. Inada goes on to argue that this "continuing and extending" (x) of tradition are the main theme of the entire work, especially as found in the story "Nodas in America."

Inada is describing the general temperature of the book, which is drastically altered by the two post–World War II stories. Critics agree that the two added stories change the tone of what was already a complete work in important ways. The first additional story, "Tomorrow Is Coming, Children," was added at the very beginning of the book. It attempts to orient the reader in Japanese America and is set in one of the camps. The story was first published in *Trek*, the Topaz Camp magazine, in 1943. Because the rest of *Yokohama, California* was written pre–World War II, the inclusion of this new story at the beginning of the book adds a whole new dimension to the collection, not the least being the relocation camp setting. What had once been an uplifting book of stories about Japanese Americans was now forced to reconfigure itself in the aftermath of the war. This new story features a grandmother recounting her history to her two grandchildren. The grandmother speaks of her pride in being a part of America and seems to be telling the children to "forgive and forget." However, in recounting her history, she is clearly instilling in her grandchildren a sense of their heritage and asking them to remember. The second added story, "Slant-Eyed Americans," deals with a family's seeing their son off to war. The reader of this story cannot help but remember that this family will soon be relocated to the camps just as Mori's family was. Unlike the sincere, hopeful, and often funny stories of the original collection, both added stories are tainted by the war. The collection as a whole was tainted by this inclusion, as well.

Several critics have noted the influence of Sherwood Anderson's *Winesburg, Ohio* on Mori's work, particularly *Yokohama, California*. Mori's title pays tribute to a work that was so important to Mori and his contemporaries, as does the way he centers his work around one specific community and its inhabitants. Mori includes a story called "Akiro Yano," which features an aspiring author who can write in the style of Anderson. Mori does not, however, reach into Anderson's realm of the "grotesque." His portraits of characters are rendered with humility, sweetness, and, often, humor, and he chooses rather ordinary people for his subjects—ordinary, that is, in the little Asian American community of Yokohama. Although Mori begins in the tradition of Anderson, locating his stories in a small community, his style and subject are all his own.

This original style and subject are partially responsible for Inada's proclamation, "This is the book—the first real Japanese-American book. . . . This is the book—by the first real Japanese-American writer. . . . This is more than a book. . . . This is the enduring strength, the embodiment of a people" (v). Mori chronicles a particular set of people in a particular time and place, Japanese Americans in his hometown of California in the late 1930s and early 1940s.

Mori does write about a particular set of people, Japanese Americans. There are rarely any white characters in Mori's books. Inada theorizes that "it is crucial to note that these are not 'minority stories' in the negative sense but 'majority' stories told from the perspective of the full self and self-determining community" ("Of Place" 256). In reading the original stories of *Yokohama, California*, one does not get the impression that the characters are working in opposition to the white community because the white community is absent. These Japanese Americans don't define themselves in relation to whiteness, nor do they depend on the white community for assistance. Yokohama is a self-contained community.

Mori's community is peopled with characters whose essences Mori effortlessly (or so he makes it seem) captures. There is the grandmother in "Tomorrow Is Coming, Children." There is Motoji Tsunoda, a laundryman who fancies himself a philosopher. There is Hatsuye, who is in love with Clark Gable, who "is hopeful in spite of the fact she is hopeless" (165). There is "The Woman Who Makes Swell Doughnuts," a section that has no plot, character development, or movement of any kind. Inada labels this story a "tribute" or an "anthem" to the woman's way of life. This unusual narrative move is one of the things most worth studying in Mori's works.

The particular and even peculiar style of Toshio Mori is difficult to describe, as various critics have discovered. To be sure, one cannot help but notice Mori's pervasive humor. In the new Introduction to *Yokohama, California*, Inada writes, "It might be said that this book is in the time-honored shibai tradition of folk drama and humorous skits" (vi). The humorous situations serve to stimulate learning, through showing in a humorous manner how various characters fail to communicate, for instance, Mori teaches the reader how to communicate. Inada continues, "Toshio Mori is an exemplary teacher, and a writer of great compassion. There is not a mean bone in all of *Yokohama, California*. His is the gentle humor of respect, not the cynical laughter of ridicule" (vi). All critics agree that humor is key to Mori's writing but that there is something else, something inexplicable, that runs deeper than the humor to create sincere and poignant moments for the reader.

CRITICAL RECEPTION

As a Japanese American writer after World War II, Toshio Mori faced insurmountable obstacles; no one wanted to read works written by and about Japanese Americans. As already mentioned, Mori's first collection of short stories was accepted for publication in 1941, but it was not published until after the war. As Lawson Fusao Inada notes in the Introduction to the 1985 edition, "By its very nature, [*Yokohama, California*] was destined for obscurity; it had to be one of the most unwanted books in history" (xx). One could see the fact that it overcame the obstacle of anti-Japanese sentiment and was ever published at all as testament to its unquestionable literary merit. Even in the aftermath of World War II, the publisher could not deny that Mori had something unique and valuable to offer. *Yokohama, California* was finally printed in 1949 and reprinted in 1985, but it received scant attention until the early 1990s. Only after critics began reclaiming "lost" authors who were once marginalized for one reason or another but now are valued for their unique qualities did Mori begin to receive notable critical attention. In the face of an unmoved and unmoving readership, Mori continued to write. Mori's other books, *The Chauvinist and Other Stories* and *Woman from Hiroshima*, were published in 1979 but are now out of print.

Mori was never widely reviewed. In fact, contemporary reviewers tended to ignore him completely. Once interest in "lost" authors arose, most critics were concerned with reclaiming Mori and offering him belated membership in the canon of American literature. The majority of critics champion Mori, painting him as a wronged man who deserves attention both for the quality of his writing and as a sort of recompense for allowing him to live and die in obscurity. The only critic who outwardly criticizes Mori is William Saroyan, in his Introduction to the first edition of *Yokohama, California*, written long before the collection is published: "It will be better for [Mori] when [he] learns to be more lucid" (1). Later critics have questioned exactly which aspect of Mori's writing Saroyan is responding to. Some, such as Inada, suggest that Saroyan is merely treating Mori as he himself was treated when he appeared on the literary scene (Introduction xxvi).

Not only was Mori ignored by critics, but he was ignored by the very people he wrote for and about, as well. In the new Introduction, Inada chides,

There is a very expensive lesson to be learned here. It might have been funny to some that Toshio Mori, the nurseryman down the street, spent all of his spare time, spent his entire life, actually, trying to be, of all things, a legitimate American writer. He considered himself to be a writer, but his writing career was pathetic, a noncareer; his own people ignored, rejected the art that he produced. . . . No one took him seriously; he died as he lived—in obscurity. . . . His literature is Japanese-American; he was committed to his people, he lived up to his people, he saw his people as the stuff of great art. He took the responsibility of founding and maintaining the tradition of Japanese-American literature. Toshio Mori did not fail; others failed him. (viii)

Inada's response is representative of the general feeling among recent critics. Surely it is only a matter of time before his second collection of short stories and his only novel, *Woman from Hiroshima*, are again made available to the public. Based on his previous efforts and his obvious dedication to the art of writing, one can only guess what Mori, given the full support of readers, critics, and publishers, might have accomplished.

BIBLIOGRAPHY

Works by Toshio Mori

Novel

Woman from Hiroshima. San Jose, CA: Isthmus Press, 1979.

Short Stories

Yokohama, California. Caldwell, OH: Caxton Printers, 1949. 2nd ed., Seattle: University of Washington Press, 1985.
The Chauvinist and Other Stories. Los Angeles: Asian American Studies Center, University of California, 1979.

Studies of Toshio Mori

Bedrosian, Margaret. "Toshio Mori's California Koans." *MELUS: The Journal of the Society for the Study of Multi-Ethnic Literature of the United States* 15.2 (1988): 47–55.

Inada, Lawson Fusao. "Of Place and Displacement: The Range of Japanese-American Literature." In *Three American Literatures: Essays in Chicano, Native American and Asian-American Literature for Teachers of American Literature.* Ed. Houston A. Baker. New York: Modern Language Association of America, 1982. 254–65.

———. "Standing on Seventh Street." Introduction. In *Yokohama, California.* 1985 ed. Seattle: University of Washington Press, 1985. v–xxvii.

Mayer, David R. "Akegarasu and Emerson: Kindred Spirits of Toshio Mori's "The Seventh Street Philosopher.' " *Amerasia Journal* 16.2 (1990): 1–10.

———. "The Philosopher in Search of a Voice: Toshio Mori's Japanese-Influenced Narrator." *AALA Journal* 2 (1995): 12–24.

———. "The Short Stories of Toshio Mori." *Fu Jen Studies: Literature and Linguistics* 21 (1988): 73–87.

———. "Toshio Mori and Loneliness." *Nanzan Review of American Studies* 15 (1993): 20–32.

———. "Toshio Mori's Neighborhood Settings: Inner and Outer Oakland." *Fu Jen Studies: Literature and Linguistics* 23 (1993): 100–115.

Palomino, Harue. "Japanese Americans in Books or in Reality? Three Writers for Young Adults Who Tell a Different Story." In *How Much Truth Do We Tell Children? The Politics of Children's Literature.* Ed. Betty Bacon. Minneapolis: Marxist Educational Press, 1988. 125–34.

Palumbo Liu, David. "The Minority Self as Other: Problematics of Representation in Asian-American Literature." *Cultural Critique* 28 (1994): 75–102.

———. "Toshio Mori and the Attachments of Spirit: A Response to David R. Mayer." *Amerasia Journal* 17.3 (1991): 41–47.

———. "Universalisms and Minority Culture." *Differences: A Journal of Feminist Cultural Studies* 7.1 (1995): 188–208.

Saroyan, William. "Introduction." In *Yokohama, California.* Caldwell, OH: Caxton Printers, 1949. 1–4.

Bharati Mukherjee
(1940–   )

Jaspal Kaur Singh

BIOGRAPHY

Bharati Mukherjee was born in Calcutta, India, in 1940 in a Bengali Brahmin family. She studied at the University of Calcutta and Baroda, where she graduated with a master's degree in English and ancient Indian culture. In 1961 she attended the Writers Workshop in Iowa and earned her master's degree in fine arts and her doctorate in English from the University of Iowa. She met Canadian author Clark Blaise in Iowa and married him in 1963, immigrating to Canada soon after and becoming a naturalized citizen in 1972. She taught at McGill University in Montreal and wrote fiction until she found life as an immigrant in Canada unbearable, so she moved with her husband to the United States and became an American citizen. She is currently a professor of English at the University of California at Berkeley. Before this, she taught creative writing at Columbia University, New York University, and Queens College.

Mukherjee has authored five novels—*Wife* in 1975, *The Tiger's Daughter* in 1971, *Jasmine* in 1989, *The Holder of the World* in 1993, and *Leave It to Me* in 1997—has coauthored two works of nonfiction with Clark Blaise—*The Sorrow and the Terror* and *Days and Nights in Calcutta*— and has written two short story collections—*Darkness* and *The Middleman and Other Stories*. *The Middleman and Other Stories* won the National Book Critic Award in 1988.

Mukherjee spoke Bengali for the first few years of her life, then went to English schools in England and Switzerland, and, when she returned, she was educated at Loreto House Convent School run by Irish nuns. She writes about her sense of alienation in *Days and Nights in Calcutta*. Even in early childhood, the two worldviews of her home and school life clashed. She wrote that her "imagination created two distinct systems of cartography [where] multiheaded serpents who were also cosmic oceans and anthropomorphic gods did not stand a chance of survival" against the mapping of the "New Testament" (*Days and Nights* 171). With her father's growing success as a chemist and industrialist, the family moved away from the joint-family household into an exclusive, Westernized neighborhood, where a group of security personnel always guarded the compound gates, regulating and checking unwanted visitors. This alienation was further complicated when Mukherjee married and went to live in Canada, where she was "simultaneously invisible" as a writer "and overexposed" ("An Invisible Woman" 36) as a racial minority until she came to live in the United States as a naturalized citizen.

MAJOR WORKS AND THEMES

In Mukherjee's texts, we see her rejection of the tradition-bound society of the East as she reaches out for the more empowering, individualistic society of the West. This reconstruction is not without struggle or loss, which she addresses in a number of novels, but in *Wife*, we see the psychic trauma of an immigrant who is caught between two cultures. The protagonist's resistance to both the hegemonic discourses of East and West leads to violence.

The Tiger's Daughter, an earlier novel of Mukherjee, deals with the return of the immigrant from the New World to the geographic space of the Old. Mukherjee's changing imagination is textualized in ways that indicate the weakening grip of the hegemony of the Old World. She describes her upper-class, convent-educated friends as a dying class, living the lives of decadence and material comforts that signify spiritual death. Although they appear to live liberated lifestyles of Westernized Indians, Mukherjee draws attention to the fact that they still believe in the traditional arranged marriage where parents initiate marriage plans with foreign-educated and brilliant boys, as they are called, from the same caste and class. The protagonist, Tara, after seven years in liberal Western institutions such as Vassar and the University of Wisconsin at Madison, seems to fall prey to the passive and fatalistic attitudes of the Indian community. This novel contains many of the author's own misgivings about India and the Indian community and its inability or unwillingness to adapt to the changing times—a world she had left behind when she relocated to the West.

In later novels such as *Jasmine*. Mukherjee shows the possibilities of remaking oneself in the New World. In this novel, written after she immmigrated to the West, she explores the possibilities for liberation through transformation—especially for oppressed, middle-class women—in the New World. Mukherjee maps the immigrant experience of a protagonist who finds the West exciting and full of possibilities; Jasmine transforms herself by finding an authentic American identity. We see epistemological violence in *Jasmine* when Jasmine reinvents herself. Jasmine, an illegal immigrant, a young widow, transforms herself from Jyoti, to Jasmine, to Jassy, to Jase, and to Jane in the United States, moving rapidly from one locale to another: starting from rural India (Hasnapur), proceeding to a city in Punjab (Jullundhar), arriving in Florida, moving to Queens, then to Manhattan, and ultimately settling for some time in Iowa. Jasmine does not transform herself gradually; she reinvents herself by killing her old selves: "There are no harmless, compassionate ways to make oneself. We murder who we were so we can rebirth ourselves in the images of dreams" (*Jasmine* 25). Jasmine's desire to come to the United States stems from the desire to commit sati on the campus where her now-deceased husband, a victim of Sikh terrorism, was supposed to attend engineering school in Florida. She buys a fake visa to the United States; when she arrives in Florida after a nightmarish journey, she is attacked by a white man who rapes her. After she stabs her rapist in the guise of Kali, she sets her clothes and her husband's clothes (which she was supposed to burn along with herself at the campus) on fire in a dumpster. At this point, she is symbolically free to find a new identity for herself in the New World. While Mukherjee investigates the possibilities offered by the New World for reconstructions of identity, her representations of the Old World draw criticism from many postcolonial critics.

When Jasmine burns her clothes in the trash bin, she symbolically trashes the old traditions and, hence, her traditional identity, as the act of rape frees her from the old notions of purity and impurity, she becomes liberated and therefore can construct a new American identity for herself.

Mukherjee discusses the problem of identity politics for the English-speaking postcolonial writer in *Days and Nights*:

I am a late-blooming colonial who writes in a borrowed tongue (English), lives permanently in an alien country (Canada), and publishes in and is read, when read at all, in another alien country, the United States. My Indianness is fragile; it has to be professed and fought for even though I look so unmistakably Indian. Language transforms our way of apprehending the world; I fear that my decades-long use of English as a first language has cut me off from my *desh* (country). (170)

By the end of her year in India, when Mukherjee finally prepares to leave, she realizes she does not need to "discard [her] Western education in order to retrieve the dim shape of [her] Indian one"; in the future, she would return to India but would see it as "just another Asian country," and she would be "just another knowledgeable but desolate tourist," believing that if she stayed on, "the country [would] fail [her] more than [she] had by settling abroad" (284). In *The Tiger's Daughter*, Tara cannot wait to go back to the United States and to her white American husband, David. In *Days and Nights*, Mukherjee, even though she acknowledges a sense of loss at not ever having a *desh*, celebrates the possibilities of the writer's ability to "demolish and reinvent" a homeland: "It was hard to give up my faintly Chekovian image of India. But if that was about to disappear, could I not invent a more exciting—perhaps a more psychologically accurate—a more precisely metaphoric India: many more Indias?" (285). While Mukherjee may be writing to redefine herself in new terms, her unfortunate representations of India as chaotic, passive, helpless, fatalistic have dragged her into the charged debates taking place in postcolonial criticism. Critics accuse many Anglophone writers such as Mukherjee of valorizing the West as rational and suggest that they still continue to think and write in a manner that is Orientalist.

Mukherjee writes about India and uses "Indianness," shows the author's affinity with the Indian nation, and points to a colonized past, while forming a postcolonial present in the United States. As Anindyo Roy writes,

[T]o assign a specific tradition to the literature written by and about the new Indian diaspora is also to acknowledge that this tradition is marked by the presence of a "postcolonial" discourse. The terms "diaspora" and "postcolonial" belong to a specific historical condition that is released by India's emergence as a "free" nation and by her entry into a new transnational geopolitical sphere. (127)

Roy's terms, "postcolonial" and "diaspora," point to the temporal and spatial components of Mukherjee's *Wife* where she writes about Dimple Dasgupta, a young Bengali wife who immigrates to the United States—an opposition to Tara in *The Tiger's Daughter*, who returns to the nation of origin. Although *Wife* was published before *Days and Nights*, it can be situated around the time that Mukherjee starts to completely affiliate herself with the West. *Days and Nights* was published in 1977; Mukherjee landed in India for the year on a "Sunday morning, May 13, 1973" (10) with her husband and children. While *The Tiger's Daughter* maps Mukherjee's slow disassociation and withdrawal from the Old World, *Jasmine* represents the possibilities of the New World for the immigrant.

In an interview published in *Iowa Review*, Mukherjee states,

The kind of women I write about, and I'm not generalizing about women in the South Asian community here, but the kinds of women who attract me, who intrigue me, are those who are adaptable . . . and that adaptability is working to the women's advantage when we come over here as immigrants. The males function very well as engineers or doctors or whatever, and they earn good money, but they have locked their hearts against mainstream culture. . . . For an Indian woman to learn to drive, put on pants, cash checks, is a big leap. They are exhilarated by that change. They are no longer having to do what mother-in-law tyrannically forced them to. (17)

Though her argument is somewhat reductive, Mukherjee here points to the fact that national identity is obviously a privilege that economically independent males can lay claim to, but for Indian women, who must negotiate their identities outside the traditional Indian family, it becomes difficult, but exhilarating.

From Tara to Dimple to Jasmine, we see a slow transformation of the female characters who negotiate their identities in the New World, although this transformation is not without violence in which one self seems to annihilate another. Mukherjee seems to suggest that when the old subjectivity and the new subjectivity collide, psychological violence is inevitable. Such violence takes textual forms in many different ways. We see this in *The Tiger's Daughter* when Tara is sexually assaulted by the old politician; in *Wife* when Dimple aborts her fetus and when she stabs her husband; and in *Jasmine* when Jasmine reconstructs herself as Kali in order to avenge her rape by slicing her tongue and then killing her rapist.

In *The Middleman and Other Stories*, Mukherjee writes about a new America, an America whose landscape was changing due to the presence of a large number of immigrants from all over the world. Mukherjee's point in all these stories, according to Fakrul Alam, "is to focus our attention on the energies or potential unleashed even in people as timid as Mr. Vendetesan by their diasporic experience" (91). While she shows an awareness of the complexities faced by the immigrant in the New World, she "highlights the fluid morality America's newest citizens almost inevitably exhibit as they struggle to root themselves in the continent" (91). The new immigrants may appear nontraditional to many old Americans, but ultimately they will come to accept them as "an inescapable and even desirable part of their society" (91).

While most of the stories share the theme of the "impact of the United States on its new immigrants and the effect they were having on older Americans" (82), Alam divides the stories into four different groups: "In the first group are 'The Management of Grief,' 'A Wife's Story,' and 'The Tenant.' " These stories deal with the issue of immigration and the impact of American culture on the female protagonist's consciousness. In the second group, Alam puts "The Middleman," "Danny's Girls," "Jasmine," and "Buried Life." In these stories, the protagonists are placed in the "shadowy world of illegal immigrants or are involved in disreputable actions" (82). The third group consists of "Loose Ends" and "Fighting for the Rebound," two stories of white Americans who are unable or unwilling to associate or interact with the new immigrants. In the final group, Alam places "Orbiting" and "Fathering," and their themes, too, are about white Americans' response to the New Americans.

We find the presence of many diasporic subjects from various countries, such as India, Afghanistan, Vietnam, Lebanon, the Philippines, Sri Lanka, Italy, and the Caribbean, in *The Middleman and Other Stories*. In many of the stories Mukherjee crosses cultural boundaries and tries to interrogate the trauma of dislocation and alienation for the diasporic subjects.

Mukherjee's fifth novel, *Leave It to Me*, is a story about Debby DiMartino, who is saved from death as a baby by Gray Nuns at a remote Indian outpost called Devigaon. She is later adopted by Manfred and Serena DiMartino of Schenectady, New York. At twenty-three she decides to find her biological parents, as she feels she was "just a garbage sack thrown out on the hippie trail" (13) and must reinvent herself. She knows only that her mother was a California hippie called Clear Water Iris and that her father was an "Asian national" serving a life sentence in an Indian prison. She feels robbed of an Asian childhood by "the California hippie who'd fucked a Eurasian thug so I could be born in that place, over there, where nightmare and poem merge" (26). In this text, too,

Mukherjee's signature theme of reinvention and renaming occurs. As the protagonist drives out of New York toward San Francisco, "Debby DiMartino [dies] and Devi Dee [births] herself on the Donner Pass at the precise moment a top-down Spider Veloce with DEVI vanities" cuts her off in front of the Welcome to California Fruit Inspector Barrier (62). Again, as in *Jasmine*, such reconstructions are to bring empowerment. The protagonist tells us, "Devi arm-wrestled Debby. I was quicker, stronger as Devi; my intuitions were sharper, my impulsiveness rowdier. As Devi, I came into possession of my mystery genes. Thank you Clear Water. And you, too, thank you, 'Asian National' " (64). The hybrid that is Devi Dee decides that "when you inherit nothing, you are entitled to everything" (67) and decides that the "American way" is "self-invention" (183). She envies Jess, her bio-mom's "eternity of makeovers" (185) from Jess DuPree (a successful Bay Area businesswoman), to Jeanne Jellineau (a citizen of France), to Sigrid Schlant (a West German), to Veronica Alexandra Taylor (of South Africa), to Magda Lukacs (a displaced person born in a German camp), to Margaret Rose Smith (a British citizen born in Port of Spain, Trinidad).

The text is liberally peppered with diasporic and displaced subjects from all over the world. For example, Linda, Devi's "psychic neighbor," was "born in a displaced-persons camp in Germany, spoke her first word (*cuidado!*) in Argentina, married a Japanese doctor in Brazil and divorced him in Chile, then found fulfillment as a psychic in the Haight" (118). Mukherjee throws in concepts like male "suttee" (164), female genital mutilation (117), and the Somalian practice of polygamy (189), and as Grewal claims in another context, such representations, "extracted from relations of power and property," render them meaningless (188). Ellen Friedman summarizes the plot of this uncanny text aptly in a review:

Devi Dee . . . is a female looking for her mother. In San Francisco she finds the ex-hippie flower child whom she presumes is her "Bio-Mom" and, Electra-like, abets her murder, as well as has sex with the man she believes is her "Bio-Dad." When he is ax-murdered by the mother's former lover who has also killed her mother, she returns the favor. As the police make their way to the crime scene, an earthquake diverts their attention and she escapes them. She rides out the earthquake bobbing up and down in the crime scene, a boat in the waters off Sausalito, the location from which she begins to tell her story. (232)

Friedman likens the text to a Hollywood thriller fantasy, a masala (meaning a mixture of spices) of East and West.

CRITICAL RECEPTION

Mukherjee's celebration of the United States and her continuing use of "Indianness" in texts that are published and consumed predominantly in the West continue to be a matter of a critical postcolonial debate. Feroza Jussawalla points out that Mukherjee celebrates the "exuberance" that an immigrant feels at the melting pot theory of assimilation in the United States (591). This exuberance gets complicated with Mukherjee's identity politics. When Mukherjee continues to write about the Indian experience and "Indianness" in her texts, which are then read as "authentic" Indian representations for a predominantly Western audience, the debate regarding the politics of representations becomes more complex. In an interview with Ameena Meer, Mukherjee affirms, "I totally consider myself an American writer. . . . Now my roots are here and my emotions are here in North America" (28). Mukherjee's statements draw criticism from Jussawalla, who finds in postcolonial writers like Mukherjee

a new hegemonic discourse of those who see themselves as assimilated and assimilable. The irony is that in separating themselves from other South Asian immigrants and in hoping to be accepted among the mainstream of the majority, these writers only extend and perpetuate a new colonial mentality. (590)

Although Jussawalla's criticism of Mukherjee appears justified, Mukherjee herself, after her naturalization as a U.S. citizen in 1988, locates herself in the mainstream American tradition but in a special space. She sees the New World full of potential where negotiations between gendered and national identities occur in an alien world. Although she has written extensively about immigrant experiences of people from all over the world in her later works, the work that focuses on Indian immigrants seems more popular. Although she claims that *The Tiger's Daughter* is not autobiographical, moments in the text reflect the author's own experience. Mukherjee herself seems to attest to these moments when she states, "There were just so many aspects of India that I disliked by then. So a lot of my stories since are really about transformation—psychological—especially among women" (Connell et al. 15).

Other critics claim that Mukherjee's representation of India and Indian customs reinforces the idea of India as backward and tradition-bound. In one of the examples from her texts, Jasmine tries to commit sati after her husband's death in *Jasmine*. In her discussion of *Jasmine*, Gurleen Grewal castigates Mukherjee for her serious omission in situating the Western audience and trivializing the practice of sati:

In fact, the novel seems to suggest there are women who might travel halfway across the globe to the United States to commit sati. Jasmine has no other motive [than to commit sati]. . . . Mukherjee fosters a gross misconception. Reading *Jasmine*, one might think sati was being practiced as a matter of routine and choice by contemporary Hindu widows. . . . Mukherjee's protagonist is neither coerced by relatives avaricious for her husband's money, nor so bereft of options that death is her only alternative. Extricated from relations of power and property, the practice of sati, as an arena of both oppression and of women's resistance to oppression, is rendered meaningless in *Jasmine*. (188)

Also, in her representation of Jasmine as an assimilationist protagonist who rejects tradition-bound culture, nation, and her gendered identity, Mukherjee is accused of reinforcing imperialist constructs of Indian women as oppressed and brutalized. Critics claim that Mukherjee is clearly limited in her conceptualization of liberation due to her class status. Though "Mukherjee is . . . careful to suggest that America is no Eden: it is a brave new world that includes the violence of rape, murder, and suicide" (Grewal 187), she shows Jasmine can become "American" by simply rejecting the old and claiming the new.

The exuberance of immigration evident in the stories of *Darkness* is more pronounced in her later collection, *Middleman*. Of these short stories and their protagonists, critic Jonathan Raban states, "Their diaspora is a haphazard, pepperpot dispersal. . . . With no Lower East Side to keep the manner and morals of the old world alive, they're on their own and on the make" (22). He feels that the stories are a romance with America, "a place where the laws of physics are suspended, where people can defy gravity, where magic is a remarkable part of everyday life" (16). Mukherjee's characters are always mobile, always willing and eager to explore the romance of the frontier.

In *Leave It to Me*, the romance and magic of America take nightmarish form. Mukherjee's signature characters, who have destructive as well as transformative powers, are very much present in this text. As Marni Jackson points out in a review,

Mukherjee treats a whole generation—the sons and daughters of the Seventies—as historical foundlings, orphaned by the Vietnam War and the sexual revolution. She portrays them as shape-shifters, able to imagine themselves into any lives—and just as quick to detach themselves again. Uprooted from history, her characters have a dangerous potential for creation, or destruction. (55)

Mukherjee rushes through the "cartoon plot" of this "quick and complicated" text (Friedman 233). The protagonist—"modern mongrel—part Electra, part avenging goddess from an Indian fairy tale, and part all-American Tarantino waif on a killing spree" (Jackson 55)—and the "multiraced cast of characters" are read as "postmodern, post-Freudian, new-millennium" and the novel itself as a novel of "new realism, postfeminism and postcanonical" (Friedman 233). Others find that Mukherjee's moral stance in this novel undermines the story and makes it less fun. For example, Devi defines herself and others of her generation as "Vietnam's war-bastards and democracy's love children" (141). The protagonist claims that she does not understand how one could protest a war by doing dope on an alien continent and feels that people of her generation are "still coping with what they did, what they saw, what they salvaged, what they mangled and dumped on that Saigon rooftop that maniacal afternoon" (141). The "hybrids"—cultural and racial—are represented as negotiating and redefining identities for empowerment; however, in the reading of the text, one sees just despair and destruction, and one is left wondering how Devi is empowered in the end.

Most of the criticism of Mukherjee's work centers around the politics of representation, as her texts are published, read, and taught predominantly in the United States. Indian critics are particularly uncomfortable with her representations, as she persistently shows India and Indianness in a stereotypical and reductive manner. What most people find disturbing about Mukherjee in view of her use of Indian themes and Indianness is her refusal to be considered an Indian or even an Asian American writer. However, her novels are consistently inserted and taught in academe in multicultural undergraduate classes as representing the Indian or the Asian American experience and are then read as "authentic" due to the author's background. If one does not situate Mukherjee as a postcolonial subject and her texts as coming out of an era when Western-educated and middle-class women writers were resisting gender identity construction in purely Western terms, misreading and stereotyping can occur.

However, despite the often severe criticism one encounters from many postcolonial critics regarding Mukherjee's representations of India and Indianness, her fiction remains popular. It is because, as Alam contends, Mukherjee has created "original and valuable fiction about the immigrant experience in North America. . . . At her best, she has been able to bring to her firsthand experience of exile, expatriation, and immigration her considerable narrative skills and a lively imagination to produce memorable and colorful tales of excitement as well as the trauma of adjusting to a new world" (147). At her worst, she is considered a "sellout" and is then placed into a category of writers who use their ethnicity simply to enhance and sell their work regardless of the (perceived) damage that is done to one's own culture or ethnic background.

BIBLIOGRAPHY

Works by Bharati Mukherjee

Fiction

The Tiger's Daughter. Boston: Houghton Mifflin, 1971.
Wife. Boston: Houghton Mifflin, 1975.
Darkness. Markham, Ontario: Penguin, 1985.
The Middleman and Other Stories. New York: Viking Penguin, 1988.
Jasmine. New York: Viking Penguin, 1989.
Holder of the World. New York: Fawcett Columbine, 1993.
Leave It to Me. New York: Fawcett Columbine, 1997.

Nonfiction

(With Clark Blaise). *Days and Nights in Calcutta.* Garden City, NY: Doubleday, 1977.
(With Robert Boyers). "A Conversation with V. S. Naipaul." *Salmagundi* 54 (Fall 1981): 4–22.
"An Invisible Woman." *Saturday Night* (March 1981): 36–40.
(With Clark Blaise). *The Sorrow and the Terror: The Haunting Legacy of the Air India Tragedy.* Markhan, Ontario: Viking Penguin, 1987.

"Immigrant Writing: Give Us Your Maximalists!" *New York Times Book Review* (August 28, 1988): 1, 28–29.

"Prophet and Loss: Salman Rushdie's Migration of Souls." *Village Voice Literary Supplement* 72 (March 1989): 9–12.

(With Clark Blaise). "After the Fatwa." *Mother Jones* 15.3 (April/May 1990): 29–31, 61–65.

"A Four-Hundred-Year-Old Woman." In *The Writer on Her Work.* Ed. Hanet Sternberg. Vol. 2. New York: W. W. Norton, 1991. 33–38.

"Orbiting." In *Braided Lives: An Anthology of Multicultural American Writing.* Ed. Minnesota Humanities Commission Staff. St. Paul: Minnesota Humanities Commission, 1991. 237–52.

Studies of Bharati Mukherjee

Alam, Fakrul. *Bharati Mukherjee.* New York: G.K. Hall, 1996.

Boxill, Anthony. "Women and Migration in Some Short Stories of Bharati Mukherjee and Neil Bissoondath." *Literary Half-Yearly* 32.2 (July 1991): 43–50.

Chua, C. L. "Passages from India: Migrating to America in the Fiction of V. S. Naipaul and Bharati Mukherjee." In *Rewording: The Literature of the Indian Diaspora.* Ed. Emmanuel S. Nelson. Westport, CT: Greenwood Press, 1992. 51–61.

Connell, Michael, Jessie Grearson, and Tom Grimes. "An Interview with Bharati Mukherjee." *Iowa Review* 20.3 (1990): 7–32.

Dayal, Samir. "Creating, Preserving, Destroying: Violence in Bharati Mukherjee's *Jasmine.*" In *Bharati Mukherjee: Critical Perspectives.* Ed. Emmanuel S. Nelson. New York: Garland, 1993. 65–88.

Friedman, Ellen G. Rev. of *Leave It to Me. Review of Contemporary Fiction* (Fall 1997): 232–33.

Grewal, Gurleen. "Born Again American: The Immigrant Consciousness in *Jasmine.*" In *Bharati Mukherjee: Critical Perspectives.* Ed. Emmanuel S. Nelson. New York: Garland, 1993. 181–96.

Jackson, Marni. Rev. of *Leave It to Me.* Maclean's 110–29 (July 1997): 55.

Jussawalla, Feroza. "Chiffon Saris: The Plight of South Asian Immigrants in the New World." *The Massachusetts Review* 29.4 (1988): 583–95.

Knippling, Alpana Sharma. "Toward an Investigation of the Subaltern in Bharati Mukherjee's *The Middleman and Other Stories* and *Jasmine.* In *Bharati Mukherjee: Critical Perspectives.* Ed. Emmanuel S. Nelson. New York: Garland, 1993. 143–60.

Leong, Liew-Geok. "Bharati Mukherjee." In *International Literature in English: Essays on the Modern Writers.* Ed. Robert L. Ross. New York: St. James Press, 1991. 487–500.

Meer, Ameena. "Bharati Mukherjee." *BOMB* 29 (1989): 26–27.

Nelson, Emmanuel. "Kamala Markandaya, Bharati Mukherjee, and the Indian Immigrant Experience." *Toronto South Asian Review* 9.2 (Winter 1991): 1–9.

Pandya, Sudha. "Bharati Mukherjee's Darkness: Exploring the Hyphenated Identity." *Quill* 2.2 (December 1990): 68–73.

Raban, Jonathan. Rev. of Middleman and Other Stories. *New York Times Book Review* June 19, 1988. 1.

Rajan, Gita. "Bharati Mukherjee (1940–)." In *Writers of the Diaspora: A Bio-Bibliographical Critical Sourcebook*. Ed. Emmanuel S. Nelson. Westport, CT.: Greenwood Press, 1993. 235–42.

Roy, Anindyo. "The Aesthetics of an (Un)willing Immigrant: Bharati Mukherjee's *Days and Nights in Calcutta* and *Jasmine*. In *Bharati Mukherjee: Critical Perspectives*. Ed. Emmanuel S. Nelson. New York: Garland, 1993. 127–42.

Rustomji-Kerns, Roshni. "Expatriates, Immigrants and Literature: Three South Asian Women Writers." *The Massachusetts Review* 29.4 (1988): 655–65.

St. Andrews, B. A. "Co-Wanderers Kogawa and Mukherjee: New Immigrant Writers." *World Literature Today* 66.1 (1992): 56–58.

Tapping, Craig. "South Asian/North American: New Dwellings and the Past." In *Reworlding: The Literature of the Indian Diaspora*. Ed. Emmanuel S. Nelson. Westport, CT: Greenwood Press, 1992. 35–49.

Milton Murayama

(1923–　)

Seri Luangphinith

BIOGRAPHY

Milton Murayama was born on April 10, 1923, in Lahaina, Maui, to Japanese immigrants from Kyushu. When he was in sixth grade, his family moved to a plantation camp at Puʻukoliʻi, his experiences of which provide the setting for his works.[1] After graduating from Lahainaluna in 1941, he went to the University of Hawaiʻi. He served in the Territorial Guard following the bombing of Pearl Harbor but was abruptly discharged with other Japanese Americans. Murayama soon volunteered for Military Intelligence, which was seeking native speakers of Japanese. Inducted in 1944, he was assigned to the China-Burma-India Theater and was sent to Taiwan, where he helped facilitate the surrender and repatriation of Japanese troops. He came home in 1946, received his B.A. in English and philosophy from the University of Hawaiʻi in 1947, and went on under the G.I. bill to obtain his master's in Chinese and Japanese at Columbia University in 1950.

During his studies at Columbia, Murayama began work as a creative writer. By the time he completed his master's, he had also finished a draft of *All I Asking for Is My Body*. He moved to Washington, D.C., and worked for the Armed Forces Medical Library from 1952 to 1956. However, feeling the need for more time for his writing, Murayama moved to San Francisco, where he worked at the public library before becoming an import specialist with the U.S. Customs Office. At this time "I'll Crack Your Head *Kotsun*" (which later became the first chapter in *All I Asking for Is My Body*) made its debut in the *Arizona Quarterly* in 1959, followed by an appearance in *The Spell of Hawaii* (1968), an anthology of Hawaii's literature.

The next three decades proved busy for Murayama. Despite the success of his short stories, Murayama encountered difficulty finding a publisher for *All I Asking for Is My Body*, which was rejected due to a lack of interest in Asian American experiences. As a result, Murayama and his wife, Dawn, formed Supa Press. Ironically, the book became a success, and in 1980 Murayama received the American Book Award of the Before Columbus Foundation. In 1982 a local theater company called Kumu Kahua performed Murayama's play *Yoshitsune*, which the author recalls as not very well done. Nevertheless, Murayama's continued interest in prose provided the basis for later novels like *Five Years on a Rock*. Retirement has not slowed down this energetic writer: apart from occasional visits to the racetracks, Murayama has devoted much of his time to his writing career. In 1991 Murayama received the Hawai'i Award for Literature. In 1994 the University of Hawai'i Press published *Five Years on a Rock*, followed by the 1998 release of *Plantation Boy*. The writer is currently looking forward to Kumu Kahua's production of *All I Asking for Is My Body*.

Unlike many writers from Hawai'i who remain on the islands, Murayama is among the few who prefer life on the mainland. While he loves Hawai'i, he nevertheless finds the weather of his adopted San Francisco to be much more conducive to writing. But Murayama's desire to keep Hawaii's past alive is a strong link to his origins, which he plans to continue to visit in his writing for years to come.

MAJOR WORKS AND THEMES

All I Asking for Is My Body, Five Years on a Rock, and *Plantation Boy* are novels devoted to capturing different perspectives of the Oyama clan, a plantation family that struggles with the irreconcilable differences between Japanese traditions and the culture of its adopted home. This conflict serves as the thematic basis for Murayama's writing.

All I Asking for Is My Body focuses on the problems of class and ethnic difference on the plantation. In the opening story of Makot Suzuki, the narrator Kiyoshi Oyama is warned by his mother to avoid such *chorimbo* (bums) and *hoitobo* (beggars) who bring shame or "sickness" to those around them (2–3). The narrator acknowledges that there is "something funny" about Makot's folks. Unlike other Japanese who live together, the Suzukis live in the Filipino camp—the father owns a Model T (a "white" luxury), and the mother wears bright red lipstick in public, "which no other Japanese mother did" (10). Toward the end of the chapter, this "strangeness" is exposed: when Kiyoshi goes to his friend's house to break all relations, he sees Mrs. Suzuki "entertaining" Filipino men. The reasons behind alienating the Suzukis become clear—Makot's mother is a prostitute, and as a result her family is exiled from the Japanese community. The social politics of the plantation community, where class and ethnic divisions are distinct and bound by expectations concerning cultural propriety and family loyalties, become clear. The Japanese don't associate with Filipinos and other "lesser" individuals; those who do are *chorimbo*, and for such reasons obedience to one's parents is of utmost priority lest one invite shame or risk contamination.

Such "traditional" Japanese expectations form the basis for the belief that "there's a proper way to do everything" (13). However, propriety, which is used to govern everything from serving rice at the dinner table to eating oranges, is also the driving force behind the perpetual cycle of poverty among these immigrants because it makes children liable for their parents. Kiyoshi's parents came to Hawai'i to help the Oyama patriarch out of bankruptcy; they, in turn, must rely on their sons to help them out of their $6,000 debt. Toshio and Kiyoshi are thus forced to work the plantation for $2 a day—a frustrating and seemingly hopeless condition that "drains one's life with nothing to show for it" (86).

The negotiation between the reverence for, and the criticism of, traditional beliefs is further developed in *Five Years on a Rock*; however, in Murayama's second novel, the reader sees the situation from the mother's perspective. While Kiyoshi and his elder brother, Toshio, see their parents as symbols of oppression, Sawa Oyama's experiences reveal how certain beliefs are not always imposed on the individual. Sawa's story begins in Kyushu, where her parents are faced with dwindling resources. Her father offers his daughter in marriage to Isao Oyama, a proposition that will supposedly pay $500. But Sawa is not forced by her parents to accept Oyama; rather, Sawa makes her own decision to go, believing that she will be on this rock for only five years. However, once she arrives in the islands, her circumstances change in such a way that "traditional" Japanese beliefs become a means of emotional survival. Sawa must help the family in the daily chores, she and her husband must relinquish his pay to the Oyama family, and she must bear the accusations of theft by the Oyama matriarch. Sawa confesses her exhaustion to Aunt Kitano, who replies, "You'll get over it. It's a Japanese disease . . . they pile up too much on us, and we tend to *gaman* [endure] too much" (82). Sawa soon embraces this "disease"; her ability to *gaman* turns the endless stream of duties into a comforting routine that blocks out their growing debt, the necessary sacrifice of their children, the family's continual lack of food and rest, and the fact that the Japanese are rumored to be involved in the killing of a white child and the rape of an American officer's wife.

With *Plantation Boy*, the body of the narrator Toshio has already crumbled. While the younger son Kiyoshi in *All I Asking for Is My Body* is able to escape the plantation, enlist in the army, and win $6,000 in a poker match to pay off the family debt, Toshio is rejected by the military for having a "busted" eardrum. Lacking physical "perfection," Toshio has few opportunities: boxing takes him nowhere, and dying on the plantation as a truck driver hauling bagasse is not acceptable. This leaves him with the promise of *gaman*—to endure, to work hard, and to get an education with the hopes of becoming something better than a garbage collector. On a certain level, *Plantation Boy* can be read as a success story: the Japanese work ethic enables Toshio to pursue his correspondence studies and to maintain his dream of leaving the plantation.

However, the "model minority" myth—that immigrants and their progeny invariably overcome poverty and succeed in America—is complicated by Murayama in *Plantation Boy*. Whereas *All I Asking for Is My Body* and *Five Years on a Rock* concentrate on the inability of plantation Japanese to get ahead in life due to cultural conflicts, *Plantation Boy* offers a much more politicized critique of this social paralysis. While his spendthrift family continually plague Toshio, the book follows his ongoing realization of other factors, built into Hawaii's "plantation" society, that function to keep the working-class poor in their place. Toshio observes that the civil service system "is just like the plantation" because an individual "cannot stay if [he] got any push" (85). He also begrudges the fact that big haole (white) business owners are "just like plantation bosses" who hire Orientals to do their "dirty work" without adequate pay or recognition (91); and he bemoans certain older nisei who become successful and turn into "Uncle Toms" by "spout[ing] the haole party line" (177). These observations make clear that even in leaving the cane fields, Hawaii's Japanese do not necessarily escape the plantation mentality, which inscribes racial difference and ethnic conflict. In fact, the text argues that a professional status does not guarantee freedom from discrimination due to the fact that the political and social reality of the islands promotes the disparity between whites and the Japanese, and the fragmentation of the Japanese into successful "Uncle Toms" and those who struggle in opposing the system. *Plantation Boy* ends ambivalently on this issue—Toshio receives his architect's license, rejects his boss' offer of a 70/30 partnership, and sets up his own company; but unfortunately, he finds himself without work and facing starvation because established white architects have a monopoly on contracts.

CRITICAL RECEPTION

The critical attention paid to Murayama's works has been considerable, especially among scholars in Asian American studies and Hawaii's local literature; however, reasons for appreciating Murayama's contribution are varied. Up until the early 1990s, favorable reception of Murayama's work focused on the author's ability to provide an accurate and authentic portrayal of the Japanese experience on the islands. In the 1968 publication of the anthology *The Spell of Hawaii*, which featured "I'll Crack Your Head *Kotsun*," editors A. Grove Day and Carl Stroven note that Murayama's "fresh and appealing story . . . gives evidence that young people of Oriental ancestry brought up in Hawaii are becoming aware of their background as a source of unique literary material" (323). Similarly, in her review of *Five Years on a Rock*, Denise Perry Donovin feels that Murayama offers a glimpse of Japanese culture and history that is not often available to the everyday person.

Criticism has fortunately not been limited to the value of revealing "experience" to be found in Murayama's work. Current scholars have abandoned notions of the "striptease" value of cultural writing and have begun to critically address Murayama's "ethnic" approach to language, craft, and character development. For contemporary Asian American scholars such as Elaine Kim, Sauling Cynthia Wong, and Stephen Sumida, the value of Murayama's craft lies in the "oppositional" nature of his narratives. Specifically, Kim argues that *All I Asking for Is My Body* duplicates multiple hierarchies (such as the plantation town Pepelau and the Oyama family), which are negotiated by the character who yearns for his individuality and his freedom: what ensues are the complete rejection of such institutions and the subsequent freedom of the main character and the author (144–47). Wong's analysis of Murayama similarly recognizes the competition between hierarchy and the "rhetoric of social mobility" in *All I Am Asking for Is My Body*, but she also argues that hierarchy and social mobility are both ultimately rejected because Kiyo can solve the family's problems only by winning $6,000 in a crap game, not through hard work (161–62). Wong's argument implies that Murayama's first novel deconstructs the plantation status quo and the romanticized American success story. For Stephen Sumida, Murayama's writing offers a more "local" benefit—Sumida argues that Murayama's use of the childhood perspective and the "talk story" conventions of speech and dialogue produces distinctly local literary forms that displace exoticized, tourist notions of Hawaiian culture and identity. This trend in reading Murayama suggests that future scholars will see Murayama's works as less of a cultural source and more as a cultural critique.

NOTE

1. The contemporary revival of the study of Hawaiian language and literature has witnessed increased attention to "accurate" spellings of Hawaiian words using linguistic markers such as the *'okina* (the glottal stop signified by '). Out of respect for Native Hawaiian concerns regarding language usage, I use the *'okina* in Hawaiian words such as Hawai'i and Pu'ukoli'i; however, I omit the marker for Anglicized words such as "Hawaiian" or "Hawaii's" and in instances where I cite a writer who does not use such spellings.

BIBLIOGRAPHY

Works by Milton Murayama

Novels

All I Asking for Is My Body. Honolulu: University of Hawai'i Press, 1988.
Five Years on a Rock. Honolulu: University of Hawai'i Press, 1994.
Plantation Boy. Honolulu: University of Hawai'i Press, 1998.

Short Stories

"I'll Crack Your Head *Kotsun*." In *The Spell of Hawaii*. Ed. A. Grove Day and Carl Stroven. Honolulu: Mutual, 1968.

Drama

Yoshitsune. Typescript. 1977.

Essays/Articles

"Author Discusses How to Write Pidgin." *Honolulu Star-Bulletin*, November 25, 1976, L-24.

"A Christmas Memory." *Honolulu Star-Bulletin*, December 21, 1980, C1.

"Remarks." *Writers of Hawaii: A Focus on Our Literary Heritage.* Proceedings from the Writers of Hawaii Conference, October 1980. Ed. Eric Chock and Judy Manabe. Honolulu: Bamboo Ridge, 1981. 59–61.

Studies of Milton Murayama

Bowman, Pierre. "An Unclear 'Yoshitsune.' " *Honolulu Star-Bulletin*, May 12, 1982, B11.

Donovin, Denise Perry. Rev. of *Five Years on a Rock*. *Booklist* (December 1, 1994): 655.

Hiura, Arnold. "Comments on Milton Murayama," Proceedings from the Writers of Hawaii Conference, October 1980. *Writers of Hawaii: A Focus on Our Literary Heritage.* Ed. Eric Chock and Jody Manabe. Honolulu: Bamboo Ridge, 1981. 65–70.

Kim, Elaine. *Asian American Literature: An Introduction to the Writings and Their Social Context*. Philadelphia: Temple University Press, 1982.

Odo, Franklin S. Rev. of *All I Asking for Is My Body*. *The Nation* (September 21, 1992): 293.

Rozmiarek, Joseph T. " 'Yoshitsune' Needs Classical Trappings." *Honolulu Star-Bulletin*, May 11, 1982, B4.

Sumida, Stephen H. *And the View from the Shore: Literary Traditions of Hawai'i*. Seattle: University of Washington Press, 1991.

Wilson, Rob. "The Language of Confinement and Liberation of Milton Murayama's *All I Asking for Is My Body*." Proceedings from the Writers of Hawaii Conference, October 1980. *Writers of Hawaii: A Focus on Our Literary Heritage.* Ed.Eric Chock and Jody Manabe. Honolulu: Bamboo Ridge, 1981. 62–65.

Wong, Sau-ling Cynthia. *Reading Asian American Literature: From Necessity to Extravagance*. Princeton: Princeton University Press, 1993.

Kirin Narayan
(1959–   )

Maya M. Sharma

BIOGRAPHY

Kirin Narayan, the youngest of four children, was born in November 1959 in
Bombay. Her German American mother, Didi Kinzinger, is an artist, decorator,
and builder of sustainable housing. Kirin's maternal grandparents were artists
who came as refugees from Germany in the 1930s and taught at Baylor University in Texas. Her paternal grandfather was from a family of temple builders
and contractors in Kutch, Gujerat. Her South Asian father, Narayan Ramji, went
to a Parsi school in Nasik, Gujerat, where he was registered under the occupa-
tional name Contractor. Kirin would later take Narayan as her legal name. Narayan Ramji Contractor studied civil engineering at the University of Colorado
at Boulder, where he met Didi Kinzinger, an art student, and broke off an
arranged engagement to marry her in 1950.

The women in Kirin Narayan's family were strong and capable. They fostered
her creativity and imagination. Her maternal grandmother, who moved to Bombay to be near her daughter's growing family, taught Kirin to read at the very
early age of two and encouraged her to read and write. One of the first books
that she remembers reading is Louisa May Alcott's *Little Women*; Jo, the protagonist of this novel, fired her ambition to become a writer. Her paternal grandmother, Kamalabai Ramji, with her sense of adventure and storytelling flair, was
an equally strong influence. On her many pilgrimages, Kamalabai met a variety
of religious personalities and told stories of these *darshans* (holy audiences)
with great dramatic flair.

The house where Kirin Narayan grew up in Bombay was always full of
guests—journalists, filmmakers, scientists, foreign scholars, hippies, religious
seekers. This rich home culture enables Kirin to assess, analyze, and present

characters with the bicultural insight of the participating insider. In much of her anthropological research she focuses on storytelling as a medium for entertainment and edification. The desire to delight and also teach is evident in her fiction. Storytelling connects her scholarship with her fiction.

MAJOR WORKS AND THEMES

Love, Stars, and All That follows folklorist Gita Das from graduate school at Berkeley, through a visiting assistant professorship in New England, to tenure track at Austin and the submission of her first book to a publisher; from prudish convent school virginity, through a brief American marriage and an equally brief Indian engagement, to the beginning of her first love affair. Behind the scenes stands the Bombay auntie who helped to raise her, a wealthy, intelligent, humorous woman who, it is hinted, was her father's lover from their days in the Communist Party.

Love, Stars is about the coming-of-age, the sexual awakening, of an Indian woman in America. The cultural conflict is very real. Nevertheless, it must be noted that the protagonist, Gita, grew up under the influence of a singularly liberated woman who had been a revolutionary and had had a lover before she had married and who refused the white weeds of widowhood. As a friend puts it, "These people were rich; even their grandparents were English speakers. They could challenge traditions" (273).

It is a novel of university life, though a singularly gentle one. The relationship between the distinguished professor and the graduate student/research assistant would normally be seen as exploitation on one side and opportunism on the other. Her marriage, after all, brings Gita into the charmed circle of the academic elite. Both Gita and Norvin Weinstein are treated with affectionate humor, and neither is seen to be using the other. There is a great deal of satire of the dominant modes of discourse involving concepts of critical theory, postmodernism, subalternity, and the like, but again this is good-natured and without ideological malice.

Most importantly, perhaps *Love, Stars* deals with very complex questions of personal, cultural, national, and racial identity. Ideology and critical theory tend to oversimplify these questions, in the process marginalizing human beings like Narayan and her characters who do not fit their stereotypes. At the end of the book Gita remarks to Firoze Ganjifrockwalla, a cousin brother of a school friend of hers, "People like us are this impossible collage, aren't we?" They are cycling through the New England countryside. "Tell me about it," he replies (304). In the best traditions of the Bombay talkie they are soon overtaken by a cloudburst and become lovers.

Finally *Love, Stars* is about storytelling. Gita keeps remembering her ayah's stories as a reference point of her life, and the novel concludes with her retelling one to her friends. In 1989 Narayan had published her anthropological study of storytelling by "Swamiji," a religious teacher, in her father's hometown, Nasik.

In 1991 she began a collaboration with Urmilaji, a woman from the Himalayan foothills village where her American mother had settled over a decade before. There she lived in her mother's house and recorded, transcribed, translated, and retold the stories told by this friend, aiming at the widest possible audience. The result was *Mondays on the Dark Side of the Moon* (1997).

The Preface to *Mondays* concludes with "A Note to My Colleagues," in which she states that "scholars trained in academic disciplines would do well to dismantle the wall between the vivid stories and intellectual conversations between narrated insights we would share with friends and family and rigorous analyses we would address to fellow specialists" (xi). In her collaboration with Urmilaji she was greatly encouraged by the late A. K. Ramanujan, a poet translator and folklorist who wrote in English and Kannada.

The final section of the "Afterword" to *Mondays* is of very general import: "If there is a central moral to this long story about Urmilaji's stories it is this: stories arise out of relationships, they are about relationships, and they forge relationships. From her I have learned afresh the value of remembering and retelling the stories handed over by loved people. Retelling their stories we keep alive their nurturing presence and at the same time we deepen ties with the people we now address" (221). In her relationships with "Swamiji" and Urmilaji, Kirin Narayan was inspired and empowered to become the teller of her own tales, of which *Love, Stars, and All That* was the first.

CRITICAL RECEPTION

Love, Stars was well received by reviewers in both India and America, who point to its strengths as a novel without canonizing it as a text in gender studies or cultural studies. In a generally positive review, "One Girl's Invention of an American Self" in the *Los Angeles Times*, Elaine Kendall finds the book "a satiric delight" but, apparently missing the author's ironic view of the communicative style adopted by Indian intellectuals, finds some of the dialogue "a bit didactic." She finds the ending "rushed and anteclimactic [sic]," which it would be if the book was really about the quest for a soul mate, and if Firoze Ganjifrockwalla were indeed intended to be indubitably he.

A lengthy review by R.T Both in the *Milwaukee Journal* is entirely laudatory. According to Both, Narayan "blends her exploration of gender politics, the day-to-day life of Indian upper classes, and the contemporary American academic scene with the skill of an experienced cook creating a delicious curry."

Writing in *India Today*, Dom Moraes takes a dim view of the existing genre of Indian expatriate fiction before finding hope in Narayan's fresh start: "So far, Indian expatriate fiction that I have read has not quite managed to fit the pieces together: the journey is often clumsy: the general impression left by the characters is that they do not quite know who they are or what they want: there is a joyless generality about them caught between two cultures." The catena of colons is the mark of a severe critic indeed. But for Moraes, *Love, Stars* marks a new beginning: "This is a novel well received and achieved. It is witty and sometimes very funny: it is also intelligent, excellently written, and revelatory of what it is like to be an American born [*sic*] in India, and it is full of promise. It makes one feel that Narayan is that very rare bird, a born writer, and that she may fly far."

BIBLIOGRAPHY

Works by Kirin Narayan

Storytellers, Saints and Scoundrels: Folk Narrative in Hindu Religious Teaching. Philadelphia: University of Pennsylvania Press, 1989.
" 'According to Their Feelings': Teaching and Healing with Stories." *The Lives Stories Tell: Narratives and Dialogue in Education*. Ed. Carol Witherell and Nell Noddings. New York: Teachers College Press, 1991. 113–35.
Love, Stars, and All That. New York: Washington Square Press, 1995.
Mondays on the Dark Night of the Moon: Himalayan Foothills Folktales. New York: Oxford University Press, 1997.

Studies of Kirin Narayan

Reviews of Love, Stars and All That.

Both, R. T. "A Searching of the Soul." *Milwaukee Journal*, January 30, 1994, E8.
Fine, Mary. "Novel Delves Deep into Cuisine of Culture." *West Palm Beach Post*, May 1, 1994, J6.
Kendall, Elaine. "One Girl's Invention of an American Self." *Los Angeles Times*, 4 March 4, 1994, E4.
Moraes, Dom. "Coming of Age." *India Today* (July 31, 1994): 95.

Fae Myenne Ng
(1957–)

Xiaoping Yen

BIOGRAPHY

Fae Myenne Ng was born into a Chinese immigrant family in San Francisco. Her mother worked as a seamstress, and her father as a laborer. Fae Myenne Ng attended University of California-Berkeley and Columbia University, where she received a master's degree. Her first novel, *Bone*, drew on the collective memories of generations of Chinese immigrants as well as her personal experiences growing up in San Francisco's Chinatown. While writing the novel, she supported herself by working as a waitress and at temporary jobs. When the novel was published in 1993, it received widespread and favorable critical attention. Fae Myenne Ng now lives in New York. She is working on her second novel.

MAJOR WORK AND THEMES

Bone is the story of a Chinese immigrant family in San Francisco, Leon, Mah, and their three daughters, Leila, Ona, and Nina. Leila, the eldest daughter, is the narrator of the story.

Leon immigrates to America thanks to a "paper father" who has no blood relation to him but agrees to sponsor him for $5,000 and Leon's promise to send the old man's bones back to China after he dies. Mah comes to San Francisco with her first husband, Dulcie Fu, who tells her that she deserves better than muddy roads and "water-carrying villages" (187). When Mah is pregnant with Leila, her husband decides to go to Australia, "the new gold mountain," with a promise to send for Mah once he settles down in the new country. He never sends for his wife or his daughter. After six years of waiting, Mah decides to marry Leon Leong because he has a green card. They have two daughters: Ona and Nina.

Mah toils at a sweatshop as a seamstress, and Leon is a seaman who is away from home most of the time. Born a dreamer, Leon tries several times to set up his own businesses. The business he puts all his savings in and pins all his hopes on is the Ong & Leong Laundry, a partnership with a slick friend, Luciano Ong. During the period when both families work at the laundry, Ona and Luciano's oldest son, Osvaldo, fall in love. While the romance flourishes, the business has to close because Luciano fails to pay rent, utilities, and other bills. Emotionally and financially hurt, Leon orders Ona to break up with Osvaldo. Soon after, Ona jumps off the thirteenth floor of a housing project named Peaceful Gardens.

One important theme of the story is what critic Heather R. Miller calls "America the Big Lie" (425). Leon and Mah came to America to search for "the gold and the easy life" (187), but after working hard for their whole lives, they feel cheated. According to Leila, his father "had kept his end of the bargain: he'd worked hard. Two jobs, three. Day and night. Overtime. Assistant laundry presser/Prep cook. Busboy. Waiter. Porter. But where was his happiness?" So Leon bitterly complains, "America, this lie of a country!" (104).

After Ona dies, Mah visits her native land for the first time since coming to America. She has no success story to share with her relatives and friends. Instead, she searches for sympathy and solace.

Twenty-five years in the land of gold and good fortune, and then she returned to tell her story: the years spent in sweatshops, the prince of the Golden Mountain turned into a toad, and three daughters: one unmarried, another who-cares-where, one dead. I could hear the hushed tone of their questions: "Why? What happened? Too sad!" (24)

Another theme of the story is the deep sense of alienation from their families and their native land that many Chinese immigrants feel. At the beginning of the story, Leila describes an old man who has got lost and who finds himself in San Fran, a bachelor hotel. When asked where he came from, the old man whispers with downcast eyes, "Don't know. Don't remember" (6). In fact, the ancient and lonely bachelor hotel provides a poignant leitmotiv to the whole novel. Leon's "paper father" dies at the hotel. After he hears of Mah's affair with her boss, Leon seeks refuge at the hotel. When Ona commits suicide, Leon moves into the hotel again. He stashes all his money in a brown bag hidden in his tiny room, which he longingly calls his "going-back to China fund" (6).

Bones are the most significant symbol of alienation in the story. Leon blames all the unhappiness in his family on his failure to send the bones of his "paper father" back to China. In an interview with Nancy Stetson, Fae Myenne Ng discusses why she chose *Bone* as the title of the book. For a long time, discriminatory laws forbade Chinese laborers who came to work in America from bringing their wives. As a result, the workers saw America only as a place of work, and they planned to return to China after they earned enough money. However, because of wars and revolutions in China, many of them were unable to return, so their wish was to have their bones sent back to China for burial after their death.

It was very important to make this journey back home after death. They [the old generation of laborers] talked about it. It was dreamed of. That moved me. I called the book *Bone* to honor that tradition. I'm not able to send bones back to China, to send this generation of men, to give them back what they missed out on in their lives. But somehow, creating this book . . . was a way of giving a resting place to my memories of them. (Stetson)

Another symbol of alienation is Leon's suitcase of neatly ordered documents. They include a marriage affidavit, pay stubs, job rejection letters, and newspaper clippings. Leon and Mah have no independent identity in America. The papers *are* their identities. Leon came to American through a "paper father," and Mah married Leon for his green card. Immigration, disability, Social Security, and even a visit to the cemetery where Leon's "paper father" is buried all require proper papers. Leon likes to tell his friends, "In this country, paper is more important than blood" (9). As critic Lisa Lowe points out, the papers are at once "the 'conversion' of Chinese into 'Americans' " and "a loss of history" (124–125).

The conflict between the Chinese tradition of filial loyalty and American individualism is another theme of the novel. Mah and Leon, like many other first-generation immigrants, have a very difficult life in America. However, their daughters have better education and more opportunities. In an article titled "False Gold: My Father's American Journey," Fae Myenne Ng calls her father's immigration to America a "sacrificial" journey. "Now, at the end of his life, he calls it a bitter, no luck life. I have always lived with his question, Was it worth it? As a child, I saw the bill-by-bill payback and I felt my own unpayable emotional debt. Obedience and obligation: the Confucian curse" (12).

The three daughters deal with this emotional debt in very different ways. Ona, the middle daughter, is the most sensitive, and she feels the closest to Leon. "When she was little, she'd be weepy for days after Leon left for a voyage, and she'd wait for him, shadowy and pensive, counting off the days till he came home." She comforts her father after he hears of Mah's affair. She accompanies Leon when he looks for a job. "Every time he lost a job, she went into a depression with him. When he got high on some scheme, she was drunk on it, too" (171–172). When Leon, deeply hurt by the failure of the Ong & Leong Laundry, threatens to disown her if she continues her romance with Osvaldo, she is torn between her filial loyalty and her love. Suicide is her way of escaping from the conflict.

Nina, the youngest daughter, has the cleanest break with the family. "She yelled back, she said things, she left" (25). She lives in New York, works as a flight attendant, dates non-Chinese men, and has an abortion. She tells Leila, "I hardly ever use chopsticks anymore. At home I eat my rice on a plate, with a fork, I only used chopsticks to hold my hair up" (27). Her answer to the Confucian tradition is unambiguous: "I know about *should*, I know about *have to*. We should, we want to do more, we want to do everything. But I've learned this: I *can't*" (33).

Leila, the oldest daughter, takes a more nuanced approach. She shuffles between her parents and Mason Louie, her boyfriend, who lives on the other side of town. She takes care of her parents and is always "on standby for them" (33). As a result, Nina comments that Leila has the peace of heart, knowing she has done her share for Mah and Leon (32). On the other hand, against the wishes of her mother and the Chinese tradition, she cohabits with Mason without getting married. She wants to test the relationship first before committing herself. Her mother married her first husband to escape China and then married Leon for his green card, but Leila wants a marriage of love. Another gesture of rebellion from Leila is marrying Mason at City Hall in New York without the pomp, crowd, and banquet Mah always wanted.

At the end of the story (since the story employs a reverse chronological order, the end of the story is also the beginning of the book), Leila and Nina are able to reconcile with their history in their own ways, Nina, for all her disdain for San Francisco's Chinatown, ends up working as a tour guide for American tourists to China. Leila works in a school as a community relations specialist, visiting immigrant families. Like her own parents, the parents of her students work too hard, know little English, and have no time for their children. "[T]he parents seem more in need than the kids" (17). When she was young, Leila hated dealing with government red tape for Mah and Leon. Now she is more generous. The parents need her help. "A call to the tax man, a quick letter to the unemployment agency. I do what I can. What's an extra hour?" (17).

CRITICAL RECEPTION

Bone was reviewed by more than twenty newspapers and magazines when it was published in 1993. The reviews were mostly positive and enthusiastic, and some critics saw the debut of a new talent.

Cristina Garcia praises the novel in the *Washington Post* for capturing "the profound loneliness at the heart of immigration experience, of the immigrant family itself—a cutting off from the past, a furious remaking of the present, febrile hopes for the future." However, she argues that Ona, the middle daughter who killed herself, is not adequately developed in the story. Although much of the story revolves around the aftermath of Ona's suicide, and although Leila spends much time analyzing the event, "Ona remains a cipher throughout, barely convincing even as a memory."

Many critics see the cultural and the generational conflict inherent in the immigration experience as a central theme of the story. For example, in a review in the *New York Times*, Michiko Kakutani points out that all three sisters "feel at once suffocated by Mah and Leon's provincialism and guilty about the freedoms and luxuries they take for granted as young American women; at once resentful of their parents' enslavement to the past and wistful about the history that eludes them here in the United States."

To Richard Eder of the *Los Angeles Times*, the strength and surprise of the book are the portraits of Mah and Leon. Leon and Mah are the "real rebels" against the past. They come to America in search of a better life, and they toil at menial jobs to give their children more opportunities. They also rebel against their marriage of convenience in their own ways. Leon's seafaring journeys, like his moving into the bachelor hotel, are a way of escaping from its troubles, and Mah's affair with her boss is an unconscious protest. On the other hand, Eder believes that the portrayal of Mason Louie, Leila's boyfriend, is "facile and sentimental." He is too much of "a perfect prince."

Heather Ross Miller argues in *The Southern Review* that *Bone* puts on trial a false American ideal. "To be American, our national dream insists, is to live redeemed, freed from a burdensome past" (422). However, through its description of what Ng calls "the personal and spiritual cost of leaving one life in order to make another" (87), the story shows what is sacrificed in the process of becoming an American. According to Louis B. Jones' review published in *The New York Times Book Review*, what makes the book authentic are its "ambivalence and ambiguities far removed from the good-against-evil moral structure one finds in the traditional tales of older societies" (9).

One feature of the story is the reverse chronology of the narrative. Telling a story backward is a technique often used in mystery and detective stories. The diagnostic structure motivates the readers to continue reading until they find the culprit and the cause of the crime. Lisa Lowe, in an article published in 1996 on four Asian American novelists, points out that the structure in *Bone* is employed for thematic purposes. The beginning of the book seems to suggest that the discord in the Leong family is a result of Ona's suicide, but as we read on, we realize that the discord precedes the death. "[W]hen the event of the suicide is at last reached, it dissolves, apprehensible not as an origin but as a symptom of the Leong family's collective condition" (122).

Critics have also commended the spare and minimal style of the story. According to Louis B. Jones, *Bone* has "the sort of profound restraint that first strikes the reader as deceptively simple, but on closer inspection, it seems an example of that rarer quality, simplicity itself" (7). Suzanne Samuel, writing for *The Women's Review of Books*, agrees: "Ng is a master storyteller. Her gift for observation and language makes *Bone* truly extraordinary."

BIBLIOGRAPHY

Works by Fae Myenne Ng

Novel

Bone. New York: Hyperion, 1993.

Short Stories and Articles

"Last Night." *City Lights Review* 1 (1987): 24–29.
"Backdaire." *Harper's* 278.1667 (April 1989): 64–68.
"False Gold: My Father's American Journey." *The New Republic* 19 (July 1993): 12–13.
"Farewell." *Granta* 54 (Summer 1996): 209–213.

Studies of Fae Myenne Ng

Brostrom, Jennifer. Interview. *Contemporary Literary Criticism* 81 (1993): 87–88.

Eder, Richard. "A Gritty Story of Assimilation." Rev. of *Bone*. *Los Angeles Times*, January 14, 1993, E5.

Garcia, Cristina. "Reading Chinese Fortunes." Rev. of *Bone*. *Washington Post*, January 10, 1993, 8.

Jones, B. Louis. "Dying to Be an American." Rev. of *Bone*. *The New York Times Book Review* (February 7, 1993): 7, 9.

Kakutani, Michiko. "Building on the Pain of a Past in China." Rev. of *Bone*. *New York Times*, January 29, 1993, C26.

Lowe, Lisa. "Decolonization, Displacement, and Disindentification: Asian American 'Novels' and the Question of History." In *Cultural Institutions of the Novel*. Ed. Deidre Lynch and William B. Warner. Durham, NC: Duke University Press, 1996. 96–128.

Miller, Heather Ross. Rev. of *Bone*. *The Southern Review* 29.2 (Spring 1993): 420–30.

Samuel, Suzanne. "Time Heals No Wounds." Rev. of *Bone*. *The Women's Review of Books* 10.8 (May 1993): 27.

Stetson, Nancy. "Honoring Her Forebears." Rev. of *Bone*. *Chicago Tribune*, April 4, 1993, 3.

Mei Ng
(1967–   )

Sarah Catlin Barnhart

BIOGRAPHY

Mei Ng is the third and youngest child of Chinese parents who immigrated to the United States. Growing up, her family was one of a few Chinese families in Queen's Village, New York. She describes herself as "kind of a goody two-shoes" as a young girl (Cryer). Her older brother and sister were stifled by their parents' expectations; as Ng explains: "There was just a lot of conflict because of [my parents] having grown up there in China and having different expectations. They wanted us [children] to be home studying" (Cryer). Ng might not have always been at home, but she did study: "I liked to read anything I could get my hands on, whatever random books were around. I read encyclopedias. I was in the library a lot" (Cryer). To this day, Ng cannot read or speak Chinese, although she did once attempt to learn it through a college adult education course. Her parents spoke Chinese at home, but, as Ng relates, they "really didn't speak to us [children] in Chinese. It was a little bit of a secret language between them" (Cryer). Ng eventually graduated from Martin Van Buren High School and enrolled in classes at Columbia University, planning to major in journalism. She completed a degree in women's studies in 1988 and retired to Key West, where she indulged what she calls her "slacker side" as long as she could afford it (Cryer). She then returned to New York and began working for a temporary employment agency. A resident of Park Slope, Ng was a student at Brooklyn College's graduate program in fiction writing. She was "discovered" when a one-page excerpt of her work was published in *Interview* magazine. In light of the successful publication of her first novel, she has given up temping for a job as a counselor for the New York City Gay and Lesbian Anti-Violence Project, which assists victims of violence.

MAJOR WORK AND THEMES

To date, Mei Ng has written one novel, the widely reviewed *Eating Chinese Food Naked*. Released in 1998, Ng reports that it took her seven years to complete the novel. It is the story of Ruby Lee, a young woman who returns home to Queens after receiving a degree in women's studies from Columbia University (much to her father's chagrin). She moves back into her parents' apartment behind the family-run laundry while she decides what to do with her life. Her indecision about the direction her life should take extends into her love life. Ruby has been seeing her Jewish lover, Nick, for four years. He adores her, even though she repeatedly cheats on him with strange men and dreams of intimacy with women.

Also problematic is Ruby's relationship with her parents. She is protective of her mother, Bell, although the nature of their relationship is conveyed through details, not conversation. For instance, Bell places choice pieces of meat on Ruby's plate when she thinks her daughter isn't looking. Ruby's father is even more difficult to know. In addition to her parents, Ruby also has a loser for a brother and a sister who is unhappy in her marriage.

The novel is driven not by plot but by the development of Ruby's character over the duration of one summer. She's struggling with making a place for herself as a second-generation Chinese American, being poor, dealing with her parents' loveless marriage, and settling questions about her own sexuality. In fact, Carole Morin believes that it is not so much Ng's nationality that causes her anguish as her guilt about being middle-class while her parents are clearly poor. This is a departure from the average response to the novel, which focuses on the Chinese American heritage of both Ng and Ruby Lee as the defining characteristic of the work.

Katherine Forestier notes that the novel is exceptional in another way, viewing it as an attack on Chinese stereotypes. The eldest brother, Van, is far from a "responsible family man." "Ruby's sister, Lily, is also unattractively selfish and dysfunctional." Forestier lauds Ng for creating Asian American characters who are not "upwardly mobile and superior in culture and intelligence to other Americans," who are, instead, individuals with real flaws, faults, and problems.

Creating well-developed, individual characters seems to be one of Ng's strengths. When asked if she considers herself to be a Chinese American author, Mei Ng responds, "I guess I am. I'm also just a writer. We all get categorized. Sometimes it's annoying that I can only be compared to Amy Tan* or Maxine Hong Kingston.* We do have common themes, but there's more that isn't common" (Cryer). Looking at her reviews, one quickly sees that Ng's complaint does have some foundation. Although she is most often compared to Kingston and Tan, her writing has also been compared to M.F.K. Fisher, Banana Yoshimoto, Rachel Cusk, and the early works of Martin Amis. Kingston does happen to be one of Ng's favorite authors, but she also likes Toni Morrison and Carson McCullers (Cryer).

CRITICAL RECEPTION

Eating Chinese Food Naked was met with mixed reviews. Many critics loved the hook; others were alienated by its dependence on character development and description instead of plot. This dissatisfaction caused a few reviewers to use words like "banal" and "flat" to describe the novel, although even these reviewers had positive things to say, as well.

The feature of the novel most commented on by reviewers is the relationship between Ruby and her mother. Katherine Forestier observes, "Ng is at her strongest in developing the relationship between daughter and parents." Many readers objected to the cold, demystified nature of Ruby's sexual encounters, but Forestier argues that the mystery has merely been relocated to the relationship between Ruby and her mother. In a similar way, Jennifer Yancy notes, "[Ruby] is protective of her mother, Bell, whom she feels is mistreated by her father. She dreams of taking Bell away from her hard life in Queens . . . and finds it easier to focus on improving her mother's life than figuring out her own." Yancy concludes that "Ng's strength lies in the realistic mother–daughter relationship, but perhaps this is also her weakness: She has created something so genuine it almost reads in real time." Lynn Karpen describes the relationship with a bit more intensity, describing Ruby's feelings as "fierce love" and her attitude as "intensely protective." Carole Morin has the most extreme view of the situation. She believes that Ruby returns home due to her "longing for her mother." She goes on to write,

Saving the novel from the ordinary is Ruby's passion for her mother. She does not just love Bell, she is in love with her. She is afraid to leave her boyfriend and confront her desire for women, which is really a perverted lust for her mother.

Ruby wants to take Bell to Florida on a twisted Freudian honeymoon, then to live with her in Manhattan, a borough away from [her husband] and his demands for sex.

Bell cannot bear to lose her inverted Electra so forces her to leave home.

Whereas most reviewers do not describe the relationship in this way, it does point to the possibility of an alternative reading of the novel that Ng herself might appreciate.

Ng notes, "Someone read my book and said it was kind of grim. That's the kind of esthetic I relate to. I don't like a happy Hollywood ending. I'm more interested in that sick world, that twisted-up stuff that's underneath family relations" (Cryer). So perhaps Morin's Freudian reading of the story is not so extreme, after all.

Although the reviews of this first novel by Mei Ng were mixed, they were generally favorable. Almost all reviewers stated that the novel was a good first effort for a young writer. In spite of a smattering of constructive criticism, *Eating Chinese Food Naked* has left readers and reviewers clamoring for more.

BIBLIOGRAPHY

Work by Mei Ng

Novel

Eating Chinese Food Naked. New York: Scribner, 1998.

Studies of Mei Ng

Brownrigg, Sylvia. Rev. of *Eating Chinese Food Naked. The Guardian* (London) March 5, 1998. 14.

Chai, May-Lee. Rev. of *Eating Chinese Food Naked. San Francisco Chronicle*, January 13, 1998, E5.

Cryer, Dan. Rev. of *Eating Chinese Food Naked. Newsday* (January 11, 1998): B11.

Forestier, Katherine. Rev. of *Eating Chinese Food Naked. Saturday Review* (March 14, 1998) 8.

Karpen, Lynn. Rev. of *Eating Chinese Food Naked. New York Times*, March 1, 1998, sec. 7: 21.

Morin, Carol. Rev. of *Eating Chinese Food Naked. The Scotsman* (March 7, 1998): 14.

Rev. of *Eating Chinese Food Naked. Publishers Weekly* 244 (December 8, 1998): 56.

Vivinetto, Gina. Rev. of *Eating Chinese Food Naked. St. Petersburg Times*, January 25, 1998, D5.

Wax, Emily. Rev. of *Eating Chinese Food Naked. Newsday* (May 10, 1998): Queens ed. G1.

Wullschlager, Jackie. Rev. of *Eating Chinese Food Naked. (London) Financial Times*, January 3, 1998, 5.

Yancy, Jennifer. Rev. of *Eating Chinese Food Naked. San Diego Union-Tribute*, February 1, 1998, Books 4.

Hualing Nieh
(1925–)

Hailing Xiao

BIOGRAPHY

Hualing Nieh was born in Hubei Province, China, in 1925. She attended middle school in Chongqing, Sichuan Province, and received her B.A. in English from the Western Languages Department of National Central University in 1948. A year later, she went to Taiwan and became a literary editor and member of the editorial board of the fortnightly *Free China*, a popular magazine for intellectuals striving for reform and freedom from the period of 1949 to 1960. Later she became an instructor in creative writing at National Taiwan University. During her stay in Taiwan, she published *Creeper (Ge Teng)*, a novella; *The Lost Golden Bell (Shi Qu de Jin Ling Zi)*, her first novel; two collections of short stories in Chinese, *Jade Cat (Fei Cui Mao)* and *A Little White Flower (Yi Duo Xiao Bai Hua)*; and a collection of short stories in English, *The Purse*. In addition, she translated *Selected American Stories* and *Madame de Mauves* from English to Chinese.

Nieh came to the United States as a writer in residence in the Writer's Workshop at the University of Iowa in 1964 and got an M.F.A. in Creative Writing from the same university two years later. In 1967 Nieh cofounded the International Writing Program at the University of Iowa with Paul Engle, whom she married in 1971 and with whom she worked as codirector of the program until 1988. Due to their significant contribution to the promotion of the exchange among international writers, Nieh and her husband were both nominated for the Nobel Peace Prize in 1976. Moreover, Nieh was a codirector of the Translation Workshop and established an M.F.A. in Translation with Daniel Weissbort. She received several honorary doctorates as well as an award for Distinguished Service to the Arts from the governors of the fifty states of America in 1982.

Nieh continued to publish many novels, collections of short stories, memoirs, and translations during her teaching career at Iowa. In 1972 she published a translation of *Poems of Mao Tse-tung*, which she cotranslated with Paul Engle, and in 1981 two volumes of *Literature of the Hundred Flowers*, a selection of Chinese literary works written in the 1950s. Her most famous novel, *Mulberry and Peach: Two Women of China* (*Sang Qing Yu Tao Hong*), which was issued in China, Taiwan, Hong Kong, England, the Netherlands, Hungary, and Korea, was published in 1989 in the United States and won the 1990 American Book Award for fiction. *Far Away, a River* (*Qian Shan Wai, Shui Chang Liu*), her recent novel in Chinese, depicts one of the themes that are often reflected in her novels—the search for identity and Chinese roots.

As a novelist, editor, critic, and translator, Nieh has traveled extensively in Asia and Europe and has lectured in some major universities in the United States as well as many leading universities in China.

MAJOR WORKS AND THEMES

Nieh's over twenty published books include novels, short stories, essays, memoirs, literary criticism, and translations, most of which were written in her native Chinese language. As one of the most famous contemporary Chinese overseas writers, Nieh's works, to a great extent, demonstrate her in-depth knowledge and great concern for the Chinese history and culture in the past century. During an interview with Peter Nazareth, Nieh mentioned that she is "even more obsessed and involved with the Chinese now than at any other time" (Nazareth 11). Most of the protagonists in her novels are constantly recalling their lives in the past in China and comparing their past lives with their present situation in the new land; thus, the search for identity and memories of the historical and personal situation function as major threads in many of her novels and short stories.

The Lost Golden Bell, Nieh's first novel, was written while she was working as a literary editor in Taiwan. The novel begins with the memories of Lingzi, the female protagonist, of her small hometown that she left five years ago. The heroine's bildungsroman is depicted through the eighteen-year-old Lingzi's relationship with Aunt Qiao and Uncle Yinzhi by utilizing symbols and lyrical description. Nieh's short story "The Several Blessings of Wang Danian" deals with Wang's wishful thinking and unrealistic dreams of getting rich through raising fish. Wang and his former classmate nicknamed Sage are often lost in their dreams of their youthful days during their school years. Moreover, the story again demonstrates Nieh's skillful adoption of symbols and images to reflect the political situation in Taiwan (Yu 132).

The best-known novel Nieh wrote while she was the director of the International Writing Program at the University of Iowa is *Mulberry and Peach: Two Women of China*, which has been published in Hong Kong, Taiwan, and China with six different Chinese editions and has been translated into eight languages.

The heroine, Mulberry, narrates the events that happened to her life as if it is about another dead woman named Peach. Peach describes the differences between herself and Mulberry as follows, "Mulberry is Mulberry and Peach is Peach. They're not the same at all. Their thoughts, manners, interests, and even the way they look are completely different" (3). The novel covers Mulberry's flight from China to Taiwan and then the United States from 1945, when she is sixteen, to 1970, when she becomes an acute schizophrenic. Nieh's incisive exposition of the detrimental effects of the political turmoils and oppression on Mulberry's psychological development caused the censorship of the book in both Taiwan and China in the 1970s. The split personality of the protagonist, according to Nieh, is about the Chinese in the twentieth century, and the book is "a kind of fable about the Chinese situation" (Nazareth, "Interview" 11). Mulberry's present life is constantly intertwined with the memories of the struggles of her past life, and her life story is a reflection of the histories of Taiwan and China.

Far Away, a River, Nieh's most recent novel, depicts the story of Lotus, who is the daughter of a Chinese female student, Fenglian, and an American reporter, Bill Brown. In search of her father's identity, Lotus experiences a series of cultural shocks and goes through a period of identity crisis in Iowa City. However, unlike Mulberry, who suffers from despair of life and a split personality, Lotus achieves an understanding of her past and attains a positive attitude toward life with the help of Dr. Lin and her cousin Billy. Through the memories of her mother, Lotus tells her story against the background of the turbulent history of China from the Sino-Japanese War to the Cultural Revolution.

Nieh once mentioned, "Fiction is my strong point. So if I write fiction, I cannot write in English. I cannot write in English. I have to write in Chinese. And I still have to write about Chinese" (Nazareth, "Interview" 17). Nieh's personal life experiences in, and her knowledge of, the cultural, social, and political events of China, Taiwan, and the United States often provide rich materials and inspiration for her creative writing. Just as Ruoxi Chen points out that "nativism is the essence of overseas literature" (13), most of Nieh's novels deal with the theme of Chinese people's life in China and Taiwan or a Chinese's search for one's identity and roots that covers the span of time from the 1940s to the present.

CRITICAL RECEPTION

Nieh's writings, like those of most of the other Chinese overseas writers of the mid-twentieth century, received critical attention mostly from Chinese-speaking countries such as Hong Kong, Taiwan, and China. Summarizing her own writings published before she came to the United States, Nieh says, "The characters of the fiction I published in Taiwan in the 1950s were all rootless, hopeless, nostalgic people" (qtd. in "In Search of" 55).

The most comprehensive survey and criticism of Nieh's fiction in English are conducted by Shiao-ling Yu in her essay "The Themes of Exile and Identity Crisis in Nie Hualing's Fiction." According to Yu, Nieh's short story "The Several Blessings of Wang Danian" represents Nieh's successful depiction of the themes of exiles in many of her writings (127). Like Yu, Chinese critic Ye Weilian also points out that Nieh's symbolic and realistic treatment of Wang's life is a typical feature of Nieh's fiction (Yu 129). Yu mentioned that the shaky chair of Wang serves as an excellent example to illustrate Nieh's technique of "delayed revelation" (129). The reader comes to the realization about "Danian's plan and Taiwan's precarious situation" (Yu 129) at the end of the story with Nieh's brilliant use of symbolic techniques.

Nieh's excellent use of symbolism is demonstrated again in her novel *The Lost Golden Bell*, in which "the golden bell stands for a kind of longing felt by Lingzi" (Yu 133). However, Yu also notes that both Ye Weilian and Xu Yu notice that Nieh is "less successful with her characters" (137), and Nieh's portrayal of the female protagonist Lingzi appears to be more mature than her actual age (Yu 137).

Of all of Nieh's novels, *Mulberry and Peach; Two Women of China* receives the most critical attention in the United States. Though most of Nieh's stories are "ironic studies of the frustrations of the mainlanders in Taiwan" (210), Pai Hsien-yung states that *Mulberry and Peach* is the novel that "has elaborated the theme of exile to its fullest extent" (210). The novel is praised for its successful depiction of the exile of "Mulberry and Peach, the two personalities locked within the heroine" (Yu 137), which also "symbolize a divided country and divided people" (Yu 137). Nieh herself once mentioned,

I myself am a split personality . . . split between being an artist and being a Chinese. . . . I want, myself, to write as an artist. And I appreciate writers as artists. On the other side, I'm Chinese, so I am thinking of the country, of Chinese history. (Nazareth, "Interview" 16)

The *Publishers Weekly* reviewer points out that *Mulberry and Peach* is a "disquieting study of psychological and cultural schizophrenia" and that "the novel provocatively juxtaposes events from American history with China's upheavals." Yu also observes that Nieh often associates the fate of her characters in the novel with the turmoils of the history of China (138). Kirk Denton, in his review of *Mulberry and Peach: Two Women of China*, reiterates Nieh's skillful use of symbolism in the novel: "Though in some respects this is a psychological novel about mental disintegration, *Mulberry and Peach* is essentially a novel in a symbolic mode" (136). Denton further points out that the novel represents "the literature of exile which is based on a paradox: the longing for freedom from one's past and the psychological need to define one's self in terms of that past" (137).

Similarly, Hsin-sheng C. Kao points out that Nieh's *Far Away, a River* demonstrates "the intricate interplays between self and family, and action and reaction to history" (4). The reviewer of *The Asiaweek Literary Review* notes that *Far Away, a River* shows Nieh's "partial return to the old tradition of realism and epic poetry" ("In Search" 56). Also, Yu argues that both *Far Away, a River* and *Mulberry and Peach: Two Women of China* focus on "the fate of the Chinese exiles against a background of modern Chinese history. . . . However, they differ in narrative technique. Whereas *Two Women* is all 'showing,' *A River* is mostly 'telling' " (152).

As Chen observes that the literature of overseas writers has become a bridge between East and West (12), Nieh's novels, to a certain extent, have contributed to people's understanding of the similarities and differences of social, historical, and cultural situations between the East and West.

BIBLIOGRAPHY

Works by Hualing Nieh

Novels

Creeper (Ge Teng). Taipei: Free China Magazine, 1953.
The Lost Golden Bell (*Shi Qu de Jin Ling Zi*). Taipei: Xue Sheng Chu Ban She, 1960.
Mulberry and Peach: Two Women of China (*Sang Qing Yu Tao Hong*). Hong Kong: You Lian Chu Ban She, 1976.
Far Away, a River (*Qian Shan Wai, Shui Chang Liu*). Si Chuan: Ren Min Chu Ban She, 1984.
Mulberry and Peach: Two Women of China. Trans. Jane Parish Yang and Linda Lappin. Boston: Beacon Press, 1988.

Short Stories

Jade Cat (*Fei Cui Mao*). Taipei: Minghua Shuju, 1959.
The Purse. A Collection of Short Stories Written in English. Hong Kong: Heritage, 1959.
A Little White Flower (*Yi Duo Xiao Bai Hua*). Taipei: World Book, 1963.
The Several Blessings of Wang Danian (*Wang Danian De Ji Jian Xi Shi*). Hong Kong: Hai Yang Wen Yi She, 1980.
Stories of Taiwan (*Taiwan Yi Shi*). Beijing: Beijing Chubanshe, 1980.
Tales from the Deer Garden. Shanghai: Shanghai Literary Press, 1996.

Nonfiction Prose

The Valley of Dreams (*Meng Gu Ji*). Hong Kong: Chengwen Chubanshe, 1965.
Black, Black, the Most Beautiful Color (*Hei Se, Hei Se, Zui Mei Li De Yan Se*). Hong Kong: Joint, 1983.
Iowa Notes: After Thirty Years (*Ai He Hua Zha Ji: San Shi Nian Hou*). Hong Kong: Joint, 1983.
People in the 20th Century (*Ren Zai Er Shi Shi Ji*). Singapore: Global, 1990.

Translations

Madame de Mauves, by Henry James. Taipei: World Book, 1959.
Selected American Stories. Taipei: World Book, 1960.

Eight Stories by Chinese Women. Hong Kong: Heritage Press, 1963.

(Cotranslated with Paul Engle). *Poems of Mao Tse-tung.* New York: Simon and Schuster, 1972.

Literature of the Hundred Flowers. New York: Columbia University Press, 1981

Other

A Critical Biography of Shen Ts'ung-wen. Boston: Twayne Press, 1972.

(Coedited with Paul Engle). *Writing from the World.* Iowa City: University of Iowa Press, 1976.

Studies of Hualing Nieh

Chen, Ruoxi. "Prologue: Chinese Overseas Writers and Nativism." *Nativism Overseas: Contemporary Chinese Women Writers.* Ed. Hsin-sheng C. Kao. New York: State University of New York Press, 1993. 9–19.

Denton, Kirk. "A Review of *Mulberry and Peach: Two Women of China.*" *Journal of the Chinese Language Teachers' Association* (May 1989): 135–38.

"In Search of Chinese Roots." *The Asiaweek Literary Review* (February 8, 1985): 55–56.

Kao, Hsin-sheng C., ed. *Nativism Overseas: Contemporary Chinese Women Writers.* New York: State University of New York Press, 1993.

Link, Perry. "Review of Literature of the Hundred Flowers." *Chinese Literature: Essays, Articles, Reviews* 6 (1984): 185–91.

Rev. of *Mulberry and Peach: Two Women of China Publishers Weekly* (October 28, 1988): 56.

Nazareth, Peter. "An Interview with Chinese Author Hua-ling Nieh." *World Literature Today* (Winter 1981): 10–18.

———. "A Review of *Two Women of China: Mulberry and Peach.*" *World Literature Today* (Spring 1982): 403–4.

Pai, Hsien-yung. "The Wandering Chinese: The Theme of Exile in Taiwan Fiction." In *Nativism Overseas: Contemporary Chinese Women Writers.* Ed. Hsin-sheng C. Kao. New York: State University of New York Press, 1993. 205–12.

Quach, Gianna. Rev. of *Mulberry and Peach: Two Women of China. Modern Chinese Literature* (Spring 1993): 1–3.

Yu, Shiao-ling. "The Themes of Exile and Identity Crisis in Nie Hualing's Fiction." In *Nativism Overseas: Contemporary Chinese Women Writers.* Ed. Hsin-sheng C. Kao. New York: State University of New York Press, 1993. 127–56.

Sanjay Nigam
(1959–   )

Jaina C. Sanga

BIOGRAPHY

Sanjay Kumar Nigam was born in 1959 in Delhi, India. While still an infant, his parents immigrated to the United States. He grew up in Arizona, where, among a sizable Hispanic and Native American minority population, being an Asian American was particularly unusual. In an article in *Natural History* ("Five Stories") Nigam writes, "I had to point out my differences to avoid confusion . . . the quest for my identity as a brown man in a white world, although not without a little pain, was exciting—possibly the defining experience of my life" (55).

Nigam has published short stories in *Grand Street* and *The Kenyon Review*, and his first novel, *The Snake Charmer*, was published in 1998. Although residing in the United States, Nigam visited India several times; his grandparents lived in Delhi, and for a while he attended school in Bangalore and Udaipur. Hence there is a significantly accurate detailing of Indian culture and its idiosyncrasies in the novel. Even the title of the novel, which seems at first to resonate with Orientalist images of an exotic India, is actually Nigam's attempt to recast and rewrite that image from a genuinely Indian perspective.

Writing short stories and novels is not, however, Nigam's first profession. He is currently associate professor of medicine at Harvard Medical School, where he works as a physician and researcher. He has published extensively in scientific journals. Nigam began writing fiction while doing his residency at Parkland Hospital in Dallas, Texas, and claims that some of his literary favorites include the "big" Russian novelists and the Latin American magic realists.

MAJOR WORK AND THEMES

Nigam's novel, *The Snake Charmer*, is based on his short story "Charming," which was published in *Grand Street*. Set in Delhi, the novel tells the story of a snake charmer, Sonalal, who, on the day the novel opens, is performing in front of Humayun's Tomb. Sonalal performs with his cobra, Raju, all day long to audiences that emerge from Delhi tourist buses. Although having earned more than his usual sum of money for the day, Sonalal coaxes his cobra into one more dance. The music emanating from Sonalal's *been* is so powerful that even the snake is completely entranced. Barely able to move, the cobra raises himself one more time. Suddenly, Sonalal hits a false note; the snake, tired and angry, bites Sonalal's leg. A totally humiliated Sonalal, in a fit of anger, bites and kills his own snake: "Sonalal felt no pity. His eyes became wild. He bent down, grabbed the listless snake by the head and tail, and stretched it to its full length. Then he closed his eyes, growled, and opened his mouth wide. All Sonalal's rage concentrated in his jaws. He bit. Two wriggling cobra halves fell and squirmed on the ground. Then they became still" (9).

After this act of violence, Sonalal's life is changed forever. The event brings him instant fame and fortune as journalists come to his house to interview him, and word of his incredible act spreads around the world. Sonalal, however, is filled with remorse and self-hatred; he thinks he will never be able to replace Raju, and he will never be able to play such divinely inspired music again. Plagued with guilt, middle-aged Sonalal loses his sexual drive and his gift for playing music; he begins quarreling with his wife, Sarita; he has nightmares; and he begins incessantly biting his tongue. His self-esteem irrevocably damaged, Sonalal embarks on a quest for redemption. He seeks the counsel of doctors, whom Nigam, a doctor himself, depicts with great satire. First there is the Nietzsche-quoting Dr. Seth, a "crackpot" doctor whose diagnosis for many of his patients is that they are homosexual. Dr. Seth also explains how Kekule, a scientist, dreamed the chemical structure of benzene to be that of a snake biting its own tail—this becomes one of the controlling metaphors of the book. Then there is Dr. Basu, who, after performing a physical examination of Sonalal, concludes that Sonalal suffers from guilt. Sonalal's disillusionment with modern scientific medicine leads him to conclude that American doctors know nothing about the symptoms of guilt because they are wholly biased by science. Nigam's satiric comparisons of Indian and American doctors, of traditional and modern medicine, are depicted with genuine insight and become the main strengths of the novel.

On one level the novel is a rendition of Sonalal's quest for some sort of perfection either in life or in art. His obsessive and ultimately frustrating recollections of his music on the apocalyptic day reinforce in his own mind that perfection in art is possible. His wish that people would remember him for his music rather than for his violent act of biting the cobra finally prompts Sonalal to assume that the world rewards all the wrong things. By the end of the novel, then, Sonalal realizes, and to some extent redeems himself in the belief, that through his art, he did, in fact, experience a fleeting moment of perfection.

CRITICAL RECEPTION

On the whole, Nigam's debut novel has received favorable reviews. The *New York Times* writes that "while Nigam's story of the Delhi streets zips along like a bicycle rickshaw, it passes through what is actually some pretty serious cultural and intellectual traffic" (Bernstein). According to a *Booklist* reviewer, the novel is "stunning" in its portrayal of the central character (Caso). The *Montreal Gazette* claims the novel is "captivating" and that Sonalal's "mental and moral wanderings are chronicled unflinchingly, but with compassion" (Viswanathan). This is, indeed, generous praise for a first novel. Other newspapers, the *Dallas Morning News*, the *Los Angeles Times*, the *San Francisco Chronicle*, the *Toronto Globe and Mail*, and *USA Today*, have applauded the novel for being simple and lyrical, engaging in its treatment of character and story, and intensely compelling in its rendition of modern India.

Some reviewers, however, have been more critical in their assessment of *The Snake Charmer*. According to *India Star*, an on-line review of books, "Nigam is at his best when he is subtly satirizing contemporary society," but "the novel weakens some when summary becomes necessary to show the passage of time" (Sethi). Some sharp words have come from *Publishers Weekly*, which writes that the novel is "overexpanded," and while it may appeal to a Western audience, the novel's "self-consciously elegant prose is uncomfortably at odds with the teeming slums it so prettily describes" (Rev.). *Library Journal* calls it a "largely bleak novel" in which "climactic moments occur at odd times" (Dwyer). *The New York Times Book Review* writes that the plot, after the brilliantly construed opening chapters, "meanders, losing its urgency in a welter of metaphors that far too quickly become far too predictable" (Lowenthal). Despite these reviewers' harsh comments of Nigam's work, *The Snake Charmer* is a well-imagined tale, exhibiting a sense of quiet wisdom. In rendering one man's quest for perfection, Nigam invites the reader to confront life as it is, with all its ambiguities and imperfections, and the novel succeeds, finally, not only because it is simple and lyrical and charmingly satiric but because it is told from the heart.

India Today, describing Nigam's first public reading of the novel at a Barnes and Noble bookstore in New York, reports that Nigam will attempt to write a bigger book that focuses on the interaction between Indians in the United States. If Nigam continues writing, judging from the generally positive responses to his first novel, he is going to be an important new voice in Indian American literature.

BIBLIOGRAPHY

Works by Sanjay Nigam

Novel

The Snake Charmer. New York: William Morrow, 1998.

Short Stories

"Charming." *Grand Street* 9. 3 (Spring 1990): 13–22.
"Levitating." *The Kenyon Review* 12. 4 (Fall 1990): 54–62.
"Amrish Bound." *The Kenyon Review* 18. 3–4 (Summer–Fall 1996): 56–66.

Essay

"Five Stories." *Natural History* 107. 2 (March 1998): 50–57.

Studies of Sanjay Nigam

Bernstein, Richard. Rev. of *The Snake Charmer*. *New York Times*, July 6, 1998, E6.
Caso, Frank. Rev. of *The Snake Charmer*. *Booklist* 94 (April 15, 1998): 1429.
Dwyer, Janet Ingraham. Rev. of *The Snake Charmer*. *Library Journal* 123 (April 15, 1998): 114.
Lowenthal, Michael. Rev. of *The Snake Charmer*. *The New York Times Book Review* 103 (August 9, 1998): 19.
Pais, Arthur. Rev. of *The Snake Charmer*. *India Today* (July 27, 1998): 41.
Rev. of *The Snake Charmer*. *Publishers Weekly* 245 (April 6, 1998): 56.
Sethi, Robbie Clipper. Rev. of *The Snake Charmer*. *India Star* www.indiastar.com.
Viswanathan, Padma. Rev. of *The Snake Charmer*. *The Montreal Gazette*, December 19, 1998, J5.

John Okada
(1923–1971)

Fu-jen Chen

BIOGRAPHY

Born in the old Merchants Hotel in the Pioneer Square area of Seattle, where his parents owned a boarding hotel, John Okada, the eldest of three sons, went to Bailey Gatzert Elementary, Broadway High, and the University of Washington, where he received bachelor's degrees in English and in library science. Later, he earned a master's degree in English from Columbia University, where he met his wife, Dorothy. During World War II, he and his family were evacuated from Seattle and interned at Minidoka, Idaho. He soon volunteered for military duty, serving as a sergeant in the U.S. Air Force until he was discharged in 1946. After the war, Okada married Dorothy, with whom he had a daughter and a son. He worked first in the Seattle Public Library and then in the Detroit Public Library; thereafter, he worked as a technical writer in Detroit and Los Angeles. When working as librarian in the early 1950s, Okada started writing his *No-No Boy*, which, according to Frank Chin,* was based on a real-life story of a no-no boy named Hajiime Jim Akutsu. Okada completed the manuscript in 1955 and published it two years later. Before he died of a heart attack in Los Angeles in 1971, he had almost finished the draft of a second novel, in which, he claimed, he had a strong urge to "faithfully describe the experiences of the immigrant Japanese in the United States" before they speedily vanished (Chin, "Afterword" 256–57). Unfortunately, shortly after his death, his wife burned the draft of the story about the issei as well as all his other manuscripts and notes. *No-No Boy* is Okada's only published work of fiction.

MAJOR WORK AND THEMES

Set just after the end of World War II, *No-No Boy* begins with Ichiro Yamada's return to the Japanese American community in Seattle from a two-year prison term. A twenty-five-year-old nisei, Ichiro was imprisoned for refusing the draft and answering "no-no" on the loyalty oath to the following two questions issued by the War Department in 1943. The first question asks: "Are you willing to serve in the armed forces of the United States on combat duty whenever ordered?" The other reads: "Will you swear unqualified allegiance to the United States of America and faithfully defend the United States from any or all attack by foreign or domestic forces, and foreswear any form of allegiance or obedience to the Japanese emperor, to any foreign government, power, or organization?" Ichiro's double negative to both the inquiries regarding his loyalty and willingness to undertake combat duty made him an outcast in the Japanese American community and a traitor to the country. He was labeled a "no-no boy." *No-No Boy* depicts Ichiro's reunion with his family and a rapid sequence of encounters with friends, neighbors, and strangers. Ichiro's rejection of his mother, the mother's suicide, his brother's betrayal and departure for the army, confrontations with "yes-yes" Japanese Americans, friendships with other "no-no" boys as well as a Japanese American veteran, a love affair with a Japanese American girl, and the search for a job—all these illustrate Ichiro's step from the trauma of being a no-no boy to his journey to reestablish an identity out of fragments. Ichiro's quest for a sense of self exposes the disfiguring effects of racism and the internment not only on the individual psyche but on the family as well as the community. The exposure of a people's sufferings further overshadows the American spirit of equality.

In the pursuit of his true identity, Ichiro first tries to analyze why he said, "No-s." After two years in jail, he is still uncertain about his actions, and his sense of selfhood has been shattered by his internalization of "No-no." Ichiro's probing begins with his reunion with the family. Fractured and disjointed by the war, it includes a patriotic and maniac mother, an ineffectual and alcoholic father, and a rebellious and malicious brother. Through examining his relationships with them and tracing his development from childhood into adulthood, Ichiro gradually understands the formation of himself as a no-no boy. Introducing the mother as having few feminine features—"a small, flat-chested, shapeless woman" (10)—Ichiro sees her as a "rock" (12) and recognizes in her an "unreckoning force" (20). Ichiro declares that her power forces him to say "No-s." Identifying with the mother, Ichiro had tried to be a Japanese like her and acted according to her will. Because the mother claimed to be loyal to the Japanese emperor and called "traitors" those Japanese Americans who enlisted in the U.S. military, Ichiro refused the draft and said "no" to the judge. In the novel, the mother is the only one who is proud of him as a no-no boy. Her repeated praise and affirmation—"You are my son"—embody what gave him existence before the war. Ichiro recalls: "There was a time when I was your son. There was a time. . . . You used to smile a mother's smile and tell me stories. . . . [W]e were Japanese with Japanese feelings and Japanese pride and Japanese thoughts" (15). The mother was half of him, and the half almost became the whole of him (16).

In the novel the disfiguring effects of war and racism on the family are shown by a Japanese American family in which no one acts like a typical Japanese: a mother is driven mad and commits suicide, a father becomes effeminate, children turn against their parents, and a brother behaves as a bitter foe. Clinging to her fanatical loyalty to Japan, the mother cannot admit the Japanese defeat in the war. Unable to accept the outcome of the war, the mother isolates herself socially and psychologically. When neighbors gossip about her madness, the mother willfully interprets their talk as a sign of envy of her strength, "the strength of Japan" (41). She finally collapses, however, when her own family denies her and can no longer tolerate her delusions. Ichiro calls her "crazy woman," her second son, Taro, leaves home for the army, and her husband reads her a letter from her sister in Japan who writes to beg for food and describes the desperate situation in Japan after the war. Because the letter divulges a secret shared only by her and her sister in childhood, the mother can hardly reject it as mere political propaganda against Japan. As a result, no longer able to live in a fantasy filled with Japan's glorious victory and her eventual return to Japan, the mother stops eating and compulsively repeats some actions: she precisely ranges cans on a shelf and knocks them down to do it again. Several days later, as if responding to her husband's begging—"Mama, eat or you will take sick. Eat or you will die" (175)—she drowns herself in a tub full of water. Although regarding the mother as a crazy woman, Ichiro asks, Was she really crazy and wrong when she turned all hopes toward Japan when America "repeatedly refused to accept her or her sons unquestioningly?" (104). Who is crazy? The mother? Or those who were so delirious as to fight for a country that denied them? Ichiro wonders.

In contrast to the mother as a "rock" who usurps the head of the family, Ichiro's father is a "round and fat and cheerful-looking" man. When conversing with his son, the old man is so nervous as to ceaselessly go back and forth as if his pants were creeping with ants (9). He is called by Ichiro "a baby," "a fool," and even "a goddamned, fat, grinning, spineless nobody" (120). Of his father, says Ichiro, "He should have been a woman. He should have been Ma" (112). In addition to this eccentric Japanese father, Taro, Ichiro's younger brother, feels shame for his parents' "Japaneseness" and his brother's "no-no" status. On his eighteenth birthday, he waits no longer to join the "American" army to prove his loyalty. In order to show his disassociation with Ichiro's treason and gain acceptance of his peers, Taro betrays his brother, leading Ichiro to be beaten by his friends. Taro hates his brother and also his parents because of the "thing" in Ichiro and because of the "thing" created by his parents representing "Japaneseness" in physical, cultural, and mental terms (19). Unwilling to be a "Japanese" brother or a "Japanese" son, Taro desires an identity—an American one—separate from his parents' and his brother's.

As Ichiro's family is torn by binary oppositions—American versus Japanese, yes-yes versus no-no—so the postwar community is wrenched by similarly polarized choices. It is a community full of self-abhorrence, guilt, agony, suicide, conflict, combustion, and hatred. The uncompromising distinctions aggravated by the war prove that the issei's insistence on maintaining Japanese culture is a mistake and the nisei's belief in American nativity, acquisition of English, and education as guarantees for an American identity turns out to be wishful thinking. After all, during the war they were all seen as "enemy aliens." Caught in this imbroglio, the community gives vent to their anguish and despair in targeting "no-no boys." No-no boys are seen as discredits to the race, as shameful reminders of disloyalty, and as emblems of "Jap lovers." At the opening of the novel, Ichiro on the way home is greeted with spit and curses by Eto, an old acquaintance in an Eisenhower jacket. Freddie, also a no-no boy, confronts ceaseless bullying and tragically is killed at the story's end. Another no-no boy, Gary, is well aware of his status, saying, "I don't blame them one bit for not hesitating to kill us" since no-no boys are "big, black marks" (228). Gary turns to find comfort in art.

In contrast to no-no boys, Kenji Kanno, representing the people who say "yes-yes," acts as a foil to Ichiro throughout the novel. Driving a new Oldsmobile, Kenji is a war hero, winning the Silver Star. Unlike Ichiro, he is a credit to the community; unlike Ichiro's father, Kenji's father, six feet tall and strong, is "a moderate and good man"; unlike Ichiro, whose home makes him feel like "puking," Kenji lives in a house decorated with a polished mahogany table, new lamps, and a big television set; unlike the meals Ichiro eats at home—eggs with soy sauce, boiled cabbage, tea, and rice—what Kenji has at home are coffee, milk, pop, cookies, or ice cream. Ichiro's no-no decision and embodiment of Japaneseness are all set off by Kenji's yes-yes choice and manifestation of Americanness. Though characterized by their opposition, Ichiro and Kenji share one thing in common: they both suffer pains either in the mind or in the body. While Ichiro is severely wounded by his guilt for being the no-no boy that makes him "nobody," "only an empty shell," or at best "only half man," Kenji lost a leg in the war and is dying slowly because of its rottenness. Although the missing leg won him a car, a badge of courage, and a proof of loyalty and made him an idol of his peers, Kenji suffers from losing inches of his leg little by little and finally his "manhood." Because of the loss of his manhood, Kenji passes on to Ichiro a Japanese American girl he is asked to look after by his friend Ralph, who reenlists in the army. "I'm only half a man," Kenji admits, "and when my leg starts aching, even that half is no good" (89). Ironically, whether answering "no-no" or declaring "yes-yes," they both end up being "incomplete" and "half."

In the novel not only Japanese Americans but also other ethnic groups suffer from being excluded from the mainstream of America. The Negroes, the Japanese, the Chinese, the Mexicans, the Filipinos, and the Jews all strive for recognition as complete persons, namely, as Americans. But being American in the novel is characterized by a practice of inclusion and exclusion. In the constitution of an American subject, "race" is one of the main signifiers that define American identity. As the ethnic groups cannot assume its attribute (e.g., white skin), they can never cross "the unseen walls" to become Americans (104). In agonies of unfulfillment, they turn against one another and impose racial discrimination on other groups. Racism is not just the whites' prejudice against the blacks or against the Asians but is a problem among minority groups, which use the same racial hierarchy to attack one another. In the novel the blacks ask the "Japs" to go back to Tokyo; in turn, the Japanese despise the "Negroes" and feel superior to the "Chins," who may see themselves as "better" Asians since China was America's ally during the war. Racism gnaws at the heart of each ethnic American, disfigures the spirit of every community, and finally damages the nation as a whole. When expelling the Japanese from the West Coast is claimed as an "evacuation," when the concentration camps become "relocation centers," and when racism is practiced in the excuse of an assurance of safety, the national conscience is eroded away, and the American ideal of democracy is marred.

Beginning with Ichiro's return home—the onset of a quest for an identity—*No-No Boy* ends with his still-ongoing search for the meaning of his existence. Constantly examining his "half of self," either Japanese or American, Ichiro hesitates to accomplish his passage and to be seen as a stabilized subject. Obsessed with recurrent guilt as a no-no boy who is worthy of nothing, Ichiro turns down two jobs, a chance to go back to the university, and love from Emi. Although concluding with a note of "hope," the novel emphatically depicts Ichiro as a solitary seeker who is still compulsively journeying to an indefinite destination:

He walked along, thinking, searching, thinking and probing, and, in the darkness of the alley of the community that was a tiny bit of America, he chased that faint and elusive insinuation of promise as it continued to take shape in mind and in heart. (251)

CRITICAL RECEPTION

Since rediscovered as a classic of Asian American literature, John Okada's *No-No Boy* has been widely examined in anthologies, literary history, Asian American studies, and scholarly journals at home and abroad. Part of it is anthologized in *Aiiieeeee! An Anthology of Asian-American Writers* (1974), *The Heath Anthology of American Literature* (1990), and *The Big Aiiieeeee!* (1991), notably introduced in *Columbia Literary History of the United States* (1988) as well as *The Columbia History of the American Novel* (1991), and significantly recognized in a series of Asian American literary studies, including *Ethnic Literatures since 1776* (1976), *Three American Literatures* (1982), *Asian American Literature: An Introduction to the Writings and Their Social Context* (1982), *Frontiers of Asian American Studies* (1989), *Reading the Literatures of Asian America* (1992), *An Interethnic Companion to Asian American Literature* (1997), and *Immigrant Subjectivities in Asian American and Asian Diaspora Literature* (1998). Besides, the novel is thoroughly explored in such ethnic journals as *Amerasia* as well as *MELUS* and in such mainstream journals as *American Literature*; it is, moreover, discussed in France and Japan.

Ironically, before rediscovery by Frank Chin and other Asian American writers in the mid-1970s, *No-No Boy* had been ignored for almost two decades. When first published in 1957, the novel was not only neglected by the American public but also rejected by the Japanese American community. Its first edition of 1,500 copies had not sold out when John Okada died in obscurity in 1971. The negative response to the novel surprised its publisher, Charles E. Tuttle, who assumed that the Japanese American community "would be enthusiastic about it"; on the contrary, they "were not only disinterested but actually rejected the book" (Chin et al. xxxix). In the Afterword of the second edition in 1976, Frank Chin writes that he "got the impression [Okada's] family was ashamed of the book" (256). After Okada's death, his wife wanted to offer all of his manuscripts to the Japanese-American Research Project at the University of California at Los Angeles (UCLA), but the manuscripts were rejected, and his wife was even encouraged to destroy the papers. In fact, in dealing with such a taboo as "no-no," the novel itself becomes a "thing" in the Japanese American community. Silence concerning the novel reveals not only the American public's unreadiness to face the historical fact that America once confined its own people in camps without legal reasons or procedures, but also the Japanese Americans' unwillingness to be reminded of the psychological wound—the wrenching experiences of the interment, the humiliation of the racial discrimination, and the disgrace of "no-no." Because the novel was first published in an era of Cold War, the time when the American public strove to construct a national consensus against communism, when the Japanese Americans could not wait to start their lives over again, it would not be difficult to understand why the novel had been ignored for almost two decades.

Since the novel's rescue from oblivion, critics have examined many aspects: its social context, use of language, distinctions of gender, use of autobiography and folklore, and focus on such issues as generational conflicts, double consciousness, dual identity, and binary patterns. No matter which aspect or issue was investigated, most readings in the 1970s through the 1980s defined the novel as a "redemptive" journey of a fragmented protagonist's search for "wholeness," emphasizing the "hopeful" ending and the transformation of Ichiro from a "no-no" boy to one saying "yes" to the future through a practice of exclusion of "Japaneseness" and inclusion of "Americanness" in terms of polarized opposition (McDonald; Inada; Chin; Chin et al.; Kim). Since then, however, critical readings have been more skeptical about the optimism of the novel, questioned the compulsion of the passage of "redemption," and even affirmed an underlying subversive and problematic texture. In "Discourse and Dislocation: Rhetorical Strategies of Asian-American Exclusion and Confinement" (1990), David Palumbo-Liu first pointed out "the lure of redemption held forth by the legal body of America" (2). In 1992 Gayle K. Fujita Sato also noticed the problematic nature of Ichiro's journey and the doubt of his return. Reading the process of journey in the novel as "a cycle of rebirth" (131), William Yeh in 1993 asserted that "Ichiro rejects all the alternatives presented to him" (129), and instead of dissolving into either pole of the binary opposition, Ichiro had to create his own category, his unique character and personality. In 1995, echoing Yen's statements, Jinqi Ling in his essay "Race, Power, and Cultural Politics in John Okada's *No-No Boy*," published in the premier journal *American Literature* in 1995, stressed that "the novel ultimately transcends the ideological fatalism" and that Ichiro "is never entirely dissolved into the social roles defined for him by the dominant discourse" (363); Ling claimed, "Okada transformed the conventional novel by making it subversively unfamiliar and problematic" (375). In 1996, Stan Yogi in *MELUS* argued that through Ichiro's journey to establish an identity, "Okada explores the gray area between the opposition that develops around polarized definitions of 'Japanese' and 'American,' individuality and community, assimilation and cultural maintenance" (64). Moreover, Yogi shows how these oppositions Okada unveils "are false and how polarized notions that divide the community tend to collapse in upon themselves" (64). In *Immigrant Subjectivities in Asian American and Asian Diaspora Literature*, published in 1998, Sheng-mei Ma argues that "Okada is entirely ethnic with the wisdom of hindsight, but his sense of identity is problematized by the historical fact of being designated as 'enemy alien' and interned during World War II" (73). Ma briefly mentions the significance of the sharp contrast between the "repugnant physical attribute" of Ichiro's immigrant mother and the embodiment of Americanness of Ichiro's Japanese American girlfriend, Emi. Currently, because of the eminence of postcolonial discourse and its emphasis on a new diasporic or exilic identity in Asian American writing, *No-No Boy* is seen as an important novel "situated at the juncture of immigrant and ethnic literary tradition" (Ma 73).

BIBLIOGRAPHY

Work by John Okada

No-No Boy. 1957. Seattle: University of Washington Press 1976.

Studies of John Okada

Chan, Jeffery Paul, et al., eds. *The Big Aiiieeeee! An Anthology of Chinese American and Japanese American Literature*. New York: Meridian, 1991.

Cheung, King-Kok, ed. *An Interethnic Companion to Asian American Literature*. Cambridge: Cambridge University Press 1997.

Chin, Frank. "Afterword." In *No-No Boy*. Seattle: University of Washington Press, 1976. 253–60.

———, et al., eds. *Aiiieeeee! An Anthology of Asian American Writers*. Washington, DC: Howard University Press, 1974.

Elliott, Emory, et al., eds. *The Columbia History of the American Novel*. New York: Columbia University Press, 1991, 405, 463, 500, 799.

———. *Columbia Literary History of the United States*. New York: Columbia University Press, 1988, 814, 818.

Fujita Sato, Gayle K. "Momotaro's Exile: John Okada's *No-No Boy*." In *Reading the Literature of Asian America*. Ed. Shirley Geoklin and Amy Ling. Philadelphia: Temple University Press, 1992.

Inada, Lawson Fusao. "Introduction." In *No-No Boy*. Seattle: University of Washington Press, 1976. iii–vi.

———. "Of Place and Displacement: The Range of Japanese-American Literature." In *Three American Literature: Essays in Chicano, Native American, and Asian-American Literature for Teachers of American Literature*. Ed. Houston A. Baker Jr. New York: Modern Language Association, 1982. 254–65.

Kim, Elaine H. *Asian American Literature: An Introduction to the Writings and Their Social Context*. Philadelphia: Temple University Press, 1982.

Lauter, Paul, et al., eds. *The Heath Anthology of American Literature*. 2 vols. Lexington, MA: D. C. Heath, 1990. 1900–12.

Ling, Jinqi. "Race, Power, and Cultural Politics in John Okada's *No-No Boy*." *American Literature* 67.2 (1995): 359–81.

Ma, Sheng-mei. *Immigrant Subjectivities in Asian American and Asian Diaspora Literature*. New York: State University of New York Press, 1998.

McDonald, Dorothy Ritsuko. "After Imprisonment: Ichiro's Search for Redemption in *No-No Boy*." *MELUS* 6.3 (1979): 19–26.

Palumbo-Liu, David. "Discourse and Dislocation: Rhetorical Strategies of Asian-American Exclusion and Confinement." *Literature Interpretation Theory* 2 (1990): 1–7.

Rigal Cellard, Bernadette. "*No-No Boy* de John Okada (1957): Les Japoais Nisei apres la deuxieme guerre mondiale et les affres de l'americanisation." In *Seminaires*. Talence: Centre de Recherches sur l'Amer. Anglophone, 1986. 89–104.

Sumida, Stephen H. "Japanese American Moral Dilemmas in John Okada's *No-No Boy* and Milton Murayama's *All I Asking for Is My Body*." In *Frontiers of Asian American Studies*. Ed. Gail M. Nomura et al. Washington: Washington State University Press, 1989. 224–26.

Usui, Masami. "An Issei Woman's Suffering, Silence, and Suicide in John Okada's *No-No Boy*." *Chu Shikoku Studies in American Literature* 33 (1997): 43–61.

Wang, Qun. " 'Double Consciousness.' Sociological Imagination, and the Asian American Experience." *Race, Gender & Class* 4.3: 88–94.

Yeh, William. "To Belong or Not to Belong: The Liminality of John Okada's *No-No Boy*." *Amerasia Journal* 19.1 (1993): 121–33.

Yogi, Stan. "The Collapse of Difference: Dysfunctional and Inverted Celebrations in John Okada's *No-No Boy*." *Revue Francaise d'Etudes Americanes* 53 (1992): 233–44.

———. " 'You Had to Be One or the Other': Opposition and Reconciliation in John Okada's *No-No Boy*." *MELUS* 21.2 (1996): 63–77.

Michael Ondaatje
(1943–)

Cynthia F. Wong

BIOGRAPHY

Michael Ondaatje still refers to his homeland of Sri Lanka as Ceylon, evoking the colonialism associated with the place. Philip Michael was born there on September 12, 1943, to Philip Mervyn Ondaatje and Enid Gratiaen Ondaatje, and his parents figure prominently in his unsentimental autobiography, *Running in the Family* (1982). The family line is Dutch, Sinhalese, and Tamil, though one critic has indicated that "the family was solidly British colonial in outlook" (Jewinski 23).

Best known as an international writer of the Booker Prize-winning *The English Patient* (1992), Ondaatje's achievements as a poet are sometimes overlooked as critics focus on the way he blurs generic distinctions between poetry and prose, factual verisimilitude and fictional reconstruction.

Ondaatje's early schooling in Colombo, Sri Lanka, was followed by formal education at Dulwich College in England and Bishop's University in Quebec, Canada, where he met his first wife, artist and photographer Kim Jones; in 1964 he transferred to University College in Toronto, where he completed his B.A. a year later. With his wife's encouragement, he earned an M.A. degree in 1967 at Queen's University in Kingston. Early literary prizes in poetry helped secure his first teaching post at the University of Western Ontario. In a relatively brief time, Ondaatje established himself as father (of two children), husband, poet, and academic professor in Canada.

Ondaatje's first published poems appeared in *New Wave Canada* (1966), and these were followed by the book-length *The Dainty Monsters* (1967), which Coach House Press invited him to submit. Ondaatje's interest in drama led to his next work of poetry, *the man with seven toes* (1969), to be performed as a dramatic reading in Vancouver (1968) and Stratford (1969). Other stage adaptations and original films followed in this period, including *The Clinton Special* and *Sons of Captain Poetry*.

His first major book, *The Collected Works of Billy the Kid* (1970), is a sustained work of poetry that he completed at the same time as his critical study of *Leonard Cohen* for McClelland and Stewart's Canadian Writers Series. Although Ondaatje continued to publish poetry, including *The Broken Ark* (1972), *Rat Jelly* (1980) *Elimination Dance* (1978), and *There's a Trick with a Knife I'm Learning to Do* (1979), *Billy the Kid* represents an important transition in Ondaatje's development as a writer of novels.

The montage of fact and history that Ondaatje collected for *Billy the Kid* is replicated in the way he gathered material for his subsequent novels, *Coming through Slaughter* (1976), *In the Skin of the Lion* (1987), and *The English Patient*.

Each of his fictional texts has won major literary prizes in Canada and abroad, including the Canadian Governor General's Award, *Books in Canada* First Novel Award, du Maurier Award for Poetry, Trillium Book Award, and the coveted Booker Prize. Ondaatje continues to write both poetry and fiction while teaching at Glendon College, York University, where he has been with the Department of English since 1971.

MAJOR WORKS AND THEMES

Classifying Ondaatje's body of works represents a distinct challenge, especially to readers familiar with postmodern literary strategies. Not properly a novel, Ondaatje's first major work, *The Collected Works of Billy the Kid*, emerges as a series of poetic, prosaic, and physical snapshots of a legendary figure. By contrast, *Coming through Slaughter* borrows from the fragmented and improvisational reconstruction that had characterized *Billy the Kid*, but that text about the jazz musician Buddy Bolden is more coherently a prose narrative. His subsequent prose works, *In the Skin of the Lion* and *The English Patient*, strike readers as being more distinct in novel form, but these, too, exploit the more conventional aspects of literature to produce a unique signature.

Each of the preceding works may be characterized by Ondaatje's attempts to produce a full and novelistic story on the basis of a few factual bits of information. There really were a Billy the Kid in the American West, a jazz musician called Bolden, who went mad during an American parade march, a community of immigrant Macedonians who built the Bloor Street Viaduct and the Victoria Park filtration system in Canada, and a Count Ladislaus de Almasy, who was an explorer and possibly a spy during World War II when he lost his face and identity. But those brief snatches of information provide enough impetus for Ondaatje's fictionalization. The author's way of reformulating identity and reconstructing a believable tale and his manner of evoking emotion from his characterizations contribute to postmodern indeterminacy: How do we know—much less know for certain—who anyone is? How much faith can we have in the facts that help contribute to identity?

This query about identity also appears in the autobiographical text *Running in the Family*, which Ondaatje himself warns is "not a history but a portrait or 'gesture.' " Indeed, Ondaatje's concerns are not with producing linear and enclosed life histories but with emphasizing the discontinuities and lack of evidence for substantiating a story, any story. What remains in the gaps of recorded facts, documented observations, and remembered conversations constitutes the imaginative space into which Ondaatje inserts his aesthetic work. Public documents can be scant when portraying a life; an artist's rendition might consider rich textures and subtleties not ostensible from the few scraps of information. Ondaatje notes, "One of the things a novel can do is represent the unofficial story, give a personal, complicated version of things, as opposed to competing with the newspapers and giving an alternate but still simplified opinion" (cited in Barbour 179). This celebration of indeterminacy and of divergent perspectives lends innovation to otherwise static forms of history-telling.

In his reinterpretations of the characters' lives, then, Ondaatje calls attention to the very act of writing: How can words express the story of one so inarticulate (Billy the Kid), one who works in the language of music (Bolden), one who is probably a self-portrait (Patrick Lewis), or one who has lost everything we commonly associate with identity, such as a name and a face (the English patient)? Or, to express the concerns differently, how can the novelist represent the stories of those who are no longer authorized to speak on their own behalf, either because they are dead, disabled, or otherwise disfranchised?

If Ondaatje makes a fiction of the few truths he has gathered about a person or a place, the opposite is also true, that he breathes life into the very characters he creates. For example, his memorable characters Hana and Carravaggio both appear in *The Skin of the Lion* and *The English Patient*. Their appearances in those books are separated by some ten years. The nurse Hana in *The English Patient* was the young listener of the story that her adoptive father, Patrick Lewis, tells her on one long car journey to pick up her stepmother; the thief Carravaggio was Patrick's friend in prison, and when he appears at the Italian villa, he disrupts the odd tranquillity that Hana has managed to contrive with the English patient and another wartime loner, Kirpal Singh.

Ondaatje surrounds his characters in circumstances that illuminate their crises. In the physical construction of place, Ondaatje moves forward and backward in time to highlight the movement of the characters' situation: Bolden's lucid talent of the early years contrasts starkly with his growing madness; Patrick Lewis' evolving understanding of immigrant communities and their important contribution to Canadian history is expressed through the lives of other seemingly peripheral characters; and the identity of the English patient is cloaked in the mystery of his clandestine activities during World War II.

Ondaatje's intensive research produces highly innovative and sophisticated prose works. It would be simplistic to say that Ondaatje's novels are but *poetic* prose pieces. While that much is true, his works are richly complex, at times mythical and larger than life, and at others, excruciatingly precise about minute details that speak volumes of his characters and their tales.

CRITICAL RECEPTION

Canadian critics and scholars embraced Ondaatje's poetry first before the international community acclaimed his work in fiction. Outside Canada, Ondaatje is best known for the widely disseminated *The English Patient*. In his book-length critical study of Ondaatje's works, Douglas Barbour describes that 1992 novel as one "whose sensuous prose and poetic perceptions are exquisitely seductive and provocative" (206). Critical language used to discuss Ondaatje's works invariably contains reference to his accomplishments in poetry, a claim that Stephen Scobie rightfully continues to make in his most recent essay, "The Reading Lesson: Michael Ondaatje and the Patients of Desire."

Criticism appearing in Canada outnumbers that in America and Europe by a considerable margin, and it is therefore not surprising that studies of Ondaatje's works focus on technical literary aspects, such as their formal construction, narrative strategy, thematic concerns, or subject matter. Moreover, early Ondaatje criticism in Canada is heavily centered on his poetry, with the bulk of criticism of the novels emerging later and emphasizing postcolonial or postmodern traits and tendencies. In addition to analyzing the relationship of actual historical figures to their fictional counterparts, fascinating work on Ondaatje's references to place-names and social milieus is discussed in works such as Smaro Kamboureli's "The Poetics of Geography in Michael Ondaatje's *Coming through Slaughter*."

Ondaatje's evasion of generic distinctions serves as the topic of essays by Linda Hutcheon, Barry Maxwell, Constance Rooke, Sam Solecki, and Stephen Scobie. Postcolonial tendencies in Ondaatje's fictions form the basis of arguments by Arun Mukherjee and Ajay Heble. Themes of death and violence appear in discussions by J. M. Kertzer, and Christian Bok.

Marilyn Jones' review of *Essays on Canadian Writing: Michael Ondaatje Issue*, edited by Karen E. Smythe, provides an informative view of Ondaatje criticism up until 1995. Essays appearing in that volume are mostly on the fiction, but their variety reflects Ondaatje's evolving thematic and technical concerns. Jones notes that the praise for Ondaatje's work is more subdued than in an earlier collection of essays (*Spider Blues: Essays on Michael Ondaatje*, edited by Sam Solecki), and their aims appear more politically inclined and theoretically sophisticated.

The literary excitement fostered by Ondaatje's writing cannot be understated, however, despite what appears to be the emergence of harsher negative critiques about Ondaatje's stance on political issues, such as postcolonialism, or his seemingly flippant attitude about physical and aesthetic forms of violence in his works. If critics such as Arun Mukherjee denounce Ondaatje's lack of social or political proselytizing, what Christian Bok calls Ondaatje's ability to "energize a collective, social vision that resists specific forms of ideological authority" (122) may be closer to the author's aesthetic aims. For Ondaatje, capturing the elusiveness of history entails such myriad experimentation and ambivalent reactions from readers and critics.

The rich diversity of criticism generated by Ondaatje's work—first in poetry and more recently in fiction—should continue to flourish and cultivate new debate about Ondaatje's writing.

BIBLIOGRAPHY

Works by Michael Ondaatje

Novels

Coming through Slaughter. New York: Norton; Toronto: House of Anansi, 1976; London: Marion Boyars, 1979.
In the Skin of the Lion. New York: Knopf; Toronto: McClelland and Stewart, 1987.
The English Patient. New York: Knopf; Toronto: McClelland and Stewart, 1992.

Poetry

The Dainty Monsters. Toronto: Coach House Press, 1967.
the man with seven toes. Toronto: Coach House Press, 1969.
The Collected Works of Billy the Kid: Left Handed Poems. New York: Norton; Toronto: House of Anansi, 1970.
The Broken Ark: A Book of Beasts. Illus. Tony Urguhart. Ottowa: Oberon Press, 1971.
Rat Jelly. Toronto: Coach House Press, 1973.
Elimination Dance. Ilderton, Ontario: Nairn, 1978.
There's a Trick with a Knife I'm Learning to Do: Poems 1963–1978. New York: Norton; Toronto: McClelland and Stewart, 1979.
Rat Jelly and Other Poems: 1963–1978. London: Marion Boyers, 1980.
Tin Roof. Lantzville, British Colombia: Island, 1982.
Secular Love. Toronto: Coach House Press, 1984.
The Cinnamon Peeler: Selected Poems. London: Pan Books, 1989; New York: Knopf, 1991; Toronto: McClelland and Stewart, 1992.

Dramatic Works/Films and Screenplays

the man with seven toes. Produced at the Vancouver Festival, 1968.
Sons of Captain Poetry. Mongrel Films, 1970.
The Collected Works of Billy the Kid. Produced at St. Lawrence Centre, Toronto. April 23, 1971.
Carry on Crime and Punishment. Mongrel Films, 1972.
The Clinton Special. Mongrel Films/Canadian Film-Makers Distribution Centre, 1972.
Coming through Slaughter. Produced at Theatre Passe Muraille, Toronto, January 5–27, 1980.
"The William Dawe Badlands Expedition 1916." *Descant* 14 (1983): 51–73.

Love Clinic. Canadian Centre for Advanced Film Studies, 1990. *Border Crossings* 9 (1990): 14–19.

Autobiography

Running in the Family. New York: Norton; Toronto: McClelland and Stewart, 1982.

Literary Criticism and Editing

"O'Hagan's Rough-Edged Chronicle." *Canadian Literature* 61 (1974): 24–31.

Personal Fictions: Stories by Munro, Wiebe, Thomas, and Blaise. Toronto: Oxford University Press, 1977.

"Garcia Marquez and the Bus to Aracataca." In *Figures in a Ground: Canadian Essays on Modern Literature Collected in Honor of Sheila Watson.* Ed. Diane Bessai and David Jackel. Saskatoon: Western Producer Prairie Books, 1978: 19–31.

The Long Poem Anthology. Toronto: Coach House Press, 1979.

From Ink Lake: Canadian Stories Selected by Michael Ondaatje. New York: Penguin; Toronto: Lester and Orpen Dennys; London: Faber and Faber, 1990.

Leonard Cohen. Toronto: McClelland and Stewart, 1970.

Studies of Michael Ondaatje

Barbour, Douglas. *Michael Ondaatje.* New York: Twayne, 1993.

Bjerring, Nancy E. "Deconstructing the 'Desert of Facts': Detection and Antidetection in *Coming through Slaughter.*" *English Studies in Canada* 16 (1990): 325–38.

Bok, Christian. "Destructive Creation: The Politicization of Violence in the Works of Michael Ondaatje." *Canadian Literature* 132 (1992): 109–24.

Butterfield, Martha. "The One Lighted Room: *In the Skin of the Lion.*" *Canadian Literature* 119 (1988): 162–67.

Clarke, George. "Michael Ondaatje and the Production of Myth." *Studies in Canadian Literature* 16 (1991): 1–21.

Greenstein, Michael. "Ondaatje's Metamorphoses: *In the Skin of the Lion. Canadian Literature* 126 (1990): 116–30.

Heble, Ajay. "Michael Ondaatje and the Problem of History." *CLIO* 19 (1990): 97–110.

Heighton, Stephen. "Approaching 'That Perfect Edge': Kinetic Techniques in the Poetry and Fiction of Michael Ondaatje." *Studies in Canadian Literature* 13 (1988): 223–43.

Hutcheon, Linda. "*Running in the Family*: The Postmodernist Challenge." Reprinted in *The Canadian Postmodern.* Toronto: Oxford University Press, 1988: 81–106.

Jewinski, Ed. *Michael Ondaatje: Express Yourself Beautifully.* Toronto: ECW Press, 1994.

Kamboureli, Smaro. "The Poetics of Geography in Michael Ondaatje's *Coming through Slaughter.*" *Descant* 14 (1983): 112–26.

Kertzer, J.M. "On Death and Dying: *The Collected Works of Billy the Kid.*" *English Studies* 1 (1975): 88–96.

Jones, Marilyn. Rev. of *Essays in Canadian Writing: Michael Ondaatje Issue. Canadian Literature* 152 (1996): 9–15.

MacFarland, Susan. "Picking Up the Pieces: *Coming through Slaughter*: As Paragram." *Open Letter* 6 (1989): 72–83.

Maxwell, Barry. "Surrealistic Aspects of Michael Ondaatje's *Coming Through Slaughter*." *CLIO* 19.2 (Winter 1990): 97–110.

Mukherjee, Arun. "The Poetry of Michael Ondaatje and Cyril Dabydeen." *Journal of Commonwealth Literature* 20.1 (1985): 49–67.

Mundwiler, Leslie. *Michael Ondaatje: Word, Image, Imagination.* Vancouver: Talonbooks, 1984.

Rooke, Constance. "Dog in a Grey Room: The Happy Ending of *Coming through Slaughter*." In *Spider Blues.* Ed. Sam Solecki. Montreal: Véhicule Press, 1985: 268–92.

Scobie, Stephen. "*Coming through Slaughter*: Fictional Magnets and Spiders Webbs." *Essays on Canadian Writing* 12 (1978): 5–23.

———. "The Reading Lesson: Michael Ondaatje and the Patients of Desire." In *Essays on Canadian Writing: Michael Ondaatje Issue.* Toronto: ECW Press, 1994.

Smythe, Karen E., ed. *Essays on Canadian Writing: Michael Ondaatje Issue.* Toronto: ECW Press, 1994.

Solecki, Sam. "Making and Destroying: Michael Ondaatje's *Coming through Slaughter* and Extremist Art." *Essays on Canadian Writing* 12 (1978): 24–47.

———. "Michael Ondaatje." *Descant* 14 (1983): 77–88.

———. *Spider Blues: Essays on Michael Ondaatje.* Montreal: Véhicule Press, 1985.

Van Wart, Alice. "The Evolution of Form in Michael Ondaatje's *The Collected Works of Billy the Kid* and *Coming through Slaughter*." *Canadian Poetry* 17 (1985): 1–28.

Wilson, Ann. "*Coming through Slaughter*: Storyville Twice Told." *Descant* 14 (1983): 99–111.

Nahid Rachlin

(1947–   )

Maya M. Sharma

BIOGRAPHY

Nahid Rachlin came to the United States from Iran in 1964 to attend college. Her father had valued education enough to have tutors for his child bride, but he was not prepared to allow his daughter to study abroad. His reluctance was softened by a full scholarship to Lindenwood, a rigidly supervised women's college in Missouri.

Nahid earned a B.A. in psychology in 1968, met Howard Rachlin at the New School of Social Research, and married him. In the fall of 1968, she began doctoral studies in English literature at Boston University; Howard was studying at Harvard. Their daughter, Leila, was born in 1969.

Nahid was born in Abadan in June 1947, the daughter of a lawyer who resigned as judge there to practice law in Ahvaz. While pregnant, her mother promised her to a childless older sister. In West Asia this is the preferred way of adoption. At nine months her grandmother took her to her aunt in Tehran. Her aunt was widowed and remarried, then divorced, and severely depressed. Nahid was very happy with her. Her birth parents were but two of the numerous relatives who came visiting. The ambience in the aunt's home was rigidly orthodox, but Nahid attended a select private school and enjoyed the privileges of an only child. Her first nine years were her happiest.

Nahid's father appeared in her tenth year, with no warning or explanation, and took her from her school playground to the door of her house to collect her suitcases. She cried on the plane all the way to Ahvaz and did not stop. Her mother did not wipe away her tears and could not bond with her. When her aunt came to visit a few months later, they could make no claims on each other. This was profoundly wrenching for both. Nahid became a perpetual rebel and avoided addressing her mother formally and avoided eye contact. When she needed something, Nahid would position herself in front of her mother, state her need, and stand until it was met. An older sister, Pari, was her only ally. After high school, Pari married a wealthy older man who ground out lit cigarettes on her skin. She had to give up her own son when she sued for divorce. Pari married a second time to escape her parents' recriminations. Soon she suffered a mental breakdown requiring hospitalization in Tehran. Pari's illness brought the second marriage to an end. Nahid notes: "Our closeness was ruptured by a tragedy that remains painfully in the background of my life" (*Veils* 143). Pari's hospitalization was "a horrible fate for me to come to terms with. . . . in a period of relative calm and lucidity, she asked me, 'Are you still writing? Will you send me the last thing you wrote?' " (*Veils* 142–143). "Would I have become a writer without Pari's encouragement?" (*Veils* 146) Rachlin asks.

She like myself was always looking for escape from the circumscribed roles set for her as a woman in a culture that discriminated against them so grossly. In what ways do her flights of mental illness correspond into the fantasy world of fiction? For though I draw upon experience, much of what I write still has to be imagined, fabricated, distorted. When Pari looks at her hand and says, "It's turning black from the lotion you sent me" or when she burns any money she gets hold of, "I can always make more of them," is she trying to say something else? (*Veils* 146)

The experiences of the women in Nahid's family provide themes that run through her fiction. Her marriage allowed her to explore the stories stuffed away in the chest of memory. The stories of the chained mad woman, the illiterate servant, and the woman who abandoned her blind son in the desert were written for a class at Columbia University with Richard Humphries; the tale based on the death of her little sister for one with Donald Bartheleme at City College. These early works won her the Stegner Fellowship, on which she wrote *Foreigner*. For this novel she drew on her return to Iran in 1976 for the first time in twelve years.

MAJOR WORKS AND THEMES

Rachlin has written three novels and a book of short stories. *Foreigner* appeared in 1977, *Married to a Stranger* in 1983, *Veils* in 1992, and *The Heart's Desire* in 1995. Ruth Prawer Jhabwala notes that *Foreigner* illuminates "present-day everyday Iran" in a style that puts our fingers on the pulse of Iranian life. In prose that is spare and clean like Hemingway's, the author exposes the nightmarish life of her heroine, Feri Mehri McIntosh. Her marriage to Tony McIntosh protected her from exilic nostalgia for Iran, but his infidelity triggers awareness of impoverishment that alters her vision and brings into focus the mystery of Iran. This vision impels a journey that brings her into the bosom of the family she had left fourteen years ago.

The opening chapter sets the mood. She is not met at the airport because of a mixup over the time. The only cab driver willing to go to her neighborhood demands an exorbitant fare. As she waits to be admitted, she is stoned by a child. Her father, Akbar, greets her with a grimace and cool, shy words. Her stepmother, Ziba's, disapproval is unchanged, her stepbrother's smile still disconnected from his eyes. Her gifts are taken for granted. The family, discovering that she was not married by *aghounds*—Iranian priests—tell her she is not married at all.

"Now in Iran, things had quietly reversed—what had seemed mysterious was menacing and what had seemed sterile in the States appeared to be orderly, almost peaceful"(38). Feri's response is to run back to Boston. She decides to leave before her two weeks are up. As she is headed out the door for the visa office, her father says that she is no better than her mother, who had left him for another man; she had been told that her mother had left to devote herself to God.

She learns that she needs her husband's permission to leave but cannot get in touch with him. She then sets out to see her mother. She arrives by bus in ancient Kashan in pain from an undiagnosed ulcer. Her mother looks after her. As Feri recovers, her mother tells the story of her affair and her new life. As she begins to understand, a sickness of soul suppressed for twenty years is mitigated.

She spends a carefree day with the attractive Dr. Majid and finds Tony, who has come to take her home. She is faced with choices again. He embodies work done to deadlines—all the time he is in Iran he is busy with his reading and writing. Feri is inspired to resign her job as a research biologist, and immediately her scientific creativity begins to flow. When she goes back to Kashan, Dr. Majid is easy to love and makes her feel comforted and secure.

a real conflict remained: he kept drifting in and out of a stage of my life that I had rejected and wanted to regain; he embodied the same pain, the same elusiveness. . . . It would be self-defeating to begin to depend on him just as I wanted to pull so many strings together, think things through. (187–188)

She needs to face the fact that she cannot live with her "identity and sense of belonging suddenly reversed . . . blurred" (165). She knows that her need to define herself requires separation from both Tony and Majid, who has rejected America. Her way of separation is to go on a pilgrimage with her mother. This closes the gap between the past and the present, providing a space where she can begin to know herself. In a tent, in a moon-flooded field at the shrine of a poetess saint, Feri reflects: "I knew soon I would have to make decisions, think beyond the day, but for the moment I lay there. Tranquil"(192).

Feri finds space and time to be in and gains strength to make the decisions necessary to her happiness. When she accepts that she is a stranger both at home and abroad, she is truly liberated to make decisions outside the two cultures that set the boundaries of her existence.

In *Married to a Stranger* Minou, the daughter of a prosperous lawyer of Ahvaz, will not submit to an arranged marriage with a much older man. Afraid that she will not marry, the family refuses to allow her to study in Tehran (32). She has a crush on a teacher, Javad Partovi. She tells him of her frustration, and he tells her about the soul-deadening job he has in Abadan. Minou feels electrified by these confidences and goes home elated that she has done something daring. Javad proposes to her and sends his mother to make arrangements.

As Minou gets ready for her bridal day at the baths, she hears women discussing their relationships: "Love always ended in disgrace for a woman, sometimes for a man as well" (37). However, the worst that can happen to a man is that he might realize he has married the wrong woman. But once women lose their virginity, lovers abandon them, and they become prostitutes. "Romantic love is ruin" is the recurrent theme in Iranian movies (39).

The model of marriage provided by her parents, in which her father visits low dives and preys on the maid where his daughter can see him, is not to her taste. If she is not allowed to go to college, at least she will choose her own man. She does not know that Javad has had an affair with Pari, the wife of his close friend and sister-in-law of the leader of the anti-Western, chauvinistic Moral Majority Party.

When Pari becomes the illustrator of the literary magazine that Minou edits and publishes, merchants won't stock it, and all copies are dumped at Minou's front door. When Minou finds out that she is sharing Javad with her as well as his political work, she decides to go to the United States and start afresh. As she leaves for Ahvaz, she watches Pari running to escape a stoning for adultery. When her father finds out about Pari and Javad, he is angry at his daughter for shaming the family and has no thought for her hurt. Her mother's reaction is typical: "I accepted the bad with the good in my marriage. You'll have to the same thing . . . you insisted on marrying him. It was your own choice. All men run around, what do you expect?" (200).

If Minou chose Javad, she can also leave him. When Javad sends Minou his permission to leave and money for her ticket, her father is disbelieving. He asks: "What's this fancy life that you are imaging for yourself, can you explain to me?" (207). When she says that it's not a fancy life that she seeks but freedom from the prison that Ahvaz and Abadan represent, her father responds heatedly: "You may as well go away. . . . I can see you will cause trouble if you are kept around here too long. You might become a communist the way you talk. You might get involved with destructive things" (207). Relenting, he lets her know that he will provide for her in America.

Before she leaves, Minou burns her wedding dress and a composition she had written for Javad. Six years later she comes back from America. The country has changed. The Iran–Iraq War has ruined Abadan and Ahvaz, and Minou finds no comfort in her homecoming.

Veils, ten stories and an autobiographical sketch, was published in 1992. Many of these stories are set against the backdrop of the Iran–Iraq War. The stories in this book, dedicated to her sister Pari and set on the ancient street of Ghanat Abad Avenue and its side streets, which give the work spatial cohesion, present men and women shuttling between the United States and Iran, caught in the violent clash between the old cultural conventions and the enduring forces of transformations: war and tyranny.

Heart's Desire (1995) fleshes out the theme of the expatriate's disenchantment and return to the familiar. Karim Sahary is married to Jennifer, an American, and they have a small son, Darius. It is 1989—the year of Khomeni. By going on "holiday' in Iran and immersing himself in his uncle's affairs, Karim risks his job, his wife, and his son. While he accompanies his uncle to a job interview, he finds that he, too, can find work and make a new life in Iran. He follows his uncle, spending time with prostitutes, becoming acquainted with Iranian female sexuality. The breakdown of the telephone service symbolizes the breakdown between Jennifer and Karim.

Back in Tehran, Jennifer becomes desperate about Darius' health. When she goes for exit visas, her mother-in-law takes Darius to the holy city of Qom without her permission. Following them, Jennifer is captured by the notorious *pasdars*, the morality police, for exposed hair and taken into custody as a suspected spy. She escapes out a bathroom window, finds her way to her mother-in-law, and rescues her son from the religious school in the Blue Mosque. Back in Tehran, she learns that Karim and his uncle have been in a car accident, and the family has gone to join them. Three sordid and exhilarating days with the doctor who had helped with her visa crystallize the separation she feels from Karim. Her experiences in Qom sensitize her to his sufferings in America. Once back in Ohio, Darius' symptoms disappear, and Jennifer adjusts to life without Karim. She will not go back to Iran; and he finds it increasingly difficult to leave. Each wants the other's love and companionship, but they cannot any longer share the same landscape.

CRITICAL RECEPTION

There is a consensus among Rachlin's reviewers that her style is cool, pure, spare, minimal, and deceptively simple. Most serious critics have concentrated on *Foreigner*. Anne Tyler notes that Rachlin dares to give the reader "a rare intimate look at Iranians who are poorer and less educated and more strictly observant." Ramin P. Jaleshgari notes, "Some Iranian-Americans criticize Rachlin for exposing very private culturally accepted habits to critical misunderstanding Western eyes" (59), and because it strips the culture bare "her work has not been translated into Farsi" (59). This might not bother Rachlin very much; for Rachlin, it has always been a language of censorship (56). In *Among the Believers*, V. S. Naipaul reminds us that *Foreigner* was the first book written in English by an Iranian. He says this book "avoids political comment. Its protest is more oblique; the political constriction drives the passions deeper, . . . with all its air of innocence, it is a novel of violation, helplessness, and defeat" (14). This is a subjective reading. In the end Feri is not defeated. She transcends both sorts of nostalgia that alternately reterritorialize her consciousness. Hamid Naficy notes that in her novel of exile, "Rachlin . . . defying Freud, Lacan and Rumi, stages not only the return of an Iranian . . . woman to her motherland but also her reunion with her long lost biological mother" (300). He thinks that *Foreigner* suffers from Rachlin's "unproblematical staging of such a complete and total reunion" (300). Naficy bases his assessment on the definition that "exile is a dream . . . remains alluring only as long as it remains unrealized" (286). Thus, his note on Rachlin's being able to stage two kinds of return is ironic. If we interpret the conclusion of *Foreigner* using the concept of exile as processual (299), we might be closer to understanding the transformation of Feri's consciousness. In "Iranian-America Literature," Nasrin Rahimieh says that Feri "has always played the image of Iran against that of America . . . [and is] now confronted with her own duplicity" (119). It is how Feri deals with this self-knowledge that defies Freud, Lacan, and Rumi. There is, indeed, a growing body of critical appreciation of Iranian American writing, and except for her first book, Rachlin's work has not received the critical attention it deserves.

BIBLIOGRAPHY

Works by Nahid Rachlin

Foreigner. New York: W. W. Norton, 1977.
Married to a Stranger. San Francisco: City Lights, 1983.
Veils: Short Stories. San Francisco: City Lights, 1992.
The Heart's Desire: A Novel. San Francisco: City Lights, 1995.

Studies of Nahid Rachlin

Filbin, Thomas. "Lost and Found." Rev. of *The Heart's Desire. Chanteh* (Summer 1996): 43–44.
Helou, Paul. "Ancient Tehran Area Forms Setting for Stony Brook Author" Rev. of *Veils. New York Times*, October 3, 1993, C 10.
Jaleshgari, Ramin P. "The Liberation of Language." *Poets & Writers* 26.5 (September–October 1998): 56–59.
Kaufmann, Bruce. "Book Offers Glimpse behind Iranian Veil." Rev. of *Married to a Stranger. Catskill Mountain News*, September 22, 1993, B1.
Morrissett Davidon, Ann. "A Woman Surviving Iran's Chaos." Rev. of *Married to a Stranger. Philadelphia Inquirer*, March 5, 1984, E4.
Naficy, Hamid. "The Poetics and Practice of Iranian Nostalgia." *Diaspora* 1.3 (1991): 285–302.
Naipaul, V. S. *Among the Believers.* New York: Alfred A. Knopf, 1982. 13–15.
———. "Our Universal Civilization." *New York Times*, November 5, 1990, Op-Ed. page.

Rahimieh, Nasrin. "Iranian-American Literature." In *New Immigrant Literatures in the United States*. Ed. Alpana Sharma Knippling. Westport, CT: Greenwood Press, 1996. 119–20.

See, Carolyn. "A Woman's Book but in a Man's World." Rev. of *Married to a Stranger*. *Los Angeles Times*, September 16, 1983, 20.

Southgate, Minoo. "Out of Iran: Escapes to Nowhere." Rev. of *Foreigner*. *Village Voice* (November 22, 1978): 105.

Tyler, Anne. Rev. of *Foreigner*. *New York Times Book Review* (February 18, 1979) 35.

Wright, Carolyne. Rev. of *Veils*. *Harvard Review* (Spring 1993): 1–2.

Balachandra Rajan

(1920–   )

Uppinder Mehan

BIOGRAPHY

Balachandra Rajan was born March 24, 1920, in Toungoo, Burma. After Presidency College, Madras, Rajan continued his studies at Trinity College, Cambridge. From 1941 to 1946 he received his B.A., M.A., and Ph.D. and served as a lecturer in modern poetry at his alma mater until 1948, when he left to serve as a member of the Indian Foreign Service. Shortly after India's independence from Britain, Rajan held various important diplomatic posts, including the Permanent Mission of India to the United Nations, chairman of the Executive Board of United Nations International Children's Emergency Fund (UNICEF) and India's representative to the Atomic Energy Agency. Near the end of his career with the Indian Foreign Service Rajan published his two novels, *The Dark Dancer* (1958) and *Too Long in the West* (1961). In 1961 he left politics for academe and joined Delhi University, where he taught until 1964. After a brief stint in the United States, he joined the University of Western Ontario in London, Canada, in 1966 and has continued to teach there since. Over the course of five decades of teaching Rajan has made a name for himself as a Miltonist and as an important scholar of Yeats and T. S. Eliot.

Balachandra Rajan was named Honoured Scholar of the Milton Society in 1979 and received a fellowship in the Royal Society of Canada in 1983. Since 1985 Rajan has been professor emeritus in the English Department. Rajan shows no signs of slowing down his critical and scholarly activity. The year 1999 saw the publication of *Under Western Eyes: India from Milton to MacAulay* (Durham, NC: Duke University Press, 1999) and a coedited work, *Milton and the Imperial Vision* (Pittsburgh: Duquesne University Press, 1999).

MAJOR WORKS AND THEMES

The artistic response by most Indian writers to the cataclysm of partition has been tragedy, and Rajan is no exception. *The Dark Dancer* is Rajan's attempt to understand the psychology of acceptance in the face of personal and national violence. In the gently satiric *Too Long in the West* Rajan continues his exploration of acceptance when it is no longer driven by the tragic drama of the battlefield. Although the motivating action in each novel is the prospect of an arranged marriage for a young Indian recently returned from abroad. *The Dark Dancer* makes the marriage into an allegory for the education of the hero, while *Too Long in the West* treats it as a comedy of manners.

The Dark Dancer starts with Krishnan's return from studies in England. His parents immediately set to finding him a wife (Kamala) and a government job, which they do, in that order. Sometime later Krishnan leaves Kamala in order to have an affair with Cynthia, a Cambridge friend who has come to India. He realizes that Cynthia cannot give him the sense of belonging he so desperately needs and goes back to Kamala. The partition riots have meanwhile started, and Kamala has gone into the most devastated northern towns to help with the refugees. Krishnan comes back to her in time to work with her and to understand her emotional and social commitment to the philosophy and practices of non-violence shortly before she is killed in a communal altercation.

Too Long in the West starts with the annual reestablishment of Sambasivan's comic misrule for three summer months in Mudalur. The harried professor (Sambasivan) arrives along with his shrewish wife Lakshmi, and their intelligent daughter, Nalini, and idiot son, Gopal, to take up the position of a tin god. Nalini is sent to Columbia for further studies and returns ready for marriage, according to her mother. Sambasivan places an ad in the newspapers that attracts an assortment of odd characters: Kalyanasundaram, whose project is to expose the evils of arranged marriages; Viswakarman, a journalist who, in seeking to master style, has "successfully imitated all the Noble Prize winners" and is now "maturing from early to late Eliot" (89); Satyamurti, a foundling, who sees himself as the new, classless man of independent India; Kubera, a cosmetics manufacturer who wants to marry Nalini so she can be an advertisement for his products; and Ernest, an old friend from Columbia working his way through India with the Peace Corps spraying DDT. Kubera's failed attempt to have the villagers make a dangerous climb to get the legendary mangoes atop the local fabled hill for his cosmetic dreams finally gives the Marxist barber Raman the excuse to be rid of Sambasivan's feudal rule. After many satirical observations and plot twists, the novel ends by creating Mudalur as a hidden paradise from which no one wants to return. Mudalur becomes the comic realization of the India promised by the combination of Nehru's five-year plans and Gandhi's idyll of village life.

The Dark Dancer is the tragic rendering of the arranged marriage as a symbol of "true" Indian culture, and *Too Long in the West* is its comic aspect. In an essay on Indian writing in English, Rajan stresses the importance of accident in the work of R. K. Narayan. Calling Narayan's fiction characteristically Indian, Rajan appeals to the brutal life of many of India's poor: "Endurance becomes the principal weapon and accident the main means of deliverance. The tragic is too close to need aesthetic underlining. It is the comic frustration which provides the welcome catharsis" (Balachandra Rajan, "India," in *Literatures of the World in English*, ed. Bruce King [London: Routledge, 1974], 92).

In Rajan's fiction endurance and frustration are explored as elements of the necessity of acceptance. *The Dark Dancer* opens with young Krishnan recently returned from England struggling to feel as though he has, indeed, arrived home: "It was where he was born, but where he was born didn't matter. There was nothing in the cracked, arid earth to suggest that he belonged to it, or in the river, shrunk away from the banks, that seemed almost to wrench its way through the landscape, startling the brown anger into green" (1). Seeking to recover his lost identity, Krishnan agrees to marry Kamala, in whom he sees the acceptance of "the temple pool, the pitiless mirror, the unclouded truth that would yield him that reflection" (20). Such Advaita Vedantic musings are a misstep for Krishnan.

The crux of *The Dark Dancer* is the state of being an in-between—a state of social, cultural, biological, or psychological hybridity that continues to be a major theme in much Indian writing in English, indeed, in much postcolonial writing. As an in-between who has had his sense of received Indian identity shaken by a metropolitan education, Krishnan finds it impossible to function as a coherent self.

Krishnan projects onto Kamala his own passive acceptance as emblematic of India. He projects onto Cynthia his own determination and certainty: Kamala is the inscrutable East; Cynthia the pragmatic West. Rajan risks such an over-simplification because Krishnan needs to realize that true acceptance does not mean abstracting Indianness into trite Vedantic aphorisms or forcing women to be representations of cultural idealizations; rather, acceptance lies in understanding that social and political categories are only approximations and never a substitute for true feeling, that, in the terms of the novel, nonviolence *and* the battlefield are aspects of India and being.

The title of *The Dark Dancer* alludes to Shiva in his phase as Nataraj, whose cosmic dance of destruction brings the end of the world and makes possible the creation of a new one. Rajan makes the dance apply psychologically to Krishnan and politically to the country: the partition riots are depicted as a fever that needs to run its course; Krishnan needs to purge himself of his abstracted notions of Indianness in order to think for himself.

Rajan shows in *Too Long in the West* the kind of metropolitan education that would have better served Krishnan. Lakshmi fears that Nalini has "been too long in the West. She's forgotten our language and will turn up her nose at our food. . . . And worst of all she'll talk back to her husband' " (29). Of course, the last and worst fear is ironic since Lakshmi, who detests moving even within

India, let alone sojourning in the West, talks back (and forth) to her husband. Upon meeting her intellectual idol at Columbia University (in a satirical, yet touching, "stranger-in-a-strange-land" chapter). Nalini puts "her work before him, devoutly in his image, in the exact words his learning had picked out, letting it live in the mould of his own brilliance" (57). Instead of blessing the effort, as Nalini expects, he destroys "the dedicated mimicry of many months" (57) and urges her to view her mind as a "light, shining into the facts and revealing their pattern. Look after your intelligence and learn to use it responsibly. It's the little core of difference that makes you yourself. If you don't own it, then everything else would own you" (59). Rajan leads the reader to expect that Nalini will either wreak havoc in her controlling family back home in India, or succumb to their wishes and lose herself in the process. As it turns out, all the major characters use their idiosyncratic lights quite effectively and detect their own particular patterns.

What prevents chaos in *Too Long in the West*, as in *The Dark Dancer*, is the social dimension. The characters' individualism has to find a way to express itself through acceptable social means, a way that allows the expression of the Janus twins of stability and change or destruction and creation.

CRITICAL RECEPTION

The most substantial review of Rajan's novels is by Uma Parameswaran (1976), in which she tells us that British and U.S. critics, unlike Indian ones, found much to like in *The Dark Dancer* and that almost no one has paid attention to *Too Long in the West*. The West focuses on the content: the East on the style. There have been some more reviews since Parameswaran's study, but again mostly of *The Dark Dancer*.

William Walsh finds *The Dark Dancer* "a distinctly literary and sophisticated novel . . . [but] a degree too remote, too civilized" (100). K. D. Verma applauds Rajan's grasp and portrayal of the social and historical dimensions of a complicated moment in Indian history: the violent transition from a colonized country to an independent one. Harrex and Woodcock both read Rajan's creative work through his scholarly work. Harrex focuses on the ways in which *The Dark Dancer* is thematically and formally expressive of Rajan's work on T. S. Eliot. Woodcock shows the ways in which Rajan's novels incorporate Yeats' sense of overcoming isolation, Milton's loss and recovery of paradise, and Eliot's drama of cycles. Harrex and Woodcock suggest that Rajan's novels are structurally and thematically more complex than has earlier been noted.

Parameswaran speculates that Rajan may have stopped writing after only two novels because his work has been ignored. Woodcock is more charitable of Rajan as an artist: "One may . . . speculate that a realization that the pattern was complete at the end of the second novel may be one of the reasons why, twenty years ago, Rajan seems to have abandoned fiction" (445). My feeling is that Anne C. Bolgan, in her laudatory review of Rajan's *The Overwhelming Question* (a major study of Eliot), comes closest to the mark. She suggests that for Rajan critical writing *is* creative writing. "He is not so much elucidating Eliot's poetry in those chapters [on *Ash Wednesday* and *Four Quartets*] as writing prose essays on the same subject-matter and writing them, moreover, in a manner fully as capable as is Eliot's own of transforming observations into states of mind and ideas into sensations" (452).

BIBLIOGRAPHY

Works by Balachandra Rajan

Novels

The Dark Dancer. New York: Simon and Schuster, 1958.
Too Long in the West. London: Heinemann, 1961.

Studies of Balachandra Rajan

Bolgan, Anne C. "Balachandra Rajan, *The Overwhelming Question*." *English Studies in Canada* 4(1978): 447–90.
Harrex, S. C. "Dancing in the Dark: Balachandra Rajan and T. S. Eliot." *World Literature Written in English* 14 (1975): 310–21.
McCutchion, David. "Le Style C'est L'Homme." *Writers Workshop* (May–June 1961): 20–21.
Narasimhaiah, C. D. "Why This Animus?" *Literary Criterion* (Summer 1966): 15–16.
Parameswaran, Uma. "Balachandra Rajan." *A Study of Representative Indo-English Novelists*. Delhi: Vikas, 1976.
Verma, K. D. "Balachandra Rajan's *The Dark Dancer*: A Critical Reading." *Journal of South Asian Literature* 22 (1987): 60–76.
Walsh, William. *Indian Literature in English*. New York: Longman, 1990.
Woodcock, George. "Balachandra Rajan: The Critic as Novelist." *World Literature Written in English* 23 (1984): 442–51.

Ninotchka Rosca
(1946–   )

Shannon T. Leonard

BIOGRAPHY

Activist, journalist, and acclaimed fiction writer, Ninotchka Rosca was born in 1946 in Manila, Philippines. She graduated from the University of the Philippines in 1975 with a B.A. in comparative literature. At the same university, Rosca enrolled in graduate studies, concentrating on Khmer civilization. During and after her student years, she served as managing editor of Manila-based *Graphic* magazine. As a result of the hard-core political reporting in *Graphic* and her involvement in political activist organizations, Rosca was detained for six months when Ferdinand Marcos declared martial law in 1972. She eluded another arrest in 1976, when she relocated to the United States to participate in the University of Iowa's International Writing Program. The persistence of dictatorship in the Philippines suspended her return to the Philippines, so she remained expatriated and taught Tagalog in the Department of Indo-Pacific Languages at the University of Hawai'i at Manoa, Honolulu. In the early 1980s, Rosca moved to New York, where she lives and works today. Rosca's many psychic and physical displacements finally surprised her when, upon return to Manila after Marcos' removal from office, she "discovered [she] had become a New Yorker," because, according to her friends in Manila, she "was unbearably rude and direct, stating outright what [she] needed and . . . thought" (Mangaliman 15).

Rosca's awards and honors include a fellowship in the International Writers Program, University of Iowa in 1977; fellowships from the New York Foundation for the Arts in 1986–1987 and again in 1991; award for magazine writing from the Women's Political Caucus in 1987; designation as one of the twelve Asian American Women of Hope by the Bread and Roses Cultural Project; 1993

American Book Award for *Twice Blessed*. Of her various roles, she sits on the Board of Directors of PEN International Women's Committee and PEN American Center, as well as the board of the Survivors Committee, a network of former political prisoners and human rights activists. Currently, she is most visible as the founder and a board member of GABRIELA, a Philippine-U.S. women's solidarity organization dedicated to resisting sex tourism, the mail-order bride industry, and the sex trafficking of women from the Philippines to foreign nations, the United States included.

At present, Rosca has five books and numerous magazine and newspaper articles on her extensive list of credits. Her first book, a collection of short stories, *Bitter Country and Other Stories* in 1970, preceded her experience as political prisoner. The stories of *The Monsoon Collection*, which appeared in 1983, were composed in the years following her imprisonment. Rosca claims that while the stories were written years afterward, in disparate locales—New York, Hawai'i, and Manila—she conceived the collection's form during her internment in the Camp Crame Detention Center in 1973. Training in, and commitment to, journalism led to the composition of *Endgame: The Fall of Marcos*, which appeared in 1987, one short year after the Aquino administration took seat. In her two novels, *State of War* (1988) and *Twice Blessed* (1992), Rosca revisits her literary talents and fictionalizes Philippine politics. Her stories have been collected in several anthologies, among them *1986 Best 100 Short Stories in the U.S.* and the *Missouri Review Anthology*. Rosca frequently contributes to *Ms. Magazine*, *The Nation*, *Village Voice*, and other worldwide periodicals. Significantly, all of Rosca's major writings after *Bitter Country and Other Stories*, after her prison sentence, have been published outside the Philippines.

MAJOR WORKS AND THEMES

Scenes of violence, tyranny, greed, and resistance occupy Ninotchka Rosca's literary imagination. Clearly, the central concerns of her novels are dictated by her sense of sociopolitical justice and her firsthand experience with political activism, tyranny, and persecution. Rosca's novels, like the writing of Linda Ty-Casper,* take place in the Philippines and narrate the author's sense of historical events refracted through literary lenses. *State of War* and *Twice Blessed* detail lives of people involved with martial rule in the Philippines.

State of War, Rosca's first novel, charts a complex relationship between three characters and their relation to the nation's political scene and personal as well as national histories. Each character epitomizes a different aspect of Philippine life in time of war: Adrian Banyaga is a member of one of the Philippines' distinguished families; Eliza Hansen, the daughter of a prostitute, is the mistress of the novel's tyrannical figure, Colonel Amor (also known ironically as the "Loved One"); and Anna Villaverde, widowed by the political events, was, in turn, persecuted and detained by the military. As the story retreats into dreamy renditions of colonial history in the Philippines, the personal histories of the three characters are expanded, and their connections to each other are tightened. National history and family history are paralleled and braided, leading to a final scene of terrifying violence when the resistance and Establishment meet. The novel's setting on an unnamed Philippine island during a festival serves as stage to scenes of bacchanalian excess and political drama, which are suggested, finally, to be one and the same.

Whereas *State of War* deals centrally with resistances to martial law, *Twice Blessed* displays satirical caricatures of martial law's central ruling players—the Marcoses. Twins Hector Basbas and Katerina Basbas Gloriosa call to mind Imelda and Ferdinand Marcos as they claw their way out of poverty toward political domination and shoe-filled closets. Rosca spares no detail in disclosing ruthless, self-serving corruption.

CRITICAL RECEPTION

We can render Ninotchka Rosca's critical reception in the image of a teeter-totter where journalistic reporting supporters sit on one side, with literary enthusiasts on the other. Rosca's attempts at both journalism and history-based fiction motivate the teeter-totter's movement. All in all, Rosca's reception is highly favorable. The few complaints that reviewers log for Rosca's fictional work typically bespeak a favoritism for her journalistic skills. For instance, *Kirkus* considers *State of War* "flawed" and in the same breath states that Rosca's "best work to date remains her nonfiction *Endgame*" (Rev.).

Reviewers for *Kirkus* are consistently critical of Rosca's novels, characterizing *State of War* and *Twice Blessed*, respectively, as "flawed" and "less than compelling." Supposed flaws and yawn-summoners—unbelievable connections and events, lack of "real or even interesting characters," and failed "attempts at surreal humor and magic realism" (Rev. *Twice, Kirkus*)—might be understood better, however, as oppositive to stranger-than-fiction Filipino politics rather than critical of Rosca's abilities. A review of *State of War* echoes this favoring of the journalistic, the supposed "real," over creativity: "One wishes Rosca had used less allegory and more realistic detail; often the unique situation in the Philippines is lost in her somewhat mannered style"—a style the same reviewer later calls "Kafkaesque" (*Publishers Weekly*). This review's final words on Rosca's *State of War* reference this literary style and say that such "erratic, Kafkaesque brilliance [is what] makes this first novel a powerful piece of literature."

Aside from relatively superficial book reviews, Rosca's oeuvre remains understudied, especially by Asian American. Philippine scholars have taken the most note of Rosca's literary achievement. Leonard Casper, well-known literary critic of Philippine literature, adds her work to his interest in literature of the Marcos regime. Casper takes up Rosca's work in a way that certainly melds the historical and literary, the journalistic and the creative. Further, Casper situates Rosca within the literary history of the Philippines. Likewise, Cristina Hidalgo focuses her brief study of Rosca on the author's status within the canon of Philippine literature and places special emphasis on Rosca's feminism. Hidalgo's article questions the future of Philippine feminist literature in 1975, well before, as Hidalgo also recognizes, Rosca had a substantial corpus of writing.

Oscar Campomanes' seminal studies contextualize Filipino writing in English within the field of Asian American studies. Campomanes challenges how the field's reigning paradigm prioritizes Asian immigration and settlement in the United States and introduces the historically more appropriate category of exile in order to analyze the writing of Filipinos in the United States. Campomanes groups Rosca with Linda Ty-Casper and Michelle Skinner, thereby delineating an emergent generation of Filipino political expatriate authors in the United States whose literary and political concerns are located in the Philippines.

That two recent critical studies of Rosca's *State of War* have appeared in *Critical Mass*, a small, but important, Asian American journal of cultural criticism, is testament to Rosca's extensive future within Asian American literary studies. Nguyen fuses queer theory, postcolonial studies, and a close reading of *State of War* to reveal the intricate interplay of discourses on sexuality and (post)colonialism. Balce-Cortes pairs *State of War* with Jessica Hagedorn's* novel *Dogeaters* and contextualizes both novels within Asian American studies broadly. Balce-Cortes carefully contemplates the trend of Filipino writing in the United States to take up Philippine landscapes and Philippine history by unpacking the categories of history, memory, narration, postcolonialism, and postmodernism.

BIBLIOGRAPHY

Works by Ninotchka Rosca

Novels

State of War. New York: Norton, 1988.
Twice Blessed. New York: Norton, 1992.

Short Stories

Bitter Country and Other Stories. Quezon City, Philippines: Malaya Books, 1970.
The Monsoon Collection. Santa Lucia and New York: University of Queensland Press, 1983.
"Generations." 1983. *Brown River, White Ocean: An Anthology of Twentieth-Century Philippine Literature in English*. Ed. Luis H. Francia. New Brunswick, NJ: Rutgers University Press, 1993. 193–99.
"Sugar and Salt." In *Charlie Chan Is Dead: An Anthology of Contemporary Asian American Fiction*. Ed. Jessica Hagedorn. New York: Penguin, 1993. 399–406.
"Fugitive Colors." In *Flippin': Filipinos in America*. Ed. Luis H. Francia and Eric Gamalinda. New York: Asian American Writers Workshop, 1996. 64–69.

Nonfiction

Endgame: The Fall of Marcos. New York: Franklin Watts, 1987.

Studies of Ninotchka Rosca

Bacho, Peter. "Windows on Philippine Women, Politics, and Life." Rev. of *Twice Blessed. Christian Science Monitor* 84 (1992): 11.

Balce-Cortes, Nerissa. "Imagining the Neocolony." *Critical Mass: A Journal of Asian American Cultural Criticism*, Special Issue on U.S. Filipino Literature and Culture 2.2 (1995): 95–120.

Batty, Barbara. Rev. of *Endgame: The Fall of Marcos. Library Journal* 112 (1987): 85.

Betty, John Domini. "Exile and Detention." Rev. of *The Monsoon Collection. New York Times Book Review* (January 1, 1984, late ed): 14.

Bumas, Ethan. Rev. of *State of War. Library Journal* 113 (1988): 144.

Campomanes, Oscar V. "Filipinos in the United States and Their Literature of Exile." In *Reading the Literatures of Asian America.* Ed. Shirley Geok-lin Lim and Amy Ling. Philadelphia: Temple University Press, 1992. 49–78.

Casper, Leonard. "Minoring in History: Rosca as Ninotchka." *Amerasia Journal* 16.1 (1990): 201–10.

———. *The Opposing Thumb: Decoding Literature of the Marcos Regime.* Quezon City, Philippines: Giraffe Books, 1995. 47–49.

———. "Social Realism in the Stories of Edilberto Tiempo and Ninotchka Rosca." *Solidarity* 8.1 (1973): 68–74.

Hidalgo, Cristina P. "Now That Dear Kerima, Carmen, Gilda, and Ninotchka Have Come, Can Our Simone de Beauvoir Be Far Behind?" *Manila Review* 1.1 (1976): 104–13.

Howard, Jennifer. Rev. of *Twice Blessed. Book World* 22 (1992): 11.

Levy, Francis. Rev. of *State of War. New York Times Book Review* (September 25, 1988) late ed.: 30.

Nguyen, Viet Thanh. "The Postcolonial State of Desire: Homosexuality and Tranvestitism in Ninotchka Rosca's *State of War.*" *Critical Mass: A Journal of Asian American Cultural Criticism*, Special Issue on U.S. Filipino Literature and Culture 2.2 (1995): 67–93.

Rev. of *Endgame: The Fall of Marcos. Kirkus Reviews* 55 (1987): 1302.

Rev. of *Endgame: The Fall of Marcos. School Library Journal* 35 (1988): 214.

Rev. of *The Monsoon Collection. Publishers Weekly* 224 (1983): 383.

Rev. of *The Monsoon Collection. World Literature Today* 58.3 (1984): 477.

Rev. of *State of War. Booklist* 84 (1988): 1573.

Rev. of *State of War. Kirkus Reviews* 56 (1988): 398.

Rev. of *State of War. Publishers Weekly* 233 (1988): 75.

Rev. of *Twice Blessed. Kirkus Reviews* 60 (1992): 16.

Rev. of *Twice Blessed. Library Journal* 117 (1992): 197.

Rev. of *Twice Blessed. Publishers Weekly* 239 (1992): 46.

Patsy Sumie Saiki
(1915–)

Seri Luangphinith

BIOGRAPHY

Patsy Sumie Saiki was born in Ahualoa, on the Island of Hawai'i, on March 12, 1915, to Japanese immigrants from Hiroshima who became independent homesteaders after working on the plantation.[1] She left the "Big Island" for Honolulu, where she attended McKinley High School in 1931; however, just prior to her graduation, Saiki's mother passed away. Memories of her parents have since served as the core of Saiki's writing. Following marriage and the birth of her four children, Saiki went on to pursue studies in education at the University of Hawai'i: she graduated with a bachelor's in 1954, followed by a master's in 1959. While studying at the university, Saiki's interest in the Japanese prompted her to write short stories and dramas.

In 1960 Saiki received a Wall Street Journalism Fellowship to study at the University of Wisconsin. She returned home and became a supervisor for practice teachers at the University of Hawai'i Lab School but returned to the mainland to obtain a doctorate from Teachers' College at Columbia University in 1967. After serving as assistant professor at the University of Hawai'i, she became an administrator in the Hawai'i State Department of Education. Saiki continued writing, and in 1978 she published the novel *Sachie: A Daughter of Hawaii*. This was followed by a number of more historically inclined works in the 1980s and 1990s. Saiki has since retired from public service; however, she continues to contribute to the study of Hawaii's Japanese.

MAJOR WORK AND THEMES

By her own account, Patsy Sumie Saiki's writing has been prolific. However, all of her works have a unified purpose—to promote an awareness of Hawaii's

Japanese Americans and their hardships. Survival is the main theme in *Sachie: A Daughter of Hawaii*, which portrays the Himeno family facing alienation and racial discrimination.

Although *Sachie* is narrated by thirteen-year-old Sachie Himeno, this novel is not an idyllic childhood memoir nor a romanticized immigrant success story. The story immediately portrays the inherent violence of plantation society. In Chapter 1, "Not Wanted, Sugar Plantation White Man," the Fraserville plantation *luna* (supervisor) Mr. Bachman comes to offer the elder daughter, Hanako, a position as maid in his household. Sachie, who has been sitting in a locquat tree eating "the most golden of the ripe yellow fruit," yells "Abunai—danger! White man!" to her brothers, who scramble for a knife and shotgun (10–11). The family is noticeably on edge as Bachman makes his offer—Hanako has gone into hiding, the mother feigns an inability to speak English, and the brothers practice knife-throwing. Bachman's request is denied because of rumors that all the girls who served at the Bachman residence have gotten pregnant. The episode ends as Bachman storms off, leaving the father to fret over the need to marry his daughter off. Thus, despite the fact that Sachie can play in the orchard and eat of its "golden" fruit, the plantation that exists just a few miles from the family farm represents a sinister authority that seemingly condones differences in social status according to race and arbitrarily exercises the power to seduce/rape women.

Responding to the social disparity between haoles (whites) and Japanese creates conflict between Sachie and her parents. Mr. Himeno's experiences lead him to view the homestead as a refuge. As a field-worker, Mr. Himeno witnessed a *luna* beating a Japanese laborer. In his friend's defense, Mr. Himeno attacks the *luna* and flees the plantation to Kekala, where he has since managed an independent homestead (21–22). "Hiding" from the white man and disengaging from the plantation system are believed by Sachie's father to be the best method of survival. However, her family's isolationist policy and their acceptance of otherness are questioned by Sachie, who feels this attitude is cowardly because it reinforces the belief that the "Japanese people have no guts. . . . they obey, even when [they] know it's not right" (19). She further argues that because the Japanese are "yes-yes people" who never stand up for their rights, they will always be immigrants instead of Americans, laborers instead of bosses.

Sachie's criticism of her parents reflects larger problems of self-hate and confusion, which continually disrupt the narrative. She wishes she had "been born to a rich Caucasian doctor or dentist" (20). She resents her "blackness" and having "straight black hair . . . stiff hair, like the horse's tail, [and] slant eyes" (31). So while Sachie berates the Japanese for being too "Asian," she herself longs to be white and "American." In turn, the continual juxtaposition of Japanese and American becomes a constant source of frustration for her because racial identity simultaneously seems both powerful and ludicrous. During a dance, Sachie observes how the "melting pot" ideal is dispelled by the whites' occupation of the dance floor, with Hawaiians and Portuguese on the periphery, while the Japanese, Chinese, and Filipinos are left on the sidewalk (56). However, this social hierarchy does not prevent Laurie Higgins, an upper-class haole, from becoming Sachie's best friend. Recurring contradictions continue to plague Sachie because no lasting definition of racial identity can be formed: neither whites nor Japanese can be continually demonized, nor can they be perpetually exalted.

Sachie's confusion inevitably keeps the novel from finding a positive resolution of racial ambivalence. The inability to posit an absolute definition of either white or Japanese leads Sachie to continually desire to escape from the things she can't explain or understand. For Sachie, the only comfort lies in childhood and in her preoccupation with fairy tales within which the bad are always punished, and the good, "no matter how ugly, how awkward, [or] how weak they are," have a chance to succeed (48). Unlike reality, where "good" and "bad" are almost impossible to distinguish, especially in terms of racial conflict, the fairy tale allows for clear-cut distinctions between binary opposites. This "comfort" is perhaps one reason that the novel, until the very end, persists in maintaining the childhood perspective and that "want[ing] to be a child a little longer" is the only solution possible for the narrator (140).

CRITICAL RECEPTION

Patsy Sumie Saiki's work has received very little critical attention. The *Star-Bulletin* once commented on Saiki's skill as a fiction writer by calling her short story "A Letter to a Daughter," in *Early Japanese Immigrants in Hawaii*, a "charming" tale that shows the "continu[ing] circle of compassion [and] creativity" between immigrants and their children (Enomoto C6). Among academics, scholarship has been limited to the works of Stephen H. Sumida. He identifies Saiki as part of a post–World War II flourishing of Hawaii's ethnic writers, who are responsible for engaging immigrant experiences and local cultural sensibilities in the production of a regionally unique style of literature.

Specifically, Sumida values Saiki's work for its ability to resist canonical, continental American notions of literature. Sumida argues that Saiki's complex use of the pastoral makes possible the movement beyond "the entrenched *simple* pastoral notions of Hawai'i" and the opposition to "sentimentalized, false, and meaningless" visions of a tourist paradise (*And the View* 270). Likewise, Sumida claims that in *Sachie* the "congruence of visions and values between her immigrant characters and the culture of the Hawaiians on whose lands they have come to settle" is an example of how Hawaii's local and polyethnic writers do not preempt the long-standing history and culture of the indigenous population but instead offer models that repudiate the colonial views of outsiders like Mark Twain and James A. Michener ("Sense of Place" 226–28).

NOTE

1. The contemporary revival of Hawaiian language and literary studies has witnessed increased attention to "accurate" spellings of Hawaiian words using linguistic markers such as the '*okina* (the glottal stop signified by'). Out of respect for Native Hawaiian concerns regarding language usage, I use the '*okina* in Hawaiian words such as Hawai'i; however, I omit the marker for Anglicized words, such as "Hawaiian" or "Hawaii's," and in instances where I cite a writer who does not use such spellings.

BIBLIOGRAPHY

Work by Patsy Sumie Saiki

Novel

Sachie: A Daughter of Hawaii. Honolulu: Kisaku, 1977.

Short Stories

Ganbare: An Example of Japanese Spirit. Honolulu: Kisaku, 1982.
Japanese Women in Hawaii: The First 100 Years. Honolulu: Kisaku, 1985.
Early Japanese Immigrants in Hawaii. Honolulu: Kisaku, 1993.

Drama

"The Return." Typescript. *University of Hawaii Plays* 2 (1959): 97–111.
"The Second Choice." Typescript. *University of Hawaii Plays* 2 (1959): 91–96.
"The Return of Sam Patch." Typescript. *Theatre Group Plays.* 12 (1966–1967): 20–33.

Studies of Patsy Sumie Saiki

Enomoto, Catherine Kekoa. "Author Continues Circle of Compassion, Creativity." *Star-Bulletin*, September 26, 1997: C6.
Sumida, Stephen H. "Sense of Place, History, and the Concept of 'Local' in Hawaii's Asian/Pacific American Literature." In *Reading the Literatures of Asian America.* Ed. Shirley Geok-lin Lim and Amy Ling. Philadelphia: Temple University Press, 1992. 215–37.
———. *And the View from the Shore: Literary Traditions of Hawai'i.* Seattle: University of Washington Press, 1991.

Bienvenido N. Santos
(1911–1996)

Anita Mannur

BIOGRAPHY

Bienvenido N. Santos was born on March 22, 1911, in Tondo, a poor neighborhood in Manila. During his life, he moved back and forth between the United States and the Philippines. In 1941 Santos came to the United States on a Philippine government scholarship. He studied at Columbia and Harvard Universities and earned his master's degree in English from the University of Illinois. When the Philippines was invaded by Japan in World War II, his studies were interrupted. Like many other *pensionados* (Filipinos sponsored by the U.S. government to study in the United States) he began working for the Philippine government in exile in Washington. His wife and children, however, were still living in the Japanese-occupied Philippines. According to one critic, the anxiety of this separation brought him closer to fellow exiles (Casper, *Firewalkers* 147) he met when asked by the U.S. Department of Education to lecture to Americans on the spirit of Philippine resistance and on the value of having Filipinos as allies. After the war, he published *The Volcano*, a novel dealing with the rise of anti-American sentiments in the Philippines.

Santos's first novel was published in 1965, but whether this was *Villa Magdalena* or *Volcano* is unclear. Both were published in 1965, and, as one critic notes, "both claim, on their wrappers, to be Santos's first novel" (Casper, *Firewalkers* 21). Apparently, although *Villa Magdalena* was completed first, the idea of *Volcano* was conceived earlier.

In the 1970s Santos' novel *The Praying Man* was serialized by the Manila-based magazine *Solidarity*. This was a particularly courageous act because of the polemical nature of the novel, which deals with political corruption in the Philippines. *The Praying Man* was banned by the government of Ferdinand E.

Marcos, presumably because it seemed to incite anti-Marcos sentiment. After the ban, Santos went into voluntary exile in the United States and became an American citizen in 1976. Only in 1981, after martial law was lifted in the Philippines, did he make his first visit home from exile.

For much of his literary career, Santos was affiliated with several universities in both the Philippines and the United States. From 1961 to 1966 he was dean and vice president of the University of Nueva Caceres in the Philippines. From 1973 to 1982 Santos served as writer in residence at Wichita State University. He has also taught at Ohio State University and the Aspen Creative Writing Workshop in the United States and at De La Salle University in the Philippines.

Santos has received numerous prestigious awards in both the United States and the Philippines. He was a Rockefeller Foundation fellow and Fulbright professor at the University of Iowa. (While he was supported by the Rockefeller Fellowship, he worked on one of his first novels, *Villa Magdalena*.) Later, he received a Guggenheim Foundation Fellowship to work on *The Volcano*. In addition, Santos has received the American Book Award and the Philippine Republic Cultural Heritage Award.

In later years, he alternated between homes in Greeley, Colorado, and the Philippines. He eventually moved back to the Philippines and took up residence in his family home in Sagpon, Daraga, Albay in the Philippines. A few years before his death, Santos completed his memoirs, *Memory's Fictions*, which was published in 1993.

MAJOR WORKS AND THEMES

The literary oeuvre of Bienvenido Santos can be subdivided into two major categories. On one hand are the novels that specifically engage the Philippines. Included in this category are his first two novels, *Villa Magdalena* and *Volcano*, as well as the novel that earned him notoriety, *The Praying Man*. The second category includes works such as *The Man Who (Thought He) Looked like Robert Taylor*, *What the Hell For You Left Your Heart in San Francisco?*, *Memory's Fictions*, and *You Lovely People*, all of which deal specifically with the Filipino experience in the United States. A unifying theme in many of these works is the sense of alienation and ambivalence felt by many Filipinos as they move between the Philippines and the United States in search of a place to call home.

Santos' short fiction provides almost paradigmatic instances of the experiences of immigrants in the United States. The stories that make up *You Lovely People* deal with the experiences of Filipinos who have lived in the United States but who think of the Philippines as "home." Linked by the character Ambo, the stories in this collection center around the experiences of various American born Filipinos in the United States and the Philippines. The tension between belonging and not-belonging to both spaces is consistently foregrounded. The first story in the collection, "The Wise Man Who Was Not There," tells the story of Ben, a student who has just arrived from the Philippines and is spending Christmas with friends. The coldness of the wintry air in Chicago is contrasted with Ben's memories of "home" in the Philippines: "home to me then was a little rambling house with windows open to the hills and Mount Mayon. There was a porch cool with wind and fragrant with papaya blossoms" (1).

In contrast to this is the final story in the collection, "For These Ruins." While both stories address a particular nostalgia for "home," the narrator of the first story is nostalgic for the Philippines, and the narrator of the final story, who lives in the Philippines, is nostalgic for his life in the United States. The work as a whole offers an insightful look into the ways "home" is negotiated for persons who feel that they simultaneously belong to more than one national space. As Francisco Arcellana observes, the work's strength lies in its unique thematic organization. He notes, "When the book opens, a Filipino in America is homesick for Filipinas. When the book closes, a Filipino in the Philippines is "homesick" for America. The circle closes" (717).

"Immigration Blues," the story of a widower, Alpino, cuts across different generations of Filipino immigrants. Alpino, the protagonist, gradually becomes involved in the plight of Monica, a Filipina who is desperately trying to remain in the United States. When Alpino is asked to marry Monica so that she can remain in the United States, he is reminded that his first marriage began in the same vein. Santos effectively examines how the process of immigration affects people's lives in poignant and at times traumatic ways. Originally published in *The Scent of Apples*, this story was recently anthologized in a collection of contemporary Asian American authors, *Charlie Chan Is Dead*, edited by Jessica Hagedorn.*

Among his notable longer works that pivot around these themes are his autobiographical narrative, *Memory's Fiction*, and *What the Hell For You Left Your Heart in San Francisco*? Certain critics have suggested that the latter text perfectly encapsulates the Filipino American experience, discussed later. In *Memory's Fictions*, Santos disrupts narrative chronology, oscillating between his life in the Philippines and that in the United States. The narrative foregrounds Santos' own story, echoing some of the sentiments found in his short fiction. He talks, for example, about feeling "homesick" and wanting to fly "back to San Francisco" (199), only to admit shortly thereafter that "many times we wished we were back home, where we knew almost everyone in the community in the towns at the foot of Mount Mayon" (207).

The dual problem of remembering and re-membering acquires a certain urgency in this text. The text has a recurring, self-reflexive tone as Santos questions why he is writing his autobiography. Throughout the narrative, the author addresses the issues of where to begin, how to begin, and how to put things together after a lifetime of experiences in two continents.

CRITICAL RECEPTION

Bienvenido N. Santos is seen as an important first-generation writer from the Philippines located in the United States, and his work has been discussed at length by many scholars of Asian American literature. Rather than examining these various arguments in summary fashion, I have selected a few representative responses that discuss Santos' work in relation to the larger corpus of Asian American literature. In the chapter on "Filipino American Literature" in King-Kok Cheung's *Interethnic Companion to Asian American Literature*, N.V.M. Gonzalez cites *What the Hell For You Left Your Heart in San Francisco?* as the "quintessential Filipino American novel" not only because of its "American setting" but also because "its characters and the attitudes and values that they cling to or pervert in the course of their lives" are also "American" (70). The essay, coauthored by Gonzalez and Oscar V. Campomanes, discusses Santos' writings in relation to those of several generations of writers who can be considered Filipino American, albeit in markedly different ways. Francisco Arcellana views *You Lovely People* in a positive light because it finds a way to chronicle the diverse experiences of Filipinos who have lived in the United States.

This observation runs parallel to Emmanuel Nelson's observation that *What the Hell For You Left Your Heart in San Francisco?* is a "moving exploration of the recent Filipino-American immigrant experience." Nelson, however, notes that although Santos chronicles the experience of dislocation and nostalgia experienced by immigrants in a useful manner, his "treatment of these themes is not particularly new." This raises an important question, What makes Santos' writing valuable? Nelson suggests that "the compelling clarity" and "haunting poignancy of his prose" render the novel memorable. Discussing the notion that Santos is the most "Asian American" (according to Asian American literary critics) of several Filipino American authors, N.V.M. Gonzalez Oscar V. Campomanes suggest that Santos has been accorded an important status in the canon of Asian American literature because of "the recognizably 'American' thematics of his stories and some of his novels" (81).

Not all critics of Bienvenido N. Santos, however, have responded positively to his work. Leonard Casper, who has written extensively on Santos' literary oeuvre, somewhat harshly criticizes Santos' style of writing. In "Paperboat Novels: The Later Bienvenido N. Santos," he comments on Santos' style, noting that "one does not think of Santos as among the Philippines' foremost experimenters" (163). Although this is at odds with other reviews of Santos' work, Casper poses an important question, Does Santos deserve his reputation as one of the most important writers from the Philippines, and, moreover, how has he been able to maintain this status? (164). Casper seems to think that Santos perhaps does not deserve this honor, describing his "overall indifference to chronology" and "sporadic breaks in continuity" as symptoms of a writer who, though "weak on extended form, [is] strong on short term characterization" (167–68). According to Campomanes, this disruption of linearity is precisely what makes Santos an exemplary Filipino American writer: this "nomadic narrative strategy" (101) is a common strategy in Filipino American writers who wish to foreground themes of migrancy and loss.

Overall, the consensus seems to be that the work of Bienvenido N. Santos is crucial within the larger corpus of Filipino American literature. While his style may not be as radically innovative as that of some of the writers of newer generations, Santos remains an important figure precisely because he gives voice to experiences that have been neglected in mainstream North American settings.

BIBLIOGRAPHY

Works by Bienvenido N. Santos

Novels

Villa Magdalena. Manila: Erewhon, 1965.
The Volcano. Quezon City: Phoenix Publishing House, 1965.
The Praying Man. Quezon City: New Day, 1982.
The Man Who (Thought He) Looked like Robert Taylor. Quezon City: New Day, 1983.
What the Hell For You Left Your Heart in San Francisco. Quezon City: New Day, 1987.

Poetry/Drama

The Wounded Stag. Manila: Capitol Publishing House, 1956.
The Bishop's Pet: One Act Play. Manila: Philippines Free Press, 1966.
Distances—In Time: Selected Poems. Quezon City: Ateneo de Manila University Press, 1983.

Short Stories

You Lovely People. Manila: Benipayo Press, 1955.
Brother, My Brother. Manila: Benipayo Press, 1960.
The Day the Dancers Came: Selected Prose Writings. Manila: Bookmark, 1967.
Scent of Apples: A Collection of Short Stories. Seattle: University of Washington Press, 1967.

Autobiography

Memory's Fictions. Quezon City: New Day, 1993.

Prose Nonfiction

"The Filipino Novel in English." In *Brown Heritage: Essays on Philippine Cultural Tradition and Literature.* Ed. Antonio G. Manuud. Quezon City: Ateneo de Manila University Press, 1967. 634–47.
"The Personal Saga of a 'Straggler' in Philippine Literature." *WLWE—World Literature Written-in English* 15 (1976): 398–405.
"The Filipino Writer in English as Storyteller and Translator." In *Asian Voices in English.* Ed. Mimi Chan and Roy Harris. Hong Kong: Hong Kong University Press, 1991. 43–50.

Studies of Bienvenido N. Santos

Alegre, Edilberto N. and Doreen G. Fernandez. *The Writer and His Milieu: An Oral History of First Generation Writers in English.* Manila: De La Salle University Press, 1984.

Arcellana, Francisco. "Bienvenido N. Santos." In *Brown Heritage: Essays on Philippine Cultural Tradition and Literature*. Ed. Antonio G. Manuud. Quezon City: Ateneo de Manila University Press, 1967. 714–21.

Bresnahan, Roger J. "Can These, Too, Be Midwestern? Studies of Two Filipino Writers." *Midamerica: The Yearbook of the Society for the Study of Midwestern Literature* 8 (1986): 134–47.

———. "The Midwestern Fiction of Bienvenido N. Santos." *Society for the Study of Midwestern Literature Newsletter* 13.2 (1983): 28–37.

Carpio, Rustica C. "Bienvenido Santos and *Brother, My Brother*." *Solidarity* 5.12 (1970): 58–64.

Casper, Leonard. *Firewalkers: Literary Concelebrations, 1964–1984*. Quezon City: New Day, 1987.

———. "Greater Shouting and Greater Silences: The Novels of Bienvenido Santos" *Solidarity* 3.10 (1968): 76–84.

———. "Paperboat Novels: The Later Bienvenido N. Santos." *Amerasia Journal* 13.1 (1986–1987): 163–70.

Cheung, King-Kok. "Bienvenido Santos: Filipino Old-Timers in Literature." *Markham Review* 15 (1986): 49–53.

Gonzalez, N.V.M., and Oscar V. Campomanes. "Filipino American Literature." In *An Interethnic Companion to Asian American Literature*. Ed. King-Kok Cheung. Cambridge: Cambridge University Press, 1996. 62–124.

Grow, L. M. "The Christian World-View of Bienvenido N. Santos." *Aumla-Journal of the Australasian Universities Language and Literature Association* 60 (November 1983): 234–251.

———. "Modern Philippine Poetry in the Formative Years: 1920–1950." *ARIEL* 15.3. (1984): 81–98.

———. "The Poet and the Garden: The Green World of Bienvenido N. Santos." *WL WE: World Literature Written in English* 29.1 (1984): 136–45.

Manuel, Dolores de. "Marriage in Philippine-American Fiction." *Philippine Studies* 42.2 (1994): 210–16.

Nelson, Emmanuel S. Rev. of *What the Hell For You Left Your Heart in San Francisco Choice* (April 1988): 173.

Puente, Lorenzo. "Split-Level Christianity in The Praying Man." *Philippine Studies* 40.1 (1992): 111–20.

Reyes, Soledad S. "Death-in-Life in Santos's Villa Magdalena." In *Essays on the Philippine Novel in English*. Ed. Joseph A. Galdon. Quezon City: Ateneo de Manila University Press, 1979. 125–49.

Rico, Victoria S. "Themes in the Poetry of Bienvenido Santos." *Philippine Studies* 42.4 (1994): 452–74.

———. "*You Lovely People*: The Texture of Alienation." *Philippine Studies* 42.1 (1994): 91–104.

Santos, Tomas. "The Filipino Writer in America—Old and New." *WLWE, World Literature Written in English* 15.2 (1976): 406–14.

Valdez, Maria Stella. "The Myth and the Matrix in Bienvenido N. Santos' *Scent of Apples*: Searching for Harmony among Incongruities." *Dlsu Dialogue* 25.1 (1991): 73–86.

Vidal, Lourdes H. "Echoes and Reflections in *Villa Magdalena*." *Philippine Studies* 35.3 (1987): 377–82.

Lisa Lenine See
(1955–   )

Xian Liu

BIOGRAPHY

Lisa Lenine See was born on February 18, 1955, in Paris, France, to Carolyn Laws, whose ancestors were among the earliest settlers in Virginia, and Richard See, one-quarter Chinese, whose great-grandfather, Fong Dun, came to California in 1867, working on the transcontinental railroad. One-eighth Chinese herself, See embarked on a journey of Eurasian experience literally when her parents took her through France, Italy, and Yugoslavia and back to Los Angeles before she was even six weeks old. Her exposure to different cultures from then on proves to be essential to her literary works in terms of providing her with not only settings and characters but also a sense of authenticity and orientation unobtainable by those without such an experience.

Like the tumultuous Chinese American saga chronicled in *On Gold Mountain*, See's life during her tender years seemed to spin out of control at any moment. Her mother—the successful novelist Carolyn See—was then a struggling writer at the University of California at Los Angeles (UCLA), while her father, pursuing his Ph.D. in anthropology, drank heavily and constantly. Adding to their stress, her grandfather, playing the role of Chinese father-in-law, "meddled, intruded, bossed" (*Mountain* 343). Her parents divorced when she was four. She changed school seven times between the second and fourth grades, following her mother from one residence to another. But living with Carolyn did not keep her away from her father's side of the family. On the contrary, her father's relatives in Los Angeles' Chinatown "provided her with a sense of community, a place where she belonged" (Ulin). "My grandmother, Stella—a Caucasian, had taught me everything I knew about my Chineseness, about identity, about race" ("Funeral" 127). The time she spent in Chinatown eventually instilled in her a feel of real life that Chinese—fresh-off-the-boat and American-born— have lived since the railroad days. It is an understatement that See's literary career would not distinguish itself without her intimate experience with the Chinese family dynamics—the core of Chinese culture.

However, unlike many ambitious, struggling writers, See decided to write for a living only when she felt that it was a feasible approach to the life of a world traveler—living out of a suitcase and having no ties. She went back to Loyola Marymount College in 1976 after traveling for two years in Europe and switched her major from humanities to modern Greek studies, though both later helped significantly prepare her as a versatile journalist/writer.

Her prolific writing career began in 1979 with an assignment from *TV Guide*. Since then she has been a freelance reporter contributing to various magazines, journals, and newspapers, including *Sporting Times*, the *Los Angeles Times*, *Angeles Magazine*, the *San Francisco Chronicle*, and the *Washington Post*, just to name a few. Under the pseudonym of Monica Highland, she collaborated with her mother and John Espey and published *Lotus Land*, *One Hundred Ten Shanghai Road*, and *Greetings from Southern California*.

Although her literary ambition began before she went to *Publishers Weekly*, the time with the magazine was crucial to her as a career writer. From 1983 to 1996 she worked as West Coast correspondent for *Publishers Weekly*, filing on average two reports per week on everything in the publishing world west of the Mississippi. The wide range of subjects she covered included book fairs in Denver, Seattle, Los Angeles, and San Francisco, short fictions from western states, the joint printing venture between university presses, independent bookstores' new strategies for book sales, Peachpit Press' new Web site, latest trends for ethnic literature on the West Coast. In addition, See interviewed and profiled scores of writers during that period. Among them were novelists Michael Chabon, Harriet Doerr, and Cynthia Kadohata,* lawyer and courtroom thriller writer Robert K. Tanenbaum, African American science fiction writer Octavia E. Butler, short story writer Merrill Joan Gerber, gay author Paul Monette, and others. The struggle for objectivity and truth in quality journalism has helped shape both the style of her writing and the way she examines her writing.

Reports or fiction, See's works are well researched, hence faithful and fair in presentation to their subjects. Her recent longer works—*On Gold Mountain* and *Flower Net*—continue to be fine examples of quality research and truthful presentation. Threading her way through layers of memory about her family and tons of information on contemporary China that romanticize and distort the facts, See manages to portray the two eras of the Chinese American experience with a voice enviably authentic and truthful.

MAJOR WORKS AND THEMES

"Prolific" may be the word to accurately describe the number of pieces she has produced as a journalist and the number of subjects she has probed as a reporter. But "profundity" is the term to characterize her promising literary career, which debuted in 1995 with *On Gold Mountain*—a *New York Times* Notable Book—followed by *Flower Net* in 1997—another *New York Times* Notable Book. *The Interior* (working title), again set in the Sino-American corporate world, was published by HarperCollins in 1999. With cross-cultural struggles as their predominant themes, See's major works humanize the experience of the "outsiders." Whether it be Chinese coolies on the transcontinental railroad, abandoned, penniless Caucasian girls, a U.S. assistant attorney in Beijing, or China's top investigators in Los Angeles, these outsiders—past and present—overcome obstacles against all odds and accomplish their goals by developing an understanding of themselves and marginalized others. Their stories thus transcend the confines of their own culture and resonate for readers of all backgrounds.

On Gold Mountain is an enthusiastically researched chronicle of one Chinese American family from the 1860s to the present. Five years of research and personal interviews with close to 100 family relatives, friends, and associates, as well as hundreds of pages of documents from family sources, newspaper clippings, magazine files, the records of the National Archives, and the Immigration and Naturalization Service (INS) interrogation notes, are included in rendering this biography "a striking piece of social history made immediate and gripping" (Stuttaford). Starting with her great-great-grandfather's days on the transcontinental railroad, it traces generations of travail of founding a business when the Alien Land Act of 1870 forbade selling property to the Chinese, marrying Caucasians when the miscegenation laws were in full force, and securing their basic rights when the Exclusion Act of 1882 barred the Chinese from becoming citizens. Through those details of her family's daily struggles in business and for social acceptance *On Gold Mountain* eloquently chronicles this nation's ongoing struggles to redefine humanity—an effort to which readers of all ethnic backgrounds can relate.

This mesmerizing, five-generation odyssey of fears, tears, and cheers has given a human face to the Chinese American experience as a whole, but it is far from an "advocacy biography." The memoir scrupulously exposes both a despicable past of the U.S. discriminatory immigration policies against Chinese and fraudulent tactics Chinese immigrants resorted to in order to claim their legal status. The Exclusion Act of 1882 declared that no Chinese was eligible for citizenship. See writes that such a statement alone "allowed the United States to join Nazi Germany and South Africa as the only nations ever to withhold naturalization on purely racial grounds" (*Mountain* 45). In the following chapter, however, See reproaches the Chinese with the same candor for some of their maneuvers to circumvent U.S. immigration rules. Thousands of Chinese claimed their American citizenship by birth when most of the city's records and birth certificates were destroyed in San Francisco during the earthquake of 1906. If each claim had been honest, "every Chinese woman living in San Francisco would have had to have borne eight hundred sons" because "Chinese women numbered only five percent of the total Chinese population in the United States" at the time (*Mountain* 81). This family biography therefore manages to be as truthful and objective as possible while remaining fair to everyone involved.

Flower Net is a murder mystery entangled in the cultural intricacies on both sides of the Pacific. But it takes the reader far beyond forensic lab work, chase scenes in crowded Beijing streets, and dismembered bodies in Los Angeles (L.A.) Chinatown. Its expected and unexpected plot twists unfold along a simple structural parallel that juxtaposes cultural idiosyncrasies and explores cultural nuances about both modern China and America.

The thriller begins with the discovery of two young male bodies thousands of miles apart. One is a perfectly preserved American encased in the ice on the peaceful Bei Hai Lake in Beijing, while the other is a grossly decomposed Chinese floating in the tank of freshwater supply on a storm-stranded smuggling ship off the coast of California. The frozen American—son of the American ambassador—is announced by the high-pitched wail of an innocent girl skater, but the existence of the smelly Chinese body—son of China's most influential hotel tycoon—is actually found in the denial of the seasick Chinese illegal immigrants to acknowledge it on their ship. While a top female inspector in Beijing appears to have all the authority and support in the investigation, especially with her father as the deputy minister of public security, a high-principled assistant attorney in L.A. seems to fight his battle alone against corruption and conspiracy. Not surprisingly, as the "flower net" widens, this detective work becomes a study of people and their behavior. Then, the investigators' cultural knowledge, not their forensic training, begins to provide them with more and more answers. By the end of the novel, the skillfully constructed parallel, which first appears as a structural necessity, turns out to serve as an effective thematic vehicle that challenges the stereotypical view in the United States that either romanticizes or dismisses China and dispels the simplistic notion in China that America has solutions to all the social and economic ills, hence offering insights into both cultures.

By telling her stories in a well-researched context—past and present—See adds personal meaning to America's diversity history in *On Gold Mountain* and human face to the remote country known as China in *Flower Net*. In fact, her works' unique reflection of facts in fiction, past in present, and politics in personal terms not only breaks new ground in the field of ethnic literature but also distinguishes her from other Asian American writers.

CRITICAL RECEPTION

Matt Miller of the *San Diego Union-Tribune* may have gone a bit overboard when he claimed that "Amerasian lit finally is finding its voice" with the publication of *On Gold Mountain* (D-1). But it is hardly an exaggeration that each of See's publications has attracted national attention. Furthermore, *On Gold Mountain* is likely to be the basis of a planned six-hour television miniseries

(Ulin), and *Flower Net*, also on the *Los Angeles Times* Best Books List for 1997, is nominated for the Edgar Award for best first novel and rated the best thriller of the year by Amazon.com. Paramount Pictures has bought its film rights, and its foreign rights have been sold to fourteen countries. Critics and readers alike are impressed by See's exhaustive research and cross-cultural insights while intrigued by her Caucasian appearance and Chinese identity.

Well received as *On Gold Mountain* has been, critical studies and discussions of this biography are mainly in the form of book reviews and personal interviews. Most of its media coverage—three personal interviews, six reports, and twenty book reviews—appeared within a few weeks of the book's publication. The verdict is unanimously positive, or, in the words of Alice Joyce, "See composes a brilliant tapestry—a fabric enlivened by the cultural diversity of an extended family that will surely resonate for readers of all backgrounds" ("Lisa" 1927).

The engaging memoir is energetically researched, as all the book reviewers have acknowledged. But the appeal and authenticity of this chronicle lie in See's insights into both the American and Chinese heritage of her family. The biography deals with a world "neither wholly white nor wholly Chinese," according to Denise Chong, writing for the *Washington Post* (14), but with "unique crosscurrents of cultural and ethnic diversity," as Zilpha K. Snyder of the *Los Angeles Times* puts it (4). Elizabeth Tallent of the *New York Times* notes that the See family's "intricate genealogy, bravura entrepreneurship, bitter adulteries and perdurable rivalries might have intimidated a lesser chronicler into euphemism," but Fong See's red-haired great-granddaughter "proves to be a clever, conscientiously fair-minded biographer." Her depiction of the very early interracial, illegal marriage between her great-grandparents and their financial success delivers both an indictment against the five decades of discriminatory U.S. immigration laws against Chinese and a testimony to the economic possibilities for all in "Gold Mountain." As such, *On Gold Mountain* "fills a void in Chinese American history" (Fong).

The biography's accomplishments aside, few critics have failed to notice the time-honored inconsistency between red hair and Chinese identity. David Ulin, book editor of the *Los Angeles Reader*, says it best: "See's physical appearance is, on some level, a striking metaphor for the way America, at its best, integrates diverse cultures and personalities into a framework larger than themselves" (*Newsday*). Perhaps, in a not too distant future, the world as a whole will accept the racial reality that a person's appearance or even last name may and may not bear much relevance to his or her ethnic identity, as this red-haired, fair-skinned Chinese has shown through her family saga.

Stereotyped ethnic clichés are not only challenged in See's novel, *Flower Net*, but also rendered as a groundless, illogical framework of reference for detectives working in the global arena. Like See's biography, *Flower Net* has also gotten instantaneous press coverage nationwide. Two reviews and one personal interview came out before the book's publication, and thirteen of the total of eighteen reviews appeared within two months after its publication. Different from *On Gold Mountain*, this murder mystery has not received the stamp of "unanimous approval" from critics despite its greater commercial success. While book reviewers are divided in their assessment of the dialogue quality between the two main characters, they tend to applaud the book's evocative portrayal of contemporary China and underscored importance of cross-cultural understanding in the world today.

Nancy Pearl, writing for *Library Journal*, is among the reviewers most critical of the book. The otherwise insightful international thriller is, as she sees it, "marked by cardboard characters and wooden dialogue." Lydia Lum of the *Houston Chronicle* shares the observation that parts of the dialogue "come off as dissertationlike monologues dragging on . . . for more than a page" but gives the endorsement that See's characters "exemplify modern-day real life." The majority of the reviews, however, are in agreement with Maureen Corrigan of the *Washington Post* that "Lisa See begins to do for contemporary Beijing what . . . Sir Arthur Conan Doyle did for the turn-of-the-century London or Dashiell Hammett did for 1920s San Francisco." The thriller becomes more than an international police drama when the investigation begins to show the toll that the years' ideological squabbles take on everyone in China. "[B]eneath the public facade of bustling commerce and polite manners," Corrigan continues, "See's Beijing is a city where violence and long-festering hatreds cloud the air." *Flower Net*, with all of its imperfections, like contrived dialogues and even cumbersome plot, thus remains to many "a penetrating examination of modern Chinese culture, the forces that have shaped it" (Wade, Books-7).

However, the novel is not only about China's painful struggle with the side effects of the market economy. Far from one-sided, it also depicts family betrayal and government corruption in America, "suggesting that although their sources may be differently motivated, the results can turn out to be disturbingly symmetrical" (Friedman). In fact, it is in the new and unfamiliar setting, thanks to the globalization of crime, "where techno-gadgetry becomes useless and understanding of different cultural mores and motive is key" ("murder mysteries" 14). As such, *Flower Net* stands to enlighten and entertain.

BIBLIOGRAPHY

Works by Lisa Lenine See

Novels

(As Monica Highland). *Lotus Land*. New York: Coward-McCann, 1983.
(As Monica Highland). *One Hundred Ten Shanghai Road*. New York: McGraw-Hill, 1986.
(As Monica Highland). *Greetings from Southern California*. Portland, OR: Graphic Arts Center, 1988.

On Gold Mountain: The One-Hundred Year Odyssey of My Chinese-American Family.
New York: St. Martin's Press, 1995; New York: Vintage, 1996.
Flower Net. New York: HarperCollins, 1997.
The Interior. New York: HarperCollins, 1999.

Essays

"The Book Business' Billion-Dollar Baby." *Los Angeles Times Book Review* (December 16, 1990): 1.
"Signs, Co-signs and Tangents." *Los Angeles Times Book Review* (June 2, 1991): 1.
"Archaeologist, Classicist, Teller of Tales." *Los Angeles Times Book Review* (December 1, 1991): 24.
"Barbara Kingsolver." In *Writing for Your Life: With an Introduction by John F. Baker.* Ed. Sybil S. Steinberg. New York: Pushcart Press, 1992. 309–14.
"Tillie Olsen." In *Writing for Your Life: With an Introduction by John F. Baker.* Ed. Sybil S. Steinberg. New York: Pushcart Press, 1992. 381–86.
"Harriet Doerr." In *Writing for Your Life #2; With an Introduction by John F. Baker.* Ed. Sybil S. Steinberg. New York: Pushcart Press, 1995. 67–72.
"Len Deighton." In *Writing for Your Life #2; With an Introduction by John F. Baker.* Ed. Sybil S. Steinberg. New York: Pushcart Press, 1995. 55–60.
"Paul Monette." In *Writing for Your Life #2; With an Introduction by John F. Baker.* Ed. Sybil S. Steinberg. New York: Pushcart Press, 1995. 145–50.
"Anna May Speaks." In *Making More Waves: New Writing by Asian American Women: With a Foreword by Jessica Hagendorn.* Ed. Elaine H. Kim, Lilia V. Villanueva, and Asian Women United of California. Boston: Beacon Press, 1997. 195–200.
"The Funeral Banquet." In *Half and Half: Writers on Growing Up Biracial and Bicultural.* Ed. Claudine Chiawei O'Hearn. New York: Pantheon Books, 1998. 125–38.

Book Reviews

"An Epic of the Taiping Rebellion." *The Second Son of Heaven,* by C. Y. Lee. *Los Angeles Times Book Review* (July 15, 1990): 15.
"New World Symphony." Rev. of *Growing Up Asian American: An Anthology,* ed. Maria Hong. *Washington Post Book World* 24.5 (1994): 4.
"Anchee's Hour." Rev. of *Katherine,* by Anchee Min. *Harper's Bazaar* 3402 (1995): 86.
"A Journey through China and Soul." Rev. of *Moon Cakes,* by Andrea Louie. *San Francisco Chronicle,* November 26, 1995, 3.
"Survival of the Prudent." Rev. of *The Middle Heart,* by Bette Bao Lord. *New York Times Book Review* (February 11, 1996): 34.
"The Good Woman of Chinkiang." Rev. of *Pearl S. Buck: A Cultural Biography,* by Peter Conn. *Los Angeles Times Book Review* (November 17, 1996): 4+.
"The Struggle of Two Generations in 19th Century Hawaii." Rev. of *A Map of Paradise,* by Linda Ching Sledge. *San Francisco Chronicle,* August 17, 1997, 3.
"A Litany of Abuses." Rev. of *Falling Leaves: The True Story of an Unwanted Chinese Daughter,* by Adeline Yen Mah. *New York Times Book Review* (July 12, 1998): 15.
"Sex, Race and Peking Man." Rev. of *Lost in Translation,* by Nicole Mones. *New York Times Book Review* (September 20, 1998): 41.

"Melting Pot." Rev. of *The Pagoda*, by Patricia Powell. *Los Angeles Times Book Review* (September 27, 1998): 8.

Studies of Lisa Lenine See

Carlin, Margaret. "Lisa See Traces Her Roots from China to 'Gold Mountain.' " Rev. of *On Gold Mountain*. *Denver Rocky Mountain News*, October 1, 1995, 75A.

Chong, Denise. "An Asian-American Odyssey." Rev. of *On Gold Mountain*. *Washington Post Book World* (August 20, 1995): 1+.

Corrigan, Maureen. "Beijing Body Count." Rev. of *Flower Net*. *Washington Post Book World* (September 21, 1997): 5.

Donahue, Deirdre. " 'Net' Captures a Changing China: Lisa See Weaves Telling Details into Murder Mystery." Rev. of *Flower Net*. *USA Today*, October 30, 1997, final ed., 5D.

Fong, Colleen. Rev. of *On Gold Mountain*. *Journal of American Ethnic History* 17.2 (Winter 1998): 73.

Friedman, Paula. "East Meets West." Rev. of *Flower Net*. *Los Angeles Times Book Review* (September 28, 1997): 10.

Gelernter, Carey Quan. "Lisa See's 'Gold Mountain': A Pioneering Family's Dream." Rev. of *On Gold Mountain*. *Seattle Times*, July 28, 1995, final ed., G2.

Giffin, Glenn. "Seeing China's Changes: Author's Observations Turn up in Her First Try at Fiction Thriller." Rev. of *Flower Net*. *Denver Post*, August 24, 1997, 2nd ed., I–01.

Hammond, Margo. "What Are You? Dealing with Issues of Racial and Cultural Identity." *St. Petersburg Times*, September 6, 1998, 5D.

Hawkins, Barbara. "Lisa See." Rev. of *On Gold Mountain*. *School Library Journal* 42.1 (1996): 142.

Heller, Amanda. "Short Takes." Rev. of *Flower Net*. *Boston Globe*, November 2, 1997, city ed., N2.

Holt, Patricia. "The Trail the Interrogators Left." Interview with Lisa See. *San Francisco Chronicle*, August 13, 1995, 2.

Janah, Monua. "A Chinese Clan Spins Gold and Stories in California." Rev. of *On Gold Mountain*. *San Francisco Chronicle*, August 13, 1995, 3.

Joyce, Alice. "Lisa See." Rev. of *On Gold Mountain*. *Booklist* (August 1995): 1927.

———. "Upfront: Advance Reviews." Rev. of *Flower Net*. *Booklist* (August 1997): 1849.

Kavanagh, Patrick. "East West Meet in Death." Rev. of *Flower Net*. *Ottawa Citizen*, March 1, 1998, final ed., E6.

Krist, Gary. "Pacific Overtures." Rev. of *Flower Net*. *New York Times Book Review* (October 26, 1997): 14.

Lambert, Pam. Rev. of *On Gold Mountain*. *People* (November 20, 1995): 32.

Lum, Lydia. "*Flower Net* Entertains, Doesn't Thrill." Rev. of *Flower Net*. *Houston Chronicle*, November 23, 1997, star ed., 31.

Miller, Matt. "Amerasian Lit Finally Is Finding Its Voice." Rev. of *On Gold Mountain*. *San Diego Union-Tribune*, September 25, 1995, D-1+.

"Murder Mysteries: Discount the Body Count." Rev. of *Flower Net*. *Economist* 345.8047 (1997): 14–15.

Nimura, Janice P. "The Tangled Roots of a Family Tree." Rev. of *On Gold Mountain*. *Daily Yomiuri*, December 22, 1996, 6.

Noble, Dennis L. Rev. of *On Gold Mountain*. *Library Journal* (August 1995): 84.

North, John. "The Law and Its Profits." Rev. of *Flower Net*. *Toronto Star*, October 25, 1997, final ed., J19.

"Notable Books of the Year 1995." Rev. of *On Gold Mountain*. *New York Times Book Review* (December 3, 1995): 70.

"Notable Books of the Year 1997." Rev. of *Flower Net*. *New York Times Book Review* (December 7, 1997): 62.

"Notes on Current Books." Rev. of *On Gold Mountain*. *Virginia Quarterly Review* 72.1 (Winter 1996): 20.

Pearl, Nancy. Rev. of *Flower Net*. *Library Journal* (August 1997): 135.

Rawlings, Irene. "Author Casts Intriguing 'Net.' " Rev. of *Flower Net*. *Denver Rocky Mountain News*, September 28, 1997, 2E.

Reed, J. D. Rev. of *Flower Net*. *People* (November 3, 1997): 38+.

Schwartz, Eleanor. "China's Promised Land." Rev. of *On Gold Mountain*. *Far Eastern Economic Review* 159.6 (1996): 40–41.

Snyder, Zilpha Keatley. "Dynasty: Saga of Colorful Lives, Lingerie and 'LoSang.' " Rev. of *On Gold Mountain*. *Los Angeles Times Book Review* (July 23, 1995): 4+.

Solomon, Charles. *On Gold Mountain: The One-Hundred-Year Odyssey of My Chinese-American Family*. *Los Angeles Times Book Review* (November 17, 1996): 14.

Spencer, Pam. Rev. of *Flower Net*. *School Library Journal* 44.4 (1998): 159.

Steinberg, Sybil S. "Forecasts: Fiction." Rev. of *Flower Net*. *Publishers Weekly* (July 21, 1997): 181.

Stuttaford, Genevieve. "Forecasts: Nonfiction." Rev. of *On Gold Mountain*. *Publishers Weekly* (June 5, 1995): 43.

Tachibana, Judy. "New Chapters in the American Experience." Rev. of *On Gold Mountain*. *Sacramento Bee*, April 14, 1996, metro ed., EN16+.

Tallent, Elizabeth. "Chinese Roots." Rev. of *On Gold Mountain*. *New York Times Book Review* (August 27, 1995): 20.

Taylor, Annie. "Private Lives: The Difference a Day Made: Lisa See." (*London*) *Guardian*, December 1, 1997, 17.

Ulin, David L. "An American Family." Interview with Lisa See. *Newsday* (October 1, 1995): 36.

Wade, Robert. "The Thrill Isn't Gone, but Now It's in the Insight." Rev. of *Flower Net*. *San Diego Union-Tribune*, October 19, 1997, Books-7.

Wisneski, Ken. "Adventure: Thrillers Span Oceans in Tales of War-Smuggling." Rev. of *Flower Net*. (*Minneapolis*) *Star Tribune*, November 23, 1997, metro ed., 17F.

Shyam Selvadurai
(1965–)

Peter G. Christensen

BIOGRAPHY

Shyam Selvadurai was born in Colombo, Sri Lanka, in 1965, in a family with three other siblings of mixed Tamil and Sinhalese background. Soon after the 1983 riots, at the age of nineteen, he moved to Canada, and he received an undergraduate degree from York University in Toronto, where he specialized in theater and television studies. He published his first novel, *Funny Boy* in 1994, and he is currently at work in Toronto on a second novel, *Cinnamon Gardens*, set in Sri Lanka in the 1920s. *Funny Boy* won in the United States the Lambda Literary Foundation's Award for Best Gay Male Novel and the 1994 Smithbooks/Books in Canada First Novel Award. It would be wrong to read the novel as autobiographical beyond the fact that Arjie (the hero) and the author are both gay and both left Sri Lanka. However, the hero of the novel was born in 1969, not 1965, and he comes to grips with his homosexuality in Sri Lanka, not in Canada, as the author did. Whereas Arjie's parents are both Tamils, Selvadurai's father is Tamil, and his mother is Sinhalese.

In a pamphlet issued by the publisher in a review copy of *Funny Boy*, Selvadurai indicated that his father's parents were furious to find out that their son was in love with a Sinhalese woman. Having passed up more prestigious jobs, such as doctor, lawyer, and engineer, he became a tennis coach. Such a choice was not a total surprise, as he had played Davis Cup for Sri Lanka. The novelist's father also conducted wildlife safaris in the jungles of Sri Lanka. Selvadurai's mother studied at medical college. Selvadurai feels that being the son of a mixed marriage was beneficial in creating a knowledge and acceptance of difference. In his parents' families, arranged marriages within ethnic groups were the norm. Although Selvadurai was sad to leave his homeland, he feels that as an immigrant he has gained a perspective on the world helpful to him as a creative artist. Perhaps he would not have written his novel if he had stayed closer to home.

MAJOR WORK AND THEMES

So far Shyam Selvadurai has published only one major work, *Funny Boy*, a novel in the form of six semi-independent novellas, covering the period from 1977 to 1983. The novel is dedicated to his parents, Christine and David Selvadurai, for "believing that pigs can fly," and it comes with a glossary of Sri Lankan words. The novel is perhaps even better enjoyed by those who have been to Colombo, for it includes many local place-names. The politics are glimpsed fleetingly, and most readers will need some background information to the July 1983 riots.

The six chapters take place in 1977, 1978, 1979, 1982, early 1983, and summer 1983, respectively, but this chronology is not clear to those with no background in the politics of the time. In the first three stories, Arjie is seven to ten in age; and in the last three stories, thirteen to fourteen. The first half of the book concerns his awakening to his sense of difference and lack of interest in traditionally boyish pursuits. The last half deals with his first name-sex sexual activity. Since Selvadurai would have been twelve in a politically aware household in 1977, the author has to imagine politics from the point of view of a much younger, nonpolitically aware protagonist. Presumably, the novel begins in 1977 because it is a crucial election year, although it is never said directly.

The young narrator comes from an upper-middle-class Tamil family that does not speak Tamil. Arjie (Arjuna), along with his elder brother Varuna ("Diggy") and his sister Sonali, are the three children of Amma (mother) Nalini and Appa (father) Robert Chelvaratnam. The parents have no sympathy for the rebellious Tamil Tigers, and they are oblivious to the fact that the ruling Sinhalese will not let them live in peace, even though they have no radical sensibilities. The family's assimilationism turns out to be a total failure. In the July 1983 riots their house is burned and looted, and Arjie's beloved paternal grandparents, who appear prominently in the first story, are murdered in the last pages of the sixth and last story.

In the first story, "Pigs Can't Fly," Arjie, at the age of seven, is the star of the game "bride-bride" played with the girl cousins at his paternal grandparents' house on once-a-month Sunday visits. He much prefers it to cricket, the choice of his older brother. Arjie, who is nothing like Arjuna, the great warrior of the *Mahabharata*, his namesake, enjoys wearing the wedding sari and is the star of the performance until Tanuja, a bossy female cousin, daughter of Kanthi Aunty and Cyril Uncle, arrives and commandeers the show. He calls Tanuja "Her Fatness," and she calls him a "pansy" and "faggot." For most children at this age, the words refer to male effeminate behavior rather than to sexual orientation, and such is the case here.

Arjie's father is the eldest of six children, three boys and three girls. In "Radha Aunty," the second story, the dark-skinned youngest sibling, Radha Aunty, returns to Sri Lanka and is courted by a Sinhalese, Anil Jayasinghe, but her parents are violently opposed to him because of his ethnic background. Now Arjie discovers that the father of Ammachi, his paternal grandmother, had been killed by Sinhalese in the 1958 riots, just over a decade before he was born. After Radha's train with its Tamil passengers is attacked by Sinhalese, Radha is coerced into wedding the Tamil suitor, Rajan Nagendra, in an arranged marriage. The backdrop for this story of thwarted love is a rehearsal for Rodgers and Hammerstein's *The King and I*, and when Radha Aunty substitutes for the actress playing Tuptim, the beleaguered young female lover, she is thrown to the floor all too vigorously by Anil, who is playing one of the guards of the Siamese king. Here we see the further decline of Tamil/Sinhalese relations. Although Arjie had been fantasizing the story of Sakuntala, casting his Aunt as the heroine and Rajan as her beloved Mani-lal, even he can understand that something has gone wrong with his Aunt's love life. His reading of the story of Sakuntala's wedding gives him emotional solace after his eviction from the bride-bride game.

"See No Evil, Hear No Evil" takes place during the period of the Jaffna riots after passage of the sinisterly named Prevention of Terrorism Act. Arjie comes down with hepatitis, and he is recuperating while his father is away. Daryl Uncle, a Sri Lankan Dutch-descended, or "Burgher," journalist, now with an Australian newspaper, returns to the island to report on the political troubles. He had once been a suitor of Arjie's mother, and they begin an adulterous affair, which shocks Arjie, who never tells his father of it. The liaison ends when Daryl disappears doing research, and he is later found to be murdered. Arjie's mother comes to realize that the government has covered up the murder (if not worse), and when she goes to the countryside to get information, she witnesses torture of a boy by the police. Her telephone is subsequently tapped, and her own efforts to find a witness lead to nothing. Throughout this period, Arjie has moved from reading about Sakuntala to casting himself in roles in fantasies based on Alcott's *Little Women*. First he is Beth, on account of his hepatitis, and later he is Jo because of his growing maturity.

"Small Choices" takes place during the year of the government-sponsored referendum that replaces the regularly scheduled elections. Arjie's family witnesses the defacing of private property by people sent out to put up pro-referendum posters. Arjie develops a slight crush on a new employee, twenty-five-year-old Jegan Parameswaram, the son of a deceased friend of his father's. Father has recently left banking and become a hotelier. When it turns out that Jegan has previously belonged to the Tamil Tigers, he is arrested. Fortunately, Arjie's father can send him away on assignment to the Middle East, and the worst is avoided. However, after Jegan leaves, his parents find that at the polling place for the referendum, a member of Parliament arrives with thugs who hold the voting officials at gunpoint and who then proceed to stuff the

ballot box with false ballots. In this story, Arjie starts to understand that his
father is quite willing to tolerate older men picking up young men for sex on
the beach outside the hotel he owns because the sex trade brings money into
the country and the hotel (171). Thus, as the definition of "faggot" starts to turn
from effeminacy to sexual activity, we see obliquely the neocolonialist sex trade
whereby Western visitors and Westernized Sri Lankans pay for young male
bodies.

Early in 1983 Father suspects that his fourteen-year-old younger son may turn
out to be "funny" (gay) and so transfers him in "The Best School of All" from
the relatively relaxed St. Gabriel's, where there are still some Catholic priests,
to the hard-line, British-style "public school," Queen Victoria Academy, where
sparing the rod means spoiling the child. Here Arjie falls in love with the effeminate Shehan Soyza, who is rumored to be having sex with the head prefect
(232) while he supposedly goes to the lavatory (218). Soyza does nothing to
deny these rumors, and one day at school the boys kiss lightly (249). When
Arjie goes over to Soyza's house, his friend spreads himself out languidly on
the bed, but Arjie does nothing, although he feels that he has ignored a sexual
overture. Later during a game of hide-and-seek in Arjie's garage, they start deep
kissing, which is pleasurable to Arjie, but then he begins to feel dirty and violated as Soyza brutally thrusts him against the wall in order to ejaculate against
his body (260). Soon he starts to have sexual desires for Soyza and decides that
he has "scorned" his friend's love. As a counterpoint to this situation, the reader
notes that the founding myth of Sri Lanka is itself heterosexual, since Vijay,
the father of the Sinhalese nation, arrived on the island to conquer Kuveni,
Yaksha princess (279).

Meanwhile, in this story the Victoria Academy is going through a crisis, as
there is a power struggle between two school leaders over whether or not the
school will take on an increasingly Sinhalese tone. It is already a bad place for
the Tamils to be stuck in. Arjie deliberately botches a major recital of some
ridiculously sentimental nineteenth-century school poetry because one of the
masters, Black Tie, has been particularly vicious to Soyza. However, Black Tie
is the more moderate of the two masters, and Arjie believes himself to be in a
no-win situation. He has, however, perhaps acted stupidly, for he may be helping
the more ethnically intolerant master consolidate his power.

The sixth story, "Riot Journal: An Epilogue," consists of a series of entries
made between July 25 and August 27, 1983. In the summer riots the family
home is burned and looted, and his paternal grandparents are burned to death
in their car. Friendly neighbors allow Arjie's family and his mother's sister
Neliya Aunty to escape by ladder over the wall, and they decide they will have
to leave the country and move to Canada, where they have a relative. Meanwhile, Arjie and Soyza have been having sometimes passionate, sometimes
dreary sex at Soyza's house (310), and on the last day of the novel, Arjie returns
home, afraid the smell of his lovemaking will be noticeable to his family. In a
classic "good-bye to all that" ending, he takes his bicycle and goes to the top

of the road during a monsoon torrent to look at his house for the final time. The closing line reads, "For a moment I saw it, then the rain fell faster and thicker, obscuring it from my sight" (312). Unfortunately, the last chapter is something of a failure, for neither the change in the relationship with Soyza nor the overall significance of the riots is given with enough detail.

Sri Lanka was hit by violence in 1958, 1977, 1981, and 1983. Before the novel opens, Arjie's father's mother's father was killed in the 1958 anti-Tamil riots just for being a Tamil (68). The violence arose from the effects of the 1956 election in which S. W. R. D. Bandaranaike, an Anglican convert to Buddhism, won the election for the Sri Lanka Freedom Party, founded five years before, thus defeating the United National Party, which had held power since independence in 1948. In 1956 the 2,500-year anniversary of the *nirvana* of Buddha, who was said to have visited Sri Lanka three times, led to the passage of an act calling for the immediate use of Sinhala rather than English as the official national language. When Bandaranaike began to moderate his anti-Tamil stance, many Buddhists felt betrayed and prompted the anti-Tamil riots. In 1959 a young monk, Buddharakkita Thero, assassinated his former ally, the prime minister.

About two years after Arjie's birth, in 1971 there was an abortive insurrection of Sinhalese youths (mentioned ambiguously, 148), leading to state-of-emergency conditions for several years. Ceylon became the republic of Sri Lanka under a new constitution in 1972, the year that the eighteen-year-old Velupillai Prabhakaram formed the rebellious Tamil New Tigers. The island had a state-regulated economy from 1956 to 1977, the end of which is also broached in the third story of the novel (102). In 1977 the Tamils voted for secession. J. R. Jayewardene's United National Party defeated Mrs. Bandaranaike's Sri Lanka Freedom Party (which had held power since 1970), and Mrs. Bandaranaike is described in the novel as looking haggard (104), now deprived of her civil rights. The government structure was changed to a French Gaullist presidential one in the following year, with both Sinhalese and Tamil recognized as "official languages," but one had to learn Sinhala for a government job and not vice versa. The 1979 Prevention of Terrorism Act added insult to injury. In June 1979 the terrible legislation was used against Tamil rebels in the north, and Daryl Uncle called it a law for the use of state terrorism (110).

In 1982 the 1,977 members of Parliament took the unprecedented step of passing a Fourth Amendment to the new Constitution to have a December referendum, which, if they won, would keep them in office until 1989. The Referendum (207) took place in December, and the vote was 55 percent in favor and 45 percent against, a smaller victory than suggested by the novel. In July 1983 there were anti-Tamil riots, and the Jayewardane government used military force to contain the violence. This is the situation when the novel closes—bleakly. The novel is entirely on the side of the nonviolent Tamils as represented by the protagonist's family. The appealing Sinhalese characters are the powerless ones, such as Anil. Considering Sinhalese persecution of Tamils, the attitude of the novel is reasonable. There is no direct correlation between sex and politics in the novel, but it is probably true that the deteriorating political situation for the Tamils leads Arjie to sympathy for a persecuted class member and sex with him at an earlier age than may have been the case in more settled times.

CRITICAL RECEPTION

Funny Boy has received at least twenty short book reviews, according to *Book Review Index*. It was translated in 1996 into both German and Swedish under its original title. In his study of three Sri Lankan novels, Prakrti praises *Funny Boy* for its political astuteness at the expense of Michael Ondaatje's* *Running in the Family* and Romesh Gunasekera's *The Reef*. In this article's half-dozen paragraphs devoted to Selvadurai, *Funny Boy*, the author states . . . "perhaps for the first time in the history of Sri Lankan writing, very subtly critiques the value charged hierarchical masculine-feminine gender equation" (3). *Funny Boy* demonstrates the rigid typecasting set up for boys attending schools cut in the colonial style, modeled along the lines of English "public" schools. The article also praises the novel for its presentation of the Tamil–Sinhalese cultural tension.

Short notices of the book, both signed and unsigned, were generally very favorable. For example, the reviewer for *Kirkus Reviews* found that *Funny Boy* "displays a precociously assured command of structure, pace, and tone" and that Arjie is "only the most appealing of a dozen or more generously observed and vividly rendered characters" in this work of a "brilliant new writer" (21). The anonymous reviewer for *Publishers Weekly* was equally as flattering, with praise for the "deep wistful feeling" with which Selvadurai ties his story to "large themes of family and country" (80). Janet St. John in *Booklist* recommended *Funny Boy* as a "foreign, funny, and unusual" entry in the "crowded coming-of-age-category" of young adult books. Cecil Foster, writing in *Canadian Forum*, said that *Funny Boy* "chronicles the stories and emotions of a child, the same naive outlook that by the end of the novel is taking such a battering by the distrust and ethnic superiority that came to dominate Sri Lankan life and politics and that make peace still so tenuous" (41). Foster finds a "beauty" in the "crispness and sparse wording, the presentation of an ungilded world where anything is possible, where the future is full of promise" (41).

A much more negative evaluation comes from Timothy Dow Adams in *Canadian Literature*, who finds the book weak as a whole and especially bad in the last three stories. Adams writes that only "Pigs Can Fly" is capable of standing on its own, whereas each story should be able to do so, as is the case in such story-novels as Alice Munro's *Lives of Girls and Women*. Although the first three stories have charm, because they are told with a child's innocence, the last three stories, given to us by an older Arjie, appear to Adams as a set of lost opportunities. In "Small Choices" and "The Best School of All" Arjie "seems particularly slow in understanding either his growing homosexuality or the increasing political unrest about him" (112). In "Riot Journal: An Epilogue," instead of "using the diary format for dramatic introspection, the author has rendered the most dramatic political portion of the novel as a bland epilogue," while the "sexual parallel" to the political tension "almost completely disappears" (112–13). Adams hopes that the promise of the early stories will be fulfilled in the author's second novel.

An examination of the reviews shows that although the novel was not apparently marketed as a coming-of-age novel, it is likely to have success in this field. Since Arjie is only fourteen years old when the novel ends, there are many things he cannot be expected to say about the political situation in Sri Lanka.

BIBLIOGRAPHY

Works by Shyam Selvadurai

Novel

Funny Boy. Toronto: McClelland and Stewart, 1994; San Diego: Harcourt, Brace, 1994; New York: Morrow, 1996.

Short Story

"Pigs Can't Fly." In *Another Part of the Forest: An Anthology of Gay Short Fiction.* Ed. Alberto Manguel and Craig Stephenson. New York: Crown Trade, 1994. 428–56.

Studies of Shyam Selvadurai

Adams, Timothy Dow. "Coming of Age." *Canadian Literature.* No. 149 (Summer 1996): 112–13.
"Conversation with Shyam Selvadurai." 5 para. [publisher's pamphlet excerpt] http://way.net/sawa/convers.html.
Foster, Cecil. "A Love beyond Bigotry." *Canadian Forum* 73, No. 836 (January–February 1995): 40–41.
Keehnen, Owen. "Sri Lankan Author Shyam Selvadurai's *Funny Boy.*" (May 1996). 24 para. Online. *Outlines: The Voice of the Gay and Lesbian Community.* Internet. November 5, 1997. http://www.suba.com/~outlines/may96/srilanka.html.
Prakrti. "'The Breech': Three Sri Lankan-Born Writers at the Crossroads." Summer 1997. 19 para. Online. *Outlook: The Weekly News Magazine.* Internet. November 5, 1997. http://www.is.lk/is/spot/sp0151/clip5.html.
Rev. of *Funny Boy. Kirkus Reviews* 64 (January 1, 1996): 21.
Rev. of *Funny Boy. Publishers Weekly* 242, No. 45 (November 6, 1995): 80.
St. John, Janet. Rev. of *Funny Boy. Booklist* 92.9–10 (January 1, 15, 1996): 792.
Thomas, Harry. "Shyam Selvadurai." 9 para. Online. http://www.emory.edu/ENGLISH/Bahri/Selva.html.

Vikram Seth

(1952–)

Anthony R. Guneratne

BIOGRAPHY

Born on June 20, 1952, two generations after Marshall McLuhan and very much
a child of the age of mass communication and international popular culture,
Vikram Seth was on the move from an early age. When he was four, his parents
migrated from Calcutta to India's capital, New Delhi. He left for Britain barely
a dozen years later and spent the next half of his life abroad but remained close
to his family. The strong-willed female characters who populate his fictions are
modeled not only on those of Jane Austen but also on his mother, a now-retired
judge who, while studying at night and raising her children, came first in the
bar exam in England. He has also incorporated other family occupations such
as peace activism and shoe manufacture into his novels (Wachtel 86–87).

Seth's studies at Corpus Christi College, Oxford, were less consequential than
his graduate work in economic demography at Stanford. It was here, shortly
after his arrival in 1975, that in seeking to supplement his education with creative writing he encountered the poets Donald Davie and Timothy Steele. The
latter continued to serve as a firm critic and mentor even after Seth had attained
some measure of literary fame, and Seth dedicates his most famous work, *The
Golden Gate*, to him.

Appropriately, Seth's first literary effort to win acclaim was a travel account.
His dissertation, on village economies in China, took him for two years to
Nanjing University, and at the conclusion of his studies there in 1981 Seth
undertook a hitchhiking journey through northwest China, Tibet, and Nepal to
his parents' home in Delhi. The book that resulted, *From Heaven Lake*, garnered
Seth the first of many awards, the Thomas Cook Travel Book Award (a Guggenheim Fellowship followed two years later). The party to celebrate the award

finds its way amusingly into the fifth chapter of *The Golden Gate*, where a publisher turns yellow on hearing that Seth's next work is to be a novel in verse.

The Golden Gate appeared in 1986 to storms of applause and howls of derision. Much of the adverse criticism of *The Golden Gate* portrays Seth as a cultural tourist in America, incapable of producing what Gore Vidal announced on the dust jacket as "the Great California novel." Seth later observed in the Introduction to the collected edition of *The Poems* (1995) that Indian critics either praised him for successfully disguising himself as a Californian (ignoring the decade he had lived there) or damned the work for lacking both Indian characters and an "Indian Sensibility" (xiv). Observant, tolerant, and fluent in a number of languages including Chinese, Seth has felt a need neither to claim a genetic affinity to Asianness (as American writers such as Siu Sin Par and Ai have done insistently) or to reject any national or ethnic affiliation in favor of a "world without boundaries" (as the Sri Lankan-born poet and novelist Michael Ondaatje)* has imaginatively attempted). Seth mentions with characteristic humor that the international settings of the poems of *All You Who Sleep Tonight* (ranging from Imperial China to Nazi Germany) restored him to the status of "Commonwealth" writer and that by the time his "prose novel," *A Suitable Boy*, appeared, he was once more embraced as a true Indian. "*Time* magazine informed me," he writes, "that I was a member of a movement, represented by the Empire-Writes-Back generation" (*The Poems* xv).

Even before *All You Who Sleep Tonight* appeared in print, Seth was spending increasing amounts of time in India researching *A Suitable Boy*. The cool reception accorded the conscious transparency of the poems in *All You Who Sleep Tonight* provoked the newly Indian Seth to write in an even more accessible fashion (both *Beastly Tales from Here and There*, modeled on the ancient Sanskrit genre of the beast fable, and *Arion and the Dolphin*, an illustrated opera libretto, have been sold as children's books). But Seth had not forgotten his training in economics, and on the strength of the popular reaction to *The Golden Gate*, he negotiated a million-dollar contract for the rights to *A Suitable Boy* (Shapiro). Until the recent success of Arundhati Roy's *The God of Small Things*, no work by a contemporary author resident in India had attracted as much international critical attention. Still a frequent traveler through disparate lands and literary genres, Seth continues to be based in Delhi.

MAJOR WORKS AND THEMES

While the work that principally concerns us here is the quintessentially San Franciscan *The Golden Gate*, many of its stylistic characteristics and central themes are shared with the rest of Seth's wide-ranging oeuvre. Seth is arguably more formally inventive and technically adventurous than any other Asian American writer. The most striking feature of *The Golden Gate* is its revival of the tetrametric sonnet form of Alexander Pushkin's verse novel *Evgeny Onegin*, which Seth succeeds in transforming into the colloquial English of the "bakery of Reagan." Yet this "tour de force of the transcendence of the mere tour de force" (Hollander 34) is only one of a number of attempts to test the limits of literary genres. In *From Heaven Lake* the traveler studies himself as well as his surroundings, occasionally breaking out into ecstatic verse; *Beastly Tales from Here and There* reworks prose fables into something akin to La Fontaine; *A Suitable Boy* (which burlesques poetic pretensions) reads like the offspring of an unlikely mating of Jane Austen and Leo Tolstoy, its length and philosophical concerns being the sum of *Pride and Prejudice* and *War and Peace*.

Far from being an obsessive exercise of virtuoso technique or a throwback to Romanticism, *The Golden Gate* translates the ironic social commentary Pushkin disguised as exoticism into an immediately familiar vocabulary—ranging from the homiletic speech to the advertising jingle—that falls comfortably into the insistent rhythms of the tetrameter. Moreover, Seth succeeds in producing a carnivalesque combination of the aracana of pop and high culture: allusions to Renaissance poets and television commercials jostle side by side, while Janet Hayakawa's last name and that of Ed's tame iguana belong, respectively, to Hollywood's most famous Asian actor of the silent period and its most famous contemporary muscle man. Poets and the reading public responded as much to Seth's impudent charm as to his unexpected rhymes and cleverly rendered dialogue.

Other factors that no doubt contributed to the work's success were its engaging and up-to-date portrayal of San Franciscan life and its avoidance of the twin banes of Asian American literature, immigrant angst and generational conflict. Seth's five protagonists are shaped not by distant memories but by the proximity of the eponymous, evocative synecdoche for the Bay Area, and they are pleased to please each other, their parents, and even their demanding pets. While some critics (notably, Iannone and Perloff) have suggested that their motivations are undeveloped and trivial, others like Hollander and Vijayasree have pointed out the ironic character of this triviality. Hollander, in fact, observes that the narrator's consistently sardonic tone, which even the authorial surrogate Kim Tarvesh cannot escape, owes even more to the author of *The Rape of the Lock* than to Pushkin (33). Paranjape, defending Seth against those who accuse him of celebrating his characters' lifestyle, attempts to summarize the novel's major themes: "[I]t is, above all, a book about love, pacifism, tolerance, and compassion . . . what emerges is a severe critique and rejection of [Yuppiedom]" (58). But Seth is always more than he appears to be, and he avoids broad condemnation as scrupulously as he does unqualified approval.

Vijayasree argues that Seth proclaims "love" as a panacea for loneliness, anomie, and a lack of direction. However, Seth's overriding concern seems to be more characteristically American, in that in all his works his characters are engaged in the fundamental prerogative of Jeffersonian freedom, the pursuit of happiness. Seth offers moral commentary in those instances in which this pursuit has become an end in itself. Thus, Amor in *The Golden Gate* is an irreverent reworking of the Platonic conviction that agape is so high a state of happiness that to achieve it may warrant a few doses of eros in various blends and concentrations.

Seth's good humor and lightness of touch do, however, conceal an earnestness that is more readily apparent in the works that followed. While in *The Golden Gate* the harsher ironies directed against self-deception and hypocrisy are tempered by the playful form of the poems, the less demanding, formal constraints of his later poetry and prose allow his addiction to paradox to sour into sarcasm, as is readily apparent in the callous self-absorption of the Auschwitz commandant of *All You Who Sleep Tonight*, the murderous hypocrisy of the crocodile in the first of the *Beastly Tales*, or the brutal political slaughters of *A Suitable Boy*.

CRITICAL RECEPTION

The extent of Seth's achievement—to write a truly popular work of verse and to attract the sustained attention of a wide spectrum of critics—should not be underestimated. Among Asian American novelists he probably has the largest readership outside classrooms. Most of the commentary on Seth is of a journalistic order, and opinions are sharply divided between those who sought to augment Hollander's early and influential endorsement and those who opted to attack Hollander, Seth, and rhyming verse by turning the occasion into a referendum on the state of poetry at the tail end of an unpoetic century.

Only a work of the innocent complexity of *The Golden Gate* could provoke a stampede of critical hobbyhorses, and many critics came to opposite conclusions about the same features of his poems. This attitude has persisted, so that while Perry found it "a tribute to the poems of *All You Who Sleep Tonight* that often they can sound a bit like Frost or Hardy" (550), Hupp insists that "this collection fails because Seth's lockstep meter and corny rhymes keep his poetry stylistically on the level of that awful stuff many of us wrote in junior high school."

Undoubtedly, the most amusing of the critical locking of horns over *The Golden Gate* occurred as a result of Mungo's review. While Hollander satisfied himself with inserting a single explanatory sonnet into his effort, Mungo responded to Seth entirely in parodic tetrametric sonnets. Sontag, donning the now dusty mantle of Prophetess of Postmodernism, at once flew to Seth's defense. In response to the response, Perloff launched into a long-winded demonstration of all the possible ways in which Seth is unequal to the source of his inspiration: coarse rhymes, faulty diction, failed comedy, "cuteness," predictability, putting nylons and pylons in the wrong places, "paper doll" characters, "Hallmark Card" mothers, inferiority to John Ashbery, and being a foreigner with a clichéd understanding of the essence of California (39–45). Perloff's torch has been carried by no less than Anita Desai, who with Towers (3) and Walker (18–19) found *A Suitable Boy* a poor substitute for the profound depths of Tolstoy, Austen, and George Eliot, a style of criticism taken to its logical extreme by Jenkyns, who uses "the Great Indian Novel" to prove that not only Seth but also Salman Rushdie and V. S. Naipaul are inferior to "the best of the postcolonial novelists . . . Patrick White."

Seth's polemical insistence on intelligibility has also drawn mixed responses. While lavishing praise on Seth's poetic gifts, Kennedy finds his emotional range limited by his tendency to preach "indirect sermons" (7). The only aspect of Seth's writing that has drawn consistently positive comment is his "vigilance," a characteristic Roland Barthes attributes to Michelangelo Antonioni. Referring to different works, Robinson speaks of Seth's being "alive to all he sees" (713), Tong of his "exact observation," Hollander of his "eye and ear for the cultural fact" (34), and Shapiro of his mastery of "vivid detail."

Strangely, the only book-length study of Seth's work to date has been Agarwalla's volume on Seth's *Search for an Indian Identity*, an attempt to claim Seth for India. In contrast, Perry finds that Seth's previous collection of lyric poems contains "little to remind us that the poet has returned to his native India" (550). Seth is undoubtedly just as Indian, American, British, and Chinese as he was when he was living in California, and he is probably best read without the help of critics.

BIBLIOGRAPHY

Works by Vikram Seth

Novels

The Golden Gate: A Novel in Verse. New York: Random House, 1986.
A Suitable Boy: A Novel. New York: HarperCollins, 1993.

Travel Narrative

From Heaven Lake: Travels through Sinkiang and Tibet. London: Chatto and Windus, 1985.

Poetry

Mappings. Calcutta: Writers Workshop, 1980.
The Humble Administrator's Garden. Manchester: Carcenet Press, 1985.
All You Who Sleep Tonight. New York: Alfred Knopf, 1990.
Beastly Tales from Here and There. New Delhi: Viking, 1992.
The Poems, 1981–1994. New York: Penguin, 1995.

Translation

Three Chinese Poets: Translations of Poems by Wang Wei, Li Bai and Du Fu. New York: HarperCollins, 1992.

Libretti

Arion and the Dolphin. New York: Dutton, 1995.

Studies of Vikram Seth

Agarwalla, Shyam. *Vikram Seth's "A Suitable Boy": Search for an Indian Identity.* New Delhi: Prestige Books, 1995.

Balliet, Whitley. "John and Liz, Phil and Ed." Rev. of *The Golden Gate. The New Yorker* (July 14, 1986): 82–83.

Desai, Anita. "Sitting Pretty." Rev. of *A Suitable Boy. New York Review of Books* (May 27, 1993): 22.

Disch, Thomas. "Sunlight, Coffee and Papers." Rev. of *The Golden Gate. The Washington Post Book News* (March 23, 1986): 7, 11.

Gross, John. Rev. of *The Golden Gate. New York Times,* April 14, 1986, 16.

Hollander, John. "Yuppie Time, in Rhyme." *New Republic* 194 (April 21, 1986): 32–34.

Hupp, Steven. Rev. of *All You Who Sleep Tonight. Library Journal* (May 15, 1990): 80.

Iannone, Carol. "Yuppies in Rhyme." Rev. of *The Golden Gate. Commentary* 82.3 (September 1986): 54–56.

Jenkyns, Richard. "As the Raj Turns." Rev. of *A Suitable Boy. The New Republic* (June 14, 1993): 41.

Kennedy, X. J. Rev. of *The Golden Gate. Los Angeles Times Book Review* (April 6, 1986): 1, 7.

Mungo, Raymond. Rev. of *The Golden Gate. The New York Times Book Review* (May 11, 1986): 11.

Paranjape, Makarand. "*The Golden Gate* and the Quest of Self-Realisation." *ACLAS Bulletin,* 8th Series, No. 1. (1989): 58–73.

Parrinder, Patrick. "Games-Playing." Rev. of *The Golden Gate. London Review of Books* 8.14 (August 7, 1986): 8–9.

Perloff, Marjorie. " 'Homeward Ho!': Silicon Valley Pushkin." Rev. of *The Golden Gate. The American Poetry Review* (November/December 1986): 37–46.

Perry, John Oliver. Rev. of *All You Who Sleep Tonight. World Literature Today* (Summer 1991): 549–50.

Ragen, Brian Abel. "Vikram Seth." In *Dictionary of Literary Biography.* Detroit: Gale Research, 1992. 281–85.

Robinson, Andrew. Rev. *From Heaven Lake. British Book News* (November 1983): 713–14.

Shapiro, Laura. *Easy Reading, Heavy Lifting.* Rev. of *A Suitable Boy. Newsweek* (May 24, 1993): 62.

Sontag, Susan. Letter to the Editor. *The New York Times Book Review* (June 8, 1986): 33.

Tong, Raymond. Rev. of *The Humble Administrator's Garden. British Book News* (September 1985): 559.

Towers, Robert. "Good Enough for Her Mother's Mother's Mother." Rev. of *A Suitable Boy. The New York Times Book Review* (May 9, 1993): 3, 16.

Vijayasree, C. "Vikram Seth (1952–)." In *Writers of the Indian Diaspora: A Bio-Bibliographic Critical Sourcebook.* Ed. Emmanuel S. Nelson. Westport, CT: Greenwood Press, 1993. 401–6.

Wachtel, Eleanor. Interview with Vikram Seth. *The Malahat Review* 107 (Summer 1994): 85–102.

Walker, J. H. "Trunks of the Banyan Tree: History, Politics and Fiction." *Island* 63 (Winter 1995): 18–26.

S. Shankar
(1962–   )

Brunda Moka-Dias

BIOGRAPHY

S. Shankar was born in Salem, Tamil Nadu, India, on July 28, 1962. The son
of a diplomat in the Indian Foreign Service, Shankar grew up in different countries as a child, mainly Germany, Nigeria, and India. Having attended boarding
school in Bombay, Shankar moved to Madras in 1981 and did his B.A. (English)
from Loyola College and M.A. (English) from Madras Christian College. Shankar's work—mainly poetry—started appearing in print from the age of twenty-
two, a career for which he had prepared since the age of fifteen. In 1987 Shankar's writing began to get noticed with the publication of a collection of poems
entitled *I as Man*. In the same year, his one-act play *After the Party* was staged
in Madras. The year 1987 continued to be an important one for the author with
the publication of his two short stories "Madness" and the award-winning "Grey
Cat." The latter story was read on German radio and won the Deutsche Welle
Prize, which included travel, stipend, and tuition at Goethe Institute in Mann-
heim.

Fueled by the desire to see the world and become a writer, Shankar came to
the United States in 1987 to do a Ph.D. in English and completed it in 1993
from the University of Texas (Austin). Shankar's dissertation on travel narratives
included a chapter on *Gulliver's Travels*, which analyzes Swift's book as a
critique of the numerous colonialist travel narratives of Europe. The influence
of Swift's novel on the author is self-evident in his debut novel, *A Map of
Where I Live*; one could even say that *Gulliver's Travels* became the author's
holy book because of its unholy treatment of social and philosophical issues, its
brilliant satire, and its creative exposé of the abuses of power. Shankar lives in
New York City and teaches as an assistant professor at Rutgers University.

MAJOR WORKS AND THEMES

In an essay titled "The Imaginative Labor of Literature," Shankar makes a case for the reconciliation of the aesthetic and the ethical, in contrast to the Kantian division of the two. In doing so he states: "As I see it, the labor of literature should really be regarded as being ennobled by the responsibilities of violating the ethical imperfection of the world and of challenging the world to perfect itself in the future" (6). To the author, this element of responsibility is connected not only with the present and the future but also with the past. In other words, it is deeply embedded in history. This sense of history and responsibility also carries over into the author's life as an "Indian writer living in the US," as is evident in the author's debut novel, which deals with that element of "responsibility" so important in social struggles for justice and equality (6).

A Map of Where I Live is a suspense-filled, original tale of two separate narratives that finally intersect in an intriguing way. The first narrative, set in 1990s Madras is told in the voice of RK, who has returned home to Madras after completing his M.A. in history in New York City. Living with his widowed mother in Krantinagar, exploring the possibilities of a career in law, RK attempts to fit into the middle-class life he does not feel a part of. While waiting to start college, RK is asked by Chandren, a family friend and editor of a Tamil political journal, to assist Carol, an American anthropologist, in her research on domestic workers unions in Madras. Carol's project leads him to eventually get involved in local politics—specifically, an election campaign between Shantamma, who organizes domestic workers in and around Kuppancherry, and the local, unscrupulous, veteran politician Sethuraman. The election process brings out the corruption, violence, and power play of dirty politics. Making journal entries through all these events, RK's character, despite realizing the value of grassroots organizing, also becomes increasingly aware of the economic differences between the classes and the power of the middle class in politics. The second narrative is told by Valur Vishweswaran, also a resident of Krantinagar in Madras but one who is totally displaced from his Indian life due to his fantastic journey to Gulliver's Lilliput. With hopes of one day returning to the countries of Blefuscu and Mildendo, Valur Vishweswaran spends most of his time writing his memoirs.

In dealing with the themes of home and travel, native locality and alien city, the migrant condition is reflected in different ways in the narratives of RK and Valur Vishweswaran. While the issues of displacement and "home" are central to both narratives, the former's narrative is about return, and the latter's is of migration. On one hand, readers encounter Valur Vishweswaran, who chooses to think of his land of voyage, Lilliput, as home, even though the natives regard him as the "other." Chained and shackled, he is first treated as an intruder and later exploited for the labor his immense body can provide. Political fascism and state control of citizens appear to be the norm in Valur Vishweswaran accounts of Lilliput; however, what he writes is overridden by his belief in the superiority of the Lilliputians. This disjunction in his memoirs is a profound statement on the reality versus fantasy of immigration. Valur Vishweswaran's tale may be seen as an allegory for the immigrant who moves from one's culture to another culture that is considered superior and ends up buying into the biases and prejudices against oneself. Shankar parodies an immigrant's dream of assimilation in Valur Vishweswaran's desire to willingly subject himself to an experiment that would reduce him to Lilliputian size. Having internalized so much of Lilliputian life, history, and culture via their language, this Indian historian is unable to deal with people of his own size upon his return to Madras and refers to everyone as "bandur" (the giant one in Lilliputian) and shrinks in horror at the thought of interaction with the locals.

On the other hand, RK's return to Madras and his unsuccessful attempts to interact with the middle-class society of Madras leave him feeling displaced and unsure of the future. In a conversation with Carol, he states: "The US was all right," but "it wasn't home. Whatever that is" (61). Shankar's RK engages with the question of home and return on a deeper level than material comforts and sanitary conditions. In his interaction with Selvi, the domestic worker, RK wonders, "What does it mean to say we [Selvi and RK] are both Indians or we are both Tamils?" thus pointing to the inevitable fact that identity is tied not only to country and region but in a very important way to class (28). RK never finds answers to his questions but continues to explore the issues, as we see in the short story titled "A Map of Where I Live," which appears at the end of the narrative. In this very cryptic story written by RK, mysterious events occur, and people and animals appear and disappear as RK waits for five people to help him draw a map of where he lives. The story ends with the map's never getting drawn, but it does point to the nature of "home" as one filled with contradictions and inequities. Drawing a map might have cast Krantinagar and Kuppancherry as separate and unequal, or not drawing it may point to the potential for fruitful coalitions; readers are left to draw their own conclusions.

Interestingly, Shankar rewrites Swift's treatment of the body (which mainly comes across as an obsession with bodily functions) in *Gulliver's Travels* to point to the role of the body and sexual behavior in the construction of "self" and "other." For example, during Queen Baatania's scientific exploration of the "monstrous body" (126), Valur Vishweswaran involuntarily ejaculates and oversteps the boundary of behavior. The due punishment for the "alien" body's misbehavior turns out to be castration, a punishment the Indian gladly agrees to. Readers are left to ponder on the issues of the "alien" body as the site of desire and hate, of rebellion and docility. In this section, the author satirizes governments around the world in his description of Mildendan ruling class and critiques political structures that put the interests of capitalism above all else.

Similarly, Shankar's treatment of Carol and RK's lovemaking in Mahabalipuram (reminiscent of Forster's Aziz and Adela), first with silence and then with a dialogue between RK and Carol, brings up issues of ethnicity, desire, and control in the context of the body. For example, RK wonders if Carol was "fucking my ethnicity" (138), and on the flip side Carol lashes out at RK about Indian men hitting on her all the time thinking that "every white woman wants to get laid" (174). RK's unexplained attraction to Carol and Carol's attitude the morning after, which RK sees as self-righteous and regretful, an attempt to police his desire toward her, bring up the complexities of a cross-racial sexual relationship. Moreover, they lead to the question, How does sex travel? In other words, how would the dynamics of this relationship have been different had this episode occurred in the United States as opposed to India? Would Carol have felt the same need to "walk up and announce her decision" to RK as if he were "some child who needed to be told things in that firm voice" (174), and how would RK have behaved about this sexual encounter in New York City or Austin?

Exploring the role of the body in the construction of self and other, native and alien also leads to another such element that marks identity: language. Language is an important aspect of the novel, and Shankar treats it with the due complexity and sensitivity that it deserves. No single language seeks dominance over the other, and there is considerable attention paid to languages, accents, and the politics of translation. Most characters are careful to identify the language in which they are speaking, thus adding realism to a story that spans classes, cultures, and lands. The author gets very creative in the Lilliputian sections of the novel by inventing words and laying down a linguistic system for the Mildendans and Blefuscudians complete with the linguistic chauvinism of High Lilliputian and its denigration of Northern Lilliputian. Humor is also a part of words such as "raiterovshit" (writer of shit), the High Lilliputian word for journalist, and "Thraivarov Puur" (Thriver of Poor), the name of a Mildendan official of labor relations. English and Tamil words sit side by side, as do the issues of accents, so important in distinguishing a "native" from a "foreigner." On his part, RK takes his job "of translating between Carol and Selvi" seriously and realizes the difficulties of translation: "I discovered that there is a whole class of words in English for which I have no corresponding words in Tamil, and vice versa. Actually, and I am appropriately shameful of this, I found myself more comfortable in English than Tamil" (27). Issues of class, race, and gender are implicit in the politics of translation. Finally, the author's economical style of writing without flowery, ostentatious language adds to the character of the book, which presents speakers of many languages from various classes and cultures.

CRITICAL RECEPTION

The majority of the reviews of *A Map of Where I Live* have been enthusiastic and favorable. On the book jacket, author Shashi Tharoor reviews it as "highly original, compelling and vivid" by a "writer of rare imagination and evident potential." Reviews have appeared in scholarly publications such as *Ariel* and *World Literature Today*. The reviewer of the former write-up compares Shankar's chronicling of South Indian life to that of R. K. Narayan's and praises him as a good "storyteller" who is "witty, satirical (without being bitter), and possesses an eye for detail" Iyer (273). In the latter review, writer Joseph John calls the novel a "minor masterpiece" and adds that "in certain ways Shankar out-Swifts Swift in invention, especially in the impressive lexicon of Lilliputian words and even sentences he builds up in the course of his narrative" (209). Reviews have also appeared in magazines such as *SAMAR* and *India Currents*.

BIBLIOGRAPHY

Works by S. Shankar

Novel

A Map of Where I Live. Portsmouth, NH: Heinemann, 1997.

Poetry

I as Man. Calcutta: Writers Workshop, 1987.
"After Konark Sun Temple, 1987." *The Massachusetts Review* 29 (1988–1989): 742–43.
"The Art of Poetry." *SAMAR* 5 (Summer 1995): 40.
"Passage to North America." In *Contours of the Heart: South Asians Map North America*. Ed. Sunaina Maira and Rajini Srikanth. New York: Asian American Writers Workshop, 1996.
"Times Square, New York, 1996 C. E." Forthcoming in *The Nuyorasian Anthology*.

Short Story

"Madness." In *I'm Not Like That and Other Stories*. Ed. Alan Maley. Madras: Orient Longman, 1987: 131–36.
"Grey Cat." *I'm Not Like That and Other Stories*. Ed. Alan Maley. Madras: Orient Longman, 1987: 137–42.

Scholarly

"Imaginative Labor of Literature." Conference Commemorating the Independence of India and Pakistan. University of Iowa, 1996.

Studies of S. Shankar

Iyer, Nalini. Rev. of *A Map of Where I Live*. *ARIEL: A Review of International English Literature* 29.1 (1998): 271–73.
John, Joseph. Rev. of *A Map of Where I Live*. *World Literature Today* 72 (1998): 209–10.
Sen, Asha. "Charting the Postcolonial Novel." Rev. of *A Map of Where I Live*. *India Currents* (April 1988): 32.
Sengupta, Promita. "Lost in Lilliput, Searching in Madras." Rev. of *A Map of Where I Live*. *SAMAR* 8 (1997): 60–62.

Bapsi Sidhwa

(1938–)

Janet M. Powers

BIOGRAPHY

A member of the Parsi community, Bapsi Sidhwa was born in Karachi, then part of India, on August 11, 1938. However, her immediate family was actually based in Lahore, in the Punjab, where she grew up. At the age of two, she became a polio victim and as a consequence received no formal schooling until she was fourteen. By that time several operations had given her greater mobility, and she was able to lead a fairly normal life. She continued, however, to spend much of her time reading virtually every book she could get her hands on, which prepared her handsomely for her later work as a writer. Married at nineteen, she bore three children in rapid succession and spent a number of years as a housewife in a privileged commercial family in Lahore. As an activist among Asian women, she represented Pakistan at the Asian Women's Congress in 1975.

Sidhwa was appointed a Bunting fellow at Radcliffe/Harvard in 1986–1987 and in 1987 was also awarded a National Endowment for the Arts Grant for Creative Writing. She taught in the graduate program at Columbia University in 1989 and prior to that at Rice University and at the University of Texas at Houston. In 1991 Bapsi Sidhwa received the *Sitara-i-Imtiaz*, the highest honor in the arts that Pakistan bestows on a citizen, as well as the *Liberatur* Prize in Germany for *Cracking India*. A Writer's Grant of $105,000 was awarded to her by the Lila Wallace-Reader's Digest Fund in 1993. Sidhwa's work has been translated into German, French, and Russian. She resides in the United States but frequently travels to Pakistan.

MAJOR WORKS AND THEMES

Her first novel, *The Bride* (1983), grew out of a true story that she first heard while on a family vacation to the Northwest Frontier Province in Pakistan. Writing secretly, so as not to seem a pretentious housewife, she retold the story of a young girl who ran away from an arranged marriage, only to be hunted down and killed as a matter of honor. An American friend helped her place the story with an agent, but she endured only a spate of publishers' rejection slips and so began writing a second novel, *The Crow Eaters* (1980) about her own ethnic community. Once again, many editors turned her work down, with the explanation that Pakistan was too far removed from the lives of Western readers. Finally, a British press, Jonathan Cape, agreed to publish her second piece of fiction, a comic novel about several generations of a Parsi family in Lahore. Publication of *The Bride* soon followed. Both novels received favorable reviews in the United States and England, although Parsees have understandably been critical of *The Crow Eaters*, which presents a somewhat caricatured version of Parsi life in late nineteenth- and early twentieth-century Lahore.

Sidhwa has won the greatest measure of success with her third novel, published under different names in England and the United States. Known as *Ice-Candy Man* (1988) in England, the title was changed to *Cracking India* (1991) for publication in the United States, ostensibly to avoid connotations of the drug culture. A mesmerizing story told in the voice of a young girl, Sidhwa's novel about the violence surrounding the partition of India and Pakistan in 1947 raises significant questions about Gandhi's role, communal responsibility, and historical events. A small portion of this novel, Sidhwa's retelling of a true partition experience, "Ranna's Story," has been anthologized in *Mirrorwork*, a recently published collection of South Asian writing in English. Although some reviewers have questioned the childlike point of view through which *Cracking India* is narrated, those who know something of what happened in the Punjab at independence will recognize the significance of this novel in coming to terms with the reprehensible actions of multiple players in the partition tragedy.

An American Brat (1993), Sidhwa's most recent novel, is a sequel to *The Crow Eaters*, chronicling further generations of the Junglewalla family. Focusing on the degree of control exercised in an Islamic state, she links the rise of Fundamentalism in Pakistan with the visit of a young Parsi girl to the United States. Although the author begins by raising important questions about the effect of Islamic values on minority religions in Pakistan, Sidhwa also explores the collision of American values with those of a more conservative Parsi family. On first reading, the novel might seem somewhat superficial, but it is far more than that and deserves greater attention as a serious study of the difficulties confronted by international students. With an unabashed Parsi sense of humor, Sidhwa also comments on the ways in which South Asian value systems tend to be modified within the context of American culture. The main character, Feroza, ultimately decides she cannot go back because her spirit requires three things she cannot enjoy in Pakistan, even as a Parsi woman: freedom, privacy, and physical space (312).

As a Westernized woman, Sidhwa is critical of traditional patriarchy and the ways in which the lives of South Asian women are controlled at every step of the way by their fathers, husbands, and sons. Nowhere in South Asia is this tradition more strictly observed than among the Muslim Pathans of Pakistan's Northwest Frontier Province, scene of *The Bride*. Long an area where no woman could safely move about without a veil, on the Northwest Frontier the honor of a man depends on the zeal with which he protects his women. Into this culture Zaitoon, rescued from the violence of partition and nurtured on her father's romanticized stories of frontier life, marries. The physical abuse meted out by her husband, Sakhi, leads her to outward subservience while firing her inner sense of self-preservation. In Sidhwa's novel, Zaitoon's wild attempt to break away from the patriarchal system succeeds, although she again comes under the protection of a man, who may treat her less cruelly than the tribesman she has left. There can be no doubt as to where Sidhwa stands on the question of women's humiliation at the hands of men.

Just as there are few respectable options for Zaitoon in *The Bride*, patriarchy in Sidhwa's other novels is inescapable but open to challenge. In *The Crow Eaters*, Putli is mortified by having to walk a step ahead of her husband at a Government House function, when she and her female ancestors, from time immemorial, have been conditioned to walk three paces behind. Speaking of the way in which Putli's daughter-in-law, Tanya, has been safeguarded since babyhood, Sidhwa is openly critical of the "gigantic conspiracy practiced by an entire society to keep its girls ridiculously 'innocent,' " this "carefully nurtured ignorance" having "a high market value in the choice of a bride" (213). Yet despite these efforts at protection, young women are still subject to the sexual whims of their male relatives, such as Tanya's cousin and Lenny's cousin in *Cracking India*. The latter novel, however, is Sidhwa's greatest indictment of patriarchy, as she gradually unveils the unspeakable evil visited on Ayah and, by extension, thousands of women by men during partition in the Punjab. Yet Sidhwa reminds us that this flagrant violation of women's bodies during a time of great crisis is linked with cultural practices introduced centuries before by Mughal rulers.

Sidhwa is among those South Asian writers who have appropriated history in an effort to make sense of events surrounding British colonialism, the independence movement, and the communal frenzy of partition. Stressing repeatedly the idea that various religious communities lived peacefully with each other prior to 1947, Sidhwa insists that the communal violence that accompanied partition in the Punjab was not a necessary consequence of independence. She illustrates this point most dramatically in *Cracking India*, which centers around a young Parsi girl who struggles to understand the unspeakable events going on around her. Described through Lenny's eyes, Ayah's admirers include a Muslim cook, a Chinaman, a Pathan, Ice-candy-man (a Muslim), Masseur (Muslim), and a Sikh. They gather for easy conversation in the park and sometimes in the kitchen, symbolizing the prepartition camaraderie of a diverse population. Servants of Lenny's family similarly include Hindus and Christians. Yet as partition approaches, the "divide and rule" tactics of the British come home to roost, aggravated by sloppy mapmaking, poor communication, and communal hatred bred by fear as well as a desire to defend one's own. Sidhwa does not mince words but describes in terms more terrible, because filtered through a child's sensibility, the violence visited upon strangers and friends alike by ordinarily peaceful people. Even Lenny, who loves her Hindu Ayah intensely, is tricked into telling the truth about her whereabouts, an act of treachery that results in the kidnapping and prostitution of India herself, for Ayah, too, is a symbol. Just that easily, implies Sidhwa, violence against neighbors occurs.

Gender and politics converge in the figure of Gandhi, whom Sidhwa presents as hypnotically feminine, with a concealed interior of ice. He spends hours talking to Punjabi women about their intestinal tracts and turns his charm off and on again at will. Gandhi was also to blame, she implies, for sowing seeds of divisiveness between Muslims and Sikhs. The Sikhs, moreover, are shown as victims of their own leader, Master Tara Singh, who resents the fact that the Sikh community has not received a communal award at partition. One peasant observes, "Hindus are being murdered in Bengal . . . Muslims in Bihar. It's strange . . . the English *Sarkar* can't seem to do anything about it." Another answers cynically, "I don't think it is because they can't . . . I think it is because the Sarkar doesn't want to" (64). It is clear that Sidhwa's personal proximity to the worst events of partition has provoked clarity of thought about their complexity. Through the elements of her story, she identifies the agents who failed and the responsibilities neglected by British and Indians alike in their dealings with rural villagers in the Punjab. Her particular brand of postcoloniality spares no one who has had a hand in the independence process but assigns ultimate culpability to those who had ruled so zealously, only to renege on their duties at the end.

In *An American Brat*, the Parsi mother, Zareen, regularly visits the tomb of a Muslim saint, and Sidhwa notes that in the Indian subcontinent, "people of all faiths flock to each other's shrines and cathedrals. They came to the fifteenth-century sufi's shrine from all over Pakistan, and before Partition they came from all over northern India" (18–19). In the same novel, Zareen's daughter, Feroza, notes parallels between her Zoroastrian religion and the domestic rituals practiced by her Jewish boyfriend, David Press. Faredoon Junglewalla of *The Crow Eaters* maintains a prayer table containing icons of the Buddha and the Virgin Mary, as well as a bookshelf filled with the sacred texts of the world's great religions. This open-mindedness toward other religious traditions lies at the heart of Sidhwa's postcolonial understanding that partition violence was unnecessary, that had the British not favored a communal approach to governance, India might still be one country.

Freddy (Faredoon Junglewalla), at the end of *The Crow Eaters*, is contemptuous of his Parsi-colleagues who have founded the Indian National Congress and joined the Quit India movement. "I tell you we are betrayed by our own kind, by our own blood! The fools will break up the country. The Hindus will have one part, Muslims the other. Sikhs, Bengalis, Tamils and God knows who else will have their share. . . . We will stay where we are . . . let Hindus, Muslims, Sikhs, or whoever rule" (262–63). Through Freddy, Sidhwa illuminates the survival tactic followed from the time that Parsees arrived in the Indian subcontinent: political naïveté. As the writer takes care to explain, Zoroastrians, though expelled from Iran by the Muslims, were granted asylum in return for their promise not to proselytize or make any bid for power. In *An American Brat*, the Parsi community in Lahore is divided over the execution of Bhutto, but his supporters are helpless to protest against it. Sidhwa makes clear in *Cracking India* that although Parsis enjoy discussing politics, they are obligated to remain neutral and present no political threat, a promise that they have kept from the outset.

Parsi ethics, however, are at work in that novel as Sidhwa presents various adults seeking to redress the balance of evil in the universe. Confronted by the specter of partition violence, Lenny's parents assist their neighbors in escaping to India. Parsi women create a safe house for women who have been kidnapped and help them find their families or, if they can't go home again, place them in domestic work. In *The Crow Eaters*, Sidhwa points out that Parsis have a reputation for honesty and propriety (24), as well as a "compelling sense of duty and obligation towards other Parsees" (22). Politically astute Feroza, in *An American Brat*, compares the "fissure at the core of America's political heart" to Zoroastrian dualism: "darkness and light—Black-and-White Right-and-Wrong Good-and-Evil—with no room for the gray that other older and poorer nations had learned to accommodate" (172). Sidhwa, however, does not merely hymn the virtues of the Parsi community; she also makes fun of it with a not-so-subtle self-deprecating humor. Names can be amusing, but she uses the most outrageous ones: Easymoney, Toddywalla, Ginwalla. Farce is often the modus operandi, farts and expectoration being indulged in with great gusto by virtually all Parsi males in her novels.

CRITICAL RECEPTION

Although Bapsi Sidhwa's work has received lukewarm reviews from the mainstream press in the United States and England, it has become the topic of scholarly attention in both venues, as well as South Asia, particularly *Cracking India* and *An American Brat*, which address issues of postcoloniality. Robert Ross responds to critics who find the child's viewpoint unbelievable in the former novel by suggesting that "what they missed or ignored was the second narrator, a shadowy adult figure who reveals herself only occasionally. . . . It is not a child writing the book after all, but the child *in* the adult, each giving the other's voice authority" ("Revisiting" 373). In her *New York Times* review of *Cracking India*, Susie Tharoor questions the accuracy of Sidhwa's politics but comments, "The author's capacity for bringing an assortment of characters vividly to life is enviable." Fawzia Afzal-Khan notes that Sidhwa's novel of partition not only shows us what history is like when seen through the eyes of women and their values but implies that "the concept of 'fate' must be challenged . . . by women, who for centuries have accepted persecution at the hands of men masquerading under the guise of 'fate' " (279–80).

An American Brat received more favorable reviews at the outset than Sidhwa's earlier novels. Adam Penenberg, writing in the *New York Times Book Review*, calls it "a coming-of-age story, a sensitive portrait of how modern America appears to a new arrival" and describes Sidhwa's writing as "brisk and funny, her characters painted so vividly you can almost hear them bickering." On the other side of the ocean, a review for *The Economist* noted that Feroza "is as often enchanted as she is appalled by the America and Americans she encounters" and "that the prevailing American culture of individualism (and aversion to traditional ways) are given intelligent attention." Sidhwa's frequently understated plots and characters often center about deeply serious issues and difficult questions. It is quite possible for reviewers who know little about South Asian culture to miss altogether the philosophical significance of her work. Issues such as the pervasive evils of patriarchy, the survival of a religious minority, moral responsibility for partition, and the oppressive Hadood Ordinance in Pakistan are at the core of Sidhwa's writing. As a stylist, she is not given to puns, brilliant wordplay, or magical realism, but nonetheless she creates solid, thought-provoking stories that cause readers to continue pondering long after the last page has been turned.

BIBLIOGRAPHY

Works by Bapsi Sidhwa

Novels

The Bride. New York: St. Martin's Press, 1983
Ice-Candy Man. London: Heinemann, 1988. (Alternate title)
Cracking India. Minneapolis: Milkweed Editions, 1991.
The Crow-Eaters. Minneapolis: Milkweed Editions, 1992.
An American Brat. New Delhi: Penguin India, 1993.

Short Story

"Ranna's Story." In *Mirrorwork: 50 Years of Indian Writing, 1947–1997.* Ed. Salman Rushdie and Elizabeth West. New York: Holt, 1997.

Studies of Bapsi Sidhwa

Abnoux, Cynthia. "A Study of the Stepfather and the Stranger in the Pakistani Novel: *The Bride* by Bapsi Sidhwa." *Commonwealth Essays and Studies* 13.1 (Autumn 1990): 68–72.
Afzal-Khan, Fawzia, "Bapsi Sidhwa." *International Literature in English.* New York: Garland, 1991. 271–81.

Baumgartner, Robert J., ed. *Creative Processes in Pakistani Fiction*. Urbana: University of Illinois Press, 1996. 231–40.

Bharucha, Nilufer E. "From behind a Fine Veil: A Feminist Reading of Three Parsi Novels." *Indian Literature* 39.5 (September–October 1996): 132–41.

Hashmi, Alamgir. "*The Crow Eaters*." *World Literature Written in English* 20.2 (Autumn 1981): 373–76.

Mehta, Nina. "From the Personal to the Political: An Interview with Pakistani Novelist Bapsi Sidhwa." *Bloomsbury Review* (June 1992): 3.

Montenegro, David. "Bapsi Sidhwa: An Interview." *Massachusetts Review* 31.4 (Winter 1990): 513–33.

———, ed. *Points of Departure: International Writers on Writing and Politics: Interviews with Bapsi Sidhwa et al.* Ann Arbor: University of Michigan Press, 1991.

Penenberg, Adam. Rev. of *An American Brat*. *New York Times Book Review* (January 16, 1994): 22.

Rev. of *An American Brat*. *The Economist* (December 11, 1993): 100.

Rev. of *The Bride*. *World Literature Today* 62 (1988): 732.

Rev. of *The Crow Eaters*. *Times Literary Supplement* (September 26, 1980): 1057.

Rev. of *Ice-Candy Man*. *London Review of Books* (September 15, 1988): 19.

Ross, Robert L. "The Emerging Myth: Partition in the Indian and Pakistani Novel." *Association for Commonwealth Literature: Indian Literature and Language Studies Bulletin* 7 (1986): 63–69.

———. "Revisiting Partition." *The World and I* (June 1992): 369–75.

Tharoor, Susie. Rev. of *Cracking India*. *New York Times Book Review* (October 6, 1991): 11.

Zaman, Niaz. "Images of Purdah in Bapsi Sidhwa's Novels." In *Erasure of Purdah in the Subcontinental Novel in English*. Ed. Jasbir Jain and Amina Amin. New Delhi: Sterling, 1995. 156–73.

Mai-mai Sze
(1905–   )

Jean Amato

BIOGRAPHY

In *Between Worlds: Women Writers of Chinese Ancestry*, the critic Amy Ling asks: "How does one define a Chinese American? At what point does an immigrant become an American?" (104) How is nationality defined in a life of transnational mobility? The works of writer and artist Mai-mai Sze, who was born in Beijing but spent the majority of her life moving between Great Britain, France, and the United States, raise important questions of ethnic and national belonging. As the daughter of a Chinese ambassador to England in 1914 and the United States in 1920, Sze was educated in elite British boarding schools, a Washington, D.C., high school, and Wellesley College, eventually settling in New York and Los Angeles (Ling 65). Active in the theater, Sze is also an accomplished artist who published a comprehensive study of Chinese painting called the *Tao of Painting* in 1946. Because she does not grant interviews, we have little information on Sze (Ling 65).

MAJOR WORKS AND THEMES

In 1945 Sze published *Echo of a Cry*, an autobiography set in China and the West. Writing during the Sino-Japanese War, her work is not overtly patriotic, but she organized the first Chinese war relief campaign in the United States and lectured on China's war efforts all over North America. In her autobiography she confronts issues such as the "patronizing condescension" of white missionaries (113) and the racial prejudice that confront people of color in the United States (163).

Sze's 1948 novel, *Silent Children*, centers on a band of homeless children displaced from an unknown war who survive by scavenging on the outskirts of a nameless city. The orphans, who come together from diverse origins without a clear nationality, carve hope out of a desolate existence by working together. In contrast, the adults who populate the city are besieged by corruption and greed. To the townspeople, who attach a higher value to a loaf of bread than a human life, the children are "rats" that need to be exterminated (9).

Toward the close of the novel, the two wandering adults who attempt to join the children are the only characters identified with a nationality. These two men, one Chinese and one American, seem to operate on an allegorical level to reflect the cultural stereotypes between the East and West that render communication almost impossible between them. In *Echo of a Cry*, Sze also wrestles with the difficult ideals of a global community and a blending of the East and West. It is a fallacy, she argues, "to associate the old with 'the East' and the new with 'the West' [since] there are no such clear divisions" (129). Yet, at the same time, her novel seems to ask why the East and West prove incapable of understanding each other.

CRITICAL RECEPTION

Amy Ling notes that *Silent Children* "is obviously unrealistic and thus hardly an outburst of nation pride" commonly found in patriotic genre of fiction by overseas Chinese writers in the early 1940s (82). Ling points to the novel's allegorical tone, which acts as an "existential parable of the conditions of life" (84), where the lost children "represent . . . the most appalling effects of war" (104). Ling finds it odd that *Silent Children*, which was published after the war, should still contain such overt pessimism, unique to its genre. Yet, the novel is filled with the unanswerable existential questions common to post–World War II world literature. A *New Yorker* reviewer calls *Silent Children* "a disturbing reminder of yet another dark sociological bloom that was nurtured by the Second World War." A reviewer in the *New York Herald Tribune* states that *Silent Children* "imprints many sharp images upon the mind. . . . Most memorable of all is [how] this little unpretentious book attacks so large a theme."

Sze's autobiography conveys the simultaneous desire to belong somewhere and to run away, while lamenting an ongoing sense of rootlessness, where there is "one part of [her] that is always lost and searching" (202). A reviewer of *Echo of a Cry* in the *Weekly Book Review* adds that "[Sze] is, like every thinking person today, a pilgrim and in a sense a stranger." The lost children in *Silent Children* lament a lost innocence or "nostalgia for something [one] might have . . . possessed" (120). A reviewer in the *New York Herald Tribune* calls it "a story of humanity uprooted." For the lost children, theirs is a homesickness with no home to go back to because the "scattered memory" from the "terrifying experience of war" (85) created "no clear recollection of home" (131). Amy Ling argues that *Silent Children* could be read as almost a morbid reworking of an earlier theme in Sze's autobiography that conveys "her own sense of a symbolic orphaned condition between worlds" (85). At the same time, the novel ends hopefully, with a few children moving on to form a new community, for "it could not be possible there was no place to go" (164).

BIBLIOGRAPHY

Works by Mai-mai Sze

Novel

Silent Children. New York: Harcourt, Brace, 1948.

Autobiography

Echo of a Cry. A Story Which Began in China. New York: Harcourt, Brace, 1945.

Nonfiction

China. Cleveland: Western Reserve University Press, 1944.
The Tao of Painting. A Study of the Ritual Disposition of Chinese Painting. 2 vols. New York: Pantheon, 1946.

Studies of Mai-mai Sze

Bicknell, John. Rev. of Silent Children. New York Times, April 18, 1948, 14.
Ling, Amy. Between Worlds: Women Writers of Chinese Ancestry. New York: Pergamon Press, 1990.
Peterson, Virgilia. Rev. of Silent Children. New York Herald Tribune Weekly Book Review (March 21, 1948): 4.
Rev. of Echo of a Cry. Weekly Book Review (November 11, 1945): 8.
Rev. of Silent Children. Booklist (April 1, 1948): 268.
Rev. of Silent Children. Time (March 22, 1948): 106.
Rev. of Silent Children. New Yorker (March 20, 1948): 117.

Lin Tai-yi (also Anor Lin or Lin Wu-shuang)
(1926–   )

Jean Amato

BIOGRAPHY

Along with her sister Adet Lin,* Lin Tai-yi was part of a group of worldly, upper-class Chinese American immigrant writers from the 1940s to the 1960s whose works revealed China to Western readers during the Sino-Japanese War and civil war. As the daughter of Dr. Lin Yu-tang, the prominent overseas Chinese writer and unofficial spokesperson for China during the 1930s and 1940s, writing was a part of Lin Yu-tang's everyday life from an early age. Born in Beijing, China, in 1926, Adet Lin was ten when she immigrated with her family to the United States. She attended Columbia University from 1946 to 1949 and taught Chinese at Yale University for a short period. After marrying a Hong Kong government official, she moved to Hong Kong, where she was editor of Hong Kong's *Reader's Digest*. Lin also spent time in England and eventually settled in Washington, D.C., with her husband and two children.

MAJOR WORKS AND THEMES

At age thirteen, Lin Tai-yi and her sisters, Adet and Mei Mei, collaborated on a 1939 collection of unedited diary entries entitled *Our Family*, where they discussed family life and impressions of Europe, the United States, and China. While generally light in tone, the work addresses complex issues of war, patriotism, class, stereotypes, and racism with candid honesty. Here one can trace the beginnings of Lin Tai-yi's imaginative, original, and direct writing style.

In 1941 Lin Tai-yi and Adet wrote a second autobiographical collection, *Dawn over Chungking*, which tells of their family's six-month visit to a small village in China. While under constant danger of Japanese bombing raids, Lin's optimistic spirit remained undaunted. After their home is bombed, this fourteen-year-old defiantly writes that the bombs could never "destroy the Chinese morale, which could only be felt in our selves and could not be seen or touched" (169). Her passion for her homeland reveals itself in this early work when she exclaims, "I wish I could hold China, feel it, see the whole of it" (191). In 1940 Lin Tai-yi and Adet translated *Girl Rebel: The Autobiography of Hsieh Ping-ying*. This translation provided Western readers with their introduction to a Chinese woman warrior while further inflaming the Lin sisters' patriotism (Ling 59).

When just seventeen, Lin wrote her first overtly patriotic novel, *War Tide*, to portray the heroic struggles of ordinary Chinese citizens during the Sino-Japanese War. The plot is centered around how the eighteen-year-old daughter of a large, extended family draws on her inner strength to keep the family together as war uproots them from their home, shatters their lives, and kills their father.

In 1946 Lin wrote her second novel, *The Golden Coin*, which also addresses the Sino-Japanese War. The novel's central theme is an almost allegorical representation of the struggle between faith and reason. It is the story of Sha, an illiterate woman rooted in folk belief who embodies an "untamed innocence," passion for life, and an idealism that is too pure for this modern world (28). The novel opens with Sha at age seven in Shanghai as one of ten children bred on "poverty and vulgarity" (10). To escape her poverty, she marries Wen Ling, a self-abnegating biology professor fifteen years her senior whose rational brain wants to crush in her what he is too weak to attain—a life force and faith. In many ways, Wen represents an intellectual class that avoids life through cynicism and logic.

Thirteen years after *Golden Coin*, Lin wrote *The Eavesdropper*, her only novel that is set in both the United States and China. The narrative, which covers the 1940s to 1950s, is told from the point of view of a male Chinese protagonist, Liang Shutung. After settling in New York, Liang begins recalling his past: starting from his childhood in Shanghai to his college experience in the United States, until his return to China for the war effort, and immigration to the United States after the communist takeover of China. He is a spiritual and antimaterialistic writer who is unable to develop his art due to economics and race. Never able to realize his potential as a writer and person, he sits outside life, always eavesdropping. "He shuttles back and forth between a chaotic China in the throes of World War II and a civil war and a materialistic inhospitable U.S." (Ling 156).

In 1960 Lin published the novel *The Lilacs Overgrow*, which covers a period later than her first two novels, namely, the end of the Japanese occupation and the establishment of the People's Republic of China. It tells the story of two daughters from a poor family who go live with their wealthy and liberal aunt in Shanghai. The sisters marry out of love, but both end up dissatisfied with their marriages. Lin's 1964 novel, *Kampoon Street*, tells the story of a poor

Chinese refugee family that resettles in Hong Kong. When the father dies, the mother struggles to support the family, only to be continually beaten down by social and economic injustice. Like *War Tide*, the novel is centered on a young daughter who must support her family by working. She is faced with a difficult moral dilemma when a rich man offers to pay her for her favors. Her most recent work is a translation of the nineteenth-century Chinese classic by Li Ju-chen, *Flowers in the Mirror*, in 1965.

CRITICAL RECEPTION

Amy Ling points to the stylistic elements in *War Tide*, where Lin effectively blends the real with the surreal, while also counterbalancing opposite emotions (71–73). Ling states that "with originality and boldness, Lin Tai-yi created the expressionistic language and grotesque imagery" necessary to convey the truths of an "unspeakable" war with a "broad vision" (73). A reviewer in the *New Yorker* comments on the novel's mixture of a "bitter realism" and "touching innocence" that conveys a clear grasp of the times (Fadiman). Some reviews of *War Tide*, such as *Book Week's* (Hendricks), take on a patronizing tone that centers on the novelty of the author's age while also expressing shock that an immigrant Chinese is even capable of writing in such "first-rate, idiomatic English." A *New York Times* review calls *War Tide* a "junior miss version of 'War and Peace'" (Kao). While centered on patriotism, the novel boldly attacks the American hypocritical trade policies toward Japan, Western misconceptions of China, and the global proliferation of greed and profit that fuels war. In Lin's fiction, argues Amy Ling, "no polite, soft-spoken, modest lotus blossom of a young girl do we find here but an ardent patriot whose indignation sets the page ablaze" (165).

Amy Ling claims that Lin's second novel, *The Golden Coin*, confronts social issues such as insurmountable class divisions that form a chasm between characters, the soul-crushing effects of poverty, the notion that a woman's body is not her own, and the myth that all women are destined for motherhood. A *New York Times* reviewer criticizes *Golden Coin*'s "confused compound" of the "affirmation" and "disillusion" found in war literature in its "falsely reassuring" story of a "blind groping toward a faith that blots out realty and denies reason" (Balakian). In contrast, Ling argues that the novel's complex ending reaffirms the reality that excessive faith and idealism are doomed, and "myth, though it may be, idealism and faith are nonetheless . . . necessary" because realism is not enough (81).

Amy Ling argues that the importance of *The Eavesdropper* lies in the protagonist's "between-world condition" and his "split loyalties" between Chinese traditional codes and the West. "He himself is superfluous—a man caught between worlds, a patriot without a country, an artist unable to make use of his talents" (156). A *New York Times* reviewer also claims that the novel successfully reveals "the problems faced by those Chinese who have absorbed some of the West without being absorbed by it" (Espey). A review from the *New York Herald Tribune Book Review* notes that the novel's characters "are well created, and they give one some feeling of what the last twenty years must have felt like to a Chinese" (Martin). A *Library Journal* review, on the other hand, sees the novel as lacking full character development with too much focus on the "hero's preoccupation with sex and self-pity" (Hopkinson).

The reviews of Lin's later novel, *The Lilacs Overgrow*, are quite mixed. A *New York Times* reviewer criticizes the novel for its lack of political breadth when he states that "though it is set in the years of the Kuomintang debacle, we are very rarely made aware of the seething turmoil sweeping through the country" (Payne). In contrast, a *New Yorker* reviewer sees the novel as "disappointing because [Lin] chooses to devote her impressive talent more to an examination of political, social and economic changes and developments than to a study of the human being." Quite a few reviewers praise the novel for its vivid and universal characterizations that represent a cross-section of Chinese people. A reviewer in the *San Francisco Chronicle* reads the novel as a successful story that is "symbolic of today's struggle between conflicting ideologies" (Johnson). A *New Yorker* review of Lin's last novel, *Kampoon Street*, also notes its thematic focus on universal ideals such as courage and "the capacity to accept life without bitterness." A review in *Book Week* notes that Lin focuses more on the everyday events of her characters than on the "great social problems illustrated by their lives" (Walsh).

BIBLIOGRAPHY

Works by Lin Tai-yi/Anor Lin/Lin Wu-shuang

Fiction

War Tide. New York: John Day, 1943.
The Golden Coin. New York: John Day, 1946.
The Eavesdropper. 1st ed. Cleveland: World, 1959, 1958.
The Lilacs Overgrow. Cleveland: World, 1960.
Kampoon Street. Cleveland: World, 1964.

Translations

(And Adet Lin). *Girl Rebel: The Autobiography of Hsieh Pingying with Extracts from Her New War Diaries*. New York: John Day, 1940.
Flowers in the Mirror (*Ching hua yüan*), by Li Ju-chen. Berkeley: University of California Press, 1965.

Autobiography

(And Adet Lin and Mei Mei Lin). *Our Family*. Ed. Lin Tai-yi. 1926. New York: John Day, 1939.

(And Adet Lin and Mei Mei Lin). *Dawn over Chungking*. New York: Van Rees Press, 1941.

Studies of Lin Tai-yi/Anor Lin/Lin Wa-shuang

Balakian, Nona. Rev. of *The Golden Coin*. *New York Times*, April 7, 1946, 12.

Espey, J. J. Rev. of *The Eavesdropper*. *New York Times*, February 15, 1959, 39.

Fadiman, Clifton. Rev. of *War Tide*. *New Yorker* (November 6, 1943): 105.

Hendricks, Walter. Rev. of *War Tide*. *Book Week* (November 14, 1943): 22.

Hopkinson, S. L. Rev. of *The Eavesdropper*. *Library Journal* (February 15, 1959): 598.

Johnson, Eva. Rev. of *The Lilacs Overgrow*. *San Francisco Chronicle*, January 29, 1961, 27.

Kao, George. Rev. of *War Tide*. *New York Times*, November 7, 1943, 18.

Ling, Amy. *Between Worlds: Women Writers of Chinese Ancestry*. New York: Pergamon Press, 1990.

Martin, S. E. Rev. of *The Eavesdropper*. *New York Herald Tribune Book Review* (February 15, 1959): 5.

Payne, Robert. Rev. of *The Lilacs Overgrow*. *New York Times Book Review* (November 27, 1960): 47.

Rev. of *Kampoon Street*. *New Yorker* (February 29, 1964):134.

Rev. of *The Lilacs Overgrow*. *Booklist* (November 15, 1960): 180.

Rev. of *The Lilacs Overgrow*. *New Yorker* (December 17, 1960): 158.

Ross, Mary. Rev. of *Our Family*. *Books* (April 16, 1939): 4.

W., K. Rev. of *Our Family*. *New York Times*, April 16, 1939, 9.

Walsh, Chad. Rev. of *Kampoon Street*. *Book Week* (March 8, 1964): 16.

Wanying, Zhao. "*The Different Notions of Heroes in the Novels of Lin Tai-yi and Maxine Hong Kingston*." Thesis, Winona State University. 1996.

Amy Tan
(1952–   )

Wenying Xu

BIOGRAPHY

Amy Tan was born in 1952 in Oakland, California, to Chinese immigrants Daisy and John Tan. She received her B.A. in English and linguistics and her M.A. in linguistics from San Jose State University. She first began to work as a language development consultant to the Alameda County Association for Retarded Citizens. Later she directed training programs for developmentally disabled children. Her writing career began when she moved into freelance business writing. Although Tan had a successful business, she felt far from fulfilled. She felt trapped and depressed. Realizing the necessity for change, she took up jazz piano and the reading of fiction by women like Isabel Allende, Alice Walker, Toni Morrison, Louise Erdrich, and Jamaica Kincaid. During this period she wrote her first story, "Endgame," about a Chinese American chess prodigy who feels overpowered by her mother. "Endgame" earned her entrance into the Squaw Valley Community of Writers. Tan describes the workshop as "intensely emotional, exhilarating" (Feldman). At the workshop she met women writers like Amy Hempel and Molly Giles, who became instrumental in Tan's rise to fame with the publication of her first novel, *The Joy Luck Club*, in 1989.

Amy Tan is one of those lucky writers whose sources for fiction come from their loved ones. Her father, the model for Jimmy Louie in *The Kitchen God's Wife* (1991), was educated as an engineer in Beijing and left China in 1947 for a new life in America. He declined a scholarship from the Massachusetts Institute of Technology and entered the Baptist ministry. When Amy was fifteen, she lost both her father and older brother, Peter, to malignant brain tumors. Her refusal to accept the death of her father became the internal conflict within Pearl in *The Kitchen God's Wife*. Convinced that their Santa Clara house was jinxed,

Amy's mother, Daisy Tan, took her two remaining children on a two-year exile to New York, Washington, and Florida before they sailed across the Atlantic to the Netherlands.

Daisy Tan's life in China and America has provided Tan with an intricately woven tapestry of women's lives that furnished characters, settings, conflicts, and themes in all of her three novels. Born into a wealthy Shanghai family complete with servants and concubines, Daisy didn't have a happy childhood. Her father died when she was very young, and afterward she and her mother were exiled to Pudong, an island off the coast of Shanghai. Her widowed mother was raped by a rich man and forced into concubinage. Her mother bore the rich man a son, who usually would guarantee security for the concubine. But when one of the rich man's favored concubines took the boy away and claimed him as her own, Daisy's mother committed suicide by swallowing a fatal amount of opium wrapped inside a New Year cake. Daisy, now nine years old, had to grow up on her own among the unrelated people in the rich man's house. This part of Daisy's life has found its embodiment in An-Mei Hsu's mother, one of the four mothers in *The Joy Luck Club*.

When Daisy became a young woman, she entered an arranged marriage with a man who soon became abusive. She gave birth to a son, who died early, and three daughters, whom she was forced to give up when she fled her husband in 1949. She had to wait twenty-nine years before she saw them again. Daisy finally succeeded in getting a divorce and emigrated to America, where she met and married John Tan. Daisy's life in China became material for the story of both Suyuan Woo in *The Joy Luck Club* and Winnie Louie in *The Kitchen God's Wife*. Tan's third novel, *The Hundred Secret Senses* (1995), moves away from the themes of mother–daughter relationship to a sisterly relationship and a death-birth-reincarnation juxtaposition. Many of Daisy Tan's talk-stories have also found their way into the settings, characters, and plot of *The Hundred Secret Senses*.

MAJOR WORKS AND THEMES

A tremendous continuity exists among Amy Tan's three novels and lies in three major themes—the conflict between the bicultural, bilingual immigrant and the thoroughly Americanized second generation, the trope of journey as discovery and reconciliation, and the dialogic and therapeutic natures of talk-story. These themes unfold as the stories move from daughters to mothers, from California to China, from the present to the past, and from this life to the previous life and back.

In the absence of the meaningful connection between mothers and daughters, Tan's women experience feelings of isolation and fragmentation. In *The Joy Luck Club*, the American-born daughters know very little about their mothers. All their lives they have tried so hard to assimilate into mainstream America that things Chinese are at best avoided, at worst shameful. By ignoring their mothers' effort to inculcate Chinese tradition into them, the daughters have frustrated the hopes of their mothers that their daughters would maintain "American circumstances and Chinese characters" (289). The price the daughters pay for their seemingly successful assimilation is "their nagging sense of unease in the identities that they have laboriously created for themselves" (Huntley 74). On the other hand, the mothers never give up the hope of imparting their Chinese character and wisdom to their daughters, something that is often perceived by their children as manipulation and control. The consequence is a complete breakdown of communication between the mothers and daughters.

Thus, mothers are estranged from their daughters, and the daughters become emotionally crippled by their mothers. In "Rice Husband," for example, Lena St. Clair complains that her mother has "the mysterious ability to see things before they happen. . . . She sees only bad things-about our family. . . . she never did anything to stop them" (161). Once when Lena is a young girl, her mother takes a look at Lena's rice bowl and comments that "your future husband have one pock mark for every rice you not finish. . . . I once know a pock mark man. Mean man, bad man" (164). This remark leads young Lena to see Arnold, a neighborhood bully, as her future husband and curse him by leaving more rice in her bowl. Many years later, when Lena reads in the paper about Arnold's death due to complications from measles, she is convinced that she is responsible for his death. Thus, when Lena finds herself in a dysfunctional marriage with Harold, she does nothing other than feel resentment, believing that Harold is her retribution and punishment for her adolescent hatred of Arnold—"we deserve what we get," Lena thinks (168).

The Kitchen God's Wife begins from Pearl's point of view and reveals a difficult relationship between her and her mother, Winnie—"Whenever my mother talks to me, she begins the conversation as if we were already in the middle of an argument" (1). It all starts with a misunderstanding due to their cultural differences. At her father's death, Pearl is unable to weep because her grief is too deep for tears. Winnie slaps the child because traditional Chinese culture measures grief by how loud one cries at the funeral. In time Pearl comes to believe that her mother loves her brother more, and Winnie is convinced that her daughter thinks that she is a bad mother. This strained relationship has kept both mother and daughter from sharing their dark secrets—Winnie's devastating marriage with Wen Fu back in China, Pearl's birth as the result of Wen Fu's rape of her, and Pearl's debilitating illness.

The theme of cultural conflict between immigrants and an Americanized second generation continues in *The Hundred Secret Senses*, but this time the gap takes place between two sisters, one born and raised in China and the other in the United States to a Chinese father and a Caucasian mother. As Olivia, the American sister, narrates her story, "she reveals that at the core of her identity lie angst and unhappiness, doubts and skepticism" (Huntley 121). As a child she is embarrassed by her immigrant sister, Kwan, who is too Chinese and too un-American in her appearance and behavior. As an adult Olivia is unkind to

Kwan, whose unceasing love and loyalty for her American sister baffle her, whose dreamlike stories about her previous existence irritate her. Yet at the moment when Olivia's marriage to Simon is about to end, Kwan comes to the rescue—she persuades both Olivia and Simon to accompany her on her journey back to China. Through this journey across time, space, and psyches Olivia learns about the magical link between her, Simon, and Kwan—literally a journey toward self and wholeness. Thus, the resolution comes when Kwan disappears mysteriously in the dark caves of Kweilin to secure the reunion between Olivia and Simon and when Olivia gives birth to a baby girl, who is suggested to be Kwan's reincarnation.

This trope of journey, most dominant in *The Hundred Secret Senses*, also serves as a major theme in the earlier novels. Jing-mei Woo at the end of *The Joy Luck Club* travels to China to meet her twin sisters, fulfilling her mother's dream as well as bringing a resolution to her own story. "For Jing-mei, the journey is an epiphany and a discovery of self: finally aware of her mother's meaning, she is able to give voice to Suyuan's story as well as to the story that they share as mother and daughter" (Huntley 48). Similarly, Pearl in *The Kitchen God's Wife*, in listening to her mother's narrative, takes a journey back into Winnie's traumatic past that has lain buried for forty-some years. This journey by means of storytelling restores love and trust between the mother and daughter, and finally Pearl is able to reveal her secret, that she is suffering from multiple sclerosis. Having divested herself of the dark secret of her past, Winnie is now able to devote herself to helping her daughter. By the end of the novel, Winnie decides that she and Pearl will travel back to China to seek a cure for Pearl's illness.

Evidenced in *The Joy Luck Club*, Chinese talk-story brings about wounds in the daughters who share little of the linguistic and cultural world of their mothers. Rose Hsu Jordon, for example, is haunted and paralyzed by childhood nightmares caused by her mother's story about Old Mr. Chou, the guardian of the dream world. When her mother tries to comfort Rose after a nightmare, "Don't pay attention to Old Mr. Chou. He is only a dream. You only have to listen to me," Rose answers in despair, "But Old Mr. Chou listens to you too" (208). In the daughters' imagination, their mothers possess the power of potent goddesses who control their daughters' identities, make impossible demands, and render their daughters powerless.

Ironically, as talk-story brings about wounds, so does it heal wounds. In all three novels, it is through talk-story that conflicts are resolved, love and trust are restored, and secrets are finally shared. Almost all of the mothers in both *The Joy Luck Club* and *The Kitchen God's Wife* resort to the power of talk-story to mend the rift between them and their thoroughly Americanized daughters. Lindo Jong in *The Joy Luck Club*, for instance, explains to her daughter, Waverly Jong, the Chinese tradition of unconditional loyalty to one's parents through the story of her own unhappy marriage arranged by her parents—"I once sacrificed my life to keep my parents' promise" (42). *The Hundred Secret*

Senses is a collage of Kwan's stories told to impress Olivia with the idea that her union with Simon is predestined by events in the distant past and that they must remain married. Kwan's talk-story, verified by Olivia's discoveries in China, brings the estranged couple back together.

The immigrant mothers' and sisters' talk-stories are dialogic in nature, for they mediate not only between speakers/writers and listeners/readers but also between oral and written language, between the linguistic and cultural modes of China and America, and between "truth" and "fiction." In *The Joy Luck Club*, for example, the mah-jongg club originates from Suyan Woo's Kweilin stories, but the club's history changes with each telling. In this manner, the club itself and the stories surrounding it deconstruct traditionally perceived oppositions between history and fiction, the experiential and the discursive. Talk-stories thus permit ample space for interpretation or misinterpretation as the Joy Luck daughters, Pearl, and Olivia have done. Being nonlinear, "irrational," feminine, and private, talk-story is not a public authorized discourse and thus is an effective resistance to the master discourse of assimilation that classifies immigrants as either happy "model minorities" or deviant and inscrutable aliens. Talk-story empowers the mothers and enlightens the daughters, something the dominant culture has failed to do, particularly for second-generation children uncertain about their identities, about their place in the culture they want to claim as their own.

CRITICAL RECEPTION

Although Amy Tan is widely taught in the classrooms of literary, ethnic, and historical studies, she has yet to receive the kind of critical attention she deserves. Most of the existent scholarship on Tan focuses on her first two novels, *The Joy Luck Club* and *The Kitchen God's Wife*. There are only two book-length studies of Amy Tan—E. D. Huntley's *Amy Tan: A Critical Companion* and *Paintbrush*'s special issue, *The World of Amy Tan* (Gately). Huntley offers a comprehensive biography of Amy Tan and detailed studies of all three novels in terms of their plot development, points of view and structures, settings, character development, literary devices, narrative structures, major themes and issues, and alternative readings. Like many critics, such as Marina Heung, Bonnie Braendlin, and E. Shelley Reid, Huntley studies "the intricacies of the relationship between mothers and daughters" in *The Joy Luck Club* and *The Kitchen God's Wife* (Huntley 99), exploring the friction, fascination, and fear between the generations engendered by their linguistic, cultural, and age divide. On *The Hundred Secret Senses* Huntley writes about several themes like love, loyalty, sisterhood, and memory, her most interesting analysis being on memory and the novel's nonlinearity. *The World of Amy Tan* presents a collection of essays whose topics range from the mother–daughter dyad, to cultural survival, to pedagogical issues on Amy Tan.

Given the multiple voices in Tan's novels, several critics have performed

Bakhtinian readings of *The Joy Luck Club* and *The Kitchen God's Wife*. For example, Stephen Souris in his " 'Only Two Kinds of Daughters': Inter-Monologue Dialogicity in *The Joy Luck Club*" focuses on "the potential for active intermingling of perspectives across utterances, with the site of the dialogicity located in the reader's experience of the narrative" (99). Souris deems *The Joy Luck Club* rich and educational, for it "allows for a rich array of dialogized perspectives within single utterances: the Chinese, the American, and the Chinese-American" (100). The dialogic nature of talk-story enables the speaker and listener to cross cultural borders in search of ways to revise history and to transfigure ethnicity. The ethnic self, as presented in Tan's works, is not a stable self predetermined by race, color, and language. Ben Xu's essay, "Memory and the Ethnic Self," explores how memories and strategic narration of the past assist the construction of a present sense of ethnic identity. However, the sense of ethnicity differs between the mothers and daughters. For the mothers, the first-generation Chinese immigrants in America, life is a "constant test of survival, to the extent that it almost becomes ethnic symbolism" (8), and the mothers define themselves by narrating their past tribulations. For the daughters, the second generation, their ethnicity is more defined by their relationship with white Americans than their relationship to the Chinese culture, about which they know little. "The return to their ethnic identity on the part of the daughters is represented . . . as realizable . . . by a narrative rivalry between 'tale of the past' and 'tale of the present' " (15).

Malini Johar Schueller points out, as have feminists of color, that both gender and ethnicity are not essences but representations, and identities are linguistically constructed. To critique liberal white feminism that "relied on notions of the singular, autonomous self" (73). Schueller draws upon Maxine Hong Kingston* and Amy Tan to illustrate the socially constructed, discursive nature of gender and ethnic identity" (74). Schueller praises Tan for subverting East-West cultural dichotomies by "appropriating (and thus questioning) the rhetoric of universalist feminism" (78) and presenting the Joy Luck daughters' cultural origins as multiple and complex.

Most people read Amy Tan's stories about the Chinese mothers straight as testimonies of the brutal patriarchal world of old China, comforted by the impression that these women lived miserable lives in China and now are safe from harm in America, if not happy. Judith Caesar's "Patriarchy, Imperialism and Knowledge in *The Kitchen God's Wife*" enlightens the reader with an allegorical reading that "questions the basic American concepts of truth and rationality" (165) and challenges the presumptuous division between the worlds of China and America. Caesar parallels the victimization of Weili with the Japanese conquest of China, Wu Fu's death as an old and respected man with the fact that the crimes of imperialism have gone unpunished, and imperialism with patriarchy. Such an allegorical reading is powerful in reminding us that "the former imperial powers . . . are both more prosperous and respected than their former victims," while the Western governments blame the human rights abuses in

China on "the ideological systems that ejected the colonial powers, not on the after-effects of imperialism itself" (168).

Wenying Xu's "A Womanist Production of Truths" is one of the few studies of mythologies used in Tan. Xu locates her argument against the background contention by the editors of *The Big Aiiieeee!*, the first anthology of Asian American writings, that writers like Maxine Hong Kingston, Amy Tan, and David Henry Hwang have faked Chinese legends and myths. Xu points out that mythologies "are one of the most appetizing, saturating, and thus most vicious components of gender ideologies, for mythologies are capable of shaping female subjects who take as their own vital survival the perpetuation of existent social and sexual order" (56). Then she proceeds to argue that Tan's revisions of the mythologies of the Moon Lady and the Kitchen God "subvert gender ideologies and gain women a measure of freedom from patriarchal domination" (58).

In recent years a large number of dissertations have taken Tan as their subject of studies. Amy Tan's works will receive more and richer critical attention in the near future.

BIOGRAPHY

Works by Amy Tan

Novels

The Joy Luck Club. New York: G. P. Putnam's Sons, 1989.
The Kitchen God's Wife. New York: G. P. Putnam's Sons, 1991.
The Hundred Secret Senses. New York: G. P. Putnam's Sons, 1995.

Children's Books

The Moon Lady. New York: Macmillan, 1992.
The Chinese Siamese Cat. New York: Macmillan, 1994.

Short Stories

"Two Kinds." *The Atlantic* 263.2 (February 1989): 11–12.
"Peanut's Fortune." *Grand Street* 10.2 (Winter 1991): 11–22.

Essays

"The Language of Discretion." In *The State of Language.* Ed. Christopher Ricks and Leonard Michaels. Berkeley: University of California Press, 1990. 25–32.
"Mother Tongue." *The Threepenny Review* (Fall 1990): 7.

Studies of Amy Tan

Braendlin, Bonnie. "Mother/Daughter Dialog(ic)s in, around, and about Amy Tan's *The Joy Luck Club.*" In *Private Voices, Public Lives: Women Speak on the Literary*

Life. Ed. Nancy Owen Nelson. Denton: University of North Texas Press, 1995. 111–24.

Caesar, Judith. "Patriarchy, Imperialism, and Knowledge in *The Kitchen God's Wife.*" *North Dakota Quarterly* 62.4 (Fall 1994): 164–74.

Cheng, Sinkwan. "Fantasizing the Jouissance of the Chinese Mother: *The Joy Luck Club* and Amy Tan's Quest for Stardom in the Market of Neo-Racism." *Savoir: Psychanalyse et analyse culturelle* 3.1–2 (1997): 95–133.

David, Rocio G. "Wisdom (Un)heeded: Chinese Mothers and American Daughters in Amy Tan's *The Joy Luck Club.*" *Cuadernos de Investigacion Filologica* 19–20 (1993–1994): 89–100.

Feldman, Gayle. "*The Joy Luck Club*: Chinese Magic, American Blessings, and a Publishing Fairy Tale." *Publishers Weekly* (July 7, 1989): 24.

Foster, M. Marie Booth. "Voice, Mind, Self: Mother–Daughter Relationships in Amy Tan's *The Joy Luck Club* and *The Kitchen God's Wife.*" In *Women of Color: Mother–Daughter Relationships in 20th Century Literature.* Ed. Elizabeth Brown-Guillory. Austin: University of Texas Press, 1996. 208–27.

Gately, Patricia. "Ten Thousand Different Ways: Inventing Mothers, Inventing Hope." *The World of Amy Tan.* Special Issue of *Paintbrush* 22 (Autumn 1995): 51–55.

Hawley, John C. "Assimilation and Resistance in Female Fiction of Immigration: Bharati Mukherjee, Amy Tan, and Christine Bell." In *Rediscovering America 1492–1992: National, Cultural, and Disciplinary Boundaries Re-Examined.* Ed. Leslie Barry et al. Baton Rouge: Louisiana State University Press, 1992. 226–34.

Heung, Marina. "Daughter-Text/Mother-Text: Matrilineage in Amy Tan's *Joy Luck Club.*" *Feminist Studies* 19 (Fall 1993): 597–616.

Ho, Wendy. "Swan-Feather Mothers and Coca-Cola Daughters: Teach Tan's *The Joy Luck Club.*" In *Teaching American Ethnic Literatures: Nineteen Essays.* Ed. John R. Maitino and David R. Peck. Albuquerque: University of New Mexico Press, 1996. 327–45.

Huntley, E. D. *Amy Tan: A Critical Companion.* Westport, CT: Greenwood, 1998.

Lim, Shirley Geok-Lin. "Feminist and Ethnic Literary Theories in Asian American Literature." *Feminist Studies* 19.3 (Fall 1993): 571–95.

Ling, Amy. *Between Worlds: Women Writers of Chinese Ancestry.* New York: Pergamon, 1990.

Mountain, Chandra Tyler. " 'The Struggle of Memory against Forgetting': Cultural Survival in Amy Tan's *The Joy Luck Club.*" In Gately, *The World of Amy Tan.* 39–50.

Olson, Carol Booth, and Pat Clark. "Using Amy Tan's '*The Moon Lady*' to Teach Analytical Writing in the Multicultural Classroom." In Gately, *The World of Amy Tan.* 85–98.

Reid, E. Shelley. " 'Our Two Faces': Balancing Mothers and Daughters in *The Joy Luck Club* and *The Kitchen God's Wife.*" In Gately, *The World of Amy Tan.* 20–38.

Schueller, Malini Johar. "Theorizing Ethnicity and Subjectivity: Maxine Hong Kingston's *Tripmaster Monkey* and Amy Tan's *The Joy Luck Club.*" *Genders* 15 (Winter 1992): 72–85.

Shear, Walter. "Generation Differences and the Diaspora in *The Joy Luck Club.*" *Critique: Studies in Contemporary Fiction* 34.3 (Spring 1993): 193–99.

Shen, Gloria. "Born of a Stranger: Mother–Daughter Relationships and Storytelling in Amy Tan's *The Joy Luck Club.*" In *International Women's Writing: New Land-*

scapes of Identity. Ed. Anne E. Brown and Marjanne E. Gooze. Westport, CT:
Greenwood, 1995. 233–44.

Smorada, Claudia Kovach. "Side-Stepping Death: Ethnic Identity, Contradiction, and the
Mother(land) in Amy Tan's Novels." *Fu Jen Studies: Literature and Linguistics*
24 (1991): 31–45.

Souris, Stephen. " 'Only Two Kinds of Daughters': Inter-Monologue Dialogicity in *The
Joy Luck Club*." *MELUS* 19.2 (Summer 1994): 99–123.

Wang, Qun. "The Dialogic Richness of *The Joy Luck Club*." In Gately, *The World of
Amy Tan*. 76–84.

Wong, Sau-ling C. *Reading Asian American Literature: From Necessity to Extravagance*.
Princeton: Princeton University Press, 1993.

———. " 'Sugar Sisterhood': Situating the Amy Tan Phenomenon." In *The Ethnic
Canon: Histories, Institutions, and Interventions*. Minneapolis: University of Minnesota Press, 1995. 174–210.

Xu, Ben. "Memory and the Ethnic Self: Reading Amy Tan's *The Joy Luck Club*." *ME-
LUS* 19.1 (Srping 1994): 3–18.

Xu, Wenying. "A Womanist production of Truths: The Use of Myths in Amy Tan." In
Gately, *The World of Amy Tan*. 56–66.

Linda Ty-Casper
(1931–   )

Shannon T. Leonard

BIOGRAPHY

Linda Ty-Casper (pronounced Tee-*Cas*-per) was born in Manila, Philippines, September 17, 1931, to Francisco Figueroa Ty (a civil engineer) and Catalina Velasquez Ty (an educator and textbook writer). She graduated from the University of the Philippines with an A.A. in 1951 and earned a law degree from the same university's College of Law in 1955. On July 14, 1956, she married Leonard Casper, renowned critic of Philippine literature, and moved later that year with him to Boston, where she eventually pursued an advanced law degree at Harvard. In 1957, while awaiting her bar exam results and feeling disheartened by the misinformation about Philippine history in Harvard's Widener Library collection, Ty-Casper rededicated herself to fiction writing. She also attributes her inspiration to tell stories to the fact that she spent much of the Japanese occupation of the Philippines with her maternal grandmother; her grandmother related to the young Ty-Casper stories of her life during the 1896 revolution and later urged her to write about collective experiences of historical, momentous occasions (Bresnahan 62). Although her career in law was eclipsed by her penchant for literary artistry, Ty-Casper's devotion to social justice has not waned. Indeed, Ty-Casper sees her writing, primarily historical fiction, as correction of common misjudgments about Philippine history.

To date, Ty-Casper has written ten novels and published several collections of short stories. One year after the publication of her first short story collection, her first novel, *The Peninsulars*, was released in 1964. Research, writing, and revision of her next novel, *The Three-Cornered Sun* (1979), occupied fifteen years, during which time she also produced several short stories, collected in *The Secret Runner and Other Stories* (1974). In 1980, the year she served as author in residence at the University of the Philippines Writing Center, another novel, *Dread Empire*, was published in Hong Kong. That same year, her short story "A Swarm of Sun" was anthologized in *Fiction by Filipinos in America*. The 1980s proved to be Ty-Casper's most prolific decade yet as she composed six more novels in quick succession: *Hazards of Distance*, 1981; *Awaiting Trespass (A Pasión)*, 1985; *Fortress in the Plaza*, 1985; *Wings of Stone*, 1986; *Ten Thousand Seeds*, 1987; and *A Small Party in a Garden*, 1988. Another collection of short stories, *Common Continent* (1991), bridges the 1980s and her weightiest novel to date, *DreamEden* in 1996. Over the years, her short stories have also appeared in *Asia Magazine*, *Antioch Review*, *Best American Stories of 1977*, *Boston Review*, *Descant*, *Kenyon Review*, *Nantucket Review*, *New Mexico Quarterly*, *Prairie Schooner*, *Southwest Review*, *Manila Review*, and *Solidarity*.

Significantly, of all of Ty-Casper's work, only three novels—*Awaiting Trespass*, *Wings of Stone*, and *DreamEden*—have been widely available to U.S. audiences. When the Philippines' political climate proved inhospitable to creative, alternative renditions of Filipino history and politics, both *Awaiting Trespass* and *Wings of Stone* were published by Readers International, a nonprofit organization in the United States and Britain dedicated to preserving endangered literature. *DreamEden* comes to U.S. audiences as a reprint of the Philippine publication, by way of University of Washington Press. Nearly all Ty-Casper's texts, U.S.- and non-U.S.-published alike, are available from the Cellar Book Shop.

In addition to writing, Ty-Casper conducts writers' workshops in the Philippines and the United States. Her honors and awards include Siliman University fellowship, 1963; Radcliffe Institute fellowship, 1974–1975; Djerassi writing fellowship, 1984; and literature award, Filipino-American Women's Network, 1985; *Awaiting Trespass* was appraised as one of the five best books by Feminist Book Fortnight of Britain and Ireland. Despite her fecundity and multiple successes, it was not until 1980, when she was invited to be a resident fictionist at the University of the Philippines Creative Writing Center, that she began to envision herself as an author, in addition to "somebody's wife, daughter or mother" (*Contemporary Authors* 449).

MAJOR WORKS AND THEMES

Linda Ty-Casper's literary corpus constitutes a broad narrative that details Philippine history. Individual stories of everyday people, not merely highly visible general or revolutionary leaders, collectively constitute a story of the nation. Ty-Casper's careful blend of national and social history with the art of fiction writing often earns her comparisons to Philippine national hero José Rizal, who wrote over a century ago against the tyranny of Spain's colonization of the Philippines. The fusion of historical narrative and creativity operates with a purpose, as a character in her novel *Three-Cornered Sun* gracefully outlines: "History as it recedes becomes confused. By raising the past to the level of imagination . . . a novel can preserve the essence of the past and give us a sense, a vision, of what we are" (166). Like nearly all contemporary Filipino authors in the United States, such as Ninotchka Rosca,* Peter Bacho, and Michelle Cruz Skinner, Ty-Casper locates her subjects in Philippine landscapes. Taken as a whole, her novels relate over 200 years of history, detailing the various colonial enterprises—Spanish, American, and Japanese—in the islands and the later similar subjugations of Filipino people under Filipino home rule. Ty-Casper's imaginative historiography, based on marginal memoirs of soldiers, legal cases, current events, and personal stories, attempts to locate the personal, the individual within the public political arena. Ty-Casper gives voice to quotidian heroes, men and women of varying nationalities and allegiances who are, as she says in the Preface to *Awaiting Trespass*, "trying to be reasonable and noble during irrational and ignoble times; to be honest and compassionate when virtues only complicate survival; to keep the faith when it is no longer clear to whom God is faithful" (n.p.).

One can sketch an outline of Philippine history with Ty-Casper's fiction at hand. The process of writing, it turns out, had as much to do with the political climate of the Philippines as the subject of her narratives. Ty-Casper's first novel, *The Peninsulars*, is a literary time machine that transports readers, characters, and concerns to the start of colonial ventures in the mid-eighteenth century, the earliest of Ty-Casper's fictionalized historical settings. *Three-Cornered Sun*, her next novel, was intended to be the first volume in a series on the Philippine revolution at the end of the nineteenth century and the Philippine-American War. Initially intending to write an epic saga of the Philippines, the eruption of martial law took precedence, compelling Ty-Casper to alter her plans for a fictionalized chronological history of foreign colonialism. Instead, Ty-Casper focused her literary attentions to making sense of current events—Ferdinand Marcos' neocolonial dictatorship.

Dread Empire's temporal setting—twenty-five years after the attainment of Philippine independence from the United States and Japan—marks the beginning of Ty-Casper's concerns with Marcos' institution of martial law in 1972. The novel's Introduction situates the novel's sociopolitical landscape of martial law within the context of larger historical frameworks, by charting the nation's experience with serial colonialisms—Spain, then the United States, then Japanese occupation during World War II. While drawing comparisons between foreign imperialisms and native tyrannies, *Dread Empire*, as with all of Ty-Casper's fiction, contemplates the repercussions of public disorders on private lives. *Dread Empire*'s protagonist, Don Paco, landlord-tyrant and former Philippine governor and statesman, characterizes the excessive, self-serving despots responsible for the perpetuation of oppression despite the apparent end of (foreign) oppressions. Written in 1980, near the midpoint of martial law's tenure in the Philippines, *Dread Empire* had to be published in Hong Kong, because of the regime's extreme antagonism to possibly inflammatory writing, fictional or otherwise.

Awaiting Trespass redirects focus to the experiences of ordinary people and the effects of martial law's tyranny on everyday lives. The novel's genre, a *pasión* or traditional "lengthy, chanted chronicle of agonies," suggests that grief, hope, and redemption are simultaneously possible, for the classic *pasión* details the death of Christ for the sake of human redemption. A three-day wake over the mysteriously closed coffin of Don Severino Gil serves as the setting for a microcosmic view of a range of possible personal reactions to life under authoritarian rule. The suspense about the condition of Don Severino's body mirrors the uncertainty of life under the Marcos regime. Tragedy, suffering, and redemption are part and parcel of the mystery surrounding the late patriarch and the conditions of his death, later revealed to be the result of brutal torture. Don Severino's niece, Telly, a forty-nine-year-old suicidal divorcée who composes unwritten poetry, and Don Severino's son, Sevi, a priest ambivalent about his calling, both find personal reconciliation during the course of the wake.

Whatever hopes for human dignity, potential, and morality *Awaiting Trespass* advances, Ty-Casper's subsequent novels *A Small Party in a Garden*, *Fortress in the Plaza*, and *Wings of Stone* doubt and unravel. *A Small Party in a Garden* portrays tragic episodes in the life of a young female lawyer who disengages herself from the pompous banality of Imelda Marcos and her entourage. Unmotivated violence—gang rape and murder of the protagonist and her father—places final grim punctuation on this novel's message about the relationship between disenchanted Filipinos and the tyrannical Establishment. *Fortress in the Plaza* recounts the bombings in Manila's Plaza Mirinda during a 1971 final campaign rally for the Liberal Party and the explosion's effects on a common family. As Leonard Casper eloquently states, with the bombing at the Plaza, "it is as if the hope of decent men for the democratic revolution has itself blown into fragments" (*Opposing* 32). Johnny Manalo, protagonist of *Wings of Stone*, leaves Manila for the United States on the day of the bombing and returns to Manila thirteen years afterward. Johnny lands on the same runway that had recently served as stage to Benigno "Ninoy" Aquino's assassination. Although Johnny is psychically disconnected from the political atmosphere of his homeland, his personal narrative and family history bind him inextricably to the fate of the country. Published in 1986, the year of Marcos' final ousting from power's seat, *Wings of Stone* remains ambivalent about the future of the country and its people as the novel ends in flames, the hiding of bodies, Johnny's undetermined feelings about remaining in the Philippines, and questions about the possibilities of love and personal connections during turbulent times. Indeed, as the novel's title suggests, the nation's predicament is so intricate and desperate as to have produced wings of stone, prohibitive to flights toward freedom.

After writing five novels about martial law, Ty-Casper's return to a linear course of fictionalized Philippine histories, set in the Philippines, reemphasizes the interdependence of local events and global politics. *Ten Thousand Seeds* narrates seven months of Philippine history, from 1898 to March 1899, through the eyes of two American honeymooners, Edward and Calista Rowbotham. The

Rowbothams visit the Philippines during the germinal stages of the Filipinos' movement toward national independence from Spain. History here is not simply localized to the Philippines but made transnational, especially as the quest for Philippine freedom echoes the novel's recent past, the U.S. Civil War. The connection between U.S. and Philippine history tightens as Ty-Casper reveals that her protagonists' family heritages directly link them to the American institution of slavery as well as what the novel foresees—the future of U.S. colonial presence in the Philippines.

In *Hazards of Distance*, Ty-Casper also links events in the Philippines to U.S. and world history. As *Hazards of Distance* contrasts self-serving Manila bureaucrats to rural family values, Ty-Casper alludes to concurrent world events, such as student riots on U.S. university campuses at Berkeley and Columbia and the support of the U.S. Embassy of the Malaysian-British position on Sabah, thus rendering portraits of the local Philippines against a backdrop of world politics. Readers of *DreamEden* recognize a similar tactic when Ty-Casper has one of her characters sympathize with the front-page story of the Challenger explosion in 1986, an event that delineated a U.S. cohort just as Kennedy's assassination marked baby boomers.

DreamEden, Ty-Casper's latest novel, interrogates the future of the Philippines by way of reflection upon the end of the Marcos era, the assumption of power by Corazon Aquino in 1986, and the numerous coup attempts in resistance to the Aquino administration. *DreamEden* maps a world of irony where the central contradiction reveals itself as the continued oppression of the Philippine people and the burgeoning of poverty—suffered indignities that were expected to cease with the end of martial law. *DreamEden* imagines the delicate intricacies of an ever-expanding suburban Manila barrio and personifies persistent and evolving national struggles via interpersonal relationships. Whereas the novel refuses to forecast the Philippines' future, readers take comfort in the successful achievement of Ty-Casper's overarching literary goal—to bring history into the realm of the imagination and therewith delineate versions of the nation's people's tales, in order to comprehend and chart Philippine collective and individual identities.

CRITICAL RECEPTION

Brief book reviews dominate critical studies of Linda Ty-Casper's oeuvre. Ty-Casper's reviewers applaud her works, naming the "scope of her historical vision" (Campomanes, "Linda" 889) and the elegance of her prose as her crowning achievements. Some reviewers, however, object and criticize her syntax and use of language as sometimes awkward, flowery, and unnecessarily symbolist. Nevertheless, all detractors agree that the "content and grandeur [of her novels'] theme[s] render such faults minor" (Rosca, 860). *Yale Review* contributor Maureen Howard expresses surprise about Ty-Casper's obscurity within American studies; Howard suggests that Ty-Casper's work be explored for depictions of colonial contexts. As well, Howard wonders why studies of the Marcos regime, so well liked by critics and readers of contemporary history as well as sensationalist tabloids that divulge the excesses in Imelda's closets, have not incorporated Ty-Casper's fictional renditions.

While Leonard Casper's more in-depth studies situate Ty-Casper's writing within a larger tradition of Philippine writing, Asian American literary criticism remains virtually silent about Ty-Casper's fiction. In part, the paucity of attention can be attributed to the difficulty in obtaining in the United States her early Philippine-published pieces. But this is not sufficient explanation. An unpacking of Asian American criticism's heavy concentration on American nativity and narratives of Asian immigration and settlement within the boundaries of the United States' fifty states might shed more light on Ty-Casper's absence from the Asian American cultural critical scene. Future critical studies of Ty-Casper will necessarily enlarge the scope of Asian American cultural criticism, through contention with the United States' (neo)colonial role in Philippine history and revision of the notion that Asian American stories are written only by and about Asians in the United States.

BIBLIOGRAPHY

Works by Linda Ty-Casper

Novels/Novellas

The Peninsulars. Manila: Bookmark, 1964.
The Three-Cornered Sun. Quezon City, Philippines: New Day, 1979.
Dread Empire. Hong Kong: Heinemann, 1980.
Hazards of Distance. Quezon City, Philippines: New Day, 1981.
Awaiting Trespass (A Pasión). New York and London: Readers International, 1985.
Fortress in the Plaza. Quezon City, Philippines: New Day, 1985.
Wings of Stone. New York and London: Readers International, 1986.
Ten Thousand Seeds. Quezon City, Philippines: Ateneo de Manila University Press, 1987.
A Small Party in a Garden. Philippines: New Day, 1988.
DreamEden. Quezon City, Philippines: Ateneo de Manila University Press, 1996; Seattle: University of Washington Press 1997.

Short Stories

The Transparent Sun and Other Stories. Manila: Alberto Florentino, 1963.
"The Outside Heart." 1968. In *Songs of Ourselves: Writings by Filipino Women in English*. Ed. Edna Zapanta Manlapaz. Manila: Anvil, 1994. 87–97.
The Secret Runner and Other Stories. Manila: Alberto Florentino, 1974.
"A Swarm of Sun." 1980. In *Fiction by Filipinos in America*. Ed. Cecilia Manguerra Brainard. Quezon City, Philippines: New Day, 1993. 10–21.
"Hills, Sky and Longing." In *Home to Stay: Asian American Women's Fiction*. Ed. Sylvia

Watanabe and Carol Bruchac. Greenfield Center, NY: Greenfield Review Press, 1990. 22–31.

Common Continent Selected Stories. Manila: Ateneo de Manila University Press, 1991.

Studies of Linda Ty-Casper

Bloom, Harold, ed. *Asian American Women Writers.* Women Writers of English and Their Work. Philadelphia: Chelsea House, 1997. 98–109.

Bresnahan, Roger J. *Angles of Vision: Conversations on Philippine Literature.* Quezon City: New Day, 1992.

Campomanes, Oscar V. "Filipinos in the United States and Their Literature of Exile." In *Reading the Literatures of Asian America.* Ed. Shirley Geok-lin Lim and Amy Ling. Philadelphia: Temple University Press, 1992. 49–78.

———. "Linda Ty-Casper." In *Oxford Companion to Women's Writing in the United States.* Ed. Cathy N. Davidson, Linda Wagner-Martin, and Elizabeth Ammons. New York: Oxford University Press, 1995. 889.

Casper, Leonard. *New Writing from the Philippines: A Critique and Anthology.* Syracuse, NY: Syracuse University Press, 1966. 134–37.

———. *The Opposing Thumb: Decoding Literature of the Marcos Regime.* Quezon City, Philippines: Giraffe Books, 1995. 31–32, 45–46.

———. "The Opposing Thumb: Recent Philippines Literature in English." *Pacific Affairs* 56.2 (1983): 301–309.

Contemporary Authors, New Revision Series (1997), 54: 448–50.

Crown, Bonnie R. Rev. of *Dread Empire. World Literature Today* 57 (1983): 351.

De Manuel, Dolores. " 'Across That Ocean Is . . . ': Trans-Oceanic Revaluations of Marriage in Filipino American Fiction." In *Privileging Positions: The Sites of Asian American Studies.* Ed. Gary Y. Okihiro et al. Pullman: Washington State University Press, 1995. 193–200.

Dietrich, Jeff. Rev. of *Awaiting Trespass (A Pasión). Los Angeles Times Book Review* (February 2, 1986): 2.

Fein, Cheri. Rev. of *Awaiting Trespass (A Pasión). New York Times Book Review* (October 27, 1985, late ed.): 40.

Fernandez, Doreen G. Rev. of *Wings of Stone. World Literature Today* 61.2 (1987): 352.

Galdon, Joseph A. Rev. of *Awaiting Trespass (A Pasión). World Literature Today* 61.1 (1987): 160–61.

———. Rev. of *Ten Thousand Seeds. World Literature Today* 62.2 (1988): 337.

Gilbert, Celia. "Transforming Fact into Fiction." *The Women's Review of Books* 3.10 (1986): 8.

Howard, Maureen. "Semi-Samizdat and Other Matters." Rev. of *Awaiting Trespass (A Pasión). Yale Review* 77.2 (1988): 243–58.

Ingoldby, Grace. "Putting on the Style." Rev. of *Awaiting Trespass (A Pasión). New Statesman* (October 18, 1985): 28–29.

Kearns, George. "Revolutionary Women and Others." Rev. of *Awaiting Trespass (A Pasión). The Hudson Review* 39 (1986): 123–34.

Knowlton, Edgar C. Rev. of *The Hazards of Distance. World Literature Today* 56 (1982): 756.

Lewis, L. M. Rev. of *Awaiting Trespass (A Pasión). Library Journal* (October 15, 1985): 104.

Lim, Jaime An. "The Three-Cornered Sun: Portraits of the Revolutionary." *Philippine Studies* 40.2 (1992): 255–66.

Martinez-Sicat, Maria Teresa. "The Exceptional Son in Linda Ty-Casper's *The Three-Cornered Sun*." In *Imagining the Nation in Four Philippine Novels*. Quezon City, Philippines: University of Philippines Press, 1994. 70–91.

Rosca, Ninotchka. Rev. of *The Three-Cornered Sun*. *Journal of Asian Studies* 40.4 (1981): 859–61.

Scott, Suzanne, and Lynne M. Constantine. "Belles Lettres Interview" with Linda Ty-Casper. *Belles Lettres* 2.5 (1987): 5, 15.

Sharrad, Paul. Rev. of *Common Continent: Selected Stories*. *World Literature Today* 67 (1993): 904.

Rev. of *Awaiting Trespass (A Pasión)*. *Booklist* (December 1, 1985): 532.

Rev. of *Awaiting Trespass (A Pasión)*. *Publishers Weekly* 228 (1985): 418.

Rev. of *Wings of Stone*. *Kirkus Reviews* 54 (September 15, 1986): 1402–3.

Rev. of *Wings of Stone*. *Publishers Weekly* 230 (1986): 82.

Holly Uyemoto
(1970–   )

Suzanne Hotte Massa

BIOGRAPHY

Holly Uyemoto, a fourth-generation Japanese American and an only child, was born on December 23, 1970, in Ithaca, New York. Her family moved to Kansas when she was seven and California when she was eight. Like many conventional teenagers, Uyemoto did not enjoy going to school. But Uyemoto was an unconventional teenager because, by the age of thirteen, she was writing seriously. Believing that she could write a book, she dropped out of high school during her junior year, when she was fifteen, to work on her novel. Her parents supported her decision and encouraged her to work toward her goal. She completed *Rebel without a Clue*, and it was published when Uyemoto was nineteen. Having proved to her parents and herself that she could successfully complete and publish a novel, Uyemoto went on to write a second novel, *Go*. Both novels are told from a teenager's perspective that seems to reflect Uyemoto's life. However, she claims that neither novel is autobiographical.

As an adult, Uyemoto returned to school at Wellesley College in Massachusetts, where she continues to write and observe. Being in a youthful environment gives her a fresh perspective that she finds useful for her writing. (Personal communication, February 28, 1999).

MAJOR WORKS AND THEMES

In both novels, Uyemoto focuses on the difficult rites of passage for contemporary youths. Uyemoto's strengths are sarcastic witticisms and realistic characterizations. The struggles her characters face are familiar; their candid dialogue is amusing. Her perspective is fresh, idealistic, and bold.

Rebel without a Clue is a coming-of-age novel as well as a morality tale that pits the allure of money and fame against unavoidable mortality. It is an AIDS story narrated by Christian Delon, who has just graduated from high school. He and his friends are enjoying their last summer of leisure before embarking on the next, and more responsible, stage of their lives. Christian, an only child, is usually home alone. His father visits the family home on occasion but makes his real home with his male lover. Christian's mom is also an absentee parent. Sometimes she is in a mental hospital; sometimes she is visiting friends; and other times she is hiding in her room, unable to face the simple day-to-day realities of life. Christian's closest friend is Thomas Bainbridge, whose sole virtue, physical beauty, helped him to launch a magnificently successful modeling and acting career. Thomas' life offstage, however, is far from perfect: he lacks depth of character; he has a problematic relationship with his father and an unhealthy relationship with his gorgeous, but loving, mother; and he is an AIDS victim. *Rebel without a Clue* is a timepiece of the generation that came of age in America in the 1980s. Christian and Thomas are facing the horror that defined their generation: AIDS. Young people have always had to face and overcome misery in order to mature. So the psychology of the young man who has to watch his close friend die before his eyes is familiar, yet new. In stark contrast to Thomas' mortality, each chapter begins with some media hype that glorifies and immortalizes Thomas.

Psychologically, these characters' problems can be easily diagnosed, but they are tragic nonetheless. They spend their money on drugs; they live in exquisite homes in an exclusive neighborhood and drive expensive cars; and they exist without rules or direction. Even Christian describes the people in his neighborhood as "a motley assortment" (33). They range from Stanford hopefuls to parent-killers. Christian, impatient with moral aberrations, considers his associates "pitiful, [but] not pitiable" (33). Uyemoto implies that irresponsible behavior is not excusable regardless of the circumstances. Even though these children are only one item on their parents' long list of material possessions, they are responsible for their own moral integrity.

Because the parents of these young adults are successful economically but dismal failures emotionally and psychologically, their children form surrogate families among their peers. The bond between Christian and Thomas is especially strong. By using flashbacks, Uyemoto familiarizes us with their importance to each other. Despite the economic privilege they enjoy, these boys are love-starved. Christian believes that Thomas satisfies that hunger for him. Thomas, on the other hand, is still searching for a satisfying love.

Although the issue of Thomas' sexuality is never directly addressed, Uyemoto plants frequent clues to his ambivalence. The question of his sexual identity has plagued his existence for quite some time. One day, after Thomas has told Adrian that he has AIDS, Thomas reminds him about the time when they saw *Peter Pan* together as youngsters: " 'If you believed in fairies, you clapped your hands and you saved Tinkerbell's life.' He glanced at me fleetingly, out of the barest corner of his eye. 'I guess that's all it takes to save a life in Never Never Land, huh?' " (84). As young men, they have both realized that the real world is not never-never land. But, also, it becomes evident that the issue of his own sexuality has caused confusion for Thomas for a long time.

As Thomas' physical beauty begins to fade, he realizes that he is losing his grip on life. Without his looks, Thomas is nothing. Uyemoto uses an interesting metaphor to express the gradual dissolution of Thomas' life: "He [Thomas] was watching himself on the screen with bored resignation and writing two- and three-letter words in smoke from the end of his cigarette, works like AT and DOG and JAR that retained their shape for a fraction of a second before dissipating lazily" (157). The smoke rings dissipated lazily, just as Thomas was dissipating, underscoring the brevity of his own life.

When Christian follows Thomas on location for his new movie, Christian gradually loses faith in Thomas' ability to be a caring human being. Thomas' reckless disregard not only for his own life but also for the lives of his uninformed sex partners is more than Christian can bear. Christian accidentally stumbles on Thomas having unprotected sex with a woman. Because Thomas is in denial about his condition, he behaves irresponsibly. Thomas' irresponsibility, ultimately, pushes Christian away, allowing him to begin his own life. There is poignant irony in the fact that Christian's life begins anew as Thomas' begins to end. Christian leaves never-never Land, while Thomas dives further into its depths.

Go is also the story about a young person's rite of passage. The title comes from a Japanese board game, which is profoundly symbolic in both positive and negative ways for Wil's extended family. Her story is complex. It explains how the various influences on her life conflict and send her into a tailspin. She has recently graduated from a university she calls Politically Correct University (PCU). Following the breakup with her boyfriend—a relationship we later discover was unfulfilling, unhealthy, and doomed to fail—Wil succumbs to the pressures that threaten her emotional stability and lands in a mental hospital. We meet Wil as she is being released. Upon reflection, she comments on the two institutions in her life: "The principal difference between the two [institutions] is that I far preferred the hospital, there were fewer drugs and fewer irritating people, and everybody wore wristbands instead of armbands" (11). Her observation reveals her troubled life and her grim outlook.

Her eccentric family, though it seems dysfunctional, provides a support system for Wil's recovery and maturation. She holds her grandparents in the highest esteem. Ojiichan, her chain-smoking grandfather, constantly told stories from his "great wicker throne" (3). Her grandmother—whose name is not mentioned—was a tireless gardener, very closely connected to the rhythms of nature. She is the person from whom Wil is most readily willing to learn and understand her heritage. Their children (Wil's mother and uncles) do not share Wil's positive opinion of their parents. As Wil's story unfolds, justification for their opinions becomes evident. Although all members of her extended family play significant roles in her life, the dominant conflict in Wil's life is the troublesome relationship with her mother, who is deeply ambivalent toward her ethnicity. It seems as though her mother is caught between cultures and, therefore, identities.

Wil comes from a family of storytellers, so it is appropriate that she tells her own story of how she learned to cope in the world, celebrate her cultural inheritance, and forge a relationship with her mother. The family uses stories to teach lessons about everything and sometimes to hide the truth. One story teaches the importance of obedience. In Wil's family, it is especially important for daughters to be obedient. So Wil's grandmother tells her what happens to a disobedient daughter (like Wil):

The mother got sick and was on her deathbed. Thinking to outwit the girl, she said, "Please bury me by the riverbank." She actually wanted to be buried in the fields, but thought her daughter would act in the opposite way as usual.

The girl, however, honored the mother's wishes, and buried her beside the river, which flooded the next year and washed the mother's grave away. The girl, so contrary and disobedient, was crushed flat beneath a falling rock. My mother often pointed her out to me, a flat stone frog that had once been a disobedient daughter. Actually, Ojiichan found the rock shaped like a frog in the Sierra Mountains, and brought it home to showcase in the garden, whereupon my grandmother provided the story for it. (80–81)

Learning obedience is a real struggle for Wil, because she and her mother—like most mothers and daughters—see the world differently. But Wil's relationship with her mother is crucial to her own well-being. Gradually, she begins to notice admirable traits in her mother. She also gains an understanding of her relatives, and that helps her to accept and appreciate them. By her twenty-first birthday (the last chapter), Wil seems to become rather comfortable with her dual inheritance as a Japanese American.

Uyemoto's blend of pertinent, timeless issues and humor makes both of her novels worth reading. They are especially relevant to the lives of those who came of age during the closing decades of the twentieth century.

CRITICAL RECEPTION

While reviews of both novels abound, there are no critical articles on either text. Reception of *Rebel without a Clue* was mixed. Not surprisingly, much attention was paid to Uyemoto's age. Sally Estes, in a review for *Booklist*, wrote that Uyemoto's book had "the authentic ring of youth." On the other hand, *Publishers Weekly*'s anonymous reviewer felt that Uyemoto's first book was too weak to "evoke much interest or emotion." Nonetheless, the book is quite relevant for young readers as well as those interested in young adult fiction. When *Go* was published, the reviews were much more favorable. Mary Ellen Sullivan wrote in *Booklist* that "Uyemoto has a real love of words, and she fills her second novel with word play, puns, and double entendres. Fortunately, the protagonist she has created is the perfect vehicle for her young, confident, and witty voice" (992).

Both Estes and Sullivan accurately describe Uyemoto's strengths. Indeed, Uyemoto's novels deserve attention for their compelling representations of certain aspects of contemporary American life.

BIBLIOGRAPHY

Works by Holly Uyemoto

Novels

Rebel without a Clue. New York: Crown, 1989.
Go. New York: Dutton, 1995.

Studies of Holly Uyemoto

Abe, Patricia. Rev. of *Go*. *Ms*. 5 (January/February 1995): 71.
Estes, Sally. Rev. of *Rebel without a Clue*. *Booklist* 86 (September 15, 1989): 146.
Hanes, Margaret. Rev. of *Go*. *Library Journal* 120 (January 1995): 139.
Monks, Merri, Rev. of *Go*. "Adult Books for Young Adults." *Booklist* 91 (February 1, 1995): 996.
Rees, Douglas. Rev. of *Rebel without a Clue*. "The Booktalker." *Wilson Library Bulletin* 64 (March 1990): 12.
Rev. of *Go*. *Kirkus Reviews* 62 (December 1, 1994): 1572.
Rev. of *Go*. *Los Angeles Times Book Review* (February 19, 1995): 2+.
Rev. of *Go*. *Publishers Weekly* 242 (January 9, 1995): 57.
Rev. of *Rebel without a Clue*. *Kirkus Reviews* 57 (July 15, 1989): 1033.
Rev. of *Rebel without a Clue*. *New York Times Book Review* (December 10, 1989): 32.
Rev. of *Rebel without a Clue*. *Publishers Weekly* 236 (August 4, 1989): 82.
Rev. of *Rebel without a Clue*. *Voice of Youth Advocates* 18 (October 1995): 210.
Rev. of *Rebel without a Clue*. *Wall Street Journal* 214 (August 30, 1989): A8.
Rev. of *Rebel without a Clue*. *Wall Street Journal* 225 (February 14, 1995): A20.
Rev. of *Rebel without a Clue*. *West Coast Review of Books* 15 (February 1989): 15.
Sullivan, Mary Ellen. Rev. of *Go*. *Booklist* 91 (February 1, 1995): 991–92.

Jade Snow Wong
(1922–   )

Leela Kapai

BIOGRAPHY

Jade Snow Wong was born in San Francisco on January 21, 1922. Her father had come from southern Canton, China, in 1903, initially with the intent of returning to his homeland. However, gradually he was able to set up a small-scale sewing factory in Chinatown and, despite harsh laws against the Asian immigrants, decided to send for his wife and two daughters. Jade Snow Wong was the fifth among eight children. Since the factory and the living quarters were in the same building in Chinatown, Jade Snow grew up under the watchful eyes of her parents and the close-knit community.

Like all Wong children, Jade Snow received instruction in Chinese language and history at home and then later at the Chinese school. Her days were tightly structured. Regular school work, followed by the Chinese school in the afternoon, in addition to household duties and homework left not an idle moment for her. As a result of this arduous schedule, she became disciplined, proficient in reading and writing Chinese, and aware of her rich heritage.

Jade Snow Wong continued to excel in her studies and lived a sheltered life where the slightest deviation from the norm of a dutiful daughter was unacceptable. "Respect and order—these were the key words of life," she wrote in *Fifth Chinese Daughter* (2). When she desired to continue her education after high school, she was told not to expect any financial assistance from her father, for he intended to use his limited funds on educating his sons, the ones to carry his family name. Disappointed but undaunted, Jade Snow did not give up; she worked and paid her way through the junior college yet could not save enough to finance her university education. Impressed by her ability, earnestness, and determination, one of her employers recommended her to the president of Mills

College in Oakland, whose assistance made it possible for her to earn a B.A. in 1942.

Jade Snow Wong worked as a secretary for the next two years before deciding to turn to writing and pottery-making for her living. It was a daring decision, for not only did the Chinese look down upon all manual work, but they could not envision a Chinese woman succeeding as a writer in the United States. She rented a small space in Chinatown for her pottery work and wrote in her spare time. She won an award for pottery at the California State Fair in 1947, a silver medal for craftsmanship in a *Mademoiselle* competition, and yet another award for enamel work from the California State Fair in 1949. Meanwhile, she was encouraged by her teachers and an editor at Harper's to write her autobiography.

Fifth Chinese Daughter was published in 1950, the same year that she married. Changed attitudes toward the Chinese after World War II contributed to the immediate success of the book and earned her a State Department-sponsored cultural tour of Asian countries. She and her husband managed a successful art gallery and a travel agency. Later on, her continued interest in her ancestral land led to her organizing tourist groups to China as the U.S. attitude toward that country began to thaw. Her second book, *No Chinese Stranger*, a mix of autobiography and an account of her travel to China in 1972, was published in 1975.

MAJOR WORKS AND THEMES

As Jade Snow Wong moved into the world outside her home, she discovered that most people knew little of the Chinese beyond the usual stereotypes. *Fifth Chinese Daughter*, she said, was written "with the purpose of creating better understanding of the Chinese culture on the part of Americans" ("Introduction" vii). She used the third person in writing about her upbringing and cultural conflicts since the Chinese literary form disapproves of using "I." This choice, though somewhat awkward, helped her present personal details objectively.

Fifth Chinese Daughter recounts the "significant episodes" in Jade Snow Wong's first twenty-four years that shaped her life ("Note" xiii). In the first section of *No Chinese Stranger*, published twenty-five years later, she continues the story of her life, again in the third person. Only after the death of her father did she begin using "I" in her autobiography: thus, the second section of the book is aptly entitled "First Person Singular." The third section of the book is a travelogue, an account of her visit to China, a fairly dry account of her impressions of life in China under the communists.

Two themes govern the narrative of her life and accomplishments. The major intent of her autobiography is to show the complexity and humanity of Chinese family life. The candid descriptions of her years of growing up in Chinatown and her parents' strict discipline and philosophy of raising children provide a close look at her family. The other theme is the conflict between the generations, not unusual in itself, but very much complicated when it is between the values of the Old World of the immigrants and those of their American children. When Jade Snow Wong discovers that she is recognized by outsiders for her ability but disparaged by her family, she rebels against her parents' oppressive behavior.

Jade Snow Wong's recounting of the scene when she first stands up for herself in defiance of her parents' commands reveals the extent to which she has been trained in the Confucian values. She wins the battle with her father in a way, but her victory is quite hollow. It is sad to observe her desperate struggle to succeed, never receive any encouragement from her parents, and yet bestow the credit of all her accomplishments on the family patriarch. Jade Snow Wong affirms repeatedly that she always "retained her deep respect for Daddy" (93). Her entire life seems to be an effort to convince her father of her worth. No honor, no victory has any significance for her until it is validated by the "great Father." When *Fifth Chinese Daughter* is a success and is to be translated into Chinese, only then does her father acknowledge the honor she has brought to their ancestors. The two autobiographical sections in *No Chinese Stranger* confirm that she continued to be in awe of her father even after his death.

CRITICAL RECEPTION

Fifth Chinese Daughter received good reviews, in part because, as Amy Ling points out in *Between Worlds*, the relations between China and America were friendly before the communist takeover (119) and in part because Wong's account lent credence to the belief that every immigrant had an equal chance of succeeding. Wong's narrative appealed to readers because it provided them a glimpse into the exotic ways of a traditional Chinese family. Contemporary reviewers admired her ability to capture the conflict between the ancient Chinese values of filial obedience and the New World emphasis on individualism. Considered an "engrossing" story (*The New Yorker*), *Fifth Chinese Daughter* also held wide appeal because it suggested that the minorities could succeed if they tried hard enough. Wong's facility with language also helped. Ernestine Evans observed that "the Chinese American artist in clay is also a craftsman in words." The State Department found the writer to be a perfect emissary to the Asian countries at a time when the racial inequities in the United States were raising doubts about its position as a world power. Her book was translated into Chinese and other languages.

With the resurgence of interest in Asian authors and the rise of feminist criticism, Jade Snow Wong's autobiography has occasionally received a closer scrutiny. Though Maxine Hong Kingston* called her "the Mother of Chinese American literature" (qtd. by Ling 120), she has often been criticized for avoiding any reference to the ill treatment of the Chinese immigrants. However, Elaine Kim explains that Wong was forced to shape her narrative to fit her editors' notion of what would sell (71). *Fifth Chinese Daughter* continues to be in print and remains a popular text for young adults.

BIBLIOGRAPHY

Works by Jade Snow Wong

Fifth Chinese Daughter. New York: Harper, 1950. Reprinted with a new introduction by the author, Seattle: University of Washington Press, 1989.

"Puritans from the Orient." In *The Immigrant Experience: The Anguish of Becoming American*. Ed. and intro. Thomas C. Wheeler. New York: Dial Press, 1971. 107–31.

No Chinese Stranger. New York: Harper and Row, 1975.

Studies of Jade Snow Wong

Blinde, Patricia Lin. "The Icicle in the Desert: Perspective and Form in the Work of Two Chinese-American Women Writers." *MELUS* 6.3 (1979): 51–71.

Evans, Ernestine. "A Chinese American Girl's Two Worlds." *New York Herald Tribune Book Review* (September 24, 1950): 4.

"*Fifth Chinese Daughter*." *The New Yorker* (October 7, 1950): 134.

Kim, Elaine. "*Fifth Chinese Daughter*." In *Asian American Literature: An Introduction to the Writings and Their Social Context*. Philadelphia: Temple University Press, 1982, 66–72.

Ling, Amy. "Jade Snow Wong and Maxine Hong Kingston." In *Between Worlds: Women Writers of Chinese Ancestry*. New York: Pergamon Press, 1990. 119–30.

Shawn Wong
(1949–   )

Chih-Ping Chen

BIOGRAPHY

Son of an engineer father and an artist mother, Shawn Wong was born in Oakland, California, and raised in Berkeley but also spent part of his childhood on the Pacific Islands and the Sierra Nevada Mountains. While studying premed at San Francisco State University, Wong found a mentor in his writing teacher, Kay Boyle, who shared his idea that writing is about belief: "That thing called belief is not only the political and personal, but also the belief that drives you to write. So that at all times in the writing of the novel you want every line, every paragraph to reflect exactly who you are" ("Reflections" 288). To discover other Asian American writers and his own voice soon became the driving force behind Wong's academic pursuits and his career as a novelist. Under Boyle's supervision, he began his first novel, *Homebase*. He also changed his major to English and finished his undergraduate study at the University of California (UC) Berkeley. He went back to San Francisco State University to work with Boyle and received a master's in creative writing in 1974. His thesis was an earlier version of *Homebase*.

Like many Asian American writers, Wong had difficulty finding publishers for this debut novel (1979), a fictionalized autobiographical novel about a young Chinese American's quest for self-knowledge. First issued by a small press run by the African American novelist and Berkeley professor Ishmael Reed, it immediately won both the 1980 Pacific Northwest Booksellers' Award and Washington State Governor's Writers Day Award. This recognition was followed by a National Endowment for the Arts Creative Fellowship in 1981. Believed to be only the third novel ever published by a Chinese American in the United States, it was reissued by mainstream publisher Plume in 1991. Wong's second novel, *American Knees*, centering on a middle-aged Chinese American's dilemma about interracial relationships, appeared in 1995. Both novels have also been translated and published in Germany.

Wong has been one of the pioneer figures in defining Asian American literature as a literary tradition and introducing Asian American literature to American readers. With writers Jeffrey Paul Chan, Frank Chin,* and Lawson Fusao, he cofounded the Combined Asian-American Resources Project (CARP) to search for, and revive, works by other members of their community. They organized the first Asian American writers' conference in 1975 and collaborated on two anthologies of Asian American literature, *Aiiieeeee!* (1974) and *The Big Aiiieeeee!* (1991). *Aiiieeeee!* included sampling works by Chinese American, Japanese American, and Filipino American writers. In their Preface to *Aiiieeeee!*, the editors explained the title to be an angry exclamation of "Asian America, so long ignored and forcibly excluded from creative participation in American culture. . . . It is fifty years of our whole voice" (viii). The anthology was much acclaimed as a landmark collection and considered by Jessica Hagedorn,* editor of *Charlie Chan Is Dead*, to be a breakthrough collection giving Asian American writers visibility and credibility (xxvi). The more ambitious *The Big Aiiieeeee!* featured works by twenty-eight Chinese American and Japanese American writers. To both these two anthologies, Wong contributed excerpts of *Homebase*. He also coedited a special issue of Asian American prose work for *Yardbird Reader* (1975). In 1996 Wong edited his own anthology, *Asian American Literature: A Brief Introduction and Anthology*.

At the age of twenty-two Wong began teaching an Asian American course at Mills College, a private women's school in Oakland. He has also taught courses on Asian American literature and history at the University of California at Santa Cruz and San Francisco State University. He became an assistant professor in the American Ethnic Studies Department in 1984, then the director of the Creative Writing Program in 1995 at the University of Washington. He has been the chairman of the English Department since 1997. Currently, he is adapting *American Knees* into a screenplay and turning his essay " 'I Miss the Person I Love Every Day' " into a nonfiction book. It is a memorial for his wife, Vicki Tsuchida, who died in 1997. Wong has also published poetry, essays, and reviews in periodicals and anthologies. He has been active in Seattle's art community, serving as Chairman of the Seattle Arts Committee, coordinator of Seattle's Bumbershoot Festival Commission, and consultant for public arts agencies, including National Endowment for the Arts. His other pursuits include professional drag racing; he won in the National Hot Rod Association Northern Pacific Division finals in 1984.

MAJOR WORKS AND THEMES

Wong sees both of his novels as basically love stories: "*American Knees* is a contemporary love story between a biracial Japanese and Irish woman and a

Chinese American man and *Homebase* is a story about a son's love for his mother and father" ("Reflections" 289). Yet for Wong's male protagonists, love and realizing their heritage are interconnected. The question "What are you?" ("Reflections" 295) haunts his major characters. Ethnic identity is more than a category established by birth. Meaning and justification of it require a quest of the mind. In the Introduction to *Asian American Literature: A Brief Introduction and Anthology*, Wong suggests that the boundaries of Asian American landscape begin "somewhere near a familiar stereotype and end with the truth being told in hidden corners of history. . . . Part of the story is heroic, legendary, and mythic, the other and more familiar part of the story is a media stereotype of fantasy, foolishness, and fakery" (1). In his novels, Wong makes it an essential task for his protagonists to explore the boundaries.

In *Homebase*, the narrator, Rainsford Chan, a fourth-generation Chinese American growing up in the 1950s, defines his orphan status at fifteen in both personal and ethnic terms: "My mother died eight years after my father and it was then that I realized I was my great-grandfather's. . . . My great-grandfather had begun a tradition of orphaned men in this country and now I realized I was the direct descendant of that original fatherless and motherless immigrant" (7). Named after the town his great-grandfather first settled in but which does not exist anymore, Rainsford embarks on a journey, both physical and symbolic, to uncover the erased and forgotten past of the Chan's men. Rainsford's narrative weaves together real and imagined letters, essays, poetry, dialogues, journal entries, and fictionalized scenes from different times, places, and people to give voice to the "hidden corners" of Asian American history, such as the building of the Pacific Railroad over the Sierra Nevada Mountains, the Exclusion Acts, the detention on Angel Island, and life in Chinatown.

Cultural stereotyping is presented as twofold—imposed by the culture and self-inflicted. The mainstream, like Rainsford's white coach in high school and the students he meets in college, marginalizes him because of his Asian body. Rainsford internalizes these constructs in his desire for false success, like his fantasy to capture America by uniting with a blondhaired dream bride. Affirmation of his ethnic identity finally comes from embracing his parents and his forefathers for who they are in spite of his personal anger and loss about his parents' early deaths and his loneliness. As the end of the novel suggests, Rainsford's dual-natured heritage has to be repossessed through reinterpretation. He must reclaim the spirits and legends of the Chinese immigrants embedded in the American landscape—"I take myths to name this country's canyons, dry riverbeds, mountains, after my father, grandfather, and great-grandfather" (95)— to mark the present, his "home base."

American Knees takes a more ironic look at the ethnic self. Wong's protagonist has aged, as the writer has aged, but the problems of identity and consequences of stereotyping do not become less agonizing. Set in present-day Los Angeles and the San Francisco Bay Area, the novel centers on Raymond Ding, a forty-year-old assistant director of minority affairs at a community college.

The title refers to a school-yard jeer that haunts Raymond—"What are you—Chinese, Japanese, or American Knees?" (12). Picturing himself as "some kind of cultural flight attendant" (119), Raymond struggles to define and articulate the dilemma between cultural consciousness and internalized racism. He marries into a big Chinese family to prove that he is a "good Chinese son" (15), only to lose his free will under the family patriarchy. Divorced, he falls in love with, and then drifts away from, his half-Irish, half-Japanese girlfriend Aurora because she is not culturally sensitive enough: "She needed to know the exact definitions of race and ethnicity, the history of the struggle, the symbols of institutionalized racism" (53). Yet he is, in turn, considered by his Vietnamese immigrant colleague and second lover as not Asian enough to share her history of abuse and abandonment.

The novel gives the reader a spectrum of educated Asian Americans, from new immigrants to long-settled professionals, who frequently feel culturally stereotyped and the lack of a sense of belonging to the larger community. Raymond's reunion with his girlfriend suggests a hope for intimacy through love, but his yearning for self-realization remains: "He wishes he could mark his life at each of these points so that he could come back later with the memory and the knowledge of how to occupy the heart in order to find solutions, discover a sense of place, reach home, explain his love" (240). The yearning, shared by all Asian American characters, echoes the desire for a "home base" in the first novel.

CRITICAL RECEPTION

Both of Wong's novels have received scant critical attention. Although generally praised for their concerns for ethnic subjectivity, they are not singled out as exceptional. *Homebase* is reviewed mostly as short paragraphs in newspapers and discussed in connection with other novels in journal articles. Most critics focus on the significance of the themes of identity and stereotype. Elaine H. Kim, for example, asserts that *Homebase* gives "a triumphant reaffirmation of the Chinese American heritage" (194). In his essay "Decolonizing America," A. Robert Lee compares *Homebase* with works that "write into American history Asian pasts seemingly all too colonized by a one-standard, western present," but he also praises Wong's experiment of style, calling the novel "lyric, spare, a deeply moving collage of memory and fact" that "typifies the process to perfection" (281). Focusing more deeply on the novel, Bill Brown connects Rainsford's Charlie McCarthy puppet to the material world in postwar America. He notes that Rainsford's ventriloquist acts of learning Chinese through the puppet offer the reader "a basic lesson in how, despite the mass-cultural homogenization of America in the 1950s, some products, significantly recoded, could become the ground from which to express ethnic individuation" (938). Patricia A. Sakurai, in her essay "The Politics of Possession," discusses the polarized significations of the female figures—the blond dream bride represents the fantasy of racial integration but also " 'negative' symbol of racism and exclusion" (163), while a Chinese American woman in Wisconsin to whom Rainsford wants to return represent a " 'positive' symbol of his finding place and home in America" (163). Race seems only male in *Homebase*. Women like the dream bride, the Wisconsin woman, and even Rainsford's mother are used as projections of his desires and to signify historical collective identity for him.

American Knees is reviewed mostly in trade journals and newspapers. Reviewers have generally positive things to say about the novel's continued exploration of ethnic issues. Charles Solomon, for example, describes the novel as a "black comedy of intercultural manners" that "attests to Wong's growing skill as a writer." Yet reviewers also give mixed comments about Wong's frequent uses of dialogue and monologues as narrative devices. Richard Potsubay in *St. Petersburg Times*, for example, critiques the dialogue for its "tendency to become bogged down with whiny, overanalytical yuppiespeak," but he also praises Wong for his colorful assortment of minor characters. Chuah Guat Eng in *New Straits Times* faults Wong for choosing to "air his concerns through interior monologues, anecdotes, and witty dialogues, rather than . . . explor[ing] them through action, plot and characterisation." On the other hand, David Wong Louie argues that the excessive talking is effective in overturning the stereotypes of silent and repressed Asians and also has a definite purpose in emphasizing the protagonist's struggle: "It's noise that distracts Raymond from his true desires."

Kris Radish seems a bit harsh in his view of *American Knees*: "It's unlikely that Wong's book will go down in history as a classic of any sort but it's a sometimes fun work that offers some interesting cultural insights." Richard Potsubay believes that Wong's distinctive strength as a writer is his "gift for tackling very complex issues without jeopardizing the accessibility of his style or the flow of the story"—issues of ethnic representation, interracial relations, gender differences, and generational concerns. For Wong, Asian American integration and identity remain problematic in spite of political and cultural changes, which he probes with good humor but also serious self-reflection. Wong is at his best examining and satirizing racial assumptions made by both mainstream and "politically correct" minority communities. His updated portraits of Asian Americans invite both criticism and self-criticism of racial sensitivities. An admiring reader would find Wong's novels, as David Wong Louie notes, "a welcome antidote to the mawkish popular fiction passed off as Asian American nowadays."

BIBLIOGRAPHY

Works by Shawn Wong

Novels

Homebase: A Novel. New York: I. Reed Books, 1979; New York: Plume, 1991.
American Knees. New York: Simon and Schuster, 1995.

Excerpts in Anthologies

from *Homebase*. "Good Luck, Happiness, and Long Life." In *Counterpoint: Perspectives on Asian America*. Ed. Emma Gee. Los Angeles: Asian American Studies Center, University of California, 1976. 464–70.

from *Homebase*. *Growing up Asian American: An Anthology*. Ed. Maria Hong. New York: William Morrow, 1993. 327–34.

from *American Knees*. "Eye Contact." In *Charlie Chang Is Dead: An Anthology of Contemporary Asian American Fiction*. Ed. Jessica Hagedorn. New York: Penguin, 1993. 500–527.

from *American Knees*. "Fear of Flying." In *Into the Fire: Asian American Prose*. Ed. Sylvia Watanabe and Carol Bruchac. New York: Greenfield Review Press, 1996. 273–85.

Nonfiction

"Beyond Bruce Lee." *Essence* (November 1993): 64–66.

"Reflections." In *Into the Fire: Asian American Prose*. Ed. Sylvia Watanabe and Carol Bruchac. New York: Greenfield Review Press, 1996. 287–97.

" 'The Chinese Man Has My Ticket.' " In *How We Want to Live: Narratives on Progress*. Ed. Susan Richards Shreve and Porter Shreve. Boston: Beacon Press, 1998. 142–49.

" 'I Miss the Person I Love Every Day.' " In *A Few Thousand Words about Love*. Ed. Mickey Pearlman. New York: St. Martin's Press, 1998. 157–73.

Edited Works

(With Jeffrey Paul Chan, Frank Chin, and Lawson Fusao Inada). *Aiiieeeee!: Anthology of Asian American Writers*. Washington, DC: Howard University Press, 1974.

(With Frank Chin). *Yardbird Reader* 3. Berkeley: Yardbird Publishing Cooperative, 1975.

(With Jeffrey Paul Chan, Frank Chin, and Lawson Fusao Inada). *The Big Aiiieeeee!: An Anthology of Chinese American and Japanese American Literature*. New York: Meridian, 1991.

(With Ishmael Reed and Kathryn Trueblood). *The Before Columbus Foundation Poetry/Fiction Anthology: Selections from the American Book Awards, 1980–1990*. 2 vols. New York: Norton, 1992.

Asian American Literature: A Brief Introduction and Anthology. New York: HarperCollins College, 1996.

Studies of Shawn Wong

Brown, Bill. "How to Do Things with Things (A Toy Story)." *Critical Inquiry* 24 (1998): 935–64.

Chiu, Monica. Rev. of *American Knees*. *MELUS* 22 (1997): 132–34.

Cowan, Peters. "Oakland Born Author Appreciates Heritage." *(Oakland) Tribune*, December 27, 1979, C1.

Eng, Chuah Guat. Rev. of *American Knees*. *New Straits Times*, January 4, 1997, 10.

Kim, Elaine H. "Shawn Hsu Wong." In *Asian American Literature: An Introduction to the Writings and Their Social Context.* Philadelphia: Temple University Press, 1982. 194–97.

Lee, A. Robert. "Decolonizing America: The Ethnicity of Ernest Gains, Josè Antonio Villarreal, Leslie Marmon Silko and Shawn Wong." In *Shades of Empire in Colonial and Post Colonial Literatures.* Ed. C. C. Barfoot and Theo D'haen. Amsterdam: Rodopi, 1993. 269–82.

Liu, Cynthia W. Rev. of *American Knees. Amerasia Journal* 22.2 (1996): 166–69.

Louie, David Wong. Rev. of *American Knees. Los Angeles Times Book Review* (September 10, 1995): 1.

Monaghan, Peter. "Writing Novels, Winning Races." *The Chronicle of Higher Education* (January 26, 1996): A5.

Olshan, Joseph. Rev. of *American Knees. Entertainment Weekly* (August 11, 1995): 48.

Potsubay, Richard. Rev. of *American Knees. St. Petersburg Times*, August 20, 1995, 6D.

Radish, Kris. Rev. of *American Knees. Milwaukee Journal Sentinel*, September 22, 1995, 6.

Rev. of *American Knees. Publishers Weekly* (June 26, 1995): 88.

Rev. of *Homebase. Washington Post Book World* (February 24, 1991): X12.

Sakurai, Patricia A. "The Politics of Possession: The Negotiation of Identity in *American in Disguise, Homebase,* and *Farewell to Manzanar.*" In *Privileging Positions: The Sites of Asian American Studies.* Ed. Gary Y. Okihiro, Marilyn Alquizola, Dorothy Fujita Rony, and K. Scott Wong. Pullman: Washington University Press, 1995. 157–70.

Solomon, Charles. Rev. of *American Knees. Los Angeles Times Book Review* (October 13, 1996): 15.

———. Rev. of *Homebase. Los Angeles Times Book Review* (January 20, 1991): 14.

Vassanji, M. G. "The Postcolonial Writer, Myth Maker and Folk Historian." In *A Meeting of Streams: South Asian Canadian Literature.* Ed. M. G. Vassanji. Toronto: TSAR, 1985. 63–68.

Lois-Ann Yamanaka

(1961–   )

Chih-Ping Chen

BIOGRAPHY

Lois-Ann Yamanaka was born on Molokai and grew up in the Hilo, Kau, and Kona districts of Hawaii. The towns she has lived in provide the settings for her fiction, and her father, a taxidermist, is the model for the father figures in her novels. A third-generation Japanese American, Yamanaka considers Hawaiian plantation culture, to which her parents belong, an important legacy. She graduated from the University of Hawaii at Manoa with a master's degree in education and became a teacher in Hawaii's public school system. Impressed by how writing helped her "at-risk" students to release emotions, she began taking writing classes at the University of Hawaii. Her teacher Faye Kicknosway encouraged her to write in her first language, pidgin. Formally known as the Hawaiian Creole English, this dialect has been considered substandard by the government, and schoolchildren, like Yamanaka, were discouraged from using it in the classroom. The liberating process of rediscovering her mother tongue soon led to this commitment: "I am devoted to telling stories the way I have experienced them—cultural identity and linguistic identity being skin and flesh to my body" (Shea 32).

Yamanaka's pidgin poems first appeared in various literary journals and anthologies and were collected into *Saturday Night at the Pahala Theatre*, a four-part verse novella focusing on, and narrated by, working-class Hawaiian teenagers. Upon publication in 1993, the book won a flurry of awards, including the Pushcart Prize, Elliot Cades Award for Literature, and Association for Asian American Studies Literature Award, and Yamanaka also received grants from the Carnegie Foundation and the National Endowment for the Arts. This debut work was followed by three novels that are loosely based on her adolescent experiences and her family history. The first novel, *Wild Meat and Bully Burgers*, inspired by Chicana writer Sandra Cisneros' story collection *The House on the Mango Street*, appeared in 1996. This is probably her most autobiographical. In a series of prose-poetry vignettes, the book chronicles the coming-of-age of a Japanese American girl living in the blue-collar Hilo community in the 1970s. *Blu's Hanging*, published in 1997, traces the adolescent struggles for self-esteem and emotional intimacy in three siblings after their mother's death. In her most recent work, *Heads by Harry*, a college student struggling with poor grades, alcohol, and drug addiction tries to regain control of her life through her passion for the art of taxidermy, her father's business.

Controversy followed Yamanaka upon publication of her first work, *Saturday Night at the Pahala Theatre*. Members of the Filipino American Caucus have continuously protested against the negative portrayal of Filipino Americans in her poetry and first two novels, especially the portrayal of Uncle Paulo as a rapist in *Blu's Hanging*. Asian American writers, including high-profile writers like Maxine Hong Kingston,* Amy Tan,* and Jessica Hagedorn,* have defended her artistic freedom. Amid the debate, Yamanaka has stood firm in her responsibility as a writer: "I am writing my truth, and we all live our individual truth" (Shea 35). Now thirty-seven, Yamanaka lives with her husband, John Inferrera, a high school health and physical education teacher, and their son, John, in Kalihi Valley, Honolulu. She is currently working on a new novel on the father–daughter relationship, a theme that has driven all her novels so far.

MAJOR WORKS AND THEMES

Centering around the emerging consciousness of female identity, Yamanaka's novels point to issues of sexuality, race, gender, class, culture, and the effects of colonialism on the islands' ethnic communities. Her heroines' insecurities are underlined by self-hatred, which Yamanaka finds prevalent in the descendants of Asian immigrants like her: "We were inundated with white images: it was agonizing the things we did as girls to makes ourselves fit in. We longed to marry someone with a white name so we could change our names. We glued and disfigured our eyes to make them resemble the eyes of white girls" (qtd. in *Publishers Weekly*, August 21, 1995). In *Wild Meat and the Bully Burgers*, the heroine, Lovey Nariyoshi, echoes such haole (Caucasian) yearning for blond ringlets and round, Shirley Temple eyes. She also fantasizes having a white husband: "Lovey Beth Cole. Mrs. Michael Cole. Wanna marry you, Dennis. Be a Cole. Be a Haole. A Japanese [*sic*] with a haole last name" (29). School becomes a place of humiliation for pidgin-speaking students, who are labeled as low-class and dumb by haole teachers.

Family is a symbol of shelter and comfort in Yamanaka's segregated community, but parents sometimes fail to protect and guide their children because they are burdened by their own pain or financial difficulties. The father in *Blu's Hanging*, for example, cannot overcome the shame of leprosy to help his children deal with the loss of their mother, leaving thirteen-year-old Ivah responsible for her brother and sister. Family ties in the novels are almost always problematic. Communication and intimacy never come easily between parent and child or between brother and sister. Yamanaka's characters usually have to fight through disappointments and pain to bridge differences or to reach compromises. Women more than men are generally the more successful protectors and nurtures. This is especially true in *Blu's Hanging*, where Ivah saves her brother, Blu, from physical and sexual abuse, and her teacher, Miss Ito, helps her sister, Maisie, struck speechless by bereavement, to speak again. Even the dead mother returns in spirit form to comfort their children in their moments of despair.

Another trial in Yamanaka's heroine's journey toward self-assertion and intimacy is sexuality. While in the first two novels, sexuality is almost always connected to male abuse and serves as a reminder of female vulnerability, in *Heads by Harry*, Yamanaka explores women's sexual experiences as means for acquiring power over men and self-confidence within themselves. Under the shadow of her pretty sister, the heroine, Toni Yagyuu, lets herself be seduced by two men she is attracted to but does not really love. Although the unexpected pregnancy brings shame to her family, it also surprisingly gives her the opportunity to dominate the two men by claiming both as fathers to her child.

Taken as a whole, Yamanaka's works are both female bildungsroman and cultural documents. Written in a poetic style, her novels include the insights of a sociologist in presenting a portrait of the islands, which is one of healing the wound of the past and present. Though a sense of belonging seems to be forever beyond the reach of her Asian American characters, they never stop striving for it. In the same spirit, Yamanaka's aim is to portray Hawaiian life in a poignant, but unsentimental, picture with a native Hawaiian pen without the distortion of mainstream media or prejudices. As the author declares, "It's nice now that we have ownership of our own stories" (Valerie Takahama).

CRITICAL RECEPTION

Yamanaka's novels are reviewed mostly in literary and trade journals, mainstream magazines, and newspapers. In general, reviewers enthusiastically praised her authentic voice and her poetic style. Commenting on Yamanaka's presentation of Hawaiian life, Diana Davenport, in *The Women's Review of Books*, describes *Wild Meat and the Bully Burgers* as "full of the authentic sights and smells of childhood in Hawaii," and the stories are "funny, poignant, scathingly authentic and often stabbingly beautiful" (37). The reviewer in *Publishers Weekly* notes the cultural significance of such presentation in *Heads by Harry*, asserting that in that book "the potency and honesty of Yamanaka's view of Hawaiian life achieves [*sic*] the haunting force of myth." Lauren Belfer in *New York Times Book Review* critiques the colloquial text of *Wild Meat and the Bully Burgers* for lacking subtlety of plot and character but praises her style: "Yamanaka delivers moments of stinging clarity, creating haunting images as she sketches Lovey's search for a spiritual home." On Yamanaka's style, Sandy M. Fernandez calls her writing "tough, pungent, vulnerable" and her use of pidgin unconventional and startling in "mixing a ridiculed language with serious and often poignant themes."

Reviewers of *Blu's Hanging* and *Heads by Harry*, in particular, pay attention to the female bildungsroman framework and the narrative skill. Johanna Stoberock in the *Seattle Times* notes that the force and inventiveness of the heroine's voice in *Blu's Hanging* carry the novel. Mindy Pennybacker in *The Nation* locates the strengths of the novel in "its rollicking black comedy and its dead-on pidgin English." Some reviewers of *Heads by Harry* notice especially its vivid details. A reviewer in *Baltimore Sun*, for example, finds the novel "earthly and exotic, occasionally macabre, often sexy." In a concluding note on Yamanaka's narrative, Renee H. Shea asserts that the Hawaiian-bred writer's work has "strong roots in the oral tradition" of storytelling and believes that "it is the honesty of her struggle for an authentic self that makes her work so powerful" (39).

With her brutally honest portraits of Hawaiian people, Yamanaka redefines her culture and reveals the power and poetry of her language. She breaks down the stereotypes of Hawaiians as "exotic" and marginalized natives of the so-called paradise and gives her community a voice that is distinct, dignified, and complex. In defending their award to Yamanaka's *Blu's Hanging*, the Association for Asian American Studies applauded the novel for its "powerful, and unflinching depiction of local cultural politics and the vagaries of Japanese-American childhood" (Shea 34). The same description can be applied to all of Yamanaka's novels so far. In her contribution to the contemporary ethnic literature, Yamanaka complicates the term "Japanese American" by presenting a community whose heritage challenges easy definitions and interpretations.

BIBLIOGRAPHY

Works by Lois-Ann Yamanaka

Novels

Wild Meat and the Bully Burgers. New York: Farrar, Straus, and Giroux, 1996.
Blu's Hanging. New York: Farrar, Straus, and Giroux: 1997.
Heads by Harry. New York: Farrar, Straus, and Giroux: 1999.

Poetry

Saturday Night at the Pahala Theatre. Honolulu, HI: Bamboo Ridge Press, 1993.

Studies of Lois-Ann Yamanaka

Belfer, Lauren. Rev. of *Wild Meat and the Bully Burgers*. *New York Times Book Review* (December 31, 1995, late ed.): sec. 7: 11.

Davenport, Diana. "Cultural Crossroads." *Women's Review of Books* (July 1996): 37–38.

Eder, Richard. Rev. of *Wild Meat and the Bully Burgers*. *Newsday*, January 25, 1996, B06.

Fernandez, Sandy M. "Lois-Ann Yamanaka: Pidgin's Revenge." *Ms. Magazine* (July–August 1996): 85.

Foote, Donna. Rev. of *Blu's Hanging*. *Newsweek* (August 17, 1998): 63.

Harlan, Megan. Rev. of *Blu's Hanging*. *New York Times Book Review* (May 4, 1997): late ed., sec. 7: 21.

James, Jamie. "This Hawaii Is Not for Tourists." *Atlantic Monthly* (February 1999): 90.

Joyce, Alice. Rev. of *Wild Meat and the Bully Burgers*. *Booklist* (December 1, 1995): 611.

Nguyen, Lan N. "Hawaiian Eye-Opener: Talking with Lois-Ann Yamanaka." *People Weekly* (May 26, 1997): 42.

Pennybacker, Mindy. Rev. of *Blu's Hanging*. *The Nation* (July 7, 1997): 33.

Ramsey, Marian. Rev. of *Wild Meat and the Bully Burgers*. *Denver Rocky Mountain News*, June 2, 1996, 31D.

Rev. of *Blu's Hanging*. *Publishers Weekly* (February 24, 1997): 62.

Rev. of *Heads by Harry*. *Baltimore Sun*, February 7, 1999; late ed.: 14F.

Rev. of *Heads by Harry*. *Publishers Weekly* (December 21, 1998): 54.

Rev. of *Wild Meat and the Bully Burgers*. *Publishers Weekly* (October 2, 1995): 51.

Rev. of *Wild Meat and the Bully Burgers*. *Publishers Weekly* (August 21, 1995): 34.

Seo, Diane. "Authentic Characters or Racist Stereotypes?" *Los Angeles Times*, July 23, 1998, E1.

Shea, Renee H. "Pidgin Politics and Paradise Revised." *Poets and Writers* 26.5 (1998): 32–39.

Stoberock, Johanna. Rev. of *Blu's Hanging*. *Seattle Times*, April 20, 1997, M3.

Takahama, Valerie. "Controversial Adventures in Paradise: Bully Burgers and Pidgin." *Orange County Register*, February 15, 1996, E01.

Karen Tei Yamashita
(1951–   )

Douglas Sugano

BIOGRAPHY

Karen Tei Yamashita was born in Oakland, California, in 1951. Her family later moved to the Los Angeles area, where she spent most of her childhood. Yamashita attended Carleton College, where she studied both English and Japanese literatures and graduated Phi Beta Kappa. During her junior year abroad, she studied in Japan at Waseda University.

Following graduation, Yamashita studied Portuguese in an intensive language program, and in 1974 Yamashita was awarded a Thomas J. Watson Fellowship to research Japanese immigration to Brazil, a study that eventually led to her novel *Brazil-Maru*. From 1974 to 1984 Yamashita lived in São Paolo, during which time she married architect/artist Ronaldo Lopes de Oliveira and had two children. While in Brazil, Yamashita turned to creative writing, and in 1975 she won several short story contests. In 1977 Yamashita was awarded a Rockefeller Playwright-in-Residence Fellowship at East West Players in Los Angeles, where her play *Omen: An American Kabuki* premiered. Two years later, Yamashita won first place in the James Clavell American-Japanese Short Story Contest for her short story "Asaka-no-Miya."

In 1984 Yamashita and her family moved to Los Angeles, where she worked at KCET, the local public television station. For fourteen years in Los Angeles she wrote poetry, prose, plays, translations (between Portuguese and Japanese), and screenplays. The year of her return to Los Angeles, East West Players produced a play in progress entitled *Hiroshima Tropical*. Two years later, Yamashita coauthored a screenplay entitled *Kusei: An Endangered Species*. From 1989 to 1996 Yamashita turned to multimedia performances of her own work: *Hannah Kuso: An American Butoh* (performed in 1989 and 1990); *Tokyo Car-*

men vs. L.A. Carmen (1990) at the Mark Taper Forum; a musical entitled *Godzilla Comes to Little Tokyo* (1991) also known as *GiLAwrecks* (1991 and 1992); and *Noh Bozos* (performed in 1993 and 1996 in Los Angeles and Minneapolis). Yamashita has also published electronically with *Circle K: Dekasegi* a series of short stories and journal entries from 1997.

Between 1991 and 1997 Yamashita received considerable recognition for her work. In 1991/1992, she received an American Book Award and the Janet Heidinger Kafka Award for her first novel, *Through the Arc of the Rain Forest*. *The Village Voice* named her second novel, *Brazil-Maru*, one of the twenty-five best books of 1992. *Tropic of Orange*, her third novel, published in 1997, was a finalist for the Paterson Fiction Prize; that same year, Yamashita received a Japan Foundation Artist Fellowship to study Brazilians living in Japan.

In 1996 the University of California at Santa Cruz (where she still teaches) hired Yamashita to teach creative writing and Asian American literature. Her current projects include researching the Asian American movement.

MAJOR WORKS AND THEMES

All three of Yamashita's novels describe a world with increasingly permeable political borders. Her works concern social dynamics, with the assumption that subtle political, environmental, and technological shifts can alter whole cultures. Her novels combine anthropology, science fiction, the picaresque, and magic realism. In brief, Yamashita delights in the combinational possibilities that change our lives.

Through the Arc of the Rain Forest (1990) begins with an epigram that notes that whatever passes through the arc of a rainbow becomes its opposite. Another prefatory note compares the ensuing novel with the Brazilian *novela*, or nightly soap opera, because of its "boundless nostalgia and terrible ruthlessness." Such is the lightly ironic tone of the novel, told by the narrator, who is a little ball that hovers near Kazumasa Ishimaru's forehead.

All of the other characters have "special" talents and thus "improve" their lives. Ishimaru's neighbors, Batista and Tania Aparecido, discover their ability to train carrier pigeons and later mass-market their pigeons; Mané da Costa Pena, an Indian, discovers the Matacão, a "magical" layer of plastic that covers his land, as well as his ability to market feathers as the newest relaxational craze; Gilberto, a poor, invalid boy healed by the rosary and television, realizes that he has a gift for pilgrimages; Chico Paco, Gilberto's friend, who discovers his gift for gaining answers to prayer, later hosts a radio talk show and develops a market for "telephone pilgrimages"; J. B. Tweep, a three-armed administrative assistant working in New York, discovers his "talent" for decision making and thus rises to the rank of chief executive officer (CEO) of a multinational corporation. Tweep's unbridled commercializing eventually brings all of the characters in contact with the Matacão.

The mysterious plastic landmass called the Matacão alters all of the characters' lives. Its magnetic properties manage to dislodge Kazumasa's hovering orb, lead to the destruction of the Aparecidos' prize pigeons as well as Mané's feather craze, and expose as a sham Gilberto's and Chico Paco's pilgrimage site. Kazumasa, who wins the national lottery and promptly gives his winnings away, is poor again at the end of the novel, not because of his generosity but because his cousin/accountant, Hiroshi, has invested heavily in the Matacão and its by-products. Yamashita's satire of capitalistic cycles, also apparent in the other novels, comes full circle when all discover that the Matacão (and Tweep's empire) is simply unrecyclable plastic sludge that can be destroyed by bacteria. Despite the undoing of so many characters, Kazumasa finds happiness at the end by marrying his true love and by raising children and tropical produce on a farm in the rain forest. The novel's close reflects upon the remains of Tweep's empire:

The old forest has returned once again, secreting its digestive juices, slowly breaking everything into edible absorbent components, pursuing the lost perfection of an organism in which digestion and excretion were once one and the same. But it will never be the same again. (212)

Just as she considers the rain forest or even the whole global, ecological system to be a single organism, Yamashita examines human interaction as a single, complex organism, much like the electronic organism that presents the nightly Brazilian *novela*.

Yamashita's focus on the matrices of human relationship continues in her next work, *Brazil-Maru*, which explores a colonial organism in an alien environment. Ostensibly a fictionalized history of an actual Japanese settlement in the Brazilian rain forest, the novel explores a Rousseauian experiment that takes place in Brazil with Japanese colonists. Each of the novel's larger sections that indicate a narrative shift opens with a passage from Rousseau that illuminates not only that narrator's essential character but also the plot of that ensuing section.

The novel follows the establishment, growth, and decline of Esperança, a colony established in the early 1920s by educated Japanese Christians with socialistic leanings. The first narrator, Ichiro Terada, is called "Émile . . . an experiment, in Brazil" (12) and notes changes in the colony as it develops from 1925 to the late 1930s. Through the eyes of this youngster, we receive an innocent viewpoint that considers simple acts such as clearing trees, starting a chicken ranch, truck farming, and playing baseball ennobling and heroic acts. Like the European American pioneers of a mythical American West, these Japanese colonists "came to create a new civilization based on the ideas of Christianity and freedom of religion" (97).

Haru's section, Part II, covers the late 1930s to the end of World War II. As the wife of the leader of the colony, Kantaro Uno, Haru reveals the colony's ungainly features: the hours of hard labor, the diseases that afflict the poultry and the people, and finally the dissention caused by Japan's war in the Pacific. According to Haru, the divided loyalties to the emperor and to Western values hasten the colony's demise.

Part III, Kantaro's account, begins with the end of World War II and ends in the late 1950s. Throughout this section, he reveals that he loves Esperança's potential but needs to realize his own potential in São Paulo, where he does his "business." Kantaro rationalizes his double life—leading an idealistic and primitive colony but living luxuriously in the city—by admitting that he needs both parts. Hence, with idealistic insouciance, Kantaro justifies keeping a house, mistress, and chauffeur; sponsoring an artist; and siphoning off Esperança's bank accounts. After Kantaro's abuses are discovered, he manages to get a new series of financiers to advance more money, which, of course, he squanders.

Genji Befu, nephew of Kantaro and son of another founder, narrates the years 1959 to 1976, a time when the colony degenerates into a dystopia. Because he does not remember Japan and because he expresses himself through painting, Genji is the real Rousseauian Emile. His naive narrative describes the end of the colony under Kantaro's leadership. Genji's habitual voyeurism (or his potential for extortion?) causes him to be banished to São Paulo, where he demonstrates his inability to adapt to urban life. Genji returns to the colony only to find it disintegrating even further. The narrative ends in 1976, when Kantaro dies in a plane crash while surveying land for a new colony.

The brief Epilogue by Guiherme, the son of an original colonist, describes what remains of Kantaro's colony and another splinter colony. It ends, ironically, with a note about the Japanese Brazilians as an underclass and a note about the death of a wild "Indian of the Lost Tribe" (Genji) who, after surviving a plane crash, was shot while stealing food. Even though Yamashita is describing events and an ethnic colony a continent away, her novel obliquely raises questions about any colonial venture and, more specifically, about the assimilation of Japanese Americans and their ability to "succeed" in North America. As in all of her novels, Yamashita problematizes terms such as "community interest," "ethnic identity," "culture," and "nationhood."

Yamashita develops these same themes in *Tropic of Orange*. The Contents as well as the "Hyper Contexts" show that our reading experience will be akin to channel-surfing through a week's worth of seven character's docuhistories that eventually blend into one plotline. The characters all live in, or migrate to, Los Angeles (L.A.) for their own reasons but are eventually drawn into the nexus of the L.A. freeway system, which is suffering from gridlock and, as such, becomes one extended marketplace or pedestrian zone. The seven characters are Rafaela, who is leaving Mazatlán for L.A.; Bobby, a Chinese immigrant from Singapore who is married to Rafaela; Emi, a Japanese American television news reporter; Buzzworm, an African American news informant who works with Emi; Manzanar, an insane, homeless Japanese American who is actually Emi's uncle; Gabriel, a Chicano who works with, and is romantically interested in, Emi; and Arcangel, a Mexican performer (fashioned after Guillermo Gomez-Penã) heading toward L.A.

For Rafaela, L.A. represents safety for her son, Sol; for Bobby, Emi, Gabriel, and Buzzworm, L.A. represents a place to make a living; but for Manzanar, the L.A. freeways and vehicles (with their swelling sounds) are orchestral instruments for him to direct, and for Arcangel (aka "El Gran Mojado"), L.A. is the site for his "Ultimate Wrestling Championship" with his archnemesis SUPER-NAFTA, a titanium robot. The match is both a wrestling match and an ideological debate as SUPERNAFTA offers the Third World "progress" and money. Arcangel loses the match to SUPERNAFTA's superior weaponry, but Bobby and Rafaela share the last laugh as (in the ring) they symbolically offer slices of their contraband orange (smuggled across the border, but from a Californian tree that was transplanted in Mazatlán) to their fallen hero. United by their love, Bobby, Rafaela, and other characters defy the political borders that separate the United States from other countries. The borders, now meaningless in a place such as L.A., are made permeable by human relationships and become redefined more simply as natural, climatic zones where any orange trees can thrive.

CRITICAL RECEPTION

Critics have approached Yamashita's work with three labels: postmodern, ecological, and Asian American. Yamashita is somewhat mystified by the first two labels, as she admits that she has since had to learn about postmodernism, and she believes that American critics have made too much of her ecological interests. Many reviewers have called her novels "ecological," but that view may be too simple. It may be more accurate to say that her characters are "attempting to live simple lives . . . enmeshed in the machine of commodity production, consumption, and environmental destruction" (Murphy 8).

Yamashita's Japanese American identity is another complex issue, for her novels are not about Japanese Americans per se. King-Kok Cheung notes: "Works that do not dwell on being Asian or Asian American . . . have also been elided in both ethnic and multicultural studies. Because American minority writers are often judged primarily by the ethnic content in their work, those interested in taking up other subjects are seldom given critical attention" (19). Cheung is correct, but it will not be long before critics of Asian American literature and postmodernism will devote more effort to Yamashita's work.

BIBLIOGRAPHY

Works by Karen Tei Yamashita

Novels

Through the Arc of the Rain Forest. Minneapolis: Coffee House Press, 1990.
Brazil-Maru. Minneapolis: Coffee House Press, 1992.
Tropic of Orange. Minneapolis: Coffee House Press, 1997.

Short Stories

"Tucano." *Rafu Shimpo* (December 20, 1975): holiday ed: 11, 35.
"Asaka-no-Miya." *Rafu Shimpo* (December 20, 1979): holiday ed.: 8–10, 16–17, 20.
"The Bath." In *The Third Woman: Minority Women Writers of the United States.* Ed. Dexter Fisher. New York: Houghton Mifflin, 1980. 505–19.
"The Dentist and the Dental Dygienist." *Asiam* 2 (1987): 66.
"The Orange." *Chicago Review* 39 (1993): 12–16.
"Madonna B." *International Examiner*, May 5–18, 1993, 17–19.
"The Last Secretary." In *2000andWhat?* San Francisco: Trip Street Press, 1996. 191–201.

Electronic Journal Publications

"Circle K." Monthly journal series for *CafeCreole*. ed. Ryuta Imafuku (http://www.ojw.or.jp/cafecreole), 1998.

Poetry

"Maceio." In *Ayumi: A Japanese-American Anthology*. San Francisco: Japanese American Anthology Committee, 1979. 253–54.
"Obasan." In *Calafia: The California Poetry*. Ed. Ishmael Reed. Berkeley: Yardbird Books, 1979. 375–77.

Studies of Karen Tei Yamashita

Backstrom, Kirsten. Rev. of *Through the Arc of the Rain Forest*. In *500 Great Books by Women*. Ed. Erica Bauermeister, Jesse Larsen, and Holly Smith. New York: Penguin, 1994. 190.
Campbell, R. B. Rev. of *Through the Arc of the Rain Forest*. *New York Times Book Review* (March 10, 1991): 16.
Cheung, King-Kok. *An Interethnic Companion to Asian American Literature*. Cambridge: Cambridge University Press, 1997. 19, 148.
Gier, Jean Vengua, and Carla Alicia Tejeda. *Jouvert: An Interview with Karen Tei Yamashita*. University of California, Berkeley. December 16, 1998 <http://social.chass.ncsu.edu/jouvert/v2i2/yamashi.htm.>.
Ho, Cathy Lang. Rev. of *Through the Arc of the Rain Forest*. *San Francisco Review of Books* 15 (1990): 33.
Kaye, Janet. Rev. of *Tropic of Orange*. *New York Times Book Review* 103 (1998): 16.
Murphy, Patrick D. "Commodification, Resistance, Inhabitation, and Identity in the Novels of Linda Hogan, Edna Escamill, and Karen Tei Yamashita." *Phoebe* 9 (1997): 1–10.
Rauch, Molly E. Rev. of *Tropic of Orange*. *The Nation* 266 (1998): 28–29.
Yang, Jeff. Rev. of *Brazil-Maru*. *Village Voice Supplement* 110 (1992): 5.

Selected Bibliography

ANTHOLOGIES

Aziz, Nurjehan, ed. *Her Mother's Ashes, and Other Stories by South Asian Women in Canada and the United States.* Toronto: TSAR, 1994.

Berson, Misha, ed. *Between Worlds: Contemporary Asian-American Plays.* New York: Theatre Communication Group, 1990.

Briscoe, Leonor Aureus, and Anita Merina, eds. *Philippine American Short Stories.* Quezon City, Philippines: Giraffe Books, 1997.

Chan, Jeffrey Paul, et al., eds. *The Big Aiiieeeee! An Anthology of Chinese American and Japanese American Literature.* New York: Meridian, 1991.

Chin, Frank, et al., eds. *Aiiieeeee! An Anthology of Asian American Writers.* Garden City, NY: Doubleday, 1974.

Hagedorn, Jessica, ed. *Charlie Chan Is Dead: An Anthology of Contemporary Asian American Fiction.* New York: Penguin, 1994.

Hong, Maria, ed. *Growing Up Asian American: An Anthology.* New York: William Morrow, 1993.

Hsu, Kai-yu, and Helen Palumbinskas, eds. *Asian-American Authors.* Boston: Houghton Mifflin, 1972.

Kadi, Joanna, ed. *Food for Our Grandmothers: Writings by Arab-American and Arab-Canadian Feminists.* Boston: South End Press, 1994.

Kim, Elaine H., et al., eds. *Making More Waves: New Writing by Asian American Women.* Boston: Beacon Press, 1997.

Kornblum, Allan, ed. *Asian American Voices.* Minneapolis: Coffee House Press, 1994.

Lim, Shirley Geok-lin, et al., eds. *The Forbidden Stitch: An Asian American Women's Anthology.* Corvallis, OR: Calyx Books, 1989.

Lim-Hing, Sharon, ed. *The Very Inside: An Anthology by Asian and Pacific Islander Lesbian and Bisexual Women.* Toronto: Sister Vision, 1994.

Ratti, Rakesh, ed. *A Lotus of Another Color: An Unfolding of the South Asian Gay and Lesbian Experience.* Boston: Alyson, 1993.

Wand, David Hsin-Fu, ed. *Asian-American Heritage: An Anthology of Prose and Poetry.* New York: Washington Square Press, 1974.

Wang, Shawn, ed. *Asian American Literature: A Brief Introduction and Anthology.* New York: HarperCollins, 1996.

Watanabe, Sylvia, and Carol Bruchac, eds. *Into the Fire: Asian American Prose.* Dexter, MI: Greenfield Review Press, 1996.

SECONDARY SOURCES

Baker, Houston, Jr., ed. *Three American Literatures.* New York: Modern Language Association, 1982.

Bloom, Harold, ed. *Asian American Women Writers.* Philadelphia: Chelsea House, 1997.

Cheung, King-Kok. *An Interethnic Companion to Asian American Literature.* New York: Cambridge University Press, 1997.

Cheung, King-Kok, and Stan Yogi, eds. *Asian American Literature: An Annotated Bibliography.* New York: Modern Language Association, 1988.

Cho, Song. *Rice: Explorations into Gay Asian Culture and Politics.* Toronto: Queer Press, 1997.

Eng, David L., and Alice Y. Horn, eds. *Q & A: Queer in Asian America.* Philadelphia: Temple University Press, 1998.

Ghymn, Esther Mikyung. *Images of Asian American Women by Asian American Women Writers.* New York: Peter Lang, 1995.

Hidalgo, Christina Pantoja. *Filipino Woman Writing: Home and Exile in the Autobiographical Narratives of Ten Writers.* Manila, Philippines: Ateno de Manila University Press, 1994.

Jinqi, Ling. *Narrating Nationalism: Ideology and Form in Asian American Literature.* New York: Oxford University Press, 1998.

Kafka, Phillipa. *(Un)doing the Missionary Position: Gender Asymmetry in Asian American Women's Writing.* Westport, CT: Greenwood Press, 1997.

Kim, Elaine H. *Asian American Literature: An Introduction to the Writings and Their Social Contexts.* Philadelphia: Temple University Press, 1982.

Knippling, Alpana Sharma, ed. *New Immigrant Literatures of the United States.* Westport, CT: Greenwood Press, 1996.

Leonard, George J., ed. *The Asian Pacific American Heritage: A Companion to Literature and Arts.* New York: Garland, 1999.

Li, David Leiwei. *Imagining the Nation: Asian American Literature and Cultural Consent.* Stanford, CA: Stanford University Press, 1998.

Lim, Shirley Geok-lin, and Amy Ling, eds. *Reading the Literatures of Asian America.* Philadelphia: Temple University Press, 1992.

Ling, Amy. *Between Worlds: Women Writers of Chinese Ancestry.* New York: Pergamon Press, 1990.

Lowe, Lisa. *Immigrant Acts: Asian American Cultural Politics.* Durham, NC: Duke University Press, 1996.

Ma, Sheng-mei. *Immigrant Subjectives in Asian American and Asian Diaspora Literatures.* Albany: State University of New York Press, 1998.

Maitano, John R., and David R. Peck, eds. *Teaching American Ethnic Literatures.* Albuquerque: University of New Mexico Press, 1996.

Nelson, Emmanuel, ed. *Bharati Mukherjee: Critical Essays*. New York: Garland, 1993.

Sumida, Stephen H. *Literary Tradition of Hawai'i*. Seattle: University of Washington Press, 1991.

Trudeau, Lawrence J., ed. *Asian American Literature: Reviews and Criticism of Works by American Writers of Asian Descent*. Detroit: Gale Research, 1999.

Wong, Sau-ling Cynthia. *Reading Asian American Literature: From Necessity to Extravagance*. Princeton: Princeton University Press, 1993.

Yamamoto, Traise. *Masking Selves, Making Subjects: Japanese American Women, Identity and the Body*. Berkeley: University of California Press, 1999.

PERIODICALS

The Asian Pacific American Journal (semiannual)

Bamboo Ridge: The Hawaii Writers' Quarterly Critical Mass (semiannual)

Disorient: An Asian Pacific American Literary Arts Journalzine (annual)

Hitting Critical Mass: A Journal of Asian American Cultural Criticism (semiannual)

Index

Page numbers for main entries appear in **boldface** type.

About the Editor and Contributors

JEAN AMATO is a doctoral candidate in Comparative Literature at the University of Oregon, Eugene, where she is completing a dissertation on Chinese American literature.

SARAH CATLIN BARNHART is a doctoral candidate in English at the University of South Carolina, Columbia.

LISA BOTSHON is Assistant Professor of English at the University of Maine, Augusta.

RHONDA BROCK-SERVAIS is a graduate student in English at the University of South Carolina, Columbia.

HARISH CHANDER is Professor of English at Shaw University.

CHIH-PING CHEN is a doctoral candidate in English at the University of Massachusetts, Amherst.

FU-JEN CHEN is a doctoral candidate in English at Northern Illinois University, De Kalb.

PETER G. CHRISTENSEN teaches in the School of Library and Information Science at the University of Wisconsin, Milwaukee.

ELIZABETH FITZPATRICK is a Reference Librarian at the W.E.B. Du Bois Library on the campus of the University of Massachusetts, Amherst.

BARRY FRUCHTER received his doctorate in English from SUNY-Stony Brook; he currently teaches at Nassau Community College.

ANTHONY R. GUNERATNE, author of *Cinehistory: The Representation of Reality in Documentary and Narrative Cinema*, is presently a Visiting Scholar at Harvard University.

JAE-NAM HAN received his Ph.D. in English from the University of Nebraska, Lincoln, where he is currently a lecturer.

JOHN C. HAWLEY, a widely published scholar, is Professor of English at Santa Clara University.

GUIYOU HUANG is Assistant Professor of English at Kutztown University.

NIKOLAS HUOT is a doctoral candidate in English at Georgia State University. His research interests include African American literature, postcolonialism, and queer theory.

YMITRI JAYASUNDERA is a doctoral candidate in English at the University of Massachusetts, Amherst.

GEOFFREY KAIN is Associate Professor in the Humanities Department at Embry-Riddle Aeronautical University, Florida. He is the editor of *R. K. Narayan: Contemporary Critical Essays* (1993) and *Ideas of Home: Literature of Asian Migration* (1997).

LEELA KAPAI is Professor of English at Prince George Community College, Maryland. She has published numerous articles on multicultural literature.

MARTIN KICH is Associate Professor of English at Wright State University— Lake Campus. He edits *Grand Lake Review*, a literary journal, and *Cyberfict*, an annual periodical devoted to cyberfictions and the electronic novel.

SARALA KRISHNAMURTHY is Associate Professor in the Postgraduate Department of English at Bangalore, India.

SHANNON T. LEONARD is a Ph.D. candidate in English at Rice University. Her dissertation focuses on the cultural productions by and about multiracial Americans of Asian descent.

KRISHNA LEWIS holds a doctorate in comparative literature from the University of Pennsylvania. She is currently Assistant Professor of English at Florida Atlantic University.

LUCHEN LI is Assistant Professor of English at Iowa State University.

YI-CHUN TRICIA LIN is Assistant Professor of English at the Borough of Manhattan Community College. She is completing a book titled *Translating Cultures as Rewriting Boundaries: Asian American Women Writing* and editing a collection of essays on Meena Alexander.

XIAN LIU is Assistant Professor of English at St. Joseph's College, Connecticut.

JAMES LIVINGSTON recently graduated from SUNY—Cortland with a degree in English.

SERI LUANGPHINITH is a doctoral candidate in English at the University of Oregon; she is completing a dissertation on Hawaii's literary history.

WENTONG MA is a doctoral candidate in comparative literature at SUNY—Binghamton.

BINDU MALIECKAL is completing her Ph.D. at Baylor University.

ANITA MANNUR is a doctoral candidate at the University of Massachusetts, Amherst.

SUZANNE HOTTE MASSA is a graduate student in English at SUNY—Cortland; she teaches multicultural literature at a private high school in Ithaca, New York.

UPPINDER MEHAN is Assistant Professor in the Department of Writing, Literature, and Publishing at Emerson College, Boston. He is a specialist in postcolonial, particularly South Asian, literatures.

BRUNDA MOKA-DIAS, a recent Ph.D. in comparative literature, teaches at Rutgers University.

EMMANUEL S. NELSON is Professor of English at SUNY—Cortland. Author of over thirty scholarly articles, he has edited a number of reference volumes, including *Winters of the Indian Diaspora* (Greenwood, 1993) and *Contemporary African American Novelists* (Greenwood, 1999).

JEFFREY PARTRIDGE teaches in the Department of English Language and Literature at the National University of Singapore.

JANET M. POWERS, who holds a doctorate from the University of Wisconsin-Madison, is Associate Professor of Interdepartmental Studies and Women's Studies at Gettysburg College.

RUBY S. RAMRAJ, a specialist in postcolonial literature, teaches in the Department of English at the University of Calgary, Canada.

CAROL ROH-SPAULDING is Assistant Professor of English at Drake University. She has published several articles on Asian American literature.

JAINA C. SANGA is Visiting Assistant Professor of English at Southern Methodist University. She is writing a book on film and literature.

MARA SCANLON is Assistant Professor of English at Mary Washington College. Her publications include articles on Afro-Caribbean poetry.

MAYA M. SHARMA is Assistant Professor of English at Hostos Community College (CUNY). She has published articles on V. S. Naipaul and Bharati Mukherjee.

JASPAL KAUR SINGH recently received her doctorate in comparative literature from the University of Oregon. She is currently a Rockefeller Foundation Humanities Residential Fellow at James S. Coleman African Studies Center, University of California, Los Angeles.

DOUGLAS SUGANO teaches British, multicultural, and Asian American literature at Whitworth College, Spokane.

ELEANOR TY is Associate Professor of English at Wilfrid Laurier University, Ontario. A widely published scholar, Ty is the author of *Empowering the Feminine: The Narratives of Mary Robinson, Jane West, and Amelia Opie* (1998).

SHUNZHU WANG teaches at Bennington College, Vermont. He has coedited and translated from English to Chinese two books on contemporary rhetoric.

CYNTHIA F. WONG is Assistant Professor of English at the University of Colorado, Denver. Her book on Kazuo Ishiguro's novels will be published shortly.

HAILING XIAO is a doctoral candidate in English at Texas Woman's University.

WENYING XU is Assistant Professor of English at Truman State University, where she teaches courses in American as well as Asian American literatures.

XIAOPING YEN teaches writing, literature, and journalism at LaGuardia Community College, New York. He is managing editor of *New York Stories*, a literary magazine, and author of *Peony Pavilion* (1999), a novel.

SU-LIN YU is a doctoral candidate in English at Northern Illinois University, De Kalb.

ISBN 0-313-30911-6

EAN

9 780313 309113

HARDCOVER BAR CODE